NEWFOUNDLAND AND LABRADOR
Pages 60–69

NEW BRUNSWICK, NOVA SCOTIA, AND PRINCE EDWARD IS.
Pages 70–93

MONTREAL
Pages 102–123

QUEBEC CITY AND THE ST. LAWRENCE RIVER
Pages 124–141

SOUTHERN AND NORTHERN QUEBEC
Pages 142–153

TORONTO
Pages 162–187

Iqaluit

QUEBEC

ATLANTIC CANADA

'ARIO

OTTAWA Montreal

St. John's

Toronto

Halifax

0 km   500

0 miles   500

OTTAWA AND EASTERN ONTARIO
Pages 188–203

DORLING KINDERSLEY *TRAVEL GUIDES*

CANADA

DORLING KINDERSLEY

LONDON • NEW YORK • SYDNEY • MOSCOW • DELHI

www.dk.com

A DORLING KINDERSLEY BOOK

www.dk.com

Produced by Duncan Baird Publishers
London, England

MANAGING EDITOR Rebecca Miles
MANAGING ART EDITOR Vanessa Marsh
EDITORS Georgina Harris, Michelle de Larrabeiti, Zoë Ross
DESIGNERS Dawn Davies-Cook, Ian Midson
DESIGN ASSISTANCE Rosie Laing, Kelvin Mullins
VISUALIZER Gary Cross
PICTURE RESEARCH Victoria Peel
DTP DESIGNER Sarah Williams

Dorling Kindersley Limited
PROJECT EDITOR Paul Hines
ART EDITOR Jane Ewart
US EDITOR Mary Sutherland
EDITOR Hugh Thompson

CONTRIBUTORS
Paul Franklin, Sam Ion, Philip Lee, Cam Norton, Lorry Patton,
Geoffrey Roy, Michael Snook, Donald Telfer, Paul Waters

PHOTOGRAPHERS
Alan Keohane, Peter Wilson, Francesca Yorke

ILLUSTRATORS
Joanna Cameron, Gary Cross, Chris Forsey,
Paul Guest, Claire Littlejohn,
Robbie Polley, Kevin Robinson, John Woodcock

Reproduced by Colourscan (Singapore)
Printed and bound in China by
Sun Fung Offset Binding Company Limited

First published in Great Britain in 2000
by Dorling Kindersley Limited
9 Henrietta Street, London WC2E 8PS

**The information in every
Dorling Kindersley Travel Guide is checked annually**.
Every effort has been made to ensure that this book is as up-
to-date as possible at the time of going to press. Some details,
however, such as telephone numbers, opening hours, prices,
gallery hanging arrangements, and travel information are liable
to change. The publishers cannot accept responsibility for any
consequences arising from the use of this book.
We value the views and suggestions of our readers very highly.
Please write to: Senior Managing Editor, Dorling Kindersley Travel
Guides, Dorling Kindersley, 9 Henrietta Street, London WC2E 8PS.

◁ **The dazzling fall foliage of Quebec's maple forests**

CONTENTS

**The historic reconstruction of
Fortress Louisbourg, Nova Scotia**

Lake Moraine in Banff National Park in the Rockies

Château Frontenac in Quebec City

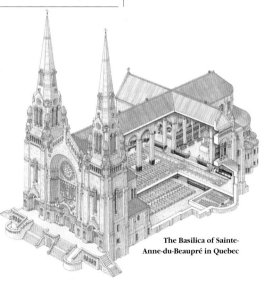
The Basilica of Sainte-
Anne-du-Beaupré in Quebec

INTRODUCING
CANADA

Putting Western and Northern Canada on the Map

Canada lies at the northern end of the American continent and covers 9,970,610 sq km (3,849,652 sq miles). More than 70 percent of this area is uninhabited because of vast tracts of frozen wilderness in the north. In contrast, British Columbia boasts Canada's only temperate rainforest.

Melville Island

Banks Island

Victoria Island

Cambridge Bay

Inuvik

NORTHWEST TERRITORIES

Great Bear Lake

Dawson City

CANADA

YUKON

Yellowknife

Whitehorse

Watson Lake

Great Slave Lake

Hay River

Fort Smith

Thelon

Dubawnt

Lake Athabasca

Fort Nelson

BRITISH COLUMBIA

Fort St. John

ALBERTA

SASKATCHEWAN

PACIFIC

Athabasca

Saskatchewan

Fli Flo

OCEAN

Queen Charlotte Islands

Prince Rupert

Prince George

Edmonton
Red Deer

Prince Albert

Saskatoon

Yorkt

Banff

Calgary

Regina

Mino

Vancouver Island

Vancouver

Victoria

Seattle

Portland

UNITED STATES OF AMERICA

KEY

✈ International airport

━ Highway

━ Major road

— Principal rail routes

━ International border

--- Provincial border

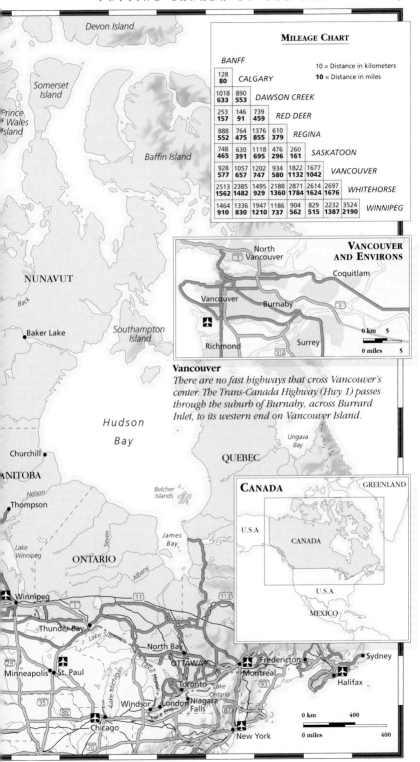

MILEAGE CHART

BANFF

10 = Distance in kilometers
10 = Distance in miles

128 **80**	CALGARY							
1018 **633**	890 **553**	DAWSON CREEK						
253 **157**	146 **91**	739 **459**	RED DEER					
888 **552**	764 **475**	1376 **855**	610 **379**	REGINA				
748 **465**	630 **391**	1118 **695**	476 **296**	260 **161**	SASKATOON			
928 **577**	1057 **657**	1202 **747**	934 **580**	1822 **1132**	1677 **1042**	VANCOUVER		
2513 **1562**	2385 **1482**	1495 **929**	2188 **1360**	2871 **1784**	2614 **1624**	2697 **1676**	WHITEHORSE	
1464 **910**	1336 **830**	1947 **1210**	1186 **737**	904 **562**	829 **515**	2232 **1387**	3524 **2190**	WINNIPEG

VANCOUVER AND ENVIRONS

North Vancouver

Coquitlam

Vancouver Burnaby

Richmond Surrey

0 km 5

0 miles 5

Vancouver

There are no fast highways that cross Vancouver's center. The Trans-Canada Highway (Hwy 1) passes through the suburb of Burnaby, across Burrard Inlet, to its western end on Vancouver Island.

Devon Island

Somerset Island

Prince of Wales Island

Baffin Island

NUNAVUT

Back

Baker Lake

Southampton Island

Churchill

Hudson Bay

Ungava Bay

QUEBEC

MANITOBA

Nelson

Thompson

Belcher Islands

James Bay

CANADA

GREENLAND

U.S.A

CANADA

U.S.A

MEXICO

Lake Winnipeg

ONTARIO

Seven

Albany

Winnipeg

Thunder Bay

Lake Superior

North Bay

OTTAWA Fredericton Sydney

Minneapolis St. Paul

Lake Michigan

Lake Huron

Montreal Halifax

Toronto Lake Ontario

Windsor London Niagara Falls

Lake Erie

Chicago

New York

0 km 400

0 miles 400

Putting Eastern Canada on the Map

M OST OF CANADA'S 30 million people live close to the US border, in a band that stretches from the east coast across to British Columbia in the west. Over 60 percent of all Canadians are concentrated in the southeast corner of the country, in the provinces of Ontario and Quebec. This is the heartland of Canadian industry, including electronics, hydro-electricity, lumber, and paper. The maritime provinces of Nova Scotia, New Brunswick, and Prince Edward Island are Canada's smallest, but the beauty of their landscapes attracts thousands of tourists each year. Newfoundland and Labrador are also known for their rugged charm.

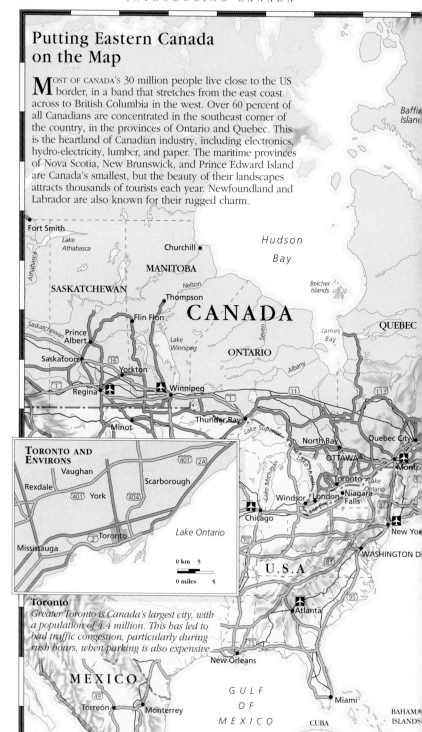

TORONTO AND ENVIRONS

Toronto
Greater Toronto is Canada's largest city, with a population of 4.4 million. This has led to bad traffic congestion, particularly during rush hours, when parking is also expensive.

MILEAGE CHART

CHARLOTTETOWN									
356 **221**	FREDERICTON								
239 **148**	473 **294**	HALIFAX							
1149 **714**	834 **518**	1003 **623**	MONTREAL						
1860 **1156**	1510 **938**	1925 **1196**	676 **420**	NIAGARA FALLS					
1339 **832**	1016 **631**	1456 **905**	200 **124**	536 **333**	OTTAWA				
954 **593**	598 **371**	1071 **665**	257 **160**	946 **588**	724 **450**	QUEBEC CITY			
1412 **877**	1267 **787**	1512 **939**	859 **534**	1569 **975**	1074 **667**	637 **396**	SEPT-ILES		
2794 **1736**	2471 **1535**	2910 **1808**	1654 **1028**	1521 **945**	1503 **934**	1963 **1220**	2613 **1624**	THUNDER BAY	
1689 **1049**	1366 **849**	1806 **1122**	549 **341**	137 **85**	399 **248**	809 **503**	1449 **900**	1384 **860**	TORONTO

10 = Distance in kilometers
10 = Distance in miles

KEY

- ✈ International airport
- ▬ Highway
- ▬ Major road
- — Principal rail routes
- ▬ International border
- --- Provincial border

0 km   500

0 miles   500

Labrador

Sea

LABRADOR

Happy Valley -
Goose Bay

Labrador
City

Sept-Iles

NEWFOUNDLAND
✈ St. John's

dericton Charlottetown
Sydney

✈
Halifax

T L A N T I C

O C E A N

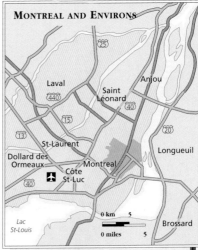

MONTREAL AND ENVIRONS

Laval

Anjou

Saint
Léonard

St-Laurent

Dollard des
Ormeaux

Côte
St-Luc

Montreal

Longueuil

Lac
St-Louis

Brossard

0 km   5

0 miles   5

Montreal
*Montreal is a well-established
transportation hub. The city is
surrounded by a network of
highways: the Trans-Canada
Highway, a hectic six-lane highway, crosses the city as number 20
or the Autoroute Métropolitain.*

A PORTRAIT OF CANADA

BLESSED *with ancient forests, rugged mountains, and large cosmopolitan cities, Canada is unimaginably vast, stretching west from the Atlantic to the Pacific and north to the Arctic Ocean. Around 20,000 years ago Canada was inhabited by aboriginal peoples but by the 19th century it had been settled by Europeans. Today, the country is noted as a liberal, multicultural society.*

In part, Canada's heritage of tolerance is a result of its conflict-ridden past. Two centuries of compromise was necessary to fully establish the country. Following fighting between the British and French armies in the 1750s, the British won control of the country in 1759. The self-governing colonies of British North America spent three years hammering out the agreement that brought them together as the Dominion of Canada in 1867. Newfoundland did not become part of the nation until 1949. Powerful regional differences, particularly between French- and English-speaking Canada meant that the country has had difficulties evolving a national identity. When Pierre Berton, one of Canada's leading commentators, was prompted to define a Canadian he evaded the question, replying: "Someone who knows how to make love in a canoe."

Inuit wooden mask

The second largest country in the world, Canada has a surface area of 9,970,610 sq km (3,849,652 sq miles). Over 40 percent of the land is north of the treeline at 60° latitude; this extraordinarily hostile and sparsely inhabited wilderness is bitterly cold in winter, averaging -30°C (-22°F), and plagued by millions of insects in summer. Not surprisingly, most

The snow-laden rooftops of Quebec City overlooking the St. Lawrence River at dusk

◁ Bull elk grazing in Jasper National Park in the Rocky Mountains

Canadians live in the more temperate regions farther to the south. Of the country's 30 million inhabitants, more than 80 percent live within 200 kilometers (124 miles) of the US border.

FLORA AND FAUNA

In the far north, the permafrost of the treeless tundra (or taiga) supports the growth of only the toughest flora, such as lichen, mosses, and a range of unusually hardy varieties of flowers and grasses. In spring and fall however, the tundra flora bursts into an impressive display of color. Animal life is abundant in this region, and includes the polar bear, arctic fox, wolf, seal, musk ox, and caribou.

Farther south, the boreal or coniferous forest covers a wide band from Newfoundland in the east to the Yukon in the west. A variety of trees here, including spruce, balsam fir, and jack pine, provides a home for those animals most typically thought of as Canadian, primarily moose, beaver, lynx, and black bear. The beaver is Canada's national symbol. It was the

Spring flower from the Bruce Peninsula

European fashion for beaver hats that created and sustained the Canadian fur trade and opened up the interior to European settlers, paving the way for the growth of the modern nation.

In the east, deciduous forests containing the emblematic maple are populated by deer, skunk, and mink. Across central Canada, the grasslands, known as the Prairies, house elk, gophers, and the few thousand buffalo which are all that remain of the vast herds that once roamed here. British Columbia's temperate rain forests are rich in wildlife such as black tail deer, brown bear, and cougar. Rare orchids and ferns grow here, among towering cedars, firs, and spruce trees.

THE FIRST NATIONS

Although thought of as a new country, Canada's prehistory dates back about 20,000 years to the end of the first Ice Age. At that time there was a land bridge joining Siberia to Alaska; Siberian hunter-nomads crossed this bridge to become the first human inhabitants of North America, and over

The bald eagle, a common sight around the Charlotte Island archipelago in British Columbia

the succeeding centuries their descendants gradually moved south. Archaeological digs in the Old Crow River Basin in the Yukon have unearthed a collection of tools believed to date to this initial period of migration. These Siberian nomads were the ancestors of the continent's native peoples, who adapted to their new environment in a variety of ways.

Inuit children at Bathurst Inlet, Northern Peninsula, Newfoundland

By the 16th century, Spanish and Portuguese traders were the first Europeans to have close dealings with the aboriginal peoples of the Americas, whom they named "Indians" in the mistaken belief that they had reached India. The "Indian" appellation stuck, and the "Red" was added by British settlers in the 17th century when they met the Beothuks of Newfoundland, who daubed themselves in red ochre to repel insects. The native peoples of the far north were also given a name they did not want – "Eskimo," literally "eaters of raw meat." Given the history, it is hardly surprising that modern-day leaders of Canada's aboriginal peoples have rejected these names in favor of others: aboriginal, native Canadians, and First Nations are all acceptable, though the people of the north prefer Inuit (meaning "the people"). Included among Canada's native peoples are the Métis, mixed race descendants of aboriginal peoples and French-speaking European traders.

SOCIETY

The joint official languages of Canada are French and English, and the interplay between Canada's two largest linguistic and cultural groups is evident in the capital city of Ottawa, where every federal speech and bill has to be delivered in both languages. Canada's population is about 24 percent French Canadian, predominantly the descendants of French settlers who came to the colony of New France in the 17th and 18th centuries (see p41). Their English-speaking compatriots are largely descended from 18th- and 19th-century British immigrants. Canada's reputation as a multicultural society began to be established in the 19th century when successive waves of immigration, along with various settlement plans, brought people from all over the world to Canada's cities and its rural areas. Today, perhaps the best way to experience modern Canada's vibrant cultural mix is to visit its three largest cities – Toronto, Montreal, and Vancouver.

View from Centre Island's parks and gardens on Lake Ontario toward Toronto's CN Tower

Changing of the Guard outside Ottawa's Parliament Building

GOVERNMENT AND POLITICS

Canada is a parliamentary democracy with a federal political system. Each province or territory has its own democratically elected provincial legislature headed by a Premier, and also sends elected representatives to the federal parliament in Ottawa. The House of Commons is the main federal legislature. The Prime Minister is the head of the political structure, as well as an elected member of the House of Commons where he must be able to command a majority. Bills passed in the Commons are forwarded to an upper

The ceremonial unveiling of the new Nunavut flag in 1999

chamber, the Senate, for ratification. At present, the Prime Minister appoints senators, although there is increasing pressure to make the upper chamber elective too. The nominal head of state is the British monarch, currently Queen Elizabeth II, and her Canadian representative is the Governor-General.

In recent years, the dominant political trend in Canadian politics has been regionalism. The provinces have sought to take back power from the center, which makes it difficult for any one political party to win majority support in all parts of the country at any one time. The most conspicuous aspect of this process has been the conflict over Quebec, where there is a strong separatist movement. Twice since 1981, the Quebecois have been asked to vote in referenda seeking their support to leave Canada and, although the electorate voted "No" on both occasions, it was a close result. Sadly, the issue of Quebec's relationship with the rest of Canada is still unresolved, and further political disputes seem inevitable.

Since the 1980s aboriginal politics has come to the fore with campaigns for constitutional, land, and mineral rights. The Assembly of First Nations have been at the forefront of the establishment of the Inuit homeland, Nunavut. Current issues include battles for self-government and schools to preserve native languages, as well as hunting and fishing rights.

Canada has played its part in the major events of the 20th century, including both world wars, and today holds a prominent position in international politics. The country is a member of NATO and one of the Group of Eight (G8) countries, which, with the US, UK, Italy, Japan, France, Germany, and Russia, decide on world trade agreements.

ART AND CULTURE

The vast and beautiful landscape of the country is a defining feature of Canadian culture. Outdoor pursuits such as hiking, skiing, and canoeing are high on the list of popular activities. Canadians are also enthusiastic sports fans, and ice hockey, baseball, and Canadian football attract huge crowds of spectators, and foster deeply felt allegiances. In addition to their passion for sports, Canadians are also enthusiastic about the arts. This is the country that has produced internationally renowned classical pianist, Glenn Gould, and whose major cities possess well-respected orchestras. Canada has also produced more than its share of international rock stars, from Joni Mitchell and Gordon Lightfoot to contemporary artists such as Celine Dion, Bryan Adams, k.d. lang, and Alanis Morissette. Canada's cosmopolitan culture also means that visitors are likely to find a wide choice of music in bars, cafés, and many other venues across the country.

International rock star, Alanis Morissette

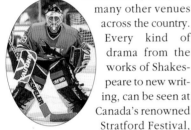

Vancouver Canucks Ice hockey game

Every kind of drama from the works of Shakespeare to new writing, can be seen at Canada's renowned Stratford Festival, which is held in Ontario every year.

Both native and European artists have looked to the wilderness as a source of inspiration. The first artist to attempt to express a sense of national identity was Tom Thomson, with his distinctive landscapes. He influenced the country's most celebrated group of painters, the Group of Seven *(see pp160–61)*, who evolved a national style of painting uniquely capable of representing Canada's wilderness, a theme developed by their contemporaries and successors, most notably Emily Carr. Canada's world-class museums and galleries represent the country's pride in its art collections: Toronto businessman Ken Thompson,

Popular TV series, the *X-Files*, was shot in Vancouver

shows a range of Canadian art in his own gallery as well as lending his support to the outstanding Art Gallery of Ontario. The marvelous array of restored forts, towns, and native villages reflect Canadian respect for both their native and European heritage.

Among Canadian writers, there are distinguished practitioners in both English and French, and an impressive list of contemporary novelists includes such prize-winning authors as Margaret Atwood, Carol Shields, Michael Ondaatje, Jacques Poulin, and Germaine Guèvremont.

The Canadian film industry is thriving, and the country's varied landscapes have proved popular locations, particularly for US film and TV producers (until 1999, the popular TV series the *X-Files* was shot in Vancouver). Behind Canada's flourishing cultural life, lies a pride in its history and cosmopolitan heritage, and an affection for the land's daunting beauty.

Landscape and Geology

CANADA IS THE LARGEST country in the world, covering an area almost as big as Europe. It was created from the world's oldest landmasses. The billion-year-old bowl-shaped Canadian Shield covers much of the country, dipping around Hudson Bay and rising to mountain ranges at its edges. The country is bordered by oceans on three sides, with a coastline 243,800 km (151,400 miles) long and an interior containing some two million lakes. Canada is well known for the impressive diversity of its interior landscapes: from the frozen, barren north that descends to the mountainous west with its forest and wheat plains, through the wooded, hilly east, and the flat, fertile lowlands of the southeast.

The Great Lakes region covers 3% of Canada's landmass, and comprises a fertile lowland bowl, vital to its agricultural economy.

The Interior Plains, including the prairies, are the principal wheat-growing areas of the country, and range southeast 2,600 km (1,600 miles) from the Cordilleras to the US border. The plains are divided into three huge steppes.

THE ROCKIES AND THE WESTERN CORDILLERA

This region is part of one of the world's longest mountain chains. In Canada, the Cordillera comprises the Pacific Coastal Mountains and forested basins. Graduated peaks and ridges reveal Ice Age erosion, as does the Columbia Icefield (see p308). The Rockies developed from continental plate movement, which began about 120 million years ago (see pp256–7).

GEOGRAPHICAL REGIONS

Characterized by its variety, Canadian landscape falls into six main areas. The north of the country offers a landscape of tundra, with the far north ice-covered for much of the year. In the west and south, the warmer, fertile lands of the Cordillera and interior plains support the rural population. To the east, the Great Lakes area is an agricultural center. The vast Canadian Shield cradles the plains and rises to form the northern Innuitian region and the Appalachians in the south.

Innuitian Region and Arctic Lowlands

The Rockies & Western Cordillera

Canadian Shield

Interior Plains

Appalachians

Great Lakes

The Appalachians' rolling landscape is two-thirds woodland and covers both arable lowland areas and the highest peaks in Quebec. These are found on the Gaspé Peninsula, the outer mountain ring of the Canadian Shield highland. Most of the Appalachian mountain chain lies in the US. They are nature's barrier between the eastern seaboard and the continental interior lowlands.

The Canadian Shield, formed of the 1,100-million-year-old bedrock of the North American continent, is the core of the country. It spreads out from Hudson Bay for 5 million sq km (1.9 million sq miles). The center is scrub and rock, and rises to steep mountains around the rim.

The Innuitian region stretches northward from the Arctic Lowlands' modest height of 100–700 m (330–2,000 ft) above sea level to the peaks of the Innuitian mountain range, at their highest on Ellesmere Island at 2,926 m (9,600 ft). Vigorous glaciation for millenia has developed deep fjords, sharp peaks, and frost patterns on the earth. This region is rich in oil, coal, and gas.

Canada's Wildlife

B Y THE TIME it emerged from the last Ice Age 10,000 years ago, Canada had developed a geography and climate that remains one of the most diverse on Earth. In the north, the Arctic weather produces a harsh, barren desert, in darkness for several months and frozen most of the year. By contrast, the country's most southerly province, Ontario, shares a latitude with northern California and offers fertile forests laced with rivers and lakes. In southern Canada, many varieties of wildlife flourish in the coniferous forest that covers the ancient rocks of the Canadian Shield. In the central plain are wheat-filled open prairies. From here, foothills lead to the Rocky Mountains, which gradually roll westward to coastal mountains and the balmy landscape of temperate rainforest along the Pacific coast.

The muskox is a gregarious herd animal and a remnant of the last Ice Age. Its thick topcoat of guard hair and undercoat of finer, fleecier hair keeps it warm even at –45°C (–50°F).

THE BOREAL FOREST

The boreal forest extends from eastern Canada, across most of Quebec and Ontario, and into the northern parts of the prairie provinces. It consists of a mix of spruce, pine, birch, and aspen, and occurs mostly on the giant rock outcrop of the Canadian Shield *(see pp18–9)*. Dotted with thousands of lakes, it is a rich habitat for some of Canada's best-known wildlife.

THE PRAIRIES

Once referred to as a "sea of grass," the Canadian prairie is now predominantly agricultural in nature, specializing in growing wheat and other grains, and ranching prime beef cattle. While little original prairie wilderness remains, this is still a land of great open spaces that supports a surprising, often rare, wildlife population.

The timber wolf, or gray wolf, was hunted almost to extinction by 1950. It has now returned to the more isolated parts of its range in the boreal forest.

The pronghorn antelope is the last of its species to survive in North America. The fastest American mammal, it can reach speeds of over 75 km (47 miles) per hour.

The loon has a haunting call that rings out over northern lakes and is symbolic of the Canadian wilderness.

The bison now exists in only two remaining wild herds in Alberta and the Northwest Territories.

CANADA'S SPORTS FISH

From the northern pike and lake trout in the north to the walleye and smallmouth bass in the south, Canada is blessed with a large number of sports fish species. Some fish that are much sought after as sport in Europe (the common carp, for example) are regarded as "trash," or undesirable, in Canada, and exist in large numbers in lakes and rivers across the Canadian Prairies. The arctic char, plentiful in the far north, is also prized for its taste.

Fly fishing is one of Canada's most popular sports and is superbly supported by 37 national parks, each containing plentiful rivers and lakes.

Salmon migrating upriver provide an annual challenge for the keen sport fisherman. Canada has half the freshwater in the world, but deep sea angling can also prove rewarding.

THE ROCKY MOUNTAINS

The Rocky Mountains begin in the foothills of western Alberta and rise into British Columbia. Along with the Columbia Mountains and the coastal mountains, they form a unique environment that ranges from heavily forested lower slopes, through alpine meadows, to snow-covered rocky peaks. This habitat is home to some of the most majestic wildlife in Canada.

THE CANADIAN ARCTIC

North of the 60th parallel of latitude, the forest yields to arctic tundra and rock. The tundra is mostly bare, and frozen year-round a few inches below the surface, the icy ground being known as permafrost. During the brief summer the top layer thaws, and the Arctic bursts into bloom. Even though the Arctic is a freezing desert with little moisture, wildlife flourishes.

The recurving horns of a mature male bighorn sheep, found in more remote spots of the Rockies, weigh as much as all its bones put together.

The great white polar bear spends most of its life alone, out on the polar ice-pack, hunting for seals.

Canada's grizzly bear stands up to 2.75 m (8.8 ft) high and weighs up to 350 kg (800 lbs). It feeds on roots, berries, and meat.

The caribou is a North American cousin of the reindeer. Caribou in the arctic migrate with the season in herds of 10,000, heading north on to the tundra in spring, south into the forest during winter.

Multicultural Canada

CANADA PRIDES ITSELF on its multiculturalism. The country has evolved a unique way of adjusting to the cultural needs of its increasingly diverse population. In contrast to the US's "melting pot," Canada has opted for what is often called the "Canadian mosaic," a model based on accepting diversity rather than assimilation. The origins of this tolerant and fruitful approach are embedded deep in Canadian history. Fearful of attack by the US in 1793, the British safeguarded the religious and civic institutions of their French-Canadian subjects in the hope that they would not ally with the Americans. This policy set the pattern of compromise that is now a hallmark of Canada. Citizens of British and French ancestry still make up the bulk of the population of 30 million, but there are around 60 significant minorities.

Young Inuit people in traditional dress huddled against the snow

NATIVE CANADIANS

TODAY THERE are approximately one million Native Canadians, though national census figures usually break this group down into three sub-sections – aboriginals (750,000), métis (Indian and French mixed race 200,000), and Inuit (50,000). Of the million, about 60 percent are known as Status Indians, which means they are officially settled on reserve land. However, over 40 percent of Status Indians now live away from reserve land, and only 900 of Canada's 2,370 reserves are still inhabited. These lands are home to 608 First Nations groups, or bands, which exercise varying degrees of self-government through their own elected councils. Since the 1970s, progressive councils have played a key role in the reinvigoration of traditional

native culture. Most non-Status Native Canadians are now integrated within the rest of Canada's population.

Rarely is the membership of a reserve descended from just one tribe. The largest band is the Six Nations of the Grand River, in Ontario, where the 19,000 inhabitants are made up of of 13 groups including the Mohawks, Delaware, and Seneca peoples.

In the far north, where white settlers have always been rare, the Inuit have a small majority. A recent result of their self-determination was the creation of Nunavut, a semi-autonomous Inuit homeland comprising 349,650 sq km (135,000 sq miles) of the eastern Arctic, created officially in April, 1999. Nunavut means "our land" in the Inuit language, and traditional skills of hunting and igloo-building are being reintroduced to this new region.

BRITISH AND IRISH CANADIANS

CANADIANS OF British and Irish descent constitute about 60 percent of the country's population. The first English settlers arrived in the wake of the fleets that fished the waters off Newfoundland in the 16th century. Thereafter, there was a steady trickle of English, Scottish, Welsh, and Irish immigrants and several mass migrations, prompted either by adverse politics at home or fresh opportunities in Canada. Thousands of Scots arrived following the defeat of Bonnie Prince Charlie at Culloden in 1746, and the Irish poured across the Atlantic during and after the potato famine (1845–49). When the Prairie provinces opened up in the 1880s and at the end of both World Wars another large-scale migration took place.

These British and Irish settlers did much to shape Canada, establishing its social and cultural norms and founding its legal and political institutions. Canada's official Head of State is still the British monarch.

British poster of the 1920s promoting emigration to Canada

FRENCH CANADIANS

CANADA'S French-speakers make up about 25 percent of the total population, and are the country's second largest ethnic group. They are mainly based in just one of the 10 provinces, Quebec, but other pockets thrive in other provinces. The French first reached the Canadian mainland in 1535 when Jacques Cartier sailed up the St. Lawrence River in search of a sea-route to Asia. Fur-traders, priests, and farmers followed in Cartier's footsteps and by the end of the 17th century, New France, as the colony was known, was well established. After the British captured New France in the Seven Years' War of 1756–63 *(see pp42–3)*, most French colonists stayed on as British subjects. The French-speakers maintained their own religious and civic institutions and a feeling of independence that has grown over time. Since the 1960s, the constitutional link between Quebec and the rest of the country has been the subject of political debate, with a strong minority of Quebecois pressing for full independence *(see p51)*.

GERMAN CANADIANS

A LTHOUGH THERE have been German-speakers in Canada since the 1660s, the first major migration came between 1850–1900, with other mass arrivals following both World Wars. On the whole, the English-speaking majority has absorbed the Germans, but distinctive pockets of German-speakers hold strong today in **German beer** Lunenburg, Nova **stein** Scotia *(see p84)*, and Kitchener-Waterloo in Ontario *(see p216)*. The rural communities surrounding Kitchener-Waterloo are strongholds of the Amish, a German-speaking religious sect, whose members shun the trappings of modern life and travel around on horse-drawn buggies wearing traditional homemade clothes.

German food and drink, especially its beer-making techniques, have added to Canadian cuisine. Ethnic restaurants in German areas still run on traditional lines.

Street scene in Chinatown, Toronto

ITALIAN CANADIANS

T HE WIDESPREAD Italian presence in Canada can prove hard to see, as, for the most part, all 600,000 immigrants have merged almost seamlessly with the English speakers. There are, however, exceptions; in Toronto, a large and flourishing "Little Italy" neighborhood delights both visitors and the city's epicurean residents. The first major influx of Italian Canadians came in the wake of the civil wars that disrupted Italy in the second half of the 19th century; another wave arrived in the 1940s and 1950s after World War II. Immigration continues into the 21st century, with two percent of Canadians today speaking Italian as their first language.

CHINESE CANADIANS

D URING THE 1850s, Chinese laborers arrived in Canada to work in the gold fields of British Columbia. Thereafter, they played a key role in the construction of the railroads, settling new towns and cities as their work progressed eastward. During this period the Chinese suffered much brutal racism, including laws that enforced statutory discrimination.

A flood of Chinese immigration took place just before the return of Hong Kong to China by the British in 1997. Most settlers chose Toronto, Montreal, and Vancouver, but recently British Columbia has gained popularity. With the Chinese focus on keeping large families together, most new arrivals today aim for an established community. About half of all Canada's new immigrants today come from Asia. Over two percent of the Canadian population claimed Chinese as their first language in the late 1990s.

UKRAINIAN CANADIANS

A LTHOUGH Ukrainians are a small fraction of the Canadian population, numbering less than three percent, they have had a strong cultural influence, especially in the Prairie Provinces where the cupolas of their churches rise above many midwestern villages. The first major wave of Ukrainian migrants arrived in the 1890s as refugees from Tsarist persecution. The Soviet regime and the aftermath of World War II caused a second influx in the 20th century.

Woman in native Ukrainian dress in Battleford, Saskatchewan

French Canada

"Free Quebec" demonstrator

MANY CANADIANS are quick to point out that Canada's origins are more French than British, that the first European Canadians were explorers from France, and therefore called *canadiens*. French Canadians have had a centuries-long history of conquest and battle to preserve their language and culture, strongest in Quebec and parts of Atlantic Canada. This has left large parts of the country with a French cultural base that lives on in language, religion, and the arts. More recently, the French-Canadian struggle for recognition in the 20th century has left unresolved the issue of Quebec's independence.

The heart of French Canada is Quebec, a province many times the size of France. Here, 85 percent of people count French as their mother tongue. French is not just the language of food, folklore, and love; it is also the language of business, government, and law.

European counterparts. Traditional food is rich and hearty. Meat pies are a specialty: *cipaille* comprizes layers of game meat under a flaky crust, and the more common *tortière* has a filling made of ground beef spiced with cloves. Salmon pie, stews made with pigs' feet, and meatballs in a rich gravy are also typical. Desserts are rich; the Acadian *tarte au sucre* (sugar pie) is popular, as well as *pudding au chomeur* (literally "unemployed pudding"), an upside-down cake with a sweet, caramelized base of sugar baked into a rich batter.

Musician Felix Leclerc, guardian of the folk music of Quebec

LANGUAGE

FRENCH IS the joint official language of Canada, but it has mutated in much the same way that North American English has. *Canadiens*, especially those in the bigger cities, have adopted some anglicisms; modern English words relating to industries and trades introduced by English-speakers are favorites. Conversely, some words that have passed out of fashion in France survive here; Canada is one of the few places where a cart remains a *charette*, for example, instead of a *tombereau*, and the *fin-de-semaine* is the time to get away for some relaxation, rather than the now-universal *le weekend*. Young Quebecois in particular are also far more free in using the informal *tu*, than more formal *vous*, than their parents would perhaps consider polite.

Wide varieties exist in the quality and style of French spoken. The Paris-influenced intonation of Montreal's college-educated *haute bourgeoisie*, for example, is quite distinct from the rhythmic

gutturals of the Acadian fishermen of the Maritimes. Residents of Quebec's Saguenay-Lac-Saint-Jean region speak a hard, clear French that must sound very like that of their Norman forbears.

Over the years Quebecois have evolved a dialect called *joual*, which is informal, slangy, and peppered with anglicisms. It is also very colorful and viewed with a mix of pride and disdain. The accent may be hard for foreigners to follow.

FOOD

CANADIENS HAVE always considered themselves the epicures of Canada, and with some justice, enjoying the delights of the table more passionately than their northern

Sugar pie, a traditional Acadian family dessert, served at celebrations

MUSIC

CHANSONIERS are the troubadours of French Canada. Rooted in the traditional music of the first settlers, their haunting songs and simple melodies, such as the ballads of Felix Leclerc, might be melancholy or upbeat, but they are almost always romantic. These folk songs, accompanied by guitar, usually reflect optimism and a deep love for the land. Quebec *chansonier* Gilles Vigneault's *Mon Pays* has become a nationalist anthem for those seeking independence. Of course, French music is not confined to the traditional; there are several successful rock, pop, and independent bands. Acadia's singers are often *chansonières*, including Edith Butler and Angèle Arseneault vividly evoking the sadness and joy of life by the sea.

Traditional Catholic church in Chéticamp, Cape Breton Island

FAITH

THE FIRST FRENCH settlers were Roman Catholic, many very devout and zealous. The founders of Montreal, Paul Chomédy Sieur de Maisonneuve and Jeanne Mance, had hoped to create a new society based on Christian principles. Much of that devotion has evaporated in the modern age, especially in Quebec, which has one of the lowest church-attendance records in the country. Past fidelity has, however, left permanent monuments. Tiny French villages in Quebec and New Brunswick often have huge, stone churches with glittering tin roofs, gilding, and ornate interiors. Some parish churches in Montreal, like the magnificent Basilique Notre-Dame-de-Montréal *(see pp108–9)*, would pass for cathedrals in US cities.

NATIONALISM

THERE HAS been a nationalist strain to most *canadien* aspirations since the founding of Modern Canada. Quebecois entered the 1867 Canadian Confederation *(see p44)* only because French leaders persuaded them that the deal would preserve their faith and language. The 1960s and 1970s took the campaign into a new phase, with the aim being the independence of Quebec, as the politics of mere survival rose to the politics of assertiveness (with French President Charles de Gaulle adding his rallying cry *"Vive le Québec – libre!"* in 1966). Acadians in New Brunswick gained real political power to preserve their unique heritage, Franco-Ontarians fought for control over their own schools, and Manitobans used the courts to force their provincial government to translate all Manitoba statutes into French.

This resurgence of national pride was felt most strongly in Quebec, where the charismatic and popular politician René Lévesque and his Parti-Québecois won the provincial election in 1976 and made outright separatism respectable. The party now regularly wins local elections and has so far held two referenda on independence. Both times Quebecois said no by the narrowest of margins, but the threat still dominates Canada's political life.

SYMBOLS

THE QUEBEC FLAG has a white cross on a blue background with a white Bourbon lily in each quarter. Acadians have created their own flag by adding a gold star to the French tricolor, which symbolizes *Stella Maris* (Star of the Sea), named after the Virgin Mary. The patron saint of French Canada is St. Jean-Baptiste (St. John the Baptist); parades and parties mark his feast day on June 24. The celebrations take on a strongly nationalist style in Quebec, where the big day is called the *Fête National*. The provincial bird of Quebec is the snowy owl, and the flower remains the white lily, both of which flourish in the province.

Quebec flag with Bourbon lilies

Demonstrators during referendum vote for independence of Quebec

Native Canadians

MOST ARCHAEOLOGISTS believe that the first inhabitants of North America crossed from Siberia to Alaska around 25,000 years ago. These hunter-nomads came in search of mammoth and bison, the ice-age animals that constituted their basic diet. The first wave of migrants was reinforced by a steady trickle of Siberian peoples over the next 15,000 years, and slowly the tribes worked their way east and south until they reached the Atlantic and South America. Over the centuries, the descendants of these hunter-nomads evolved a wide range of cultures, which were shaped by their particular environment. In the icy north or across the barren wastes of Newfoundland, life was austere; but the fertile soils of Ontario and the fish-rich shores of British Columbia nourished sophisticated societies based on fishing and farming.

Native mask from Vancouver

Europeans began to arrive *in numbers during the 17th century. In Newfoundland, the first part of Canada settled by whites, interracial relations were initially cordial but soured when new settlers encroached on ancient hunting grounds. In a pattern repeated across the continent, the native peoples, many dying from European diseases, were driven to inhospitable lands.*

THE IROQUOIS

Spread along the St. Lawrence River and the shores of the Great Lakes, were the Iroquois-speaking tribes, among whom were the Mohawks, the Huron, and the Seneca. These tribes hunted and fished, but they also cultivated beans, pumpkins, squash, and corn, growing everything in abundance for a year-round food supply. This enabled them to live in large villages, often with several hundred inhabitants. Their traditional dwelling was the longhouse, built of cedar poles bent to form a protective arch and covered with bark. These settlements were all surrounded by high palisades made of sharpened wooden stakes, a necessary precaution as warfare between the tribes was endemic.

Cornplanter, a 17th-century chief of the Seneca tribe

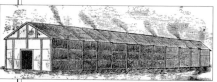

An Iroquois-built longhouse

THE PLAINS PEOPLES

War was also commonplace on the plains of southern Manitoba and Saskatchewan, where the majority Blackfoot tribe was totally reliant on the buffalo: they ate the meat, used the hide for clothes and tents, and filed the bones into tools. The first Blackfoot hunted the buffalo by means of cleverly conceived traps, herding the animals and stampeding them off steep cliffs *(see p294)*. Originally, the horse was unknown to the

Indians on horseback hunting buffalo with arrows

native peoples of the Americas – their largest beast of burden was the dog – but the Spanish conquistadores brought the horse with them when they colonized South America in the 1500s. Thereafter, horses were slowly traded north until they reached the Canadian plains. The arrival of the horse transformed Blackfoot life: it made the buffalo easy to hunt and, with a consistent food supply now assured, the tribe developed a militaristic culture, focusing particularly on the valor of their young men – the "braves."

A Blackfoot camp, showing traditional homes

PEOPLES OF THE PACIFIC COAST

The native peoples of the Pacific Coast were divided into a large number of small tribes such as the Tlingit and the Salish. The ocean was an abundant source of food; with this necessity taken care of, they developed an elaborate ceremonial life featuring large and lively feasts, the potlachs, in which clans tried to outdo each other with the magnificence of their gifts. The peoples of this region were also superb woodcarvers, their most celebrated works of art being totem poles. Each pole featured a myth from the tribe's religion; magical birds and beasts mix with semi-human figures to tell a story in carved panels rising up the pole.

Totem pole in Stanley Park

Sqylax tribal celebration in British Columbia

TERMINOLOGY

For many Canadians, the words "Eskimo" and "Red Indian" or just "Indian" are unacceptable. They are seen as terms of abuse, as they hark back to times when whites dominated the country and crushed its original population. The word "Eskimo" has been replaced by "Inuit," but modern substitutes for "Indian" are not as clear-cut. Some people choose "aboriginal" or "native," others prefer "indigenous," or speak of Canada's "First Nations." All are accept-able, and the simple rule, if in doubt, is to ask which word is preferred as this is a sensitive issue.

THE INUIT AND THE PEOPLES OF THE NORTHERN FORESTS

Stretching in a band from Alaska to Greenland, the far north was home to the Inuit, nomadic hunters who lived in skin tents in the summer and igloos in the winter. Arctic conditions and limited food supply meant that they foraged in small family groups and gathered together only in special circumstances – during the annual caribou migration, for instance. To the south of the Inuit, and also wide-spread across modern-day Canada, were the tribes of the northern forest, including the Naskapi, the Chipewyan, and the Wood Cree. These tribes were also nomadic hunters, dependent on fish and seal, or deer and moose. Successful hunters earned prestige, and the tribal priest (shaman) was expected to keep the spirit world bene-volent, but there was little other social organization.

An Inuit hunter by his igloo home

Inuit in Caribou parka, checking his harpoon

Paul Okalik, Nunavut's first Premier, at his inauguration

NATIVE CANADIAN ISSUES

Since the 1960s, Canada's native peoples have recovered some of their self-confidence. A key development was the creation of the Assembly of First Nations (AFN), an intertribal organization that has become an influential player on the national scene. In the 1980s, the AFN successfully argued for a greater degree of self-government on the reservations and tackled the federal gov-ernment on land rights, sponsoring a series of court cases that highlighted the ways the native population had been stripped of its territories. The AFN was also involved in the establish-ment of Nunavut (see p51), the new homeland for the Inuit created in 1999 from part of the former Northwest Territories. By comparison with their white compatriots, Canada's native population remains, nonetheless, poor and disadvantaged. The rectification of historic wrongs will take decades, even assuming that the political will remains strong enough to improve matters.

Art in Canada

INUIT AND OTHER First Nations groups have produced art in Canada since prehistoric times: the Inuit carved wood or antler sculptures, and other native groups were responsible for works from rock paintings to richly decorated pottery. Early European immigrants, both French and English, generally eschewed native traditions and followed European forms. Throughout the 19th and early 20th centuries, artists traveled, to Paris, London, and New York to study European art. It was in the 1900s that painters sought to develop a distinctly national style. However, one consistent subject of Canadian painting is the country itself: a preoccupation with its lush forests, stately landscapes, and expanse of freezing northern wilderness. Today, Canadian art reflects a wide range of art movements, with native art in particular fetching high prices among collectors.

(1855–1936) and Ozias Leduc (1855–1964) were the first artists to learn their craft in Canada. Watson said, "I did not know enough to have Paris or Rome in mind. ... I felt Toronto had all I needed." His canvases portray Ontarian domestic scenes.

After Confederation in 1867, the Royal Canadian Academy of Arts and the National Gallery of Canada were founded in 1883. Artists could now train at home, but many still left to study in Paris. Curtis Williamson (1867–1944) and Edmund Morris (1871–1913) returned from France determined to revitalize their tired national art. They formed the Canadian Art Club in 1907, where new schools such as Impressionism were shown. James Wilson Morrice (1865–1924), Maurice Cullen (1866–1934), and Marc Aurèle de Foy Suzor-Coté (1869–1937) were key figures in this move toward modernity.

On the Saint Lawrence (1897) oil painting by Maurice Cullen

PAINTERS IN THE NEW WORLD

IN THE 1600s French settlers in Canada either imported religious paintings or commissioned stock subjects to adorn their new churches. Only Samuel de Champlain, the "Father of New France" *(see p41)*, stands out for his sketches of the Huron tribe. After the English conquest in the 1760s, art moved from religion to matters of politics, the land, and the people. Army officers, such as Thomas Davies (1737–1812), painted fine detailed works, conveying their love of the landscape. Artists such as Robert Field (1769–1819), trained in Neo-Classicism, which was prevalent in Europe at the time,

and became very popular, as did Quebec painters Antoine Plamondon (1817–95) and Théophile Hamel (1817–70). Cornelius Krieghoff (1815–72) settled in Quebec and was famous for his snow scenes of both settlers and natives. His contemporary, Paul Kane (1810–71), recorded the lives of the First Nations on an epic journey across Canada. He then completed over 100 sketches and paintings, of which *Mah Min*, or *The Feather*, (c.1856) is one of the most impressive *(see p36)*. During the 19th century, painters focused on the Canadian landscape. Homer Watson

MODERN PAINTERS

THE INFLUENCE OF European art was criticized by perhaps the most influential set of Canadian artists, the Group of Seven *(see pp160–61)*. Before World War I, Toronto artists had objected to the lack of a national identity in art. By the 1920s the Group had defined Canadian painting in their boldly colored landscapes, such as A.Y. Jackson's *Terre Sauvage* (1913). Despite his early death, painter Tom Thomson was a founding influence. Three painters who came to prominence in the 1930s were influenced by the Group but followed highly individual muses, each of the artists were distinguished by a passion for their own province; David Milne (1882–1953), known for his still lifes, LeMoine Fitzgerald (1890–1956) for his domestic and backyard scenes, and Emily Carr (1871–1945) *(see p280)*

Lawren S. Harris, painter (1885–1970)

Skidegate, Graham Island, BC, **(1928) a later work by Emily Carr**

for her striking depiction of the west coast Salish people and their totem poles. Carr was the first woman artist to achieve high regard. A writer as well as painter, her poem *Renfrew* (1929), describes her intense relationship with nature, which was reflected in her paintings: "... in the distance receding plane after plane... cold greens, gnarled stump of gray and brown."

The strong influence of the Group of Seven provoked a reaction among successive generations of painters. John Lyman (1866–1945) rejected the group's rugged nationalism. Inspired by Matisse, he moved away from using land as the dominant subject of painting. Lyman set up the Contemporary Arts Society in Montreal and promoted new art between 1939–48; even Surrealism reached the city.

Since World War II there has been an explosion of new forms based upon abstraction. In Montreal, Paul-Emile Borduas (1905–60) and two colleagues formed the Automatists, whose inspirations were Surrealism and Abstract Impressionism. By the 1950s Canadian painters achieved international acclaim. Postwar trends were also taken up in Toronto where The Painters Eleven produced abstract paintings. Today, artists work across the range of contemporary art movements, incorporating influences from around the world and from Canada's cultural mosaic. Experimental work by painters such as Jack Bush, Greg Carnoe, and Joyce

Wieland continues strongly in the wake of ideas from the 1960s. Canada now boasts a plethora of public and private galleries, and exceptional collections of 20th-century art.

ABORIGINAL ART

THE ART OF the Inuit *(see pp324–5)* and the Northwest First Nations is highly valued in Canada. Prehistoric Inuit finds reveal beautiful objects, from sculpted figurines to carved harpoon heads, which were largely created for religious use. With the coming of the Europeans the Inuit quickly adapted their artistic skills to make objects for sale such as sculptures made from ivory, bone, and stone. Today, Inuit artists such as Aqghadluk, Qaqaq Ashoona, and Tommy Ashevak are noted for their contribution to contemporary Canadian art, especially their sculpture and

Robert Murray's *Sculpture*

The celebrated Haida sculptor Bill Reid

wallhangings. The sculpture of the Northwest coast First Nations people is known worldwide, particularly the cedar-wood carvings of Haida artist Bill Reid, the totem poles of Richard Krentz, and the Kwa Gulth Big House at Fort Rupert by Chief Tony Hunt.

Painters such as Norval Morisseau, Carl Ray, and Daphne Odjig cover a range of styles, from realism to abstract work. Native art celebrates the culture of its people, from their legendary survival skills, tales and myths, to their land and the fight for its preservation.

SCULPTURE

EUROPEAN SCULPTURE arrived in Canada with the French who created sacred figures to adorn their churches. Sculptors such as Louis Quévillon (1749–1832) carved decorative altarpieces as well as fine marble statues in Montreal. European traditions continued to dominate through the 19th century, and it was not until the 20th century that Canada's new cities began to require civic monuments. The façade of the Quebec Parliament was designed by Louis-Phillipe Hébert (1850–1917).

Native subjects were incorporated into much 20th-century sculpture, as were European styles including Art Nouveau and Art Deco. Since the 1960s, sculptors such as Armand Vaillancourt (b.1932) and Robert Murray (b.1936) have sought to develop a Canadian style. Modern materials and the influence of conceptual art inform the work of such current artists as Michael Snow. Their work can be seen not just in museums but also in new commercial and civic buildings.

Literature and Music in Canada

As the Canadian poet the Reverend Edward Hartley Dewart wrote in 1864, "A national literature is an essential element in the formation of a national character." Much Canadian literature and music is concerned with defining a national consciousness but also reflects the cultural diversity of the country. Both English and French speakers have absorbed a variety of influences from the US, Britain, and France, as well as from the other nations whose immigrants make up the population. The Europeans' relationship with First Nations peoples has also affected the style and content of much Canadian fiction and poetry, as have the often harsh realities of living in a land of vast wilderness.

Stars of the popular 1934 film *Anne of Green Gables*

New Beginnings

Much of the earliest writing in Canada (between the mid-1500s and 1700s) was by explorers, fur traders, soldiers, and missionaries. French lawyer Marc Lescarbot's *Histoire de La Nouvelle France* (1609) is an early example of pioneer commentary and is a lively record of his adventures in Nova Scotia. After the English conquest of 1760, New France was subdued, but by the 19th century, French poets began producing patriotic poems such as *Le Vieux Soldat* (1855) by Octave Cremazie (1827–79), sparking a renaissance of poetry that continues today.

English writing was concerned with man's struggle with nature and life in the new world. *Roughing it in the Bush* (1852) by Mrs. Moodie is a tale of struggles in isolated northern Ontario. British Columbia was the last region to be settled, and a captivating memoir is *A Pioneer Gentlewoman in British Columbia: the recollections of Susan Allison* (1876). Allison came from England to teach in the town of Hope and was the first European woman to make the dangerous journey across the Hope Mountains on horseback. Much 19th-century Canadian fiction romanticizes the past, such as William Kirby's (1817–1906) *Golden Dog* (1877), with its idealized view of 18th-century Quebec. Epic novels of the time focused on native lives and cultures, notably *Wacousta* (1832) by John Richardson (1796–1852). Archibald Stansfield Belaney (1888–1938) took on a new identity as an Ojibway

native named Grey Owl *(see p248)*, producing some of Canada's best-loved literature. *Pilgrims of the Wild* (1935) tells of his journey into Quebec to find sanctuary for the over-hunted beaver. *The Adventures of Sajo and her Beaver People* and *Tales of an Empty Cabin* (1935–6) are laments for the wild and lost traditions.

Classics of the early 1900s deal with domesticity. These include *Anne of Green Gables* (1908) by L.M. Montgomery (1874–1942). Humorous writing was led by Stephen Leacock *(see p216)*, and Thomas Chandler Haliburton (1796–1865), a judge who created Sam Slick, narrator of *The Clockmaker* (1876). Painter Emily Carr's *A House of all Sorts* (1944) describes her days as a landlady.

Poetry

Early English language poets Standish O'Grady (1793–1843) and Alexander McLachan (1818–76) wrote verse that reflected a colonial point of view. The genre looked critically at an iniquitous motherland (England), while praising the opportunities available in the New World. Creators of a "new" Canadian poetry in the 1870s and 80s used detailed descriptions of landscape to highlight man's efforts to conquer nature. Two notable authors were Charles Mair (1838–1927) and Isabella Velancey Crawford (1850–1887). By the 20th century the idea of the wilderness stayed at the center of Canadian poetry but was written

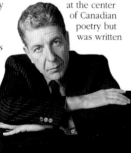

Internationally renowned poet and songwriter, Leonard Cohen

in a sparer style that mirrored the starkness of the Group of Seven's landscape paintings (*see pp160–1*). Robert Service's (1874–1958) popular ballads deal with history, and he is noted for his gold rush poems such as *The Spell of the Yukon* (1907) and the later *Rhymes of a Roughneck* (1950). John McCrae (1872–1918) wrote one of the most famous World War I poems *In Flanders Fields* (1915).

Modern English and French poetry now has a worldwide audience, with writers such as Anne Wilkinson, Irving Layton, Earle Birney, E.J. Pratt, Leonard Cohen, and Patrick Anderson, whose *Poem on Canada* (1946) looks at the impact of nature on European mentalities. The simple power of French writer Anne Hèbert's poems, such as *Le Tombeau des Rois* (The Kings' Tombs) (1953) focuses on the universal themes of childhood, memory, and death. A postwar boom in poetry and fiction was fostered by the Canada Council for the Arts.

Canadian poet Robert Service in 1942

NATIVE CANADIAN WRITING

DESPITE A powerful oral tradition – where stories are both owned and passed down through families and clans – autobiography, children's books, plays, short stories, poetry, essays, and novels have been produced by Canadian native writers since the 19th century. One of the most popular autobiographies of this period was written by Ojibway native George Copway (1818–69). Titled *The Life, History, and Travels of Kah-ge-ga-ga-bowh* (1847), it had six editions in a year. The first book to be published by a native woman is thought to be *Cogewea, The Half-Blood* (1927), by Okanagan

author Mourning Dove (1888–1936). Another Okanagan novelist, Jeanette Armstrong (b.1948), published *Slash* in 1985. The struggles of a Métis woman in modern Canada are described in the best-selling autobiography of Maria Campbell in *Halfbreed* (1973).

A mix of legend and political campaigning for native rights informs much aboriginal fiction, such as Pauline Johnson's *The White Wampum* (1895) and Beatrice Culleton's *In Search of April Raintree* (1983). The first Inuit work in English was *Harpoon of the Hunter* (1970), a story of coming of age in the northern Arctic by Markoosie (b.1942). One of Canada's top contemporary playwrights is Cree author Thompson Highway (b.1951), whose plays deal with the harsh reality of life on the reservations.

MODERN FICTION

SINCE THE 1940s, many Canadian writers have achieved international fame. Margaret Atwood (b.1939) for her poetry, novels, and criticism, while Carol Shields (b.1935) won the prestigious British Booker Prize for *The Stone Diaries* in 1996. Mordecai Richler (b.1931) and Robertson Davies (1913–95) are noted for their wry take on contemporary Canadian society. Many authors have reached a wider public through having their books adapted for the big screen. Gabrielle Roy's *Bonheur d'Occasion* (1945) became the 1982 movie *The Tin Flute*; a novel by W.P. Kinsella, *Shoeless Joe* (1982), became *Field of Dreams* starring Kevin

Michael Ondaatje, Oscar-winning author of *The English Patient*

Costner in 1989, and Michael Ondaatje's 1996 *The English Patient* won nine Oscars. There is a strong tradition of short-story writing, one master being Alice Munro (b.1931). Popular history is highly regarded; noted author Pierre Berton has written 40 books on the nation's history.

MUSIC IN CANADA

SOME OF THE biggest names in the music industry are Canadian. A strong tradition of folk and soft rock has produced such artists as Leonard Cohen, Kate and Anna McGarrigle, Joni Mitchell, and Neil Young. A new generation of singer/songwriters that have continued the tradition of reflective, melodic hits include Alanis Morissette and k.d. lang; and the Cowboy Junkies and Shania Twain play new styles of country music. Superstars such as Celine Dion and Bryan Adams have made a huge impact in Europe and the US. In the classical sphere, orchestras such as the Montréal Orchestre Symphonique are world famous, as was the pianist Glenn Gould. Jazz is represented by the pianist Oscar Peterson, and every year Montreal hosts one of the world's most famous festivals.

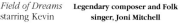

Legendary composer and Folk singer, Joni Mitchell

Sports in Canada

CANADIANS ARE avid sports fans, and most of the country's cities and towns offer visitors a chance to see year-round sports entertainment. Although the official national game is lacrosse – a First Nations game in which the ball is caught and tossed in a leather cradle on a stick – Canadians reserve their strongest enthusiasm for ice hockey. Baseball and Canadian football (similar to the US game) are also big crowd-pullers. Major cities regularly attract international stars to world-class racing, golf, and tennis tournaments. Even small towns provide the chance to watch minor professionals, amateurs, and student athletes. For visitors who prefer participating in sports, Canada offers a broad choice of activities from skiing to golf, fishing, and hiking.

National ice hockey heroes in action during a league game

ICE HOCKEY

THE POPULARITY of ice hockey in Canada knows no bounds. Every town has a rink, and every school, college, and university a team. The North American **National Hockey League** (NHL) was founded in 1917, and its principal prize, the Stanley Cup, was instituted in 1892 by Canadian Govenor General, Lord Stanley. Today, the league has 28 teams, five of which belong to Canadian cities; the Montreal Canadiens, Calgary Flames, Edmonton Oilers, Toronto Maple Leafs, and the Vancouver Canucks. The Quebec Nordiques and Winnipeg Jets are now based in the US. Although most of the players in both the US and Canada are Canadian, recent years have seen an influx of other nationalities such as Russian, American,

and Swedish atheletes playing for the top teams. Renowned for its toughness, the game usually involves a skirmish or two among the players, which often means that this 60-minute game can last up to three hours. The season runs from October to April when the play-offs for the Stanley Cup are held. Hockey stars such as Wayne Gretzky are national icons. He retired in 1999 after 20 years in the game, having captured 61 NHL scoring records.

Tickets to the major games can be hard to come by, and should be booked in advance. It is a good idea to contact the club's ticket lines, or book through **Ticketmaster**. Minor league and college games are easier to get into, and the University of Toronto and York, Concordia in Montreal, and the University of Alberta in Edmonton all have good teams. Tickets can be bought from the local playing field, or direct from the administration center, and are usually a great bargain.

BASEBALL

ALTHOUGH baseball is seen as an American sport, the game has a large following in Canada. There are two teams that play in the US's two major leagues; the well-known **Toronto Blue Jays**, who won the World Series in 1992 and 1993, and the **Montreal Expos**, who became the first Canadian team to play in a US league in 1968. Baseball is played in the summer, and the season lasts from April to September (with play-offs through October) and can be a great family day out, with its beer, popcorn, and sunshine accompaniment.

The teams play their American league rivals in two outstanding stadiums; the Jays in Toronto's SkyDome, an architectural marvel with a roof that opens and closes depending on the weather (see p169), and the Expos in Montreal's Olympic Stadium (see pp120–21). Tickets have to be booked well in advance, and it is easier to obtain them for the Montreal Expos than it is for the Jays. Seeing one of the minor league teams such as the Edmonton Trappers is also fun.

Jose Canseco from the Toronto Blue Jays steps up to the plate

FOOTBALL

T HE CANADIAN version of football (not soccer) is noted for being a more exciting version of American football. Although the best Canadian players tend to move to the US for higher salaries, the game still attracts substantial home audiences. The Canadian Football League has two divisions of four teams who each play over the July to November season.

The games tend to attract a lively family crowd and are fun, especially around the Grey Cup final. Played on the last Sunday of November, the game is preceded by a week of festivities and a big parade in the host city. Football is also played at most universities, where a Saturday afternoon game makes for an entertaining excursion. The annual college championship game is called the Vanier Cup and is played at Toronto's Skydome at the beginning of December. Tickets are relatively easy to come by and are reasonably priced.

BASKETBALL

W HAT ONCE was an American passion has now spread around the world to become one of the fastest growing international sports. The game was invented in the United States by a Canadian, Dr. James Naismith, and now enjoys huge popularity in his homeland. The **Toronto Raptors** and **Vancouver Grizzlies** both play in the National Basketball Association, the top professional league in the world, against the likes of the Chicago Bulls, Boston Celtics, Los Angeles Lakers, and New York Knicks. The season lasts from October until late spring, and it is well worth a visit to Vancouver's GM Place or Toronto's Air Canada Centre to watch a game. Most of Canada's universities have teams, and although crowds tend to be smaller than those drawn by the professionals, the competition is fierce and the atmosphere exhilarating, especially during the annual national championship tournament played in Halifax each March.

Toronto Raptors versus the L.A. Lakers basketball match

GOLF

C ANADA HOSTS two major tournaments each year (both in September), which draw large crowds of spectators, as well as the world's greatest players. The biggest is the Canadian Open, usually played at Toronto's Glen Abbey on a course designed by Jack Nicklaus. The annual Greater Vancouver Open is a regular stop on the Professional Golfers' Association tour, although the field is not as strong as that of the Open.

Golf is an immensely popular participation sport, with over 1,700 beautiful courses across the country, from the Banff Springs course in the west to the many rolling fairways of Prince Edward Island in the east.

WINTER SPORTS

F AMOUS FOR the plentiful snow and sunshine of its cold winters, Canada is one of the top places both to watch and participate in winter sports. Canadian resorts are less crowded than their European counterparts, and are set among some of the most dramatic scenery in the

world. Visitors can enjoy a range of options in resorts across the country, from Whistler in the Rockies to Mont Ste-Anne in Quebec. As well as downhill skiing, it is also possible to try snowboarding, snowmobiling, dogsledding, or even heli-skiing on pristine snow (see p387).

see p387

DIRECTORY

National Hockey League
11th Floor, 50 Bay Street, Toronto.
((416) 408 4846.

Ticketmaster
(for hockey games)
((416) 870 8000.

Baseball
Toronto Blue Jays
(*Tickets: (416) 341 1234.*
Montreal Expos
((514) 790 1245.

Football
Canadian Football League
110 Eglinton Avenue W. Toronto
((416) 322 9650.

Basketball
Toronto Raptors
(*Tickets: (416) 815 5600.*
Vancouver Grizzlies
(*Tickets: (604) 899 4667.*

Golf
Royal Canadian Golf Association
((905) 849 9700.

Snowboarder descending a slope at speed in powder snow

CANADA THROUGH THE YEAR

SEASONAL CHANGES IN Canada vary greatly across the country, but in general it is safe to say that the winters are long and cold and run from November to March, while spring and fall tend to be mild. British Columbia is the most temperate zone, with an average temperature of 5°C (40°F) in January. July and August are reliably warm and sunny in most places, even the far north, and

Native powwow in Calgary

most outdoor festivals tend to be held in the summer months. There are plenty of events held during winter, both indoors and out, some of which celebrate Canadians' ability to get the best out of the icy weather, especially activities such as dogsledding, snowmobiling, and ice-skating. A range of cultural events reflect the country's history, as well as its diverse peoples and culture.

SPRING

MARCH AND APRIL bring the country some of its most unpredictable weather, moving from snow to sunshine in a day. In the north this is a time for welcoming the end of winter, while farther south spring is the start of an array of fun festivals.

Dogsledding at Yellowknife's Caribou Carnival in spring

MARCH

The Caribou Carnival
(late March) Yellowknife. A celebration of the arrival of spring, featuring dogsledding, snowmobiling, and delicious local foods.

APRIL

Toonik Tyme *(mid-April)* Iqaluit. This week-long festival includes igloo building, traditional games, and community feasts.

Okanagan Spring Wine and Food Festival
(last weekend in April) Okanagan Valley. Wine-tastings, vineyard picnics, and orchard tours in horse-drawn carriages *(see p315)*.
Shaw Festival
(April–October) Niagara-on-the-Lake. Theater festival with classic plays by George Bernard Shaw and his contemporaries *(see p206)*.

SUMMER

WARM WEATHER across most of the country means that there is an explosion of festivals, carnivals, and cultural events, from May through August.

MAY

Canadian Tulipfest *(mid-May)* Ottawa. Colorful display of millions of tulips is the centerpiece for a variety of events.
Stratford Festival *(May–November)* Stratford. World famous theater festival featuring a range of plays from Elizabethan to contemporary works *(see p209)*.
Omingmak Frolics (May) Cambridge Bay, Nunavut. Feasts, dance, and games.
Dreamspeakers *(late May)* Edmonton. International celebration of First Nations' culture through art and film.
Shorebirds and Friends' Festival *(late May)* Wadena, Saskatchewan. Features guided bird-watching and tours of wildlife habitats.
Vancouver International Children's Festival *(last weekend in May)* Vancouver. Theater, circus, and music for children ages 3 and up.

JUNE

Grand Prix du Canada *(early June)* Montreal. Major racing stars turn out for North America's only Formula One event.
Midnight Madness *(mid-June)* Inuvik. Celebration of the summer solstice, with parties under the midnight sun.

Vividly colored tulips at Ottawa spring festival, Canadian Tulipfest

Steer wrestling competition in the *Half Million Dollar Rodeo* at Calgary's Exhibition and Stampede

Mosaic – Festival of Cultures *(first weekend in June)* Regina. Cultural events from around the world.

Banff Festival of the Arts *(mid-June to mid-August)* Banff. Two months of opera, music, drama, and dance.

Jazz Fest International *(late June–July)* Victoria. Jazz and blues musicians play in venues all over town.

Red River Exhibition *(late June–July)* Winnipeg. A huge fair with a wide choice of entertainments.

Festival International de Jazz de Montréal *(late June–July)* Montreal. Famous jazz festival with a number of free outdoor concerts.

Nova Scotia International Tattoo *(late June–July)* Halifax. There are 2,000 participants in one of the world's largest indoor shows.

JULY

Folk on the Rocks *(second weekend)* Yellowknife. Inuit drummers, dancers, and throat singers perform here.

Calgary Exhibition and Stampede *(mid-July)* Calgary. Ten-day celebration of all things western, including parades and a major rodeo competition *(see p292).*

Molson Indy *(mid-July)* Toronto. Indy car race held at Exhibition Place.

du Maurier Quebec City Summer Festival *(second week)* Quebec City. Ten days of music and dance.

Just for Laughs Festival *(July 14–25)* Montreal. Twelve-day comedy festival with more than 600 comedians from around the world.

Canadian Open Tennis Championships *(July-Aug)* Montreal. Major tennis tournament that attracts top international stars.

Antigonish Highland Games *(mid-July)* Antigonish. Oldest traditional highland games in North America, with pipe bands and dancing.

Ford race car at the Molson Indy meeting held in Toronto

AUGUST

Royal St. John's Regatta *(Aug 4)* St. John's. Noted as North America's oldest sporting event, features rowing races and a carnival.

Wikwemikong Powwow *(first weekend)* Manitoulin Island. Ojibway native festival with a dancing and drum competition *(see p222).*

Discovery Days Festival *(mid-Aug)* Dawson City. Commemorates gold rush days, with costumed parades and canoe races.

First People's Festival Victoria. *(mid-Aug)* Three days of exhibitions, dancing, and a traditional native gathering known as the potlatch.

Folklorama *(mid-Aug)* Winnipeg. Multicultural festival of food, performance, and the arts.

Victoria Park Arts and Crafts Fair *(mid-Aug)* Moncton. Atlantic Canada's largest outdoor sale of arts, antiques, and crafts.

Festival Acadien de Caraquet *(Aug 5–15)* Caraquet. Celebration of Acadian culture and history.

Halifax International Busker Festival *(second week)* Halifax. The best street entertainers from around the world.

Canadian National Exhibition *(Aug–Sep)* Toronto. Annual fair featuring spectacular air show, concerts, and a casino.

Folkfest *(mid-Aug)* Saskatoon. Saskatchewan's multicultural heritage celebrated in a variety of events.

Showjumping in the Masters equestrian event held in Calgary

FALL

C̲OOL, BUT often sunny
weather provides the best
setting for the dramatic reds
and golds of the fall foliage,
which are mostly seen in the
deciduous forests of the eastern provinces. In Ontario and
Quebec, fall signals the end
of the humid summer months
and heralds crisp days that are
perfect for outdoor pursuits.

SEPTEMBER

The Masters *(first week)*
Calgary. Equestrian event
with top international riders.
Molson Indy *(early Sep)*
Vancouver. This year's second
Molson Indy sees car racing
in downtown Vancouver.
**Toronto International
Film Festival** *(Sep)*
Toronto. Famous movie stars
and directors attend this
prestigious festival.

Flambée des Couleurs
(mid-Sep–Oct) Eastern Townships. A series of celebrations
of glorious fall leaf colors.
**Niagara Grape and Wine
Festival** *(last week)* Niagara
Falls. Vineyard tours, wine
tastings, and concerts welcome the area's grape harvest.

OCTOBER

Okanagan Wine Festival
(early-Oct) Okanagan Valley.
Tours and tastings through-
out the valley *(see p315)*.
Oktoberfest *(mid-Oct)*
Kitchener-Waterloo. Largest
Bavarian festival outside
Germany *(see p216)*.

**Traditional Bavarian costumes
and music at the Oktoberfest**

VANCOUVER

	23/73		
°C/°F 14/57	13/55	14/57	
5/41		7/45	6/43
			0/32
6 hrs	9 hrs	4 hrs	2 hrs
90 mm	39 mm	172 mm	214 mm
month Apr	Jul	Oct	Jan

TORONTO

	27/81		
		17/63	15/59
°C/°F 12/54		7/45	
3/37			
			-1/30 / -8/18
6 hrs	10 hrs	9 hrs	2 hrs
66 mm	74 mm	41 mm	66 mm
month Apr	Jul	Oct	Jan

Climate
*This vast country has
a variable climate, des-
pite being famous for
having long, cold win-
ters. Most Canadians
live in the warmer south
of the country, close to
the US border. Southern
Ontario and BC's south
and central coast are
the warmest areas,
while central and
northern Canada have
the coldest winters.*

**Average daily
maximum
temperature**

**Average daily
minimum
temperature**

**Average daily
hours of
sunshine**

**Average
monthly
rainfall**

OTTAWA

	27/81		
	14/57		
10/50		13/55	
°C/°F		3/37	
0/32			-6/21 / -16/3
6 hrs	9 hrs	4 hrs	3 hrs
69 mm	82 mm	67 mm	62 mm
month Apr	Jul	Oct	Jan

MONTREAL

	26/79		
	17/63		
11/52		13/55	
°C/°F		6/43	
2/36			-5/23 / -13/9
5 hrs	8 hrs	4 hrs	3 hrs
83 mm	98 mm	84 mm	87 mm
month Apr	Jul	Oct	Jan

HALIFAX

	23/73		
		14/57	14/57
9/48			7/45
°C/°F 1/34			0/32
			-7/19
5 hrs	8 hrs	5 hrs	3 hrs
113 mm	94 mm	120 mm	140 mm
month Apr	Jul	Oct	Jan

Celtic Colours *(mid-Oct)*
Cape Breton Island.
International Celtic music
festival held across the island.

WINTER

A PART FROM coastal British
Columbia, Canadian
winters are long and cold
with lots of snow. Events
focus on winter sports, with
some of the best skiing in
the world available at such
resorts as Whistler in British
Columbia. The Christmas holidays are a time of fun activities to cheer everyone up in
the midst of long, dark days.

NOVEMBER

**Royal Agricultural Winter
Fair** *(early–mid-Nov)*
Toronto. The world's largest
indoor agricultural fair features
the Royal Horse Show and
the Winter Garden Show.
Canadian Finals Rodeo
(mid-Nov) Edmonton.
Canada's cowboy champions
are decided at this event.
Winter Festival of Lights
(mid-Nov–mid Jan) Niagara
Falls. Spectacular light
displays and concerts.

DECEMBER

**Canadian Open Sled Dog
Race** *(Dec)* Fort St. John and
Fort Nelson. Snow sports
and family fun-days as well
as dogsled races.

PUBLIC HOLIDAYS

New Years Day (Jan 1)
Good Friday (variable)
Easter Sunday (variable)
Easter Monday (variable)
Vacation for government
offices and schools only.
Victoria Day. (Monday
before May 25)
Canada Day (July 1)
Labour Day (first Monday
in September)
Thanksgiving (second
Monday in October)
Remembrance Day
(Nov 11)
Christmas Day (Dec 25)
Boxing Day (Dec 26)

An illuminated display of
Christmas decorations

**Christmas Carolships
Parade** *(mid-Dec)*
Vancouver. Boats are
beautifully decorated with
Christmas lights, and cruise
Vancouver's waters.

JANUARY

Ice Magic *(mid-Jan)* Lake
Louise. International ice
sculpture competition.
**Techni-Cal Challenge –
Dog Sled Race** *(mid-Jan)*
Minden. Over 80 teams com-
pete in international races.
Rossland Winter Carnival
(last weekend) Rossland.
Snowboarding contests, a
torchlit parade, and lots of
music and dancing at this
weekend-long party.
Quebec Winter Carnival
(Jan-Feb) Quebec. A famous

canoe race across the St.
Lawrence River is just one
attraction at these huge
winter celebrations.
Jasper in January *(last two
weeks)* Jasper. Winter festivities include skiing parties,
races, and food fairs.
**Banff/Lake Louise Winter
Festival** *(last week)* Banff,
Lake Louise. Variety of fun
events, including skating
parties and barn dances.

FEBRUARY

**Yukon Quest International
Sled Dog Race** *(Feb)*
Whitehorse. Famous
1,600 km (1,000 mile) race
from Fairbanks, Alaska to
Whitehorse.
**Yukon Sourdough
Rendevous** *(Feb)*
Whitehorse. A "mad trapper"
competition and an array
of children's events in this
winter festival.
Frostbite Music Festival
(third weekend) Whitehorse.
Features a wide range of
music from jazz to rock.
Calgary Winter Festival
(second week) Calgary.
Winter festival with lots of
fun family activities, music,
and feasting.
Festival du Voyageur *(mid-
Feb)* Winnipeg. Celebration
of fur trade history featuring
an enormous street party.
Winterlude *(every weekend)*
Ottawa. A wide array of
activities including ice-
skating on the Rideau Canal.

Two eagle ice sculptures at Ottawa's February festival, Winterlude

THE HISTORY OF CANADA

*C*ANADA IS KNOWN *for its wild and beautiful terrain, yet with the help of the aboriginal peoples, European settlers adapted to their new land and built up a prosperous nation. Despite continuing divisions between its English- and French-speaking peoples, Canada has welcomed immigrants from around the globe and is respected as one of the most tolerant countries in the world today.*

Long before the first Europeans crossed the Atlantic in AD 986, the landscape we now know as Canada was inhabited by various civilizations. Tribes of hunters came on foot, walking across a land bridge that once joined Asia with North America as part of the ancient land mass of Laurasia.

Detail of totem pole made by Haida peoples from the west

These first inhabitants, now referred to as the First Nations, endured centuries of hardship and adaptation, eventually developing the skills, technology, and culture required to survive the rigors of life in Canada.

EARLY SURVIVAL

Across most of the country, from the Yukon to the Atlantic, there were two main groups of hunter-gatherers, the Algonquins and the Athapaskans. They lived in small nomadic bands, which developed birch bark canoes and snowshoes to travel across this vast land. Food and clothing were procured through fishing and animal trapping, traditions that gave Canada the lucrative fish and fur trades.

To the north of these two groups were the Innu people, who mastered life in the Arctic, being able to survive in a region of dark, ice-bound winters and brief summers. To the south, the Iroquois settled in forest villages where they lived in longhouses and grew corn as their staple crop.

On the western plains, other tribes depended on the bison for their livelihood, while communities living along the Pacific Coast relied on fishing and trading. Their towering totem poles indicated a rich culture and spiritual belief system.

The common bond between all the First Nations, despite their disparate lifestyles, was that they saw themselves as part of nature and not as its masters. They believed the animals they hunted had kindred spirits, and misfortune befell those who offended such spirits by gratuitous killing.

The generosity of the natives toward Europeans may have hastened their own downfall. As Canadian historian Desmond Morton points out: "Without the full... assistance of natives showing the Europeans their methods of survival, their territory, and their resources, the early explorers and settlers would have perished in even greater numbers and possibly abandoned their quest, much as the Vikings had done 500 years before."

TIMELINE

30,000 BC	20,000 BC	10,000 BC	AD1	500	1000	1500

9,000 BC Native peoples are living at least as far south as the Eramosa River near what is now Guelph, Ontario

Viking ship c.980 AD

AD 986 Bjarni Herjolfsson, a Viking sailing from Iceland to Greenland, is the first European to see the coastline of Labrador

1497 John Cabot's first voyage to North America

30,000–10,000 BC Nomadic hunters arrive in North America across a land bridge from Asia

992 Leif "the Lucky" Ericsson visits Labrador and L'Anse aux Meadows, Newfoundland

1003 Thorfinn Karlsefni starts a colony in Labrador (Vinland) to trade with the natives, but it is abandoned two years later because of fighting with the hostile aboriginals

◁ *Mah-Min* or *The Feather*, painting of an Assiniboine chief by Paul Kane c.1856

THE FIRST EUROPEANS

The Norse sagas of Northern Europe tell how Vikings from Iceland first reached the coast of Labrador in AD 986 and made a series of unsuccessful attempts to establish a colony here. Leif "the Lucky" Ericsson sailed from Greenland in 988, naming the country he found in the west Vinland after the wild grapes found growing in abundance there. Around 1000 AD Thorfinn Karlsefni tried to establish a Vinland colony. Thorfinn's group wintered in Vinland but sailed home to Greenland in the spring, convinced that a colony was impossible as there were too few colonists and the *skraelings* (aboriginals) were hostile. Remarkably, remains of this early Viking settlement were discovered in Newfoundland in 1963 *(see p67).*

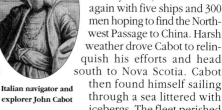

Italian navigator and explorer John Cabot

THE ENGLISH INVASION

In 1497, the Italian navigator John Cabot (1450–98), on the commission of King Henry VII of England, set sail aboard the *Matthew*, bound for America. On June 24, he found a sheltered place on Cape Breton Island. Here he went ashore with a small party to claim the land for England. He then went on to chart the eastern coastline before sailing home, where he was greeted as a hero.

In May 1498, Cabot sailed again with five ships and 300 men hoping to find the Northwest Passage to China. Harsh weather drove Cabot to relinquish his efforts and head south to Nova Scotia. Cabot then found himself sailing through a sea littered with icebergs. The fleet perished off the coast of Greenland, and English interest in the new land faded.

THE FRENCH ARRIVAL

Originally from the port of St. Malo, explorer Jacques Cartier (1491–1557) made his first voyage to Canada in 1534. He reached Labrador, Newfoundland, and the Gulf of the St. Lawrence before landing on Anticosti Island where he

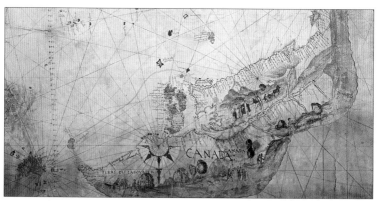

Map of the voyage of Jacques Cartier and his followers by Pierre Descaliers c.1534–1541

TIMELINE

1541 At the mouth of the Cap Rouge River, Cartier founds Charlesbourg-Royal, the first French settlement in America – it is abandoned in 1543

1567 Samuel de Champlain "Father of New France" born

1605 Samuel de Champlain and the Sieur de Roberval found Port Royal, now Annapolis, Nova Scotia

1525	1550	1575	1600

1535 Cartier sails up the St. Lawrence River to Stadacona (Quebec City) and Hochelaga (Montreal)

Jacques Cartier

1608 Champlain founds Quebec City, creating the first permanent European settlement in Canada

1610 Henry Hudson explores Hudson Bay

realized he was at the mouth of a great river. A year later, he returned and sailed up the St. Lawrence River to the site of what is now Quebec City, and then on to a native encampment at Hochelaga, which he named Montreal. In 1543, Cartier's hopes for a successful colony died when, after a bitter and barren winter, he and his dispirited group returned to France. Seventy

Champlain, "Father of New France," fighting the Iroquois

more years would pass before French colonists returned to Canada to stay.

THE FATHER OF NEW FRANCE

Samuel de Champlain (1567–1635) was a man of many parts – navigator, soldier, visionary – and first made the journey from France to Canada in 1603. While the ship that carried him across the Atlantic lay at Tadoussac, Champlain ascended the St. Lawrence River by canoe to the Lachine Rapids.

In 1605, Champlain's attempt to found a colony at Port Royal failed, but in 1608 the seeds of a first tiny French colony at Quebec City were planted, with the construction of three two-story houses, a courtyard, and a watch-tower, surrounded by a wooden wall.

The economic engine propelling Champlain was the fur trade. In its name he made alliances with the Algonquins and Hurons, fought their dreaded enemies, the Iroquois, traveled to the Huron country that is now central Ontario, and saw the Great Lakes. Champlain and the other Frenchmen who followed him not only established lasting settlements in the St. Lawrence Valley but also explored half a continent. They built a "New France" that, at its zenith, stretched south from Hudson Bay to New Orleans in Louisiana, and from Newfoundland almost as far west as the Rockies. In 1612 Champlain became French Canada's first head of government.

Champlain's efforts also helped to create the religious climate that enabled orders such as the Jesuits to establish missions. But his work also laid the seeds of conflict with the English that would last well into the next century and beyond.

Hudson's last voyage

THE HUDSON'S BAY COMPANY

In 1610, English voyager Henry Hudson landed at the bay that still bears his name. The bay's access to many key waterways and trading routes ensured the fortunes of the fur trade.

Founded in 1670, the Hudson's Bay Company won control of the lands that drained into the bay, gaining a fur-trading monopoly over the area. The company was challenged only by Scottish merchants who established the North West Company in Montreal in 1783. By 1821, these two companies amalgamated, and the Hudson's Bay Company remains Canada's largest fur trader to this day.

1629 British adventurer David Kirke captures Quebec, but it is returned to France in 1632

1648–49 The Iroquois disperse the Huron nation and Jesuit father Jean de Brébeuf is martyred during Iroquois raids on Huronia

Engraving of Iroquois

1702 French and British rivalries result in outbreak of Queen Anne's War

1625	1650	1675	1700

1629 British adventurer David Kirke captures Quebec, but it is returned to France in 1632

Raccoon pelt

1670 The Hudson's Bay Company is founded by royal charter and underwritten by a group of English merchants

1676 population of New France swelled to 8,500 by settlers.

Anglo-French Hostilities

THROUGHOUT THE 18th century, hostilities between the French and English in Europe continued to spill over into the New World. By 1713, Britain ruled Nova Scotia, Newfoundland, and the Hudson Bay region and, after the Seven Years War in 1763, all of French Canada.

Anglo-French tensions were exacerbated by religion: the English were largely Protestant and almost all of the French Catholic. This resulted in the colony of Quebec being divided in 1791 into the mainly English-speaking Upper Canada (now Ontario), and majority French-speaking Lower Canada (now Quebec).

Taking advantage of the British conflict with Napoleon in Europe, the Americans invaded Canada in 1812. They were defeated by 1814, but the threat of another invasion colored Canadian history during much of the 19th century.

The Acadian Exodus
French-speaking Acadians were ruthlessly expelled from their homes by the British in the 1750s (see pp58–9).

The Plains Of Abraham, in Quebec, were the site of victory for the British over the French.

General Isaac Brock
Brock's heroic exploits during the War of 1812, such as the capture of an American post at Detroit, buoyed the spirits of the Canadian people.

United Empire Loyalists
The surrender of British General Cornwallis effectively ended the American Revolution (1775–83). A large number of United Empire Loyalists, refugees from the newly formed United States who remained loyal to the British crown, fled to Canada. They swelled the British population by 50,000.

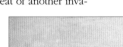

THE SEVEN YEARS WAR

The famous Battle of the Plains of Abraham in 1759 was the last between British and French forces to take place in Canada. The British launched a surprise assault from the cliffs of the St. Lawrence River at a site now known as Wolfe's Cove. Louis Joseph de Montcalm, the French commander, was defeated by General Wolfe and his army. Both generals were killed, and Quebec fell to the British. The war finally ended in 1763 with the Treaty of Paris, which ceded all French-Canadian territory to the British.

Louisbourg
The French fortress of Louisbourg on Cape Breton Island was built between 1720 and 1740, and was the head-quarters for the French fleet until it was destroyed by the British in 1758. Today, the restored fortress is a popular tourist attraction (see pp92–3).

General Wolfe
The distinguished British soldier, shown here fatally wounded at the Plains of Abraham, preceded his 1759 victory in Quebec with the taking of the French fortress, Louisbourg, in 1758.

General Wolfe's forces sailed up the St. Lawrence river overnight, allowing them to surprise the enemy at Quebec.

French Rights
In 1774 the British government passed the Quebec Act, granting French-Canadians religious and linguistic freedom and giving official recognition to French Civil Law.

Wolfe's infantry scrambled up a steep, wooded cliff. They had to defeat an enemy post before the waiting boats of soldiers could join the battle.

1755 Expulsion of the Acadians from Nova Scotia

1743 The La Vérendrye brothers discover the Rocky Mountains

1758 Louisbourg, the French fortress on Cape Breton Island, falls to the British

Sir Alexander Mackenzie

1793 English explorer and fur trader Alexander Mackenzie crosses the Rockies and reaches the Pacific Ocean by land

1720	1740	1760	1780	1800

1713 British gain control of Nova Scotia, Newfoundland, and Hudson Bay

1759 Wolfe defeats de Montcalm in the Battle of the Plains of Abraham

Medal for the British capture of Quebec 1759

1760 Montreal falls to the British

1774 The Quebec Act grants French colonists rights to their own language and religion

1812 The US at war with Britain until the Treaty of Ghent in 1814

A British Dominion

Twenty-five years after the War of 1812 ended in stalemate, violence of a different sort flared in Canada. The English wanted supremacy in voting power and to limit the influence of the Catholic Church. By 1834 the French occupied one quarter of public positions, although they made up three-quarters of the population. Rebellions in Upper and Lower Canada during 1837–38 were prompted by

Representatives meet in London to discuss terms of union

both French and British reformers, who wanted accountable government with a broader electorate. The response of the British Government was to join together the two colonies into a united Province of Canada in 1840. The newly created assembly won increased independence when, in 1849, the majority Reform Party passed an Act compensating the 1837 rebels. Although the Governor-General, Lord Elgin, disapproved, he chose not to use his veto. The Province of Canada now had "responsible government," (the right to pass laws without the sanction of the British colonial representative.)

The rest of British North America, however, remained a series of self-governing colonies that, despite their economic successes, were anxious about American ambitions. Such fears were reinforced by a series of Fenian Raids on Canadian territory between 1866–70. (The Fenians were New York Irish immigrants hoping to take advantage of French Canada's anti-British feeling to help them to secure independence for Ireland.) The issue of confederation was raised and

Northwest rebel Louis Riel

discussed at conferences held from 1864 onward. Only by uniting in the face of this common menace, said the politicians, could the British colonies hope to fend off these incursions.

The new country was born on July 1, 1867. Under the terms of the British North America Act the new provinces of Quebec (Canada East) and Ontario (Canada West) were created, and along with Nova Scotia and New Brunswick became the Dominion of Canada. The new government was based on the British parliamentary system, with a governor-general (the Crown's representative), a House of Commons, and a Senate. Parliament received power to legislate over matters of national interest; defense, criminal law, and trade, while the provinces ruled over local issues such as education.

The Métis Rebellion

Following confederation, the government purchased from the Hudson's Bay Company the area known as Rupert's Land, which extended south and west inland for thousands of kilometers from Hudson's Bay.

The Métis people (descendants of mostly French fur-traders and natives) who lived here were alarmed by the expected influx of English-speaking settlers. In 1869, local leader Louis Riel took up their cause and led the first of two uprisings. The Red River Rebellion was an attempt to defend what the Métis saw as their ancestral rights to this land. A compromise was reached in 1870 and the new province of, Manitoba was created.

Driving home the last spike of the Canadian Pacific Railroad, 1885

However, many Métis moved westward to what was to become the province of Saskatchewan in 1905.

Riel was elected to the House of Commons in 1874 but, in 1875, he emigrated to the US. The government's intention to settle the west led the Métis of Saskatchewan to call Riel home in 1884 to lead the North-West Rebellion. It was short-lived. Defeated at Batoche in May, Riel was ultimately charged with treason and hanged in Regina on November 16, 1885.

BIRTH OF A NATION

The defeat of the Métis and the building of a transcontinental railroad were crucial factors in the settlement of the west. British Columbia, a Crown colony since 1858, chose to join the Dominion in 1871 on the promise of a rail link with the rest of the country. The first train to run from Montreal to Vancouver in 1886 paved the way for hundreds of thousands of settlers in the west in the late 1800s. Prince Edward Island, Canada's smallest province, joined the Dominion in 1873.

In 1898, the northern territory of Yukon was established to ensure Canadian jurisdiction over that area during the Klondike gold rush *(see pp46–7)*. In 1905, the provinces of Saskatchewan and Alberta were created out of Rupert's Land, with the residual area becoming the Northwest Territories. Each province gained its own premier and elected assembly. By 1911 new immigrants had doubled the populations of the new provinces.

For the time being, Newfoundland preferred to remain a British colony, but in 1949 it was brought into Canada as the country's tenth province.

THE MÉTIS PEOPLE

The Métis people of central Canada were descended from native and largely French stock. Proud of their unique culture, this seminomadic group considered themselves separate from the rest of the Dominion. With their own social structure and lifestyle dependent almost entirely on buffalo hunting, they resisted integration. They responded to the unification of the country with two failed rebellions. The Métis won no land rights and were condemned to a life of poverty or enforced integration.

Métis hunt buffalo on the Prairie

Sir John MacDonald

1867 Dominion of Canada; Sir John A. Macdonald is Canada's first Prime Minister

1870 The Red River Rebellion is quashed by General Wolseley, and the the province of Manitoba is created

General Wolseley

1886 Gold found on the Forty-Mile River

| 1860 | 1870 | 1880 |

1866 The Fenians raid Canadian territory to divert British troops from Ireland

1885 Riel leads the North-West Rebellion. The Métis are defeated at Batoche, and Riel is hanged in Regina. The last spike of the transcontinental railroad is put in place

1855 Queen Victoria designates Ottawa as capital of the Province of Canada

Canadian Pacific

The Klondike Gold Rush

THERE HAD BEEN rumors of gold in the Yukon since the 1830s, but the harsh land, together with the Chilkoot Indians' guarding of their territory, kept most prospectors away. Then, on August 16, 1896 the most frenzied and fabled gold rush in Canadian history started when George Washington Carmack and two Indian friends, Snookum Jim and Tagish Charlie, found a large gold nugget in the river they later named Bonanza Creek. For the next two years at least 100,000 prospectors set out for the new gold fields.

Only about 40,000 prospectors actually made it. Most took boats as far as Skagway or Dyea, on the Alaskan Panhandle, then struggled across the Coast Mountains by the White or Chilkoot passes to reach the head-waters of the Yukon River. From here boats took them 500 km (310 miles) to the gold fields. In all, the gold rush generated Can $50 million, although few miners managed to hold onto their fortunes.

Klondike Entrepreneur
Alex McDonald, a Nova Scotian with a canny business sense, bought up the claims of discouraged miners and hired others to work them for him. Known as "King of the Klondike," he made millions.

The sternwheeler was a steamboat driven by a single paddle at the back.

Skagway, Alaska
The jumping-off point for the Klondike was the tent city of Skagway. There were saloons and swindlers on every corner, and gunfire in the streets was commonplace. The most famous con man was Jefferson Randolph "Soapy" Smith, who died in a shoot-out in 1898.

The Yukon River rises in British Columbia's Coast Mountains, winding for 3,000 km (1,900 miles) to Alaska.

The Mounties Take Control
The safety of the Klondike Gold Rush was secured by Canada's red-coated Mounties. Thanks to them, the rush was remarkably peaceful. A small force of 19 Mounties led by Inspector Charles Constantine were sent to the Yukon in 1895, but by 1898 there were 285, operating out of Fort Herchmer at Dawson.

Klondike Fever
The outside world learnt of the riches in July 1897, when miners docked in Seattle and San Francisco hauling gold. In no time, Klondike fever was an epidemic.

Dawson City
As the gold rush developed in the summer of 1897, the small tent camp at the junction of the Klondike and Yukon rivers grew to a population of 5,000. A year on it had reached 40,000, making Dawson City one of the largest cities in Canada.

Steamboats and other craft brought thousands of prospectors up the long Yukon River to Dawson, where the boats jostled for space at the dock.

Capturing the Mood
Even literature had a place in the Klondike. The gold rush inspired novels such as Call of the Wild *(1903) by Jack London (shown here) and the 1907 verses* Songs of a Sourdough *by poet Robert Service.*

CROSSING THE YUKON RIVER

The ferocious Yukon River rapids in Miles Canyon smashed so many boats to splinters that the Mounties decreed that every boat had to be guided by a competent pilot. Experienced sailors could earn up to Can$100 a trip taking boats through the canyon. Past the canyon, only one more stretch of rapids remained before the Yukon's waters grew calmer all the way to Dawson City.

TIMELINE

Klondike News 1898

1896 George Carmack and two friends, Tagish Charlie and Snookum Jim, strike it rich on Bonanza Creek. Liberal Wilfred Laurier elected as the country's first French-Canadian prime minister

1898 The Yukon is given territorial status, partly to assert British authority in the eyes of the Americans from neighboring Alaska

1896	1897	1898	1899

1897 Steamers from Alaska carry word of the strike to San Francisco and Seattle, setting off a frenzied gold rush

1899 Gold is discovered in Nome, Alaska, and Dawson begins to shrink as people leave to follow the new dream of riches farther west

New optimism and arrivals

The impact of the Klondike gold rush was felt all over Canada. It led to an expansion of cities such as Vancouver and Edmonton, and the establishment of the Yukon territory. A period of optimism was ushered in by the new Liberal government, elected in 1896 under the first French-Canadian premier, Wilfred Laurier, who firmly believed that "the 20th century will belong to Canada."

The new central Canadian provinces provided a home for European immigrants eager to farm large tracts of prairie land. By 1913, this wave of immigration had peaked at 400,000. Finally Canada began to profit from a prosperous world economy and establish itself as an industrial and agricultural power.

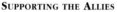

1914 poster promoting immigration to Canada

Supporting the Allies

The first test of the fledgling nation came in 1899, when the Boer War broke out in South Africa; the second in 1914, when Europe entered World War I. Initially, Laurier was cautious in his approach to the South African crisis, but pressure from the English-speaking population led to the dispatch of 1,000 soldiers to Cape Town in 1899. Before the Boer War ended in 1902, some 6,000 men had made the journey to the South African battlefields. They returned with a stronger sense of national identity than many of their compatriots at home had expected. But, while the experience of war infused some with a new sense of national unity, it also laid bare divisions. There were fights between French- and English-speaking university students, as well as disputes among Ontario conservatives and French-speaking Quebec politicians.

Before matters could come to a head, another crisis loomed. Joining the Allies in Flanders, the Canadians found renewed glory during World War I. Canadian pilot, Billy Bishop, was the Allies' greatest air ace, and another Canadian, Roy Brown, was the pilot credited with downing the Red Baron. Canadian troops were the heroes of two major battles, Ypres (1915) and Vimy Ridge (1917). When peace was declared on November 11, 1918, there were 175,000 Canadian wounded, and 60,000 had died for their country.

Independent Status

Canada had played so significant a role during World War I that it gained recognition as an independent country, winning representation in the League of Nations. This independence was confirmed in 1931 with the passing of the Statute of Westminster,

Canadians advance at Paardeberg in the Boer War, 1900

Timeline

1900	1905	1910	1915	1920

1899 The first Canadians are sent to fight in the Boer War

1911 Robert Borden and the Conservatives win federal election, defeating Liberal party leader, Wilfred Laurier on the issue of Reciprocity

1917 Munitions ship explodes in Halifax harbor wiping out 5 sq km (2 sq miles) of the town, killing 2,000, and injuring 9,000

1918 Canadians break through the German trenches at Amiens beginning "Canada's Hundred Days"

1903 Canada loses the Alaska boundary dispute when a British tribunal sides with the US

1914 Britain declares war on Germany, automatically drawing Canada into the conflict in Europe. The War Measures Act orders German and Austro-Hungarian Canadians to carry identity cards

Dr. Frederick Banting

1922 Canadians Charles Best, Frederick Banting, and John MacLeod win the Nobel Prize for the discovery of insulin

which gave Canada political independence from Britain and created a commonwealth of sovereign nations under a single crown.

However, national optimism was curtailed by the Great Depression that originated with the Wall Street Crash in 1929. Drought laid waste the farms of Alberta, Saskatchewan, and Manitoba. One in four workers was unemployed, and the sight of men riding boxcars in a fruitless search for work became common.

Soup kitchen during the Great Depression

WORLD WAR II

The need to supply the Allied armies during World War II boosted Canada out of the Depression. Canada's navy played a crucial role in winning the Battle of the Atlantic (1940–3) and thousands of Allied airmen were trained in Canada. Canadian regiments soon gained a reputation for bravery,

for example, many died in the fiercely fought 1942 raid on Dieppe. Thousands battled up the boot of Italy, while others stormed ashore at Normandy. In the bitter fighting that followed, the Second and Third Canadian Divisions took more casualties holding the beachheads than any unit under British command. It was also the Canadians who liberated much of Holland.

The Canadian prime minister of the day was the Liberal, Mackenzie King (1935–48). He ordered a plebiscite to allow the sending of conscripts overseas, monitored the building of the Alaska Highway *(see pp260–61)* and, aided by his minister of munitions and supply, he directed a massive war effort.

AN INTERNATIONAL VOICE

When peace finally came in September 1945, Canada had the third-largest navy in the world, the fourth-largest air force, and a standing army of 730,000 men. Although the price Canada had paid during World War II was high – 43,000 people died in action and the national debt quadrupled – the nation found itself in a strong position. A larger population was better able to cope with its losses and much of the debt had been spent on doubling the gross national product, creating durable industries that would power the postwar economy.

German prisoners captured by Canadian Infantry on D-Day, June 6, 1944

1925	1930	1935	1940	1945
1926 The Balfour Report defines British dominions as autonomous and equal in status		**1937** Trans-Canada Air Lines, now Air Canada, begins regular flights	**1942** Around 22,000 Japanese Canadians are stripped of non-portable possessions and interned	**1944** Canadian troops push farther inland than any other allied units on D-Day
1929 The Great Depression begins	**1931** The Statute of Westminster grants Canada full legislative authority		**1941** Hong Kong falls to the Japanese, and Canadians are taken as POWs	**1945** World War II ends. Canada joins the UN. Canada's first nuclear reactor goes on line in Chalk River, Ontario

Air Canada logo

Large Canadian grain carrier approaches the St. Lawrence Seaway in 1959 – its inaugural year

Since World War II, Canada's economy has continued to expand. This growth, combined with government social programs such as old-age security, unemployment insurance, and medicare, means Canadians have one of the world's highest standards of living and a quality of life which draws immigrants from around the world. Since 1945, those immigrants have been made up largely of southern Europeans, Asians, South Americans, and Caribbean islanders, all of whom have enriched the country's multicultural status.

Internationally, the nation's reputation and influence have grown. Canada has participated in the United Nations since its inception in 1945 and is the only nation to have taken part in almost all of the UN's major peacekeeping operations. Perhaps it is only fitting that it was a future Canadian prime minister, Lester Pearson, who fostered the peacekeeping process when he won the Nobel Peace Prize in 1957 for helping resolve the Suez Crisis. Canada is also a respected member of the British Commonwealth, la Francophonie, the Group of Eight industrialized nations, the OAS (Organization of American States), and NATO (North Atlantic Treaty Organization).

THE FRENCH–ENGLISH DIVIDE

Given all these accomplishments, it seems ironic that the last quarter of a century has also seen Canadians deal with fundamental questions of national identity and unity. The driving force of this debate continues to be the historic English–French rivalry. The best-known players of these late 20th-century events are Prime Minister Pierre Trudeau (1968–84) and Quebec Premier René Lévesque (1968–87).

When Jean Lesage was elected as Quebec Premier in 1960, he instituted the "Quiet Revolution" – a series of reforms that increased provincial power. However, this was not enough to prevent the rise of revolutionary nationalists. In October 1970, British Trade Commissioner James Cross and Quebec Labor Minister Pierre Laporte were kidnapped by the French-Canadian terrorist organization, the

Quebec Premier René Levesque and Canadian Prime Minister Pierre Trudeau during the 1980 referendum

TIMELINE

	1949 Newfoundland joins the Confederation. Canada joins NATO	1959 Prime Minister John Diefenbaker cancels the AVRO Arrow project, losing 14,000 jobs	The AVRO Arrow Delta High speed aircraft		1967 Expo '67 is held in Montreal and Canada celebrates its Centennial
	1950	**1955**	**1960**	**1965**	**1970**
1950 The Canadian Army Special Force joins UN soldiers in the Korean War		*Lester Pearson* 1957 Lester Pearson wins the Nobel Peace Prize for helping resolve the Suez Crisis	1965 Canada's new flag is inaugurated after a bitter political debate		1972 Canada wins the first hockey challenge against the Soviets, touching off a huge nationwide celebration

1990 demonstration for Quebec independence in Montreal

Front du Libération de Québec (FLQ). Cross was rescued by police but Laporte was later found murdered. Trudeau invoked the War Measures Act, sent troops into Montreal, and banned the FLQ. His actions eventually led to nearly 500 arrests.

Trudeau devoted his political life to federalism, fighting separatism, and giving Canada its own constitution. In contrast, Lesage's successor, René Lévesque, campaigned for a 1980 referendum in Quebec on whether that province should become independent. A majority voted against, but the results were far from decisive, and separatism continued to dominate the country's political agenda. However, in 1982, the Constitution Act fulfilled Trudeau's dream, entrenching federal civil rights and liberties such as female equality.

A MOVE TOWARD CONSERVATISM
In 1984 the leader of the Progressive Conservatives, Brian Mulroney, won the general election with the largest majority in Canadian history. Dismissive of Trudeau's policies, Mulroney's emphasis was on closer links with Europe and, in particular, the US. In the years that followed, two major

efforts were made to reform the constitutional system. The 1987 Meech Lake Accord aimed to recognize Quebec's claims to special status on the basis of its French culture, but Mulroney failed to implement the amendment since it did not obtain the consent of all provinces. When the Inuit began campaigning for more parliamentary representation it led to the Charlottetown Accord of 1991, which raised the issue of aboriginal self-government. The Accord was rejected in a national referendum held in 1992.

Today, many of these reforms are finally in place and hopefully aiding Canadian unity. Quebec's French heritage has official recognition, and the Inuit rule their own territory of Nunavut.

INDEPENDENCE FOR NUNAVUT

On April 1, 1999, Canada gained its newest territory, the Inuit homeland of Nunavut. The campaign for an Inuit state began in the 1960s when the Inuit desire for a political identity of their own was

Signing ceremony in Iqaluit, April 1, 1999

added to aboriginal land claims. Nunavut's first Premier is 34-year-old Paul Okalik, leader of the first-ever Inuit majority government over an 85 percent Inuit population. English is being replaced as the official language by the native Inuktitut, and traditional Inuit fishing and hunting skills are being reintroduced. By 2012, the federal government will invest over Can$1 billion in public services for Nunavut.

1976 The Olympic games are held in Montreal under tight security. René Lévesque and the separatist *Parti Québecois* win a provincial election	**1984** Aboard the US shuttle *Challenger*, Marc Garneau becomes the first Canadian in space	**1989** The Canada–US Free Trade agreement goes into effect	*Canadian & Nunavut flags*	**1999** The Inuit territory of Nunavut established

975	1980	1985	1990	1995	2000

| | **1979** 225,000 people of Mississauga, Ontario, are evacuated after a train derailment threatens to release clouds of chlorine gas | **1988** Calgary hosts the XV Winter Olympics | | **1991** Canadian forces join the battle to drive Saddam Hussein's Iraqi troops from Kuwait | **1997** A 13-km (8-mile) bridge connecting Prince Edward Island to the mainland is opened |

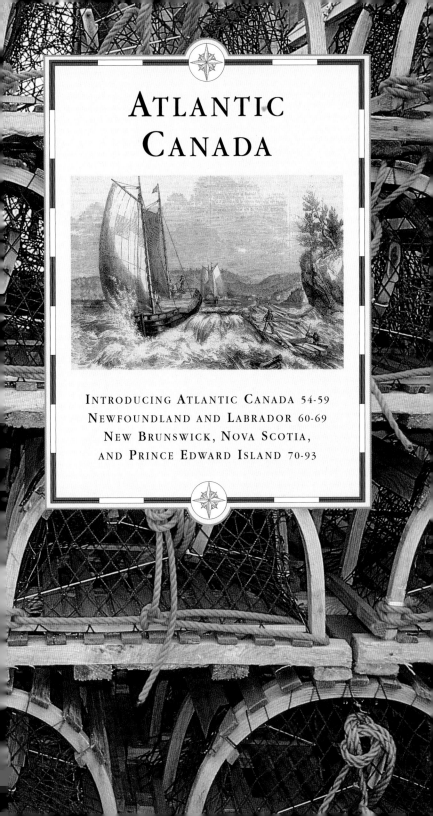

ATLANTIC CANADA

Introducing Atlantic Canada

ATLANTIC CANADA IS renowned for rocky coastlines, picturesque fishing villages, sun-warmed beaches, cozy country inns, and friendly people. Each province has a distinctive cultural flavor. In northeastern New Brunswick, French-speaking Acadian culture flourishes while the south coast offers the pristine, tide-carved beauty of the Bay of Fundy. Nova Scotia, famous for world-class attractions, such as the 18th-century Fortress Louisbourg and the stunning natural scenery of the Cabot Trail, is also home to historic towns like seafaring Lunenburg. Prince Edward Island is known for its emerald-green farmland, fine sandy beaches, and rich lobster catches. In Newfoundland, the mountains of Gros Morne National Park rise 800 m (2,625 ft) above sparkling blue fjords. Labrador offers an imposing and stunning coastal landscape, often with a backdrop of glittering icebergs.

LABRADOR SEA

●NAIN

LABRADOR

Smallwood
Reservoir

500

●CHURCHILL
FALLS

●LABRADOR CITY

Acadian homesteads still flourish after 400 years of a unique culture that dominates northeastern New Brunswick

CAMPBE.

N.
BRUN

The fresh maritime scenery of Two Islands beach, known as "The Brothers" for its twin offshore islands, in Parrsboro, Nova Scotia

GETTING AROUND

Air Canada, Air Nova, and Canadian Airlines offer regularly scheduled flights throughout the region. The Trans-Canada Highway (TCH) travels to all four provinces, but not through Newfoundland and Labrador. The new Confederation Bridge connects Prince Edward Island to Cape Tormentine, New Brunswick. Newfoundland must be accessed by air or by ferry from Sydney, Nova Scotia, to either Port aux Basques or Argentia. A ferry also travels between Nova Scotia and Bar Harbor, Maine. Bus services cross the provinces, but many areas are remote so availability should be checked.

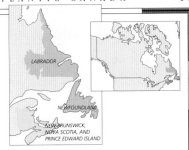

LOCATOR MAP

KEY

	Highway
	Major road
	Minor road
	River

SEE ALSO

• *Where to stay* pp344–346

• *Where to eat* pp364–366

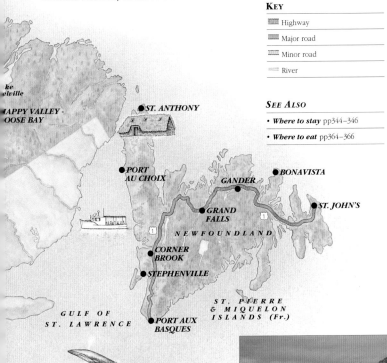

ke
elville

HAPPY VALLEY -
GOOSE BAY

ST. ANTHONY

PORT
AU CHOIX

GANDER

BONAVISTA

ST. JOHN'S

GRAND
FALLS

NEWFOUNDLAND

CORNER
BROOK

STEPHENVILLE

ST. PIERRE
& MIQUELON
ISLANDS (Fr.)

GULF OF
ST. LAWRENCE

PORT AUX
BASQUES

CAPE
BRETON ISLAND

SYDNEY

BATHURST

PRINCE
EDWARD ISLAND

BOUCTOUCHE

AMHERST

NOVA
SCOTIA

TRURO

FREDERICTON

ATLANTIC OCEAN

SAINT
JOHN

HALIFAX

DIGBY

LUNENBURG

SHELBURNE

0 km	250
0 miles	250

Perched on the Atlantic Coast, Quidi Vidi is one of the oldest villages in Newfoundland

Maritime Wildlife of Atlantic Canada

THE PROVINCES OF Atlantic Canada – Nova Scotia,
New Brunswick, and Prince Edward Island – along
with Newfoundland, the Quebec north shore of the
St. Lawrence River, and the Gaspé Peninsula, constitute a rich and diverse maritime habitat for wildlife.
The climate is dominated by the ocean, being influenced by the moderating Gulf Stream that flows north
from the Caribbean and by the southward flow of icy
waters, often bearing icebergs, from the Canadian
Arctic. The terrain of the eastern Canadian coastline
varies from rocky headlands to soft, sandy beaches.
Both sea and land mammals inhabit this coast, as
do hundreds of species of seabird.

*The piping plover is a small,
endangered shore bird that
lives and breeds along the
Atlantic coast of Canada.*

SHORELINE HABITAT

The maritime shoreline encompasses rocky
cliffs, sandy beaches, and salt-flat marshes.
Moving a little inland, the landscape shifts to
bog, forest, and meadow. It is an inviting habitat for many smaller mammals such as raccoons
and beavers, and also provides a home for
a diversity of bird life. Where the shoreline
meets the water, fertile intertidal zones are
a habitat for mollusks, algae, and invertebrae.

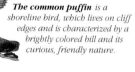

*The river otter
lives in "families,"
frequenting rivers,
lakes, and ocean
bays, in
its search
for fish.*

*The common puffin is a
shoreline bird, which lives on cliff
edges and is characterized by a
brightly colored bill and its
curious, friendly nature.*

*The raccoon, with
its ringed tail and
black-masked face,
preys upon fish,
crayfish, birds
and their eggs.*

*The beaver, symbol of Canada, lives in marshy
woodland near the coast. It gnaws down trees,
using them to build dams, its lodge, and for food.*

OCEAN HABITAT

The sea around Atlantic Canada is influenced by the cold Labrador Current flowing from the north, the Gulf Stream from the south, and the large outflow of fresh water at the mouth of the St. Lawrence River. The region is home to myriad ocean creatures, and the highest tides in the world at the nutrient-rich Bay of Fundy. Off Newfoundland lie the Grand Banks, once one of the Earth's richest fishing grounds. Over-fishing has endangered fish stocks, and quotas are now limited.

The adult blue whale is the world's largest mammal, reaching up to 30 m (100 ft) long. Today, whale-watching is a growing eco-tourism enterprise, particularly off the east coast, where this and other species congregate.

Lobster, *a favorite seafood of the area, is caught in traps set near the shore. Rigid conservation rules have been put in force to protect its dwindling numbers.*

The Atlantic salmon, *unlike its Pacific cousins, returns to its home stream to spawn several times during its lifetime. Atlantic salmon are renowned sport fish (see p21).*

Bottle-nosed dolphins, *characterized by their long beaks and "smiles," live off the east coast, in both New Brunswick and Nova Scotia.*

SEABIRDS OF THE ATLANTIC COAST

The maritime coast of eastern Canada is a perfect environment for seabirds. Rocky cliffs and headlands provide ideal rookeries. The rich coastal waters and intertidal zones ensure a generous larder for many species, including the cormorant and storm petrel. Some Atlantic Coast seabirds are at risk due to environmental changes, but puffins and razorbills, in particular, continue to thrive.

The double-crested cormorant *or "sea crow," as it is sometimes known, is a diving fishing bird, capable of capturing food as deep as 10 m (30 ft) under water.*

Leach's storm-petrel *is part of the Tubenose family of birds, whose acute sense of smell helps them navigate while out at sea.*

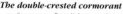

The Acadians

FEW STORIES SURROUNDING the settlement of the New World evoke as many feelings of tragedy and triumph as the tale of the Acadians. Colonizing Nova Scotia's fertile Annapolis Valley in the 1600s, 500 French settlers adopted the name Acadie, hoping to establish an ideal pastoral land. They prospered and, by 1750, numbered 14,000, becoming the dominant culture. The threat of this enclave proved too much for a province run by the British, and in 1755 the Acadians were expelled overseas, many to the US. When England and France made peace in 1763, the Acadians slowly returned. Today their French-speaking culture still thrives in coastal villages.

Acadian women play a part in summer festivals, displaying local woolcraft and linen textiles.

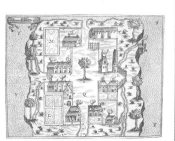

Ile Sainte-Croix *was the earliest Acadian settlement, established by the French in New Brunswick in 1604. The neat, spacious layout of the village is typical.*

ACADIAN FARMING

As hardworking farmers, Acadians cleared the land of the Annapolis Valley, built villages, and developed an extensive system of dikes to reclaim the rich farmland from tidal waters. Summer crops were carefully harvested for the winter; potatoes and vegetables were put in cellars, and hay stored to feed cattle and goats. By the 19th century, Acadian farmers had expanded their crop range to include tobacco and flax.

An important crop, hay was raked into "*chafauds,*" spiked haystacks that dried in the fields for use as winter animal feed.

The Embarkation of the Acadians took place in August 1755. British troops brutally rounded up the Acadians for enforced deportation. Over 6,000 Acadians were put on boats, some bound for the US, where they became the Cajuns of today. Others returned in later years, and today their descendants live in villages throughout Atlantic Canada.

The Acadian people *maintained a traditional farming and fishing lifestyle for centuries, re-created today at the Village Historique Acadien (see p75).*

The Church of Saint Anne *in Sainte-Anne-du-Ruisseau represents Acadian style in its fresh simplicity and elegance. Catholicism was very important to the Acadians, who turned to their priests for succour during the 1755 diaspora.*

Acadian musicians *have reflected their culture since the 17th century. Playing lively violin and guitar folk music, they are known for their upbeat tunes and ballads of unrequited love and social dispossession.*

Acadian life revolved around the farmsteads in each community. Men tilled the fields and fished while women helped with the annual harvest.

HENRY WADSWORTH LONGFELLOW

One of the most popular poets of the 19th century, both in the US and Europe, the American Henry Longfellow (1807–82) is best known for his long, bittersweet narrative poems. Based on the trials and injustices of the Acadian civilization, *Evangeline*, published in 1847, traces the paths of a young Acadian couple. The poem, now regarded as a classic, stirringly records Evangeline's tragic loss in this land intended as an idyll when their love was destroyed through the upheavals and expulsion of the 18th century: "Loud from its rocky caverns, the deep-faced neighbouring ocean [sings], List to the mournful tradition sung by the pines of the Forest, ... List to a Tale of Love in Acadie, home of the happy."

NEWFOUNDLAND AND LABRADOR

WITH TOWERING peaks, vast landscapes, and 17,000 kms (10,500 miles) of rugged coastline, Newfoundland and Labrador displays wild, open spaces and grand spectacles of nature. In this captivating land, massive icebergs drift lazily along the coast, whales swim in sparkling bays, and moose graze placidly in flat open marshes. Newfoundland's west coast offers some of the most dramatic landscapes east of the Rockies. The granite mountains of Gros Morne National Park shelter deep fjords, while the eastern part of the island has a more rounded terrain, featuring the bays and inlets of Terra Nova National Park. Part of the area's appeal is retracing the history of past cultures that have settled here, including Maritime Archaic Indians at Port au Choix, Vikings at L'Anse-Aux-Meadows, and Basque whalers at Red Bay in the Labrador Straits.

SIGHTS AT A GLANCE

Historic Towns and Cities
Gander **9**
Happy Valley-
  Goose Bay **16**
Labrador City **18**

Nain **15**
St. John's **1**
Trinity **6**

National Parks
Gros Morne National Park **11**
Terra Nova National Park **7**

**Historic Sites and Areas
of Natural Beauty**
Avalon Peninsula **2**
Battle Harbour **14**

Bonavista Peninsula **5**
Burin Peninsula **3**
Churchill Falls **17**
Labrador Straits **13**
Northern Peninsula **12**
Notre Dame Bay **8**
Saint-Pierre and Miquelon
  Islands **4**
The Southwest Coast **10**

KEY

✈ International airport

▬ Major road

— Major rail routes

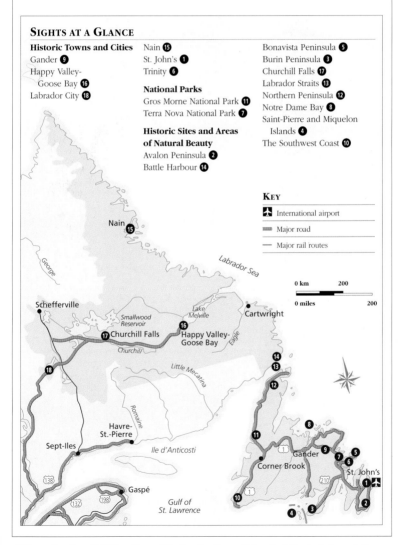

◁ **The weathered seaside fishing villages of Newfoundland have relied on the fishing trade for centuries**

St. John's ❶

ITALIAN EXPLORER John Cabot *(see p40)* aroused great interest in Newfoundland (after his 1497 voyage on behalf of Henry VII of England) when he described "a sea so full of fish that a basket thrown overboard is hauled back brimming with cod." Cabot started a rush to the New World that made St. John's a center of the fishing industry, and North America's oldest and liveliest settlement. Today, St. John's still bustles with the commerce of the sea: fishing, oil exploration, and the ships of a hundred nations waiting to be serviced. The people of St. John's are known for their friendliness, a delightful counterpoint to the harsh, rugged beauty that surrounds this historic town.

Pendant in local museum

Downtown St. John's, seen from the approach by sea

Exploring St. John's

The capital of Newfoundland is easily explored on foot. Most of the sights are within a short distance of each other moving east along Water Street. Approaching by sea offers the best view of the harbor, in particular the steep cliff-lined passage on the east side where pastel-colored old houses cling to the rocks.

⚐ Murray Premises

cnr Water St. & Beck's Cove. 【 (709) 738 8111. ◯ 8am–10:30pm daily. ♿

At the west end of Water Street stands Murray Premises. Built in 1846, these rambling brick and timberframe buildings are the last remaining examples of the large mercantile and fish-processing premises that were common on the St. John's waterfront. Murray Premises once bustled with the work of shipping cod to world markets. The complex narrowly escaped destruction in a huge fire that engulfed much of the city in 1892, and the buildings mark the western boundary of the fire's devastation. Now a National Historic Site, the restored buildings are home to several boutiques, offices, and a fine seafood restaurant, hung with photographs that recall the busy town of the 1900s.

⚐ Newfoundland Museum

285 Duckworth St. 【 (709) 729 2329. ◯ 9am–5pm Tue, Wed, Fri; 9am–9pm Thu; 10am–6pm Sat & Sun. ◐ Mon.

This museum illustrates the province's history over the past 9,000 years. The prehistory of Newfoundland is illustrated with artifacts excavated locally. Focusing on colonial times, restorations range from humble fishing cottages to the elegant drawing rooms of early townspeople. There is also a popular gallery of native Indian art.

⚐ The Waterfront

Water St. 【 (709) 576 8106. ♿

Tracing the edge of St. John's waterfront, Water Street is the oldest public thoroughfare in North America, dating to the late 1500s when trading first started in the town. Once a brawling wharfside lane of gin mills and brothels, Water Street and Duckworth Street now offer an array of colorful gift shops, art galleries, and some of Newfoundland's top restaurants. Also along the waterfront is Harbour Drive, a great place to stroll or relax. Nearby George Street is the hub of the city's nightlife.

⚐ East End

King's Bridge Rd. ℹ (709) 576 8106.

The East End is one of St. John's most architecturally rich neighborhoods, with narrow, cobblestone streets and elegant homes. Commissariat House, built in 1836, was once the home of 19th-century British officials. This simple but elegant historic dwelling is now a provincial museum. Nearby Government House, built during the 1820s, is the official residence of the province's Lieutenant Governor.

⚐ The Battery

Battery Rd. ℹ (709) 576 8106.

The colorful houses clinging to sheer cliffs at the entrance to the Harbour are known as the Battery. With the look and feel of a 19th-century fishing village, this is one of St. John's most photographed sites. The community is named for the military fortifications built here over centuries to defend the harbor. Local residents used the battery's guns in 1763 to fight off Dutch pirate ships.

⚐ Signal Hill

Signal Hill Rd. 【 (709) 772 5367. ◯ Interpretation Centre: Jun–Sep: 8:30am–8pm; Sep–May: 8:30am–4:30pm. 🏷 ♿

This lofty rise of land presents spectacular views of the open Atlantic, the rocky harbor entrance, and the city of St. John's curled in historic splendor around the town harbor.

View of Signal Hill from St. John's picturesque fishing harbor

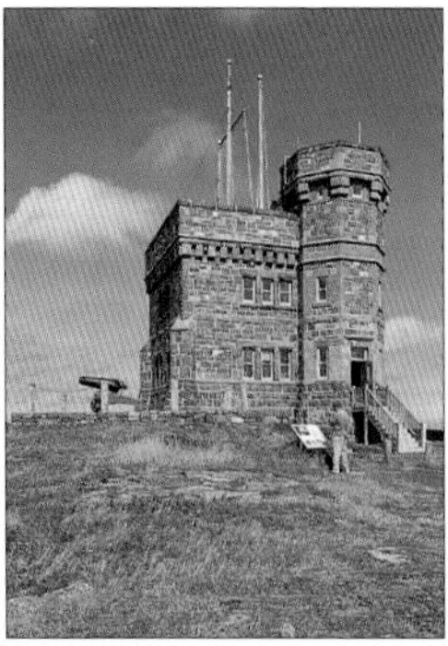

The Cabot Tower as it rises above Signal Hill over the harbor

🏛 Cabot Tower

Signal Hill Rd. ☎ *(709) 772 5367.* 🕒 *Jun–Sep: 8:30am–8:30pm; Sep–May: 8:30am–4:30pm.* ♿

The building of Cabot Tower at the top of Signal Hill began in 1897 to celebrate the 400th anniversary of Cabot's arrival. On summer weekends, soldiers in period dress perform 19th-century marching drills, with firing muskets and cannon. It was here that another Italian, Guglielmo Marconi, received the first transatlantic wireless signal in 1901.

🏛 Quidi Vidi Village

Quidi Vidi Village Rd. ☎ *(709) 729 2977.* 🕒 *daily.*

On the other side of Signal Hill, the weathered buildings of ancient Quidi Vidi Village nestle around a small harbor. Visitors can browse through the eclectic collection of antiques for sale at Mallard Cottage, dating back to the 1750s. Above the village, the Quidi Vidi Battery was a fortified gun emplacement built in 1762 to defend the entrance of Quidi Vidi Harbour. Today, the site is a reconstruction of the small barracks that soldiers lived in. Guides in period military dress are on hand to relate tales of their lives and hardships.

🍁 Pippy Park

Nagles Place. ☎ *(709) 737 3655.* 🕒 *daily.* ♿

Visitors are sometimes startled to see moose roaming free in St. John's, but it happens often in this 1,400-ha (3,460-acre) nature park, 4 km (2 miles) from the town center. The park is also home to the ponds and gardens of the local Botanical Gardens. The only Fluvarium in North America is based here too, featuring nine underwater windows that look onto the natural activity of a rushing freshwater trout stream.

> **VISITORS' CHECKLIST**
>
> 👥 *102,000.* ✈ *6km (4 miles) N of the city.* 🚌 *Memorial University.* ⛴ *Argentia 130 km (80 miles) SE.* ℹ *St. John's City Hall, New Gower St. (709) 576 8196.* 🎉 *St. John's Days Celebrations (Jun); Signal Hill Tattoo (Jul-Aug); Royal St. John's Regatta (Aug).*

🏛 Cape Spear Lighthouse

☎ *(709) 772 5367.* 🕒 *mid-May–mid-Oct: daily.* 🎟 ♿

Ten km (6 miles) southeast of town, the Cape Spear National Historic Site marks the most easterly point in North America. Set atop seaside cliffs, as the ocean pounds rocks below, the majestic Cape Spear Lighthouse has long been a symbol of Newfoundland's independence. Two lighthouses sit here. The original, built in 1836 and the oldest in Newfoundland, stands beside a graceful, modern, automated lighthouse, added in 1955.

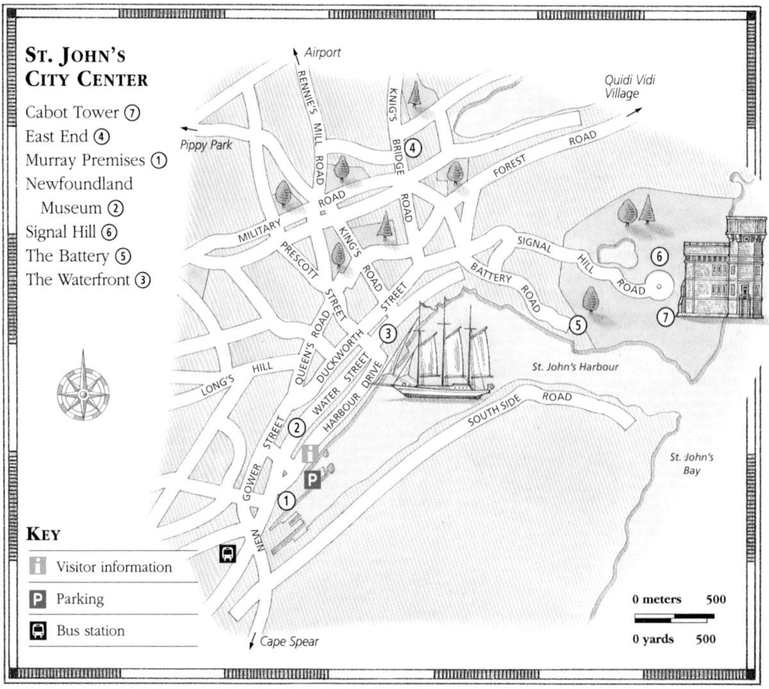
ST. JOHN'S CITY CENTER
Cabot Tower ⑦
East End ④
Murray Premises ①
Newfoundland Museum ②
Signal Hill ⑥
The Battery ⑤
The Waterfront ③
Airport
Pippy Park
Quidi Vidi Village
RENNIE'S MILL ROAD
KING'S BRIDGE ROAD
FOREST ROAD
MILITARY ROAD
PRESCOTT STREET
KING'S ROAD
SIGNAL HILL ROAD
BATTERY ROAD
QUEEN'S ROAD
DUCKWORTH STREET
WATER STREET
HARBOUR DRIVE
LONG'S HILL
GOWER STREET
NEW GOWER
SOUTH SIDE ROAD
St. John's Harbour
St. John's Bay
Cape Spear
KEY
Visitor information
Parking
Bus station
0 meters 500
0 yards 500

Whale- and bird-watching boats tour the Avalon Peninsula frequently

Avalon Peninsula ❷

🚉 St. John's. ⚓ Argentia. ℹ️ Dept. of Tourism, Confederation Building, St. John's (709) 729 2830.

THE PICTURESQUE community of Ferryland on the Avalon Peninsula is the site of a large-scale archeological excavation of Colony Avalon, a settlement founded by English explorer Lord Baltimore and 11 settlers in 1621. This was Baltimore's first New World venture, intended

Boat-tour sign in Witless Bay

to be a self-sufficient colony engaged in fishing, agriculture, and trade, with firm principles of religious tolerance.

By the end of the following year there were 32 settlers. The population continued to grow, and for many years it was the only successful colony in the area. Although excavations to date have unearthed only five percent of the colony, it has proved to be one of the richest sources of artifacts from any early European settlement in North America. Over half a million pieces have been recovered, such as pottery, clay pipes, household implements, and structural parts of many buildings, including defensive works, a smithy, and a waterfront commercial complex. An interpretive center tells the story of the colony and a guided tour includes the chance to watch archeologists working on site and in the laboratory.

At the southern end of the peninsula, **Cape St. Mary's Ecological Reserve** is the only nesting seabird colony in the province that can be approached on foot. A short trail leads along spectacular seacliffs to a site where over 8,000 golden-headed gannets nest on a rock just a few yards over the cliff.

On the southwest side of the peninsula, overlooking the entrance to the historic French town of Placentia, visitors can stroll through **Castle Hill National Historic Site**. These French fortifications dating back to 1632 protected the town, and the site of the remains offers fine coastal views.

🐦 Cape St. Mary's Ecological Reserve
off Route 100. 📞 (709) 729 2431. ⏱ year round. **Interpretive Centre** ⏱ daily, May–Oct. 🖼 ♿

🏰 Castle Hill National Historic Site
Jerseyside, Placentia Bay. 📞 (709) 227 2401. ⏱ Sep–mid-Jun: 8:30am–4:30pm; late Jun–Aug: 8:30am–8pm. 🖼 ♿ 🎫

Burin Peninsula ❸

🚉 St. John's. ⚓ Argentia. ℹ️ Columbia Drive, Marystown (709) 279 1211.

THE BURIN PENINSULA presents some of the most dramatic and impressive scenery in Newfoundland. Short, craggy peaks rise above a patchwork green carpet of heather, dotted by scores of glittering lakes. In the fishing town of Grand Bank, the **Southern Newfoundland Seaman's Museum** is a memorial to Newfoundland seamen who perished at sea. The nearby town of Fortune offers a ferry to the French-ruled islands of Saint-Pierre and Miquelon.

🏛 The Southern Newfoundland Seaman's Museum
Marine Drive. 📞 (709) 832 1484. ⏱ May–Oct: daily. ♿ limited. 🎫

Saint-Pierre and Miquelon ❹

👥 6,400. ✈ ⊠ ⚓ ℹ️ 4274 Place de General DeGaulle (508) 41 23 84.

THESE TWO SMALL islands are not Canadian but French, and have been under Gallic rule since 1783. Saint-Pierre, the only town on the island of the same name, is a charming French seaside village, complete with gendarmes, bicycles, and fine French bakeries where people line up every morning for fresh baguettes. The **Saint-Pierre Museum** details the history of the islands, including their lively role as a bootlegger's haven during Prohibition in the 1930s when over 3 million cases of liquor passed

The Newfoundland Ferry collects visitors for Saint-Pierre and Miquelon

Cape Bonavista Lighthouse, built on the spot believed to be John Cabot's first landing place in the New World

through this tiny port annually. Many of the harborfront warehouses originally built for this trade are still standing.

A daily ferry leaves Saint-Pierre for the smaller village of Miquelon. Miquelon Island is made up of two smaller islands, Langlade and Grand Miquelon, joined by a narrow, 12-km (7-mile) long strand. The road across this sandy isthmus crosses grassy dunes where wild horses graze and surf pounds sandy beaches.

🏛 **Saint-Pierre Museum**
Rue du 11 Novembre. **℃** *011 508 41 35 70.* ⭘ *2–5pm daily.* 🎫 ⭘

Bonavista Peninsula ❺

⭘ *St. John's.* ⭘ *Argentia.*
ℹ *Clarenville (709) 466 3100.*

BONAVISTA Peninsula juts out into the Atlantic ocean, a rugged coastal landscape of seacliffs, harbor inlets, and enchanting small villages such as Birchy Cove and Trouty.

The town of Bonavista is believed to be the point at which Italian explorer John Cabot *(see p40)* first stepped ashore in the New World. A monument to the explorer stands on a high, rocky promontory, near the Cape Bonavista Lighthouse, built in 1843.

Along the Bonavista waterfront, the huge 19th-century buildings of Ryan Premises,

once a busy fish merchants' processing facility, are now restored as a National Historic Site. Ryan Premises include three large buildings where fish were dried, stored, and packed for shipping, and displays on the history of the fisheries in North America. The waterfront salt house offers local music.

Trinity ❻

🏃 *300.* ℹ *Trinity Interpretation Centre, West St. (709) 464 2042.*

THE CHARMING village of Trinity, with its colorful 19th-century buildings overlooking the blue waters of Trinity Bay, is easily one of the most beautiful Newfoundland communities. Best explored on foot, Trinity has a range of craft shops and restaurants. The **Trinity Museum** contains over 2,000 artifacts, illustrating the town's past.

Also here is Hiscock House, a turn-of-the-century home, restored to the style of 1910, where merchant Emma Hiscock ran the village store, forge, and post office while raising her six children.

🏛 **Trinity Museum**
Church Rd. **℃** *(709) 464 2244.* ⭘ *mid-Jun–mid-Sep: 10am–6pm daily.* 🎫 ⭘

Terra Nova National Park ❼

Trans-Canada Hwy. ⭘ *from St. John's.* ⭘ *Jun–mid-Oct: daily.* ⭘ ⭘ *limited.* ℹ *Glovertown (709) 533 2801.*

THE GENTLY rolling forested hills and deep fjords of northeastern Newfoundland are the setting for Terra Nova National Park. The park's Marine Interpretation Centre offers excellent displays on the local marine flora and fauna, including a fascinating underwater video monitor that broadcasts the busy life of the bay's seafloor. Whale-watching tours are also available.

A lookout over Terra Nova National Park

Notre Dame Bay ❽

🏠 Gander. 🚢 Port-aux-Basques.
ℹ️ Notre Dame Junction, Rte 1 (709)
535 8547.

O N THE EAST side of Notre
Dame Bay, traditional
Newfoundland outports maintain a way of life that echoes
their history. The **Twillingate
Museum**, located in an
elegant Edwardian rectory in
Twillingate, has several rooms
furnished with period antiques.
Also on display are aboriginal
artifacts collected from nearby
sites, and marine memorabilia
recounting the region's
fascinating shipping history.

Boat tours take passengers
out into the bay for a close-
up look at the huge icebergs
that float by in spring and
summer, and to see the many
whales that roam about offshore. Nearby Wild Cove and
Durrell are romantic villages.

**The elegant Edwardian rectory
that houses the Twillingate Museum**

Gander ❾

🏃 1,300. 🛬 ✈️ ℹ️ 109 Trans-
Canada Hwy (709) 256 7110.

B EST KNOWN for its illustrious
aviation history, Gander is
a small town and a useful
tourist center for fuel and food.
In Grand Falls-Windsor, 50 km
(31 miles) west
of Gander,

A mamateek dwelling reveals a past way of life in Grand Falls Indian village

the Mary March Regional
Museum, named after the last
survivor of the now extinct
Beothuk people, traces 5,000
years of human habitation in
the Exploits Valley. Throughout
Newfoundland, the Beothuks
were decimated by disease
and genocide between 1750
and 1829. Behind the museum,
visitors can take a guided tour
through the historic village.

The Southwest Coast ❿

🏠 Ferry dock terminal. 🚢 Port-aux-
Basques. ℹ️ Port-aux-Basques (709)
695 2262.

I N SOUTHERN Newfoundland
a 45-km (28-mile) coastal
drive along Route 470 from
Channel Port-aux-Basques to
Rose Blanche leads through a
landscape of ancient, jagged,
green mountains and along a
rocky, surf-carved shoreline.
Near Rose Blanche, a 500-m
(545-yd) boardwalk trail winds
through bright wildflower-
strewn heath to the impressive Barachois Falls. There is
a charming picnic spot at the
foot of the 55 m (180 ft) falls.
The Rose Blanche Lighthouse,

built in 1873, stands in defiant
splendor atop the harbor
headland. The peninsula road
offers marvelous scenery,
especially near Petit Jardin.

Gros Morne National Park ⓫

📞 (709) 458 2417. 🚃 Corner
Brook. 🚢 St. Barbe. ⏰ daily.
🖼️ ♿ 🚻

A UNITED NATIONS World
Heritage Site, Gros Morne
is Newfoundland's scenic
masterpiece. Here the Long
Range Mountains rise 700 m
(2,000 ft) above blue fjords
that cut into the coastal range.
Some of the world's oldest
mountains, these are pre-
Cambrian and several million
years older than the Rockies.

The best way to see the park
is on a boat tour along Western
Brook Pond, a narrow fjord
cradled between soaring cliffs
where waterfalls vaporize as
they tumble from great heights.
Wildlife, including
moose, caribou,
and eagles, is
frequently
seen and
heard.

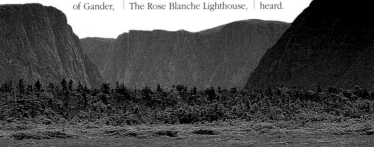

The Long Range Mountains in Gros Morne National Park, seen from a walkway in the park

Northern Peninsula Tour ⓬

Viking Trail
Road sign on Hwy 430

A LAND OF LEGENDS and mystery, the Northern Peninsula of Newfoundland offers adventurous travelers the chance to experience over 40 centuries of human history, from early aboriginal people through colonization to today's modern fishing life. The road north travels along a harsh and rocky coast. Along the way, important historic sites, such as L'Anse-aux-Meadows, tell the story of the earlier cultures who chose this wild land as their home.

TIPS FOR DRIVERS

Tour length: *690 km (430 miles) along Hwy 430.*
Starting point: *Deer Lake, at junction of Hwy 1.*
Stopping off points: *Gros Morne's Wiltondale Visitors' Centre and Tablelands; Port au Choix National Historic Site; Grenfell Museum in St. Anthony.*

Port au Choix ⑤
This historic site is dedicated to exhibitions of Maritime Archaic Indians and Dorset Eskimos who lived here in 2000 BC and AD 500.

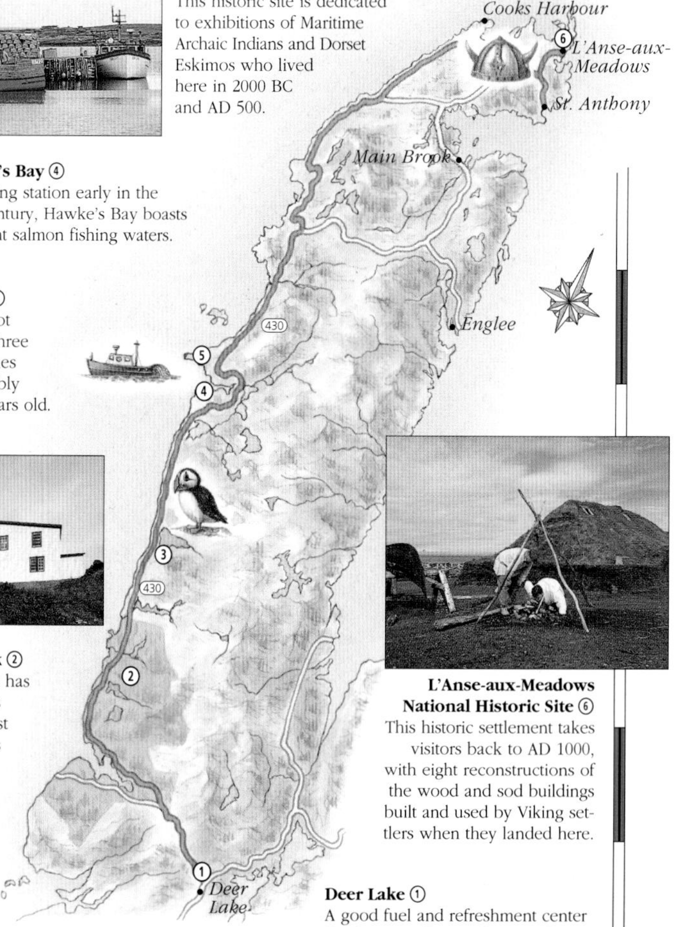
Cooks Harbour
L'Anse-aux-Meadows
St. Anthony
Main Brook
Englee
430
430
Deer Lake

Hawke's Bay ④
A whaling station early in the 20th century, Hawke's Bay boasts excellent salmon fishing waters.

The Arches ③
This lovely spot is named for three limestone arches that are probably 400 million years old.

Gros Morne National Park ②
This fine place has a reputation as one of the most beautiful parks in the whole of Canada.

L'Anse-aux-Meadows National Historic Site ⑥
This historic settlement takes visitors back to AD 1000, with eight reconstructions of the wood and sod buildings built and used by Viking settlers when they landed here.

Deer Lake ①
A good fuel and refreshment center for those starting on the tour, Deer Lake and its surrounding area is remarkable for its jagged landscape, glittering seas, wildlife, and tiny friendly fishing villages.

KEY

- Tour route
- Other roads
- Viewpoint

0 km 25
0 miles 25

Fishermen's huts in the village of Red Bay on the coast of Labrador

Labrador Straits ⓭

🚤 *Blanc Sablon.* ℹ️ *Labrador Straits Historical Development Association, Forteau (709) 927 5825.*

H AUNTINGLY beautiful coastal landscapes explain why the Labrador Straits is a popular place to visit in this province. A summer ferry service crosses the straits from Newfoundland to Blanc Sablon, Quebec, just a few kilometers from the Labrador border. From there, an 85-km (53-mile) road leads along the coast through a wild countryside of high, barren hills, thinly carpeted by heath and wind-twisted spruce.

The Labrador Straits was an important steamship route in the mid-19th century. To aid navigation in the often treacherous waters, the Point Amour Lighthouse was built in 1854 near L'Anse-Amour. Now a Provincial Historic Site, this 30-m (109-ft) tower is the second-tallest lighthouse in Canada. Visitors can ascend the tower for stunning views of the Labrador coast.

Along the road to the lighthouse is a monument that marks the site of the Maritime Archaic Burial Mound National Historic Site, North America's oldest burial mound, where a Maritime Archaic Indian child was laid to rest 7,500 years ago.

At the end of Rte. 510 lies **Red Bay National Historic Site**. Here visitors can take a short boat ride to an island where 16th-century Basque whalers operated the first factory in the New World. A tour around the island leads past the foundations of the shanties, shipworks, and cooper shops

where as many as 1,500 men worked each season, rendering whale oil for lamps in Europe.

⛵ Red Bay National Historic Site
Route 510. ☎️ *(709) 920 2142.* ⭕ *mid-Jun–mid-Oct: daily.* 💰 ♿

Battle Harbour ⓮

🗙 🚤 ℹ️ *Mary's Harbour, Newfoundland. (709) 921 6216.*

O NCE CONSIDERED the unofficial capital of Labrador (from the 1870s to the 1930s), Battle Harbour, a small settlement on an island just off the southern coast of Labrador, was a thriving fishing community during the late 18th and 19th centuries. In 1966, the dwindling population was relocated to St. Mary's on the mainland, but all of the town's buildings,

many of which date back 200 years, were left standing, and in the 1990s the town was restored. Today, visitors can tour the island and get a taste of the way life was in coastal Labrador a century ago.

Nain ⓯

🚶 *1,000.* 🗙 🚤 ℹ️ *Town Council, Nain (709) 922 2842.*

T RAVELING NORTH, Nain is the final community of more than a few hundred people. The town can be reached by a coastal boat service that carries passengers and freight, but no cars. A large part of Nain's small population is Inuit, and Piulimatsivik (The Nain Museum) contains valuable artifacts from early Inuit culture. Nain is home to many of Labrador's most prominent Inuit artists. There are also exhibits highlighting the important role that the Moravian Missionaries, an evangelical Christian movement active in the late 18th century, played in bringing education and health care to this wilderness region.

Nearby Hopedale was the site of one of the many Moravian Missions built in Labrador. Today the main feature here is the **Hopedale Mission National Historic Site**. Visitors can tour the Mission, constructed in 1782, which is the oldest woodframe building in Atlantic Canada. Both the Mission and

Inuit children in Nain

Battle Harbour Island with icebergs on the horizon

A snowy street in Nain during the long winter

other structures were built in Germany, shipped across the Atlantic, and reassembled here.

⛪ Hopedale Mission National Historic Site

Agvituk Historical Society, Hopedale. 📞 (709) 933 3777. 🕐 daily. 📷

The Moravian Church in Happy Valley-Goose Bay

Happy Valley-Goose Bay ⑯

🏃 8,600. 🛬 ✈ ⚓ ℹ Labrador North Chamber of Commerce (709) 896 8787. 📷 obligatory, book ahead.

THE LARGEST town in the wilderness of Central Labrador, Happy Valley-Goose Bay was a strategically important stopover for transatlantic flights during World War II. A Canadian military base now tests fighter planes in the area.

Today, the town is home to the Labrador Heritage Museum, where exhibitions depict Labrador's fascinating history. The museum pays particular attention to the life of trappers, with displays that include samples of animal furs, trapper's tools, and a traditional tilt (wilderness shelter).

Churchill Falls ⑰

ℹ Churchill Falls Development Corporation (709) 925 3335. 📷 obligatory, book ahead.

THE TOWN of Churchill Falls is ideally placed for visitors to stock up on supplies, fill up with gas, and check tyres as there are no service stations between Happy Valley-Goose Bay and Labrador City. Churchill Falls is famous as the site of one of the largest hydroelectric power stations in the world. Built in the early 1970s, the plant is an extraordinary feat of engineering, diverting the Churchill River (it is Labrador's largest) and its incredible volume of water to power the underground turbines that produce 5,225 megawatts of power – enough to supply the needs of a small country. Guided tours are available of this impressive complex.

Labrador City ⑱

🏃 9,000. ✈ 🚌 🚍 ℹ Labrador North Tourism Development Corporation (709) 944 7631.

IN THE MIDST of ancient tundra, Labrador City is a mining town that shows the modern, industrial face of Canada. The town is home to the largest open-pit iron mine in the world and the community has largely grown up around it since the late 1950s. The historic building that once held the town's first bank is now the Height of Land Heritage Centre, a museum of photographs, artifacts, and displays dedicated to preserving the history of the development of Labrador.

The vast open wilderness surrounding Labrador City, with its myriad pristine lakes and rivers, is renowned as a sportsman's paradise that attracts hunters and anglers from around the world. Every March, this region sponsors the Labrador 150 Dogsled Race, which has become one of the world's top dogsledding competitions. The western Labrador wilderness is also home to the 700,000 caribou of the George River herd. The herd moves freely through the area for most of the year, grazing the tundra in small bands. Professional outfitters take groups of visitors out to track the herd through the region. Many tourists make the trip to admire the animals.

THE LABRADOR COASTAL FERRY

The Labrador Coastal Ferry is the primary mode of transportation for many communities along the Coast. Departing from St. Anthony in northern Newfoundland, the ferry round-trip takes 12 days, visiting up to 48 communities, delivering goods, passengers, and supplies in each port. Half the passenger space is for tourists, half for locals. Along the way, the ferry calls at the historic port of Battle Harbour and travels into fjords. Icebergs are a common sight.

New Brunswick, Nova Scotia, and Prince Edward Island

THE BEAUTY AND lure of the sea is always close at hand here. Stunning coastal scenery, picturesque centuries-old villages, world-class historic sites, and a wealth of family attractions have turned these three Maritime Provinces into one of Canada's top vacation destinations. New Brunswick's ruggedly beautiful Bay of Fundy is matched by the gently rolling landscape of Acadian villages tucked into quiet coves and long sandy beaches. With its sparkling bays and ancient weathered fishing towns, Nova Scotia embodies the romance of the sea. Elegant country inns and historic sites bring the past to life. Canada's smallest province, Prince Edward Island, is best known for its vibrant green farmlands, red bluffs, and deep blue waters, enjoyed by cyclists, anglers, and hikers.

SIGHTS AT A GLANCE

Historic Towns and Cities
Amherst **11**
Annapolis Royal **16**
Bouctouche **8**
Digby **17**
Fredericton **4**
Grand Falls **5**
Halifax **22**
Lunenburg **19**
Mahone Bay **20**
Parrsboro **13**
Peggy's Cove **21**
Shelburne **18**

Saint John **2**
Truro **12**
Windsor **14**
Wolfville **15**

National Parks
Fundy National Park **1**
Kouchibouguac
    National Park **7**

Historic Sites and Areas of Natural Beauty
Acadian Peninsula **6**
Cape Breton Island **24**

Eastern Shore **23**
Passamaquoddy Bay **3**
Prince Edward Island **10**
Village Historique Acadien **9**

KEY

✈ International airport

═ Highway

▬ Major road

— Major rail routes

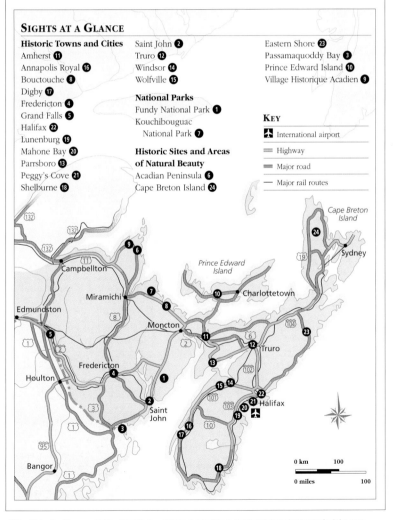

◁ The Fisheries Museum of The Atlantic, Lunenburg, housed in a wooden fishing hut typical of the area

Humpback whales at play in the Bay of Fundy

Fundy National Park ❶

📞 (506) 887 6000. 🚂 Moncton.
🚌 Sussex. ⛴ Saint John. ◯ daily.
📅 Jun–Sep. ♿ ✔

ALONG New Brunswick's
eastern shore, the tremendous tides of the Bay of Fundy
are a powerful feature of
everyday life. Twice
a day, over 100
billion tons of
water swirl into and
out of the bay, creating a tidal shift of
up to 15 m (48 ft)
and carving out a
stunning wild and
rocky shoreline.
    One of the best
places to experience
these world-famous
tidal wonders is at Fundy
National Park. Here at low
tide, visitors can walk out over
the Hopewell Rocks, looking
for marine treasures. The Bay
is a favorite with naturalists.
Swirling tides make for
nutrient-rich waters that attract
the world's largest population
of whales, including minke,
humpback, finback, and even
the rare right whale.

Moose in Fundy National Park

Saint John ❷

🏙 125,000. ✈ 🚂 ⛴ 🛈 City
Hall, King St. (506) 658 2990.

NEW BRUNSWICK'S largest
city, Saint John, still
retains the charm of a small
town. In 1785, 14,000 loyalists
escaping the turmoil of the
American Revolution built
Saint John in under a year.

More recently, restoration
has made Saint John's historic
center a delightful place to
explore. The Old City Market
is a working public market,
with colorful produce stacked
high, fresh seafood vendors,
cafés, and an excellent traditional fish restaurant.
    In nearby Market Square, an
airy atrium links buildings that
were once the city's center of
commerce. Here
visitors will find
upscale restaurants
and stores. Market
Square is also the
home of the lively
**New Brunswick
Museum**. Three
floors offer clever
and entertaining
exhibits on New
Brunswick's geological, cultural,
and natural history. Children
particularly enjoy the Hall of
Whales and the three-level
Tidal Tube in which
water rises and falls,
re-creating the height
of the tides roaring
away just outside.
    Nearby, the Loyalist
House Museum is located in an impressive
Georgian house built
by Loyalist David
Merritt in around 1810.
Inside, the house has
been renovated to
reflect the lifestyle of a
wealthy family of that
time, with authentic
period furnishings.

🏛 **New Brunswick Museum**
Market Square. 📞 (506)
643 2300. ◯ daily.
⬤ Dec 25. 📷 ♿

Passamaquoddy Bay ❸

🚗 St. Stephen. ⛴ Black's Harbour
& Letete. 🛈 St. Stephen (506) 466
7390.

THERE IS A genteel historic
charm to the villages
surrounding the island-filled
waters of Passamaquoddy
Bay, and none is more
charming or intriguing than
the lovely holiday town of
St. Andrews-by-the-Sea. Overlooking the town, the beautifully maintained Algonquin
Resort, with its elegant grounds
and 27-hole golf course, recalls
early 20th-century days when
St. Andrews was renowned as
an exclusive getaway of the
rich and powerful.
    In town, Water Street is lined
with intriguing boutiques,
craft shops, and fine restaurants housed in century-old
buildings. At the town dock,
tour companies offer numerous sailing, whale-watching,
and kayaking adventures.
Nearby, the elegant Georgian
home built for Loyalist Harris
Hatch in 1824 is now the location of the **Ross Memorial
Museum** which contains
an extensive collection of
antiques and art assembled
early in the 20th century.
    Two ferries leave from
the St. George area nearby
for Campobello and Grand
Manan Islands, 20 km (12
miles) and 30 km (18 miles)
south respectively of St.

Saint John town from the Saint John River

The charming Victorian vista of Fredericton seen from across the Saint John River

Andrews. The Roosevelt Campobello International Park is a 1,135-ha (2,800-acre) pre-serve on Campobello Island built around the elegant summer home of US President Franklin D. Roosevelt. The 34-room Roosevelt Cottage has been restored, and includes historic and personal artifacts belonging to Roosevelt and his family.

Renowned for its rugged coastal beauty, Grand Manan Island has high rocky cliffs, picturesque fishing villages, and brightly painted boats resting against weathered piers. It is popular with bird-watchers as it attracts large flocks of seabirds annually.

🏛 The Ross Memorial Museum
188 Montague St. 【 (506) 529 5124. ◯ late Jun–Sep: Mon–Sat; Sep & Oct: Tue–Sat. ♿

Fredericton ❹

🏚 44,000. ✕ 🖃 ℹ City Hall, Queen St. (506) 460 2041.

STRADDLING THE Saint John River, Fredericton is New Brunswick's provincial capital. Its Victorian homes and water-front church make it one of the prettiest small cities in Atlantic Canada. Several historic build-ings reflect the town's early role as a British military post. The **Beaverbrook Art Gallery** contains an impressive col-lection of 19th- and 20th-century paintings, including Salvador Dali's masterpiece *Santiago el Grande* (1957).

King's Landing Historical Settlement, 37 km (22 miles) west of Fredericton is a living history museum that re-creates daily life in a rural New Bruns-wick village of the mid-1800s. Over a hundred costumed workers bring villagers' homes, church, and school to life.

🏛 Beaverbrook Art Gallery
703 Queen St. 【 (506) 458 8545. ◯ Jun–Oct: daily; late Oct–Jun: Tue–Sun. 🅿 ♿ 🖾
🎪 King's Landing Historical Settlement
Rte 2, W of Fredericton. 【 (506) 363 4999. ◯ Jun–mid-Oct: 10am–5pm daily. 🅿 ♿ partial.

Grand Falls ❺

🏚 6,100. 🖃 ℹ Malabeam Reception Centre (506) 475 7788. 🅿

FROM FREDERICTON to Edmundston, the Saint John River flows through a pastoral valley of rolling hills, woods, and farmland. The

little town of Grand Falls consists of one well-appointed main street, which is a useful refreshment stop. The town was named Grand Falls for the mighty cataract the Saint John's River creates as it tum-bles through Grand Falls Gorge. Framed by parkland, the surge of water drops more than 25 m (40 ft). Over time it has carved a gorge 1.5 km (1 mile) long, with steep sides 70 m (200 ft) high in places.

Upriver north through the valley, the town of Edmund-ston offers the **New Bruns-wick Botanical Gardens**. Garden paths lead through eight theme gardens and two arboretums that offer a dazzling input for the senses. Bright colors, delicate scents, and even soft classical music emanating from hidden cor-ners delight visitors.

🌺 New Brunswick Botanical Gardens
Saint-Jacques, Edmundston. 【 (506) 739 6335. ◯ Jun–Oct: 9am–dusk

The deep waterfall valley of Grand Falls Gorge

Endless sandy beaches stretch to the horizon at Kouchibouguac National Park

The Acadian Peninsula **6**

🏠 Bathurst. 🚌 Bathurst.
🚢 Dalhousie. 🛈 Water St.,
Campbellton (506) 789 2367.

THE QUIET coastal villages, beaches, and gentle surf of the Acadian peninsula have made it a favorite vacation destination for years. Established here since the 1600s, the Acadians have long enjoyed a reputation for prosperous farming centered around pretty villages and a strong folk music tradition (see pp58–9).

In Shippagan, the small fishing town at the tip of the mainland, the **Marine Centre and Aquarium** holds tanks with over 3,000 specimens of Atlantic sealife and displays on local fishing industries.

Nearby, the Lamèque and Miscou islands are connected by causeways to the mainland. On Miscou Island, a 1-km (0.5-mile) boardwalk leads through a peat bog with interpretive signs about this unique ecosystem. Nearby, the 35-m (85-ft) high Miscou Lighthouse is the oldest operating wooden lighthouse in Canada.

Home to many Acadian artists, Caraquet is the busy cultural center of the peninsula. On the waterfront, adventure centers offer guided kayak trips on the Baie des Chaleurs. For those wanting an introduction to the story of the Acadians, the **Acadian Wax Museum** features a self-guided audio tour past 23 tableaus from Acadian history. The scenes begin with the founding of the

"Order of the Good Times" at Annapolis Royal in 1604 and focus on the expulsion of 1755.

🚤 **Marine Centre and Aquarium**
Rte 113, Shippagan. 📞 (506) 336 3013. ⏰ mid-May–mid-Oct: 10am–6pm daily. 🅿️ ♿
🏛 **Acadian Wax Museum**
Rte 11, Caraquet. 📞 (506) 727 6424. ⏰ Jun–Sep: daily. 🅿️ ♿

Kouchibouguac National Park **7**

📞 (506) 876 2443. 🏠 Newcastle.
🚌 Newcastle. 🚢 Miramichi. ⏰ daily.

THE NAME of this park comes from the native Mi'kmaq word for "River of Long Tides." The park's 238 sq km (92 sq miles) encompass a salt-spray world of wind-sculpted dunes, salt marshes packed with wild life, and 25 km (16 miles) of fine sand beaches, as well as excellent terrain for cyclists. One of the park's most popular activities is the Voyager Marine

Adventure, a three-hour canoe paddle to offshore sandbanks where hundreds of gray seals relax in the warm sun.

Bouctouche **8**

🏃 2,350. 🚌 🛈 14 Acadia St.
(506) 743 8811.

A SEASIDE TOWN with a strong Acadian heritage, Bouctouche is home to **Le Pays de la Sagouine**. This theme village is named for La Sagouine, the wise washerwoman created by Acadian authoress Antonine Maillet (b. 1929), very much part of Canadian popular heritage. Ongoing theatrical shows here act out Maillet's tales.

Nearby, the Irving Eco-Centre studies and protects the beautiful 12-km (8-mile) network of dunes, saltmarshes, and beach that extend along the entrance to Bouctouche Harbour.

🎭 **Le Pays de la Sagouine**
57 Acadia St. 📞 1 800 561 9188.
⏰ mid-Jun–Sep: 10am–6pm daily.

The raised boardwalk at the Irving Eco-Centre, La Dune de Bouctouche

Village Historique Acadien ⑨

AFTER THE TRAGIC deportation of 1755–63 (see p58–9), Acadians slowly returned to the Maritimes, clearing new farmlands and rebuilding their way of life. The Village Historique Acadien portrays a rural Acadian community between 1770 and 1890. The village's 45 restored historic buildings, including several working farms, cover 364 ha (900 acres). Throughout the village, period-costumed bilingual guides re-create the daily activities of the 19th century. Visitors can ride in a horse-drawn wagon, watch the work of the blacksmith, print shop, or gristmill, and also tour working farms and homes where women are busy spinning, weaving, and cooking.

VISITORS' CHECKLIST

Route 11, 10 km (6 miles) W of Caraquet. ((506) 726 2600. ☐ from Bathurst. ☐ Jun–Oct: 10am–6pm daily. ● late Oct–May. ⌨ ◙ ♿ ⚟ ⛨ ⅰⅰ

School and Chapel
Through centuries of turmoil, Catholicism was a vital mainstay of the Acadian people. Priests were also schoolteachers; education was highly prized by the community.

Men in horse-drawn cart
Traditional methods are used on the farms; tilled by local people arriving each day, the harvest is moved in carts to barns for winter.

COOPER'S SHOP
TINSMITH
LOBSTER POUND

The Chapel was built by pioneer Acadians and dates from 1831.

Doucet Farm was first built in 1840 and has been fully restored to its original appearance.

Mazerolle Farm sells fresh bread and rolls, which are baked daily in a large oven in the farmhouse.

Poirier Tavern

Savoie House Education Centre

Robin shed

Godin House

Forge
In many ways the center of the community, the blacksmith was a feature of every Acadian village, repairing farm equipment and shoeing horses for the people of the area.

The Visitors' Reception Centre offers an audiovisual presentation, and typical Acadian food in its restaurant.

0 m   100

0 yards   100

Prince Edward Island ⑩

B EAUTIFUL AND PASTORAL, Prince Edward Island is famous for its lush landscapes. Wherever you look, the island's rich colors, emerald green farmlands, red-clay roads, and sapphire sea, seem to combine and recombine in endless patterns to please the eye. The island is also a popular destination for golfers who come to tee off on some of Canada's best courses, as well as a haven for sun worshipers who revel in the sandy beaches that ring the island. Prince Edward Island seems made for exploring at a leisurely pace. Meandering coastal roads present an ever-changing panorama of sea, sand, and sky. Small historic towns are home to elegant country inns and art galleries. In the evenings, the island's famous lobster suppers await, caught fresh daily from the Atlantic Ocean.

Green Gables House
Set amid leafy green paths, this 19th-century home was the setting for the popular Anne of Green Gables *tales.*

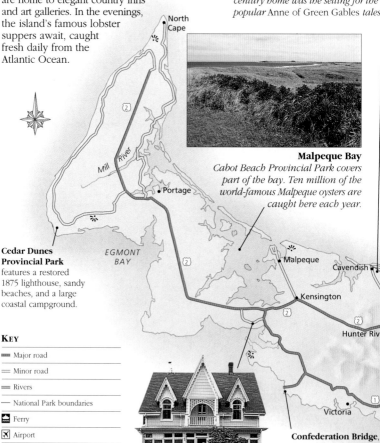

Malpeque Bay
Cabot Beach Provincial Park covers part of the bay. Ten million of the world-famous Malpeque oysters are caught here each year.

Cedar Dunes Provincial Park
features a restored 1875 lighthouse, sandy beaches, and a large coastal campground.

Main street, Summerside
This quiet city with its attractive tree-lined streets is known for its Lobster Carnival each July.

Confederation Bridge,
opened in 1997 at a total cost of Can$900m, runs for 13 km (8 miles) to the mainland.

KEY

▬▬ Major road

═══ Minor road

══ Rivers

─── National Park boundaries

⛴ Ferry

✕ Airport

☀ Viewpoint

STAR SIGHTS

★ **PEI National Park**

★ **Charlottetown**

0 km	100
0 miles	100

★ Prince Edward Island National Park

Characterized by 40 km (25 miles) of coastline leading onto red cliffs, pink and white sand beaches, and mild seas, this park offers unbeatable sport and vacationing facilities and has an educational Visitors' Centre for those interested in its marine wildlife.

VISITORS' CHECKLIST

ℹ Water St., Charlottetown. *(902) 368 4444.* ✈ *Charlotte-town.* 🚢 *to Wood Islands, Borden-Carleton.* 🚌 *to Wood Islands, Borden-Carleton, Souris.*

East Point Lighthouse
The island's easternmost point is home to a 19th-century light-house with a restored radio room. Now unmanned and fully auto-matic, it is open to visitors.

★ Charlottetown

Elegant 19th-century row houses characterize the streets of this sleepy town, the smallest of Canada's provincial capitals; in 1867 the Confederation of Canada was decided here.

St. Peter's

Souris

TO MAGDALEN ISLANDS

Hillsborough River

Georgetown

Valleyfield River

Orwell

NORTHUMBERLAND STRAIT

Red Point Beach
Characteristic red rocks lead down to wide beaches; the sand here mysteriously squeaks underfoot, much to the delight of vacationing children.

Brudenell River Provincial Park is surrounded by rocky coastlines and fine sea views.

TO NOVA SCOTIA

Panmure Island

Exploring Prince Edward Island

THE SMALLEST PROVINCE in Canada, Prince Edward Island's concentration of activity means every corner of the island is accessible. Charlottetown, known as the birthplace of Canada, is centrally located, and its tree-lined streets make a gentle start to exploring the outlying country. Red clay roads guide the visitor through farms and fishing villages to tiny provincial parks scattered throughout the island. Traveling the north coast takes in the splendid rolling green scenery of PEI National Park, with its famous beaches, while southward, warm swimming spots abound.

Fishing huts overlooking French River near Cavendish

Cavendish

This is such a busy little town that it can be hard to see the gentle, pastoral home of the *Anne of Green Gables* novels. The best place to get in touch with its charm is at the site of **Lucy Maud Montgomery's Cavendish Home**, where the author lived for many years, a simple and authentic site. The town is also the location of **Green Gables,** the novels' fictional 19th-century home.

🚻 Lucy Maud Montgomery's Cavendish Home
Route 6. 📞 *(902) 963 2231.*
⭘ *Jun–Oct: 10am–5pm daily.* 🖼 ♿

🚻 Green Gables
Route 6. 📞 *(902) 672 6350.*
⭘ *May–Oct: 9am–8pm daily.* ♿
Cavendish
Routes 6 & 13. ℹ *(902) 963 7830.*

Prince Edward Island National Park
Green Gables is part of Prince Edward Island National Park, whose western entrance is in Cavendish. This is the park's busier side. The soft sand and gentle surf of Cavendish Beach make it one of the most popular beaches in the province. The park's coastal road leads to North Rustico Beach, which is a favorite with sightseers. At the park's western end, the Homestead Trail leads for 8 km (5 miles) through rustic green woodlands and meadows.

The park's quieter eastern side features a long stretch of pristine beach and dunes, and a coastal road that makes a scenic drive. The Reeds and Rushes Trail is a lovely short boardwalk track that leads to a freshwater marsh pond where local species of geese and duck nest and feed.

🌿 Prince Edward Island National Park
🚉 *Charlottetown.* ⛴ *Wood Islands.*
ℹ *(902) 672 6350.* ⭘ *daily.* 🖼 ♿

The South Coast
Enchanting vistas of farmland and seashore are found along the roads of the south shore, between Confederation Bridge and Charlottetown. This is also where visitors will find Victoria-by-the-Sea, a small village that is home to some of the island's most interesting craftshops.

En route to Charlottetown, visitors can make a short detour to **Fort Amherst-Port-la-Joye National Historic Site**. It was here, in 1720, that the French built the island's first permanent settlement. The British captured it in 1758, and built Fort Amherst to protect the entrance to Charlottetown Harbour. While the fort is long gone, the earthworks can still be seen in the park-like surroundings.

🚻 Fort Amherst-Port-la-Joye National Historic Site
Rocky Point. 📞 *(902) 566 7626.*
⭘ *May–Oct: daily.* 🖼 ♿

The red bluffs of Cavendish Beach, one of the most favored spots in Prince Edward Island National Park

View of 19th-century church at Orwell Corners Historic Village

Panmure Island
The natural beauty of the island's eastern area is easy to experience on Panmure Island, south of Georgetown. Level roads make it popular with cyclists. In summer, the octagonal wooden **Panmure Island Lighthouse** is open, and the view from the top takes in a long vista of the island's beaches, saltmarshes, and woodlands. The lighthouse still guides ships into port as it did when it was first built in 1853.

🚩 **Panmure Island Lighthouse**
Panmure Island. 📞 (902) 838 3568. 🕐 Jul–Aug: 9am–6pm daily. 🅿

Orwell Corners Historic Village
Just outside of the small hamlet of Orwell, Orwell Corners Historic Village re-creates the day-to-day life of a small 19th-century crossroads community. Orwell Corners was thriving until well into the 20th century, when changes in transportation and commerce lessened the importance of the settlement. Restored and opened in 1973, this small historic village radiates charm. Visitors can see several buildings including a blacksmith's, church, schoolhouse, and Clarke's store, the social center of the village. Upstairs is the workshop of Clarke's seamstresses, who made dresses for local ladies.
Just 1 km (0.5 mile) away is the **Sir Andrew Macphail Homestead**. This Victorian house and its surroundings were the much-loved home of Macphail, a local doctor, journalist, teacher, and soldier who counted among his friends prime ministers and acclaimed writers such as Kipling. The house features many exhibits dealing with Macphail's life. Outside, trails wind through deep woodlands.

🚩 **Orwell Corners Historic Village**
Orwell. 📞 (902) 651 2013. 🕐 May–Oct: daily. 🅿 🅿

🚩 **Sir Andrew Macphail Homestead**
off Rte 1, Orwell. 📞 (902) 651 2789. 🕐 Jun–Sep: 10am–5pm daily. 🅿 🅿

Charlottetown
The birthplace of Canada is a charming small city. Along Peake's Quay, sailboats lie snug against marina piers, and the waterside buildings are home to numerous intriguing shops and restaurants. The elegant **Confederation Centre of the Arts** hosts an array of shows including the popular musical of *Anne of Green Gables*.
Province House National Historic Site is where the 1864 Charlottetown Conference was held (see p46), which led to the formation of Canada as a nation. Several rooms have been meticulously restored to their 19th-century character. **Ardgowan National Historic Site** was once the elegant home of William Pope, one of the Fathers of Confederation.

🏛 **Confederation Centre of the Arts**
145 Richmond St. 📞 (902) 628 1864. 🕐 daily. 🅿

🚩 **Province House National Historic Site**
165 Richmond St. 📞 (902) 566 7626. 🕐 daily; call ahead for hours. 🅿

🚩 **Ardgowan National Historic Site**
Mount Edward Rd. 📞 (902) 566 7050. 🕐 daily. 🅿

Charlottetown
ℹ Water St. (902) 368 4444.

Historic homes in Great George Street, Charlottetown

LUCY MAUD MONTGOMERY
The island's most famous author, Lucy Maud Montgomery, was born in Cavendish in 1874. Nearby Green Gables House became the setting of her internationally best-selling novel, *Anne of Green Gables* (1908), set in the late 19th century. The manuscript was accepted only on the sixth attempt. To date, millions of copies of *Anne* have been published, in 16 languages. In 1911, Lucy married and moved to Ontario, where she raised two sons. She continued to write, producing 17 more books, ten of which feature Anne, with all but one set on Prince Edward Island. She died in 1942 and was buried overlooking the farms and fields of her beloved native Cavendish, the Avonlea of which she wrote so often.

Author Lucy Maud Montgomery

Amherst ⓫

🚶 *9,700.* 🚌 ℹ️ *Rte 104, exit 1 (902) 667 8429.*

A BUSY COMMERCIAL and agricultural town right in the center of Atlantic Canada, Amherst overlooks the world's largest marsh, the beautiful Tantramar. Along the edge of the marsh, hayfields grow on land reclaimed by Acadian dikes during the 18th century. **The Cumberland County Museum** in central Amherst is located in the family home of Senator R.B. Dickey, one of the Fathers of Confederation. The museum focuses on the region's industrial development, local, and natural history. Particularly interesting are examples of goods once made in the town's busy factories.

🏛 **Cumberland County Museum**
150 Church St. 📞 *(902) 667 2561.* 🕐 *Jun–Sep: daily.* 📷 ♿

Truro ⓬

🚶 *11,700.* 🚌 🚉 ℹ️ *Victoria Square (902) 893 2922.*

A PROSPEROUS TOWN at the hub of Nova Scotia's major transportation routes, Truro is also the site of a unique geographical phenomenon, the tidal bore. As the Great Fundy tides return landward, sweeping into the Minas Basin, they generate a wave or "bore" that is driven for several kilometers up the rivers that empty into the back of the basin. An information display next to the Salmon River explains each process and posts the

Façade of Haliburton House in Windsor, home of the famous humorist

tidal times. On the nearby Shubenacadie River, visitors can ride the bore in rafts. The waves generated can reach 2 m (7 ft) in height, particularly on the new and full moons, creating a churn of whitewater that the rafts race through as they follow it for miles upstream.

Parrsboro ⓭

🚶 *1,600.* ℹ️ *Main St. (902) 254 3266.*

L OCATED ON the north shore of the Minas Basin, Parrsboro is famous as the home of the world's highest tides, which reach over 15 m (50 ft) in height. Rockhounds are drawn to the Minas Basin whose beaches are scattered with semiprecious gems and fossils. The excellent displays at **Fundy Geological Museum** in Parrsboro feature superb examples of the amethysts found locally. There are also dinosaur footprints and bones.

Prosauropod dinosaur skull from Fundy Museum

🏛 **The Fundy Geological Museum**
6 Two Islands Rd. 📞 *(902) 254 3814.* 🕐 *Jun–mid-Oct: daily; late Oct–May: Tue–Sun.* 📷 ♿

Windsor ⓮

🚶 *3,600.* 🚌 ℹ️ *Hwy 101, exit 6 (902) 798 2690.*

A QUIET TOWN whose elegant Victorian homes overlook the Avon River, Windsor was the home of Judge Thomas Chandler Haliburton, lawyer, historian, and the author of the Canadian "Sam Slick" stories, which achieved enormous popularity in the mid-1800s. Haliburton was one of the first widely recognized humorists in North America. His clever, fast-talking character Sam Slick was a Yankee clock peddler who coined idiomatic terms such as "the early bird gets the worm," and "raining cats and dogs." His elegant home is now the **Haliburton House Provincial Museum**. Surrounded by gardens that Haliburton tended and loved, the house is furnished in Victorian period antiques and contains many of his personal possessions, including his writing desk.

🏛 **Haliburton House Provincial Museum**
414 Clifton Ave. 📞 *(902) 798 2915.* 🕐 *Jun–mid-Oct: daily.* ♿ *limited.*

Two Island Beach in Parrsboro, famous for the two large rock outcrops known as the "Brothers Parrsboro"

Wolfville ⑮

🚶 3,500. ℹ️ Willow Park (902) 542 7000.

THE HOME of the acclaimed Acadia University, Wolfville and the surrounding countryside radiate a truly gracious charm. Here the green and fertile Annapolis Valley meets the shore of the Minas Basin, and keen visitors can follow country roads past lush farmlands, sun-warmed orchards, gentle tidal flats, and wildlife-filled salt marshes.

Much of the valley's rich farmland was created by dikes built by the Acadians in the 1700s. When the Acadians were deported in the Great Expulsion of 1755, the British offered the land to struggling New England villagers on the condition that the entire village would relocate. These hardworking settlers, known as Planters, proved so successful that the towns of the Annapolis Valley flourished.

Wolfville is a pretty town of tree-lined streets and inviting shops and restaurants. Nearby, the town's Visitor Information Center marks the beginning of a beautiful 5-km (3-mile) trail along the Acadian dikes to the graceful church at the **Grand Pré National Historic Site**. When the British marched into the Acadian village of Grand Pré in August 1755, it marked the beginning of the Great Uprooting, *Le Grand Dérangement*, which eventually forced thousands of peace-loving Acadians from Nova Scotia *(see pp58–9)*. In 1921 a beautiful stone church modeled after French country churches was built on the site of the old village of Grand Pré as a memorial to this tragedy. Today, visitors tour the church and stroll around the garden grounds where a statue of Evangeline, the heroine of Longfellow's epic poem about the Acadians, stands waiting for her lover, Gabriel. The site's information center features exhibits on the Acadians, their deportation and eventual resettlement in

Longfellow's Evangeline

the Maritimes. Many families hid locally, but even deportees returned in the 18th century.

🏛 Grand Pré National Historic Site

Hwy 101, exit 10. ℹ️ (902) 542 3631. ⏰ daily. ♿ ♿

Annapolis Royal ⑯

🚶 630. 🚌 ℹ️ Prince Albert Rd. (902) 532 5769.

AT THE EASTERN end of the Annapolis Valley lies the historic and picturesque town of Annapolis Royal. It was near here that Samuel de Champlain built the fur trading post of Port Royal in 1605 *(see p41)*. A purely commercial venture, this was the first European settlement in the New World north of Florida. **The Port Royal National Historic Site** is an exact replica of the original colony, based on French farms of the period, from plans drawn by Champlain.

Kejimkujik Park entrance sign

An hour's drive inland from Annapolis Royal lies **Kejimkujik National Park**, which covers 381 square km (148 sq miles) of inland wilderness laced with sparkling lakes and rivers. Throughout the park there are numerous paddling routes and 15 hiking trails, ranging from short walks to a 60-km (37-mile) perimeter wilderness and wildlife trail.

🏛 Port Royal National Historic Site

15 km W. of Annapolis Royal. ℹ️ (902) 532 2898. ⏰ May–Oct: 9am–5pm. 🅿️ ♿

🌲 Kejimkujik National Park

Hwy 8. ℹ️ (902) 682 2772. ⏰ daily. 🅿️ mid-May–Oct. ♿

Digby ⑰

🚶 2,300. ✈️ 🚌 ⛴ ℹ️ Shore Rd (902) 245 2201.

THE HARDWORKING fishing town of Digby is virtually synonymous with the plump, juicy scallops that are the prime quarry of the town's extensive fishing fleet. The area around Digby also offers splendid scenery and is the starting place for a scenic trip along Digby Neck to the rocky coastal landscape of beautiful Long and Brier Islands.

The waters off Long and Brier Islands brim with finback, minke, and humpback whales, and whale-watching tours are one of the region's favorite pastimes. Some visitors may even glimpse the rare right whale, as about 200 of the 350 left in the world spend their summers basking and breeding in the warm Bay of Fundy.

Children having fun in a canoeing lake at Kejimkujik National Park

Riverfront houses at Bridgewater near Lunenburg, Nova Scotia ▷

The Dory Shop Museum in Shelburne, center of local boat-building

Shelburne ⑱

🏚 2,250. 🚃 ℹ️ Dock St. (902) 875 4547.

A QUIET HISTORIC town nestled on the shore of a deep harbor, Shelburne was founded hastily by 3,000 United Empire Loyalists fleeing persecution after the American Revolution in 1775. More loyalists followed over the next few years, and Shelburne's population swelled to 16,000, making it at the time the largest town in British North America. Many of these settlers were wealthy merchants who were unprepared for the rigors of living in a primitive land. Over time, many relocated to Halifax or returned to England, leaving behind the fine 18th-century homes they had built.

Today, a walk along Water Street leads past some of the town's most attractive historic homes to the **Dory Shop Museum**. This two-storey waterfront structure has been a commercial dory (flat-bottomed) boat building shop since its founding in 1880. During the days of the Grand Banks schooner fleet,

Shelburne dories were famous for their strength and seaworthiness, and the town boasted seven shops that built thousands of boats each year. The museum's first floor features displays on the industry and the salt-cod fishery. Upstairs, skilled shipwrights demonstrate the techniques of dory building that have changed little in a century.

🏛 **Dory Shop Museum**
Dock St. 📞 (902) 875 3219.
🕐 Jun–Sep: daily. 🎟 ♿ limited.

Lunenburg ⑲

🏚 2,800. 🚃 ℹ️ Waterfront (902) 634 8100.

No TOWN CAPTURES the seafaring romance of Nova Scotia as much as Lunenburg. In the mid-1700s the British, eager for another loyal settlement, laid out a town plan for Lunenburg. They then offered the land to Protestant settlers from Germany. Although these settlers were mainly farmers, they soon turned to shipbuilding and harvesting the wealth of the

sea. In 1996 the town was declared a UNESCO World Heritage Site, representing one of the best-preserved examples of a planned British settlement in the New World.

The **Fisheries Museum of the Atlantic** fills several historic buildings along the waterfront. The museum docks are home to many ships including the *Theresa E. Conner*, the last of the Grand Banks Schooners.

🏛 **Fisheries Museum of the Atlantic**
Bluenose Dr. 📞 (902) 634 4794.
🕐 mid-May–mid-Oct: daily; late Oct–May: Mon–Fri. 🎟 ♿ limited.

One of Mahone Bay's three waterfront churches

Mahone Bay ⑳

🏚 1,100. 🚃 ℹ️ Hwy 3 (902) 624 6151.

THE SMALL seaside town of Mahone Bay has been called the "prettiest town in Canada." Tucked into the shores of the bay that shares its name, the waterfront is lined with historic homes dating to the 1700s, and at

View of the Lunenberg Fisheries Museum of the Atlantic along the town's romantic waterfront

the back of the harbor three stately churches cast their reflection into the still waters.

The town has attracted some of Canada's finest artists and craftspeople, whose colorful shops line the main street. The small **Settlers Museum** offers exhibits and artifacts relating the town's settlement by foreign Protestants in 1754, and its prominence as a boat-building center. The museum's most popular exhibit is a collection of 18th- and 19th-century ceramics and antiques.

🏛 **Settlers Museum**
578 Main St. ☎ (902) 624 6263.
⏰ May–Sep: Tue–Sun.

Peggy's Cove ㉑

🎣 60. 🍴 Sou'wester Restaurant (902) 823 2561/1074.

THE GRACEFUL Peggy's Cove Lighthouse stands atop wave-worn granite rocks and is one of the most photo-graphed sights in Canada, a symbol of Nova Scotia's enduring bond with the sea. The village, with its colorful houses clinging to the rocks, and small harbor lined with weathered piers and fish sheds, has certainly earned its reputa-tion as one of the province's most picturesque fishing vil-lages. This is a delightful place to stroll through, but visitors may want to avoid midday in summer, when the number of tour buses can be a dis-traction. Early morning and late afternoon are the best times to walk peacefully along the smooth granite headland, with its salty sea breezes and captivating coastal views.

The village was also the home of well-known marine artist and sculptor, William E. deGarthe (1907–83). Just above the harbor, the deGarthe Gallery has a permanent exhi-bition of 65 of his best-known paintings and sculptures.

Right outside the gallery, the Memorial is a 30-m (90-ft) sculpture created by deGarthe as his monument to Nova Scotian Fishermen. Carved into an outcropping of native granite rock, the sculpture depicts 32 fishermen, and

The best-known symbol of Atlantic Canada, Peggy's Cove Lighthouse

their wives and children. The large angel in the sculpture is the original Peggy, sole survivor of a terrible 19th-century shipwreck, for whom the village was named.

Halifax ㉒

See pp86–7.

The Eastern Shore ㉓

🚌 Halifax. ✈ Antigonish. 🚢 Pictou.
ℹ Canso (902) 366 2170.

A TOUR ALONG the Eastern Shore is a trip through old-world Nova Scotia, through towns and villages where life has changed little since the turn of the 20th century. The tiny house and farm that comprise the Fisher-man's Life Museum in Jeddore, Oyster Ponds (60 km/37 miles east of Halifax) was the home of an inshore fisherman, his

wife, and 13 daughters around 1900. Today, the home-stead is a living-history mus-eum where guides in period costume (many of them wives of local fishermen) reenact the simple daily life of an inshore fishing family, still the heart of Nova Scotia culture. Visitors who arrive at midday may be invited to share lunch cooked over a woodburning stove. There are also daily demonstrations that include rug-hooking, quilting, and knitting, and visitors can tour the fishing stage where salted fish were stored.

Sherbrooke Village is the largest living-history museum in Nova Scotia. Between 1860 and 1890, this was a gold and lumber boomtown. As the gold ran out, Sherbrooke once again became a sleepy rural village. In the early 1970s, 25 of Sherbrooke's most historic buildings were restored. Within the village, scores of costumed guides bring 19th-century Nova Scotia to life. A ride on a horse-drawn wagon offers an overview of the town; the drivers share bits of local his-tory as the horses trot along the village roads. At the Apothecary, visitors can watch the careful mixing of patent medicines, and those interest-ed in the Ambrotype Studio can dress in period costumes, sitting very still while the vin-tage camera records their im-age on glass. Just outside town a massive waterwheel turns, powering the Lumber Mill.

♨ **Sherbrooke Village**
off Hwy 7. ☎ (902) 522 2400.
⏰ Jun–Oct: daily. 📷

The Apothecary at the living history museum Sherbooke Village

Halifax ❷

WITH ITS GLEAMING waterfront, pretty parks, and unique blend of modern and historic architecture, Halifax is a romantic and fascinating small city. Its cultured flavor belies Halifax's 250-year history as a lusty, brawling, military town. Founded in 1749 by General George Cornwallis and 2,500 English settlers, Halifax was planned as Britain's military center north of Boston. The city has a long history of adventure, being the town where swash-buckling legalized pirates, or privateers, brought captured ships to be shared with the crown, at a time when men made huge fortunes from sea trading. Today, Halifax is best known as Canada's foremost center of higher learning and has many colleges and five universities.

Town memorial to merchant seamen

Exploring Halifax

This is an easy town to explore on foot, as many of the better museums, historic sites, shops, and restaurants are located within the fairly contained historic core.

Downtown, leading west from Brunswick Street, is hilly and green, ideal for a leisurely walk to appreciate the old-style architecture. Citadel Hill offers excellent views of the town as it stretches out over the water.

🏛 Historic Properties

1869 Upper Water St. ☎ (902) 429 0530. ◯ daily. ♿ limited.
The Historic Properties are a wharfside collection of elegant stone and timber-frame struc-tures, which were originally built in the 19th century to hold the booty captured by privateers. Today, they house an intriguing collection of specialty and gift shops, pubs, and fine restaurants. This is the one of the city's favorite gathering spots on warm summer nights, with crowds of strollers enjoying the lights of the harbor and music drifting from nearby pubs, or placing bets at the Sheraton Casino.

🏛 Maritime Museum of the Atlantic

1675 Lower Water St. ☎ (902) 424 7490. ◯ daily. 🎟 summer. ♿ 🏪 on request.
This harborfront museum offers extensive displays on Nova Scotia's seafaring history, including small craft, a restored chandlery, and, at the dock outside, the elegantly refitted 1921 research vessel *Acadia*. The museum's most popular exhibit is the *Titanic* display, which offers artifacts recovered from the ship. There is also a grand staircase, a replica of the original, which was built for the 1997 movie, *Titanic*, partly filmed in Halifax. After the 1912 catastrophe, many of the bodies that were recov-ered were brought to Halifax, and 150 are buried in the town.

🏛 Harbourfront

ℹ (902) 490 5946.
The Harbourfront Walkway, features interesting gift shops, cafés, and restaurants in his-toric settings along the board-walk. This delightful promen-ade leads to the Dartmouth Ferry, North America's oldest town ferry. A trip round the harbor is an inexpensive way to enjoy a panorama of Halifax.

🏛 Government House

1200 Barrington St.
The current home of Nova Scotia's lieutenant-general, this beautiful building is not open to the public but well worth exterior inspection for its historic and architectural interest. Its Georgian façade lends an urban grandeur. Completed in 1807, Govern-ment House cost over £30,000 (Can$72,000), a huge amount for a humble fishing village.

The bandstand of Halifax Public Gardens, framed in flowers

🌷 Halifax Public Gardens

Spring Garden Rd. ☎ (902) 490 5946. ◯ daily. ♿ limited.
Created in 1836, the Public Gardens are a beautiful 7-ha (17-acre) oasis of Victorian greenery and color in the midst of the bustling city. This is a peaceful place to stroll. The gardens' paths wind past duck ponds, foun-tains, and a seemingly endless array of vivid flowerbeds. In the center of the gardens, an ornate bandstand is the site of Sunday concerts. On week-ends, craftspeople gather outside the park's cast-iron fence to display their varied and colorful wares.

The waterfront of Halifax, seen from the town ferry

🏛 Halifax Citadel National Historic Site

Citadel Hill. ☎ *(902) 426 5080.*
🕐 *May–Oct: daily.* 👥 *summer.*
♿ ☞

Overlooking the city, this huge star-shaped fortress has a commanding view of the world's second-largest natural harbor. Built between 1828 and 1856, the citadel, along with its outlying fortifications, created such a formidable defense that the city was never attacked. Today visitors can stroll the broad parade grounds where the kilted regiment of the 78th Highlanders perform with twice-daily musket drills. Inside, children enjoy exploring the powder magazines and dark tunnels leading to secret firing rooms.

🏛 Old Town Clock

Citadel Hill.

At the base of Citadel Hill stands the city's most recognized landmark, the Old Town Clock. The clock was a gift in

Halifax's famous town clock, built in 1803 as a gift from British royalty

1803 from Edward, the British Duke of Kent and then military commander, who had a passion for punctuality. He designed the clock with four faces, one for each direction, so that both the army and town citizens would arrive at their appointed destinations on time. Not open to the public, the base of the clock was once a home for its clock keepers.

> **VISITORS' CHECKLIST**
>
> 👥 *115,000.* ✈ *35 km (22 miles) N of the city.* 🚆 *CN Station.* 🚌 *6040 Almon St.* ℹ *Halifax International Visitors' Centre, 1595 Barrington St. (902) 490 5946.* 🎭 *Nova Scotia International Tattoo (Jul); Atlantic Jazz Festival (Jul).*

🏛 Province House

1726 Hollis St. ☎ *(902) 424 4661.*
☞ *daily.* ♿

Begun in 1811 and finished in 1819, Nova Scotia's Province House is the oldest seat of government in Canada. What the building may lack in size it makes up for in elegance of design and for the momentous decisions reached within its walls. In 1864 the Fathers of Confederation held two days of meetings here on the formation of Canada *(see p44)*. Visitors can tour the rooms where these plans were laid.

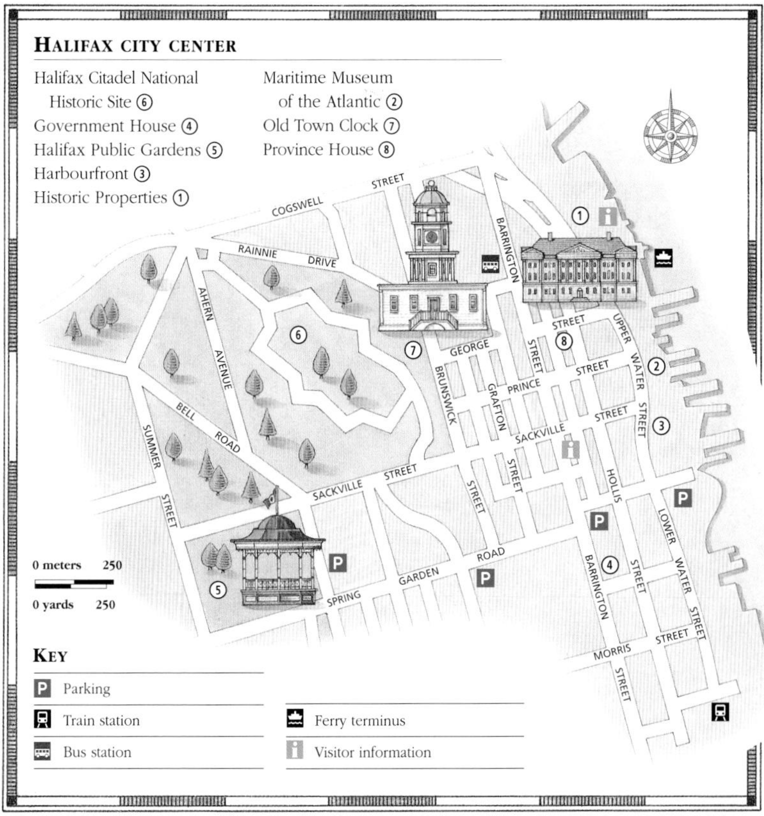
HALIFAX CITY CENTER
Halifax Citadel National Historic Site 6
Government House 4
Halifax Public Gardens 5
Harbourfront 3
Historic Properties 1
Maritime Museum of the Atlantic 2
Old Town Clock 7
Province House 8
COGSWELL STREET
RAINNIE DRIVE
AHERN AVENUE
BELL ROAD
SUMMER STREET
SACKVILLE STREET
SPRING GARDEN ROAD
BRUNSWICK STREET
GEORGE STREET
GRAFTON STREET
PRINCE STREET
BARRINGTON STREET
HOLLIS STREET
UPPER WATER STREET
LOWER WATER STREET
MORRIS STREET
0 meters 250
0 yards 250
KEY
Parking
Train station
Bus station
Ferry terminus
Visitor information

Cape Breton Island ㉔

MAGNIFICENT NATURAL BEAUTY is the attraction on Cape Breton. Every year thousands of people travel the famous Cabot Trail through the craggy splendor of Cape Breton Highlands National Park *(see p90–1)*. But Cape Breton's beauty is not limited to these two renowned sights; it can be found along inviting country roads and in the less explored corners of this green, fertile island. Particularly stunning are the Mabou Highlands, which cradle the gentle waters of Lake Ainslee, Bras d'Or Lake where eagles soar over scenic shores, and romantic coastal villages such as windswept Gabarus. The reconstructed 18th-century French garrison and village, Fortress Louisbourg, is also highly popular.

Glenora Whisky

Cabot Trail Highway
This sublime 300-km (186-mile) drive around the island's northwest and its national park attracts more visitors each year.

St. Pierre Church at Cheticamp
Built in 1883, the silver spire of this church is typical of Catholic style. The church is in the center of the town of Cheticamp, which offers whale-watching opportunites and is the focus of the 3,000-strong local Acadian community.

Margaree Harbour

Mabou

105

Port Hastings

104

St.

Isle Madame

Lake Ainslee
This tranquil lake, encircled by scenic roads, attracts many bird species, such as ospreys and loons, which feed on its shores.

KEY

▬▬	Major road
══	Minor road
▬▬	Scenic route
—	Rivers
ℹ	Visitor information
☼	Viewpoint
✈	Airport
—	National Park boundary
⛴	Ferry

0 km   15

0 miles   15

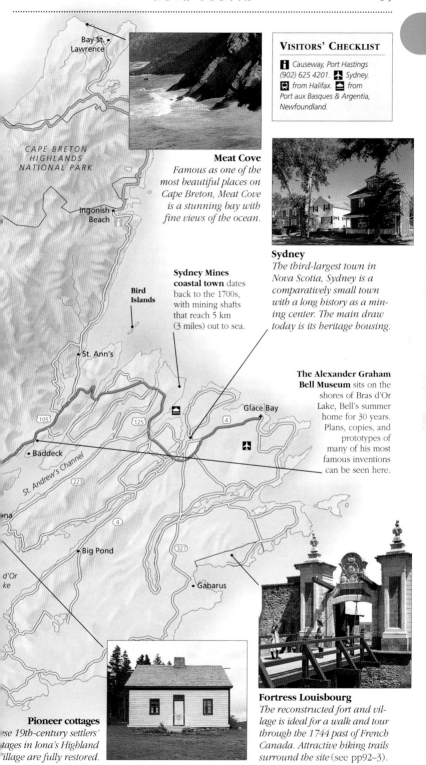

Meat Cove
*Famous as one of the
most beautiful places on
Cape Breton, Meat Cove
is a stunning bay with
fine views of the ocean.*

CAPE BRETON
HIGHLANDS
NATIONAL PARK

Ingonish
Beach

Sydney
*The third-largest town in
Nova Scotia, Sydney is a
comparatively small town
with a long history as a mining center. The main draw
today is its heritage housing.*

**Sydney Mines
coastal town** dates
back to the 1700s,
with mining shafts
that reach 5 km
(3 miles) out to sea.

Bird
Islands

St. Ann's

**The Alexander Graham
Bell Museum** sits on the
shores of Bras d'Or
Lake, Bell's summer
home for 30 years.
Plans, copies, and
prototypes of
many of his most
famous inventions
can be seen here.

105

125

Glace Bay

4

Baddeck

St. Andrew's Channel

223

na

4

Big Pond

327

d'Or
ke

Gabarus

Fortress Louisbourg
*The reconstructed fort and vil-
lage is ideal for a walk and tour
through the 1744 past of French
Canada. Attractive hiking trails
surround the site (see pp92–3).*

Pioneer cottages
*se 19th-century settlers'
tages in Iona's Highland
illage are fully restored.*

Exploring Cape Breton Island

Cape Breton fresh lobster

THE LARGEST ISLAND in Nova Scotia, Cape Breton has a wild beauty and grandeur that makes for some of the most impressive scenery in Canada. From the rolling highlands, sprinkled with sparkling streams, to fine sandy beaches, the island's 300-km (200-mile) Cabot Trail provides one of the most memorable tours in Canada. Other inviting country roads lead to the stunning Mabou Hills, surrounding Lake Ainslee, and to romantic little towns including Baddeck and the Acadian settlement of Cheticamp near the green Margaree Valley.

Lobster fishing boats in the Main à Dieu harbor on Cape Breton Island

Cape Breton Highlands National Park

In the 1930s the Canadian Government set aside the 958 sq km (370 sq miles) of magnificent highlands in the northern tip of Cape Breton Island to form Cape Breton Highlands National Park. The park contains some of Canada's most famous scenery, with its mountains, green wilderness, and windswept coastal beauty. The best-known feature of the park is the spectacular 106-km (66-mile) section of the Cabot Trail highway, which traces much of the park's boundary in a loop from Cheticamp to Ingonish.

The Cabot Trail is the primary route through the park, and most attractions are found along it. Entering the park, the trail ascends along the flanks of the coastal mountains. Several viewpoints on this stretch present far-reaching views of the highlands rising from the sea. Continuing inland, the trail travels across the highland plateau. Just past French Lake, the short Bog Walk is a boardwalk trail

through marshes, with educational panels that describe this unique bog-bound ecosystem, which is home to rare orchids. Visitors may even catch a glimpse of the park's many moose grazing here in a wetland marsh.

Crossing the French and Mackenzie Mountains, the trail descends dramatically to the charming old community of Pleasant Bay. It then re-enters the highlands, crossing

Picturesque Ingonish Beach on Cape Breton Island

North Mountain, which, at 475 m (1,560 ft), is the highest point in the park. The trail descends into the Aspy River Valley, where a side road leads to the base of the 30-m (100-ft) high Beulach Ban Falls.

At Cape North, another side road leads to the scenic whale-watching destination of Bay St. Lawrence just outside the park and the stunningly pretty road to Meat Cove. Farther on, the Scenic Loop breaks away from the Cabot Trail and follows the coast, offering awesome views as it descends to White Point. This road rejoins the Cabot Trail to the east, where it reaches the resort town of Ingonish. The Highland Links Golf Course here is ranked among the top golf courses in Canada.

♣ Cape Breton Highlands National Park

ℹ Ingonish Beach. **【** (902) 285 2691. ◯ daily. 🅿 🔥 limited.

Baddeck

Across the lake from the estate of Alexander Graham Bell, who loved the little town, Baddeck lies in rich farmland and is very much the island's premier resort destination. Set on the northwest side of Bras d'Or Lake, Baddeck is still the small, friendly town that charmed visitors in the 19th century. All amenities are within walking distance. The town's main street follows the waterfront and is lined with shops, cafés, and restaurants. Boat cruises around the lake are available from several places on Water Street by the shore.

The town's top attraction is the **Alexander Graham Bell National Historic Site**. The museum here contains the world's largest collection of photographs, artifacts, and documents about the life of this famous humanitarian and inventor. There are early telephones and several of his later inventions, including a copy of his HD-4 Hydrofoil.

Baddeck

ℹ Chebucto St. (902) 295 1911.
🏛 Alexander Graham Bell National Historic Site
559 Chebucto St. **【** (902) 295 2069. ◯ daily. 🅿 🔥

A fly-fisher tries his hand in the salmon- and trout-filled waters of the Margaree River

Margaree River Valley

Small and emerald green, the Margaree River Valley is in a delightful world of its own. The river has attracted salmon and trout anglers in large numbers since the mid-19th century. Today the region is also a favorite with hikers, antique-hunters, and sightseers.

In the little town of North East Margaree, the tiny but elegant **Margaree Salmon Museum** will fascinate even non-anglers with its beautiful historic rods and reels.

Paved and gravel roads follow the Margaree River upstream to the scenic spot of Big Intervale, where the headwaters come tumbling out of the highlands. This area is ideal for a long hike, fishing, or cycling, and is dazzling when the hillsides are carpeted in the flaming colors of fall.

Margaree Valley
Margaree Fork (902) 248 2803.
Margaree Salmon Museum
60 E. Big Interval Rd. (902) 248 2848. mid-Jun–mid-Oct: 9am–5pm daily. limited.

Cheticamp

This vibrant town is the largest Acadian community in Nova Scotia. Its beautiful Saint Pierre Church is visible from miles out at sea. The Acadians of Cape Breton are skilled craftspeople, and the town's seven cooperatives produce pottery and hooked rugs. Cheticamp's best-known rug hooker was Elizabeth Le-Fort, whose large and intricate works depicting prominent moments in history have hung in the Vatican and in the White House. Several of her finest rugs are on display at the **Dr. Elizabeth LeFort Museum** at Les Trois Pignons.

Cheticamp is also a popular whale-watching destination; tours are available for seeing many varieties of whale.

Dr. Elizabeth LeFort Museum
1584 Main St. (902) 224 2642.
May–Oct: daily.

Sydney

The only city on Cape Breton Island, Sydney is the third-largest town in Nova Scotia. Boasting the biggest steel plant in North America, the town is the region's industrial center. Despite this, Sydney has a small, attractive historic district around the Esplanade, with several restored buildings, such as Cossit House and Jost House, both dating from the 1870s. Downtown, boutiques, stores, and restaurants can be found along the town's main drag, Charlotte Street.

Sydney
Sydney (902) 539 9876.

ALEXANDER GRAHAM BELL

Alexander Graham Bell

Alexander Graham Bell was born in 1847 in Scotland. Bell's mother was deaf and, as a child, he became fascinated by speech and communication. In 1870, Bell and his family moved to Ontario (*see p216*). His work involved transmitting the voice electronically, and he began experimenting with variations of the technology used by the tele-graph. In 1876 he transmitted the world's first telephone message, "Watson, come here, I want you." With the patenting of his invention, Bell secured his role as one of the men who changed the world. In 1877, Bell married Mabel Hubbard, one of his deaf students. In 1885, the couple visited Cape Breton, where Bell later built his beautiful estate, Beinn Bhreagh, by Bras d'Or Lake. There he lived and worked each summer until he died in 1922. In Baddeck, the Alexander Graham Bell Museum focuses on his life and varied work.

Fortress Louisbourg

Costumed interpreter

BUILT BETWEEN 1713 AND 1744, the magnificent Fortress Louisbourg was France's bastion of military strength in the New World. Today, it is the largest military reconstruction in North America. Visitors stepping through the fortress gate enter the year 1744, when war had just been declared between France and England. Inside, scores of historically costumed guides bring the excitement of an 18th-century French trading town to life. The streets and buildings are peopled with merchants, soldiers, fishmongers, and washerwomen, all going about the daily business of the 1700s. From the lowliest fisherman's cottage to the elegant home of the Chief Military Engineer, attention to detail throughout is superb. The costumed interpreters offer information about the fortress, its history, and the lives of people they portray.

Overview of the Fortress
The seat of government and the central command of French military power in the New World, the Fortress was home to a town of thousands.

0 meters   50

0 yards   50

The Quay and Frederic Gate
The Quay was the center of commercial activity in the town. It is still central to the fort, as many activities now take place at the Gate's imposing yellow arch.

STAR FEATURES

★ King's Bastion

★ Engineer's Residence

★ **The Engineer's Residence**
Responsible for all public construction projects at the fortress, the engineer was one of the most important and powerful men in the community.

VISITORS' CHECKLIST

Rte. 22 SW of Louisbourg.
📞 (902) 733 2280. 🕐 May,
Jun, Sep & Oct: 9:30am–5pm
daily; Jul & Aug: 9am–7pm daily.
🔲 🅿 🚻 🏛 🅿 🍴 ✓

★ King's Bastion
The largest building in the Citadel, the King's Bastion Barracks was home to the 500 French soldiers who lived, ate, and slept here.

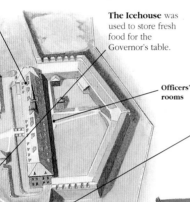

The Icehouse was used to store fresh food for the Governor's table.

Officers' rooms

King's Bakery
Visitors can buy warm bread from this working bakery that produced the soldiers' daily rations.

The Forge
Traditional skills are in evidence here, with costumed workers demonstrating exactly the carefully learned craft of the 18th century.

The Guardhouse held the vital human line of defense; guards were stationed here while on duty.

The Dauphin Gate
Soldiers in historic uniforms at the gate challenge visitors, just as they would have in 1744. The gate's artistic details are based on archeological relics from the original gate recovered in the 1960s.

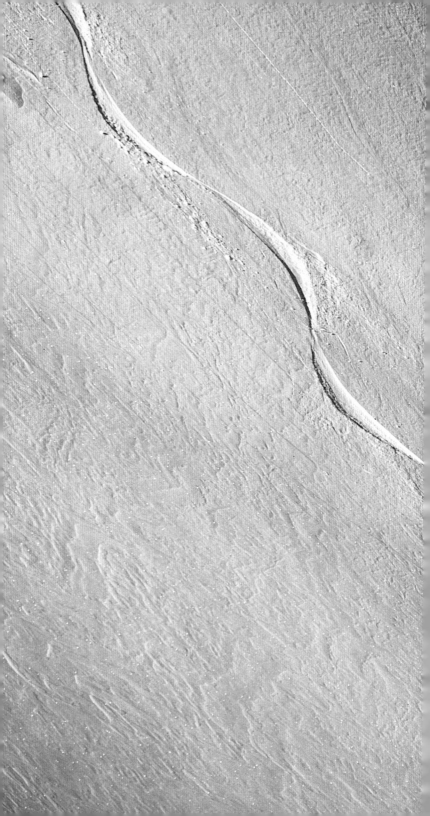

QUEBEC

Introducing Quebec

QUEBEC IS THE LARGEST of Canada's provinces and the biggest French-speaking territory in the world, with many of its seven million citizens holding firm to the language and culture inherited from their French ancestors. Landscapes range from pastoral valleys and villages along the American border, to vast expanses of tundra on the shores of Hudson Bay. At Quebec's heart is the St. Lawrence River. Its north shore begins with the scenic Charlevoix region edging a wilderness of lakes, forest, and tundra that stretches to the Hudson Strait, past one of the world's largest power projects at James Bay. To the south lies the mountainous Gaspé Peninsula. There are two major cities; multiethnic Montreal, and Quebec City, the provincial capital and North America's only walled city.

The picturesque lakeside resort of St-Jovite in the Laurentian Mountains set amid a backdrop of magnificent fall colors

Hudson Strait

Hudson Bay

VAL D'OR

0 km   100

0 miles   100

KEY

▓ Highway

▓ Major road

═ River

SEE ALSO

Quebec's largest city, Montreal, has a vibrant downtown area that comes to life after dark

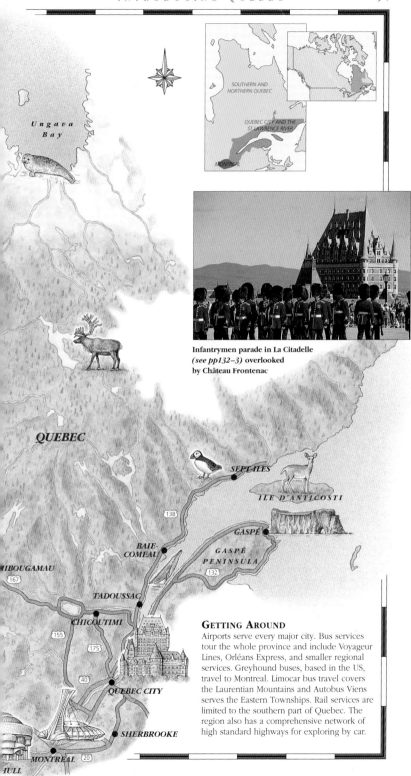

SOUTHERN AND
NORTHERN QUEBEC

QUEBEC CITY AND THE
ST LAWRENCE RIVER

MONTREAL

*Ungava
Bay*

**Infantrymen parade in La Citadelle
(see pp132–3) overlooked
by Château Frontenac**

QUEBEC

SEPT-ILES

ILE D'ANTICOSTI

138

GASPÉ

BAIE-
COMEAU

GASPÉ
PENINSULA

132

CHIBOUGAMAU

167

TADOUSSAC

CHICOUTIMI

155

175

40

QUEBEC CITY

SHERBROOKE

MONTREAL 20

HULL

GETTING AROUND

Airports serve every major city. Bus services
tour the whole province and include Voyageur
Lines, Orléans Express, and smaller regional
services. Greyhound buses, based in the US,
travel to Montreal. Limocar bus travel covers
the Laurentian Mountains and Autobus Viens
serves the Eastern Townships. Rail services are
limited to the southern part of Quebec. The
region also has a comprehensive network of
high standard highways for exploring by car.

Maple Forests

The red maple leaf of Canada

LONG THE PRIDE of Quebec and Ontario, there is more to Canada's ancient maple forests than their annual display of beauty. Every fall, turning leaves splash crimson and orange across the south, but it is in springtime that the trees give up their most famous product: maple syrup. Extracting techniques which were developed by native peoples were passed to Europeans in the 17th century. Traditional methods changed little until the 1940s, when part of the process was mechanized. Many age-old methods remain, however, including the final hand-stirring of the syrup.

Maple trees, either red maple *(Acer rubrum)* or sugar maple *(Acer saccharum)*, grow to heights of well over 30 m (100 ft), with thick trunks a meter (3 ft) in diameter. While their main product is the syrup, the hard wood is used for furniture and, of course, the leaf itself is the national symbol of Canada, officially established on the flag in 1965.

Collecting sap from trees *by tapping maple trunks is the first step. Cuts are made low in the wood in spring as sap rises.*

Transporting the sap *in large barrels on a horse-drawn sleigh through the snowy forests is traditional. In the 1970s this was largely replaced by a network of plastic tubing that take the sap directly from tree trunks to the sugar shacks.*

Sugar shacks *are built in the forest in the center of the sugar bush, the cluster of maple trees that are producing sap. Men and women alike work long hours at slowly evaporating the sap, reducing it to syrup. Quebecois have their own rite of spring: when the first syrup is ready, it is poured onto the crisp snow outside the shacks to make a tasty frozen taffy.*

MAPLE SYRUP PRODUCTS

Although 80 percent of Canada's annual maple harvest eventually becomes maple syrup, there is more to the industry than simply a sweet sauce. Boiled for longer, the syrup hardens into a pale golden sugar that can be used to sweeten coffee or eaten like candy. Maple butter, which is whipped with sugar, is also popular. Savory products benefit too; ham and bacon can be cured in syrup, which is delicious. The sweet-toothed people of Quebec use the

Maple products are used in a variety of foods, both sweet and savory

syrup to make sugar pie, a tart with a sweet, fudge filling.

Maple syrup

Syrup is graded according to quality; clear golden fluid, produced at the start of the season, is the most prized, and is generally bottled. Later, darker syrup is used in cooking, and the final, even darker, batch makes a base for synthetic flavors or syrups. Over Can$100 million is spent annually on maple products.

THE STORY OF MAPLE SYRUP

The first maple-sugar farmers were native Canadians. Long before European settlers arrived in the 16th century, tribes all over Northeast America sweetened savory dishes with syrup. An Iroquois legend tells the story of a chief in ancient times who, hurling an ax at a tree, found it stuck in the trunk at the end of the next day, dripping sweet fluid. That night the chief's wife boiled the day's hunt in the sap, and the syrup was born. Folk tales apart, it is certain that native people discovered the sap and techniques for refining it, few of which have changed, and passed their knowledge to Europeans freely.

Boiling maple sap involves 40 liters (88 pts) of sap to create one liter (2.2 pts) of syrup. The gold color and maple flavor develop as distillation takes place. The paler first syrup of the season is the most valuable.

Transforming sap into maple syrup takes place very slowly. The sap bubbles over a wood fire (maple wood is prefered) until about 98 percent of its water content evaporates. Modern processes use mechanized evaporators to boil the sap and draw off the steam, but even hi-tech methods still require a final hand-stirred simmering.

The St. Lawrence Seaway

Extending from the Gulf of St. Lawrence on the Atlantic coast to Duluth at the western end of Lake Superior in Minnesota, the St. Lawrence Seaway and Great Lakes System flows across North America for over 3,700 km (2,300 miles). The St. Lawrence Seaway itself stretches 553 km (344 miles) from Montreal to Lake Erie and covers 245,750 square km (95,000 sq miles) of navigable water. Open from March to December, it is the world's longest deep-draft inland waterway. Ships carry a huge quantity of domestic traffic, but over 60 per cent of the total freight travels to and from overseas ports, mainly from Europe, the Middle East, and Africa. Traffic varies: cargoes of grain travel in superships alongside pleasure boats.

LOCATOR MAP

☐ *The St. Lawrence Seaway*

THE HISTORY OF THE SEAWAY

The Seaway has ancient beginnings: in 1680, French monk Dollier de Casson started a campaign to build a mile-long canal linking Lac St. Louis and Montreal, which was finally opened in 1824 as the Lachine Canal. In 1833, the first Welland Canal (from Lake Ontario to Lake Erie) opened. The fourth Welland Canal was the first modern part of the Seaway to be built in 1932. 1951 brought US and Canadian cooperation to bear on a new seaway, which began in Canada in 1954. On April 25, 1959, the Seaway opened, linking the Great Lakes to the world.

The *D'Iberville*, first ship to cross the Seaway

Pleasure boats *cruise the Seaway near the Thousand Islands by Kingston, Ontario. Each summer, small craft take advantage of the excellent sailing and waterskiing available in this section of the Seaway.*

Otta

O N T A R I O

Kingston

Toronto

Lake Ontario

✦ LAKE HURON

U N I T E D

S T A T E S

Lake Erie

| 0 km | 100 |
| 0 miles | 100 |

KEY

⚓ Lock

Montreal is the historic beginning of the Seaway. It was here that the first link was built to the lakes during the 18th century, opening up pathways to the center of North America. The Seaway is open nine months each year, despite much freezing weather.

GULF OF ST. LAWRENCE

Quebec City

Q U E B E C

Cargo ships carry iron ore, grain, coal, and other bulk commodities through the waterway: more than 2 billion tons of cargo have been shipped since 1959. Canada's heavy industry could not continue without the Seaway.

St. Lambert Lock bypasses the Lachine Rapids west of Montreal. The Seaway is a watery staircase to America's heartland. The process involves raising and lowering the ships the height of a 60-story building.

Montreal

CONSTRUCTION OF THE SEAWAY

In 1895, the US and Canadian governments appointed a Deep Waterways Commission to study the feasibility of what was to become today's St. Lawrence Seaway; it reported in favor of the project two years later. After 50 years of intercountry wrangling, the jointly financed project was begun on August 10, 1954 – in the words of Canadian Prime Minister Louis St. Laurent "a bond rather than a barrier between Americans and Canadians." The massive undertaking was beset with problems not previously encountered, especially the discovery of ancient rock formations so hard that new machinery had to be created to dig through them. All work, including relocating villages and dredging the existing canals, had to be carried out with minimum disruption to the daily boat, rail, and car traffic of major cities. Nonetheless, the four-year construction was completed almost to the day.

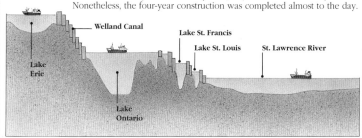

The Seaway in profile with locks and rising water levels

MONTREAL

M**ONTREAL IS** *the second largest city in Canada, and the only French-speaking one in the Americas. The pious 17th-century French founders of this vibrant island metropolis might be a little surprised to have produced a place that revels so much in its reputation for joie de vivre, but at least their edifices remain; the spires of some of Canada's finest churches still rise above the skyline.*

Montreal's location at the convergence of the St. Lawrence and Ottawa rivers made it Canada's first great trading center. It was founded in 1642 by a group of French Catholics as a Christian community and port. Much of its economic power has now moved west to Toronto, and what makes Montreal interesting today is a cultural, rather than a geographical, confluence. About 70 percent of its 3 million residents are of French descent, another 15 percent have British origins, and the rest represent nearly every major ethnic group. Many speak three or more languages. The communities form a kind of mosaic, with the anglophones in the west, the francophones in the east, and other ethnic communities in pockets all over the island. There is nothing rigid about these divisions: Anglophones eat and drink in the restaurants and bistros of the historic French district, and francophones visit the traditionally English area. The most interesting neighborhoods sprawl along the southern slopes of Mont-Royal – the 234-m (767-ft) hill from which the city derives its name. Vieux-Montréal's network of narrow, cobblestone streets huddles near the waterfront, while the main shopping area is farther north along Rue Sainte-Catherine. It extends below the city's surface in the maze of tunnels that connect the Underground City, the complex of homes, stores, and leisure venues that spreads out beneath the bustling city. Other modern attractions include the Olympic Park stadium and the Musée d'Art Contemporain, built in the 1990s to complement Montreal's fine historic museums.

Visitors admiring the skyline of Montreal

◁ **Waiters posing outside a typically French traditonal bistro in downtown Montreal**

Exploring Montreal

MONTREAL SHARES A 50-kilometer (30-mile) long island in the St. Lawrence River with the 28 other municipalities that make up the Communauté Urbaine de Montréal (Montreal Urban Community). The city core lies between Mont-Royal and the river, and streets follow a fairly consistent grid pattern, with Boulevard Saint-Laurent, known as The Main, splitting the city into its western and eastern halves. Montreal is a large city but getting around is easy.

The skyscrapers of downtown Montreal at dusk

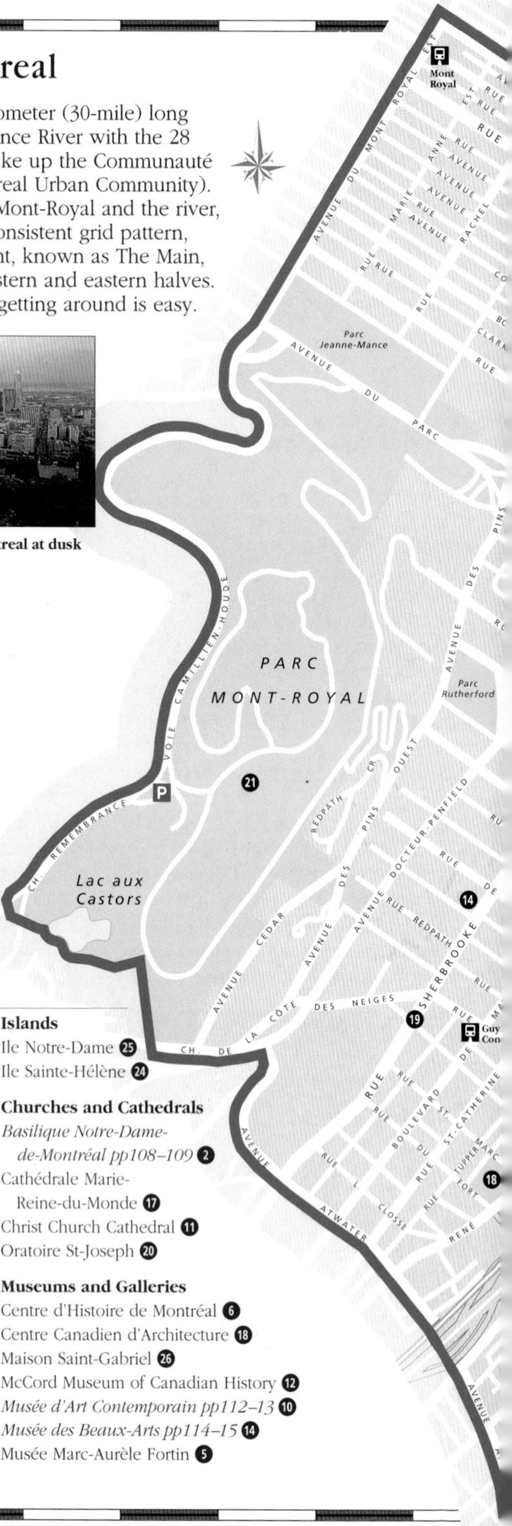

KEY

- ▒ Street-by-street: *see pp106–107*
- ✈ International airport
- 🚆 Railroad station
- 🚌 Bus terminus
- ⛴ Ferry boarding point
- ℹ Visitor information
- [P] Parking
- 🚇 Métro station
- ▬ Highway
- ▬ Major road
- ┅ Pedestrian walkway

SIGHTS AT A GLANCE

Historic Buildings and Areas

Château Ramezay 3
Chinatown 7
Lachine 27
McGill University 13
Place des Arts 9
Plateau Mont-Royal 8
Sir George Etienne-Carter National Historic Site 4
Square Dorchester and Place du Canada 16
Rue Sherbrooke 19
Underground City 15
Vieux Port 1

Parks and Gardens

Jardin Botanique de Montréal 23
Olympic Park pp120–21 22
Parc Mont-Royal 21

Islands

Ile Notre-Dame 25
Ile Sainte-Hélène 24

Churches and Cathedrals

Basilique Notre-Dame-de-Montréal pp108–109 2
Cathédrale Marie-Reine-du-Monde 17
Christ Church Cathedral 11
Oratoire St-Joseph 20

Museums and Galleries

Centre d'Histoire de Montréal 6
Centre Canadien d'Architecture 18
Maison Saint-Gabriel 26
McCord Museum of Canadian History 12
Musée d'Art Contemporain pp112–13 10
Musée des Beaux-Arts pp114–15 14
Musée Marc-Aurèle Fortin 5

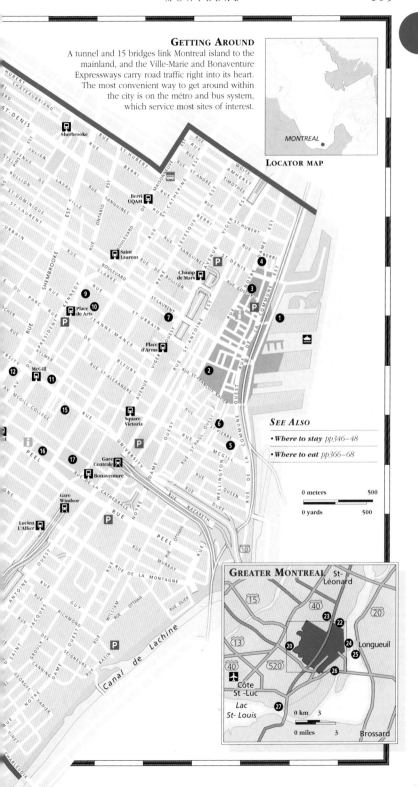

GETTING AROUND

A tunnel and 15 bridges link Montreal island to the mainland, and the Ville-Marie and Bonaventure Expressways carry road traffic right into its heart. The most convenient way to get around within the city is on the métro and bus system, which service most sites of interest.

LOCATOR MAP

MONTREAL

Sherbrooke

Berri
UQAM

Saint
Laurent

Champ
de Mars

Place
de Arts

Place
d'Arms

McGill

Square
Victoria

Gare
Centrale

Bonaventure

Gare
Windsor

Lucien
L'Allier

SEE ALSO

• *Where to stay* pp346–48

• *Where to eat* pp366–68

| 0 meters | 500 |
| 0 yards | 500 |

Canal de Lachine

GREATER MONTREAL

St-
Léonard

Longueuil

Côte
St-Luc

Lac
St-Louis

Brossard

0 km   3

0 miles   3

Street-by-Street: Vieux-Montréal

MONTREAL'S FOUNDERS, led by Paul de Cho:médy and Sieur de Maisonneuve, built the Catholic village that was to become Vieux-Montréal by the Lachine Rapids in 1642. Missionary efforts failed to flourish, but the settlement blossomed into a prosperous fur-trading town with fine homes and a stone stockade. As Montreal expanded in the 19th century, the old city, Vieux-Montréal, fell into decline. In the 1960s, however, the district underwent a renaissance. The remaining 18th-century buildings were renovated and transformed into the restaurants, bistros, and boutiques that are so fashionable today, especially those of rue Notre-Dame and rue St-Paul.

View from the river
This clutch of historic streets leading down to the great St. Lawrence River is a district of romance and charm in the midst of this modern city.

★ Basilique Notre-Dame
One of the most splendid churches in North America, the city's 1829 Catholic showpiece has a richly decorated and colorful interior ❷

**Pointe-à-Callière
Archeological Museum**
An underground tour here leads visitors past excavated ruins and early water systems dating from the 17th century.

STAR SIGHTS

★ **Basilique Notre-Dame**

★ **Château Ramezay**

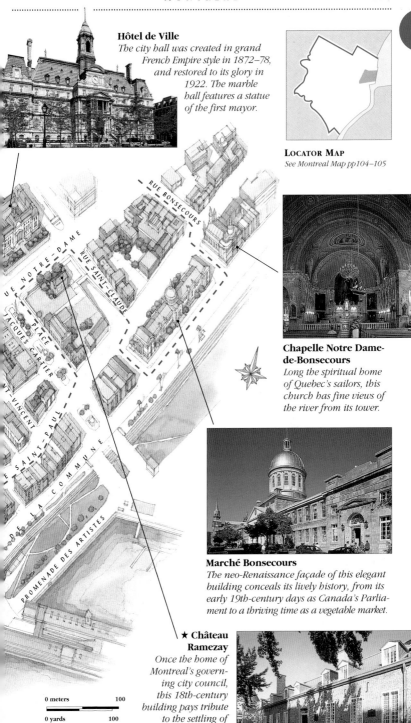

Hôtel de Ville
The city hall was created in grand French Empire style in 1872–78, and restored to its glory in 1922. The marble hall features a statue of the first mayor.

LOCATOR MAP
See Montreal Map pp104–105

Chapelle Notre Dame-de-Bonsecours
Long the spiritual home of Quebec's sailors, this church has fine views of the river from its tower.

Marché Bonsecours
The neo-Renaissance façade of this elegant building conceals its lively history, from its early 19th-century days as Canada's Parliament to a thriving time as a vegetable market.

★ Château Ramezay
Once the home of Montreal's governing city council, this 18th-century building pays tribute to the settling of Quebec with its fine museum of early tools and artifacts ❸

0 meters 100

0 yards 100

KEY

– – – Suggested route

Vieux-Port ➊

333 Rue de la Commune.
📞 *(514) 496 7678.* 🚇 *Central Station.* 🚌 *55.* 🚍 *Terminus Voyageur.* 🚇 *Square Victoria.*

IN ITS GLORY DAYS of the 19th century, the Vieux-Port of Montreal was one of the most important inland harbors in North America, but it declined with the introduction of mega-ships and the airplane in the early 20th century. By the late 1980s, the Canadian government had begun to transform it into one of the most popular parks in Montreal. Its 12.5 km (9 miles) of waterside walk-ways and open grassy fields blend almost seamlessly into

Cyclists enjoying the waterfront promenade, Vieux-Port

the lovely streets of Vieux-Montréal, giving the old city a wide window onto the river.

The port has a bustling, recreational atmosphere. On summer afternoons, visitors and Montrealers alike stroll, cycle, or in-line skate along the Promenade du Vieux Port.

Château Ramezay ➌

280 Rue Notre Dame E. 📞 *(514) 861 3708.* 🚆 *VIA Rail.* 🚌 *14, 55.* 🚍 *Terminus Voyageur.* 🚇 *Champ-de-Mars.* 🕐 *Jun–Sep: 10am–6pm daily; Oct–May: 10am–4:30pm Tue–Sun.* ⚫ *Dec 25, Jan 1.* 📷 ♿ 🎁

WHEN MONTREAL'S 11th governor, Claude de Ramezay, arrived in the city in 1702, he was homesick for Normandy and decided to build a residence for himself that was reminiscent of the châteaux back home, with stone walls, dormer windows, and copper roof. The squat round towers, added in the

Basilique Notre-Dame-de-Montréal ➋

IN THE CENTER OF PLACE D'ARMES sits the Basilica, Montreal's oldest and grandest Catholic church. Originally built in the 17th century, a new building was commissioned in 1829. American architect James O'Donnell excelled himself with a vast vaulted cavern that combined elements of Neo-Classical and Neo-Gothic design, and provides 3,800 seats in the nave and two tiers of balconies. Splendidly redecorated in the 1870s, the intricate wood-carving and stained glass are the work of Canadian craftsman Victor Bourgeau.

The main altar is surrounded by delicate pine and walnut woodcarving.

The nave is illuminated by a rose window under an azure ceiling.

★ **Reredos**
The focus of the nave is backed by azure, beneath a golden starry sky.

STAR SIGHTS

★ **Reredos**

★ **Pulpit**

★ **Pulpit**
This ornate construction was sculpted by Philippe Hébert. The prophets Ezekiel and Jeremiah stand at its base.

19th century, reinforce the effect. Many of de Ramezay's governor successors lived here. Château Ramezay is one of the most impressive remnants of the French regime open to the public in Montreal.

The château has been restored to the style of Governor de Ramezay's day. Of particular interest is the Nantes Salon, with its 18th-century carved paneling by the French architect Germain Boffrand.

Uniforms, documents, and furniture on the main floor reflect the life of New France's ruling classes, while the cellars depict the doings of humbler colonists. The scarlet automobile, made for the city's first motorist, is an interesting sight.

Sir George-Etienne Cartier National Historic Site ❹

458 Rue Notre Dame. 🄲 *(514) 283 2282.* 🚇 *Central Station.* 🚌 🚇 *Terminus Voyager.* 🚇 *Champ-de-Mars.* 🄾 *mid-May–Aug: daily; Sep–Dec & Mar–mid-May: Wed–Sun.* ⬤ *Jan & Feb.* 📷 🚻 🎦

G EORGE-ETIENNE Cartier (1814–73) was a Father of Confederation *(see p44)* and one of the most important French-Canadian politicians of his day. This national historic site comprises two adjoining graystone

Ormolu clock at the Etienne-Cartier

houses owned by the Cartiers on the eastern edge of the old town. One is dedicated to Cartier's career as a lawyer, politician, and railroad-builder. In this house, you can sit at a round table and listen in either French or English to a very good summary of the political founding of modern Canada.

The second house focuses on the Cartiers' domestic life and the functioning of a Victorian upper middle-class family. Visitors can wander through formal rooms full of rich furniture and listen to snatches of taped conversation from "servants" talking about their lives.

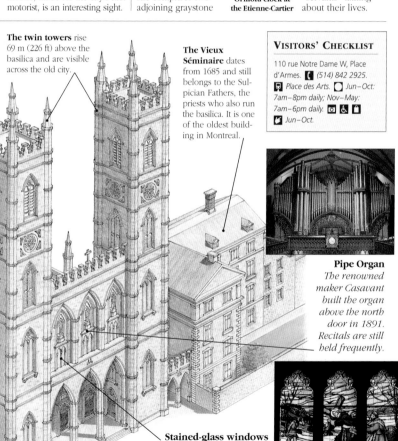

The twin towers rise 69 m (226 ft) above the basilica and are visible across the old city.

The Vieux Séminaire dates from 1685 and still belongs to the Sulpician Fathers, the priests who also run the basilica. It is one of the oldest buildings in Montreal.

VISITORS' CHECKLIST

110 rue Notre Dame W, Place d'Armes. 🄲 *(514) 842 2925.* 🚇 *Place des Arts.* 🄾 *Jun–Oct: 7am–8pm daily; Nov–May: 7am–6pm daily.* 📷 🚻 🛗 🎦 *Jun–Oct.*

Pipe Organ
The renowned maker Casavant built the organ above the north door in 1891. Recitals are still held frequently.

Stained-glass windows
The basilica's beautiful windows were imported from Limoges in 1930. Each tells a story of Montreal's past; this shows New World pioneer Maisonneuve climbing Mont Royal in 1643.

Musée Marc-Aurèle Fortin ❺

118 Rue Saint-Pierre. 🛈 (514) 845
6108. 🚉 Central Station. 🚌 Terminus
Voyageur. Ⓜ Square Victoria.
⭘ 11am–5pm Tue–Sun. 🖼 ♿

T HIS MUSEUM, housed in
an old stone warehouse
belonging to an ancient order
of nuns, has an extensive
collection of Fortin's work,
and it also mounts exhibitions
of new painting by local artists.
Marc-Aurèle Fortin trans-
formed landscape painting in
Canada. He was born in 1888,
when European styles dominated North American art.
Fortin loved the light of his
native province, and used
many unusual techniques. To
capture the "warm light of
Quebec," for example, he
painted some of his pictures
over gray backgrounds. By the
time he died in 1970, he left
behind not only a staggering
amount of work but a whole
new way of looking at nature,
especially the various rural
areas of his native Quebec.

**Gray stone façade of the Musée
Marc-Aurèle Fortin**

Centre d'Histoire de Montréal ❻

335 Place d'Youville. 🛈 (514) 872
3207. 🚌 61. Ⓜ Square Victoria.
⭘ mid-May–Aug: daily; Sep–May:
Tue–Sun. ⬤ mid-Dec–mid-Jan. 🖼

T HIS MUSEUM is housed in a
handsome, red-brick fire
station, which has a gracefully
gabled roof built in 1903. The
exhibits trace the history of
Montreal from the first Indian
settlements to the modern age,
with the focus on everyday
life. A dummy 19th-century
town crier, for example,
warns residents of the penalties for letting their pigs and

Centre d'Histoire de Montréal

sheep run loose. Particularly
interesting is the second floor,
which depicts life in the 1930s
and 1940s. Visitors can relax
in a period living room and
listen to snippets of Canadian
radio broadcasts (ranging
from a hockey game to the
recitation of the rosary), or
step into a phone booth and
eavesdrop on a factory worker
making a date with his shop-
clerk girlfriend. A simulated
ride in a city tram brings visitors back into modern times.

Chinatown ❼

Ⓜ Champ-de-Mars; Place-des-Arts.

T HE NAME IS becoming a
little anachronistic. Many
of the restaurants and shops
in this 18-block district just
northeast of the Old City are
now owned by Vietnamese

and Thai immigrants,
who arrived in Mont-
real in the wake of
20th-century up-
heavals in Southeast
Asia. The Chinese,
however, were here
first. They began
arriving in large
numbers after 1880,
along with many
European immi-
grants, and stuck
together in this
corner of the city in
an attempt to avoid
discrimination.
As they grew more
prosperous, many of
the descendants of
the first immigrants
moved to wealthier
areas, leaving Chinatown to
the old and to the newly
arrived. Many thousands of
them now return on week-
ends, and the narrow streets
are busy with people shopping
for silk, souvenirs, vegetables,
records, and barbecued meat.
Restaurants specialize in
a range of cuisines, serving
Szechuan, Cantonese, Thai,
Vietnamese, and Korean food,
and the air is fragrant with the
smell of hot barbecued pork
and aromatic noodles.
For those seeking respite
from the bustle, there is a
lovely little garden dedicated
to the charismatic Chinese
leader Sun Yat-sen on Clarke
Street. Other features of the
area include two large,
Chinese-style arches which
span de la Gauchetière Street,
and a pair of authentic
pagodas on the roof of the
modern Holiday Inn hotel.

A brightly colored market stall in vibrant Chinatown

Locals picknicking in the leisurely atmosphere of the Parc Lafontaine in Plateau Mont-Royal

Plateau Mont-Royal ❽

❦ *Tourisme Plateau Mont-Royal: (514) 840 0926.* **Ⓜ** *Sherbrooke; Mont-Royal.*

No NEIGHBORHOOD captures the essence of Montreal more fully than the Plateau. Its main thoroughfares are lined with bistros, bookstores, boutiques, and sidewalk cafés. Nightclubs veer from the eccentric to the classic, and eateries from snack bars and sandwich shops to some of the best dining locations in the city. Jazz bars, too, are popular in this area and range from the decorous to the distinctly shady.

The area's residents are a mix of students, working-class French-speakers, trendy young professionals, and ethnic families with roots in Europe and Latin America. They congregate either in Parc Lafontaine, a neighborly expanse of green with an outdoor theater, or in "Balconville," a distinctly Montrealer institution linked to the duplexes and triplexes that many residents live in. To save interior space, these stacks of single-floor flats are studded with balconies linked to the street by fanciful, wrought-iron stairways. Although treacherous in winter, in summer they are decked with flowers and barbecue grills, and become centers for parties, family gatherings, and picnics.

The large working-class families for whom these homes were built in the early part of the century lived very modestly, but they managed to amass enough money to build impressively large and beautiful parish churches, notably the Eglise Saint-Jean-Baptiste. The Catholic bourgeoisie lived just a little farther south, in gracious Second-Empire homes on Rue Saint-Denis or Carré Saint-Louis, one of the prettiest squares in the city.

Place des Arts ❾

183 Rue Ste.-Catherine W. **❦** *(514) 842 2112.* **Ⓜ** *Place des Arts.*

This complex of halls and theaters is Montreal's prime center for the performing arts. Both the Opéra de Montréal (Montreal Opera) and the Orchéstre Symphonique de Montréal (Montreal Symphony Orchestra) make their home in the Salle Wilfrid Pelletier. This is the largest of the center's five halls, and has 2,982 seats. The buildings of Place des Arts share a modern, spacious central plaza with the outstanding Musée d'art contemporain *(see pp112–13).*

Place des Arts, Montreal's top entertainment venue

Musée d'Art Contemporain ➓

OPENED IN 1964, THE MUSEUM of Contemporary Art is the only institution in Canada dedicated exclusively to modern art. Located in downtown Montreal, more than 60 percent of the approximately 6,000 paintings, drawings, photographs, videos, and installations in the permanent collection are by Quebec artists. Works date from 1939, but the emphasis is on the contemporary. There are also works by innovative international talents, such as the controversial Bill Viola, Louise Bourgeois, and Andrès Serrano. The exhibits are in wide, well-lit galleries whose elegance helped to earn the Musée a Grand Prix from Montreal Council. The exhibition space is built around a rotunda, which runs up through the core of the building.

Les Dentelles de Montmirail
Young artist Natalie Roy's 1995 landscape (detail shown) is part of a large collection of new Quebec art.

First floor

★ **Niagara Sandstone Circle** *(1981)*
English sculptor Richard Long's work is literally ground breaking. Using materials from the natural environment, which itself is the theme of the work, his careful geometric placing acts as a spur to meditation.

Street Level

Entrance Hall
The museum uses this airy modern space, hung in places with pieces from its collection, for special events and receptions. A pleasant first-floor restaurant overlooks the hall.

KEY

- ☐ Permanent exhibition space
- ☐ Temporary exhibition space
- ☐ Pierre Granche sculpture
- ☐ Movie theater
- ☐ Video gallery
- ☐ Multimedia gallery
- ☐ Theater/Seminar hall
- ☐ Art workshops
- ☐ Nonexhibition space

STAR EXHIBITORS

★ **Pierre Granche**

★ **Richard Long**

MUSEUM GUIDE

Only a small proportion of the exhibits in the museum are on permanent display. They occupy the upper floor space along with rotating and visiting items. There is also a sculpture garden, accessible from the main museum building, that has rotating exhibits and is a good spot to rest during a tour of the galleries.

★ **Comme si le temps ... de la rue** (1991–2)
Pierre Granche's permanent outdoor installation is based on Egyptian mythological figures whose shapes symbolize Montreal. Created to contrast with its urban milieu, the work exudes humor and poetry.

Main Entrance

Museum façade
Built in the 1990s, the MAC building shows 320 artworks, taken from their much larger rotating collection.

Christ Church Cathedral ⓫

1444 Union Ave. 📞 (514) 843 6577. 🚇 Central Station. 🚌 15. 🚇 McGill. ⏱ 8am–5:30pm daily. ♿

ARCHITECT Frank Wills completed Christ Church in 1859 as the seat of the Anglican bishop of Montreal. This graceful Gothic limestone building, with a triple portal and a tall slender spire, has exterior walls decorated with gargoyles. The church was too heavy for the land, and the stone spire was replaced in 1940 with a treated aluminum steeple. Many local workers find respite at noon concerts in the cathedral's cool, dim interior with its pointed arched nave and magnificent stained-glass windows, some from the William Morris studio in London.

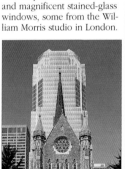

Christ Church Cathedral, based on a 14th-century English design

McCord Museum of Canadian History ⓬

690 Rue Sherbrooke W. 📞 (514) 398 7100. 🚇 Central Station. 🚌 24. 🚇 McGill. ⏱ 10am–6pm Tue–Fri; 10am–5pm Sat & Sun. ● Mon. ♿

LAWYER DAVID Ross McCord (1844–1930) was an avid collector of virtually everything that had to do with life in Canada, including books, photographs, jewelry, furniture, clothing, documents, papers,

paintings, toys, and porcelain. In 1919, he gave his considerable acquisitions to McGill University with a view to establishing a museum of Canadian social history. That collection, now more than 90,000 artifacts, is housed in a stately limestone building that was once a social center for McGill students. The museum has a good section of early history, as well as exceptional folk art. A particularly fine collection of Indian and Inuit items features clothing, weapons, jewelry, furs, and pottery. A separate room is devoted to the social history of Montreal. The museum's most celebrated possession is the collection of 700,000 photographs, that painstakingly chronicle every detail of daily life in 19th-century Montreal.

Inuit slippers at the McCord Museum

McGill University ⓭

845 Rue Sherbrooke W. 📞 (514) 398 4455. 🚇 Central Station. 🚌 24. 🚇 McGill. ⏱ 9am–6pm Mon–Fri. 🎦 book in advance. ♿

WHEN IT was founded in 1821, Canada's oldest university was set on land left for the purpose by fur trader and land speculator James McGill (1744–1813). The university's main entrance is guarded by the Classical Roddick Gates. Behind them an avenue leads to the domed Neoclassical Arts Building, which is the oldest structure on campus.

The rest of the 70 or so buildings range from the ornately Victorian to the starkly concrete. One of the loveliest is the **Redpath Museum of Natural History**, which holds one of the city's most eclectic and eccentric collections. A huge number of fossils, including a dinosaur skeleton, sit alongside African art, Roman coins, and a shrunken head.

🏛 **Redpath Museum of Natural History**
859 Rue Sherbrooke W. 📞 (514) 398 4086. ⏱ 9am–5pm Mon–Thu; 1pm–5pm Sun. ● Fri & Sat. ♿

Musée des Beaux Arts ⑭

THE OLDEST AND LARGEST art collection in Quebec is housed in two dramatically different buildings that face each other across Rue Sherbrooke. On the north side is the Benaiah Gibb Pavilion with white marble pillars; on the south side is the huge concrete arch and tilting glass front of the Jean-Noël Desmarais Pavilion.

The galleries in the Desmarais Pavilion focus on European art from the Middle Ages to the 20th century, especially the Renaissance. Linking the two pavilions is the gallery of ancient cultures, with rich collections of artifacts, including Roman vases and Chinese incense boxes. The Benaiah Gibb Pavilion galleries focus on Canadiana, with Inuit art, furniture, and church silver from early settlers, and paintings from the 18th century to the 1960s.

Façade of Jean-Noël Desmarais Pavilion
Opened in 1991, the larger pavilion contains a collection that has grown from 1,860 to about 26,000 pieces.

★ Portrait of a Young Woman *(c.1665)*
This famous work originated in Rembrandt's native Holland. Painted in characteristically realist style, the sitter's pensive concentration is thrown into sharper relief by the deep black background.

BENAIAH GIBB PAVILION

Named after a 19th-century benefactor, the Benaiah Gibb Pavilion is connected to the southern side by an underground tunnel that contains the gallery of ancient cultures. Dedicated to pre-1960 America, the Benaiah Gibb has Meso-American, Inuit, and Amerindian art, as well as early European-style furniture, domestic silver, and decorative art. Later galleries follow the history of Canadian painting, from church sacred art to early native studies by wandering artist Paul Kane and the impressionism of James Wilson Morrice. The Group of Seven and Paul-Emile Borduas are among those representing the 20th century.

18th-century silver teapot

Level 3

STAR EXHIBITS

_____

★ **Man of the House of Leiva by El Greco**

★ **Portrait of a Young Woman by Rembrandt**

Access to the Benaiah Gibb Pavilion

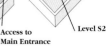

Access to Main Entrance

Level S2

VISITORS' CHECKLIST

1379–1380 Rue Sherbrooke W.
(514) 285 2000. Central
Station. 24. Guy
Concordia. 11am–6pm, Tue,
Thu–Sun; 11am–9pm, Wed.
Mon. for special
exhibitions.

Level 4

★ **Man of the House of Leiva** *(1590)*
El Greco's haunting portrayals of the Spanish aristocracy are a Renaissance highlight.

GALLERY GUIDE
The exceptional painting collections are contained on both levels 3 and 4 of the Desmarais Pavilion. Levels 1 and 2 offer a fine café and shop. Level S2 continues the connecting tunnel display of ancient cultures. Access to the main entrance is available from the elevators situated on every exhibit level.

KEY

- ☐ Contemporary art
- ☐ Art of ancient cultures
- ☐ 19th-century European art
- ☐ 20th-century European art
- ☐ European Decorative arts
- ☐ Old Masters
- ☐ Temporary exhibitions
- ☐ Nonexhibition space

A street-level entrance to the labyrinthine Underground City

Underground City 🟊

Central Station. Terminus Voyager. Place des Arts.

WHEN MONTREAL OPENED its first métro (or subway) lines in 1966, it inadvertently created a whole new layer of urban life – the Underground City. It is theoretically possible to lead a rich life in Montreal without once stepping outside. The first métro stations had underground links to just the two main train stations, a few hotels, and the shopping mall under the Place Ville-Marie office tower. This has turned into a vast network of over 30 km (19 miles) of well-lit, boutique-lined passages that includes more than 1,600 shops, 200 restaurants, hotels, film theaters, and concert halls.

Square Dorchester and Place du Canada 🟊

1001 Rue Square Dorchester.
(514) 873 2015. Central
Station. Terminus Voyager.

THESE TWO open squares create a green oasis in central downtown Montreal. On the north side of Boulevard René-Lévesque, statues including Canada's first French-Canadian prime minister, Sir Wilfrid Laurier, share the shade of Square Dorchester's trees with a war memorial. On Place du Canada a statue of the country's first prime minister, Sir John A. Macdonald, looks out over the stately Boulevard René-Lévesque.

The buildings surrounding the park are eclectic. The mix includes a Gothic church, a shiny, black bank tower and the Sun Life Building (1933), a huge stone fortress that housed the British Crown Jewels during World War II.

Varied architecture, from historic to post-modern, in Square Dorchester

Montreal skyline at night ▷

Marie-Reine-du-Monde façade with statues of Montreal's patron saints

Cathédrale Marie-Reine-du-Monde ⑰

1085 Rue Cathédrale. 📞 *(514) 866 1661.* 🚇 *Central Station.* 🚌 *Terminus Voyager.* 🚇 *Bonaventure.* 🕐 *6:30am–7:30pm Mon–Fri, 7:30am–8:30pm Sat, 8:30am–7:30pm Sun.* ♿

W HEN MONTREAL'S first Catholic cathedral burned down in 1852, Bishop Ignace Bourget decided to demonstrate the importance of the Catholic Church in Canada by building a new one in a district dominated at the time by the English Protestant commercial elite. To show his flock's loyalty to the Pope, he modeled his new church on St. Peter's Basilica in Rome.

The cathedral, which was completed in 1894, has dimensions that are a quarter of those of St. Peter's. The statues on the roof represent the patron saints of all the parishes that constituted the Montreal diocese in 1890. The magnificent altar canopy, a replica of the one Bernini made for St. Peter's, was cast in copper and gold leaf. Another reminder of Bourget's loyalty to Rome can be found on the pillar in the northeast corner of the church. Here lies a marble plaque listing the names of all the Montrealers who served in the Papal armies during the Italian war of independence in the 1850s.

The altar canopy in the cathedral

Centre Canadien d'Architecture ⑱

1920 Rue Baille. 📞 *(514) 939 7026.* 🚇 *Central.* 🚌 *Terminus Voyager.* 🚇 *Guy Concordia.* 🕐 *Jun–Sep: 11am–6pm Tue, Wed, Fri–Sun, 11am–9pm Thu; Oct–May: 11am–5pm Tue, Wed, Fri–Sun, 11am–9pm Thu.* ● *Mon.* ♿ 📷 *on request.*

V ISITORS ENTER through an unobtrusive glass door in an almost windowless façade of gray limestone that fronts this large U-shaped building. Well-lit exhibition rooms house a series of rotating displays. While some can be fairly academic, others focus on the whimsical: doll's houses and miniature villages have been featured. The two arms of the modern building embrace the ornate, grand Shaughnessy Mansion, which faces Boulevard René-Lévesque Ouest. Now part of the Centre, the house was built in 1874 for the president of the Canadian Pacific Railway, Sir Thomas Shaughnessy, and has an art-nouveau conservatory with an intricately decorated ceiling.

The Centre is also a major scholarly institution. Its collection of architectural plans, drawings, models, and photographs is the most important of its kind anywhere. The library alone has over 165,000 volumes on the world's most significant buildings.

Rue Sherbrooke ⑲

🚇 *Central Station.* 🚌 *Terminus Voyager.* 🚇 *Sherbrooke.*

I N THE LATTER HALF of the 19th century, Montreal was one of the most important cities in the British Empire. Its traders and industrialists controlled about 70 percent of Canada's wealth, and many built themselves fine homes on the slopes of Mont Royal in an area that became known as the Golden, or Square, Mile. Rue Sherbrooke between Guy and University was their Main Street, and its shops, hotels, and churches were the most elegant in the country.

Some of that elegance survived the modernizing bulldozers of the 1960s. Holt Renfrew, Montreal's upscale department store, and the stately Ritz-Carlton Hotel still stand. So do two exquisite churches, the Presbyterian St. Andrew and St. Paul, and the Erskine American United at the corner of avenue du Musée, which boasts stained-glass windows by Tiffany. Boutiques, bookstores, and galleries fill many of the rows of graystone townhouses. Millionaires not quite wealthy enough to make it into the Square Mile built graceful row homes on rues de la Montagne, Crescent, and Bishop nearby. Many of these now house trendy shops and bistros.

Farther west is the Grande Seminaire, where Montreal's Roman Catholic archdiocese still trains its priests.

Historic home on Rue Sherbrooke, the "Golden Square Mile"

Montreal's largest shrine, Oratoire Saint-Joseph, showing the steps climbed annually by pilgrims

Oratoire Saint-Joseph ⑳

3800 Chemin Queen Mary. ((514) 733 8211. 🚇 Central Station. 🚌 Terminus Voyager. 🚇 Côte-des-Neiges. ◯ 7am–9pm daily. ♿

EVERY YEAR, thousands of pilgrims climb the 300 steps to the entrance of this enormous church on their knees. Their devotion would no doubt please Brother André (1845–1937), the truly remarkable man responsible for building this shrine to the husband of the Virgin Mary. It began when he built a hillside chapel to St. Joseph in his spare time. Montreal's sick and disabled joined him at his prayers, and soon there were reports of miraculous cures. Brother André began to draw pilgrims, and the present oratory was built to receive them. He is buried here and was beatified in 1982.

The octagonal copper dome on the top of the church is one of the biggest in the world – 44.5 m (146 ft) high and 38 m (125 ft) in diameter. The interior is starkly modern; the elongated wooden statues of the apostles in the transepts are the work of Henri Charlier, who was also responsible for the main altar and the huge crucifix. The striking stained-glass windows were made by Marius Plamondon. The main building houses a museum depicting André's life and a crypt church, ablaze with hundreds of flickering candles lit by hopeful pilgrims, where daily masses are said.

Parc Mont-Royal ㉑

((514) 844 4928. 🚇 Central Station. 🚌 11. 🚇 Mont-Royal. ◯ 6am–midnight daily. ♿

THE STEEP GREEN bump that rises above the city center is only 234 m (767 ft) high, but Montrealers call it simply "the mountain" or "la montagne." Jacques Cartier gave the peak its name when he visited in 1535 and it, in turn, gave its name to the city. The hill became a park in 1876 when the city bought the land and hired Frederick Law Olmsted, the man responsible for designing New York's Central Park, to landscape it. Olmsted tried to keep it natural, building a few lookouts linked by footpaths. Succeeding generations have added a manmade pond (Beaver Lake), a 30-m high (98-ft) cross made of steel girders, and the Voie Camilien Houde, a thoroughfare that cuts through the park from east to west.

The mountain's 101 ha (250 acres) of meadows and hardwood forests still offer Montrealers a precious escape from urban life, as well as spectacular views of the city. The wide terrace in front of the Chalet du Mont-Royal pavilion looks out over the skyscrapers of the down-town core. The northern boundary of the park abuts two huge cemeteries, the Catholic Notre-Dame-Des-Neiges and the old and stately Protestant Mount Royal Cemetery, where many of Canada's finest rest.

A typical view of Montreal from the top of lofty Parc Mont-Royal

Olympic Park ②

ᴰESIGNED FOR the 1976 Olympic Games, Montreal's Olympic Park showpieces a number of stunning modern buildings. Paris architect Roger Taillibert created the Stadium, now known to many Montrealers as "The Big Owe," a reference not only to its round shape but the Can$695 million it cost to build. The stadium, seating 56,000, is used today for concerts by international stars, major league baseball and big exhibitions, and as a modern attraction in a historic city. Arching up the side of the stadium is the Montreal Tower, with its fine views. Nearby, the Biodome environmental museum replicates four world climates.

Penguin at the Biodome

Aerial view of Olympic Park
An exceptional tourist attraction, the park can be toured fully during the day. Another popular way to visit is for a concert or ballgame.

The Biodome was first used as a velodrome for the 1976 Olympics – hence the unusual cycling hat design of its roof.

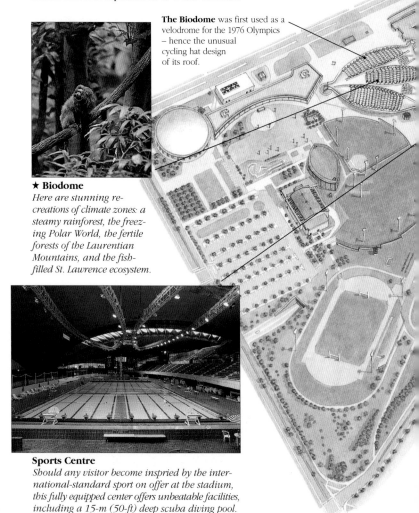

★ Biodome
Here are stunning re-creations of climate zones: a steamy rainforest, the freezing Polar World, the fertile forests of the Laurentian Mountains, and the fish-filled St. Lawrence ecosystem.

Sports Centre
Should any visitor become inspried by the international-standard sport on offer at the stadium, this fully equipped center offers unbeatable facilities, including a 15-m (50-ft) deep scuba diving pool.

★ Olympic Stadium
Finished in 1976, this magnificent hall does justice to the world stars and players who perform here.

The stadium roof was originally intended to be retractable. However, due to structural problems, it was replaced in 1998 by a detached, permanently closed roof.

★ Montreal Tower
At 175 m (575 ft) this is the world's tallest inclined tower. It arches over the stadium and overhangs it in a graceful sweep. A cable car takes 76 visitors at a time up the side of the tower to its large viewing deck. The trip takes less than two minutes.

Viewing Deck
This glass platform provides some stunning views of the city. Signs point out sights of interest that can be as far as 80 km (50 miles) away.

A cable car shoots up the side of the tower at speed; tickets can be combined with a guided tour of the stadium or Biodome.

0 meters 50
0 yards 50

STAR SIGHTS

★ Olympic Stadium

★ Montreal Tower

★ Biodome

PLAN OF THE OLYMPIC PARK AREA

1 Sports Field
2 Sports Arena
3 Maurice-Richard Centre
4 Biodome
5 Olympic Stadium
6 Botanical Gardens

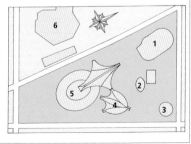

The Jardin Botanique is an oasis of calm away from the rush of the city

Jardin Botanique de Montréal ㉓

4101 Rue Sherbrooke E. 📞 *(514) 872 1400.* 🚇 *Pius-X.* ⏱ *May–Oct: 9am–9pm daily; Nov–Apr: 9am–5pm daily.* 🎫 ♿

MONTREAL'S botanical garden is among the largest in the world, a fine accomplishment for this northern city with a brutal climate. Its 73 ha (181 acres) enclose 30 outdoor gardens, 10 greenhouses, a popular display of poisonous plants, the largest collection of bonsai trees outside Asia, and a bug-shaped Insectarium full of creepy-crawlies, both dead and alive. Its most peaceful havens are the 2.5-ha (6-acre) Montreal–Shanghai Dream Lake Garden, a delightful replica of a 14th-century Ming garden, and the exquisite Japanese Garden and Pavilion where visitors can relax and appreciate the scenery.

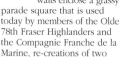

Bonsai tree at the Jardin Botanique

Ile-Sainte-Hélène ㉔

20 Chemin Tour de Lille. 📞 *(514) 844 5400.* 🚇 *Ile-Ste-Hélène.* ⛴ *Vieux-Port.* ⏱ *10am–5pm Wed–Tue.* 🎫 ♿ 🎥 *groups only.*

THIS SMALL forested island in the middle of the St. Lawrence River has played a major role in Montreal's emergence as a modern city. Originally named after

Samuel de Champlain's wife *(see pp41)*, Ile-Sainte-Hélène was the site of Expo '67, the world fair that brought millions of visitors to the city in the summer of 1967.

Several reminders of those days remain – most notably La Ronde, the fair's amusement park, and the dome that served as the United States Pavilion. This is now the Biosphere, an interpretive center that examines the Great Lakes and St. Lawrence River system. Between the dome and the roller coasters is the Fort de l'Ile-Sainte-Hélène, built in 1825 to protect Montreal from a potential American attack. Its red stone walls enclose a grassy parade square that is used today by members of the Olde 78th Fraser Highlanders and the Compagnie Franche de la Marine, re-creations of two 18th-century regimental military formations that fought each other over the future of New France until 1759. The fort also houses the **Musée David A. Stewart**, a small and excellent museum of social and military history.

🏛 **Musée David A. Stewart**
20 Chemin Tour de Lille. 📞 *(514) 861 6701.* ⏱ *10am–5pm Wed–Mon.* ⬤ *Tue; Dec 25, Jan 1.* 🎫

Ile-Notre-Dame ㉕

110 Rue Notre-Dame. 📞 *(514) 842 2925.* 🚉 *Central Station.* 🚌 *Terminus Voyager.* 🚇 *Place d'Armes.* ⏱ *late Jun–Aug: 7am–8pm daily; Sep–Jun: 7am–6pm daily.* ♿ 🎫 *for a charge.*

THIS 116-ha (286-acre) wedge of land encircled by the St. Lawrence Seaway did not exist until 1967, when it was created with rock excavated for the Montreal métro system. It shared Expo '67 with Ile-Sainte-Hélène, and today the two islands constitute the Parc-des-Iles. Ile-Notre-Dame's most popular attraction by far is the monumental Casino de Montréal, a province-owned gambling hall housed in the old French and Quebec pavilions. Every day, thousands line up at its tables and slot machines. The casino never closes. There are more refined entertainments – a rowing basin, excavated for the 1976 Olympics, superb floral gardens, and a carefully filtered body of water, which is the site of the city's only swimming beach.

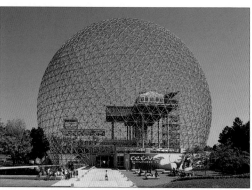

Built for Expo '67, the Biosphere has displays on Canadian river systems

The province-owned Casino on Ile-Notre-Dame is open to the hopeful 24 hours a day

Ile-Notre-Dame's Circuit Gilles Villeneuve, named for the Canadian champion, plays host to Canada's Formula 1 Grand Prix every June.

Maison Saint-Gabriel ㉖

2146 Place de Dublin. **(** *(514) 935 8136.* **🚇** *Charlevoix.* **🚌** *57.* **◯** *late Jun–Aug: daily; Sep–Jun: Tue–Sun.* 📷 ♿ 🎫 *obligatory.*

THIS ISOLATED little fragment of New France at first appears lost among the apartment buildings of working-class Pointe-Saint-Charles. It was a farm when the formidable Marguerite Bourgeoys, Montreal's first schoolteacher and now a canonized saint, bought it in 1668 as a residence for the religious order she had founded in 1655.

The house, rebuilt in 1698 after a fire, is a fine example of 17th-century architecture, with thick stone walls and a steeply pitched roof built on an intricate frame of original heavy wooden timbers.

Marguerite Bourgeoys and her tireless sisters worked the farm and ran a school on the property for native and colonial children. They also housed and trained the *filles du roy* (the "king's daughters"),

orphaned young girls sent abroad to be the women of his new colony. The house's chapel, kitchen, dormitory, and drawing rooms are full of artifacts dating from the 17th century. These include a writing desk the saint used herself and a magnificent vestment and cope, embroidered in silk, silver, and gold by a wealthy hermit who lived in a hut on the property.

Lachine ㉗

Blvd. St. Joseph. **(** *(514) 873 2015.* **🚇** *Lionel Groulx.* **🚌** *191.*

LACHINE COMPRISES a suburb of southwest Montreal and includes a small island of the same name along the shore west of the Lachine Rapids, where the St. Lawrence River widens to form Lac-Saint-Louis. Lachine is now part of Montreal, but has a long history of its own, and the old town along Blvd. Saint-Joseph is charming. Many of its fine old homes have become restaurants and bistros with outdoor terraces that overlook Parc René-Lévesque and the lake. One of the oldest houses, built by merchants in 1670, is now the **Musée de Lachine**, a historical museum and art gallery. The **Fur Trade at**

Lachine National Historic Site is a building dedicated to the fur trade, which for years was Montreal's main support.

The Lachine Canal, built in the 19th century to bypass the rapids, links the town directly to the Vieux-Port. The canal itself is now blocked to shipping, but the land along its banks has been turned into parkland with a bicycle trail.

🏛 **Musée de Lachine**
110 Chemin de LaSalle. **(** *(514) 634 3471.* **◯** *Mar–Dec: 11:30am–4:30pm Wed–Sun.* 🎫 *reserve.*
🏛 **Fur Trade at Lachine National Historic Site**
1255 Blvd. St. Joseph. **(** *(514) 637 7433.* **◯** *Apr–Oct: daily.* 📷 ♿ 🎫

A view of the historical Musée de Lachine from the reclaimed canal

QUEBEC CITY AND THE ST. LAWRENCE RIVER

T HE HEART AND soul of French Canada, Quebec City sits overlooking the St. Lawrence River on the cliffs of Cap Diamant. As provincial capital, the city is the seat of regional government, and nowadays is the heart of French-Canadian nationalism. Parisian in atmosphere, with every tiny street worth visiting, Quebec City is almost entirely French-speaking. The European ambiance, architecture, and the city's crucial historical importance all contributed to it being named as a United Nations World Heritage Site in 1985. One of the world's great waterways, the St. Lawrence River is home to rare marine wildlife. Right and minke whales swim as far upstream as Tadoussac and feed at the mouth of the Saguenay River. The Laurentian Mountains rise up above the St. Lawrence on the north shore, a year-round natural playground. Nearer Quebec City, the rich scenery of the Charlevoix region is among the most beautiful in the country, contrasting with the soaring cliffs and wilderness of the Gaspé Peninsula. Offshore, Ile d' Anticosti is a stunning nature preserve.

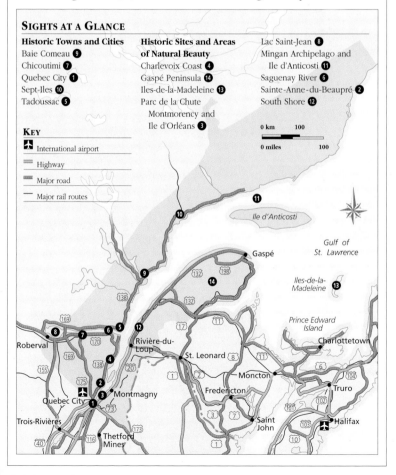

SIGHTS AT A GLANCE

Historic Towns and Cities
Baie Comeau **9**
Chicoutimi **7**
Quebec City **1**
Sept-Iles **10**
Tadoussac **5**

Historic Sites and Areas of Natural Beauty
Charlevoix Coast **4**
Gaspé Peninsula **14**
Iles-de-la-Madeleine **13**
Parc de la Chute Montmorency and Ile d'Orléans **3**

Lac Saint-Jean **8**
Mingan Archipelago and Ile d'Anticosti **11**
Saguenay River **6**
Sainte-Anne-du-Beaupré **2**
South Shore **12**

KEY

✈ International airport

═ Highway

═ Major road

─ Major rail routes

0 km   100
0 miles   100

Ile d'Anticosti

Gulf of St. Lawrence

Gaspé

Iles-de-la-Madeleine **13**

Prince Edward Island

Charlottetown

Roberval

Rivière-du-Loup

St. Leonard

Moncton

Fredericton

Truro

Quebec City

Montmagny

Saint John

Halifax

Trois-Rivières

Thetford Mines

◁ **The historic architecture of Quebec City's Lower Town**

Street-by-Street: Quebec City ❶

ONE OF THE OLDEST communities on the American continent, Quebec City was discovered as an Iroquois village by the French explorer Jacques Cartier and founded as a city in 1608 by explorer Samuel de Champlain (*see p41*). The British gained dominance over the city and the rest of the province at the Plains of Abraham battle just outside the city walls in 1759. Today the town is renowned as the heart of French Canada. The oldest part of the city is Basse-Ville, or Lower Town, which was renovated in the 1970s. With its winding staircases and cafés, it is a charming destination.

★ **Basilique Notre-Dame-de-Québec**
This 1647 cathedral provides a rich setting for relics from early French rule in Quebec, and Old Master paintings.

Musée du Fort
Military history is brought to life here in sound-and-light shows reenacting six Quebec sieges and battles, and numerous war relics.

Holy Trinity Anglican Cathedral
An elegant 1804 stone Neo-Classical façade conceals an English oak interior.

Château Frontenac
Quebec City's best-known landmark has risen over the city since 1893, and has 600 luxurious guest rooms.

| 0 meters | 100 |
| 0 yards | 100 |

KEY

– – – Suggested route

Musée de la Civilisation
Human history through the ages is explored in this airy modern building linked to historic houses in the rest of the town, including Maison Chevalier.

VISITORS' CHECKLIST

167,500. ✈ 16 km (10 miles) west of the city. 🚂 450 Rue de Gare-du-Palais. 🚌 320 Rue Abraham-Martin. ⛴ 10 Rue des Praversiers. ℹ 835 Avenue Wilfrid-Laurier (418) 649 2608. 🎭 Winter Carnival (Feb); Summer Festival (Jul).

★ Place Royale
A virtual microcosm of Canadian history, Place Royale has experienced a renaissance, and the surrounding streets, with their 18th- and 19th-century architecture, have been sandblasted back to their original glory.

PORT DAUPHIN
RUE DU SAULT AU MATELOT
RUE SAINT-PIERRE
COTE DE LA MONTAGNE
RUE NOTRE-DAME
RUE SAINT-PIERRE

The funicular travels from Terrasse Dufferin to Lower Town, providing excellent aerial views of the historic city center.

STAR SIGHTS

★ **Place Royale**

★ **Basilique Notre-Dame**

Maison Chevalier
Linked with the Musée de la Civilisation, this home built for an 18th-century merchant showcases the decorative arts. Quebec furniture and the famous Quebec silverware feature in every room, as well as exhibits showing how well-to-do families lived in the 18th and 19th centuries.

Quebec City

CONTAINING THE ONLY WALLED city north of the Rio
Grande, Quebec City has narrow cobblestone
streets and 18th-century buildings that lend a European
air to this small provincial capital, just 93 square km (36
square miles). Most of the sights are packed into one
accessible corner, above and below the Cap Diamant
cliffs, with the Citadel rising up protectively at the top
of the cliff. As Quebec's capital, the city is home to the
provincial parliament, the Assemblée Nationale, which
conducts its debates almost entirely in French in
splendid chambers behind the ornate early 19th-
century façade of the grandiose Hôtel du Parlement.

Château Frontenac dominates the skyline of Quebec City

Exploring Quebec City

Most of the main sights are
easily reached on foot. The city
can conveniently be divided
into three parts. Basse-Ville,
or Lower Town, is the oldest
part, and rambles along the St.
Lawrence River at the foot of
Cap Diamant. Above lies the
walled city, Haute-Ville, or
Upper Town. This area is
full of shops and restau-
rants, similar to the
Basse-Ville, but both
Catholic and Protestant
cathedrals are here, as
is the imposing Château
Frontenac. Beyond the
walls stretches Grande
Allée, with the Hôtel du
Parlement where the
provincial parlia-
ment of Quebec sits.

☗ Terrasse Dufferin

Sweeping along the top of
Cap Diamant from Château
Frontenac to the edge of the
Citadel, this boardwalk is well
equiped with benches and
kiosks, and offers unmatched
views of the St. Lawrence River,
the Laurentian Mountains, and
Ile d'Orleans. During the

freezing Quebec winter, the
municipal authorities install
an ice slide for toboggans
on the terrace, known as
Les Glissades de la Terrasse.

♣ Parc des Champs-de-Bataille

835 Ave. Wilfrid Laurier. ☏ (418)
648 4071. ◯ daily. ♿

Once a battlefield where the
future of Canada was decided, the National Battlefields
Park is now a delightful grassy
recreation ground, with
grand monuments
and a dedicated
fountain the only
clues to the area's
bloody and drama-
tic history. On
September 13,
1759, British reg-
ulars under Gen-
eral James Wolfe
defeated the
French army on this clifftop
field, the Plains of Abraham,
just outside the walls of
Quebec (see pp42–3), establishing permanent British rule
in Canada. In 1908, the 100-
ha (250-acre) battlefield was
turned into one of the largest
urban parks in North America.

Joan of Arc at Parc-des-Champs de Bataille

☗ Assemblée Nationale

Ave. Honoré-Mercier & Grande Allée E.
☏ (418) 643 7239. ◪ late Jun–early
Sep: daily; late Sep–Jun: Mon–Fri. ♿
The Assemblée Nationale,
Quebec's provincial parliament,
meets just outside the walls of
the Old City in this graceful
Second-Empire building, completed in 1886 as a showcase
of provincial history. Niches
along the imposing façade and
up the sides of the tall central
tower display 22 bronze figures, each representing a person who played a vital role in
Quebec's development. The
first inhabitants of the territory
are honored in a bronze ren-
dition of a native Indian family
by the main door. Inside, the
blue chamber is the hub of
Quebec's political activity.

☗ Fortifications de Québec

☏ (418) 648 7016. ◯ Apr–Oct:
daily. ♿♿
After a century of peace, the
fortifications that had secured
Quebec since their completion by the British in 1760
were transformed in the 1870s
from a grim military necessity
into this popular attraction.
On the city's northern and
eastern edges, low ramparts
studded with cannon defend
the clifftop, with the walls on
the western side reaching 2.5
m (10 ft). Two elegant gates,
the Saint-Jean and the Saint-
Louis, pierce the western
stretch. Visitors can walk
along the top of the walls
for 4 km (3 miles).

Quebec's 18th-century fortifications in the Parc d'Artillerie

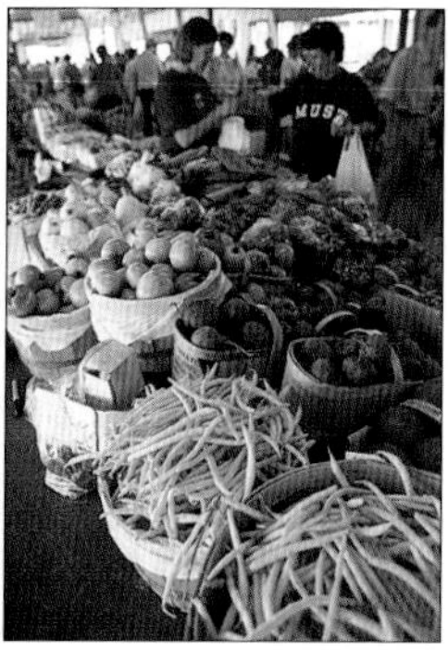

Abundant produce stalls draw crowds at the market in Vieux Port

🏛 Vieux Port

[i] *100 Quai Saint Andre.* ☎ *(418) 648 3300.* ♿

This delightful area has its focus around the old harbor northeast of the walled city. In contrast to the crammed heritage of much of the Lower Town, Vieux Port is an airy riverside walking site, full of new and restored modern attractions. Boat cruises which lead gently downriver to the Chute Montmorency waterfalls are available. Waterfront walks pass chic boutiques, apartment blocks, the city's concert stadium, and shops in trendy warehouse settings.

🏛 Musée de la Civilisation

85 Rue Dalhousie. ☎ *(418) 643 2158.* 🕒 *late Jun–early Sep: daily; late Sep–early Jun: Tue–Sun.* 🚫📷 ♿

Top contemporary Canadian architect Moshe Safdie designed this modern limestone and glass building in Basse-Ville to house Quebec's new museum of history and culture. Although highly up-to-date in feel, the construction has won several prizes for blending in well with its historic surroundings. Three heritage buildings are part of the museum's structure including Maison d'Estebe, an 18th-century merchant's house. The museum also uses another nearby 18th-century house, Maison Chevalier, for displaying Quebec architecture and furniture in period setting.

Museum exhibits include a collection of Chinese imperial furniture and the remains of a 250-year-old French flat-bottomed boat. *Mémoires*, a permanent exhibit on the third floor, provides a real insight into 400 years of Quebec history with a collection of items from everyday life including tools, folk art, toys, carriages, and many religious articles.

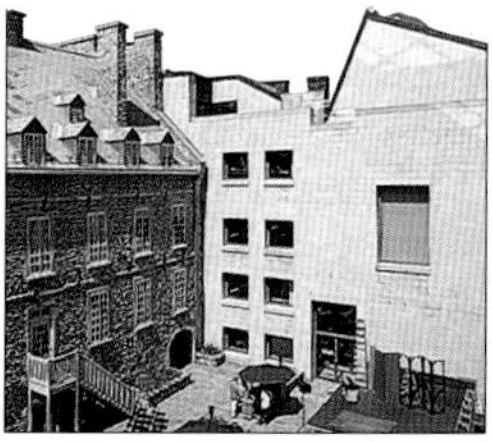

Antique and modern architecture of the Musée de la Civilisation

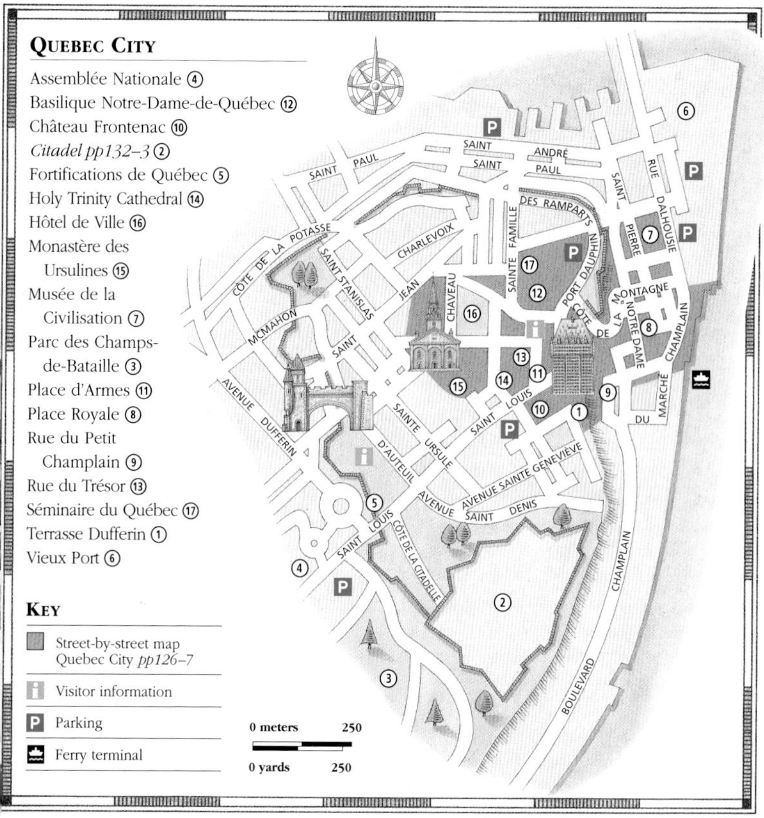
QUEBEC CITY
Assemblée Nationale 4
Basilique Notre-Dame-de-Québec 12
Château Frontenac 10
Citadel pp132–3 2
Fortifications de Québec 5
Holy Trinity Cathedral 14
Hôtel de Ville 16
Monastère des Ursulines 15
Musée de la Civilisation 7
Parc des Champs-de-Bataille 3
Place d'Armes 11
Place Royale 8
Rue du Petit Champlain 9
Rue du Trésor 13
Séminaire du Québec 17
Terrasse Dufferin 1
Vieux Port 6
KEY
Street-by-street map Quebec City *pp126–7*
Visitor information
Parking
Ferry terminal
0 meters 250
0 yards 250
SAINT PAUL
SAINT ANDRÉ
SAINT PAUL
DES RAMPARTS
RUE SAINT PIERRE
DALHOUSIE
CÔTE DE LA POTASSE
SAINT STANISLAS
CHARLEVOIX
SAINTE FAMILLE
PORT DAUPHIN
CHAUVEAU
JEAN
MCMAHON
SAINT
CÔTE DE LA MONTAGNE
NOTRE DAME
CHAMPLAIN
AVENUE DUFFERIN
SAINTE URSULE
D'AUTEUIL
SAINT LOUIS
DU MARCHÉ
AVENUE SAINTE GENEVIÈVE
AVENUE SAINT DENIS
SAINT LOUIS
CÔTE DE LA CITADELLE
CHAMPLAIN
BOULEVARD

⊞ Place Royale
Rue Saint Pierre.

Of all the squares in Canada, Place Royale has undoubtedly the most history. Samuel de Champlain, the founder of Quebec, planted his garden on this site, and the French colonial governor Frontenac turned it into a market in 1673. A bust of Louis XIV was installed in 1686, and the square was named Place Royale.

Today it remains much as it did in the 18th century, exuding an air of elegance and delicate grandeur. A cobblestone court in the center of Basse-Ville, Place Royale is surrounded by steep-roofed early 18th-century buildings with pastel-colored shutters that were once the homes of wealthy traders. The square declined in the 19th century but is now fully restored and a favorite for street performers.

Rue du Petit Champlain bustling with shoppers

🏛 Rue du Petit Champlain
below Dufferin Terrace in Old City.
【 (418) 692 2613. ♿ partial.

The rather aptly named Escalier Casse-Cou, or Breakneck Stairs, descends from Haute-Ville past several levels of gift shops to end on this narrow little walkway in the oldest part of the town. French artisans built homes along here as early as the 1680s, and Irish dockworkers moved to the area in the 19th century. Much of the historic architecture remained, but the area fell into decline early in the 20th century. Now fully refurbished, the workers' homes are transformed into shops and restaurants, and the short pedestrian walkway has become one of the liveliest spots in old Quebec City. While often crowded, some interesting boutiques can be found.

A familiar landmark of the city, the 600-room Château Frontenac hotel

⊞ Place d'Armes
French colonial soldiers once used this attractive, grassy square just north of Château Frontenac as a parade ground, but its uses today are more congenial. Open horse-drawn carriages wait here to offer visitors a journey that reveals the square in all its charm. In the center, the Monument de la Foi commemorates the 300th anniversary of the 1615 arrival of Catholic Recollet missionaries. On the southwest corner next to the fine Anglican cathedral, lies the grand early 19th-century Palais de Justice. The Musée du Fort opposite contains a large scale model of Quebec City in the 19th century.

⊞ Château Frontenac
1 Rue des Carrières. 【 (418) 692 3861.

The steep, green copper-roofed landmark that dominates the skyline of Old Quebec is a luxury hotel, built by the Canadian Pacific Railway on the heights overlooking the St. Lawrence River. In the 19th century, US architect Bruce Price designed the hotel as a French-style château on a huge scale, with dozens of turrets, towers, and a high copper roof studded with rows of dormer windows. Building continued for almost a century after the first section of the hotel was opened in 1893, with a final part completed in 1983. Made from brick and stone, the hotel now has over 600 rooms. The public salons are sumptuous and elegant; Salon Verchère and the Champlain are the most visited.

♦ Basilique Notre-Dame-de-Québec
Place de l'Hôtel de Ville. 【 (418) 694 0665. ◯ 7:30am–4:30pm daily. ♿

This magnificent cathedral is the principal seat of the Roman Catholic archbishop of Quebec, whose diocese once stretched from here to Mexico. Fire destroyed the first two churches on the site before 1640, and the first cathedral built here was torn down by the British in 1759. A fourth version burned down in 1922. The present cathedral replaced it in the style of the 1647 original. Some building materials, including concrete, steel, and plaster, have been used to re-create the light feel; glowing stained-glass windows, richly gilded decoration, and the graceful baldachin over the main altar add to the effect.

Imposing façade of the Basilique-Notre-Dame-de-Quebec

⚜ Rue du Trésor

off Place d'Armes.
This tiny alley just across rue
de Buade from Holy Trinity
cathedral is something of a
Quebecois institution. Closed
to cars, the little street is packed in summer with visitors
eager to have their portraits
drawn, painted, or caricatured
by the dozens of street artists
who gather here. Browsing
for sketches and watercolors
of Quebec scenes can be fun.

⛪ Holy Trinity Anglican Cathedral

31 Rue des Jardins. **(** (418) 692
2193. ⭘ daily. &
After worshiping for nearly a
century in the city's Catholic
churches, in 1804 the Anglicans
of Quebec finally had their
own cathedral built at state
expense. Their new mother
church was the first
Anglican cathedral
outside Britain and
is modeled on
London's huge Neo-
Classical St. Martin's
in the Fields. To this
day, gifts from
England remain,
including the prayer
book and Bible don-
ated by the British
King George III. Cut from
the King's Windsor Forest in
England, the pews are of oak,
and the eight-bell peal is the
oldest in Canada. In the summer artists and artisans fill the
verdant church grounds.

Reliquary from the Ursuline Convent

⛪ Monastère des Ursulines

Rue Donnacona. **(** (418) 694 0694.
⭘ daily. &
In 1639, Mère Marie de
l'Incarnation brought the Ursuline order of nuns to Quebec
and oversaw the construction
in 1641 of the nunnery here,
which later burned down.
Today, visitors can see the
Saint-Augustin and Saint-
Famille wings, which date from
a period of rebuilding between
1685 and 1715. Surrounded
by fruit orchards, the charming
complex has gradually evolved
over the past four centuries.
One of the buildings is North
America's oldest girls' school.
Nearly a hundred nuns still
live and work here, so access
is limited. The beautifully
decorated chapel and French

The Hôtel de Ville seen from the small park in its grounds

antiques, including Louis XIII
furniture, antique scientific
tools and instruments, paintings, and embroid-
eries are displayed
in the Musée des
Ursulines within
the monastery. The
museum also tells
the story of the nuns'
educational and mis-
sionary achievements
in the province. Mère
Marie completed the
first native Algonquin
and Iroquois dictionaries, and
these can be seen here, alongside native art and artifacts.

⚜ Hôtel de Ville

Côte de la Fabrique. **(** (418) 691
4606. ⭘ Interpretive Centre: late
Jun–Sep: daily; Oct–Jun: Tue–Sun. &
This imposing building stands
at the western end of the rue
de Buade, a popular gathering
place for Quebec artists offering their wares. Built in 1833,
and still the town hall to the
city, it is the grounds that are

the focus for the city's people.
The small park here holds
theater performances in the
summertime and is a meeting
place for festival-goers.

⚜ Séminaire de Québec

2 Côte de la Fabrique. **(** (418) 692
2843. ⭘ summer. ⚐ obligatory. &
In 1663, the first bishop of
Quebec, Francois Laval, built
a seminary next to his cathedral to train Catholic priests
for his huge diocese. Over the
centuries the school has been
added to and now forms a
graceful complex of historic
17th-, 18th-, and 19th-century
buildings centered on a peaceful grassy courtyard.
Within the seminary, visitors
can admire the excellent 18th-
century paneling that covers
the walls of the chapel. The
Musée de l'Amérique Française
is part of the complex and
has a wonderfully eclectic collection, including a converted
chapel decorated with fascinating wooden *trompe l'oeils*.

The 19th-century interior of the chapel at the Séminaire de Québec

La Citadelle

BOTH THE FRENCH and British armies contributed to the building of this magnificent fort. The French started construction in 1750, with work completed in 1831 by the British. The purpose of the fort was to defend Quebec against an American attack that never came.

Regimental stained glass beaver badge

Today the fortifications are a pleasant walkway that provides a tour around the star-shaped fortress. The Citadel is home to the famous French Canadian regiment the Royal 22-ème (Van Doos). Because the Citadel is still a working military barracks, visitors can see the regiment perform their daily tasks as well as their parade drill.

The Fortifications
From the mid-19th century, the Citadel served as the eastern flank of Quebec City's defenses.

Old Military Prison

Cap Diamant is the highest point of the Cape Diamond cliffs, from which the Lower Town descends.

Governor-General's residence
This splendid mansion with its double central staircase and marble hall has been the official home of Canada's governors-general since the 19th century.

Trenches
around the Citadel have always been key defensive structures.

Cape Diamond Redoubt
The oldest building in the Citadel, the Redoubt dates back to 1693 when it was built under the leadership of the French Count Frontenac as a first citadel for Quebec. Now home to relics of war, the Redoubt offers fine views of the St. Lawrence River.

The Vimy Cross was erected in memory of the Canadians who fell at the WWI battle of Vimy Ridge in 1917.

Chapel
A key part of the fortress, this private chapel used to be a British powder magazine and is now used for ceremonial purposes.

★ Changing of the Guard, Parade Square
Every day from June to Labour Day, the Changing of the Guard takes place. The ceremonial dress of the 22-ème, scarlet tunic and blue trousers, is of British design.

The Barracks
As a fully operational military site, the barracks is home to Canada's most dashing regiment, the 22-ème, who fought with bravery in both world wars.

The Prince of Wales Bastion contains a now disused powder magazine. Built in 1750, it once stored 2,388 barrels of gunpowder.

0 meters 25
0 yards 25

STAR SIGHTS

★ Changing of the Guard

★ Dalhousie Gate

★ Dalhousie Gate
One of the original structures remaining from the 19th century, Dalhousie Gate is surrounded by portholes and gun fittings. These helped the four-pointed fortress to cover its north, south, and west flanks with defensive fire.

Sainte-Anne-de-Beaupré ●

O NE OF CANADA'S most sacred places, the shrine to
the mother of the Virgin Mary was originally built
in the 17th century by a group of grateful sailors who
landed here after narrowly surviving a shipwreck. Over
1.5 million sightseers and pilgrims now visit every year,
including an annual pilgrimage on the Saint's Day in July.
The focus of their homage is the ornate medieval-style
basilica, which was built in the 1920s. Inside the entrance
stand two columns of crutches, testimony to the faith of
generations of Roman Catholics.
Rows of thick columns divide the
interior into five naves, and the
dome-vaulted ceiling is decorated
with gold mosaics portraying the
life of Saint Anne. She is represented in a large gilt statue in the
transept, cradling the Virgin Mary.

Statue of Saint Anne
*The focus of the upper floor,
the richly decorated statue
sits in front of the relic
of Saint Anne,
presented to the
shrine by Pope John
XXIII in 1960.*

PLAN OF THE SHRINE

1 Basilica　　4 Museum
2 Monastery　5 Blessing Office
3 Seminary

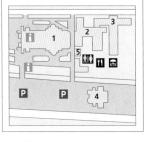

**Stained-glass
windows** show
the progress of
pilgrims through
the shrine, with
the rose window
as centerpiece.

THE BASILICA
*In 1876, Saint Anne was
proclaimed patron saint of
Quebec, and in 1887 the
existing church was granted
basilica status. The
Redemptorist order
of Catholic priests
took charge of the
shrine in 1878.*

**Entrance
to Basilica's
upper floor**

**Bright mosaic
floor tiles echo
ceiling patterns**

★ **The Basilica**
*There has been a church on this
site since 1658. In 1922, the
previous basilica burned down.
Today's version was built in 1923
and consecrated in 1976.*

STAR SIGHTS

★ **The Basilica**

★ **Pietà**

★ **Pietà**
*A faithful copy of Michel-
angelo's original in St.
Peter's, Rome,
this shows
Christ at
his death.*

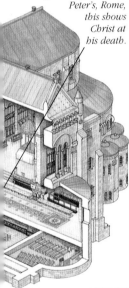

Basilica interior
*Lit by sun streaming through
the stained-glass windows,
the cream and gold interior
is decorated in every corner.*

Montmorency Falls at Ile d'Orléans, Quebec's most dramatic waterfall

Parc de la Chute Montmorency and Ile d'Orléans ❸

Montmorency Falls (418) 663 3330.
8:30am–11pm daily.
Ile d'Orléans Tourist Centre, 490
Cote du Pont, St. Pierre (418) 828 9411.

LOCATED 7 KM (4.5 miles) east of Quebec City, Montmorency Falls is Quebec's most celebrated waterfall. Higher than Niagara Falls, the cascade is created as the Montmorency River empties out into the St. Lawrence River – a total of 30 m (100 ft) higher than the 56-m (175-ft) plunge of Niagara Falls from the Niagara River to Lake Ontario. The park surrounding the Falls offers several ways to view the cascade; a suspension bridge, an aerial tram, and, for the fit and fearless, a series of trails that climb the surrounding cliffs.

A spidery modern bridge nearby crosses the river to the Ile d'Orléans. This richly fertile island is covered with flowers, strawberry fields, and flourishing farmland. Sprinkled with villages, it gives a fascinating look at the traditional Quebec routine of peaceful rural life.

Charlevoix Coast ❹

166 Blvd. de Comporte, La
Malbaie (418) 665 4454.

THE CHARLEVOIX coast runs 200 km (130 miles) along the north shore of the St. Lawrence River, from Sainte-Anne-de-Beaupré in the west to the mouth of the Saguenay. A

UNESCO World Biosphere Reserve because of its fine examples of boreal forest, the area is a slim band of flowery rural beauty on the southern edge of tundra that stretches northward. Gentle valleys protect old towns reaching to the river, with coastal villages sheltering beneath tall cliffs. Lying in a fertile valley is the exception-ally pretty Baie-Saint-Paul, its streets lined with historic houses and inns.

Just 35 km (21 miles) north of Baie-Saint-Paul lies the **Parc des Grands Jardins**, a vast expanse of lakes and black-spruce evergreen taiga forest with a herd of caribou. Small mountains offer walking and hiking. Farther downstream is the tiny and tranquil island Ile-aux-Coudres. The lush, green farmland here is sprinkled with historic farms and a windmill.

Parc des Grands Jardins
Rte. 381. (418) 846 2057. May–
Oct: daily; Nov–Apr: Sat & Sun.

Moulin de L'Ile-aux-Coudres, in the Charlevoix region

The town of Tadoussac at the confluence of the St. Lawrence and Saguenay rivers

Tadoussac ❺

🏃 *850.* 🚍 ⛴ ℹ️ *196 Rue des Pionniers (418) 235 4977.*

L INED WITH boutiques, the old streets of this little town make a gentle start to exploring the local stretch of the St. Lawrence River. In 1600, French traders picked the village as the site of the first fur-trading post in Canada, noticing that for generations native Indians had held meetings here to trade and parley. In the 19th century, even while the fur trade was still a force, steamships began to transport well-heeled tourists to the village for a taste of its wilderness beauty.

Justifying two centuries of tourism, the scenery here is magnificent. Backed by rocky cliffs and towering sand dunes, Tadoussac's waterfront faces over the estuary at the confluence of the St. Lawrence and Saguenay rivers. In the town, the re-creation of the original 17th-century fur-trading post and the oldest wooden church in Canada, the Petite Chapelle built in 1747, are popular.

However, the main attraction in Tadoussac lies offshore. Whale-watching tours offer trips into the estuary to see many species at close quarters. The thriving natural conditions in the estuary support a permanent colony of white beluga whales, which are joined in summer by minke, fin, and blue whales.

Saguenay River ❻

🚋 *Jonquière.* 🚍 *Chicoutimi.* ℹ️ *198 Rue Racine East (418) 543 9778.*

T HE SAGUENAY River flows through the world's south-ernmost natural fjord. This was formed from a retreating glacier splitting a deep crack in the Earth's crust during the last Ice Age, 10,000 years ago. Inky waters, 300 m (985 ft) deep in places, run for 155 km (95 miles) beneath cliffs that average 450 m (1,500 ft) in height. Due to the exceptional depth, ocean liners can travel up to Chicoutimi on the river.

Running from Lac St. Jean to the St. Lawrence estuary, the Saguenay is best known for its lush borderlands and the

wildlife that thrives in its lower reaches. Much of the pretty Bas Saguenay, the southern half of the river, is a federal marine park. Most visitors take a tour to view the colony of a thousand whales that have chosen the fjord as their home.

Beautiful views of the length of the fjord are available on the western shore at Cap Trinité, a cliff that rises 320 m (1,050 ft) over the channel, with a well-known 10-m (33-ft) statue of the Virgin Mary surveying the scenery from the lowest ledge.

Chicoutimi ❼

🏃 *64,600.* ℹ️ *198 Rue Racine East (418) 543 9778.*

S NUG IN THE crook of moun-tains on the western shore of the Saguenay, Chicoutimi is one of northern Quebec's most expansive towns, despite its modest population. The cultural and economic center of the Saguenay region, its waterfront district has now been restored. A stroll along the riverside offers good views of the surrounding mountains and the confluence of the Chicoutimi, Du-Moulin, and Saguenay rivers.

Once a center for the paper trade, Chicoutimi still features a large pulp mill, the **Pulperie de Chicoutimi**. Although no longer operational, the plant can be toured, and an adjacent museum shows visitors the intricacies of this long-standing Quebecois industry, which once supplied most of North America's paper needs.

🏛 **Pulperie de Chicoutimi**
300 Dubuc. 🄲 *(418) 698 3100.*
🄾 *late Jun–Sep: 9am–6pm daily.* ♿

Waterside view of a section of the deep Saguenay fjord

A Tour of Lac-Saint-Jean ❽

IN THE MIDST OF THE ROCKY, spruce-covered wilderness that characterizes central Quebec, Lac-Saint-Jean is an oasis of tranquillity. Dairy farms, charming villages such as Chambord, and warm sandy beaches border the lake itself, which covers 1,350 sq km (520 sq miles). The lake and its rolling green landscape fill a crater-sized basin left by advancing glaciers at the end of the last Ice Age. Tiny rivers flow to the lake and tumble dramatically down the basin's steep walls into the blue waters, to be reborn as the source of the Saguenay River.

Tips for Drivers

Starting point: *Chambord.*
Length: *180 km (112 miles).*
Getting around: *This is a long, though relaxed drive, and the road is well maintained. Inns and restaurants offer rest on the way in most towns and villages, including Mashteuiatsh. Small side roads make peaceful diversions.*

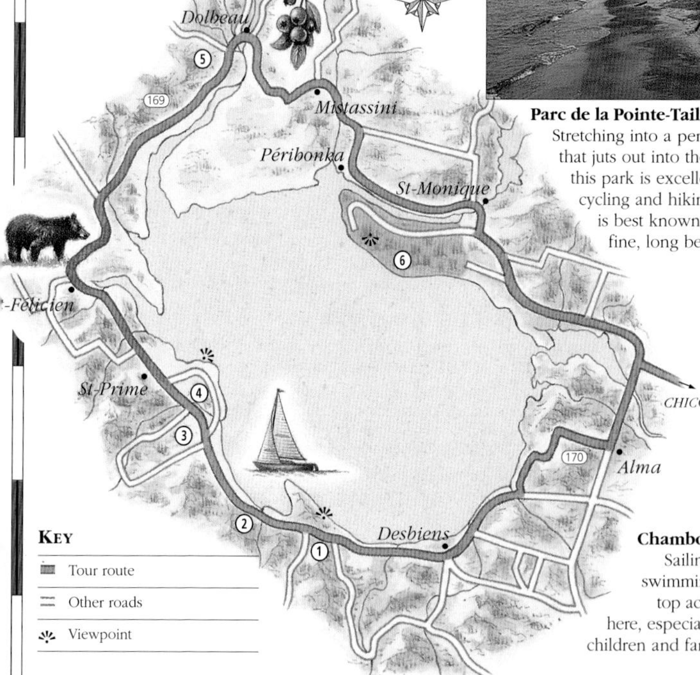
0 km 10
0 miles 10
Dolbeau
169
Mistassini
Péribonka
St-Monique
-Félicien
St-Prime
CHICOUTIMI
170
Alma
Desbiens
Key
Tour route
Other roads
Viewpoint

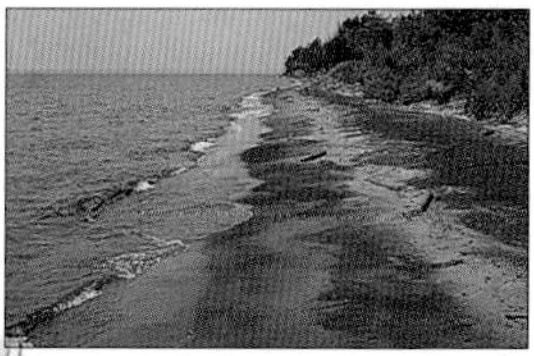

Parc de la Pointe-Taillon ⑥
Stretching into a peninsula that juts out into the lake, this park is excellent for cycling and hiking, but is best known for its fine, long beaches.

Chambord ①
Sailing and swimming are top activities here, especially for children and families.

Dolbeau ⑤
Most visitors to Dolbeau arrive in July for the ten-day Western Festival, which features rodeos and cowboys in Stetsons.

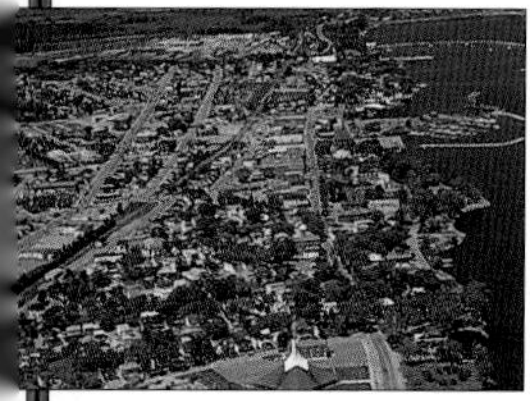

Mashteuiatsh, Pointe Bleu ④
This Montagnais Indian village is open to visitors who can see at first hand age-old methods of carving, hunting, weaving, and cooking.

Roberval ③
This little village has a charming waterfront, from which spectators can see the finish of the swimming contest to cross the lake, which has taken place each July since 1946.

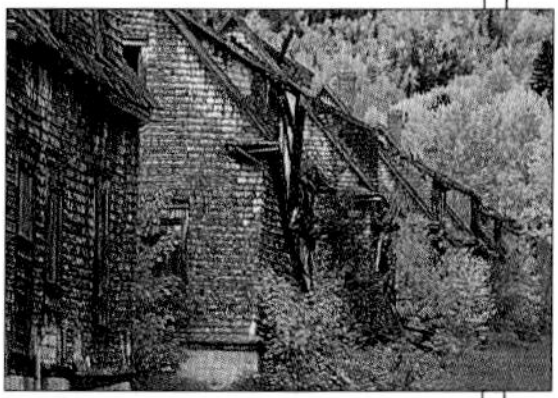

Val-Jalbert ②
This small town is dominated by the 70-m (200-ft) Ouiatchouan waterfall in the center, which once acted as power for a pulp mill here in the 1920s.

Manic Côte Nord, a hydroelectric power plant north of Baie-Comeau

Baie-Comeau ❾

🏃 26,700. ☒ 🚂 🛳 ℹ️ 337 La Salle (418) 294 2345.

THIS SMALL town owes its entire existence to the US newspaper, the *Chicago Tribune*, which in 1936 built a mill near the mouth of the Manicougan River to supply its newspaper presses with paper. Declared a historic district in 1985, Baie-Comeau's oldest area is the Quartier Amélie, with rows of fine homes and an impressive hotel dating from the 1930s.

Paper production remains a vital industry in this area, but Baie-Comeau is most important today as a gateway to the enormous Manic-Outardes hydroelectric power complex, situated along Hwy 389, from 22 km (14 miles) to 200 km (130 miles) north of town. The most spectacular example is Manic-5, 190 km (115 miles) from Baie-Comeau. Its gracefully arched Daniel Johnson Dam holds back a vast reservoir that fills a crater geophysicists believe might have been created by a meteorite several millennia ago.

Sept-Iles ❿

🏃 26,000. 🚂 🚂 🛳 ℹ️ 312 Ave. Brochu (418) 962 0808.

UNTIL THE 1950s, Sept-Iles led a quiet existence as a historic, sleepy fishing village. However, after World War II, the little settlement, set on the shores of a large, circular bay, drew the attention of large companies to use as a base for expanding the iron mining industry in northern Quebec. Now the largest town along the north shore of the Gulf of St. Lawrence, Sept-Iles has turned into Canada's second largest port as part of the St. Lawrence Seaway. A boardwalk along the waterfront offers visitors the chance to see the large ships in action, and to observe close-up the workings of a busy modern dock.

Although boasting the best of modern marine technology, the town also offers a reminder of its long-standing history. Vieux Poste near the center of the town is a fine reconstruction of a native trading post, where the original inhabitants of the area met to barter furs with French merchants. A small museum with aboriginal art and artifacts sells native crafts.

Despite its industrial importance, Sept-Iles is an area of considerable natural beauty.

Sept-Iles from the air, showing the bustling dock in action

Miles of sandy beaches rim the nearby coastline, and the salmon-rich Moisie River flows into the Gulf of St. Lawrence just 20 km (12 miles) east of the town. The seven rocky islands that gave the city its name make up the Sept-Iles Archipelago Park.

Ideal for campers and hikers with its beaches and nature trails, one of the seven islands, Ile Grand-Basque, is a popular local camping spot. Another small island, Ile du Corossol, has been turned into a bird sanctuary that teems with gulls, terns, and puffins, and can be toured with a guide. Cruises are available for guided trips between islands.

Mingan Archipelago and Ile d'Anticosti ⓫

🚂 Sept-Iles. 🛳 Sept-Iles. ℹ️ 312 Ave. Brochu, Sept-Iles (418) 962 0808.

BARELY VISITED until recently, this unspoiled and unsettled area is fast gaining in popularity for its harsh landscape, rich wildlife, and untouched ecosystems. In 1984, the Mingan Archipelago islands became Canada's first insular national park. Puffins, terns, and several gull species find refuge in the Mingan Archipelago Wildlife Park, which comprises all 40 of the Mingan Islands that scatter along the north shore of the Gulf of St. Lawrence. Gray, harbor, and harp seals all cluster along the tiny coves and bays, and fin whales are occasional visitors. As well as the abundant wildlife, the islands are famous for their bizarre monoliths. Eroded over many centuries by the sea, these limestone carvings have surreal shapes. The best-known rocks look strikingly like flowerpots, with grasses sprouting from their peaks. Visitors can book a trip to admire this unique manifestation of nature by boat.

Until 1974, the Ile d'Anticosti, east of the archipelago, was private property – all 8,000 sq km (3,090 sq miles) of it. The past owner, French chocolate tycoon Henri Menier, bought

"Flowerpot" limestone monoliths at Mingan Archipelago National Park

the island in 1895 and stocked it with a herd of white-tailed deer for his friends to hunt. Now numbering 120,000, the deer herd is firmly ensconced but can still be hunted. Wildlife abounds; over 150 species of bird live happily in the relatively unspoiled forest and on the beaches. A lone village on the island, Port Menier, has 300 residents and acts as the local ferry terminus and lodging center.

Seal at Ile d'Anticosti

South Shore ⓬

🏠 *Rivière-du-Loup.* 🚉 *Rivière-du-Loup.* ⛴ *Rivière-du-Loup.*
🛈 *Rivière-du-Loup (418) 867 3015.*

COMMUNITIES here can trace their roots back to the old 18th-century settlers of New France. Dotted along the flat, fertile farmland of the south shore of the St. Lawrence River west of Gaspé and inland toward Montreal, the villages cover the area between the region's largest towns of Montmagny and Rimouski. Rivière-du-Loup, a seemingly unremarkable town in this stretch, provides for many people a taste of true Quebec. Featuring an ancient stone church that rears above the skyline, the old town rambles

along hilly streets, and its old 18th-century cottages have an appealing French atmosphere. From the peak of the old town, views across the river valley are lovely. Other villages in this area feature unusual attractions. Farther along the main Route 32, Trois-Pistoles boasts a history that goes back to 1580, when Basque whalers arrived. The offshore Ile-aux-Basques was a whaling station in the 16th century, and today can be visited to tour the nature preserve in its place. Toward the region's commercial center, Rimouski, lies Parc Bic, a small preserve of 33 square km (13 square miles) dedicated to the two forest zones, deciduous and boreal, it encloses, and its varied coastal wildlife.

Iles-de-la-Madeleine ⓭

🛈 *128 Chemin du Debarcadere, Cap-aux-Meules (418) 986 2245.*

THE FEW FISHING families who make their homes on this remote archipelago in the middle of the huge gulf of St. Lawrence have taken to painting their cottages in a bright and beautiful assortment of mauves, yellows, and reds. The river gives striking views of the little communities on their low-lying, windswept islands, but the islands themselves have more to offer the visitor who makes the boat trip to see them. As well as the charming ancient villages, they are home to what are reputed to be some of the most relaxing beaches in Canada, celebrated for their fine sand and sheltered position.

Painted fisherman's cottage on L' Ile-du-Havre-Aubert, Iles-de-la-Madeleine

Gaspé Peninsula Tour ⑭

POPULARLY KNOWN as La Gaspésie, the Gaspé Peninsula stretches out north of New Brunswick to offer Quebec's wildest and most appealing scenery. As the peninsula spreads east, clumps of trees become dense pine forests, and the landscape becomes rough and rocky; cliffs along the northern coast reach 500 m (1,500 ft). The Chic-Choc mountains reach heights of 1,300 m (4,000 ft) and provide some of the province's best hiking. Shielded by the mountains, the southern coast harbors 18th-century fishing villages, inland fruit farms, exotic gardens, and wilderness national parks.

Parc de la Gaspésie ③
Here, over 800 sq km (300 sq miles) of rough, mossy terrain mark a change from boreal to subalpine forest.

Cap Chat ②
Named for a cat-shaped rock, Cap Chat boasts the tallest windmill in the world at 110 m (160 ft).

Grand Métis ①
This small town is home to one of Canada's most beautiful gardens, an exotic haven of over 1,000 rare species.

QUEBEC CITY

RÉSERVE FAUNIQUE DE MATANE

Matane

Amqui

Saint-Zénon-du-Lac-Humqui

Causapscal

Routhierville

0 km   20

0 miles   20

Vallée de la Matapédia ⑨
Starting at the confluence of two excellent salmon-fishing rivers, the picturesque Matapédia Valley is crisscrossed by covered bridges dating from the 18th century. Concealing long-established fruit farms, the valley's elm and maple trees show stunning fall colors.

Carleton ⑧
Founded in 1756 by Acadians fleeing the Great Expulsion in Nova Scotia (see pp58–9), Carleton today is a pleasant, relaxed resort town. Quality hotels and restaurants line the airy streets, and many visitors enjoy the mild coastal climate.

Sainte-Anne-des-Montes ④
The entrance to Gaspé's park and the wildlife reserves of the Chic-Chocs, this 19th-century village has fine restaurants, and good salmon fishing nearby.

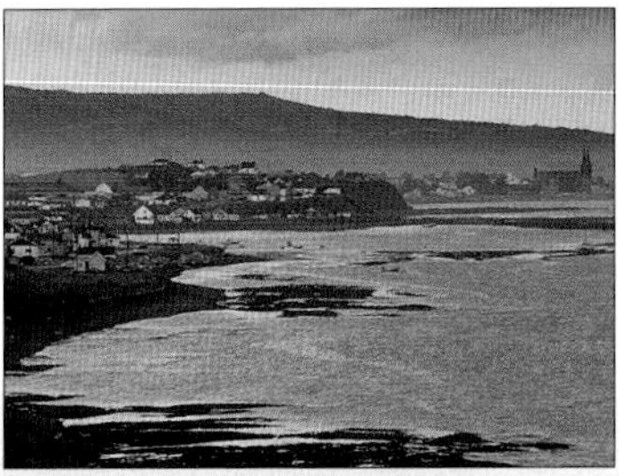

Tips for Drivers

The main road on this tour is Hwy 132, which follows the coastline from Grand Métis along the peninsula in a round trip. While too long to complete in a day, the journey can be broken in many of the local villages. Trips into the interior on the secondary road 299 are ideal for seeing the rocky wilderness.

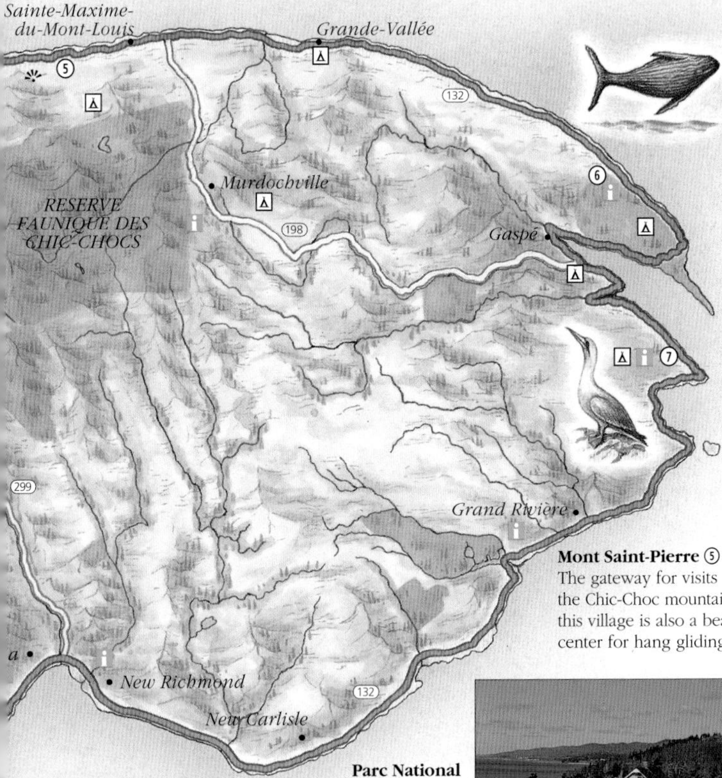
Sainte-Maxime-du-Mont-Louis
Grande-Vallée
5
132
Murdochville
RESERVE FAUNIQUE DES CHIC-CHOCS
198
6
Gaspé
7
299
Grand Rivière
New Richmond
132
New Carlisle

Mont Saint-Pierre ⑤
The gateway for visits to the Chic-Choc mountains, this village is also a beach center for hang gliding.

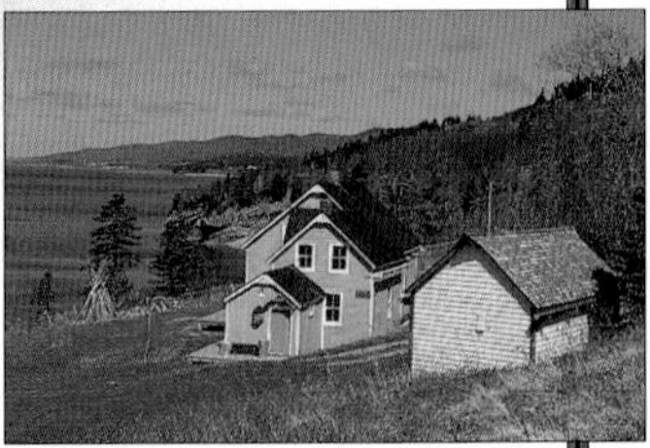

Parc National Forillon ⑥
The park contains the tail end of the Appalachian Mountains, now cliffs worn into rugged formations by the sea.

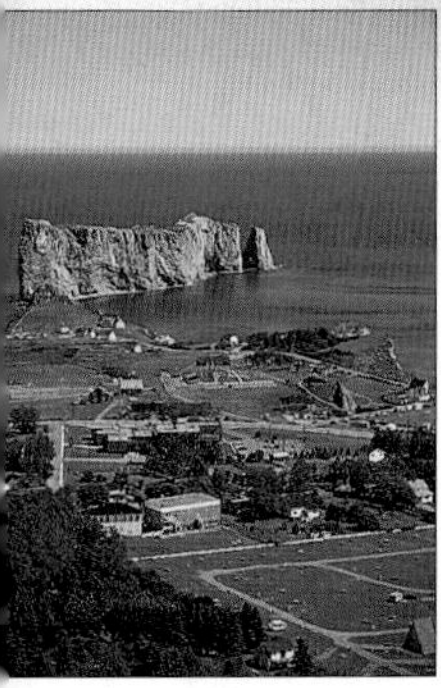

Rocher Percé ⑦
Situated out to sea south of the small town of Percé, this famous pierced landmark is the result of tidal erosion. In the 1930s, Percé became a popular spot for Canadian artists and still contains many galleries.

Key

- Tour route
- Other roads
- [⛺] Camp grounds
- [i] Visitor information
- Viewpoint

SOUTHERN AND NORTHERN QUEBEC

THE VAST AREA of land that stretches across Quebec from the Ontario boundary to historic Quebec City is rewarding in its diversity. In the south, the rich hilly farmland of the Appalachians and scarlet forests of maple trees attract many visitors each year, while the stark beauty of Nunavik's icy northern coniferous forests bursts into a profusion of wildflowers in spring, alongside the largest hydroelectric projects in the world. The center of the region is Quebec's natural playground, the Laurentian Mountains, a pristine lake-filled landscape offering fine skiing on ancient mountains. Populated by native people until Europeans arrived in the 16th century, the area was fought over by the French and British until the British gained power in 1759. Today French-speakers dominate.

SIGHTS AT A GLANCE

National Parks
Parc National de la Mauricie **5**

Historic Towns and Cities
Hull **12**
Joliette **7**
Oka **9**
Rouyn-Noranda **15**

Sherbrooke **2**
Sainte-Croix **3**
Terrebonne **8**
Trois Rivières **6**
Val d'Or **14**

Historic Sites and Areas of Natural Beauty
Lac Memphrémagog **1**
Laurentian Mountains **11**
Nunavik *(not shown on map)* **17**
Reserve Faunique La Vérendrye **13**

Richelieu Valley **4**
James Bay **16**
Sucrerie de la Montagne **10**

KEY

✈ International airport
═ Highway
▬ Major road
— Major rail routes

0 km   100
0 miles   100

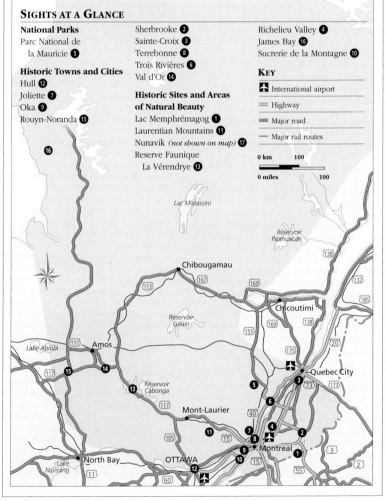

◁ **Colorful houses in St. Jovite, with the Laurentian Mountains rising behind**

Church by Lac Memphrémagog

Lac Memphrémagog **❶**

🏠 Magog. 🚂 Magog. ℹ 55
Cabana St., Magog 1 (800) 267 2744.

T HIS AREA belongs to the
Eastern Townships, or the
"Garden of Quebec" that
stretches from the Richelieu
River valley to the Maine,
New Hampshire and Vermont
borders in the US. Set among
rolling hills, farmland, woods,
and lakes in a landscape
similar to the Appalachians,
the Townships are among
Canada's top maple syrup
producers (see pp98–99).

Lac Memphrémagog itself is
long, narrow, and surrounded
by mountains. It even boasts
its own monster, a creature
named Memphré, first spotted
in 1798. The lake's southern
quarter dips into the state of
Vermont, so it is no surprise
that the British Loyalists fleeing
the American Revolution were
this region's first settlers. Their
influence can be seen in the
charming late 19th-century red-
brick and wood-frame homes
of lakeside villages such as enchanting Georgeville and Vale
Perkins, and in the resort city
of Magog that sits at the northern end of the scenic lake.

Benedictine monks from
France bought one of the lake's
most beautiful sites in 1912
and established the Abbaye
Saint-Benoît-du-Lac. Today
the monks produce cider and
a celebrated blue cheese called
l'Ermite. They are also renowned for Gregorian chant, and
visitors can hear them sing
mass in the abbey church.

Sherbrooke **❷**

🏃 77,500. ✈ 🚌 ⛴ ℹ 3010
King St. W. 1 (800) 561 8331.

T HE SELF-STYLED "Queen of
the Eastern Townships,"
Sherbrooke is indeed this
region's industrial, commercial, and cultural center. The
city lies in a steep-sided valley,
with the historic quarter delightfully situated among the
rolling farmlands of the Saint-
François and Magog Rivers.
The first settlers were British
Loyalists from the New
England states. Although
their heritage survives in
the fine old homes
and gardens of
Sherbrooke's
North Ward and
in street names,
today the city is
overwhelmingly French
speaking. The cen-
ter of town is the
starting point of the
Riverside Trail, a
lovely waterfront park with 20
km (12 miles) of cycling and
walking trails along the banks
of the Magog River.

Sainte-Croix **❸**

🏃 2,600. ℹ 6375 rue Garneau
(418) 926 2620.

A CHARMING, wooden manor
house with bold sweeping
front steps, pillars, and carved
curlicues is the grandest old
house in this pretty riverside
town. It is the centerpiece of
Domaine Joly-De-Lotbinière,
a stunning estate built in 1851
by the local squire
(seigneur). The house is
surrounded by banks of
geraniums and terraces
of walnut trees stretching
down to the river. Rare
plant finds include 20
red oaks estimated to be
more than 250 years old.
The gardens are best
known, however, for
cultivating blue potatoes.

**♿ Domaine Joly-De-
Lotbinière**
Rte. de Pointe-Platon. 📞 (418)
926 2462. ⭕ Jun–Sep: daily;
Oct–May: 10am–6pm Sat &
Sun. 📷 ♿ partial.

Richelieu Valley **❹**

ℹ 1080 Chemin des Patriotes Nord,
Mont Saint-Hilaire (450) 536 0395.

T HIS FERTILE VALLEY follows
the 130-km (80-mile)
Richelieu River north from
Chambly to Saint-Denis. **Fort
Chambly**, also known as Fort
St. Louis, in the industrial
town of Chambly along the
valley on the Montreal Plain,
is the best preserved of a
series of ancient buildings
that the French erected to
defend this vital
waterway from
Dutch and British
attack. Built from
solid stone in 1709
to replace the
wooden fortificat-
ions that the original
settlers set up in
1655, the fort is very well
preserved and is a
popular attraction.
A museum in Saint-
Denis commemor-
ates Quebecois patriots who
fought in the failed 1837
rebellion against British rule.

**A sign to Fort Chambly
in the Richelieu Valley**

Today the river flows past
attractive villages surrounded
by orchards and vineyards;
Mont Saint-Hilaire affords fine
views of Montreal, and is
famed for its apple plantations.
Its 19th-century church was
declared a historic site in 1965
and features paintings by Canadian Ozias Leduc (see p28).

♿ Fort Chambly
2 Richelieu St., Chambly. 📞 (450)
658. ⭕ Mar–mid-Jun: 10am–5pm
Wed–Sun; mid-Jun–Sep: 10am–6pm
daily. ● Nov–Feb. 📷

Mont Saint-Hilaire, Richelieu Valley

Canoeists on Lac Wapizagonke in Parc National de la Mauricie

Parc National de la Mauricie ❺

off Hwy 155 N. Shawinigan.
📞 (819) 536 2638. 🚉 Shawinigan.
🚌 Shawinigan. 🕐 daily. 📷
♿ partial. 🎫 for a fee.

Campers, hikers, canoeists, and cross-country skiers love this 536-sq km (207-sq mile) stretch of forest, lakes, and pink Precambrian granite. The park includes part of the Laurentian Mountains (see p147), which are part of the Canadian Shield, and were formed between 950 and 1,400 million years ago. La Mauricie's rugged beauty is also accessible to motorists, who can take the winding 63-km (40-mile) road between Saint-Mathieu and Saint-Jean-de-Piles.

Another great drive starts at Saint-Jean-de-Piles and has good views of the narrow Lac Wapizagonke Valley. With trout and pike in the lake, the area is an angler's delight. Moose and bear roam wild in the park.

Trois-Rivières ❻

🏛 51,800. ✈ 🚉 🚌 ⛴ 🛈 5775 Blvd. Jean XXIII (819) 375 1222.

Quebec is one of the major paper producers in North America, and Trois-Rivières, a pulp and paper town, is a main center of that industry in the province. This fact often hides the rich historical interest that Trois-Rivières has to offer. The first colonists arrived here in 1634 from France and, although not many of the colonial dwellings remain, the city's charming old section has a number of 18th- and 19th-century houses and shops, many of which have been recently converted into cafés and bars.

Ursuline nuns have been working in the city since 1697, and the core of the old city is the **Monastère des Ursulines**, a rambling complex with a central dome, a chapel, and a little garden that is now a public park. Rue des Ursulines features several little old houses with varying architectural styles, which can be viewed on a stroll around

The church of the Monastère des Ursulines in Trois-Rivières

the area. Also here is an 18th-century manor house, the 1730 Manoir Boucher-de-Niverville, which contains the local chamber of commerce and rotates displays on the rich history of the area around the Eastern Townships.

🏛 Monastère des Ursulines
734 Ursulines. 📞 (819) 375 7922.
🕐 Mar & Apr: Wed–Sun; May–Oct: Tue–Sun; Nov–Feb: call ahead. 📷

Joliette ❼

🏛 31,100. 🚉 🛈 500 rue Dollard (450) 759 5013.

Two catholic priests are responsible for turning the industrial town of Joliette on the Assomption River into a cultural center. In the 1920s, Father Wilfrid Corbeil founded the Musée d'Art de Joliette, whose permanent collection ranges from medieval religious art to modern works. In 1974, Father Fernand Lindsay started the Festival International de Lanaudière, a series of summer concerts by some of the world's best-known musicians.

The nearby town of Rawdon, 18 km (11 miles) west, has a deserved reputation as a place of great natural beauty. Trails wind away from the small town alongside the Ouareau River, leading to the picturesque, rushing Dorwin Falls.

Terrebonne ⓭

🚶 36,680. 🚌 🚆 🏛 ℹ *3643 Queen Street (450) 834 2535.*

JUST NORTHWEST of the outer fringe of Montreal's suburbs, this historic little town on the Mille-Iles River was founded in 1673, but a fire in 1922 engulfed many of its original buildings. However, some graceful 19th-century homes remain, on rue Saint-François-Xavier and rue Sainte-Marie, many of them converted into lively restaurants and bistros. The town's real gem is the **Ile-des-Moulins**, a pre-industrial complex of living history in the middle of the Mille-Iles River, with water-powered mills for grinding grain, carding wool, and sawing lumber. One of the biggest buildings on the site is the three-floor factory that was the first large-scale bakery in Canada. It was built by the Northwest Company in 1803 to make the saltless ship's biscuits that sustained the *voyageurs* who paddled west every year to collect furs for the company.

Terrebonne is also the center of Quebec's horse-riding culture. Popular with locals, rodeo and ranching events take place regularly.

🏚 Ile-des-Moulins
Autoroute 25, exit 22 E. 🄲 *(450) 471 0619.* ⭘ *Jun–Sep: 1–9 pm daily.* ♿

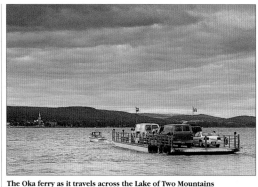
The Oka ferry as it travels across the Lake of Two Mountains

Rue-St-Louis Church in Terrebonne

Oka ⓮

🚶 3,840. 🚌 🚆 ℹ *183 rue des Anges (450) 479 8337.*

THE PRETTIEST WAY to approach this village north of Montreal is on the small ferry that chugs across the Lake of Two Mountains from Hudson. Framed by mountains and orchards, from the water the small Neo-Romanesque 1878 church is visible through the trees. Oka's best-known religious building is the **Abbaye Cistercienne**, founded by a group of monks who moved to Canada from France in 1881. The decor of the abbey church is somewhat stark, in the Cistercian tradition, but the Neo-Romanesque architecture is gracefully simple and the gardens peaceful. The abbey shop sells the soft Oka cheese that the monks have developed. Nearby, the Parc d'Oka covers about 20 sq kms (7 sq miles) of ponds and forests. It features the best beach and campground in the Montreal area, attracting sports lovers and visitors year-round.

⛪ Abbaye Cistercienne
1600 Chemin d'Oka. 🄲 *(450) 479 8361.* ⭘ *8am–8pm Mon–Sat.* 🕙 *lunchtimes; Sun.*

Sucrerie de la Montagne ⓯

10 km South of Rigaud. 🚌 🄲 *(450) 451 0831.* ⭘ *year round but call ahead.* ♿ 🄵 *obligatory.* 🅿

THIS TYPICALLY Canadian treat is set in a 50-ha (120-acre) maple forest on top of Rigaud Mountain near Rang Saint-Georges, Rigaud. It is entirely devoted to the many delights of Quebec's most famous commodity, the maple tree and its produce *(see pp98–99)*. The site features a reconstructed 19th-century sugar shack, where collected maple sap is distilled and boiled in large kettles to produce the internationally renowned syrup. Over 20 rustic buildings house a fine bakery, a general store, and comfortable cabins for overnight guests. The heart of the complex is a huge 500-seat restaurant that serves traditional banquets of ham, pea soup, baked beans, pork rinds (called *oreilles du Christ*, or Christ's ears), and pickles, and dozens of maple-based products, including syrup, sugar, candies, taffy, muffins, and bread. Folk music accompanies the nightly feast. The tour includes a thorough guided explanation of the maple syrup-making process, which is generally thought to have originated with the native people. They later imparted their secrets to European settlers, whose traditional methods are still in use today.

Quebecois Maple Syrup

Laurentian Mountains Tour [11]

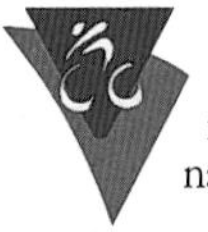

Cycle sign

THIS WHOLE region, from the lively resort of Saint-Sauveur-des-Monts in the south to north of Sainte Jovite, is nature's own amusement park, full of beautiful lakes, rivers, hiking and cycling trails, and ski runs visited all through the year. The mountains are part of the ancient Laurentian Shield and are a billion years old. Dotted with pretty, old French-style towns, this is a superb area to relax in or indulge in some vigorous sports in the many national parks.

TIPS FOR DRIVERS

Although the 175-km round tour of the Laurentian Mountains can be made from Montreal in a day on Hwy 15, the region is best seen and enjoyed by taking advantage of the slower, but more scenic, Hwy 117. There may be traffic congestion at the peak times of July through August and from December to March.

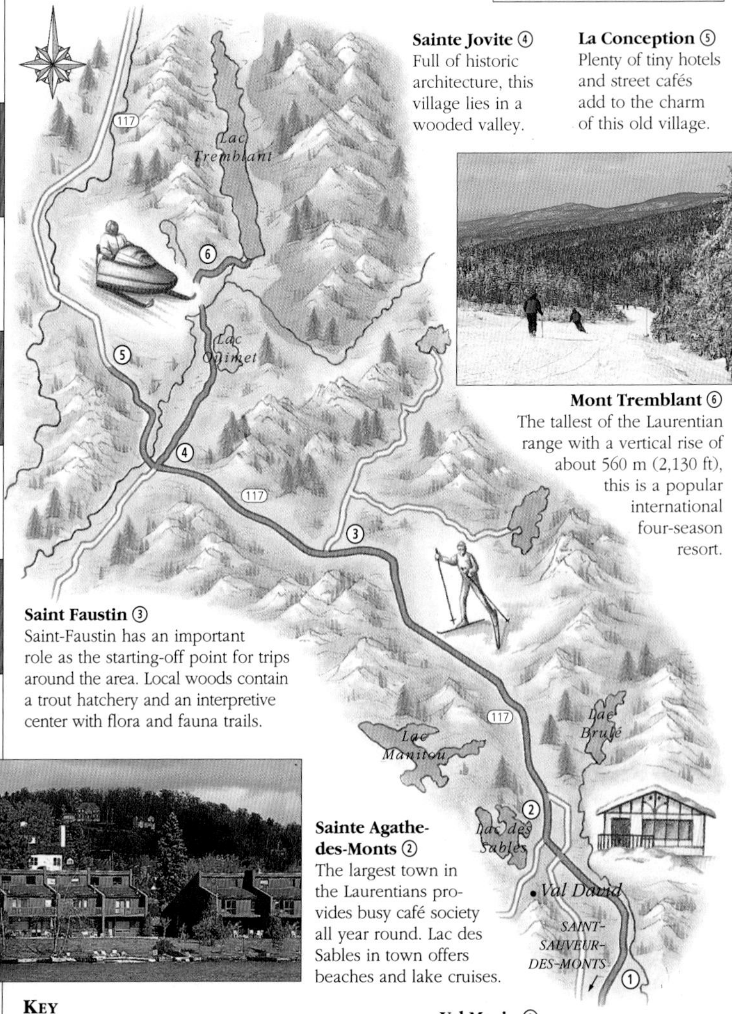

Sainte Jovite 4
Full of historic architecture, this village lies in a wooded valley.

La Conception 5
Plenty of tiny hotels and street cafés add to the charm of this old village.

Mont Tremblant 6
The tallest of the Laurentian range with a vertical rise of about 560 m (2,130 ft), this is a popular international four-season resort.

Saint Faustin 3
Saint-Faustin has an important role as the starting-off point for trips around the area. Local woods contain a trout hatchery and an interpretive center with flora and fauna trails.

Sainte Agathe-des-Monts 2
The largest town in the Laurentians provides busy café society all year round. Lac des Sables in town offers beaches and lake cruises.

KEY

Tour route

Other roads

0 km 3

0 miles 3

Val Morin 1
This enchanting village is a charming introduction to the area, with traditional French homes and churches.

The impressive beauty of Quebec's thundering Montmorency Falls ▷

Hull ⑫

Meditation center

Hull's links to the province of Ontario often appear stronger than its ties to its county position as the main city of Western Quebec. The town is based just across the river from Ottawa, and, as a result, many federal bureaucracies have their headquarters here. For years Hull has been a more relaxed and fun-loving counterpart to the capital, an attitude that reveals itself even in its officialdom – City Hall, for instance, boasts a meditation center. From Hull's establishment in 1800 until very recently, the city's liquor laws were far more lenient than Ottawa's, and this was where Ottawa politicians came to party. Hull contains one of Canada's best museums, the Museum of Civilization, which has a fascinating tour of Canada's history over the past 1,000 years.

🍃 Gatemeau Park

Hwy 5. 📞 (819) 827 2020. ⏰ daily.
This 360 sq km (140 sq miles) oasis of lakes and rolling hills between the Gatineau and Ottawa Rivers is a weekend playground for city residents. The park contains fragments of Gothic buildings, collected by the former Prime Minister, William Lyon MacKenzie-King, from demolition sites.

Casino de Hull

1 Casino Blvd. 📞 (819) 772 2100. ⏰ 11am–3am daily. ♿
Four million visitors a year are lured to this glittering Casino, which is equipped with 1,300 slot machines and 45 gaming

Gaming room in the Casino de Hull

tables. Owned by the Quebec Government, the Casino opened in 1996 and is set in a park full of flowers and fountains.

🚏 Alexandra Bridge

Built in 1900, this handsome steel-framed bridge spans the Ottawa River and links Ontario

to Quebec. From footpaths, drivers' lanes, and cycle routes, the bridge offers fine views of the river, the modern Museum of Civilization, and the Parliament Buildings in Ottawa.

🚏 Maison du Citoyen

25 Laurier St. 📞 (819) 595 7175. ⏰ 8am–5pm Mon–Fri. ● public holidays. ♿
The heart of this modern complex is a vast atrium, the Agora, meant to serve as an all-weather gathering place for Hull's citizens, as well as an airy meditation center for the city's workers. Opening from it are City Hall, a library, a theater, and an art gallery.

🚏 Promenade du Portage

Linked with the city bridges, this main route downtown is a good shopping center with large stores and lively cafés. After dark the area and nearby Place Aubry become the focus of the city's excellent nightlife.

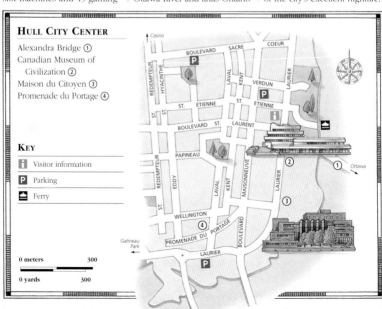

HULL CITY CENTER

Alexandra Bridge ①
Canadian Museum of
   Civilization ②
Maison du Citoyen ③
Promenade du Portage ④

KEY

🛈   Visitor information

🅿   Parking

⛴   Ferry

0 meters   300

0 yards   300

Canadian Museum of Civilization

THIS MUSEUM ON THE BANKS of the Ottawa River was built in the 1980s to be the storehouse of Canada's human history. The architect, Douglas Cardinal, wanted the undulating façades of both buildings to reflect the Canadian landscape. The more curved hall is the Canadian Shield Wing, home to the museum's offices. The Glacier Wing displays the exhibits. Its entry is stunning; the dramatic interior of the Grand Hall contains a forest of totem poles. Canada Hall traces the progress of the Canadian people from the Vikings through early settlers to the present day. The Children's Museum is delightfully diverting.

VISITORS' CHECKLIST

100 Laurier St. (819) 776 7000. May–Sept: 9am–6pm daily. www.civilization.ca

The museum façade echoes the rolling Quebec landscape

Canada Hall is a mazelike journey that traces the country's history from Norse settlers and colonial times to Acadian and Victorian villages.

Upper Level

David M. Stewart Salon

Street Level

Main Entrance

The Children's Museum
This extremely popular space contains a "world tour" of interactive exhibits, a busy international market, and this brightly decorated Pakistani trolleybus.

Lower Level

Library

KEY TO FLOOR PLAN

- ☐ Children's Museum
- ☐ Grand Hall
- ☐ Canada Hall
- ☐ River Gallery
- ☐ Art Gallery
- ☐ Temporary exhibition halls
- ☐ Permanent exhibition galleries
- ☐ W.E. Taylor Research Gallery
- ☐ Marius Barbeau Salon
- ☐ IMAX/OMNIMAX™ movie theater
- ☐ Nonexhibition space

★ **The Grand Hall**
Lit by windows three stories high, totem poles from the West Coast line the Grand Hall; each pole tells a native myth in wood carving.

STAR SIGHT

★ **The Grand Hall**

The wildlife preserve of La Vérendrye, seen from the air

Reserve Faunique La Vérendrye 🔞

🔘 *(819) 736 7431.* 🔲 *Maniwaki.*
🔘 *summer.* 🔲 *partial.*

THIS WILDLIFE preserve is situated approximately 190 km (120 miles) to the northwest of Montreal on Hwy 117. It is celebrated for long, meandering waterways and streams and, with thousands of kilometers of canoe trails, is a legend among canoeists. Its rivers are usually gentle, and the 13,000 sq km (5,000 sq miles) of wilderness are home to large numbers of moose, bear, deer, and beaver. The land is practically untouched, but there are several campgrounds here for those who seek a truly peaceful break. In season, anglers can try for walleye, pike, lake trout, and bass. Hwy 117 traverses the park, providing access to many of its lakes and rivers, and is the starting point of hiking trails.

Val d'Or 🔞

🔘 *25,000.* 🔲 🔘 *20 3rd Ave. E. (819) 824 9646.*

VAL D'OR IS principally a mining town and is the major center in the northwestern part of Quebec. The town sights here are not architectural but vivid living history attractions of mines and historic villages from the area's heritage of lumber trade and mining. Miners have been digging gold, silver, and copper out of the ground around Val d'Or since the 1920s. A climb to the top of the 18-m (60-ft) Tour Rotary on the edge of town shows 10 still-active mineheads.

The Lamaque Goldmine, now abandoned, used to be one of the richest sources of gold in the area. In its heyday of the early 20th century, the mine had its very own small town-site with a hospital, a boarding house for all single workers, and neat streets lined with little log cabins for married men and their families. The mine managers had more elaborate homes nearby, and there was a sumptuous guesthouse for visiting executives. Much of this remains intact. The townsite and mine, **Village Minier de Bourlamaque** and **La Cité de l'Or**, were declared historic sites in 1979 and are a reconstruction of gold rush times of the 1850s. Visitors can tour the village, the old laboratories, and the minehead. For the brave there is a ride 90 m (300 ft) underground to see mining techniques through history.

A moose at La Vérendrye

🏛 Village Minier de Bourlamaque, La Cité de l'Or
123 Ave. Perrault. 🔘 *(816) 825 7616.* 🔘 *Jun–Sep: 9am–6pm daily.*
🔲 🔲 *partial.*

Rouyn-Noranda 🔞

🏃 *26,450.* 🔲 🔘 *191 Ave. du Lac (819) 727 1242.*

As WITH ALL developed areas in the north of Quebec, towns here are based on heavy industry. Rouyn and Noranda sprang up virtually overnight in the 1920s when prospectors found copper in the region. They merged into one city in 1986 but are quite different places. Noranda on the north shore of Lake Osisko is a carefully planned company town with its own churches and schools, built to house the employees of the now-defunct Noranda copper mine. The lawns and tree-lined streets have an almost English air. Nowadays its residents are likely to be employed in surrounding mines. The Horne Smelter, one of the biggest in the world, is based just outside the center of town and can be visited by arrangement.

Rouyn, on the south shore of the lake, is less structured and more commercial. It is also where Noranda residents used to go for recreation, and it is useful as a refreshment and fuel center for those traveling to the northern wilderness. The **Maison Dumulon**, a reconstruction of Rouyn's first post office and general store, celebrates its pioneer spirit with displays on the first settlers.

🏛 Maison Dumulon
191 Ave. du Lac. 🔘 *(819) 797 7125.*
🔘 *Jun–Sep: daily; Oct–Jun: Mon–Fri.*
🔘 *Dec 25, Jan 1.* 🔲 🔲

Copper being smelted into huge nuggets for export, Noranda

Herds of caribou migrate south in summer across the Hudson Bay area into Nunavik

James Bay 16

ℹ️ *Federation des Pourvoyeurs du Quebec, Jonquiere (418) 877 5191.*

THE THINLY populated municipality of James Bay is roughly the size of Germany, which makes it much larger than most other municipalities in the region – about 350,000 square km (135,000 square miles). Its landscape, lakes, scrubby trees, and early pre-Cambrian rock is hardly urban, changing from forest to taiga to tundra and becoming gradually more inaccessible in the frozen northern parts. However, what the region lacks in infrastructure it makes up for amply in power capacity. Its six major rivers, which all flow into the Bay, can produce enough electricity to light up the whole of North America. So far, the Quebec government has spent over Can$20 billion in building a third of the number of dams for what is already one of the biggest hydroelectric projects in the world. Five power plants produce nearly 16,000 megawatts of electricity to power much of Quebec and parts of the northeastern US. Le Grand 2 (known as LG 2) is the biggest dam and underground generating station in the world.

The main town in the area is the small settlement of Radisson. A functional but useful tourist center, Radisson also offers good views of the surrounding country. Not all of the Bay's 215 dams and dikes can be seen, but the massive dams and series of reservoirs, especially LG 2, which is just east of town, are visible from above.

One of the vast power stations at James Bay

Nunavik 17

ℹ️ *Association touristique du Nunavik (819) 964 2876.*

IN THE FAR NORTH of Quebec, the municipality of Nunavik covers an area slightly larger than continental Spain. Its inhabitants number about 7,000, nearly all of them Inuit, who live in 14 communities along the shores of Hudson Bay, the Hudson Strait, and Ungava Bay. Nunavik is Quebec's last frontier, a wild and beautiful land that is virtually inaccessible except by airplane. Caribou herds, polar bears, and musk oxen roam the taiga coniferous forest and frozen Arctic tundra that covers this region. Seals and beluga whales can be found swimming in its icy waters.

Kuujjuaq, near Ungava Bay, is Nunavik's largest district, with a population of just over 1,400. This is a good jumping-off point for expeditions to the beautiful valley of Kangiqsujuaq near Wakeham Bay and the rugged mountains around Salluit.

Visitors come to Nunavik and Kuujjuaq to appreciate the many varieties of wildlife which roam freely in their natural setting. Summer is the best time for a trip; temperatures rise, but the ground remains frozen all year round. The region has no railroads (and hardly any roads) and should be explored only in the company of a seasoned and reliable guide. Many Inuit groups and communities offer guide services and the opportunity to experience life on the land with Inuit families. Visitors should be prepared for a very warm welcome and the chance to sample traditional Inuit foods and hospitality.

ONTARIO

Introducing Ontario

THE SHEER SIZE OF ONTARIO is daunting. It is Canada's second-largest province, covering over one million square miles and stretching all the way from the Great Lakes on the US border to the frozen shores of Hudson Bay. Northern Ontario is relatively inaccessible, but this wild and stunningly beautiful region of turbulent rivers, deep forests, and Arctic tundra can be reached by air, and by the occasional scenic road and railroad. Much of the north is also sparsely populated, in striking contrast to the fertile lands farther south, and bordering Lake Ontario, which have attracted many thousands of immigrants. Both Toronto, Canada's biggest city, and Niagara Falls, the country's leading tourist destination, are here.

The world's tallest free-standing structure, Toronto's CN Tower is illuminated at night

0 km 150

0 miles 150

A tour boat approaches the spectacular Horseshoe Falls at Niagara

GETTING AROUND

Among several highways skirting the northern shore of Lake Ontario, the most important are Hwy 401, heading east from Toronto to Montreal, and the Queen Elizabeth Way (QEW), running south from Toronto to Niagara Falls. Niagara Falls, Toronto, and Ottawa, are connected by bus and VIA Rail. Traveling north from Toronto, Hwy 400 becomes part of the Trans-Canada Highway which travels west to Lake Superior. Trains and buses also cover many northerly routes.

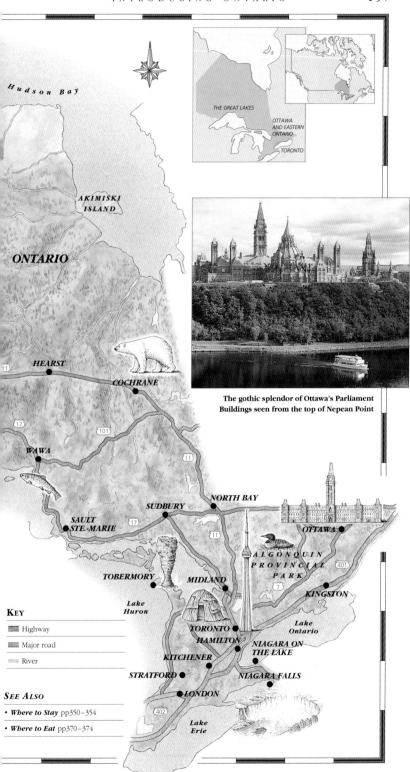

Hudson Bay

THE GREAT LAKES

OTTAWA AND EASTERN ONTARIO

TORONTO

AKIMISKI ISLAND

ONTARIO

The gothic splendor of Ottawa's Parliament Buildings seen from the top of Nepean Point

HEARST

COCHRANE

WAWA

SUDBURY

NORTH BAY

SAULT STE.-MARIE

OTTAWA

ALGONQUIN PROVINCIAL PARK

TOBERMORY

MIDLAND

KINGSTON

Lake Huron

TORONTO

HAMILTON

NIAGARA ON THE LAKE

KITCHENER

STRATFORD

NIAGARA FALLS

LONDON

Lake Ontario

Lake Erie

KEY

Highway

Major road

River

SEE ALSO

The Hudson's Bay Company

The Hudson's
Bay Co. crest

THE HUDSON'S BAY COMPANY was incorporated by King Charles II of England on May 2, 1670. His decision was prompted by the successful voyage of the British ship *Nonsuch*, which returned from the recently discovered Hudson's Bay crammed with precious beaver furs. The king granted the new company wide powers, including a monopoly of trading rights to a huge block of territory bordering the Bay, then known as Rupert's Land. The Company was ordered to develop links with the native Americans of Rupert's Land, and trade took off swiftly. Here fashion played a part: the ladies and gentlemen of 18th-century Europe were gripped by a passion for the beaver hat, and the demand for beaver pelts became almost insatiable.

European fur couriers rapidly built up a roaring trade with native fur trappers, which came to follow a seasonal pattern.

Fort Yukon
1846-1869

Fort Good
Hope 1821

Fort Simpson
1821

Fort St. James
1821

Edmonton
1795

Cumberland
House 1774

Fort Victoria
1843

LANDS AND TRADING POSTS

From 1670 onward, trading goods were dispatched from England to the Company's main trading sites around Hudson Bay, modest stockaded settlements with safe stores for the merchandise. Larger outposts gradually became self-sufficient, catering to newer, smaller posts as the Company moved ever westward. By 1750, HBC camps were established at the mouths of all the major rivers flowing into Hudson Bay. James Bay's Fort Albany had a jail, a hospital, a smithy, a cooperage, a canoe-building jetty, and sheep and cattle barns, while gallant efforts were made to grow crops. Main trading posts serviced a network of smaller seasonal outposts. They continued their expansion west until the transfer of land rights to the new country of Canada in 1870.

KEY

🏠	Trading post
– –	Trading route
══	1670 boundary of Rupert's Land

The Sevenoaks Massacre of June 1816 in Ontario occurred when HBC workers clashed with the rival North West Company, and 20 men were killed. The two companies agreed in 1820 to join territories and increased in power.

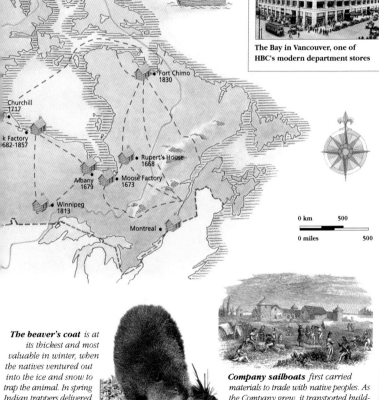

English traders *assembled a variety of goods to trade with local tribes in return for the winter's supply of pelts. Transported by ship in spring, the merchandise ranged from trinkets to more substantial items including blankets, knives, and guns.*

THE CHANGING FORTUNES OF HBC

Until the 1840s HBC reigned supreme in Canada, but civil disobedience led the British to relinquish claims to Washington State and Oregon in 1846, establishing the US border. Unable to continue enforcing its monopoly, HBC sold its land to Canada in 1870, retaining only areas around the trading posts. Since they were in key locations, this boosted HBC's expansion into real estate and retail in the 20th century. Today HBC is one of Canada's top companies and chain stores.

The Bay in Vancouver, one of HBC's modern department stores

Fort Chimo
1830

Churchill
1717

k Factory
682-1857

Rupert's House
1668

Albany
1679

Moose Factory
1673

Winnipeg
1813

Montreal

| 0 km | 500 |
| 0 miles | 500 |

The beaver's coat *is at its thickest and most valuable in winter, when the natives ventured out into the ice and snow to trap the animal. In spring Indian trappers delivered bundles of soft pelts to the Company's trading posts, in exchange for goods.*

Company sailboats *first carried materials to trade with native peoples. As the Company grew, it transported building materials, food, and seeds to set up what became sizeable settlements. Ships returned with up to 16,000 beaver pelts.*

The Group of Seven

FORMED IN 1920, the Group of Seven revolutionized Canadian art. Mostly commercial artists working in an Ontario art firm, this small band of painters was inspired by a colleague, Tom Thomson. An avid outdoorsman, Thomson started making trips in 1912 into the wilderness of northern Ontario to produce dozens of brightly colored, impressionistic sketches. His friends realized that he was taking Canadian art in a new direction – these landscapes of their country were largely free of the rigid European focus that had characterized painting until then and a nationalist movement had begun. After World War I and the death of Thomson in 1917, these same friends started the Group and held their first exhibition in Toronto in 1920. Many of the paintings shown depicted Nova Scotian, Ontarian and Quebec wildernesses; a new art was born that forged a sense of national pride between the people and their land in this young country.

Tom Thomson, (1877–1917)

The Red Maple is A.Y. Jackson's vibrant landmark of 1914, embodying the Group aim of creating a national consciousness.

Edge of the Forest (1919) by Frank Johnston is just one of the Group's works that illustrates their statement: "Art must grow and flower in the land before the country will be a real home for its people." Using the impressive surroundings of their homeland, the Group painters developed a spontaneous technique.

Above Lake Superior was produced by Lawren Harris in 1922. Known for his simple, heroic images, Harris captures the harsh, exhilarating climate of the Great Lakes region in winter, known as "the mystic north." Harris believed that spiritual fulfillment could best be obtained by studying landscape. The Group also held the ethos that truly meaningful expression was accomplished only when the the subject of the work was one the viewer shared with the artist, in this case local landscape.

Falls, Montreal River
*(1920) was painted by
J. E. H. MacDonald, who
chose Algoma as his work
base. Each of the Group
had a preferred individual
region in which they
found most inspiration,
mostly in Ontario.
Sketching trips regularly
took place in summer, with
painters showing each
other favorite areas.*

THE GROUP OF SEVEN

Based in a converted railway boxcar, the
members hiked and boated to favorite places
in Algonquin Park, Georgian Bay, Algoma,
and Lake Superior to produce new art for
their country. Following the 1920 exhibition,
entitled The Group of Seven, their striking
paintings immediately became popular and
the Group went on to exhibit together almost
every year. Native inspiration was vital to
the Group's subject and technique. The
apparently raw and coarse methods were a
rejection of the heavy, realist oils produced
in Europe at the time. Luminous colors and
visible brushstrokes led one critic to remark
that the Group had "thrown [their] paint pots
in the face of the public." The Group held
their final show in 1931 and disbanded the
following year to make way for a wider
group of painters from across Canada, the
Canadian Group of Painters. Founders of a
distinctive Canadian art movement based on
a love of their country's natural beauty, the
Group of Seven painters remain particularly
celebrated in Canada and are still given
prominence in top galleries across Ontario
and the rest of the country today.

The photograph below, taken at Toronto's
Arts & Letters Club in 1920, shows, from left
to right: Varley, Jackson, Harris, Barker Fairley
(a friend and writer), Johnston, Lismer and
MacDonald. Carmichael was not present.

AUTUMN, ALGOMA *(1920)*
This richly decorated canvas shows the
extraordinary evening colors of the fall in
Ontario. Algoma was J.E.H. MacDonald's
chosen region, a Canadian Eden in northern Ontario that acted as his inspiration
and where he regularly made sketching
trips. MacDonald records uniquely Canadian
subjects in this painting; the blazing foliage
and looming pines serve to record and
thus establish a Canadian identity. Influenced by the stark landscapes produced in
Scandinavia from around 1900, MacDonald
focuses on the chill drama in this scene to
add a grandeur to his beloved landscape.

The Group of Seven in 1920

TORONTO

ORONTO HAS SHED *its prim, colonial image to become one of North America's most dynamic cities, a cosmopolitan mix of nearly 4 million inhabitants drawn from over one hundred ethnic groups. Reveling in its position as the richest city in the country's most prosperous region, Toronto is the financial and commercial center of Canada, with fine art museums, suave café-bars, and luxury stores.*

Toronto is an enterprising city. Located on the banks of Lake Ontario, it was originally a native Indian settlement dating from the 17th century, and, after 1720, a French fur-trading post. Fought over by the US and Britain in the War of 1812 *(see p41)*, Toronto has since been a peaceful city, growing dramatically after World War II with the arrival of over 500,000 immigrants, especially Italians, and, most recently, Chinese.

The first place to start a visit must be the CN Tower, the third-tallest building in the world and the city's most famous tourist attraction. From the top it is easy to pick out the sights of the city, and from the bottom a short stroll leads to the Skydome stadium or the banking district. To the north of downtown is the boisterous street-life of Chinatown and the superb paintings of the world-renowned Art Gallery of Ontario. Beyond sits the University of Toronto on whose perimeters lies the fine Royal Ontario Museum and also two delightful specialty collections, the historic Gardiner Museum of Ceramic Art and the contemporary Bata Shoe Museum. A quick subway ride takes the visitor north to both Casa Loma, an eccentric Edwardian mansion that richly merits a visit, and Spadina House, the elegant Victorian villa next door. Many more attractions are scattered around the peripheries of Toronto, including Toronto Zoo and the Ontario Science Centre. The McMichael Art Collection, in nearby Kleinburg, contains an outstanding collection of paintings by the Group of Seven in a modernist setting.

Toronto's café society doing what it does best in the downtown area

◁ **The spire of the CN Tower rearing above the city reflected in an office building**

Exploring Toronto

Toronto is a large, sprawling metropolis that covers over 259 sq km (100 sq miles) on the north shore of Lake Ontario. The suburbs are divided into satellite townships such as Etobicoke and Scarborough that, together with the city, form the GTA or Greater Toronto Area. The center consists of a series of interlocking neighborhoods such as the banking district between Front and Queen Streets (west of Yonge Street). Yonge Street is the main artery, bisecting the city from north to south.

SIGHTS AT A GLANCE

Historic Areas and Buildings
Casa Loma **21**
Chinatown **12**
First Post Office **8**
Fort York **23**
Little Italy **24**
Ontario Parliament
  Buildings **16**
Queen Street West **9**
Royal Alexandra Theatre **7**
Royal York Hotel **3**
Spadina House **22**
Toronto City Hall **11**
University of Toronto **14**
Yorkville **20**

Parks and Gardens
Ontario Place **25**
Queen's Park **16**
Toronto Zoo **28**

Islands and Beaches
Toronto Island **26**
The Beaches and
  Scarborough Bluffs **27**

Museums and Galleries
Art Gallery of Ontario
  pp174–5 **10**
The Bata Shoe Museum **19**
Black Creek
  Pioneer Village **30**
George R. Gardiner Museum
  of Ceramic Art **17**
Hockey Hall of Fame **4**
Hummingbird Centre for
  the Performing Arts **5**
McMichael Art Collection **29**
Ontario Science Centre **29**
Royal Ontario Museum
  pp182–3 **18**
Toronto Dominion Gallery
  of Inuit Art **6**

Modern Architecture
CN Tower p168 **1**
SkyDome **2**

Shopping Areas
Kensington Market **13**

GETTING AROUND

Toronto's public transportation system is excellent. One of the subway's three lines carries passengers east to west, while the other two run north to south. Buses and streetcars leave each subway station to service the surrounding area. Rush-hour traffic is heavy downtown.

GREATER TORONTO

North York

Vaughan

Scarborough

Rexdale

Mississauga

Lake Ontario

0 km   5

0 miles   5

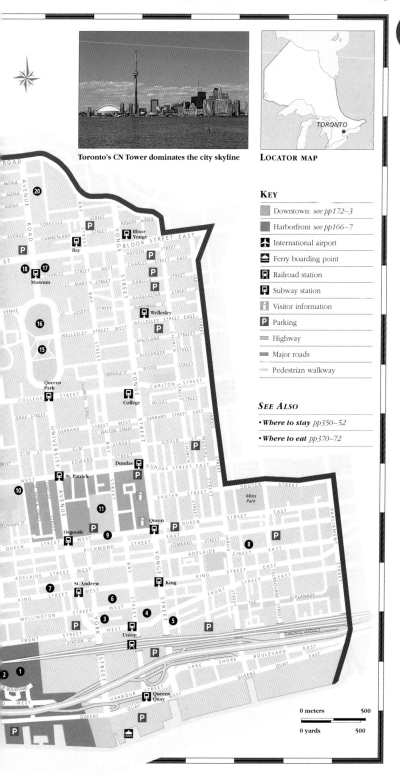

Toronto's CN Tower dominates the city skyline

LOCATOR MAP

KEY

	Downtown: *see pp172–3*
	Harborfront *see pp166–7*
✈	International airport
⛴	Ferry boarding point
🚉	Railroad station
🚇	Subway station
ℹ	Visitor information
P	Parking
▬	Highway
▬	Major roads
▬	Pedestrian walkway

SEE ALSO

• **Where to stay** *pp350–52*

• **Where to eat** *pp370–72*

0 meters 500

0 yards 500

Street-by-Street: Harborfront

Toronto's HARBORFRONT has had a varied history. Lake Ontario once lapped against Front Street, but the Victorians reclaimed 3 km (1.5 miles) of land to accommodate their railroad yards and warehouses. Ontario's exports and imports were funneled through this industrial strip until the 1960s, when trade declined. In the 1980s the harborfront had a new lease on life, when planners orchestrated the redevelopment of what has now become 10 sq km (4 sq miles) of reclaimed land. It now boasts grassy parks, walkways, smart apartments, many of the city's best hotels, and a cluster of tourist sights in and around the Harbourfront Centre.

★ **View of the CN Tower**
The highest free-standing tower in the world offers views of up to 160 km (100 miles) over Ontario, and a glass floor for those with iron nerves ❶

Convention Centre
Split into north and south arenas, the center is used for large-scale business shows as well as trade and consumer exhibitions for the public.

★ **SkyDome**
Using enough electricity to light the province of Prince Edward Island, a performance at the vast SkyDome stadium is an unforgettable experience

Charter boats
Sailing out into Lake Ontario and around the three Toronto Islands provides fine views of the city. Small sailboats, motorboats, and tours are available.

KEY

– – – Suggested route

0 m   150

0 yards   150

Toronto Harborfront
The harborfront is a pleasing and relaxing addition to the city. Modern attractions consolidate Toronto's standing as the third-largest theater and dance center in the world.

LOCATOR MAP
See pp164–5

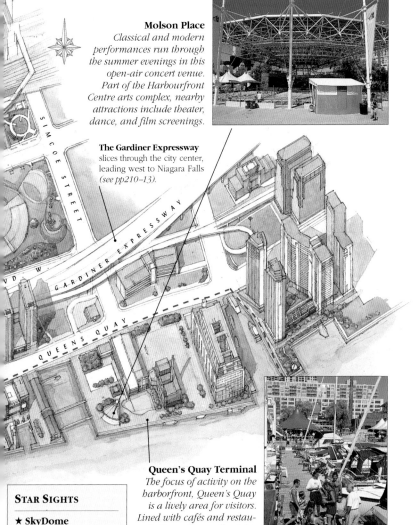

Molson Place
Classical and modern performances run through the summer evenings in this open-air concert venue. Part of the Harbourfront Centre arts complex, nearby attractions include theater, dance, and film screenings.

The Gardiner Expressway
slices through the city center, leading west to Niagara Falls
(*see pp210–13*).

SIMCOE STREET

GARDINER EXPRESSWAY

VD W

QUEENS QUAY

Queen's Quay Terminal
The focus of activity on the harborfront, Queen's Quay is a lively area for visitors. Lined with cafés and restaurants, the walkway offers lakeside views as well as street performers and gift shops.

STAR SIGHTS

★ **SkyDome**

★ **CN Tower**

CN Tower ❶

No less than 553 m (1,815 ft) high, the CN Tower is the tallest free-standing structure in the world. In the 1970s, the Canadian Broadcasting Company (CBC) decided to build a new transmission mast in partnership with Canadian National (CN), the railroad conglomerate. The CN Tower was not originally designed as the world's tallest spire, but it so overwhelmed the city's visitors that it soon became one of Canada's prime tourist attractions. The tower houses the largest revolving restaurant in the world, which rotates fully every 72 minutes.

VISITORS' CHECKLIST

301 Front St. W. 🛈 (416) 868 6937. 🅦 www.cntower.ca
🕐 Oct–May: 9am–10pm; Jun–Sep: 9am–11pm. 🕐 Dec 25.

The Sky Pod is reached by its own elevator and is the highest accessible point on the tower at 447 m (1,465 ft).

The 360 Restaurant
Top-quality cuisine is available here as the restaurant revolves, allowing diners a spectacular view while they dine.

The exterior lookout level is protected by steel grilles and illustrates how high the tower is, especially in windy weather.

The interior lookout level offers visitors the chance to observe the city in comfort, away from the wind; signs identify main Toronto landmarks.

The CN Tower from the Lake
The tower offers fantastic views in every direction. On a clear day it is possible to see as far south as Niagara Falls (see pp210–13).

Glass Floor
The ground is over 300 m (1,000 ft) beneath this thick layer of reinforced glass, and even the courageous may feel a little daunted.

The outside elevators are glass-fronted and take visitors shooting up the outside of the Tower to the upper levels. Speeds take your breath away and make your ears pop; the elevators can reach the top in under a minute.

The inside staircase is the longest in the world, with 1,769 steps. Visitors would climb down only in an emergency. Even 70 major storms each year have no effect on the elevators.

View of the City from the Lookout Level
At 346 m (1,136 ft) above the city, the Lookout Level provides panoramas of Toronto from exterior and interior galleries.

SkyDome ❷

1 Blue Jay Way. 📞 *(416) 341 3663.*
🚇 *Union Station.* 🚌 *Bay St. Terminal.*
🚉 *Union.* ⬜ *daily.* 🎥 ♿ ✅

OPENED IN 1989, the Sky-Dome was the first sports stadium in the world to have a fully rectractable roof. In good weather, the stadium is open to the elements, but in poor conditions the roof moves into position, protecting players and crowd alike. This remarkable feat of engineering is based on simple principles; four gigantic roof panels are mounted on rails and take just twenty minutes to cover the playing area. The design is certainly innovative and eminently practical, but the end result looks sort of like a giant hazelnut. However, the building's looks are partially redeemed by a matching pair of giant-sized cartoon-sculptures on the outside wall showing spectators at an imaginary game, the creation of a popular contemporary artist, Michael Snow.

The SkyDome is home to two major sports teams, the Toronto Argonauts from the Canadian Football League, and the Toronto Blue Jays of Major League Baseball. The Skydome is also used for special events and concerts. Guided tours allow a close look at the mechanics of the roof and include a 20-minute film outlining the story of its ground-breaking construction.

Lavish interior lobby of the Royal York

Royal York ❸

100 Front St. W. 📞 *(416) 368 2511.*
🚇 *Union Station.* 🚌 *Bay St. Terminal.*
🚉 *Union.* 🛏 *121+.* ♿

DATING FROM 1929, the Royal York was once Toronto's preeminent hotel, its plush luxury easily outshining its rivals. It was built opposite the city's main train station for the convenience of visiting dignitaries, but for thousands of immigrants the hotel was the first thing they saw of their new city, giving it a landmark resonance beyond its immediate commercial purpose. The Royal York was designed by the Montreal architects Ross and Macdonald in Beaux Arts contemporary style with a tumbling, irregular façade that resembles a large French château. Inside, the public areas are lavish and ornate with slender galleries providing extra grace and charm. Recently revamped, the Royal York remains a favorite with high-powered visitors, although other, newer hotels threaten to usurp its long-established position. Union Station, across the street from the Royal York, was also designed by Ross and Macdonald. The earlier building of the two, it shares a similar Beaux Arts style. The long and imposing stone exterior is punctuated by stone columns, and on the inside the cavernous main hall has a grand coffered ceiling supported by 22 sturdy marble pillars.

Doorman of the Royal York

The retractable roof of the SkyDome rears above the playing field, site of many famous ballgames

The Hummingbird Centre, home to the National Ballet and Opera

Hockey Hall of Fame **❹**

BCE Place, 30 Yonge St. 📞 *(416) 360 7735.* 🚇 *Union Station.* 🚌 *Bay Street Terminal.* 🚊 *Union Station.* 🕐 *10am–5pm Mon–Fri, 9:30am–6pm Sat, 10:30am–5pm Sun.* ♿ &

T**HE HOCKEY HALL** of Fame is a lavish tribute to Canada's national sport, ice hockey *(see p32).* Hockey, both ice and grass, originated in Canada; from its simple winter beginnings on frozen lakes and ponds, the game now ignites Canadian passions like no other. The Hall of Fame's ultra-modern exhibition area is inventive and resourceful, and features different sections devoted to particular aspects of the game. There are displays on everything from the jerseys of the great players, including Wayne Gretsky and Ray Ferraro, to a replica of the Montréal Canadiens' locker room, and antique hockey sticks and skates.

Another section traces the development of the goalie's mask from its beginnings to the elaborately painted versions of today. Interactive displays abound, and visitors can practice their shooting on a mini-ice rink. A small theater shows films of hockey's most celebrated games. A separate area at the front of the Hall displays a collection of trophies, including the Stanley Cup, hockey's premier award, donated by Lord Stanley in 1893.

The Stanley Cup at the Hockey Hall of Fame

Hummingbird Centre for the Performing Arts **❺**

1 Front St. E. 📞 *(416) 393 7474.* 🚇 *Union Station.* 🚌 *Bay Street Terminal.* 🚊 *Union Station.* ♿

O**WNED AND** operated by City Hall, the Hummingbird Centre is one of Toronto's largest performing arts venues, with over 3,000 seats in the single large theater. It was known as the O'Keefe Centre until 1996 when the Hummingbird software company donated several million dollars to have the place refurbished. Now with a cavernous modern interior, it is home to both the Canadian Opera Company and the National Ballet of Canada. The Hummingbird also offers a wide-ranging program including light comedy shows, and childrens' entertainments, not to mention musicians famous worldwide. Recent productions have included Houston Ballet's *Dracula* and *The Nutcracker.* Top artists come from all over the world to the center – pop performers and classical musicians regularly star here. Despite this, the accoustics here have often been criticized, and many people try to avoid sitting in the front rows.

Toronto Dominion Gallery of Inuit Art **❻**

Wellington St. 📞 *(416) 982 8473.* 🚇 *Union Station.* 🚇 *Union Station.* 🚊 *Union Station.* 🕐 *8am–6pm Mon–Fri, 10am–4pm Sat & Sun.* ♿

T**HE TORONTO** Dominion Centre consists of five jet-black skyscrapers, a huge modern tribute to the money-making skills of the Toronto Dominion Bank. The southern tower displays a strong collection of Inuit Art on two levels of its foyer. The exhibits were assembled on behalf of the bank by a panel of art experts in the 1960s. They bought over 100 pieces in a variety of materials, including caribou antler and walrus ivory, but the kernel of the collection is the stone carving. Soapstone sculptures on display, mostly 30–60cm (1–2 ft) high, show mythological beasts and spirits as well as scenes from everyday life. Some of the finest were carved by Johnny Inukpuk (b.1911), whose *Mother Feeding Child* (1962) and *Tattooed Woman* (1958) have a raw, elemental force.

Royal Alexandra Theatre **❼**

260 King St. W. 📞 *(416) 872 1212.* 🚇 *Union Station.* 🚌 *Bay Street Terminal.* 🚊 *St. Andrew.* ♿

I**N** THE 1960s, the Royal Alexandra Theatre was about to be flattened by modernizing bulldozers when a flamboyant Toronto retail

Façade of the Edwardian Royal Alexandra Theatre

Toronto's fashionable café society on Queen Street West

entrepreneur by the name of "Honest Ed" Mirvish, the king of the bargain store, came to the rescue. Mirvish saved a fine Edwardian theater, whose luxurious interior of red velvet, green marble, gold brocade, and flowing scrollwork once made it the most fashionable place in Toronto. Nowadays, the Royal Alex puts on block-buster plays but specializes in big-hit Broadway musicals, which are often held over for months at a time. Evening performances are extremely popular; theater-goers stand in line to admire the interior as much as the show, and booking promptly is recommended. Early arrivals can enjoy the original Edwardian features in the bar before the show.

First Post Office ❽

260 Adelaide St. E. 📞 (416) 865 1833. 🚉 Union Station. 🚌 Bay Street Terminal. 🚇 Yonge St. 🕐 9am–4pm Mon–Fri, 10am–4pm Sat & Sun. ♿ 📷 by arrangement.

I N THE EARLY Victorian era, the British Empire needed good communications for all its colonies. In 1829, the British House of Commons founded their colonial postal service and five years later established a post office in a far-flung outpost of the newly created town of Toronto.

Remarkably, Toronto's First Post Office has survived, weathering various municipal attempts by the city to have it demolished. The only remaining example in the world of a post office dating from the British North American postal era still in operation, the First Post Office functions fully. Visitors make the trip to write a letter with a quill pen and have it sealed with hot wax by a clerk wearing period dress. Today's mail, however, is processed by the national service, Canada Post. After a devastating fire in 1978, the building was entirely restored and refurbished to its former carved and decorated appearance using old documents and historical city archive records.

Young visitors on Queen Street West

Queen Street West ❾

🚉 Union Station. 🚌 Bay Street Terminal. 🚇 Queen.

T HROUGH the day and into the small hours of the morning, Queen Street West buzzes. Students and trend-setters reinvigorated this old warehouse area in the 1980s, but nowadays the street is more varied, with chic designer stores, downbeat bars, and stylish cafés mixed in with more main-stream offerings from the big chain stores. The chief merrymaking is concentrated between University and Spadina, a good place for budget restaurants and bars.

Worker at Toronto's First Post Office stamping mail by hand

Street-by-Street: Downtown

Throughout the 19th century, Yonge Street was the commercial focus of Toronto, lined with scores of shops and suppliers. It also separated the city ethnically. In 1964, with the building of the new City Hall and Nathan Phillips Square just across from Old City Hall, Toronto's center of gravity shifted to Queen Street. South of Queen Street lay the banking district, where old Victorian buildings were replaced from the 1960s onward by gleaming concrete-and-glass tower blocks. The re-invigorated Harbourfront, with its yachts and cafés, provides light relief from the busy atmosphere. Yonge Street is now best known for the Eaton Centre emporium, one of the world's biggest malls.

Textile Museum
Based in a downtown office building, this collection features fabrics, embroidery, and clothing through the ages.

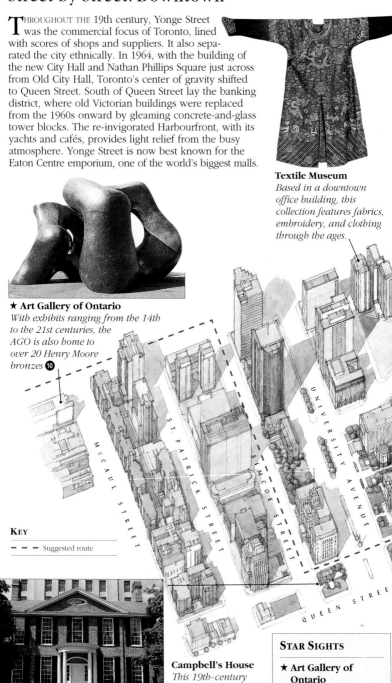

★ Art Gallery of Ontario
With exhibits ranging from the 14th to the 21st centuries, the AGO is also home to over 20 Henry Moore bronzes ⑩

KEY

– – – Suggested route

McCAUL STREET

ST. PATRICK STREET

SIMCOE STREET

UNIVERSITY AVENUE

QUEEN STREET

Campbell's House
This 19th-century home is a period piece from the days of the Victorian bourgeoisie.

STAR SIGHTS

★ Art Gallery of Ontario

★ Toronto City Hall

Eaton Centre
If Toronto has a specific core it would be outside the Eaton Centre shopping mall at the Yonge and Dundas intersection. The Eaton Centre boasts that it sells anything available in the world.

LOCATOR MAP
See Toronto Map pp164–5

Yonge Street is the main north-south thoroughfare of the city.

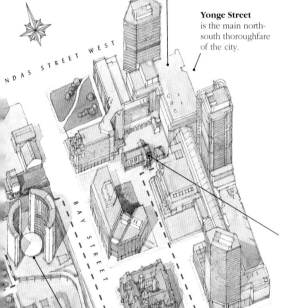

Church of the Holy Trinity
This charming Catholic church was built in the 19th century and features an elegant interior.

Nathan Phillips Square is a center of the town's activity and is a popular rendezvous for young people.

★ Toronto City Hall
Built in 1964, this controversial development has slowly become popular with locals, who use the plaza as a skating rink in winter ⑪

Old City Hall
In sharp contrast to its ultra-modern replacement across the street, the elegant 19th-century Old City Hall now houses Toronto's Law Courts and the Justice Department.

Art Gallery of Ontario ⑩

Founded in 1900, the Art Gallery of Ontario holds one of Canada's most extensive collections of fine art and modern sculpture. Its first permanent home was The Grange, an English-style manor built in 1817 and left to the gallery in 1913. In 1973 The Grange was restored in 1830s style and opened to the public as a historic house which is now connected to the main gallery building. This modern structure houses European Art ranging from Rembrandt to Picasso, a superb collection of Canadian painting including Group of Seven work *(see pp 160–1)*, Inuit art, and an entire gallery of Henry Moore sculptures.

Hina and Fatu (1892), Paul Gauguin

Henry Moore Sculpture Centre

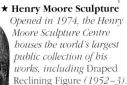

★ Henry Moore Sculpture
Opened in 1974, the Henry Moore Sculpture Centre houses the world's largest public collection of his works, including Draped Reclining Figure *(1952–3).*

Upper Level

Floor Burger *(1962)*
Claes Oldenburg's giant hamburger is made of painted sailcloth and foam rubber and is an iconic work of the Pop Art movement.

Street Level

Street level Entrance

Gallery Façade
The gallery was reopened in 1993 after four years of architectural renovation that unified a range of styles, from Georgian to Modernist. Outside, the stern Henry Moore bronze, Large Two Forms *(1966–9), dominates the forecourt.*

STAR SIGHTS

★ **The West Wind by Tom Thomson**

★ **Henry Moore Sculpture Centre**

★ **Inuit Collection**

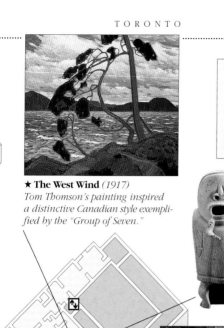

VISITORS' CHECKLIST

317 Dundas St. W. **☎** *(416) 979 6648.* **W** *www.ago.net*
◷ *11am–6pm Tue, Thu, Fri; 11am–8:30pm Wed; 10am–5:30pm Sat & Sun.* **●** *Mon.*

★ **The West Wind** *(1917)*
Tom Thomson's painting inspired a distinctive Canadian style exemplified by the "Group of Seven."

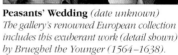

★ **Inuit Collection**
The gallery houses the world's third-largest collection of Inuit art. Made from soapstone, whalebone, and sinew, this piece, Shaman with Spirit Helper *(1972) is by Karoo Ashevak.*

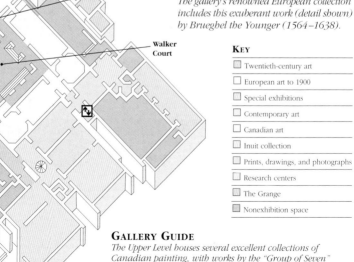

Peasants' Wedding *(date unknown)*
The gallery's renowned European collection includes this exuberant work (detail shown) by Brueghel the Younger (1564–1638).

Walker Court

KEY

- ☐ Twentieth-century art
- ☐ European art to 1900
- ☐ Special exhibitions
- ☐ Contemporary art
- ☐ Canadian art
- ☐ Inuit collection
- ☐ Prints, drawings, and photographs
- ☐ Research centers
- ☐ The Grange
- ☐ Nonexhibition space

GALLERY GUIDE

The Upper Level houses several excellent collections of Canadian painting, with works by the "Group of Seven" (see pp160–1), and Inuit art. The Upper Level also houses the Henry Moore Centre, which is home to Moore's sculptures, bronzes, and plaster casts, as well as over 700 prints and drawings. European art is found on the ground floor.

Built in the 1960s, the ultra-modern design of Toronto City Hall has proved controversial

Toronto City Hall ⓫

Queen St. W. & Bay St. 📞 *(416) 392 7341.* 🚇 *Union Station.* 🚌 *Bay Street Terminal.* 🚋 *Queen St.* 🕐 *8:30am–4:30pm Mon–Fri.* ♿

COMPLETED IN 1964, Toronto's City Hall was designed by the award-winning Finnish architect Viljo Revell. At the official opening, the Prime Minister Lester Pearson announced, "It is an edifice as modern as tomorrow," but for many cityfolk tomorrow had come too soon and there were howls of protests from several quarters. Even now, after nearly 40 years, the building appears uncompromisingly modern. It is the epitome of 1960s urban planning, with two curved concrete and glass towers framing a central circular building where the Toronto councils meet. Nearby, the Old City Hall is a grand 19th-century neo-Romanesque edifice whose towers and columns are carved with intricate curling patterns.

Chinatown ⓬

🚇 *Union Station.* 🚌 *Bay Street Terminal.* 🚋 *505, 77.*

THE CHINESE community in Toronto numbers around 250,000, six percent of the city's total population. There have been several waves of Chinese migration to Canada, the first to British Columbia in the late 1850s during the gold rush. The first Chinese to arrive in Toronto came at the end of the 19th century as workers on the Canadian Pacific Railway, settling in towns along the rail route. The Chinese found work in the Toronto laundries, factories, and on the railways. The last immigration wave saw prosperous Hong Kong Chinese come to live in Toronto in the 1990s. Chinese Canadians inhabit every part of the city but are concentrated in four Chinatowns, the largest and liveliest of which is focused on Spadina Avenue, between Queen and College streets, and along Dundas Street, west of the Art Gallery of Ontario. These few city blocks are immediately different from their surroundings. The sights, sounds, and aromatic smells of the neighborhood are reminiscent not of Toronto but of Hong Kong. Everywhere, stores and stalls spill over the sidewalks, offering a bewildering variety of Chinese delicacies, and at night bright neon signs advertise dozens of delicious restaurants.

Vivid restaurant signs in Chinatown

Kensington Market ⓭

Baldwin St. & Augusta Ave. 🚇 *Union Station.* 🚌 *Bay Street Terminal.* 🚋 *510.*

KENSINGTON MARKET is one of Toronto's most distinctive and ethnically diverse residential areas. It was founded at the turn of the 20th century by East European immigrants, who crowded into the patchwork of modest houses near the junction of Spadina Avenue and Dundas Street, and then spilled out into the narrow streets to sell their wares. The bazaar they established in their small 1930s houses has been the main feature of the area ever since. Today, Jewish, Polish, and Russian stall owners and shopkeepers rub shoulders with Portuguese, Jamaican, East Indian, Chinese, and Vietnamese traders in a vibrant street scene that always excites the senses. The focal point of this open-air market is Kensington Avenue, whose lower half, just off Dundas Street, is crammed with thrift shops selling all manner of trendy retro bargains, from original punk gear to flares. Kensington Avenue's upper half is packed with fresh food stores filled with produce from every corner of the globe, ranging from iced fish to stacks of cheeses and exotic fruits.

A Torontonian samples exotic nuts in the bazaar of Kensington Market

Façade of the Ontario Parliament Building, home of the provincial legislature since 1893

University of Toronto ⑭

27 King's College Circle. ☎ (416) 978 2011. 🚇 Union Station. 🚌 Bay Street Terminal. 🚇 St. George. ♿

THE UNIVERSITY of Toronto, an interdenominational institute, opened in 1850 after opposition from some religious quarters for being seen as challenging church control of education. The new institution weathered accusations of god-lessness and proceeded to swallow its rivals, becoming in the process one of Canada's most prestigious universities.

This unusual history explains the rambling layout of the present campus, a leafy area sprinkled with colleges. The best-looking university buildings are near the west end of Wellesley Street. Here, on Hart House Circle, lie the delightful quadrangles and ivy-clad walls of Hart House (1919), built in imitation of some of the colleges of Oxford and Cambridge universities in Britain, and the Soldiers' Tower, a neo-Gothic memorial to those students who died in both world wars. Nearby, King's College Circle contains University College, an imposing neo-Romanesque edifice dating from 1859, Knox College with its rough gray sandstone masonry, and the fine rotunda of the university's

Convocation Hall. A visit to the campus can be peacefully rounded off by a short stroll along Philosophers' Walk, where the manicured lawns lead to Bloor Street West.

Reminiscent of old British universities, the University of Toronto

Ontario Parliament Building ⑮

Queen's Park. ☎ (416) 325 7500. 🚇 Union Station. 🚌 Bay Street Terminal. 🚇 Queen's Park. 🚌 97B. ○ May–Sep: 9am–4pm daily; Sep–May: 9am–4pm Mon–Fri. ♿

THERE IS NOTHING modest about the Ontario Parliament Building, a vast pink sandstone edifice built in 1893 that dominates the end of

University Avenue. Ontario's elected representatives had a point to make. The province might have been a small (and exceedingly loyal) part of the British Empire, but it clamored to make its mark and had the money to do this in style. Consequently, the Members of Provincial Parliament (MPPs) commissioned this immensely expensive structure in the Romanesque Revival style. Finished in 1892, its main façade is a panoply of towers, arches, and rose windows decorated with relief carvings and set beneath a series of high-pitched roofs.

The interior is of matching grandeur. Gilded classical columns frame the main stair-case and enormous stained-glass windows illuminate long and richly timbered galleries. The chamber is a lavish affair, with a wealth of fine wooden carving that carries epithets urging good behavior, such as "Boldly and Rightly," and "By Courage, not by Craft."

In 1909, a fire razed the west wing, which was rebuilt in Italian marble. The stone was very expensive, so the MPPs were annoyed to find that a large amount of the marble was blemished by dinosaur fossils, which can still be seen today in the west hallway. Visitors can sometimes watch the parliament in session.

The Parliament Buildings, viewed from inner-city Queen's Park

Queen's Park ⑯

College St. & University Ave. **(** (416) 325 7500. 🚉 Union Station. 🚌 Bay St. Terminal. 🚋 506. 🚌 Queen's Park. ♿

JUST BEYOND the Parliament Buildings lies Queen's Park, a pleasant grassy space for those wishing to stroll and relax in between the closely packed sights in this area. It is fringed to the west by the 19th-century buildings of the University and offers views of the historic campus, from where walking tours regularly depart in the summer.

In June each year a spectacular parade passses by the north of the park on Gay Pride Day. Toronto has a sizable gay and lesbian community, and the gay lifestyle is celebrated in flamboyant fashion in this yearly weekend festival, which started in the 1970s.

George R. Gardiner Museum of Ceramic Art ⑰

111 Queen's Park. **(** (416) 586 8080. 🚉 Union Station. 🚌 Bay St. Terminal. 🚋 Museum. 🕙 11am–7pm Mon–Fri, 11am–5pm Sat & Sun. ● Jan 1, Dec 25, 31. 📷 ♿

OPENED IN 1984, the Gardiner Museum of Ceramic Art is the only showcase of its kind in North America dedicated solely to pottery and porcelain. Skillfully displayed, the collection traces the history of ceramics, with a detailed focus on its principal developmental stages. These start with Pre-Columbian pottery, and the museum has fascinating displays of ancient pieces from Peru and Mexico that incorporate several grimacing fertility gods.

The Greeting Harlequin Meissen ceramic figure

Examples of brightly colored *maiolica* (glazed, porous pottery), includes painted pots made first in Mallorca, then Italy, from the 13th to the 16th centuries. Cheerfully decorated everyday wares are complemented by later Renaissance pieces relating classical myths and history. English delftware (tin-glazed earthenware) is also well represented, but the most memorable exhibits are Renaissance pieces gathered from Italy, Germany, and England – particularly the collection of

commedia dell'arte figures. These are derived from the Italian theatrical tradition of comic improvisation with a set of stock characters, notably the fun-loving practical joker Harlequin. Intricately decorated in rainbow colors, these figurines were placed on dinner tables by the aristocracy to delight, impress, or even to woo their special guests.

Porcelain here is stunning, with many examples of exquisite Meissen from 1700 to 1780. Packed in its own specially made leather carrying case to accompany a fine lady owner on her travels, a special feature is the embellished tea and chocolate service dating from the early 18th century. Each tiny cup reveals individual, intricate sailing scenes surrounded in gold. The porcelain collection also contains over 100 carved or molded scent bottles from all over Europe.

Royal Ontario Museum ⑱

See pp182–183.

The Bata Shoe Museum ⑲

327 Bloor St. W. **(** (416) 979 7799. 🚉 Union Station. 🚌 Bay St. Terminal. 🚋 St. George. 🕙 10am–5pm Tue–Sat, noon–5pm Sun. ● Jan 1, Good Friday, Jul 1, Dec 25. 📷 ♿

THE BATA SHOE MUSEUM was opened in 1995 to display the extraordinary range of footwear collected by Sonja Bata, the current director of the eponymous shoe manufacturing family, a worldwide concern that sells footwear in 60 countries. To be sure her collection was seen to best effect, Sonja had the prestigious contemporary Canadian architect Raymond Moriyama design the building, an angular modern affair complete with unlikely nooks and

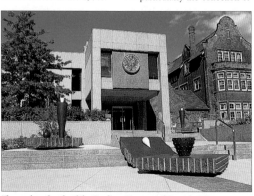

The modern façade of the Gardiner Museum of Ceramic Art

crannies created to look like a chic shoebox. The collection is spread over several small floors and features temporary exhibitions developing a particular theme, for instance "Japanese Footgear and Pādukā: Feet and Footwear in the Indian Tradition," as well as regularly rotated items selected from the museum's substantial permanent collection.

One fixed feature in the museum is the exhibition entitled "All About Shoes," which provides the visitor with an overview of the functions and evolution of footwear. It begins with a plaster cast of the earliest known footprint, discovered 4,000,000 years after it was made in Tanzania, and has an interesting section on medieval pointed shoes. A second permanent feature is the section on celebrity footwear. This displays all kinds of eccentric performance wear, from Elvis Presley's blue-and-white patent-leather loafers and a pair of Elton John's platforms to Michael Johnson's gold lamé sprinting shoes and ex-Canadian Prime Minister Pierre Trudeau's battered sandals.

There is also a display of unusual and improbable footwear including unique French chestnut-crushing boots, Venetian platform shoes dating from the 16th century, and a pair of US army boots made for use in the Vietnam War, whose sole is shaped to imitate the footprint of an enemy Vietcong irregular.

Other fascinating items on display feature the importance of First Nations and Inuit

A lazy Sunday afternoon at Café Nervosa in trendy Yorkville

bootmaking skills. The development of snowshoes is generally credited with aiding the Inuit to settle in the very far north of Canada.

Yorkville ⑳

🚇 Union Station. 🚌 Bay St. Terminal. 🚇 Bay.

IN THE 1960s tiny Yorkville, in the center of the city, was the favorite haunt of Toronto's hippies. With regular appearances by countercultural figures such as Joni Mitchell, it was similar to London's Chelsea or New York's Greenwich Village. The hippies have now moved on, and Yorkville's modest brick and timber terrace houses have either been colonized by upscale shops and fashionable restaurants, or converted into bijou townhouses. Designer boutiques, specialty bookstores, private

art galleries, fine jewelers, wine stores, and quality shoe stores all jam into the neighborhood, attracting shoppers in droves. The area is a lovely place to sit at an outdoor café, nursing a cappuccino and watching the crowds. Yorkville and Cumberland Avenues are the center of all this big spending, as are the elegant and discreet shopping complexes that lead off them, especially the deluxe Hazelton Lanes, at the corner of Yorkville Avenue and The Avenue, with its Ralph Lauren and Versace boutiques. The dropout philosophy has been thoroughly replaced by very chic stores – some of the most exclusive retail outlets in the country are found here. Although the recession in the 1990s affected trade somewhat, the area is still prosperous and thriving. Café society really takes off at night, even so Yorkville can be an expensive place to have fun.

The Bata Shoe Museum lobby displays enticing footwear

Replica dressing room in BCE Hockey Hall of Fame, Toronto ▷

Royal Ontario Museum ⑱

Ming headrest in the Chinese Gallery

Founded in 1912, the Royal Ontario Museum (ROM) holds a vast and extraordinarily wide-ranging collection drawn from the fields of fine and applied art, the natural sciences, and archaeology. The museum is far too large to absorb in one visit, and merits several trips to appreciate its many treasures. Special highlights include a room full of dinosaur skeletons from around the world and the fabulous Far East collection. The latter features the best display outside China of Imperial Chinese artifacts, such as dainty ceramic head cushions, and the Ming Tomb of a grandee, reassembled this century after 300 years and the only complete example in the West.

Third Level

★ Dinosaur Gallery

The most popular gallery in the ROM, 13 dinosaur skeletons are set in simulations of the Jurassic Age. Animation techniques as used in the 1990s blockbuster Jurassic Park *draw children and adults alike.*

Second Level

Street Level

Museum façade

Based in a handsome early 20th-century building, the ROM is the largest museum in Canada. It was finished in 1914 to house 19th-century collections from Toronto University.

Main Entrance

★ Ming Tomb

The ROM's Chinese galleries include this splendid imperial tomb thought to be part of an enormous 17th-century complex that may have been the burial site of a Ming general.

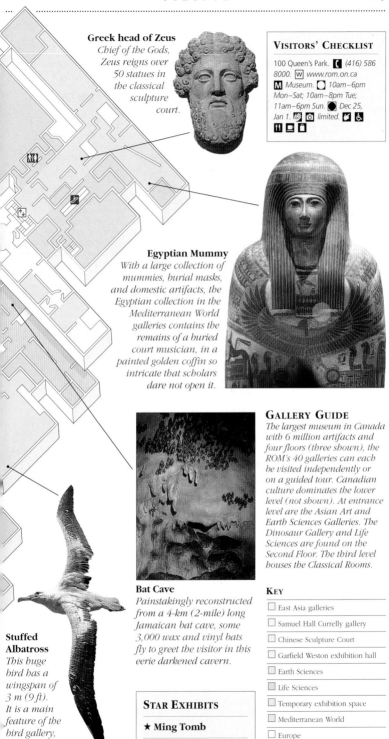

Greek head of Zeus
Chief of the Gods, Zeus reigns over 50 statues in the classical sculpture court.

VISITORS' CHECKLIST

100 Queen's Park. ☎ (416) 586 8000. 🔲 www.rom.on.ca
Ⓜ Museum. ⊙ 10am–6pm Mon–Sat; 10am–8pm Tue; 11am–6pm Sun. ⬤ Dec 25, Jan 1. 🅿 🄾 limited. ♿ 🅿
🚻 🍴 🛍 📷

Egyptian Mummy
With a large collection of mummies, burial masks, and domestic artifacts, the Egyptian collection in the Mediterranean World galleries contains the remains of a buried court musician, in a painted golden coffin so intricate that scholars dare not open it.

GALLERY GUIDE
The largest museum in Canada with 6 million artifacts and four floors (three shown), the ROM's 40 galleries can each be visited independently or on a guided tour. Canadian culture dominates the lower level (not shown). At entrance level are the Asian Art and Earth Sciences Galleries. The Dinosaur Gallery and Life Sciences are found on the Second Floor. The third level houses the Classical Rooms.

Bat Cave
Painstakingly reconstructed from a 4-km (2-mile) long Jamaican bat cave, some 3,000 wax and vinyl bats fly to greet the visitor in this eerie darkened cavern.

Stuffed Albatross
This huge bird has a wingspan of 3 m (9 ft). It is a main feature of the bird gallery, which offers interactive exhibits.

KEY

☐ East Asia galleries

☐ Samuel Hall Currelly gallery

☐ Chinese Sculpture Court

☐ Garfield Weston exhibition hall

☐ Earth Sciences

☐ Life Sciences

☐ Temporary exhibition space

☐ Mediterranean World

☐ Europe

☐ Nonexhibition space

STAR EXHIBITS

★ **Ming Tomb**

★ **Dinosaur Gallery**

Spadina House ㉑

285 Spadina Rd. 📞 (416) 392 6910.
🚇 Union Station. 🚌 77+, 127.
🚇 Dupont. 🕐 Jan–Mar: noon–5pm
Sat & Sun; Apr–Aug: noon–5pm, Tue–
Sun; Sep–Dec: noon–4pm, Tue–Fri;
noon–5pm, Sat & Sun. ⬤ Mon; Dec
25, 26, Jan 1. ♿ 🅿 obligatory.

J AMES AUSTIN, first president of
the Toronto Dominion Bank
in the 1860s, had this elegant
Victorian family home, Spadina
House, built on the bluff overlooking Spadina Avenue in
1866. The last of the Austins,
Anna, moved out in 1982. She
left the building, its contents
and gardens intact, to the Historical Board of Toronto, and,
as a result, Spadina House is
an authentic family home
illustrating the decorative tastes
of four generations of well-to-
do Canadians. The general
ambience appeals here, but
there are several particularly
enjoyable features, notably the
Art Nouveau frieze in the bill-
iard room and a trap door in
the conservatory that allowed
gardeners to tend to the plants
unseen by the family.

**The front door of Spadina House
with garlanded Victorian columns**

Fort York ㉓

Garrison Rd. 📞 (416) 392 6907.
🚇 Union Station. 🚋 7. 🕐 Tue–Sun.
⬤ Mon; Good Fri, Dec 18–Jan 2
approx. ♿ 🅿

T HE BRITISH built Fort York
in 1793 to reinforce their
control of Lake Ontario and
to protect the city that is now
Toronto. Modestly sized, the
weaknesses of the fort were
exposed when the Americans
overran it after a long battle
in the War of 1812 *(see p43)*.
After the war, the British
strengthened the fort, and its
garrison gave a boost to the
local economy. Fort York's
military compound has been
painstakingly restored, and its
barracks, old powder magazine, and officers' quarters
make for a pleasant visit.

Casa Loma ㉒

T HIS UNUSUAL FAIRY-TALE building was designed
by E.J. Lennox, the man responsible for
Toronto's Old City Hall. It has no claim to the
history of a stately home and architecturally
it is a novelty, but it is a remarkable tribute
to the foibles of one man, Sir Henry Pellatt
(1859–1939). He made a fortune in hydro-
power during the early 1900s, harnessing the
strength of Niagara Falls for electricity. In 1911, Pellatt decided to build
himself a castle in Toronto. Three
years and Can$3.5 million later,
Casa Loma was built in a mixture
of styles – medieval fantasy meets
early 20th-century technology.

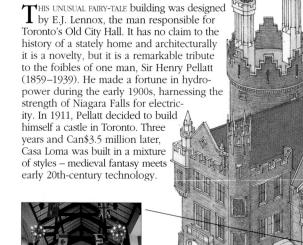

The Study hid secret
doors in its wooden
panels, one
leading to
Sir Henry's
wine cellar.

★ **The Great Hall**
*Oak beams support a ceiling
18-m (60-ft) high, with cary-
atid sculptures and a 12-m
(40-ft) tall bay window.*

The Terrace looks over
delightful formal gardens
and a fountain against a
backdrop of hills and
rhododendron forest.

The Bathroom was designed by Sir
Henry for his personal use. He built a
free-standing shower with six heads
and indulged in lavish decoration.

Fresh vegetables on sale in Little Italy

Little Italy

St. Clair Ave. W. ⊠ *Union Station.* ⊟ *Bay St. Terminal.* ⊞ *512.* ⓘ *207 Queen's Quay W. (416) 203 2500.*

THERE ARE half a million people of Italian descent resident in Toronto. The first major wave of Italian migrants arrived between 1885 and 1924. Italians have been in Toronto since 1830, and their sense of community, together with the instability of Italy after World War II, led to another large influx in the 1940s and 1950s. Italians live and work in every corner of the city, but there is a focus for the community in the lively "Corso Italia," or Little Italy, whose assorted stores, cafés, and restaurants run along St. Clair Avenue West.

Though the architecture is at best unremarkable, many houses are brightly painted in the traditional colors of red, green, and white. More European touches appear in the proliferation of espresso bars, and cinemas showing Italian films. The typically Mediterranean food offered by the many sidewalk cafés is terrific.

Ontario Place ㉕

955 Lakeshore Blvd. W. ☎ *(416) 314 9900.* ⊠ *Union Station.* ⊞ *511.* ◯ *mid-May–Sep: 10am–midnight.*

AN EXCELLENT theme park, this waterfront complex on Lake Ontario is built on three artificial islets. It provides family entertainment, with rides both tame and terrifying. Inside, the Children's Village is equipped with playgrounds and swimming pools, long water slides, computer games, and bumper boats, while Cinesphere is a huge dome housing a giant IMAX cinema. The HMCS *Haida* is an old World War II destroyer that has been converted into a floating museum to show the layout and naval machinery of a historic ship.

Façade of house and formal gardens
Five acres of garden add to the charm of the estate with perennial borders, roses, lawns, and woodland.

★ Conservatory
White walls clad with Ontario marble offset the Victorian stained-glass dome. The marble flowerbeds conceal steam pipes for the rare plants.

VISITORS' CHECKLIST
1 Austin Terrace. ☎ *(416) 923 1171.* ⊠ *Dupont.* ◯ *9:30am–4pm daily.* ● *Dec 25, Jan 1.*

STAR SIGHTS
★ **The Great Hall**
★ **Conservatory**

Visitors on the bicycling paths on the Toronto Islands

The Toronto Islands ㉖

🚇 Union Station. 🚌 Bay St. Terminal.
🚋 6, 75. ⛴ Queen's Quay. 🚶 207
Queen's Quay W. (416) 203 2500.

I N LAKE ONTARIO, just offshore
from the city, the three low-lying Toronto Islands, which are connected by footbridges, shelter Toronto's harbor and provide some easy-going recreation in a car-free environment. Here, amid the cool lake breezes, visitors can escape the extremes of the summer heat, which can reach up to 35°C (95°F). In good weather there are fine views of the top of the CN Tower (see p168).

It takes about half an hour to walk from one end of the islands to the other. In the east is Ward's Island, a sleepy residential area with parkland and wilderness; Centre Island, home to the Centreville Amusement Park for children, is in the middle, and to the west lies the isle of Hanlan's Point with the Islands' best beach.

The Beaches and Scarborough Bluffs ㉗

🚇 Union Station. 🚌 Bay St. Terminal.
🚋 Queen St. E. routes. 🚶 207
Queen's Quay W. (416) 203 2500.

T HE BEACHES is one of
Toronto's most beguiling neighborhoods, its narrow leafy streets running up from the lakeshore and lined by

attractive brick houses with verandas. The area lies to the east of downtown between Woodbine Avenue and Victoria Park Avenue. Queen Street East, the main thoroughfare, is liberally sprinkled with excellent cafés and designer clothes shops. Until very recently, the Beaches was a restrained and quiet neighborhood, but its long sandy beach and boardwalk have made it extremely fashionable – and real estate prices have risen dramatically in recent years. Rollerblading and cycling are popular here – a 3-km (2-mile) path travels through the area and is very busy in summer, as is the large public swimming pool. The polluted waters of Lake Ontario are not ideal for swimming, nevertheless many take the risk and surfboards can be rented easily.

At its eastern end, the Beaches borders Scarborough, the large suburb whose principal attraction is also along the rocky lakeshore. Here, the striking Scarborough Bluffs, outcrops of rock made from ancient sands and clay, track along Lake Ontario for 16 km (10 miles). A series of parks provides access: Scarborough Bluffs and the Cathedral Bluffs parks offer great views of jagged cliffs, and Bluffers Park is ideal for

picnics and beach trips. Layers of sediment from five different geological periods can be seen in the rocks around the park.

Toronto Zoo ㉘

361A Old Finch Ave., Scarborough.
📞 (416) 392 5900. 🚇 Scarborough.
🚌 Kennedy. 🚋 86A. 🕐 mid-May–
Sep: 9am–7:30pm daily; mid-Mar–
mid-May & Sep–mid-Oct: 9am–6pm
daily; mid-Oct–mid-Mar: 9:30am–
4:30pm. ● Dec 25. 📷 ♿ 🛒

T ORONTO can claim to have
one of the world's best zoos. It occupies a large slice of the Rouge River Valley, and is easily accessible by public transportation and car.

The animals are grouped according to their natural habitats, both outside, amid the mixed forest and flatlands of the river valley, and inside within a series of large, climate-controlled pavilions.

Visitors can tour the zoo by choosing one of the carefully-marked trails, or hop aboard the Zoomobile, a 30-minute ride with commentary, which gives an excellent overview. It takes about four hours to see a good selection of animals, including such Canadian species as moose, caribou, and grizzly bear. The Children's Web area has a playground, and child-friendly exhibits.

A mother and baby orangutan at Toronto Zoo

A tinsmith takes a break outside his store in Black Creek Pioneer Village

Ontario Science Centre ㉙

770 Don Mills Rd. (416) 696 3177.
Oriole. Eglinton or Pape.
Eglinton Ave. E. routes. 10am–
5pm daily. Dec 25.

ONE OF TORONTO'S most popular sights, the Ontario Science Centre attracts children in droves. They come for the center's interactive displays and hands-on exhibits exploring and investigating all manner of phenomena, which are divided into 12 categories. These include the Living Earth, Matter-Energy-Change, the Information Highway, and the Human Body. Visitors can land on the moon, travel to the end of the universe, or have hair-raising fun on a Van de Graaff generator.

Black Creek Pioneer Village ㉚

cnr Steeles Ave. W. & Jane St. (416) 736 1733. Jane. 35b.
May & Jun: 9:30am–4:30pm Mon–Fri, 10am–5pm Sat & Sun; Jul–Sep:10am–5pm daily; Oct–Dec: 9:30–4pm Mon–Fri, 10am–4:30pm Sat & Sun. Jan–May; Dec 25.

OVER THE YEARS, some 40 19th-century buildings have been moved to historic Black Creek Pioneer Village in the northwest of the city from other parts of Ontario. Inevitably, the end result is not entirely realistic – no Ontario village ever looked quite like this – but this living history showpiece is still great fun. Staff in period costume demonstrate traditional skills such as candlemaking, baking, and printing. Among the more interesting buildings are the elegant Doctor's House from 1860, and the Lasky Emporium general store, which is open and trading, selling baking products to visitors. The Tinsmith Shop is manned by skilled craftsmen, and there is a Masonic Lodge meeting room too.

Four buildings are credited to Daniel Stong, a 19th-century pioneer; his pig house, smoke house, and two contrasting homes – the first and earlier dwelling is a crude log shack, the second a civilized house with a brick fireplace, outside of which is a herb garden.

McMichael Art Collection ㉛

10365 Islington Ave., Kleinburg.
(905) 893 1121. Yorkdale.
TTC 37. daily. Dec 25.

ON THE EDGE OF Kleinburg, about 30 minutes' drive north of downtown Toronto, Robert and Signe McMichael built themselves a fine log-and-stone dwelling overlooking the forests of the Humber River Valley. The McMichaels were also avid collectors of Canadian art, and in 1965 they donated their house and paintings to the government. Since then, the art collection has been greatly increased and is now one of the most extensive in the province, with over 6,000 pieces.

Most of the McMichael is devoted to the work of the Group of Seven (see pp160–61), with a whole series of rooms devoted to an eclectic selection of their works. The keynote paintings are characteristically raw and forceful landscapes illustrating the wonders of the Canadian wilderness. Each of the group has been allocated a separate area, and both Tom Thomson (a famous precursor of the group) and talented Group of Seven member Lawren Harris, are particularly well represented. The McMichael also has fascinating sections devoted to contemporary Inuit and Native American art, including the sculpture Bases Stolen from the Cleveland Indians and a Captured Yankee (1989) by the well-known contemporary artist Gerald McMaster (b.1953).

Bill Vazan's "Shibagau Shard" at the McMichael

The log and stone façade of the McMichael Art Collection building

Ottawa and Eastern Ontario

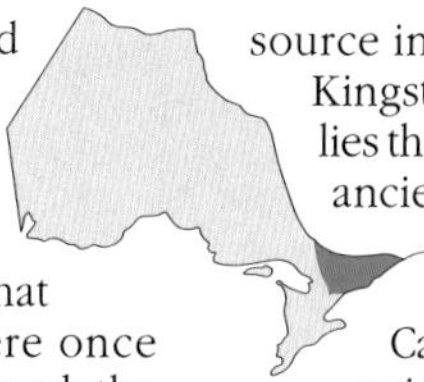

One of the most visited regions in Canada, Eastern Ontario is justly famous for its history and natural beauty. The myiad lakes and waterways that dominate the landscape here once served as trade highways through the wilderness for native people and explorers. Today they form a beautiful natural playground, with spectacular opportunities for outdoor activities such as boating, fishing, hiking, and skiing. The St. Lawrence is one of the world's great waterways and has its source in the historic small city of Kingston. North of Lake Ontario lies the Canadian Shield, with the ancient lakes, rocks, and forest that epitomize Canada. A big favorite with many Canadian vacationers, Algonquin Provincial Park is one of the country's most famous wilderness areas. Also popular is the picturesque Kawartha Lakes region. Rising majestically over the Ottawa River, Canada's capital is a storehouse of national history and stately architecture that attracts over five million visitors each year.

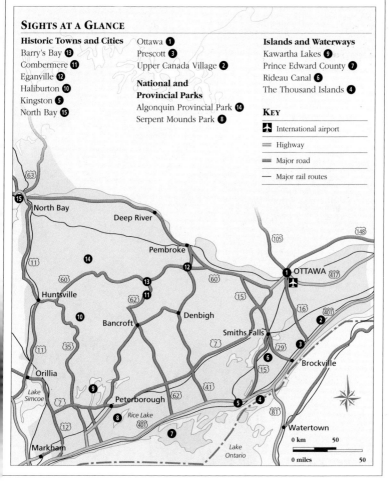

Sights at a Glance

Historic Towns and Cities

Barry's Bay 13
Combermere 11
Eganville 12
Haliburton 10
Kingston 5
North Bay 15
Ottawa 1
Prescott 3
Upper Canada Village 2

National and Provincial Parks

Algonquin Provincial Park 14
Serpent Mounds Park 8

Islands and Waterways

Kawartha Lakes 9
Prince Edward County 7
Rideau Canal 6
The Thousand Islands 4

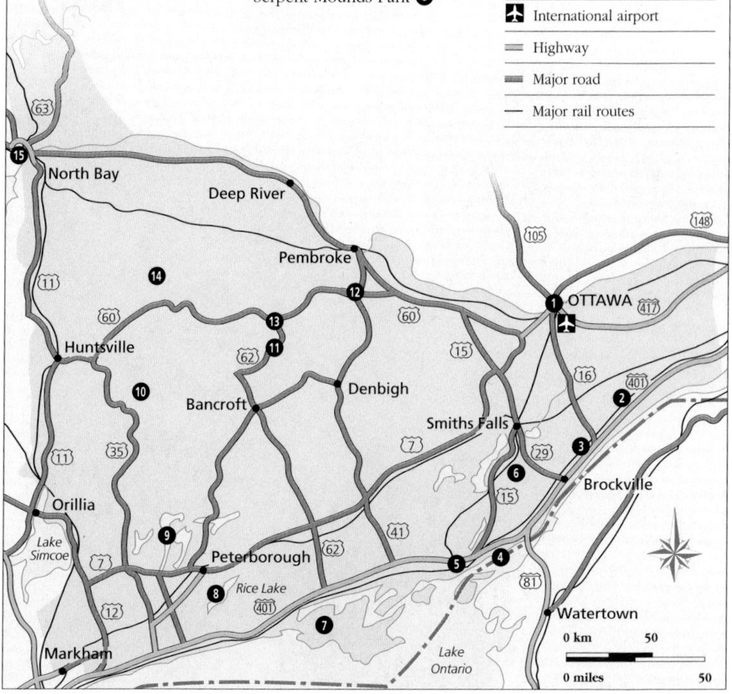
Key
International airport
Highway
Major road
Major rail routes
North Bay
Deep River
Pembroke
OTTAWA
Huntsville
Bancroft
Denbigh
Smiths Falls
Brockville
Orillia
Lake Simcoe
Peterborough
Rice Lake
Markham
Lake Ontario
Watertown
0 km 50
0 miles 50

Pleasure boats on the Rideau Canal at night overlooked by Ottawa's imposing Parliament Buildings

Street-by-Street: Ottawa **❶**

OTTAWA WAS A COMPROMISE choice for Canada's capital, picked in part because of the rivalry between the English and French and the cities that grew into today's urban giants, Toronto and Montreal. This compromise has from its foundation in 1826, grown into a city with an identity all its own. Named capital of the Province of Canada in 1855, Ottawa has a fine setting on the banks of the Ottawa and Rideau rivers. Far more than just the political capital, the city has grown into a mix of English and French residents and historic and modern buildings with plenty of attractions to keep its 4 million annual visitors busy.

A member of the RCMP leading his horse by the Parliament buildings

★ Parliament Buildings
The Changing of the Guard takes place outside daily in July and August. The spectacular cere-mony adds to the grandeur of this seat of government.

The Peace Tower has recently been renovated and forms a striking city landmark.

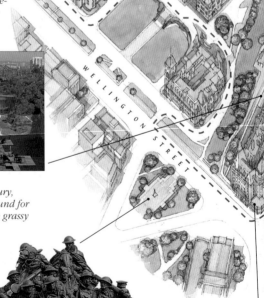

Rideau Canal
Built in the early 19th century, the Canal is now a playground for visitors, its banks lined with grassy cycling and walking paths.

National War Memorial
Annually, on November 11, a memorial service takes place here to honor Canada's war dead. The Centennial Flame is also here. First lit in 1967 to commemorate a century of Confederation, it burns continually.

Chateau Laurier is a luxury hotel, and arguably Canada's most famous. It has been offer-ing sumptuous accommodation to Canada's great and good since it was built in 1901.

Nepean Point

This stunning viewpoint is marked by a statue of a native Canadian at the foot of a monument to Samuel de Champlain (see p41). From here, the whole of central Ottawa can be seen.

The Canadian War Museum houses Canada's largest collection of militaria and war art, focusing on World Wars I and II.

VISITORS' CHECKLIST

🏙 315,000. ✈ 18 km (12 miles) south of the city. 🚌 265 Catherine St. 🚆 VIA Rail Station, 200 Tremblay Rd. ℹ Canada's Capital Information Centre, 14 Metcalfe St. (613) 239 5000. 🎭 Winterlude (Feb), Canadian Tulip Festival (May).

0 meters 100

0 yards 100

KEY

– – – Suggested route

Royal Canadian Mint

This Can$20 Olympic skiing coin was created by the Mint as a souvenir for the 1986 Winter Olympic Games in Calgary. The mint produces only special edition and investment pieces.

Major's Hill Park is a peaceful open-air space in the heart of the busy capital.

★ **National Gallery**
Now featuring more than 25,000 artworks, this is the country's premier collection of the fine arts, housed in this outstanding 1988 granite building.

STAR SIGHTS

★ **National Gallery**

★ **Parliament Buildings**

Exploring Ottawa

Tⁿᴴᴱ CORE OF THE capital is relatively contained, and many of the top sights can be easily accessed on foot. Traveling south through the city, the Rideau Canal is Ottawa's recreation ground year round, from boating and strolling during summer to skating across its icy surface in the freezing Canadian winter. The National Arts Centre is a focus for theater, opera, and ballet; history and art buffs can spend days visiting museums and galleries, both large and small. Ottawa is a city of festivals too; notably Winterlude, a three-weekend February celebration, while in spring the Canadian Tulip Festival transforms the city into a sea of flowers. Canada Day celebrations, on July 1, also attract thousands of visitors.

Antique doll's dress, Bytown

Away from downtown, it sometimes seems that the suburban National Capital Region is overflowing with museums for every enthusiast. Attractions include the Central Experimental Farm and the National Aviation Museum.

Cash register from a 19th-century shop at the Bytown Museum

Ottawa's Gothic Parliament Buildings rise over the city in majestic style

view of the Ottawa River. The Parliament Buildings are distinctly reminiscent of London's Westminster, both in their Victorian gothic style and in their position. Partly destroyed in a fire in 1916, all the buildings are now restored to their former grandeur.

The Parliament Buildings can be toured while the Government, Commons, and Senate are in session. Hand-carved sandstone and limestone characterizes the interior of the government chambers. The Library, with its wood and wrought-iron decorations, is a must. In the summertime Mounties patrol the neat grassy grounds outside the Parliament, where visitors mingle and spot politicians.

⚜ Parliament Buildings

Parliament Hill. 🅲 1 (800) 465 1867. ⬜ daily. ⬤ July 1. 🈹

Dominating the skyline, the country's government buildings overlook downtown Ottawa in a stately manner. Undaunted by the tall buildings that have crept up around them in the 150 years since they became Ottawa's center of power, the East and West Blocks glow green above the city because of their copper roofing. The gothic sandstone buildings were completed in 1860. Located on a 50-m (165-ft) hill, the Parliament offers a

🏛 Bytown Museum

Ottawa Locks. 🅲 (613) 234 4570. ⬜ May–Oct: daily. 🈹

Bytown, the capital's original name, changed to Ottawa in 1855. Located east of Parliament Hill and beside the Rideau Canal, in Ottawa's oldest stone building (1827),

KEY

🅿	Parking
ℹ	Visitor information
⬛	Ottawa street-by-street *see pp190–91*

the Bytown Museum is a well-appointed place to learn more about local history. Colonel John By, the officer in charge of building the Rideau Canal, set up his headquarters here in 1826. While work was underway, the building, also known as the Bytown, was used to store military equipment and cash. The ground floor houses an

The elegant Zoë's Lounge bar at the Château Laurier Hotel

exhibit on the construction of the Rideau Canal. Also very enjoyable is the focus on domestic life of the early 19th century, with a wide variety of homey artifacts on display.

🏛 Château Laurier Hotel

1 Rideau St. 📞 (613) 241 1414. FAX (613) 562 7031. ♿

This wonderful stone replica of a French château is a fine example of the establishments built by railroad companies in the early 1900s. It has attracted both the great and the good since it opened as a hotel in 1912. Centrally located at the foot of Parliament Hill, its interior features large rooms with high ceilings,

decorated with Louis XV-style reproductions. The hotel attracts an upscale clientele, and it is well worth a visit to rub shoulders with celebrities and government mandarins. Within the hotel, Zoë's Lounge, a restaurant with soaring columns, chandeliers and palms, lit by an atrium, is a wonderful place for lunch, as is the larger restaurant, Wilfred's.

🏛 Canadian War Museum

330 Sussex Dr. 📞 (819) 776 8600. 🔵 May–mid-Sep: daily. 🎫 ♿

Canadians may have a reputation as a peaceful people but they have seen their share of the world's battlefields. This aspect of their history is well represented in a museum that houses the country's largest military collection. Highlights include a life-size replica of a World War I trench, displays on the American invasion of 1775, the Normandy Landings (1944), and the Canadian Navy's role in the 1942 Battle of the Atlantic, where Allied sailors fought bravely to secure Britain against German U-boats, often against incredible odds. World War II memorabilia continues, in the form of Goering's personal car, which is riddled with bullet holes; disappointingly, these were added by a past owner trying to increase its value. A gallery is devoted to weapons from clubs to machine-guns. Also worth seeing is the collection of war art, much of it representing both world wars.

Demob sign at the War Museum

National Museum of Science & Technology

♦ Royal Canadian Mint

320 Sussex Dr. **(** (613) 991 5853.
◯ daily. **▨ ➍ ✸** obligatory.
Founded in 1908 as a branch
of the British Royal Mint, this
no longer produces regular
Canadian cash currency.
Instead, it strikes many special-
edition coins and Maple Leaf
bullion investment coins. The
mint also processes about 70
percent of the country's gold
in its refinery, which is among
the largest in North America.

The building was refurbished
fully in the 1980s and now
offers guided tours. These are
available daily, but coinage
fanatics must make reservations
in advance to see the process
that turns sheets of metal into
bags of shiny gold coins.

The façade of Ottawa's imposing
Cathédrale Notre Dame

♦ Cathédrale Notre Dame

Cnr Sussex Dr. & St. Patrick St.
((613) 241 7496. **◯** daily. **➍**
Built in 1839, Notre Dame,
with its twin spires, is Ottawa's
best-known Catholic church.
It is situated in the Byward
Market area and features a
spectacular Gothic-style ceiling. The windows, carvings,
and the huge pipe organ are
also well worth seeing (and
hearing). Philippe Parizeau
(1852–1938) carved the wood-
work in mahogany. In niches
around the sanctuary, there
are wooden etchings of prophets and apostles, crafted by
Louis-Philippe Hebert (1850–
1917), now painted to look
like stone. Joseph Eugene
Guiges, the first bishop of
Ottawa, oversaw the completion of Notre Dame, and his
statue is outside the basilica.

Byward Market is known as a
lively area of Ottawa

♦ Byward Market

Ward St. **(** (613) 244 4410.
◯ Jan–Apr & late Oct–Nov: Tue–
Sun; May–mid-Oct & Dec: daily.
● Dec 25, 26, Jan 1. **➍** limited.
This neighborhood bustles all
year round; outdoors in the
summer, inside in winter. The
area is located just east of Parliament Hill, across the Rideau
Canal, and offers a colorful
collection of craft shops, cafés,
boutiques, bistros, nightclubs,
and farmers' market stalls.
Special attractions include the
artisans' stalls in the Byward
Market Building on George
Street, and the cobblestoned
Sussex Courtyards. The cafés
are among Ottawa's most
popular places to lunch.

♦ Laurier House

335 Laurier Ave. **(** (613) 992 8142.
◯ 9am–5pm Tue–Sat; 2pm–5pm
Sun. **●** Mon. **▨ ➍**
Now a national historic site,
Laurier House, a Victorian town
house built in 1878, served as
the chief residence of two
notable Canadian prime ministers, Sir Wilfrid Laurier and

Mackenzie King. Beautifully
furnished throughout, it
houses memorabilia, papers,
and personal possessions of
both former national leaders.

Rideau Canal

ℹ 1 (800) 230 0016.
Built in the mid-19th century,
the Rideau Canal is a man-
made construction that travels
through lakes and canals from
Ottawa to the city of Kingston
(see p198). The canal flows
through the capital, providing
an attractive pastoral sight
with its walking and cycling
paths bordering the water.
Once used for shipping, the
canal is now a recreational
area. In summer visitors stroll
along its banks, while through
Ottawa's freezing winter the
canal turns into the city's skating rink, popular with locals
during the winter festival.

♦ Central Experimental Farm

Experimental Farm Dr. **(** (613)
991 3044. **◯** 9am–5pm daily.
● Dec 25. **▨ ➍ ✸**
The CEF is a national project
researching all aspects of farming and horticulture. It also
offers some of the best floral
displays in the country, including a spectacular chrysanthe-
mum show every November.
There is also an ornamental
flower show and an arboretum
with over 2,000 varieties of
trees and shrubs. The farm's
livestock barns and show
cattle herds are especially
popular with children, and
everybody loves the tours of
the 500-ha (1,200-acre) site in
wagons drawn by huge, magnificent Clydesdale horses.

Children can get close to animals at the Central Experimental Farm

The waterside restaurant at the National Arts Centre, seen from the Rideau Canal

🏛 National Arts Centre

53 Elgin St. 🎟 (613) 996 5051.
⬤ daily. 🗓 ✅ obligatory. ♿

Completed in 1969, the National Arts Centre has three stages, an elegant canal-side restaurant, and a summer terrace. The building, designed by noted Canadian architect Fred Neubold, comprises three interlocking hexagons opening onto good views of the Ottawa River and the Rideau Canal. Many exponents of Canadian and international dance, theater, and musical forms, including the National Arts Centre Orchestra, perform here regularly. The center's Opera auditorium seats 2,300; the Theatre, with its innovative apron stage, seats 950; the Studio, a marvelous venue for experimental productions, comfortably seats 350. Visitors should note that the center is extremely popular and reserving well in advance is recommended, especially for top international shows.

🏛 Currency Museum

245 Sparks St. 🎟 (613) 782 8914
⬤ May–Sep: 10:30am–5pm Mon–Sat; 1pm–5pm Sun: Oct–Apr: 10:30am–5pm Tue–Sat; 1pm–5pm Sun.

Based in the Bank of Canada, displays in the Currency Museum trace the history of money through the ages. This is a fascinating place to learn about the unusual variety of things used as Canadian currency over the years – whales' teeth, glass beads, grain, paper, and metal. The emphasis of the exhibition is on Canadian currency in all its forms. Visitors can also see the workings of the National Bank. Staff are on hand to answer queries.

🏛 National Museum of Science and Technology

1867 St. Laurent Blvd. 🎟 (613) 991 3044. ⬤ May–Sep: 9am–6pm daily; Oct–Apr: 9am–5pm Tue–Sun. 🗓

Discover a whole new world at this interactive museum whose permanent exhibits include a wide range of fascinating displays exploring Canada's space history, transportation through the ages, and modern and industrial technology. A vintage steam locomotive can be boarded, and the more modern-minded may enter a mini-control room and pull levers to launch a make-believe rocket. Children and adults can also join in a mission to save a colony on Mars. More down-to-earth, the biology section includes live chicks incubating.

🏛 National Aviation Museum

Aviation & Rockcliffe Parkways.
🎟 (613) 993 2010. ⬤ May–Sep: daily; Oct–Apr: Tue–Sun. 🗓

This huge building near Rockcliffe Airport houses more than 100 aircraft, which have flown both in war and peace. The famous 1909 *Silver Dart*, one of the world's earliest flying machines, is here, as is the nose cone from the *Avro Arrow*, the supersonic superfighter that created a political crisis in Canada when the government halted its development in the 1970s. The *Spitfire*, valiant friend of the Allies in World War II, features alongside historic bush planes such as the *Beaver* and early passenger carrier jets. Displays detail the exploits of Canadian war heroes, including World War I ace Billy Bishop, while the audiovisual Walkway of Time traces the history of world aviation.

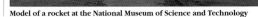

Model of a rocket at the National Museum of Science and Technology

National Gallery of Canada

OPENED IN 1988, the National Gallery of Canada provides a spectacular home for the country's impressive collections of art. Located near the heart of the capital, architect Moshe Safdie's memorable pink granite and glass edifice is architecture as art in its own right. The National Gallery is one of the three largest museums in the country, and is Canada's top art gallery, with excellent collections of both national and international exhibits. The museum is a short stroll from the Rideau Canal and Major's Hill Park.

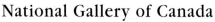

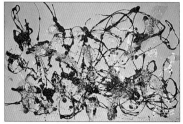

Library

Level 2

No.29 (1950)
A vivid example of Jackson Pollock's idiosyncratic drip technique, this was part of an enormous canvas carefully cut into sections, hence its title, No. 29.

Café

★ **Rideau Street Chapel**
Set in a peaceful inner courtyard, this 1888 chapel was saved from bulldozers nearby and moved here for safety.

GALLERY GUIDE
On its first level the gallery houses the world's largest collection of Canadian art. It also features international displays and major traveling exhibitions. The second level contains the European and American Galleries alongside Asiatic art and the gallery of prints, drawings, and photographs. Visitors can relax in the two courtyards or in the fine café.

KEY

☐ Special exhibition space

☐ Canadian gallery

☐ Contemporary art

☐ European and American galleries

☐ Asiatic art

☐ Prints, drawings, and photographs

☐ Inuit art

☐ Nonexhibition space

STAR EXHIBITS

★ **Rideau Street Chapel**

★ **The Jack Pine by Tom Thomson**

Inuit sculpture
This is represented in ancient and modern forms; Aurora Borealis decapitating a young man *dates from 1965.*

National Gallery façade
In addition to displays of painting, prints, architecture, and photography, the gallery holds regular events for the performing arts, including movies, lectures, and concerts.

VISITORS' CHECKLIST

380 Sussex Dr. ☎ (613) 990
1985. FAX (613) 990 9824.
W http://national.gallery.ca
🚌 3, 306. ◯ May–Oct: 10am–
6pm Fri–Wed, 10am–8pm Thu;
Oct–Apr: 10am–5pm Wed,
Fri–Sun, 10am–8pm Thu. ●
Mon, Tue, Dec 26, Jan 1. 🎫 for
special exhibitions. 📷 in some
areas. 🕐 11am & 2pm. 🅿 🚻

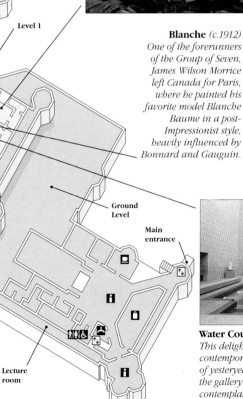

Level 1

★ The Jack Pine *(1916)*
In many ways the father of Canada's nationalist art movement of the early 20th century, the Group of Seven, Tom Thomson first attracted notice with his vivid, sketchy, impressionist paintings of Ontario landscape, here shown with a brightly colored oil of a provincial tree framed in wilderness.

Blanche *(c.1912)*
One of the forerunners of the Group of Seven, James Wilson Morrice left Canada for Paris, where he painted his favorite model Blanche Baume in a post-Impressionist style, heavily influenced by Bonnard and Gauguin.

Ground
Level

Main
entrance

Lecture
room

Water Court
This delightful airy space is a sharp contemporary contrast to the treasures of yesteryear that abound in the rest of the gallery. Water Court is used as a contemplative gallery for sculpture.

Upper Canada Village ➋

🚌 Cornwall. 🚐 ℹ️ Morrisburg
1 (800) 437 2233.

THIS LITTLE country town was relocated 11 km (7 miles) west of Morrisburg to save it from the rising waters of the St. Lawrence River during construction of the Seaway in the 1950s. Today, it is preserved as a tourist attraction and is a colorful reminder of the province's social history with its collection of 40 authentic pre-Confederation (1867) buildings. Costumed villagers work in the blacksmith's forge and the sawmill while tinsmiths and cabinetmakers employ the tools and skills of the 1860s. A bakery and general store are both in operation. History is also reflected in nearby **Battle of Crysler's Farm Visitor Centre**, a memorial to those who died in the War of 1812.

🏛 **Battle of Crysler's Farm Visitor Centre**
Exit 758 off Hwy 401. 📞 (613) 543 3704. 🕐 mid-May–mid-Oct: 9:30am–5pm daily. 📷 ♿

Prescott ➌

🏠 4,000. 🚌 🚐 ℹ️ 360 Dibble St. (613) 925 2812.

THE MAJOR attractions in this 19th-century town are its architecture and access to the St. Lawrence River. Prescott's recently refurbished waterfront area and its busy marina make for a pleasant waterside stroll.

The 1838 lighthouse overlooks the pleasure boats of Prescott's marina

The town is full of 19th-century homes and is the site for the road bridge to New York State in the US. **Fort Wellington National Historic Site**, east from the center of town, attracts many visitors. Originally built during the War of 1812 and rebuilt in 1838, four walls and some buildings remain. These include a stone blockhouse which is now a military museum, incorporating refurbished officers' quarters. Guides in period uniform give tours during the summer, and in July a military pageant includes mock battles.

🏛 **Fort Wellington**
Prescott. 📞 (613) 925 2896. 🕐 late May–mid-Oct: daily. ♿

The Thousand Islands ➍

ℹ️ 2 King St. East, Gananoque (613) 382 3250.

THE St. Lawrence River, one of the world's great waterways, is a gateway for ocean-going vessels traveling through the Great Lakes. Few stretches of the trip compare in charm or beauty to the Thousand Islands, an area that contains a scattering of over a thousand tiny islands, stretching from just below Kingston downriver to the waterside towns and cities of Gananoque, Brockville, Ivy Lea, and Rockport. Cruising opportunities abound from the Kingston boarding site.
River sights include the curious Boldt's Castle, a folly built on one of the islands by millionaire hotelier Boldt and abandoned in grief when his wife died in 1904. It was Oscar, Boldt's head chef at the Waldorf Astoria who, entertaining summer guests at the castle, concocted Thousand Island salad dressing. Landlubbers will enjoy the scenery

A sailboat travels the Thousand Islands

from the Thousand Islands Parkway, which runs from the pretty town of Gananoque to Mallorytown Landing.

Kingston ➎

🏠 141,000. ✈️ 🚌 🚐 ⛴
ℹ️ 209 Ontario St. (613) 548 4415.

ONCE A center for ship building and the fur trade, Kingston was briefly (1841–44) the capital of the United Province of Canada (see pp45). Constructed by generations of shipbuilders, the city's handsome limestone buildings reflect a dignified lineage.
The host of the 1976 Olympic Games regatta, Kingston is still one of the freshwater sailing capitals of North America and the embarkation point for many local cruises. Kingston is home to more museums than any other town in Ontario. Universally popular, the restored British bastion **Old Fort Henry** is a living military museum brought to life by guards in bright scarlet period uniforms who are trained in drills, artillery exercises, and traditional fife and drum music of the 1860s. Canada's top Army

Guard at Old Fort Henry

Training University is also based in the city and The Royal Military College Museum, housed in a 1846 Martello Tower, tells the story of today's cadets and their forebears.

West of the downtown area lies the **Marine Museum of the Great Lakes**. There are displays on the history of the Great Lakes and the ships that sailed on them, including the first ship built for the Lakes here in 1678. The museum also contains a 3,000-tonne icebreaker which has found a new vocation as a delightfully appointed bed-and-breakfast. Modern-day technology is explored at Kingston Mills, the lock station at the southern end of the Rideau Canal, where boats are lifted 4 m (13 ft).

Historic house along the main street of Picton in peaceful Quinte's Isle

⚔ Old Fort Henry
Kingston. 🕻 *(613) 542 7388.*
⬜ *mid-May– late Sep: daily.* 🧩 ♿
🏛 Marine Museum of the Great Lakes
55 Ontario St. 🕻 *(613) 542 2261.*
⬜ *Jun–Oct: 10am–5pm daily; Nov–May: 10am–4pm Mon–Fri.* 🧩 🖥

Rideau Canal ❻

ℹ *34a Beckwith St. South,
Smiths Falls (613) 283 5170.*

THE RIDEAU CANAL, originally a defensive barrier protecting Canada against the Americans and finished in 1832, stretches for 200 km (125 miles). The best way to enjoy this sparkling necklace of scenic waterway is by boat. A great feat of 19th-century

A view of the Rideau Canal as it travels through Westport village

engineering, which includes 47 locks and 24 dams, the system allows boaters to float through tranquil woods and farmland, scenic lakes, and to stop in quaint villages, as well as visit the **Canal Museum** at Smith's Falls. The canal north of Kingston also contains a number of provincial parks which offer canoe trails. Also popular is the 400-km (250-mile) Rideau Trail, a hiking system linking Kingston and Canada's capital city, Ottawa.

🏛 Canal Museum
34 Beckwith St. S. 🕻 *(613) 284 0505.* ⬜ *mid-Jun–mid-Oct: daily; mid-Oct–mid-Jun: Tue–Sun.* 🧩 ♿

Prince Edward County ❼

ℹ *116 Main St., Picton.*
🕻 *(613) 476 2421.*

CHARMING AND KNOWN for its relaxed pace and old-fashioned hospitality, Prince Edward County is surrounded by Lake Ontario and the Bay of Quinte, and is sometimes referred to as Quinte's Isle. The island is renowned for its two camping and sunbathing beaches in Sandbanks Provincial Park. There, mountains of fine sand reach 25 m (82 ft) and are considered one of the most significant fresh-water dune systems in the world.

United Empire Loyalists (*see p42*) settled in the County following the American Revolution (1775), founding engaging small towns and a strong farming industry.

Visitors can absorb the local historic architecture by traveling along the country roads and the Loyalist Parkway, either cycling or by car, pausing to appreciate the island's charming views.

Serpent Mounds Park ❽

Rural route 3. 🕻 *(705) 295 6879.*
🚌 *Coburg.* 🚌 *Peterborough.*
⬜ *mid-May–mid-Oct: 9am–8pm daily.* 🧩 ♿

SITUATED ON the shore of Rice Lake, Serpent Mounds is a historic native Indian burial ground. A grove of aging oak encloses nine burial mounds of an ancient people who gathered here more than 2,000 years ago. The only one of its kind in Canada, the largest mound has an unusual zigzag appearance, said to represent the shape of a moving snake. The site is still sacred to native people. Rice Lake, which offers shady picnic spots and excellent fishing, provides a pleasant backdrop.

On the tiny Indian River 9 km (5 miles) away, Lang Pioneer Village is a more traditional representation of Canada's past, featuring 20 restored 19th-century buildings, heritage gardens, and farmyard animals. Visitors can watch an ancient restored grist mill in action, and workers in period costumes display ancient skills. Blacksmiths and tinsmiths ply their trade in an authentic smithy and will give lessons.

Lush bullrushes surround a pond in Petroglyphs Provincial Park

Kawartha Lakes ⑨

🛈 Peterborough (705) 742 2201.
🚌 Peterborough. 🚃 Cobourg.

THE KAWARTHA LAKES are part of the 386-km (240-mile) Trent–Severn Waterway that runs from Lake Ontario to Georgian Bay and was originally built in the 19th century. Today the area is a playground for vacationers, with water-based activities including cruises and superb fishing. Renting a houseboat from one of the coastal villages is a popular way of exploring the locality. At the center of the region lies the friendly little city of Peterborough, notable for its university, pleasing waterfront parks, and the world's largest hydraulic liftlock. Thirty-four km (21 miles) north lies the Curve Lake Indian Reserve's famous Whetung Gallery, one of the best places locally for native arts and crafts.

Petroglyphs Provincial Park, 30 km (19 miles) to the north of Peterborough, is better known to locals as the "teaching rocks" for the 900-plus aboriginal rock carvings cut into the park's white limestone outcrops. Rediscovered in 1954, these wonderfully preserved symbols and figures of animals, boats, spirits, and people were made to teach the story of life to aboriginal males. After each lesson, the elders would cover the stones with moss to preserve them. Today, the carvings are under glass to protect them from acid rain. The stones remain respectfully regarded to this day as a sacred site by native peoples.

🍁 **Petroglyphs Provincial Park**
Northey's Bay Rd. off Hwy 28.
📞 (705) 877 2552. 🕐 May–Oct: 10am–5pm daily. 🈳 ♿

The Haliburton Highlands ⑩

🛈 Haliburton (705) 457 2871.

THE HALIBURTON Highlands are one of Ontario's year-round outdoor destinations, renowned for their forests, lakes, and spectacular scenery. In the summer, thousands of visitors enjoy boating, fishing, and swimming in this region. In fall, busloads of tourists travel to appreciate the celebrated seasonal colors; other visitors come for the deer hunting. Winter brings skiers, snowboarders, and many snowmobiles.

The village of Haliburton is found along scenic Highway 35, which winds its way through exceptional scenery from Minden north to the considerable charms of Dorset. The fire tower atop a rock cliff overlooking the village gives spectacular views of the Lake of Bays and the surrounding area. This spot is a fantastic viewing point for the myriad colors of Ontario's fall trees with their lovely bright red and orange shades.

Combemere ⑪

🚶 250. 🛈 Ottawa Valley Tourist Association, 9 International Dr., Pembroke (613) 732 4364.

THE VILLAGE of Combemere is a central point for people heading to a number of provincial parks in Eastern Ontario, including Algonquin (*see pp202–203*), Carson Lake, and Opeongo River. It is a good tourist center for fuel and refreshments. A few kilometers south of Combemere lies the **Madonna House Pioneer Museum**. Founded by Catherine Doherty, this Catholic lay community has grown to have mission outposts around the world. It is managed by volunteers, who survive from its cooperative farm, and who dedicate themselves to fundraising. Since 1963, a recycling program has been raising money for the world's poor.

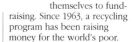

The Madonna at Pioneer Museum

🏛 **Madonna House Pioneer Museum**
Hwy 517. 📞 (613) 756 0103.
🕐 mid-May–mid-Oct: 10am–5pm Tue–Sat.

Golfers take a break between games to enjoy the Haliburton scenery

Farm cottages outside Barry's Bay, home to many Ontarian craftspeople

Eganville ⓬

1,300. Ottawa Valley Tourist Association, 9 International Dr., Pembroke (613) 732 4364.

THIS HIGHWAY 60 village with its little restaurants and gas station provides a handy tourist center for visitors to this picturesque region. Local attractions include the **Bonnechere Caves**, 8 km (5 miles) away. The caves were at the bottom of a tropical sea 500 million years ago. Gradually raised over millennia from the ocean bed, they are covered with fossils of primitive life forms. The privately owned site is open for tours in summer.

Bonnechere Caves
(613) 628 2283. May–early Sep: daily; late Sep–Oct: Sat & Sun.

Barry's Bay ⓭

1,100. Ottawa Valley Tourist Association, 9 International Dr., Pembroke (613) 732 4364.

AN ATTRACTIVE LITTLE town, Barry's Bay has a sizeable Polish population, as does its neighbor Wilno, site of the first Polish settlement in Canada. The area is home to many craftspeople and artisans, who sell their wares in the local villages. Barry's Bay is also popular for stores selling outdoor gear and watersport equipment. Year-round sports facilities can be found at nearby Kamaniskeg Lake and Redcliffe Hills, both of which are popular places for renting cottages. Perched high on a hill, nearby Wilno overlooks scenic river valleys and boasts the fine church and grotto of St. Mary's.

Algonquin Provincial Park ⓮

See pp202-203

North Bay ⓯

56,000. 1375 Seymour St. (705) 472 8480.

BILLING ITSELF as the Gateway to the Near North, North Bay sits at the eastern end of Lake Nippissing, 350 km (217 miles) north of Toronto. The region's most famous natives are undoubtedly the Dionne quintuplets. Born in 1934, the Quints' original modest family homestead has been relocated and now forms the town's popular **Dionne Homestead Museum**.

Lake Nippissing nearby is famous for its fishing and wilderness scenery. Boat cruises across the lake follow the old French explorers route. North Bay is a good starting-point for trips to the area's many vacation camps.

Dionne Homestead Museum
1375 Seymour St. (705) 472 8480. mid May–mid-Oct: daily.

THE DIONNE QUINTS

The hamlet of Corbeil experienced a natural miracle on May 28, 1934: the birth of the Dionne quintuplets; Annette, Emilie, Yvonne, Cecile, and Marie, the five identical girls born to Oliva and Elzire Dionne. The Quints' combined weight at birth was only 6.1 kg (13 lbs 5 oz), and the babies' lungs were so tiny that small doses of rum were required daily to help them breathe. Experts put the chances of giving birth to identical quintuplets at 1 in 57 million. The girls became international stars, attracting countless visitors to North Bay during the 1930s. A Quint industry sprang up with curiosity-seekers flocking to watch the young girls at play. The Dionne homestead was moved to North Bay in 1985, and visitors can travel back over 60 years to marvel anew at the birth of the Quints in this small farmhouse.

Algonquin Provincial Park ⑭

"Moose Crossing"

To many Canadians, Algonquin, with its lush maple and fir woods, sparkling lakes, and plentiful wildlife, is as familiar a symbol of Canada as is Niagara Falls.

Founded in 1893, Algonquin Provincial Park is the oldest and most famous park in Ontario, stretching across 7,725 square km (3,000 square miles) of wilderness. Wildlife abounds; visitors have a chance to see beavers, moose, and bear in their natural habitats, and the park echoes with the hauntingly beautiful call of the loon, heard often in northern Ontario. Every August, nightly "wolf howls" are organized whereby visitors attempt to elicit answers from these native animals by imitating their cries. Opportunities for outdoor activities are plentiful; most visitors like to try one of the 1,500-km (932-miles) of canoe routes through the forested interior.

Killarney Lodge
One of the park's rental lodges, these rustic buildings are popular places to stay during their summer and fall season.

The Algonquin Gallery
exhibits various international art displays, with a focus on nature and wildlife. Painters featured have included Tom Thomson, precursor of the famous Group of Seven *(see pp160–1).*

Moose near Highway 60
Visitors can usually spot a few moose each day, especially near lakes and salty puddles by roadsides, which these huge animals seem to love.

Canoe Lake
Almost a thousand miles of canoe trails lace the park. They range from beginner and family routes, some as short as 6 km (4 miles), to 70-km (50-mile) treks for the experienced. Routes are well planned and marked.

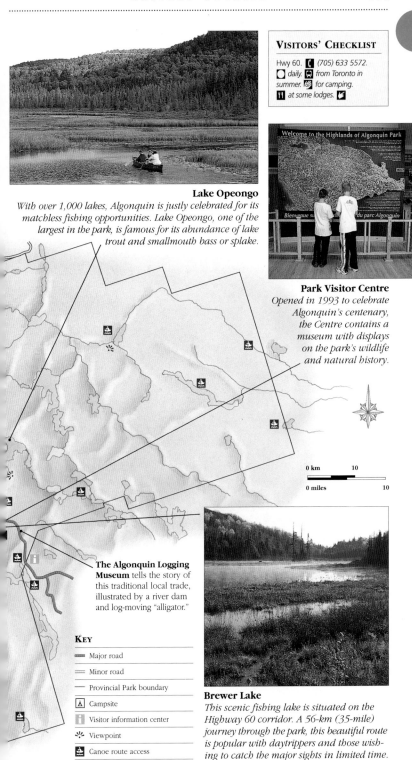

VISITORS' CHECKLIST

Hwy 60. ☎ (705) 633 5572.
○ daily. 🚌 from Toronto in
summer. 🚐 for camping.
🍴 at some lodges. 🅿

Lake Opeongo

With over 1,000 lakes, Algonquin is justly celebrated for its matchless fishing opportunities. Lake Opeongo, one of the largest in the park, is famous for its abundance of lake trout and smallmouth bass or splake.

Park Visitor Centre

Opened in 1993 to celebrate Algonquin's centenary, the Centre contains a museum with displays on the park's wildlife and natural history.

0 km 10

0 miles 10

The Algonquin Logging Museum tells the story of this traditional local trade, illustrated by a river dam and log-moving "alligator."

KEY

▬▬ Major road

═══ Minor road

—— Provincial Park boundary

△ Campsite

ℹ Visitor information center

☀ Viewpoint

⛴ Canoe route access

Brewer Lake

This scenic fishing lake is situated on the Highway 60 corridor. A 56-km (35-mile) journey through the park, this beautiful route is popular with daytrippers and those wishing to catch the major sights in limited time.

The Great Lakes

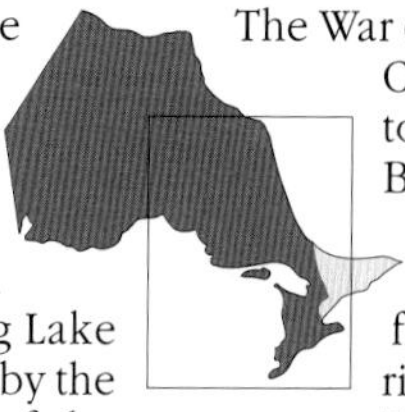

The varied charms of the Canadian Great Lakes region, from the sleepy little farming towns bordering Lake Erie to the island-studded bays of Lake Huron and the wilderness encircling Lake Superior, tend to be obscured by the fame of Niagara Falls. One of the world's most famous sights, the falls occur where the Niagara River tumbles 50 meters (164 ft) between Lakes Erie and Ontario. Native tribes once lived on the fertile land around the area's lakes and rivers, but fur traders used the lakes as a vital waterway. The War of 1812 resulted in British Canada securing trade rights to the northern lakeshores. Between 1820 and 1850 settlers established farms, and mining and forestry flourished in Canada's then richest province. Today, the Trans-Canada Highway follows the northern shores of Lakes Huron and Superior for over 1,000 km (620 miles), traveling through the untamed scenery of Killarney Park, past picturesque old towns such as Sault Ste. Marie, and eventually reaching the bustling port of Thunder Bay.

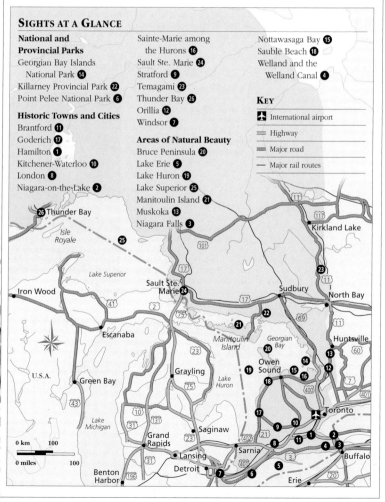

Sights at a Glance

National and Provincial Parks

Georgian Bay Islands National Park 14
Killarney Provincial Park 22
Point Pelee National Park 6

Historic Towns and Cities

Brantford 11
Goderich 17
Hamilton 1
Kitchener-Waterloo 10
London 8
Niagara-on-the-Lake 2
Sainte-Marie among the Hurons 16
Sault Ste. Marie 24
Stratford 9
Temagami 23
Thunder Bay 26
Orillia 12
Windsor 7

Areas of Natural Beauty

Bruce Peninsula 20
Lake Erie 5
Lake Huron 19
Lake Superior 25
Manitoulin Island 21
Muskoka 13
Niagara Falls 3
Nottawasaga Bay 15
Sauble Beach 18
Welland and the Welland Canal 4

Key

✈ International airport
Highway
Major road
Major rail routes

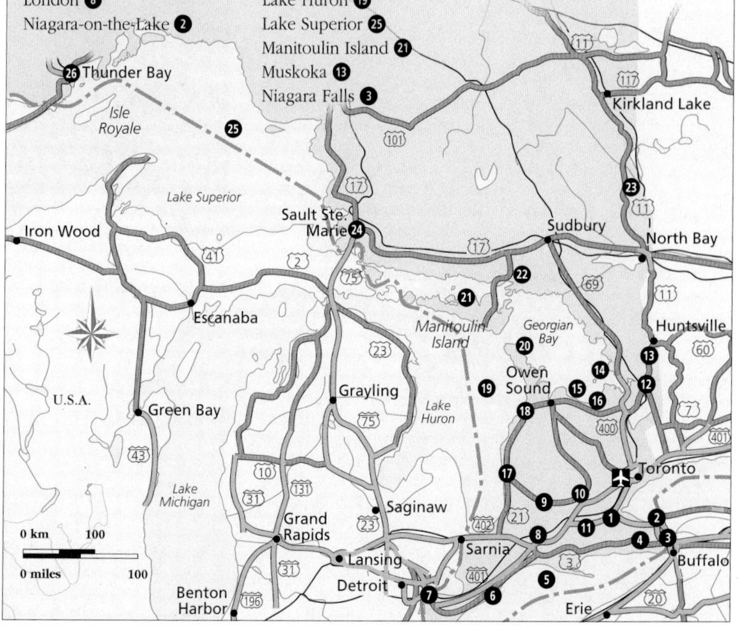

◁ **The warm colors of Killarney Provincial Park reflected in the tranquil waters of Cranberry Lake**

The imposing façade of Dundurn Castle in Hamilton

Hamilton ❶

🚶 322,350. ⊠ ✈ 🚌 🚆 ℹ 127 King St. East (905) 546 2666.

THE CITY OF Hamilton sits at the extreme western end of Lake Ontario, some 70 km (44 miles) from Toronto. Its specialty is steel, and the city's mills churn out around 60 per cent of Canada's total production. Despite the town's industrial bias, it possesses some enjoyable attractions. **Dundurn Castle** is a Regency villa dating from the 1830s, whose interior holds a fine collection of period furnishings. It was built for the McNabs, one of the most influential families in Ontario, who included in their number Sir Allan Napier McNab, Prime Minister of Canada from 1854–6.

Another sight is the **Royal Botanical Gardens**, comprising forests, marshes, and small lakes over some 1,093 ha (2,700 acres) on the north side of Hamilton harbor. Trails crisscrossing the lakeshore conduct visitors to several special gardens, notably a fine Rose Garden, the Laking Garden with its peonies and irises, and the heavily perfumed Lilac Garden. The Mediterranean Garden occupies a large conservatory and contains plants found in this climate zone drawn from every corner of the globe.

Also in town, the Canadian Warplane Heritage Museum has a display of more than 30 operational aircraft dating from World War II to the jet age.

Rose in the Royal Botanical Gardens

🏛 **Dundurn Castle**
610 York Blvd. 📞 (905) 546 2872. ⏰ mid-May–early Sep: 10am–4pm daily; late Sep–mid-May: noon–4pm Tue–Sun. 📷 ♿ partial.
🌷 **Royal Botanical Gardens**
680 Plains Rd. West. 📞 (905) 527 1158. ⏰ daily. 📷 ♿ partial.

Niagara-on-the-Lake ❷

🚶 13,000. 🚆 ℹ 153 King St. (905) 468 4263.

NIAGARA-ON-THE-LAKE is a charming little town of elegant clapboard mansions and leafy streets set where the mouth of the Niagara River empties into Lake Ontario. The town was originally known as Newark and under this name it became the capital of Upper Canada (as Ontario was then known) in 1792. It was to be a temporary honor. Just four years later, the British decided to move the capital farther away from the US border, and chose York (now Toronto) instead. It was a wise decision. In 1813, the Americans crossed the Niagara River and destroyed Newark in the War of 1812 (see pp42–43). The British returned after the war to rebuild their homes, and the Georgian town they constructed has survived pretty much intact.

Today, visitors take pleasure in exploring the town's lovely streets, but there is one major attraction, **Fort George**, a carefully restored British

---

stockade built in the 1790s just southeast of town. The earth and timber palisade encircles ten replica buildings including three blockhouses, the barracks, a guard house, and the officers' quarters. There is also a powder magazine store, where all the fittings were wood or brass, and the men donned special shoes without buckles to reduce the chance of an unwanted explosion. Guides in old-style British military uniforms describe life in the fort in the 19th century.

Niagara-on-the-Lake is also home to the annual Shaw Festival, a prestigious theatrical season featuring the plays of George Bernard Shaw and other playwrights, which runs from April to November.

🏛 **Fort George**
Queen's Parade, Niagara Pkwy. 📞 (905) 468 4257. ⏰ 9:30am–5:30pm daily. 📷 ♿

Gardens in front of an early 19th-century inn at Niagara-on-the-Lake

Niagara Falls ❸

(See pp210–13)

Welland and The Welland Canal ❹

🚶 48,000. ⊠ 🚌 ℹ Seaway Mall, 800 Niagara St. (905) 735 8696.

AN IMPORTANT steel town, Welland is bisected by the famous Welland Canal, which was built to solve the problem of Niagara Falls. The Falls presented an obstacle that made

Aerial view of the small village of Long Point on the shore of Lake Erie

it impossible for boats to pass between lakes Ontario and Erie. Consequently, goods had to be unloaded on one side of the Falls and then carted to the other, a time-consuming and expensive process. To solve the problem, local entrepreneurs dug a canal across the 45-km (28-mile) isthmus separating the lakes early in the 19th century, choosing a route to the west of the Niagara River.

The first **Welland Canal** was a crude affair, but subsequent improvements have created today's version, which has eight giant locks adjusting the water level by no less than 99 m (324 feet). A remarkable feat of engineering, the canal is capable of accommodating the largest of ships. It is possible to drive alongside the northerly half of the canal, on Government Road from Lake Ontario

to Thorold, where seven of the eight locks are situated. The viewing platform at Lock No.3 provides a great vantage point and has an information center detailing the canal's history.

Welland boasts another eye-catching attraction: 28 giant murals decorate some of the city's downtown buildings.

Lake Erie ❺

ℹ️ 100 Goderich St., Fort Erie (905) 871 3505.

LAKE ERIE IS named after the native peoples who once lived along its shores. The Erie, or cat people, were renowned for their skills as fishermen. Some 400 km (249 miles) long and an average of 60 km (37 miles) wide, Lake Erie is the shallowest of the Great Lakes

and separates Canada from the US. Its northern shore is one of the most peaceful parts of Ontario, with a string of quiet country towns and small ports set in rolling countryside. Three peninsulas reach out from the Canadian shoreline, one of which has been conserved as the Point Pelee National Park, home to a virgin forest and, during spring and summer, thousands of migrating birds.

About 30 km (19 miles) south of Niagara Falls, the small town of Fort Erie lies where the Niagara River meets Lake Erie, facing its sprawling US neighbor, Buffalo. The massive Peace Bridge links the two, and most people cross the border without giving Fort Erie a second look. They miss one of the more impressive of the reconstructed British forts that dot the Canada-US border. Historic **Fort Erie** is a replica of the stronghold, destroyed by the Americans in the War of 1812. Entry is across a drawbridge, and the interior holds barracks, a powder magazine, officers' quarters, and a guard house. The fort became a popular posting among British soldiers. This was because it was fairly easy to desert across the river to join the US army, whose pay and conditions were thought to be better.

🏛️ **Fort Erie**
350 Lakeshore Rd. 📞 (905) 371 0254. ⭕ mid-May–Sep: daily. ♿ 👜 partial.

⌐ A merchant ship on the Welland Canal near the town of Welland

Point Pelee National Park ❻

((519) 322 2365. **▢** Windsor.
▢ Windsor. **○** daily. **▥** **&** **▯**

ALONG, FINGERLIKE isthmus, Point Pelee National Park sticks out into Lake Erie for 20 km (12 miles) and forms the southernmost tip of Canada's mainland. The park has a wide variety of habitats including marshlands, open fields, and ancient deciduous forest. These woods are a rarity, as they are one of the few places in Canada where many of the trees have never been logged. There is a profusion of species that creates a junglelike atmosphere, with red cedar, black walnut, white sassafras, hickory, sycamore, and sumac, all struggling to reach the light. Furthermore, this varied vegetation attracts thousands of birds, which visit on their spring and fall migrations. Over 350 species have been sighted in the park, and they can be observed from lookout towers and forest trails. Every fall, hosts of orange-and-black monarch butterflies can also be seen throughout the park. A marshland boardwalk trail winds through Point Pelee and has good observation spots along the way. Bikes and canoes can be rented at the start of the boardwalk, and there is a concession stand here. Farther into the park, the visitor center features displays of local flora and fauna.

Water cascades at the main entrance of Windsor's fashionable Casino

Windsor ❼

▦ 191,450. **✈** **✕** **▢** **▢** **ℹ** 333
Riverside Drive W. (519) 255 6530.

A CAR MANUFACTURING town, just like its American neighbor Detroit, Windsor and its factories produce hundreds of US-badged vehicles every day. Windsor has clean, tree-lined streets and a riverside walkway, but its most noted attraction is a trendy riverside Casino that draws thousands of visitors throughout the day and night. The city has many lively bars and cafés, the best of which are along the first three blocks of the main street, Ouellette. Also of interest, the nearby **Art Gallery of Windsor**, is noted for its excellent visiting exhibitions.

It is possible to relive the days when the town was a bootleggers' paradise by taking a guided tour of the Hiram Walker Distillery: during Prohibition millions of bottles of alcohol were smuggled from Windsor into the US across the Detroit River.

Contemporary painting at Windsor Art Gallery

From Windsor, it is an easy 20-km (12-mile) drive south along the Detroit River to the British-built Fort Malden at Amherstburg. Not much is left of the fort, but there is a neatly restored barracks dating from 1819, and the old laundry now holds an interpretation center. This relates the fort's role in the War of 1812 (*see pp42–43*), where the English plotted with the Shawnee to invade the US.

🏛 Art Gallery of Windsor
445 Riverside Dr. W. **(** (519) 969 4494. **○** daily. **▨** donation. **&**

London ❽

▦ 305,150. **✈** **✕** **▢** **▢** **ℹ** 300
Dufferin Ave. (519) 661 5000.

LIKEABLE LONDON sits in the middle of one of the most fertile parts of Ontario and is the area's most important town. It is home to the respected University of Western Ontario, which has a striking modern art gallery and a campus with dozens of Victorian mansions. In addition, the few blocks that make up the town center are notably refined and well tended. The finest buildings in the center are the two 19th-century cathedrals, St. Paul's, a red-brick Gothic Revival edifice built for the Anglicans in 1846, and the more ornate, St. Peter's Catholic Cathedral erected a few years later.

Canoeists alongside the boardwalk at Point Pelee National Park

Located in the northwest of the city, the Museum of Archeology focuses on the 1,100-year history of the settlement of the area. The adjacent Lawson Indian Village is a popular attraction here. This reconstruction of a 500-year-old village, once occupied by the Neutral Indians, has elm longhouses and cedarwood palisades.

Reconstruction of a 500-year-old house at Lawson Indian Village

THE UNDERGROUND RAILROAD

Neither underground nor a railroad, the name "Underground Railroad" (UGRR) was founded by abolitionists in the 1820s. The UGRR helped slaves from the southern United States to escape to both Canada and the free northern states. It was a secretive organization, especially in the South where the penalties for helping a slave to escape were severe. Slaves were moved north from safe house to safe house right up to the end of the American Civil War in 1865. Reverend Josiah Henson was one of those who escaped on the UGRR, and later founded a school for ex-slaves. Harriet Beecher Stowe's 1851 abolitionist novel *Uncle Tom's Cabin* was based on his life story.

Reverend Josiah Henson

Stratford ❾

🏛 *28,000.* 🚉 ℹ️ *88 Wellington St. (519) 271 5140.*

IN 1830, AN innkeeper called William Sargint opened the "Shakespeare Inn" beside one of the rough agricultural tracks that then crisscrossed southern Ontario. Those farmers who settled nearby called the local river the "Avon" and named the town that grew up here "Stratford," after William Shakespeare's home town.

In 1952 Tom Patterson, a local journalist, decided to organize a Shakespeare Festival. This first event was a humble affair held in a tent, but since those early days the festival has grown into one of Canada's most important theatrical seasons, lasting from May to early November and attracting over half a million visitors. The leading plays are still Shakespearean, but other playwrights are showcased too – including modern works.

Stratford is an attractive town with plenty of green lawns, riverside parks, and swans. The town is geared to visitors, offering over 250 guesthouses and several good restaurants. The visitor center produces a book with information and photographs of all the town's bed-and-breakfasts. They also organize heritage walks through the town, which pass its many historic buildings. One of the town's architectural highlights is the Victorian town hall with its towers and turrets. Stratford has a plethora of art galleries, and the central Gallery Indigena features an interesting collection of native works.

The Shakespearean Gardens along Ontario's River Avon are overlooked by Stratford's distinctive courthouse

Niagara Falls ❸

Alough the majesty rumble of the falls can be heard from miles away, there is no preparation for the sight itself, a great arc of hissing, frothing water crashing over a 52-m (170-ft) cliff amid dense clouds of drifting spray. There are actually two cataracts to gaze at as the speeding river is divided into twin channels by Goat Island, a tiny spray-soaked parcel of land. On one side of Goat Island is the Canadian Horseshoe Falls, and on the far side, across the border, is the smaller American Falls. Stunning close-up views of the falls are available from the vantage point of the Maid of the Mist boat trips. Even better is the walk down through a series of rocky tunnels that lead behind Horseshoe Falls, where the noise from the crashing waters is deafening.

American Falls
The Niagara River tumbles over the 30-m (98-ft) wide American Falls.

Rainbow Bridge
From the elegant span of the Rainbow Bridge there are panoramic views over the falls. The bridge itself crosses the gorge between Canada and the US. Here, on sunny days, rainbows rise through the spray.

Customs

Niagara Falls Museum
houses a collection of artifacts and photographs that record the attempts of adventurous individuals to ride the falls – in a kayak, a barrel, and a diving bell.

Clifton Hill
This street boasts a range of attractions. Ripley's Believe it or Not Museum features a dog with human teeth as just one of its offerings.

STAR SIGHTS
★ **Horseshoe Falls**
★ **Maid of the Mist boat trip**

VISITORS' CHECKLIST

130 km (80 miles) SW of Toronto. 🚌 from Toronto. 🚃 from Toronto. ℹ️ Niagara Falls Canada Visitor and Convention Bureau, 5515 Stanley Ave., Niagara Falls (905) 356 6061 or 1 (800) 563 2557.

★ Horseshoe Falls
Shaped like a horseshoe, these are the larger set of falls at Niagara and are some 800 m (2,625 ft) wide and 50 m (164 ft) high.

The Minolta Tower, like the Skylon Tower, offers panoramic views of the whole area. Three observation decks look out over the falls.

0 metres   250

0 yards   250

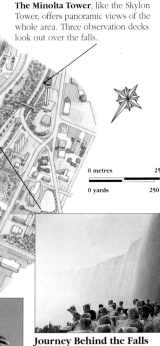

Journey Behind the Falls
An elevator from the Horseshoe Falls leads to the Journey Behind the Falls, where a series of rocky tunnels take visitors behind a wall of water so thick it blocks out daylight.

Skylon Tower
The tower has an observation deck, which gives a bird's-eye view of the falls. It is also open at night so visitors can see the floodlit waters.

★ Maid of the Mist boat trip
These intrepid vessels gets very close to the foot of the falls. Raincoats are supplied as passengers can expect to get wet on this thrilling trip.

Exploring Niagara Falls

NIAGARA FALLS IS A welcoming little town that stretches along the Niagara River for about 3 km (2 miles). Renowned as a honeymoon destination, the town is well equipped to satisfy the needs of the 14 million people who visit the falls each year. It is divided into three main sections: to the south are the falls themselves, and these are flanked by a thin strip of parkland that stretches out along the river bank as far as Clifton Hill, the glitziest street in Ontario, lined with garish amusement park attractions. To the west is the main motel strip, Lundy's Lane. To the north, on Bridge Street, lies the business district and the train and bus stations.

Horseshoe Falls
Named for their shape, the 800-m (2,625-ft) wide and 50-m (164-ft) high Horseshoe Falls are formed by the turbulent waters of the Niagara River roaring over a semicircular cliff to plunge into the bubbling cauldron below. By these means the Niagara River adjusts to the differential between the water levels of lakes Erie and Ontario, which it connects. The falls remain an awe-inspiring sight, despite the fact that the flow of the river is regulated by hydroelectric companies, which siphon off a substantial part of the river to drive their turbines. One result has been a change in the rate of erosion. By the 1900s, the falls were eroding the cliff beneath them at a rate of 1 m (3 ft) a year. Today, the rate is down to 30 cm (1 ft) a year.

The Maid of the Mist pleasure trip

🚢 Maid of The Mist
River Rd. 🅲 *(905) 358 5781.*
◯ *mid-May–Oct: daily.* 🈂️ ♿
The best way to appreciate the full force of the falls is to experience the Maid of the Mist boat trip. Boats depart from the jetty at the bottom of Clifton Hill and then struggle

upriver to the crashing waters under the falls. It is an invigorating (if wet) trip. The boat owners provide raincoats.

A wax museum and an array of other attractions at Clifton Hill

Clifton Hill
No one could say Clifton Hill is refined. This short, steep street runs up from the edge of the Niagara River gorge and is lined with a string of fast food restaurants and gaudy tourist attractions. The flashing lights and giant advertising billboards point the way to such sights as the Guinness Book of World Records, House of Frankenstein, That's Incredible Museum, Houdini's Museum and Ripley's Believe it or Not! Museum, where visitors can speak to a genie in a crystal bottle and see oddities such as a man with a greater-than-usual number of pupils in his eyes.

Great Gorge Adventure
4330 River Road. 🅲 *(905) 371 0254.*
◯ *mid-Apr–mid-Oct: daily.* 🈂️ ♿
The great force of the Niagara River's torrent is best admired from down at the bottom of the canyon. The Great Gorge

The dramatic arc of thundering waters at Horseshoe Falls

Wooden boardwalk along the Niagara River at the Great Gorge Adventure

Adventure provides this close-up view by means of an elevator and a tunnel, which lead from the top of the gorge to a riverside boardwalk. The whirlpools and rapids here are some of the most spectacular, yet treacherous, in the world.

The Old Scow

Just above the falls, stranded on the rocks in the middle of the river, is the Old Scow, a flat-bottomed barge that was shipwrecked in August 1918. It was being towed across the Niagara River by a tugboat when the lines snapped. The scow hurtled towards the falls, getting within 750 m (2,460 ft), of the brink, and the two-man crew appeared to be doomed. Luckily the boat grounded itself on this rocky ledge just in time. The crew's ordeal was, however, far from over: they had to wait another 29 hours before being finally winched to safety. The Old Scow has been rusting away on the rocks ever since.

✖ Niagara Glen Nature Reserve

3050 River Road. **[** (905) 371 0254.
◯ *daily.*
The small Niagara Glen Nature Reserve lies 7 km (4 miles) downriver from the falls. This segment of the gorge has been preserved in pristine condition, with bushes and low trees tumbling down the rocky cliffside. This is how it may have looked before the coming of the Europeans. Seven different hiking trails lead past boulders, caves, and wild flowers. The walks are easy on the way down but a steep climb on the way up.

Whirlpool Rapids

3850 River Road. **[** (905) 371 0254.
◯ *Apr–Oct: daily; Mar: Sat & Sun.* 🅿
The Niagara River makes a dramatically sharp turn about 4.5 km (3 miles) downstream from the falls, generating a vicious raging whirlpool, one of the most lethal stretches of water in the whole of North America. The effect is created when the river pushes against the northwest side of the canyon, only to be forced to turn around in the opposite direction. The most stunning view of the whirlpool rapids is from the Spanish Aero Car, a specially designed, brightly colored cable car that crosses the gorge high above the river. A different perspective of the falls can be seen from here.

✖ Niagara Parks Botanical Gardens and Butterfly Conservatory

2565 River Road. **[** (905) 371 0254.
◯ *daily.* 🅿 *for conservatory.* ⚙
The Niagara Parks Botanical Gardens are located 9 km (6 miles) downstream from the falls and comprise over 40 ha (99 acres) of beautifully maintained gardens divided into several different zones. One of the prettiest areas in summer is the rose garden, which displays over 2,000 different varieties. The extensive annual garden, which houses many rare species imported from all parts of the globe, puts on a year-round show. The gardens also include an arboretum that has examples of many different types of trees from beech and mulberry to magnolia and yew.

The butterfly conservatory is even more popular. At the beginning of a visit, a video is shown in the theater. The film explains the life cycle of a butterfly, from egg and larvae through to the emergence of the adult. The butterflies are housed in a huge heated dome that holds several thousand – one of the largest collections in the world. Visitors follow a series of pathways that pass through the dome, leading past the lush tropical flora on which the butterflies make their homes.

Butterfly at the Botanic Gardens and Conservatory

The Whirlpool Rapids are best seen from the Spanish Aero Car

Tourists get a close-up view of the magnificent frothing waters of Niagara's Horseshoe Falls ▷

Alexander Graham Bell's study at the Bell Homestead in Brantford

Kitchener-Waterloo ⑩

🚶 210,300. 🚗 🚉 ℹ️ 80 Queen
Street N. (519) 745 3536.

ORIGINALLY CALLED Berlin by
the German immigrants
who settled here in the 1820s,
the town was renamed Kitchener (after the British Empire's
leading general) during
World War I. Today, the
town is a supply center for
the surrounding farm-
ing communities
including religious
groups such as
the Mennonites
(see box). Visitors can
see the fascinating
sight of tradi-
tionally dressed
Mennonites in
their horse-drawn
buggies around **Fruit seller in Brantford**
town. These des-
cendants of German immi-
grants provide a key reason to
visit Kitchener-Waterloo. Every
year they organize the nine-day
Oktoberfest, a celebration of
German culture, with everything from sausages with sauer-
kraut to lederhosen and lager.

Brantford ⑪

🚶 85,000. ✈️ 🚗 🚉 ℹ️ 1 Sherwood
Drive (519) 751 9900.

BRANTFORD IS AN unassuming
manufacturing town that
takes its name from Joseph
Brant (1742–1807), the leader
of a confederacy of tribes
called the Six Nations. An
Iroquois chief himself, Brant
settled here in 1784. He soon
decided that the interests of
his people lay with the British,
and his braves fought alongside the Redcoats during the
American War of Independ-
ence (1775–83). Sadly, he had
chosen the losing side and,
after the war, his band was
forced to move north to
Canada, where the British
ceded the natives a piece
of land at Brantford. The
Iroquois still live in this area,
and host the Six Nations
Pow Wow, featuring tradi-
tional dances and crafts,
and held here on tribal
land every August.
Brantford is also known
for its association with
the telephone. In
1876, the first ever
long-distance call was
made from Brantford
to the neighboring
village of Paris by
Alexander Graham
Bell (1847–1922), who had
emigrated from Scotland to
Ontario in 1870. Bell's old
home has survived and, conserved as the **Bell Homestead
National Historic Museum**, is
located in the countryside on
the outskirts of town. The site
has two buildings: Bell's homestead is furnished in period
style and houses displays on
his inventions as well as telling
the story of the telephone; the
other, containing the first Bell
company office, was moved
here from Brantford in 1969.

⛪ Bell Homestead
National Historic Museum
94 Tutela Heights Rd. 📞 (519) 756
6220. 🕐 9:30am–4:30pm Tue–Sun.
⬤ Dec 25, Jan 1. 🈸 ♿

Orillia ⑫

🚶 26,000. 🚗 ℹ️ 150 Front St. S.
(705) 326 4424.

ORILLIA IS A pleasant country
town that was the home
of the novelist and humorist
Stephen Leacock (1869–1944).
Leacock's tremendously popular *Sunshine Sketches of a Little
Town* poked fun at the vani-
ties of provincial Ontario life
in the fictional town of Mari-
posa. His old lakeshore home
has been conserved as the
Stephen Leacock Museum,
containing original furnishings
as well as details of his life.
Orillia lies along a narrow
strip of water linking Lake
Couchiching to Lake Simcoe
(once a Huron fishing ground)
and is a good base from which
to cruise both lakes. On the
shore, Orillia's Centennial Park
has a marina and a long boardwalk that stretches all the way
to Couchiching beach.

🏛 Stephen Leacock Museum
50 Museum Drive, Old Brewery Bay.
📞 (705) 329 1908. 🕐 daily. 🈸 ♿

**Bethune Memorial House in the
town of Gravenhurst, Muskoka**

Muskoka ⑬

🚶 50,000. 🚗 Gravenhurst.
🚗 Huntsville. ℹ️ 295 Muskoka Rd. S.,
Gravenhurst (705) 687 4432.

MUSKOKA COMPRISES an area
north of Orillia between
the towns of Huntsville and
Gravenhurst. It comes alive in
the summer as city folk stream
north to their country cottages.
The center of this lake county
is Gravenhurst, a resort at the
south end of Lake Muskoka.

Here, a small museum is devoted to the life and work of Doctor Norman Bethune (1890–1939), who pioneered mobile blood transfusion units during the Spanish Civil War. Bethune Memorial House is the doctor's birthplace, and it has been restored and furnished in late 19th-century style.

Windsurfing off Turgean Bay Island in Georgian Bay

Georgian Bay Islands National Park ⑭

🚗 (705) 756 2415. 🚉 Midland.
🕐 daily. 🏖 summer. ♿ 🚻

THE DEEP-BLUE waters of Georgian Bay are dotted with hundreds of little islands, often no more than a chunk of rock guarded by a windblown pine. The bay is large, beautiful, and flows into Lake Huron. Sixty of its islands have been incorporated into the Georgian Bay Islands National Park. The park's center is Beausoleil Island, the hub of the area's

THE MENNONITE RELIGIOUS COMMUNITY

The Mennonite Christian sect was founded in Europe in the early 16th century. The Mennonites were persecuted because they refused to swear any oath of loyalty to the state or take any part in war. In the 17th century, a group split off to form its own, even stricter, sect. These Ammanites (or Amish) emigrated to the US and then to Ontario in 1799. The Amish own property communally and shun modern machinery and clothes, traveling around the back lanes in distinctive horse-drawn buggies and dressed in traditional clothes.

Amish couple driving a buggy

wide range of boating activities, with everything from canoeing to yachting available.

Beausoleil is also crossed by scenic hiking trails, but it is important to come properly equipped since it is a remote spot. The only way to reach the island is by water taxi from the resort of Honey Harbour. The journey takes about forty minutes. Day trips around the islands are also available.

Nottawasaga Bay ⑮

🚉 Barrie. 🚌 Wasaga Beach.
ℹ️ 550 River Rd. W., Wasaga Beach
(705) 429 2247.

PART OF SCENIC Georgian Bay, Nottawasaga Bay is one of the region's most popular vacation destinations. The Wasaga Beach resort has miles of golden sandy beach and many chalets and cottages. As well as swimming and sun-bathing there is the curious Nancy Island Historic Site,

behind Beach Area 2. The site has a museum which houses the preserved HMS *Nancy*, one of few British boats to survive the War of 1812 *(see pp42–43)*.

There are more naval relics in Penetanguishene, just to the east of Nottawasaga Bay, where Discovery Harbour is a superb reconstruction of the British naval base that was established here in 1817. Along the inlet are replicas of the barracks, blacksmiths' workshops, houses, and the original 1840 Officers' Quarters. The harbor holds a pair of sailing ships, the *Tecumseh* and the *Bee*, built to 19th-century specifications. In the summer, volunteers organize sailing trips for visitors, who are expected to lend a hand during the voyage.

To the west of Nottawasaga Bay lies Owen Sound. Once a tough Great Lakes port, this is now a quiet place with a Marine-Rail Museum devoted to the town's past. Displays include photographs of Victorian ships and sailors.

Discovery Harbour, Nottawasaga Bay's restored British naval base

Sainte-Marie among the Hurons ⑯

17th-century Iroquoian jug

Sᴀɪɴᴛᴇ-ᴍᴀʀɪᴇ ᴀᴍᴏɴɢ ᴛʜᴇ ʜᴜʀᴏɴꜱ is one of Ontario's most compelling attractions. Located 5 km (3 miles) east of the town of Midland, the site is a reconstruction of the settlement founded here among the Hurons by Jesuit priests in 1639. The village is divided into two main sections, one for Europeans (complete with a chapel and workshops), the other for Hurons, with a pair of bark-covered longhouses. Marking the boundary between the two is the small church of Saint Joseph, a simple wooden building where the Jesuits set about trying to convert the Huron to Christianity. Their efforts met with a variety of reactions, and the complex relationship between the two cultures is explored here in detail.

Exterior of Longhouse
The exterior of the longhouse had bark-covered walls built over a cedar pole frame that was bent to form an arch.

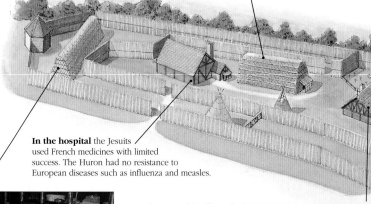

In the hospital the Jesuits used French medicines with limited success. The Huron had no resistance to European diseases such as influenza and measles.

★ Fireside Gathering
Inside the longhouse, fish, skins, and tobacco were hung from the ceiling to dry. An open fire burned through the winter. The smoke caused health problems to the Huron.

St. Joseph's Church
This is the grave site of two Jesuit priests, Jean de Bré-beuf and Gabriel Lalement, who were captured, bound to the stake, then tortured to death by the Iroquois.

Sᴛᴀʀ Fᴇᴀᴛᴜʀᴇꜱ

★ Fireside Gathering
   in Longhouse

★ Traditional Crafts

Ojibway Wigwam by the Palisades
This wigwam is built to Ojibway design and lies next to the wooden palisade which encloses the mission. It is believed that the Jesuits built these to make visiting Ojibway feel at home.

★ Traditional Crafts

The costumed guides here have been trained in the types of traditional crafts employed by both the Huron and the French, including canoe-making and blacksmith's work.

VISITORS' CHECKLIST

Hwy 12 (5 km, 3 miles east of Midland). ☎ (705) 526 7838. ◷ May–Oct: 10am–5pm daily.

The blacksmith's shop was important as Sainte-Marie needed essential items such as hinges and nails, often made by using recycled iron.

The carpenter's shop had an abundant supply of local wood, and craftsmen from France were employed by the priests to build the mission.

Interior of Chapel

The old chapel has been carefully re-created and, with the light filtering in through its timbers, it is easy to imagine what it was like for the priests as they gathered to say mass each day before dawn.

Entrance

0 meters 25

0 yards 25

Bastions helped defend the mission from attack. Built of local stone to ward off arrows and musket balls, they also served as observation towers.

The Cookhouse Garden

At Sainte-Marie, care is taken to grow crops the Huron way, with corn, beans, and squash planted in rotation. This system provided a year-round food supply, which was supplemented with meat and fish.

Goderich ⓱

🏛 7,450. ✈ ⓘ cnr Hamilton St. &
Hwy 21. 🎫 (519) 524 6600.

GODERICH IS A charming little town overlooking Lake Huron at the mouth of the River Maitland. It was founded in 1825 by the British-owned Canada Company, which had persuaded the Ontario government to part with 1 million ha (2.5 million acres) of fertile land in their province for just twelve cents an acre, a bargain of such proportions that there was talk of corruption. Eager to attract settlers, the company had the Huron Road built from Cambridge, in the east, to Goderich. The town was laid out in a formal manner, with the main streets radiating out from the striking, octagon-shaped center.

Goderich possesses two excellent museums. The first, the **Huron County Museum**, houses a large collection of antique farm implements, the most interesting of which are the cumbersome machines, such as tractors, pickers, and balers, which dominated the agricultural scene between the 1880s and the 1920s. There is also a huge, steam-driven thresher. The **Huron Historic Jail**, built between 1839 and 1842, is an authentically preserved Victorian prison. Fascinating tours are available of its dank cells, the original jailers' rooms, and the Governor's 19th-century house. The town is also renowned for its sunsets, particularly as viewed from the shore of Lake Huron.

The golden sands of Sauble Beach on the shore of Lake Huron

🚪 **Huron Historic Jail**
181 Victoria St. N. 🎫 (519) 524
2686. ⭘ May–Sep: 10am–4:30pm
Mon–Sat, 1pm–4:30pm Sun. 🅰
🏛 **Huron County Museum**
110 North St. 🎫 (519) 524 2686.
⭘ May–Sep: 10am–4:30pm Mon–
Sat, 1pm–4:30pm Sun. 🅰 ♿

Sauble Beach ⓲

⭘ Owen Sound. ⓘ RR1, Sauble
Beach (519) 422 1262, open May–Sep.

ONE OF THE finest beaches in the whole of Ontario, the golden sands of Sauble Beach stretch for 11 km (7 miles) along the shores of Lake Huron. Running behind this popular beach is a long, narrow band of campsites, cabins, and cottages. The center of the resort is at the pocket-sized village of Sauble Beach, which has a population of only five hundred. The quiet back streets of the village also offer friendly guesthouses and bed-and-breakfasts. The most attractive and tranquil camping is at Sauble Falls Provincial Park, to the north of the beach.

Lake Huron ⓳

ⓘ Sarnia, Southern shore (519) 344
7403. ⓘ Barrie, Georgian Bay (705)
725 7280. ⓘ Sault Ste. Marie, North
shore (705) 945 6941.

OF ALL THE Great Lakes, it is Lake Huron which has the most varied landscapes along its shoreline. To the south, the lake narrows to funnel past the largely industrial towns of Sarnia and Windsor on its way to Lake Erie while its southeast shore is bounded by a gentle bluff, marking the limit of one of Ontario's most productive agricultural regions. Farther north, the long, thin isthmus of Bruce Peninsula stretches out into Lake Huron, signaling a dramatic change in the character of the lakeshore. This is where the southern flatlands are left behind for the more rugged, glacier-scraped country of the Canadian Shield. This transition can be seen clearly in the area of Georgian Bay. This is an impressive shoreline of lakes, forests, beaches, and villages that attract large numbers of visitors every year. The lake's island-sprinkled waters are a popular area for water sports. Outdoor activities here include swimming, hiking, and fishing.

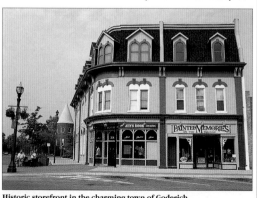
Historic storefront in the charming town of Goderich

Bruce Peninsula Tour 20

THE 100-KM (62-MILE) Bruce Peninsula divides the main body of Lake Huron from Georgian Bay and also contains some of the area's most scenic terrain. Bruce Peninsula National Park lies along the eastern shore and boasts craggy headlands and limestone cliffs with several hiking paths. Beyond the port of Tobermory, at the peninsula's tip, Fathom Five Marine National Park, comprises 19 uninhabited islands. The park is popular with divers because of its clear waters and amazing rock formations.

Tips for Drivers

Tour Route: *The route follows Hwy 6 and can be reached from Owen Sound in the south, or Tobermory in the north.*
Length: *100 km (62 miles).*
Stopping-off points: *Diving trips and tours to Flowerpot Island leave fromTobermory, which also has good accommodation.*

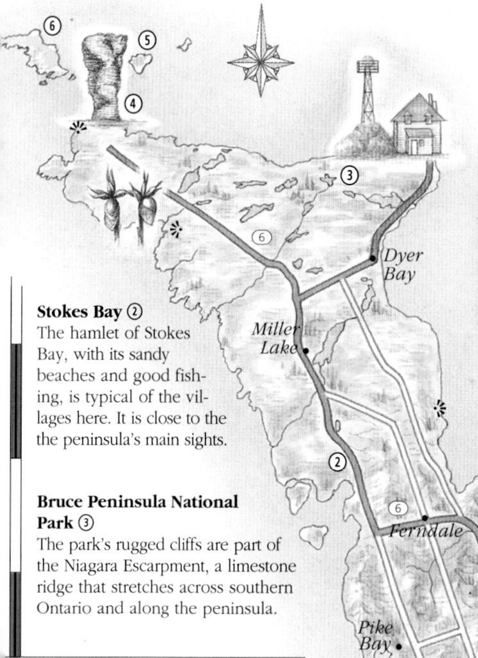
6
5
4
3
6
Dyer Bay
Miller Lake
2
6
Ferndale
Barrow Bay
1
Hope Bay
Pike Bay
6

Cape Croker 1
At the tip of Cape Croker, the Cabot Head Lighthouse and keeper's house can be reached via the scenic coast road from the village of Dyer's Bay.

Fathom Five Marine Park 6
Off the northern tip of the peninsula, the park's boundaries enclose an area around 19 islands. Divers are drawn here by the clear, calm waters and shipwrecks.

Stokes Bay 2
The hamlet of Stokes Bay, with its sandy beaches and good fishing, is typical of the villages here. It is close to the the peninsula's main sights.

Bruce Peninsula National Park 3
The park's rugged cliffs are part of the Niagara Escarpment, a limestone ridge that stretches across southern Ontario and along the peninsula.

Tobermory 4
At the northern tip of the peninsula, this small fishing village is a hub for tourist acitivities in the area. Ferries to Flowerpot Island leave from here.

Flowerpot Island 5
The only island in Fathom Five Marine Park with basic facilities, it is noted for the rock columns that dot the coastline.

0 km 5

0 miles 5

Key

Tour route

Other roads

✳ Viewpoint

Manitoulin Island ㉑

5,000. 🚌 ⓘ *Little Current (705) 368 3021.*

Hᴜɢɢɪɴɢ ᴛʜᴇ northern shores of Lake Huron, Manitoulin Island is, at 2,800 sq km (1,100 square miles), the world's largest freshwater island. A quiet place of small villages and rolling farmland, woodland, and lakes, its edges are fringed by long, deserted beaches. The lake's North Channel separates Manitoulin from the mainland, its scenic waters attracting hundreds of summer sailors, while hikers escape the city to explore the island's numerous trails.

The Ojibway people first occupied the island more than 10,000 years ago, naming it after the Great Spirit – Manitou, (Manitoulin means God's Island). First Nations peoples still constitute over a quarter of the island's population. Every August they celebrate their culture in one of Canada's largest powwows, called the Wikwemikong (Bay of the Beaver).

On the north shore, Gore Bay houses five tiny museums that focus on the island's early settlers. Nearby, the island's largest settlement is Little Current, a quiet town, where there is a handful of motels, bed and breakfasts, and restaurants.

Gore Bay on Manitoulin Island

Reflections in George Lake, Killarney Provincial Park

Killarney Provincial Park ㉒

📞 *(705) 287 2900.* 🚌 *Sudbury.* ◯ *daily.* ♿ *for some facilities.*

Kɪʟʟᴀʀɴᴇʏ ᴘʀᴏᴠɪɴᴄɪᴀʟ park is a beautiful tract of wilderness with crystal-blue lakes, pine and hardwood forests, boggy lowlands, and the spectacular La Cloche Mountains, which are known for their striking white quartzite ridges. This magnificent scenery has inspired many artists, particularly members of the Group of Seven *(see pp160–1)*, one of whom, Franklin Carmichael, saw the park as Ontario's most "challenging and gratifying landscape." The park's 100-km (62-mile) La Cloche Silhouette Trail takes between a week and ten days to complete and attracts numbers of serious hikers to its stunning views of the mountains and of Georgian Bay. Canoeists can paddle on the park's many lakes and rivers by following a network of well-marked canoe routes.

Temagami ㉓

1,000. 🚌 🚌 ⓘ *Chamber of Commerce, Lakeshore Rd. (705) 569 3344.*

Tʜᴇ ᴛɪɴʏ ʀᴇsᴏʀᴛ of Temagami and its wild surroundings have long attracted fur traders and trappers, painters, and writers, most famously Grey Owl *(see p248)*, the remarkable Englishman who posed as a Native Canadian and achieved celebrity status as a naturalist and conservationist in the 1930s. The resort sits on the distinctively shaped Lake Temagami, a deep lake with long fjords and bays as

One of Lake Temagami's numerous canoe routes

well as 1,400 islands, which are crisscrossed by numerous scenic canoe routes, hiking and mountain bike trails.

Even more remote is the Lady Evelyn Smoothwater Wilderness Park, farther to the west. The only way in is by canoe or float plane from Temagami, but the reward is some of Ontario's most stunning scenery. Much more accessible is the 30-m (98-ft) high Temagami Fire Tower lookout point, which provides panoramic views of the surrounding pine forests, and the charming Finlayson Provincial Park, a popular place to picnic and camp; both are located on Temagami's outskirts.

Sault Ste. Marie ㉔

🏙 81,500. ✕ 🚉 🚌 ℹ cnr Huron St. & Queen St. W. (705) 945 6941.

WHERE THE RAPIDS of St. Mary's River link Lake Superior to Lake Huron sits the attractive town of Sault Ste. Marie, one of Ontario's oldest European communities. The town was founded as a Jesuit mission and fur trading post by the French in 1688. Called the "Sault" (pronounced "Soo") after the French word for "rapids," the trading station prospered after 1798 when the rapids were bypassed by a canal. Since then, the canal has been upgraded time and again, and today transports the largest of container ships to the interior, thereby maintaining a thriving local economy.

Although there are regular boat trips along the canal, visitors are drawn to Sault Ste. Marie's main tourist attraction, the **Algoma Central Railway**, which offers day-long rail tours from the city into the wilderness. The train weaves north through dense forest, past secluded lakes and over yawning ravines to reach the spectacular scenery of Agawa Canyon where there is a two-hour break for lunch.

In town, the Roberta Bondar Pavilion is a huge tentlike structure decorated with murals depicting Sault's history. Named after Canada's first female astronaut, who

Canal locks at Sault Ste. Marie

was on the *Discovery* mission in 1992, the pavilion is also the venue for concerts, exhibitions, and a summer farmers' market.

🚂 Algoma Central Railway
129 Bay St. 📞 (705) 946 7300. ⏰ Jun–mid-Oct: once daily. 📷 ♿

Lake Superior ㉕

ℹ Ontario Travel Information Centre, Sault Ste. Marie (705) 945 6941.

THE LEAST POLLUTED and most westerly of the Great Lakes, Lake Superior is the world's largest body of freshwater, with a surface area of 82,000 sq km (31,700 sq miles). It is known for sudden violent storms, long a source of dread to local sailors. The lake's northern coast is a vast weather-swept stretch of untamed wilderness

dominated by dramatic granite outcrops and seemingly limitless forest. This challenging area is best experienced in Pukaskwa National Park and Lake Superior Provincial Park, both reached via the Trans-Canada Highway (Hwy 17) as it cuts a dramatic route along the lake's north shore.

Thunder Bay ㉖

🏙 114,000. ✈ ✕ 🚌 ℹ Terry Fox Information Centre, Hwy 11/17 E. (807) 983 2041.

ON THE NORTHERN shore of Lake Superior, Thunder Bay is Canada's third-largest freshwater port, its massive grain elevators dominating the city's waterfront. Grain is brought to Thunder Bay from the prairies farther west before being shipped to the rest of the world via the Great Lakes.

The town was originally established as a French trading post in 1679. These early days are celebrated at Old Fort William, a replica of the old fur trading post, with costumed traders, French explorers, and natives. Fort William was amalgamated with the adjacent town of Port Arthur to form Thunder Bay in 1970.

🏯 Old Fort William
Off Broadway Ave. 📞 (807) 473 2344. ⏰ mid-May–mid-Oct: 10am–5pm daily. 📷 ♿ partial.

Lake Superior, the world's largest freshwater lake

CENTRAL
CANADA

Exploring Central Canada

CENTRAL CANADA COVERS the provinces of Manitoba, Saskatchewan, and eastern Alberta and encompasses the most productive agricultural and energy-rich part of the country. The region is dominated by prairie, (often associated with borderless fields that stretch to the horizon) and covers a vast area of the western interior, which is the size of Mexico. The region is not all prairie, but has a variety of landscapes, from the forested aspen parkland to the west and north of the plains to the tundra of northern Manitoba and the rocky desert of the badlands in the south.

The Broadway Bridge and central Saskatoon overlook the South Saskatchewan River

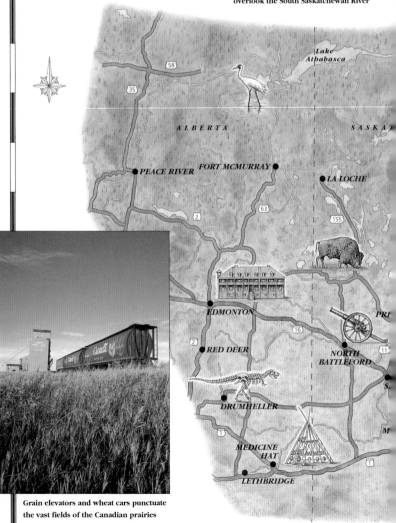

Grain elevators and wheat cars punctuate the vast fields of the Canadian prairies

GETTING AROUND

Winnipeg, Edmonton, Regina, and Saskatchewan, the four main cities of the region, are well served by public transportation, with regular air, train, and bus connections from British Columbia and other provinces. All four cities also have international airports. From Winnipeg, the Trans-Canada Highway follows the route established in the 19th century by the Canadian Pacific Railway, going 1,333 km (828 miles) west to Calgary. The more scenic Yellowhead Highway starts at the Forks in Winnipeg and runs through Yorkton and Saskatoon, reaching Edmonton at 1,301 km (808 miles), continuing on through Jasper National Park and British Columbia.

KEY

▨▨▨	Highway
▨▨▨	Major road
──	River
─ ─	Provincial boundaries

CHURCHILL ●

H u d s o n   B a y

M A N I T O B A

● LYNN LAKE

THOMPSON

106

● FLIN FLON

● THE PAS

6

60

3

10

Lake
Winnipeg

The prairies of Manitoba are one of
Canada's richest agricultural areas

0 km		150
0 miles		150

● YORKTON

● DAUPHIN

16

6

1

NA

PORTAGE
LA PRAIRIE

● WINNIPEG

SEE ALSO

• *Where to Stay* pp352–3

• *Where to Eat* pp372–3

Dinosaurs and Prehistoric Canada

IT IS EASIER TO imagine gunslingers and coyotes in the desert-like badlands of the Red Deer River Valley in Central Canada than it is to envisage the dinosaurs who once lived in this region. Over 75 million years ago the area was a tropical swamp, similar to the Florida Everglades, and the favored habitat of these huge reptiles, which dominated the Earth for some 160 million years. All the dinosaur specimens found here originate from the Cretaceous period (144–65 million years ago). Dramatic changes in the region's weather patterns, from wet and tropical to dry desert, helped to preserve an incredible number of dinosaur remains in the area. Today, the Dinosaur Provincial Park is a UN World Heritage Site.

LOCATOR MAP

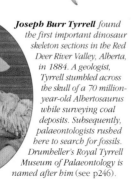

This Triceratops skull shows the dinosaur's flaring bony frill, which protected its neck from attack. Its two horns were an awesome 1 m (3 ft) long. More types of horned dinosaurs have been found here in Alberta than anywhere else.

Trained staff carefully dig out a groove around the bone while it is still in the ground. Once removed it will be carefully matched to its adjoining bone.

The Magnolia is thought to be one of Earth's first flowering plants, or angiosperms, and became widespread during the Cretaceous period.

Joseph Burr Tyrrell found the first important dinosaur skeleton sections in the Red Deer River Valley, Alberta, in 1884. A geologist, Tyrrell stumbled across the skull of a 70 million-year-old Albertosaurus while surveying coal deposits. Subsequently, palaeontologists rushed here to search for fossils. Drumheller's Royal Tyrrell Museum of Palaeontology is named after him (see p246).

An artist's re-creation of the Cretaceous landscape depicts the types of flora living at the time. Tree ferns dominated the country, and grew in large forests to heights of 18 m (60 ft). Some species still grow in the tropics.

Horseshoe Canyon lies along the Red Deer River, its high, worn hills visibly layered with ancient sediments. Ice Age glaciers eroded the layers of mud and sand that buried the remains of dinosaurs and plants. Erosion continues to form this barren, lunar landscape, exposing more bones, petrified wood, and other fossils.

This dinosaur nest on display at the Royal Tyrrell Museum was discovered at Devil's Coulee, Alberta, in 1987, and contains several embryos and eggs of the plant-eating Hadrosaur.

The Royal Tyrrell Field Station in the Dinosaur Provincial Park opened in 1987, and offers visitors interpretive displays explaining the history of the area's dinosaurs.

DINOSAUR DIG NEAR DRUMHELLER

The Royal Tyrrell Museum runs a series of different dig programs where visitors can experience the excitement of uncovering a dinosaur skeleton destined for the museum. Several trips are led by Canada's leading paleontologists, and visitors learn to use the tools of the trade, such as hammers, chisels, and brushes. Gradually uncovering fossils is a skilled business. Technicians have to record the location of every tiny piece of bone before the skeleton can be rebuilt.

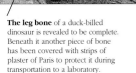

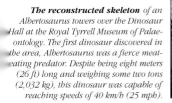

The leg bone of a duck-billed dinosaur is revealed to be complete. Beneath it another piece of bone has been covered with strips of plaster of Paris to protect it during transportation to a laboratory.

The reconstructed skeleton of an Albertosaurus towers over the Dinosaur Hall at the Royal Tyrrell Museum of Palae-ontology. The first dinosaur discovered in the area, Albertosaurus was a fierce meat-eating predator. Despite being eight meters (26 ft) long and weighing some two tons (2,032 kg), this dinosaur was capable of reaching speeds of 40 km/h (25 mph).

Canadian Mounties

Traditional Mountie

THE ROYAL CANADIAN Mounted Police are a symbol of national pride. Canada's first Prime Minister, Sir John A. Macdonald, founded the North West Mounted Police in 1873 in Ontario after violence in the west of the country (between illicit liquor dealers and local natives) reached a climax with the Cypress Hills Massacre *(see p245)*. Marching west, the Mounties reached the Oldman River, Alberta, 70 km (43 miles) west of the Cypress Hills, where they built Fort Macleod in 1874. The principal aims of the Mounties were to establish good relations with the aboriginal peoples of the Prairies and to maintain order over new settlers in the late 1800s. The Mounties won respect for their diplomacy, policing the Canadian Pacific Railroad workers and the Klondike Gold Rush in the Yukon during the 1890s. In recognition of their service they gained the Royal prefix in 1904.

The lush Cypress Hills were the site of a gruesome massacre which led to the founding of the North West Mounted Police.

The march west covered 3,135 km (1,949 miles) from Fort Dufferin, Manitoba to southern Alberta. A force of 275 men, 310 horses, and cattle, was sent to catch the illicit whiskey traders operating in the west. Battling with extreme temperatures, plagues of insects, and lack of supplies, the Mounties arrived at the Oldman River in 1874.

THE LONG MARCH

Inspector James M. Walsh sealed the Mounties' reputation for bravery when he took only six men on a parley with Sioux Chief Sitting Bull. The Sioux had retreated to the area after their defeat of US General Custer at the Battle of the Little Big Horn in 1876. Although the Sioux were the traditional enemies of the local Blackfoot and Cree Indians, there was no fighting after the arrival of the Mounties. Walsh's force succeeded in enforcing law and order across mid-west Canada, winning respect for their diplomacy. Blackfoot native chief Crowfoot praised their fairness saying, "They have protected us as the feathers of a bird protect it from winter."

Sioux Chief Sitting Bull

James M. Walsh

The adventures of the pioneering Mounties have long been a source of inspiration to countless authors and filmmakers. Square-jawed and scarlet clad, the Mountie was the perfect hero. Perhaps the best-known "Mountie" film was the 1936 "Rose Marie" starring crooner Nelson Eddy and Jeanette MacDonald.

The Skilled Horsemen of the Musical Ride are selected after two years on the force. The officers then begin seven months of intensive training.

THE MUSICAL RIDE

The Musical Ride is a thrilling spectacle of 32 riders and horses performing a series of traditional cavalry drills set to music. The drills have not changed since their original use in the British army over a century ago. Staying in tight formation, the horses do the trot, the canter, the rally, and the charge. Every summer the Ride is performed in different venues across Canada and the US.

Royal Canadian Mounted Police, Lake Louise, Canadian Rockies

As an enduring symbol of Canada the image of the Mounties has adorned everything from postage stamps and currency to this 1940s promotional tourist poster for Lake Louise in Banff National Park.

32 specially bred horses take part in the Musical Ride. A mixture of thoroughbred stallion crossed with black Hanoverian mare, the horses train for two years.

Today's Mounties are a 20,000 strong police force responsible for the enforcement of federal law across Canada. Their duties range from counting migratory birds to exposing foreign espionage. Jets, helicopters, and cars are all used by modern Mounties.

CENTRAL CANADA

CENTRAL CANADA covers a vast region of boreal forest and fertile grasslands, often known as the Prairies, which traverses Manitoba, Saskatchewan, and part of Alberta. Originally, First Nations peoples lived here, and depended on the herds of buffalo that provided them with food, shelter, and tools. By the end of the 19th century the buffalo were hunted almost to extinction. European settlers built towns and farms, some taking native wives and forming a new cultural grouping, the Métis. By the 20th century the area's economy came to rely on gas, oil, and grain. Today the Prairies, punctuated by striking, tall grain elevators, are known for the surprising variety of their landscape and the intriguing history of their towns.

SIGHTS AT A GLANCE

Historic Towns and Cities
Batoche National
  Historic Park 28
Churchill 32
Dauphin 8
Duck Lake 29
Edmonton 23
Flin Flon 31
Fort Qu'appelle 10
Gimli 5
Lethbridge 18
Maple Creek 16
Medicine Hat 17
Moose Jaw 12
North Battleford
  and Battleford 27

Portage La Prairie 6
Red Deer 21
Regina 11
Saskatoon 13
Selkirk 3
Steinbach 2
The Pas 30
Vegreville 24
Winnipeg 1
Yorkton 9

Rivers and Lakes
Lake Winnipeg 4

National and Provincial Parks
Cypress Hills Interprovincial
  Park 15
Dinosaur Provincial Park 20
Elk Island National Park 22

Grasslands National Park 14
Prince Albert National Park 26
Riding Mountain
  National Park 7
Wood Buffalo National Park 25

Museums
Royal Tyrrell Museum
  of Palaeontology 19

KEY

✈ International airport

━ Highway

━ Major road

─ Major rail routes

0 km   250

0 miles   250

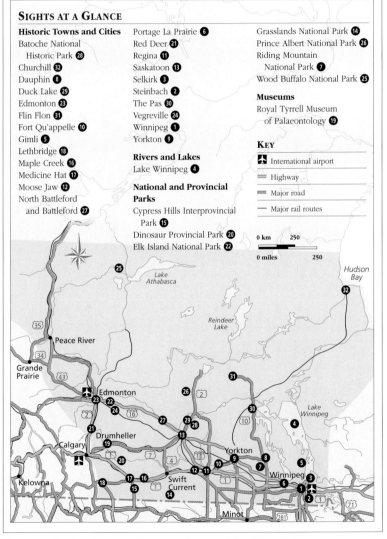

◁ A young Indian dancer in traditional costume performs a centuries-old dance in Alberta

Winnipeg ❶

WINNIPEG IS A LARGE, cosmopolitan city located at the geographic heart of Canada. Over half of Manitoba's population live here, mostly in suburbs that reflect the city's broad mix of cultures. Winnipeg's position, at the confluence of the Red and Assiniboine rivers, made it an important trading center for First Nations people going back some 6,000 years. From the 1600s Europeans settled here to trade fur. During the 1880s grain became the principal industry of the west, aided by a railroad network routed through Winnipeg. Today, this attractive city, with its museums, historic buildings, and excellent restaurants, makes for an enjoyable stay.

Exploring Winnipeg

Most of Winnipeg's sights are within easy walking distance of the downtown area. The excellent Manitoba Museum of Man and Nature and the Ukrainian Cultural Centre lie east of the Exchange District.

At the junction of the Red and Assiniboine rivers lies The Forks, a family entertainment center devoted to the city's history. At the junction of Portage and Main streets, lie the city's financial and shopping districts with their banks and malls.

🏛 St. Boniface

Cultural Centre, 340 Blvd. Provencher. 📞 (204) 233 8972. ◯ Mon–Sat. ♿ The second largest French-speaking community outside of Quebec lives in the historic district of St. Boniface. This quiet suburb faces The Forks across the Red River and was founded by priests in 1818 to care for the Métis (see p45) and the French living here. In 1844 the Grey Nuns built a hospital which now houses the St. Boniface Museum.

Priests built the Basilica of St. Boniface in 1818. Although the building was destroyed by fire in 1968, its elegant white façade is one of the city's best-loved landmarks. Métis leader Louis Riel was buried here after his execution following the rebellion at Batoche in 1881.

🏛 Manitoba Children's Museum

The Forks. 📞 (204) 956 KIDS. ◯ daily. 🎟 ♿ Located within The Forks complex, the Manitoba Children's Museum provides a series of enticing hands-on exhibits aimed at children from the ages of 3 to 11. In the All Aboard gallery children can play at being train drivers for a day on a reconstructed 1952 diesel engine while learning the history of Canada's railroad. They can also browse the internet or produce a TV show in a studio.

🏛 The Forks National Historic Site

45 Forks Market Rd. 📞 (204) 983 6757. ◯ grounds: daily; office: Mon–Fri. 🎟 special events. ♿ The Forks National Historic Site celebrates the history of the city. The river port, warehouses, and stables of this once bustling railroad terminus have now been restored.

The stable buildings, with their lofty ceilings, skylights, and connecting indoor bridges, house a flourishing market offering a wide range of specialty food, fresh produce, meat, and fish. Crafts, jewelry, and folk art are sold from the converted hayloft.

Set in 23 ha (56 acres) of parkland, The Forks

The brightly colored main entrance to the Manitoba Children's Museum

0 meters   500

0 yards   500

KEY

🚉   VIA Railroad station

🅿   Parking

ℹ️   Visitor information

Cruise boats and canoes can be hired from The Forks harbor

has an open-air amphitheater, and a tower for a spectacular six-story-high view of the Winnipeg skyline. The riverside walkway also offers splendid views of the city center and St. Boniface.

🏛 Dalnavert
61 Carlton St. 📞 *(204) 943 2835.*
🕐 *Tue–Thu, Sat, Sun.* ⬤ *Mon, Fri.*
📷 ♿
Built in 1895, this beautifully restored Victorian house is a fine example of Queen Anne Revival architecture. Its elegant red brick exterior is complemented by a long wooden veranda. The house once belonged to Sir Hugh John Macdonald, the former premier of Manitoba, and the only surviving son of Canada's first prime minister, John A. Macdonald. The interior's rich furnishings reflect the lifestyle of an affluent home in the late 19th century.

VISITORS' CHECKLIST

🏠 616,800. ✈ 12 km (8 miles) NW of city. 🚉 VIA Rail Station, cnr Main St. & Broadway. 🚌 Greyhound Canada Station, cnr Portage Ave. & Colony St. 🛈 Tourism Winnipeg, 279 Portage Ave. 📞 (204) 943 1970. 🎭 The Red River Exhibition (Jun); Folklorama (Aug); Festival Voyageur (Feb).

The Golden Boy statue adorns the dome of the Legislative Building

🏛 Legislative Building
Cnr Broadway & Osborne. 📞 *(204) 945 5813.* 🕐 *Mon–Fri for tours.* ♿
The Legislative Building is built of a rare and valuable limestone complete with the delicate remains of fossils threaded through its façade. The building is set in 12 ha (30 acres) of beautifully kept gardens dotted with statues of poets such as Robert Burns of Scotland, and Ukrainian Taras Ahevchenko, which celebrate the province's ethnic diversity.

🏛 Winnipeg Art Gallery
300 Memorial Blvd. 📞 *(204) 786 6641.* 🕐 *Tue–Sun.* 🎟 *but free Wed.*
The Winnipeg Art Gallery has the largest collection of Inuit art in the world. Over 10,000 carvings, prints, drawings, and textiles have been acquired since 1957. Especially striking is the large four-panel fabric collage wall-hanging, "Four Seasons of the Tundra" by Inuit artist Ruth Qaulluaryuk. The Gallery also contains Gothic and Renaissance altar paintings and tapestries donated by Irish peer Viscount Gore.

WINNIPEG TOWN CENTER

👑 Exchange district and Market Square

Albert St. 📞 *(204) 942 6716.*

When the Canadian Pacific Railway decided to build its transcontinental line through Winnipeg in 1881, the city experienced a boom that led to the setting up of several commodity exchanges. Named after the Winnipeg Grain Exchange, this district was soon populated with a solid array of handsome terracotta and cut stone hotels, banks, warehouses, and theaters. The Exchange District is now a National Historic Site and has been restored to its former glory. It now houses boutiques, craft stores, furniture and antique stores, galleries, artists' studios, and residential lofts.

The center of the district is Old Market Square, a popular site for staging local festivals and outdoor concerts.

🏛 Ukrainian Cultural and Educational Centre

184 Alexander Ave. E. 📞 *(204) 942 0218.* ⏰ *10am–5pm Mon–Fri, 10am–3pm Sat, 2pm–5pm Sun.* ♿

Housed in an attractive 1930s building in the Exchange District, the Ukrainian Cultural and Educational Centre celebrates the history and culture of Canada's second-largest ethnic grouping. Through its museum, gallery, and research library, the center offers a unique insight into Ukrainian history and culture.

The museum's exhibits include vibrant textiles and wood carvings, but the most popular attraction is the collection of elaborately decorated, often hand-painted, Easter Eggs, or Pysanky.

Original 19th-century walls enclose the buildings at Lower Fort Garry

👑 Lower Fort Garry

Hwy 9, nr Selkirk. 📞 *(204) 785 6050.* ⏰ *May–Sep: 10am–6pm daily.* 📷 ♿

Located 32 km (20 miles) north of Winnipeg on the banks of the Red River, Lower Fort Garry is the only original stone fur-trading post left standing in Canada. The Fort was established in 1830 by George Simpson, the governor of the Hudson's Bay Company's northern division, whose large house is now one of the fort's major attractions.

Before exploring the fort, visitors can see a film about the fort and its fur at the reception center. Several buildings have been restored, including the clerk's quarters and the store with its stacks of furs.

🏛 Royal Canadian Mint

520 Lagimodière Blvd. 📞 *(204) 257 3359.* ⏰ *May–Aug: 9am–4pm Mon–Fri.* 📷 ♿ 🚭

The Royal Canadian Mint is housed in a striking building of rose-colored glass. The mint produces more than four billion coins annually for Canadian circulation, as well as for 60 other countries including Thailand and India.

🍁 Assiniboine Park

2355 Corydon Ave. 📞 *(204) 986 5537.* ⏰ *daily.* ♿

Stretching for 153 ha (378 acres) along the south side of the Assiniboine River, Assiniboine Park is one of the largest urban parks in central Canada.

One of the park's best-loved attractions is the Leo Mol Sculpture Garden which has some 50 bronze sculptures by the celebrated local artist. The park's Conservatory offers a tropical palm house which has seasonal displays of a wide range of flowers and shrubs. The park also features an English garden, a miniature railroad, and a fine example of a French formal garden. The old refreshment pavilion is now the Pavilion Gallery, which focuses on local artists.

The Assiniboine Park Zoo contains 275 different species, specializing in cold-hardy animals from the northern latitudes and mountain ranges such as polar bears, cougars, elk, and bald eagles. The zoo houses a large statue of Winnie the Bear, which is thought to be modeled on the original Winnie the Pooh of the A.A. Milne books.

The park's numerous cycling and walking trails are popular with both visitors and locals in summer, as is cross-country skiing, skating, and tobogganing in winter.

Sculpture in the Leo Mol garden, Assiniboine park

A pink glass pyramid houses Canada's Royal Mint

Manitoba Museum of Man and Nature

OUTSTANDING DISPLAYS of the region's geography and people are imaginatively presented at this excellent museum, which opened in 1970. The visitor proceeds through chronologically organized galleries with displays that range from pre-history to the present day. Each geographical area also has its own gallery: from the Earth History Gallery, which contains fossils up to 500 million years old, to the re-creation of Winnipeg in the 1920s, including a train station, a cinema, and a dentist's office. One of the museum's biggest draws is a replica of the *Nonsuch*, a 17th-century ketch.

VISITORS' CHECKLIST

190 Rupert Ave. ☎ (204) 956 2830. 🚌 11. ◯ mid-May–Sep: 10am–6pm daily; Sep–May: 10am–4pm Tue–Fri; 10am–5pm Sat, Sun. ● Mon, Sep–May. ♿ 🅿 📷 □

KEY

- □ Orientation gallery
- □ Earth History gallery
- □ Arctic/Sub-Arctic gallery
- □ Boreal Forest gallery
- □ Grasslands gallery
- □ Discovery room
- □ Urban gallery
- □ Nonsuch gallery
- □ Hudson's Bay Company gallery
- □ Parkland/Mixed Woods gallery
- □ Temporary exhibits
- □ Nonexhibition space

Moose Diorama
A moose and her calf among the conifers of the Boreal Forest are part of a display that includes a group of Cree people rock painting and gathering food before the harsh winter sets in.

Boreal Mezzanine

Earth History Mezzanine

GALLERY GUIDE
The galleries are arranged on two levels with steps connecting to mezzanines in the Earth History and Boreal Forest galleries. Part of a three-story addition built in 1999 houses the museum's Hudson's Bay Company collection.

Main entrance

Nonsuch Gallery
This two-masted ketch, built in England in 1970, is a replica of the Nonsuch that arrived in Hudson Bay in 1688 in search of furs.

Buffalo Hunt
A Métis hunter chasing buffalo symbolizes the museum's focus on man's relationship with his environment.

Prairie fields bloom with color across Central Canada during summer ▷

Ploughing with horses at the Mennonite Heritage Village, Steinbach

Steinbach ②

⚐ 11,350. ✈ ▣ 🛈 Hwy 12N. (204) 326 9566.

ABOUT AN hour's drive southeast of Winnipeg, Steinbach is a closely knit community with impressive businesses in trucking, printing, manufacturing, and especially car dealerships. These are run largely by the Mennonites, members of a Protestant religious sect who are noted for their fair dealing.

The Mennonites arrived in Steinbach on ox-drawn carts in 1874, having fled from religious persecution in Russia. Despite not having a rail link, the town thrived as the Mennonites were good farmers and, later, car dealers (despite preferring not to use the motor car themselves). The nearby **Mennonite Heritage Village** re-creates a 19th-century Mennonite settlement with some original 100-year-old buildings and a church and school furnished to the period. Its restaurant serves home-made meals such as Mennonite borscht, a soup made with cabbage, and cream according to a traditional recipe. The general store offers locally crafted items, including Victorian candy.

🏛 **Mennonite Heritage Village**
Hwy 12 North. 🕿 (204) 326 9661.
◯ May–Sep: daily. 🎫 ♿

Steam Engine at the Mennonite Heritage Village

Selkirk ③

⚐ 9,800. ▣ 🛈 200 Eaton Ave. (204) 482 7176.

NAMED AFTER the fifth Earl of Selkirk, Thomas Douglas, whose family had an interest in the Hudson's Bay Company, Selkirk was established in 1882 when settlers arrived along the shores of the Red River. Today, on Main Street, a 7.5-m (25-ft) high statue of a catfish proclaims Selkirk as the "Catfish capital of North America." Excellent sport fishing is a year-round activity, attracting enthusiasts from across North America.

The city's main attraction is the Marine Museum of Manitoba, where six historic ships, including the 1897 S.S. *Keenora*, Manitoba's oldest steamship, have been restored.

Lake Winnipeg ④

▣ Winnipeg. 🚍 Winnipeg.
🛈 Winnipeg (204) 945 3777.

LAKE WINNIPEG is a huge stretch of water some 350 km (217 miles) long that dominates the province of Manitoba, connecting the south of the province to the north at Hudson Bay via the Nelson River. Today, the resorts that line the lake are highly popular with both locals and visitors alike.

Numerous beaches line the southeastern coast of the lake, including Winnipeg Beach, renowned for having one of the best windsurfing bays on the lake. An impressive carving of an Indian head by resident native artist Peter "Wolf" Toth stands in the local park. Called *Whispering Giant*, the wood sculpture honors the Ojibwa, Cree, and Assiniboine First Nations people of Manitoba.

Grand Beach in the **Grand Beach Provincial Park** has long powdery-white sand beaches and huge grass-topped dunes over 8 m (26 ft) high. Stretching back from the beach, the marsh, which is also known as the lagoon, is one of the park's treasures, and supports many species of birds, such as the rare and endangered Piping Plover.

Moving west from the lake, **Oak Hammock Marsh** provides an important habitat for some 280 species of birds and animals. The marsh's tall grass prairie, meadows, and aspen-oak bluffs house birds

Historic ships outside the Marine Museum of Manitoba in Selkirk

Carved cedar sculpture in the park at Winnipeg Beach

such as the ruff (a shorebird), the garganey (a duck), and the sharp-tailed sparrow.

Farther north, **Hecla Provincial Park** occupies a number of islands in the lake. A causeway links the mainland to Hecla Island, which was originally inhabited by the Anishinabe (Ojibwa) people. The first European settlers here were Icelanders who arrived in 1875. Today, the seaside village of Hecla is a pretty open-air museum featuring several restored 19th-century buildings. From Hecla there are many hiking and biking trails that lead to viewpoints for sightings of waterfowl such as great blue herons and the rare western grebe.

♣ **Grand Beach Provincial Park**
Hwy 12, nr Grand Marais. [(204) 754 2777.] daily. 🏷 🕭 partial.

♣ **Hecla Provincial Park**
Hwy 8, nr Riverton. [(204) 378 2261.] daily. 🕭

Gimli ❺

🚶 2,100. 🚌 🚹 Centre St. (204) 642 7974.

LOCATED ON the western shores of Lake Winnipeg, Gimli is the largest Icelandic community outside Iceland. The settlers arrived, having gained the rights to land, at nearby Willow Creek in 1875. They soon proclaimed an independent state, which lasted until 1897 when the government insisted that other immigrants be allowed to settle in Gimli. Today, the **New Iceland Heritage Museum** tells the story of the town's unusual history.

Gimli has a distinctly nautical atmosphere, with cobbled sidewalks leading down to a picturesque harbor and a wooden pier. At the Icelandic Festival of Manitoba, held every August, visitors can play at being Vikings, participate in games, listen to folk music, and eat Icelandic specialties.

About 25 km (15 miles) west of Gimli, the Narcisse Wildlife Management Area has been set up to preserve the habitat of thousands of red-sided garter snakes that can be seen here during the summer, on a specially designated short trail.

🏛 **New Iceland Heritage Museum**
Gimli Public School, 62 Second Ave. [(204) 642 4001.] Jul & Aug: daily; call for off-season hours. 🏷 Donation. 🕭

Portage la Prairie ❻

🚶 13,400. 🚌 🚌 🚹 11 Second St. NE (204) 857 7778.

PORTAGE LA PRAIRIE lies at the center of a rich agricultural area growing wheat, barley, and canola. The town is named after the French term for an overland detour, as Portage la Prairie lies between Lake Manitoba and the Assiniboine River, which formed a popular waterway for early travelers. Today, this thriving farming community contains the Fort La Reine Museum and Pioneer Village, on the site of the original fort built by the French explorer, La Vérendrye, in 1738. The museum offers exhibits of tools and photographs detailing 19th-century prairie life. The popular railroad display features a caboose, a watchman's shack, and the cigar-stained business car of Sir William Van Horne, founder of the Canadian Pacific Railroad. Pioneer Village successfully re-creates a 19th-century settlement with authentic stores and a church.

Statue of a Viking in the village of Gimli

Pioneer Village, part of the Fort La Reine complex at Portage la Prairie

Riding Mountain National Park ❼

Hwys 10 & 19. **(** *1 800 707 8480.*
⬤ *daily.* 📷 ♿ *partial.*

ONE OF western Manitoba's most popular attractions, Riding Mountain National Park is a vast 3,000 sq km (1,160 sq miles) wilderness. The best hiking trails and some of Manitoba's most beautiful scenery are to be found in the center of the park, where a highland plateau is covered by forests and lakes. To the east, a ridge of evergreen forest including spruce, pine, and fir trees houses moose and elk. A small herd of some 30 bison can also be found in the park near Lake Audy. Bison were reintroduced here in the 1930s after they had been hunted out at the end of the 19th century. The most developed area here is around the small settlement of Wasagaming where information on the park's network of trails for cycling, hiking, and horseback riding is available. Canoes are also available to rent for exploring the park's biggest lake, Clear Lake.

Wasagaming is the park's main settlement, and offers hotels, restaurants, and campgrounds. At nearby Anishinabe village, visitors have the opportunity to camp in traditional tipis.

One of a small herd of bison at
Riding Mountain National Park

Dauphin ❽

🏛 *8,800.* ✈ 🚆 🚌 **ℹ** *3rd Ave.*
(204) 638 4838.

A PLEASANT TREE-LINED town, Dauphin was named after the King of France's eldest son by the French explorer La Vérendrye. Located north of Riding Mountain National Park, Dauphin is a distribution-and-supply center for the farms of the fertile Vermilion River valley. The Fort Dauphin Museum in town is a replica of an 18th-century trading post. Exhibits include a trapper's birchbark canoe and several early pioneer buildings, including a school, church, and blacksmith's store.

Today, the town's distinctive onion-shaped dome of the Church of the Resurrection is a tribute to Dauphin's Ukrainian immigrants who began to arrive in 1891. A traditional Ukrainian meal, including savory stuffed dumplings (*piroggi*), forms part of a tour of the church.

Yorkton ❾

🏛 *16,700.* ✈ 🚆 **ℹ** *Jct Hwy 9 &
Hwy 16 (306) 783 8070.*

YORKTON WAS founded as a farming community in 1882, and is located in central Saskatchewan. The striking architecture of its churches, particularly the Catholic Church of St. Mary's, reflects the town's Ukrainian heritage. The church was built in 1914 and is a city landmark. Its 21-m (68-ft) high dome, icons and paintings are stunning. The Yorkton branch of the **Western Development Museum** (one of four in the province) focuses on the story of immigrants to the region.

🏛 **Western Development Museum**
Yellowhead Hwy. **(** *(306) 783 8361.*
⬤ *May–mid-Sep: daily.* 📷 ♿

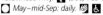
**The magnificent Dome at Saint
Mary's Catholic Church, Yorkton**

The elegant façade of Motherwell Homestead

Fort Qu'Appelle ❿

🏛 *2,000.* **ℹ** *Regina (306) 789 5099.*

NAMED AFTER an 1864 Hudson's Bay Company fur trading post, the picturesque town of Fort Qu'Appelle is located between Regina and Yorkton on Highway 10. The **Fort Qu'Appelle Museum** is built on the site of the old fort and incorporates a small outbuilding that was part of the original structure. The museum houses native artifacts such as antique beadwork and a collection of pioneer photographs.

The 430-km (267-mile) long Qu'Appelle River stretches across two-thirds of southern Saskatchewan. At Fort Qu'Appelle the river widens into a string of eight lakes bordered by several provincial parks. Scenic drives through the countryside are just one of the attractions of the valley.

About 30 km (19 miles) east of Fort Qu'Appelle is the **Motherwell Homestead National Historic Site**. Originally built by politician William R. Motherwell, this gracious stone house with extensive ornamental gardens is open to visitors. Motherwell introduced many agricultural improvements to the area and was so successful that, after living in poverty for 14 years, he rose to become agriculture minister of Saskatchewan between 1905 and 1918.

🏛 **Motherwell Homestead**
Off Hwy 22. **(** *(306) 333 2166.*
⬤ *May–Oct: daily.* 📷 ♿ *limited.*
🏛 **Fort Qu'Appelle Museum**
cnr Bay Ave. & Third St. **(** *(306)
332 6443.* ⬤ *Jul–Sept: daily.* 📷
♿ *limited.*

Regina ⑪

🚶 199,700. ✈ ⊠ 🚉 🛈 Hwy 1 E
(306) 789 5099.

REGINA IS A friendly, bustling city and the capital of Saskatchewan. The city was named for Queen Victoria by her daughter, Princess Louise, who was married to the Governor General of Canada. Regina was established in 1882 after starting life as a tent settlement called Pile O'Bones. This is a derivation of "oskana" (a Cree word meaning buffalo bones), from the piles of bones left behind after hunting.

Today, Regina is a thriving modern city whose highrise skyline contrasts with the 350,000 trees of the man-made Wascana Centre, a 930-ha (2,298-acre) urban park which contains a vast man-made lake. The lake's Willow Island is a popular site for picnics and can be reached by ferry. The park is also a haven for some 60 species of waterfowl, including large numbers of Canada geese. The **Royal Saskatchewan Museum** is housed in the park and focuses on the story of the area's First Nations peoples from earliest times to the present day. There are lectures by tribal elders on the land and its precious resources, as well as murals, sculptures, and paintings by contemporary Saskatchewan native and non-native artists.

Canadian goose in Wascana Centre Park

One of several murals on downtown buildings in Moose Jaw

The original headquarters for the North West Mounted Police lies west of the city center. Today, the Royal Canadian Mounted Police Barracks trains all Canada's Mounties and is also the site of the **RCMP Centennial Museum**. Here, the story of the Mounties is told from their beginnings following the Cyprus Hills Massacre in 1873 *(see p245)*. Among the highlights of a visit to the museum are the ceremonies and drills that are regularly performed by special trained groups of Mounties, including the Sergeant Major's Parade, the Musical Ride, and Sunset Retreat Ceremonies.

🏛 **RCMP Centennial Museum**
Dewdney Ave. W. 📞 (306) 780 5838. ◻ daily. ♿
🏛 **Royal Saskatchewan Museum**
Cnr Albert St. & College Ave. 📞 (306) 787 2815. ◻ daily. ● Dec 25. ♿

Moose Jaw ⑫

🚶 34,500. ⊠ 🚉
🛈 99 Diefenbaker Dr. (306) 693 8097.

THE QUIET TOWN of Moose Jaw was established as a railway terminus by the Canadian Pacific Railroad in 1882. A terminus for the American Soo Line from Minneapolis, Minnesota soon followed. Today, a series of murals celebrates the lives of the early railroad pioneers and homesteaders, decorating 29 buildings around downtown's 1st Avenue. Nearby, River Street has a concentration of 1920s hotels and warehouses that reflect Moose Jaw's time as "sin city" during the 1920s – when Prohibition in the United States meant that illegally produced liquor was smuggled from Canada to Chicago, by gangsters such as the infamous Al Capone.

The Moose Jaw branch of the Western Development Museum focuses on transportation, particularly the railroad.

Cadets of the Royal Canadian Mounted Police Academy in Regina are put through their paces

Traditional powwow dancer in Wanuskewin Park, Saskatoon

Saskatoon ⑬

🏙 229,750. ✈ ⊠ 🚉 🚌 ℹ 6306 Idylwyld Dr. N. (306) 242 1206.

FOUNDED IN 1882 by Ontario Methodist John Lake as a temperance colony, Saskatoon is located in the middle of prairie country. Today, the city is an agricultural and commercial hub, and a busy regional center for cattle ranchers and wheat farmers from surrounding communities. The region's history is told in Saskatoon's branch of the Western Development Museum, which focuses on the town's boom years in the 1900s, re-creating the bustling main street of a typical prairie town, including its railroad station and a hotel.

The South Saskatchewan River meanders through the city and is bounded by many lush parks, including the outstanding 120-ha (290-acre) **Wanuskewin Heritage Park**. The park is devoted to First Nations history, with many archeological sites that confirm the existence of hunter-gatherer communities some 6,000 years ago. Some of the digs are open to the public, and the excellent park interpretive center has an archeological lab explaining current research. The park's wooded hills and marshy creeks are still held to be sacred lands by the Northern Plains peoples who act as interpretive guides. Easy-to-follow trails lead the visitor past tipi rings, buffalo trails, and a buffalo jump *(see p294)*.

The riverbank also houses two fascinating museums, The Ukrainian Museum of Canada with its collection of brightly colored traditional textiles, and the Mendel Art Gallery, which houses a collection including First Nations and Inuit pottery and glassware.

🌿 **Wanuskewin Heritage Park**
Off Hwy 11. 📞 (306) 931 6767. ⭘ daily. ⬤ Good Fri, Dec 25. 🖉 limited.

Grasslands National Park ⑭

Jct Hwys 4 & 18. ℹ Val Marie (306) 298 2257. 🚌 Val Marie. ⭘ daily. ♿ partial.

SITUATED IN THE southwest corner of Saskatchewan, Grasslands National Park was set up in 1981 to preserve one of the last original prairie grasslands in North America. The park is an area of climactic extremes where summer temperatures can be as high as 40 °C (104 °F), and winter ones as low as -40 °C (-48 °F). This environment supports a range of rare wildlife, including short-horned lizards and ferruginous hawks. The rugged landscape along the Frenchman River valley is the only remaining habitat of the black-tailed prairie dog in Canada. Visitors

Black-tailed prairie dog

may hike and camp in the park, but facilities are basic.

East of the park is the striking, glacially formed landscape of the **Big Muddy Badlands**. In the early 1900s, caves of eroded sandstone and deep ravines provided hideouts for cattle thieves such as Butch Cassidy and Dutch Henry.

🏞 **Big Muddy Badlands**
Off Hwy 34. 📞 (306) 267 3312. Tours in summer from Coronach. 🖉

Buttes (isolated flat-topped hills) in the Big Muddy Badlands seen from Grasslands National Park

Cypress Hills Interprovincial Park ⑮

Hwy 41. ⓘ *(306) 662 2645.*
🚌 *Maple Creek.* ○ *daily.* ♿ *partial.*

CROSSING THE border between Saskatchewan and Alberta, the Cypress Hills Interprovincial Park offers fine views of the plains from its 1,400-m (4,593-ft) high peaks. The park's landscape is similar to the foothills of the Rocky Mountains, with its lodgepole pine forests and abundant wild flowers. Walking trails through the park offer the visitor the chance to see moose, elk, and white-tailed deer, as well as the 200 or more species of bird that stop here during migration, such as the rare trumpeter swan and mountain chickadee.

In the eastern section of the park, in Saskatchewan, **Fort Walsh National Historic Site** houses a reconstruction of Fort Walsh, which was built in 1875 by the Mounties to keep out the illicit whiskey traders who were causing trouble among the natives. Nearby, the trading posts involved in the illegal liquor trade, Farwells and Solomons, have been reconstructed. Costumed guides tell the story of the Cypress Hills Massacre.

🏛 Fort Walsh National Historic Site
Cypress Hills Interprovincial Park.
ⓒ *(306) 662 2645.* ○ *May–Oct: 9am–5pm daily.* 🎫

Maple Creek ⑯

🏚 *2,300.* 🚌 ⓘ *Hwy 1 West (306) 662 2244*

LOCATED ON THE edge of the Cypress Hills, Maple Creek is affectionately known as "Old cow town," and was established as a ranching center in 1882. The town still has a look of the Old West with trucks, trailers, and Stetson-wearing ranchers filling the downtown streets. Maple Creek's many original 19th-century storefronts include the elegant Commercial Hotel

Iron Bridge over the Oldman River, Lethbridge

with its marble-floored lobby. The oldest museum in the province, the Saskatchewan Old Timers' Museum, boasts an excellent collection of pictures and artifacts telling the story of the NWMP, the natives, and the early settlement of the area.

Medicine Hat ⑰

🏚 *46,700.* ✈ 🚌 ⓘ *8 Gekring Rd SE (403) 527 6422.*

THE SOUTH Saskatchewan River Valley is the picturesque setting for the town of Medicine Hat, the center of Alberta's gas industry. Founded in 1883, Medicine Hat is noted for Seven Persons Coulee, once a substantial native camp and buffalo jump and now one of the most important archeological sites of the northern plains. Evidence that aboriginal peoples lived here over 6,000 years ago has been garnered from finds including bones, tools, and arrowheads. Tours of the site are available.

Lethbridge ⑱

🏚 *66,050.* ✈ 🚌 ⓘ *2805 Scenic Dr. (403) 320 1222.*

COAL, OIL, AND gas are the basis of Lethbridge's success. Alberta's third-largest city was named after mine-owner William Lethbridge in 1885, but First Nations peoples such as the Blackfoot Indians have inhabited the area since prehistoric times.

Lying on the banks of the Oldman River, Lethbridge is home to the notorious Fort Whoop-up, established in 1869 by whiskey traders John Healy and Alfred Hamilton for the sole purpose of profiting from the sale of illicit, and often deadly, whiskey. Many Indians, drawn by the lure of the drink, were poisoned or even killed by the brew, which was made with substances such as tobacco and red ink. Today, a replica of Fort Whoop-up has a visitor's center that describes the history of the trading post.

Two Assiniboine Indians from an engraving made in 1844

CYPRESS HILLS MASSACRE

On June 1, 1873 a group of whiskey traders attacked an Assiniboine camp, killing several women, children, and braves in retaliation for the alleged theft of their horses by natives. Many native people had already died from drinking the traders' liquor, which was doctored with substances such as ink and strychnine. The massacre led to the formation of the North West Mounted Police. Their first post at Fort Macleod in 1874, and another at Fort Walsh in 1875, marked the end of the whiskey trade and earned the Mounties the natives' trust.

Royal Tyrrell Museum of Palaeontology ⓳

The museum's Albertosaurus logo

THE OUTSTANDING Royal Tyrrell Museum of Palaeontology was opened in 1985 and is the only museum in Canada devoted to 4.5 billion years of the Earth's history. The layout of the exhibits enables visitors to follow the course of evolution through displays of dinosaurs and fossils from different ages. The museum uses interactive computers, videos, and 3-dimensional dioramas to re-create distinct prehistoric landscapes, bringing the age of the dinosaurs to life.

VISITORS' CHECKLIST

Hwy 858, 6 km NW of Drumheller.
📞 (403) 823 7707. ✈ Calgary.
🕐 May–Aug: 9am–9pm daily; Sep & Oct: 10am–5pm daily; Nov–Apr: 10am–5pm Tue–Sun. 🎫 📷 ♿ ♿

KEY

- ☐ Science hall
- ☐ Extreme theropod
- ☐ Discoveries
- ☐ Burgess Shale
- ☐ Dinosaur hall
- ☐ Bearpaw sea
- ☐ Age of reptiles
- ☐ Age of mammals
- ☐ Palaeoconservatory
- ☐ Terrestrial Palaeozoic
- ☐ Nova Discovery room
- ☐ Pleistocene gallery
- ☐ Nonexhibition space

Dinosaur Hall
In Dinosaur Hall, a T-rex towers over a display of some 35 complete dinosaur skeletons.

The "Introducing Fossils" part of this gallery explains fossils and their formation, from fossilized tree sap (amber) to natural molds and 500-million-year-old casts.

MUSEUM ORGANIZED DINOSAUR DIGS

Visitors on a dinosaur dig

Most of the Royal Tyrrell Museum's dinosaur remains have been found in the Alberta Badlands, a barren landscape of fluted gullies and steep bluffs. There is a variety of tours of the area, ranging from 2-hour Dig Watches to camps lasting a week or more. Participants may help the Museum paleontologists to uncover fossils and dinosaur bones.

GALLERY GUIDE

The collection is housed on several levels reached by a series of ramps. Each area contains a display on an era of geological time. Introductory exhibits on fossils and dinosaurs are followed by displays on prehistoric mammals and the Ice Ages. The largest and most popular part of the museum is the Dinosaur Hall.

Albertosaurus
A fossilized Albertosaurus was found in 1884, in the Drumheller Valley, by the museum's namesake, Dr. J.B. Tyrrell. A cousin to the meat-eating T-rex, this reptile was a fierce hunter.

Elk Island National Park's largest lake, Astotin Lake, is skirted by a popular hiking trail

Dinosaur Provincial Park ⓴

Rte 544. **☎** (403) 378 4342. ○ daily. 🖼 ♿ partial.

Two hours' drive southeast of the town of Drumheller, the UNESCO World Heritage Site of Dinosaur Provincial Park, established in 1955, contains one of the world's richest fossil beds. Located along the Red Deer River Valley, the park includes dinosaur skeletons mostly from the Cretaceous period, between about 144 and 66.4 million years ago (see pp228–9). More than 300 significant finds have been made here and more than 30 institutions worldwide have specimens from this valley on display.

From the town of Drumheller it is possible to tour the 48-km (30-mile) loop **Dinosaur Trail**, which takes visitors through the "Valley of the Dinosaurs" and features fossils and displays relating to prehistoric life, as well as stunning views of the strange badlands landscape from highpoints such as Horseshoe Canyon.

🏞 Dinosaur Trail
ℹ Drumheller (403) 823 1331.

Red Deer ⓴

🏃 63,100. 🚌 ℹ Heritage Ranch, Hwy 2: (403) 346 0180.

Located midway between Calgary and Edmonton, this bustling city was founded in 1882 by Scottish settlers as a stopover point for travelers. A modern city with good cultural and recreational facilities, Red Deer is the hub of central Alberta's rolling parkland district. The city has some interesting buildings, such as the award-winning St. Mary's Church, and the landmark Water Tower, known as the "Green Onion." The city's beautiful reserve of Waskasoo Park is located along the Red River.

Elk Island National Park ⓴

Hwy 16. **☎** (780) 992 2950. ○ daily. 🖼 ♿ partial.

Established in 1906 as Canada's first animal sanctuary, Elk Island became a national park in 1913. It offers a wilderness retreat only half-an-hour's drive from Edmonton. This 194 sq km (75 sq miles) park is exceptional for providing a habitat for large mammals such as elk, the plains bison, and the rarer, threatened wood bison. The park's landscape of transitional aspen parkland (an area of rolling meadows, woodlands, and wetlands) is, according to the World Wildlife Fund for Nature, one of the most threatened habitats in North America.

Aspen trees grow mostly on the hills, while balsam, poplar, and white birch grow near wet areas. Plants such as sedges and willows also thrive in the wetlands alongside a host of birds such as the swamp sparrow and yellow warbler.

Elk Island is a popular day trip from Edmonton as well as being a picturesque weekend picnic spot for locals. There are 13 hiking trails of varying difficulties and lengths. During the summer a wide range of activities is available in the park including swimming, canoeing, and camping. Cross-country skiing is the most popular winter activity.

Hoodoos, towers of rock sculpted by glacial erosion, near Drumheller

Ice Palace at West Edmonton Mall

Edmonton ❷❸

🏛 890,000. ✈ ⊠ 🚌 🚏 🛈
9797 Jasper Ave. (780) 496 8400.

E DMONTON SPANS the valley of the North Saskatchewan River and sits in the center of Alberta province, of which it is the capital. Established as a series of Hudson's Bay Company trading posts in 1795, this city is now the focus of Canada's thriving oil industry.

Edmonton's downtown area is centered on Jasper Avenue and Sir Winston Churchill Square, where modern glass high-rises sit among shops and restaurants. Without doubt the main attraction in Edmonton is the gigantic **West Edmonton Mall**. Billed as the world's largest shopping center, it contains over 800 stores and services, an amusement park, over 100 restaurants, a water park with its own beach and waves, a golf course, and an ice rink. In contrast, downtown also houses one of Alberta's oldest buildings, the delightful Alberta Legislature, which was opened in 1912. Overlooking the river, on the site of the old Fort Edmonton, the building has beautifully landscaped grounds filled with fountains.

Southwest of downtown, Fort Edmonton Park re-creates the original Hudson's Bay Company fort with reconstructions of street areas in 1885 and 1920. Here visitors can experience past times, wandering around original shops and businesses, as well as taking rides on a horse-drawn wagon, steam train, or street car.

🎡 **West Edmonton Mall**
170th St. & 87th Ave. 🄲 (780) 444 5200. ◯ daily. ♿

Vegreville ❷❹

🏛 5,300. 🚏 🛈 at giant Pysanka (780) 632 6800.

A LONG THE Yellowhead Hwy, heading eastward from Edmonton, lies the predominantly Ukrainian town of Vegreville. Its community is famous for producing traditionally Ukrainian, highly decorated Easter eggs (*or pysanki*). Clearly visible from the road there is a fabulously decorated giant pysanka covered with intricate bronze, gold, and silver designs that tell the story of the region's Ukrainian settlers, and celebrates their religious faith, bountiful harvests, and the protection they received from the RCMP. The egg is 7 m (23 ft) high, and is made of over 3,500 pieces of aluminum.

A giant decorated Easter egg made by Ukrainians at Vegreville

Wood Buffalo National Park ❷❺

main access: Fort Smith, NWT.
🄲 (867 872 7900). ◯ daily. 📷

T HE LARGEST national park in Canada, Wood Buffalo National Park is about the size of Denmark, covering an area of 44,807 sq km (17,474 sq miles). The park was made a UNESCO World Heritage Site in 1983 because of the range of habitat it offers for such rare species of animal as the wood bison or buffalo.

There are three different environments here: fire-scarred forest uplands; a large, poorly drained plateau filled with streams and bogs; and the Peace-Athabasca delta, full of sedge meadows, marshes, and shallow lakes. Sightings of such birds as peregrine falcons and bald eagles are common, and the park is the only natural nesting site of the rare whooping crane in the world.

THE GREY OWL STORY

Long before conservation became popular, the renowned naturalist by the name of Grey Owl, took up the cause. Inspired by his Mohawk wife, Anahareo, he wrote the first of several best-selling books, *Men of the Last Frontier*, in 1931, the same year he became the official naturalist of Prince Albert National Park. He built a cabin on the peaceful shores of Lake Ajawaan from where he ran a beaver protection program.

When Grey Owl died of pneumonia in 1938, there was uproar when a newspaper discovered that he was really an Englishman. Born in Hastings in 1888, Archibald Stansfield Belaney took on the identity of Grey Owl when he returned to Canada after World War I. He wore buckskins and wore his hair in Apache-style braids. A generation later Grey Owl's legacy remains the protection of Canada's wildlife.

Grey Owl feeding a beaver

Prince Albert National Park ㉖

ESTABLISHED IN 1927, Prince Albert National Park covers 3,875 sq km (1,500 square miles) of wilderness, which changes from the gently rolling terrain of aspen parkland in the south to the spruce and fir trees of the northern boreal forest. These distinct environments house different wildlife populations, with moose, wolf, and caribou in the forests, and elk, bison, and badger in the parkland. The center of the park, and the most accessible areas for visitors, are the hiking and canoeing trails around the Kingsmere and Waskesiu Lakes. The townsite of Waskesiu is the best place from which to begin exploring the park.

KEY

━━ Major road

══ Minor road

▪▪ Hiking route

── Rivers

⚠ Camping

🏕 Picnic area

ℹ Visitor information

♨ Viewpoint

Grey Owl's cabin by Ajawaan Lake
A popular hike in the park leads to Grey Owl's log cabin, "Beaver Lodge."

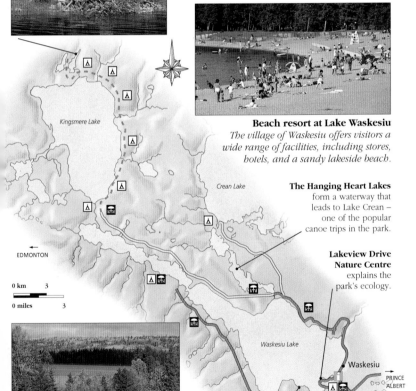

Kingsmere Lake

Crean Lake

Waskesiu Lake

Waskesiu

EDMONTON ←

→ PRINCE ALBERT

0 km 3

0 miles 3

Beach resort at Lake Waskesiu
The village of Waskesiu offers visitors a wide range of facilities, including stores, hotels, and a sandy lakeside beach.

The Hanging Heart Lakes
form a waterway that leads to Lake Crean – one of the popular canoe trips in the park.

Lakeview Drive Nature Centre
explains the park's ecology.

Kingfisher trail is a popular 13-km (8-mile) walk by Waskesiu lake.

View over Waskesiu Lake
Fall foliage across the boreal forest seen around the lake from Kingsmere Road.

Gun with carriage at Fort Battleford National Historic Site

North Battleford and Battleford ㉗

🚶 *19,500.* 🚌 ℹ️ *Visitors' center, jct Hwys 16 & 40 (306) 445 2000.*

THE COMMUNITIES of North Battleford and Battleford, together known as The Battlefords, face each other across the North Saskatchewan River Valley. Named after a ford in the Battle River, the area was the site of age-old conflicts between the Blackfoot and Cree. An important early settlement in the West, Battleford was chosen as the seat of the North-West Territories government from 1876 to 1882. Today, the communities are thriving industrial centers, although the North Battleford branch of the Western Development Museum focuses on the rural life of the prairies.

One of the most popular attractions in The Battlefords is the **Allan Sapp Gallery**,

housed in the old municipal library. Allan Sapp is one of Canada's best-loved contemporary artists. His work celebrates the traditions of the Northern Plains Cree community in simple, delicately colored paintings and drawings.

Across the river, just south of Battleford, the **Fort Battleford National Historic Site** contains a well-restored North-West Mounted Police post. The stockade has original buildings such as the Sick Horse Stable, where the Mounties' horses were taken to recover from the rugged life of the prairies. Costumed guides tell the story of the time when 500 settlers took refuge in the stockade during the North-West Rebellion.

🏛️ **Allan Sapp Gallery**
1091 100th St. ℂ *(306) 445 1760.* ○ *1pm–5pm daily.* ♿ *limited.*
⛺ **Fort Battleford National Historic Site**
Off Hwy 4. ℂ *(306) 937 2621.* ○ *mid-May–mid-Oct: daily.* 📷 ♿

Batoche National Historic Park ㉘

Rte 225 off Hwy 312. ℂ *(306) 423 6227.* ○ *May–Oct: daily.* 📷 ♿

THE ORIGINAL village of Batoche was the site of the Métis's last stand against the Canadian Militia, led by Louis Riel and Gabriel Dumont in 1885 *(see p45).*

From the 17th century, white fur traders in the west had married Indian wives and adopted tribal languages and customs. The resulting mixed raced peoples, known as the Métis, had originally rebeled in 1869 in the Winnipeg area when it seemed the federal government might deprive them of their land rights. When history began to repeat itself in 1885, Métis rebels recalled Riel from exile in Montana to declare a provisional government at Batoche. Violence erupted on May 9, 1885 into what was to become known as the North-West Rebellion. Riel surrendered, was tried for treason, and hanged in Regina.

Today, the Batoche National Historic Park occupies the site of the village and battlefield. The 648-ha (1,600-acre) park houses the bullet-ridden St. Antoine de Padou Church and Rectory as well as the cemetery where the Métis leaders are buried. An interpretive center features an audio-visual presentation telling the history of Batoche and the rebellion through the eyes of the Métis.

St. Antoine de Padou Church and Rectory at Batoche National Historic Park

POLAR BEARS

Known as the "Lord of the Arctic," the magnificent polar bear can weigh as much as 650 kg (1,433 lb). In the fall the bears begin to congregate along the bay east of Churchill waiting for ice to form in order to hunt seals. Their acute sense of smell can detect a scent up to 32 km (20 miles) away and pick up the presence of seals under 1 m (3 ft) of snow and ice.

Up to 150 bears pass by and through Churchill during the season. The best way to view them is in a tundra buggy, a large buslike vehicle that is warm, safe, and elevated over 2 m (6.5 ft) from the ground.

The majestic polar bear

Duck Lake ㉙

🏚 670. 🚗 ℹ️ 301 Front St. (306) 467 2277.

A LITTLE TO THE WEST of the small farming village of Duck Lake lies a plaque commemorating the first shots fired in the North-West Rebellion. On March 26, 1885, a police interpreter and a Cree emissary scuffled during a parley, and the officer was killed. During the ensuing battle, 12 NWMP officers and six Métis died. The Battle of Duck Lake is depicted in a series of murals at the town's visitors' center.

The Pas ㉚

🏚 5,900. 🚗 ✈️ ℹ️ 324 Ross Ave. (204) 623 7256.

ONCE A KEY fur-trading post dating back some 300 years, The Pas is now a major industrial distribution and transportation center for Manitoba's northwest. Nearby Clearwater Lake Provincial Park is named for the lake itself, which is said to be so clear that it is possible to see the bottom at 11 m (35 ft). The park also offers a walking trail through "the caves," a geological phenomenon where rock masses split away from shoreline cliffs to create huge crevices that provide shelter for a number of animals, including black bears, squirrels, and weasels.

Flin Flon ㉛

🏚 7,200. ✈️ 🚗 ℹ️ Hwy 10A (204) 687 4518.

STEEP HILLY STREETS reflect the fact that Flin Flon lies on Precambrian rock (as old as the formation of the Earth's crust itself, roughly 3.8 billion years ago), and the area is famous for its distinctive greenstone. The town bears the name of a fictional character of a popular novel, *The Sunless City* by J.E.P. Murdock. The book was read by a prospector at the time he staked his claim here in 1915. Copper and gold are still mined in Flin Flon, but visitors mostly come to experience the vast wilderness of the nearby Grass River Provincial Park.

The distinctive Grass River, where strings of islands dot the countless lakes of the river system, has been a trade route for centuries, used by both natives and, later, European explorers and fur traders to travel from the northern forests to the prairies. Today, visitors may follow the historic route on guided canoe tours as well as fishing for northern pike, lake trout, turbot, and perch.

Churchill ㉜

🏚 1,100. ✈️ 🚗 ℹ️ 211 Kelsey Blvd. (204) 675 2022.

LOCATED AT THE mouth of the Churchill River on Hudson Bay, the town retains the look of a basic pioneer town, with no luxury hotels, no paved roads, and few trees. This vast Arctic landscape is snow-free only from June through to the end of August. Churchill has no road access and can be reached only by plane or train from Winnipeg, Thompson, and The Pas. Despite its remote situation, Churchill was an important point of entry into Canada for early European explorers and fur traders arriving by boat in the 18th century. The Hudson's Bay Company established an outpost for fur-trading here in 1717.

Today, visitors come to see the polar bears, beluga whales, and the splendid array of tundra flora in this region. In the spring and fall the tundra's covering of moss, lichens, and tiny flowers bursts into an array of reds, violets, and yellows. In the summer beluga whales move upriver to the warmer waters and can be seen from boat trips or on scuba dives.

Polar bear warning sign near Churchill

BRITISH COLUMBIA AND THE ROCKIES

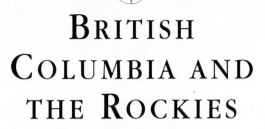

Introducing British Columbia and the Rockies

THE DRAMATIC BEAUTY OF British Columbia and the Rockies' mountain ranges, forests, and lakes make it a much visited area. There is a wide variety of landscapes available here, from the northern Rockies with their bare peaks, to the south's Okanagan Valley with its orchards and vineyards. The region's temperate climate means that BC has more species of plant and animal than anywhere else in the country.

Millions of visitors come here every year, drawn by a wide range of outdoor activities. To the west, Vancouver Island offers ancient rainforest and the impressive coastal scenery of the Pacific Rim National Park. Lying between the Pacific Ocean and the Coast Mountains, Vancouver is a stunningly attractive city, with good transportation links to the rest of the region, including Calgary in the east.

Centuries-old rainforest in the Gwaii Haanas National Park on the Queen Charlotte Islands

Illuminated by 3,000 lights, Victoria's Parliament Buildings are reflected in the waters of Inner Harbour on Vancouver Island

SEE ALSO

• **Where to Stay** pp355–59

• **Where to Eat** pp375–79

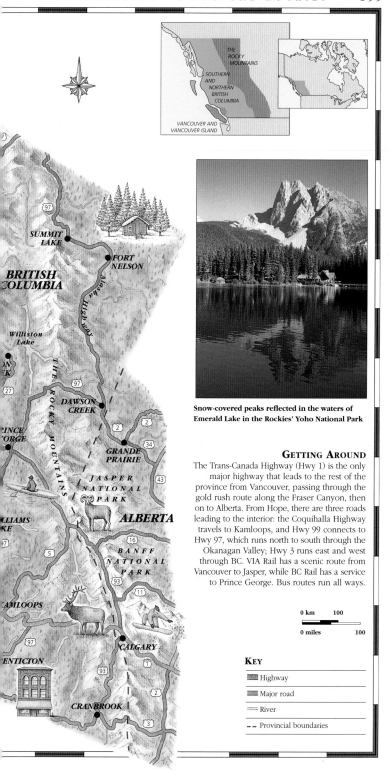

Snow-covered peaks reflected in the waters of Emerald Lake in the Rockies' Yoho National Park

GETTING AROUND

The Trans-Canada Highway (Hwy 1) is the only major highway that leads to the rest of the province from Vancouver, passing through the gold rush route along the Fraser Canyon, then on to Alberta. From Hope, there are three roads leading to the interior: the Coquihalla Highway travels to Kamloops, and Hwy 99 connects to Hwy 97, which runs north to south through the Okanagan Valley; Hwy 3 runs east and west through BC. VIA Rail has a scenic route from Vancouver to Jasper, while BC Rail has a service to Prince George. Bus routes run all ways.

0 km   100

0 miles   100

KEY

▨ Highway

▨ Major road

═ River

‑ ‑ Provincial boundaries

The Rocky Mountains

Orchid found
in the Rockies

THE CANADIAN ROCKY MOUNTAINS are a younger section of the Western Cordillera, a wide band of mountain ranges that stretch from Mexico to Canada. Formed between 120 and 20 million years ago, they include some of Canada's highest peaks, the 389-sq km (150-sq mile) Columbia Icefield, and glacial lakes. In summer wild flowers carpet the alpine meadows; in winter both visitors and locals take advantage of the snow-covered slopes to indulge in winter sports. The flora and fauna of the Canadian Rockies are protected within several National Parks; the most noted being Banff, Jasper, and Yoho (see pp298–309), which houses the renowned Burgess Shale fossil beds.

LOCATOR MAP

▨ *The Canadian Rockies*

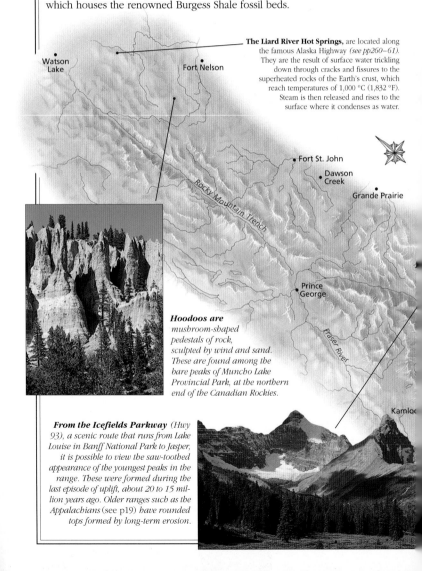

The Liard River Hot Springs, are located along the famous Alaska Highway (see pp260–61). They are the result of surface water trickling down through cracks and fissures to the superheated rocks of the Earth's crust, which reach temperatures of 1,000 °C (1,832 °F). Steam is then released and rises to the surface where it condenses as water.

Watson Lake

Fort Nelson

Fort St. John

Dawson Creek

Grande Prairie

Rocky Mountain Trench

Prince George

Fraser River

Kamlo

Hoodoos are *mushroom-shaped pedestals of rock, sculpted by wind and sand. These are found among the bare peaks of Muncho Lake Provincial Park, at the northern end of the Canadian Rockies.*

From the Icefields Parkway *(Hwy 93), a scenic route that runs from Lake Louise in Banff National Park to Jasper, it is possible to view the saw-toothed appearance of the youngest peaks in the range. These were formed during the last episode of uplift, about 20 to 15 million years ago. Older ranges such as the Appalachians (see p19) have rounded tops formed by long-term erosion.*

***Maligne Canyon** is a 50-m deep (164-ft), limestone gorge in Jasper National Park. The canyon was formed by the melt-waters of a glacier that once covered the valley. Today, the Maligne River rushes through this narrow channel, which also drains a series of underground caves.*

***The Lewis Overthrust** in Waterton Lakes National Park is a geological phenomenon. When rocks were moving east during the formation of the Rockies, a single mass composed of the lowest sedimentary layer of the Rockies – known as the Lewis Thrust – came to rest on top of the prairies.*

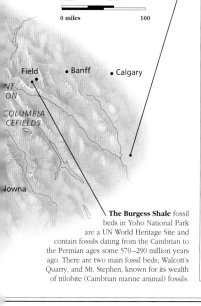

0 km   100

0 miles   100

Field   • Banff   • Calgary

NT
ON

COLUMBIA
CEFIELDS

lowna

The Burgess Shale fossil beds in Yoho National Park are a UN World Heritage Site and contain fossils dating from the Cambrian to the Permian ages some 570–290 million years ago. There are two main fossil beds; Walcott's Quarry, and Mt. Stephen, known for its wealth of trilobite (Cambrian marine animal) fossils.

THE FORMATION OF THE ROCKY MOUNTAINS

There are three main forces responsible for the formation of the Rocky Mountains. First, large areas of the Earth's crust (known as tectonic plates), constantly moving together and apart, created uplift. Second, the North American plate was subducted by the Pacific plate, which caused a chain of volcanoes to form from the molten rock of the oceanic crust. Third, erosion caused by the Ice Ages, as well as rivers and wind, deposited sedimentary rocks on the North American plate, which was then folded by more plate movement between 50 and 25 million years ago. The Rockies' jagged peaks reflect their recent formation.

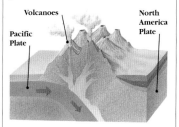

Volcanoes   North America Plate

Pacific Plate

1 Some 150 million years ago, the Pacific plate moved east, adding to the molten rock from great depths of the North American Plate. This then rose up to form the Western Cordillera Mountains.

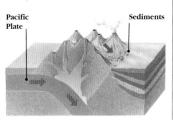

Pacific Plate   Sediments

2 The Cordillera was eroded over millions of years and during various Ice Ages. This led to sediments being deposited in the sagging, wedge-shaped crust east of the mountain range.

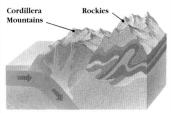

Cordillera Mountains   Rockies

3 Around 50 million years ago, the Pacific plate continued to push east, forcing the Cordillera range eastward, compressing sedimentary rocks, folding and uplifting them to form the Rockies.

Forestry and Wildlife of Coastal British Columbia

FROM ITS SOUTHERN BORDER with the United States to the northern tip of the Queen Charlotte Islands, the coastal region of British Columbia ranks as the richest ecological region in Canada. The warm waters of the north Pacific Ocean moderate the climate, creating a temperate rainforest teeming with life such as the black tail deer, black bear, and cougar. Dense forest still covers many islands, bays, and inlets along the coast, and is home to a large number of plant and animal species, including some of the tallest trees in Canada. Douglas Fir and Sitka Spruce can grow as high as 91 m (300 ft).

Trumpeter swans are so-called for their distinctive brassy call. They are found on marshes, lakes, and rivers.

TEMPERATE RAINFOREST HABITAT
High rainfall and a mild climate have created these lush forests of cedar, spruce, and pine, with their towering Douglas Firs and Sitka Spruces. Housed beneath the dripping forest canopy is a huge variety of ferns, mosses, and wild flowers, including orchids. Today, environmentalists campaign to protect these ancient forests from the threat of logging.

Bald eagles, with their distinctive white heads, can be seen in large numbers diving for fish in the ocean near the Queen Charlotte Islands. The area is noted for having the largest bald eagle population in BC.

The white black bear is unique to coastal British Columbia. It is related to the common black bear, and is an agile salmon catcher.

Harlequin ducks are small and shy, and the males have striking markings. A good swimmer, the harlequin enjoys fast-flowing rivers and the strong surf of the Pacific.

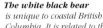

Black tail deer are found only on the north Pacific coast. They are the smallest member of the mule deer family and are preyed on by cougars in the area.

SALMON

The coastal waters of BC are home to five species of Pacific salmon: pink, coho, chinook, sockeye, and chum. Together they support one of the most important commercial food fisheries in the world. All Pacific salmon spawn in freshwater streams only once in their adult life, then die. Their offspring migrate downstream and out to sea where they feed and grow to adults ranging in size from 7 kg (15 lb) to over 45 kg (100 lb). At maturity they swim long distances upstream in order to return to the waters of their birth.

Chinook Salmon leaping while swimming upstream to spawn.

Sockeye Salmon are highly prized in BC's fishing industry for their firm, tasty flesh.

COASTLINE HABITAT

The warm waters of the north Pacific Ocean provide a habitat for more species of wildlife than any other temperate coastline. This distinctive region is characterized by having thousands of islands and inlets, which provide a home for a range of animals. Mammals such as gray, humpback, and orca whales can be seen here, as can sea otters, seals, and sea lions.

Northern sea lions live in colonies along the rocky BC coast. Large, lumbering animals, they have short "forearms" that enable them to move on land.

The glaucous gull is a large, gray-backed sea gull, which nests along coastal cliffs, and on the numerous small islands here.

Killer whales (or orcas) are found off the sheltered eastern coast of Vancouver Island and up BC's mainland coast. They are known as "killer" because they feed on other mammals.

Sea otters were hunted, almost to extinction, for their thick fur coats. Today, these playful creatures are numerous off the coast of mainland BC and Vancouver Island.

The Alaska Highway

T HE BUILDING of the Alaska Highway was an extraordinary achievement. Winding through 2,451 km
(1,523 miles) of wilderness, mountains, muskeg (moss-
covered bog), and forest, the first road was completed
in 1942, only eight months and twelve days after construction began. Linking the United States to Alaska
through British Columbia, it was built after the Japanese
attacked Pearl Harbor in 1941, as a military supply
route and to defend the northwest coast of Alaska.

Today, the original gravel road has been replaced
by a two-lane, mostly asphalt highway. The highway's
many curves are gradually being
straightened, shortening its total
length, and the present road now
covers 2,394 km (1,488 miles).

LOCATOR MAP

■ *Map area*

Kluane National Park *contains some of
the most dramatic scenery to be seen along
the highway. The Kluane Mountains are
among the highest in Canada, and icefields cover around half of the park's area.*

Whitehorse *is the
capital of the Yukon
and the center of the
province's forestry
and mining indus-
tries. The town, at
mile 910 of the high-
way, retains a frontier
atmosphere, and it is
still possible to hear
coyotes at night.*

Historical Mile 836
marks the site of the
Canol Project. This oil
pipeline was built
alongside the highway,
to aid the military
effort. The pipe runs
an incredible 965 km
(600 miles) to an oil
refinery at Whitehorse.

Teslin Lake *derives its name from the
Tlingit language, meaning "long and
narrow waters." The highway follows
the 130-km long (80-mile) stretch of
water, lined by snow-capped peaks.
Today, the area attracts anglers eager to
catch the plentiful trout, grayling, and
pike, and hunters looking for game.*

The Alaska Highway in winter is often covered in snow and affected by frost heave. Since it was opened to the public in 1949, teams of maintenance workers have ensured that the road is open year round.

CONSTRUCTION OF THE HIGHWAY

The Alaska Highway was built in under nine months by US army engineers and Canadian construction workers. The recruiting poster for workers warned: "This is no picnic... Men will have to fight swamps, rivers, ice, and cold. Mosquitoes, flies, and gnats will not only be annoying but will cause bodily harm. If you are not prepared to work under these... conditions, DO NOT APPLY."

The workers shared mobile army camps that were moved along the route as construction progressed. If a company got stuck in one of many dismal swamps, they employed such techniques as laying corduroy – where whole trees were laid side by side, then spread with gravel. In some places en route as many as five layers were required.

Bogged-down truck waits for corduroy to be laid

Watson Lake

③⑦

MUNCHO LAKE PROVINCIAL PARK

Fort Nelson

Kechika River

BRITISH COLUMBIA

KWADACHA WILDERNESS PROVINCIAL PARK

SPATSIZI PLATEAU WILDERNESS PROVINCIAL PARK

EDZIZA VINCIAL PARK

Fort St. John

Dawson Creek

Peace River

⑨⑦

The Peace River Valley section of the highway winds through fertile farmland, between Dawson Creek and Fort St. John. Before the Peace River suspension bridge was built in 1943, travelers crossed the river by ferry.

Historic Mile 588 or "Contact Creek" is the point where two teams of builders, from the north and south, met in 1942.

The Sign Post Forest *at Watson Lake has over 10,000 signs. The first was erected in 1942 by a GI missing his home-town of Danville, Illinois.*

0 km   100

0 miles   100

KEY

═══ Alaska Hwy

═══ Other roads

☐ National and Provincial Parks

– – Provincial boundaries

VANCOUVER AND VANCOUVER ISLAND

LOOKING OUT TOWARD the waters of the straits of Johnstone and Georgia, Vancouver occupies one of the most beautiful settings of any world city. The coastal mountains form a majestic backdrop for the glass towers and copper-topped skyscrapers of the city. It was Captain James Cook who claimed the area for the British when he stepped ashore at Nootka Sound, Vancouver Island, in 1778. Until then the area had been inhabited for more than 10,000 years by the Coast Salish peoples, whose cultural heritage is celebrated in two of Canada's best museums: the UBC Museum of Anthropology in Vancouver and Victoria's Royal BC Museum. Established as a city after a fire destroyed the fledgling town of Granville in 1886, Vancouver offers historic districts, lush gardens, and wilderness parks within its environs. A short ferry ride away, Vancouver Island's world-famous Pacific Rim National Park is the whale-watching center of Canada.

SIGHTS AT A GLANCE

VANCOUVER
(See pages 264–277) ❶ - ❿

VANCOUVER ISLAND
Gardens and Areas of
Natural Beauty
Butchart Gardens ㉑

Cowichan District ㉓
Port Renfrew ㉒
Telegraph Cove ㉚

Historic Towns and Cities
Campbell River ㉙
Chemainus ㉔

Gold River ㉗
Nainamo ㉕
Port Alberni ㉖
Victoria ⑳

National Parks
Pacific Rim National
  Park Reserve ㉘

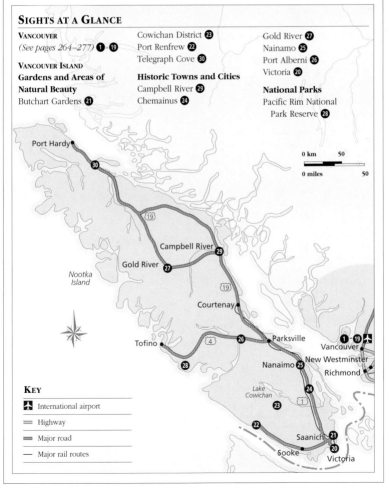

KEY

✈ International airport

═ Highway

▬ Major road

— Major rail routes

◁ **Detail from Haida totem pole carved from cedar wood representing a double-headed snake**

Exploring Vancouver

The heart of Vancouver is its downtown area, a finger of land bounded by the waters of English Bay. The city center radiates from Robson Square. The 404.7-ha (1,000-acre) Stanley Park occupies the tip of the peninsula, next to the West End. The historic Chinatown and Gastown districts are close to Main Street, the city's south to north axis.

GEORGIA
ROBSON
BARCLAY
DENMAN
COMOX
CARDERO
NICOLA
NELSON
DAVIE
BROUGHTON
JERVIS
BEACH AVENUE
PACIFIC
THURLOW
English Bay
Vanier Park
Burrard Bridge
Granville Bridge
GRANVILLE STREET
BURRARD
1ST AVENUE WEST
3RD AVENUE WEST
4TH AVENUE WEST

Sights at a Glance

Historic Streets and Buildings
Chinatown 2
Old Hastings Mill Store 12

Historic Sites
Capillano Suspension Bridge 18
Royal Hudson Steam Train 14

Parks and Gardens
Dr. Sun Yat-sen Chinese Garden 1
Grouse Mountain 17
Lighthouse Park 19
Lynn Canyon Park and Ecology Centre 16
Queen Elizabeth Park and Bloedel Conservatory 9
Stanley Park 13
Van Dusen Botanical Gardens 10

Modern Architecture
BC Place Stadium 4

Museums and Galleries
Maritime Museum 6
Science World 3
University of British Columbia Museum of Anthropology pp274–5 11
Vancouver Art Gallery 5
Vancouver Museum and Pacific Space Centre 7

Shopping Areas
Granville Island 8
Lonsdale Quay Market 15

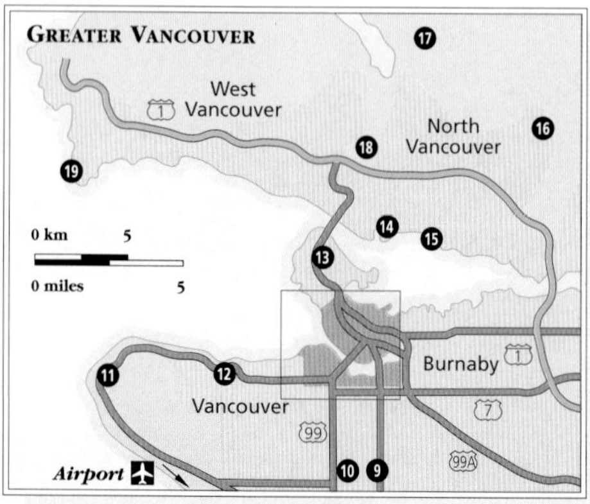
Greater Vancouver
West Vancouver
North Vancouver
Burnaby
Vancouver
Airport
0 km 5
0 miles 5

Key
- Waterfront and Gastown: *see pp266–7*
- International airport
- SkyTrain station
- Bus station
- SeaBus station
- Railroad station
- Visitor information
- Parking
- Highway
- Major road
- Pedestrian walkway

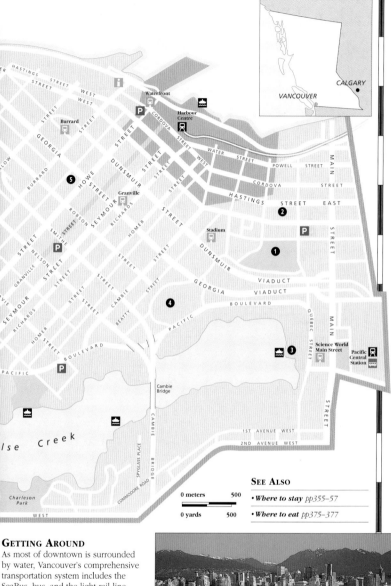

CALGARY

VANCOUVER

SEE ALSO

| 0 meters | 500 |
| 0 yards | 500 |

- *Where to stay* pp355–57
- *Where to eat* pp375–377

GETTING AROUND

As most of downtown is surrounded by water, Vancouver's comprehensive transportation system includes the SeaBus, bus, and the light-rail line, the SkyTrain, a driverless system that runs above and below ground. The SeaBus runs between Lonsdale Quay in North Vancouver and Waterfront Station downtown, where it is possible to connect with the bus and SkyTrain system. Many Vancouverites commute by car, and rush hour traffic is to be avoided because access to downtown is limited to a few bridges, including the hectic Lion's Gate Bridge.

Street-by-Street: Waterfront and Gastown

O NE OF VANCOUVER's oldest areas, Gastown faces the waters of Burrard Inlet and lies between Columbia Street in the east and Burrard Street in the west. The district grew up around a saloon, opened in 1867 by "gassy" Jack Deighton whose statue can be seen on Maple Tree Square. Today, Gastown is a charming mix of cobblestone streets, restored 19th-century public buildings, and storefronts. Chic boutiques and galleries line Powell, Carrall, and Cordova streets. Delightful restaurants and cafés fill the mews, courtyards, and passages. One popular café occupies the site of the city's first jail. On the corner of Water and Cambie streets, visitors can hear the musical chimes of the steam clock every 15 minutes, as well as be entertained by local street performers.

★ Canada Place

Canada Place is a waterside architectural marvel of white sails and glass that houses a hotel, two convention centers, and a cruise ship terminal.

The SeaBus

Stunning views of the harbor can be seen from the SeaBus, a catamaran that ferries passengers across Burrard Inlet between the central Waterfront Station and Lonsdale Quay in North Vancouver.

The Waterfront Station occupies the imposing 19th-century Canadian Pacific Railroad building.

★ Harbour Centre Tower

The Harbour Centre is a modern high-rise building best-known for its tower. Rising 167 m (550 ft) above the city, on a clear day it is possible to see as far as Victoria on Vancouver Island.

HOWE STREET

SEYMOUR STREET

HAST

STAR SIGHTS

★ Canada Place

★ Harbour Centre Tower

Water Street

Much of the quaint charm of Gastown can be seen here. Water Street boasts gas lamps and cobblestones, as well as shops, cafés, and the famous steam clock.

LOCATOR MAP
See map pp264–5

Steam Clock

Said to be the world's first steam operated clock, it was made in the 1870s, and toots every 15 minutes on the corner of Water and Cambie streets.

"Gassy" Jack Statue

Gastown is named after "Gassy" Jack Deighton, an English sailor noted both for his endless chatter and for the saloon he opened here for the local sawmill workers in 1867.

The Inuit Gallery
on Water Street offers a variety of original Inuit art such as jewelry and paintings.

TERFRONT ROAD EAST

WATER STREET

VA STREET WEST

WEST

Shopping on Powell Street
is a delightful experience with its range of small galleries and trendy boutiques.

0 meters	100
0 yards	100

Triangular Building

Reminiscent of New York's Flatiron Building, this striking structure was built in 1908–9 as a hotel and forms the corner of Alexander and Powell streets. It is now an apartment building.

KEY

– – – Suggested route

Peaceful pavilion in the Dr. Sun Yat-sen Classical Chinese Garden

Dr. Sun Yat-sen Classical Chinese Garden ❶

578 Carrall St. **[** (604) 662 3207. **[** Central Station. **[** Central Station. **[** 19, 22. **[** Downtown terminal. **[** Jun–Sep: 9:30am–7pm; Oct–May: call ahead. **[** Dec 25. **[** **[**

BUILT FOR EXPO '86, this re-creation of an 800-year-old Ming Dynasty garden offers a refuge from Vancouver's bustling city center. The garden owes its tranquillity to ancient Taoist principles, which aimed to create a healthy balance between the contrasting forces of man and nature.

Over 50 skilled craftsmen came from Suzhou, China's Garden City, to construct the garden, using only traditional techniques and tools. Pavilions and covered walkways were all built with materials from China, which included hand-fired roof tiles and the pebbles in the courtyard. Many of the plants and trees symbolize different human virtues. Willow is a symbol of feminine grace, and the plum and bamboo represent masculine strength.

Chinatown ❷

Pender St. **[** East Hastings & East Pender Sts routes.

VANCOUVER'S CHINATOWN is older than the city itself. In 1858 the first wave of Chinese immigrants was drawn to Canada by the promise of gold. The Canadian Pacific Railroad attracted even more Chinese workers in the 1880s with jobs to build the new railroad. Today Chinatown stretches from Carrall to Gore Streets and still provides a warm welcome for more recent Asian immigrants.

Declared an historic area in 1970, Chinatown has restored many of its notable houses with their elaborately decorated roofs and covered balconies. The main drag, Pender Street, is the best place to view the architectural details that decorate the upperstories of the buildings, such as highly painted wooden balconies.

Bilingual sign in Chinatown

Street signs with colorful Chinese characters add to the authentic atmosphere.

Whether buying mouth-watering duck, or watching the spicy dumplings known as won tons being made at top speed, or settling down to taste the myriad dishes available in an array of fine restaurants, the main attraction for the visitor is food. There is also a fascinating range of stores, from bakeries selling a selection of savory and sweet buns to traditional herbalists, and jewelers specializing in jade. In contrast to the bustling markets there are also several relaxing tea-rooms, as well as the nearby Dr. Sun Yat-sen Chinese Garden, which also offers tea and cakes and has weekly evening concerts of Chinese music under the soft light of lanterns throughout the summer.

Science World ❸

1455 Quebec St. **[** (604) 268 6363. **[** Central Station. **[** Central Station. **[** 10am–5pm Mon–Fri, 10am–6pm Sat & Sun. **[** Dec 25. **[** **[**

OVERLOOKING the waters of False Creek, near the Main Street Railway Station, stands the 47-m (155-ft) high steel geodesic dome that now houses Vancouver's science

The striking geodesic dome housing Vancouver's interactive Science World

museum, Science World. The dome was designed for Expo '86 by American inventor R. Buckminster Fuller, and is now one of the city's striking landmarks. The highly inter-active science museum moved into the structure in 1989.

A range of hands-on exhibits includes activities such as blowing square bubbles, wandering through the insides of a camera, and playing with magnetic liquids, all of which make this a popular day out for children. In the Sara Stern Search Gallery visitors can touch and feel fur, bones, and animal skins while the Shadow Room encourages visitors to chase their own shadows. There is also a wide spectrum of different laser presentations offered.

The museum is renowned for its Omnimax cinema, locat-ed at the top of the dome, where a huge screen shows films of flights through such epic landscapes as Mount Everest and the Grand Canyon.

BC Place Stadium ❹

777 Pacific Blvd. S. 📞 (604) 661 7373. 🚇 Stadium. 🕐 varies, depending on scheduled events. 🎧 🎥 May–Oct: Tue–Fri. ♿

S TANDING OUT from the Vancouver skyline, the white-domed roof of the BC Place Stadium has often been described as a giant mush-room. When it opened in 1983, it was the first covered stadium in Canada and the largest air-supported dome in the world. Noted for its versatility, the stadium is able to convert in a matter of hours from a football field seating 60,000 people to a more intimate concert bowl seating up to 30,000.

Among the famous guests who have visited the dome are Queen Elizabeth II and Pope John Paul II. Visitors hoping to catch a glimpse of a celebrity or two can take behind-the-scenes tours to the locker rooms, playing fields, and media lounges. The stadium also houses the **BC Sports Hall of Fame and**

The large white dome of BC Place Stadium

Museum, which chronicles the history of the region's sporting heroes.

🏛 BC Sports Hall of Fame and Museum

BC Place Stadium. 📞 (604) 687 5520. 🕐 10am–5pm daily. 🎧 ♿

Vancouver Art Gallery ❺

750 Hornby St. 📞 (604) 662 4719. 🚇 Central Station. 🚌 Central Station. 🚏 3. 🕐 daily. 🎧 ♿

W HAT WAS ONCE British Columbia's imposing provincial courthouse now houses the Vancouver Art Gallery. The building was designed in 1906 by Francis Rattenbury, an architect known for the Gothic style of Victo-ria's Parliament building and the Empress Hotel (see p278). The interior was modernized in 1983 by Arthur Erikson, another noted architect, who designed the UBC Museum of Anthropology (see pp274–5).

Decorative Victorian features on the Vancouver Art Gallery façade

Among an impressive assort-ment of historical and modern Canadian art, including works by the Group of Seven (see pp160–61), the gallery also houses the world's largest collection of paintings by one of Canada's best-loved artists, Emily Carr. Carr was born in Victoria in 1871, and studied the local native cultures, cap-turing their way of life and the scenery of the western coast-line in her sketchbook. She often depicted Haida artifacts such as totem poles in her pic-tures. Her palette is dominated by the blues, greens, and grays of the stormy west coast.

Maritime Museum ❻

1905 Ogden Ave. 📞 (604) 257 8300. 🚇 Central Station. 🚌 Central Station. 🕐 late May–Aug: daily; Sep–mid-May: Tue–Sun. ● 25 Dec. 🎧 ♿

C ELEBRATING Vancouver's history as a port and trading center, the Maritime Museum's star feature is the schooner, St. Roch, which is on permanent display. Built as a supply ship for the Mounties in 1928, in 1940–42 St. Roch was the first ship to navigate the Northwest Passage in both directions.

Other displays include Man the Oars, and Map the Coast, which tells the story of British Captain George Vancouver and the crews of the Chatham and the Discovery who charted the inlets of the coast of British Columbia in 1792. The Child-ren's Maritime Discovery Centre has a powerful tele-scope through which the city's busy port can be viewed.

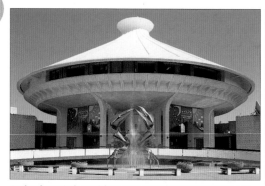

Steel sculpture in front of the Vancouver Museum's distinctive façade

Vancouver Museum and Pacific Space Centre ❼

1100 Chestnut St., Vanier Park.
 (604) 738 7827. Central
Station. Central Station. 22.
 Jul & Aug: daily; Sep–Jun:
Tue–Sun.

LOCATED IN Vanier Park near the Maritime Museum *(see p269)*, the Vancouver Museum is a distinctive addition to the city's skyline. Built in 1967, the museum's curved, white, concrete roof has been compared to a flying saucer. Outside, a stunning modern sculpture, which looks like a giant steel crab, sits in a fountain on the museum's south side.

Permanent displays here include the Orientation Gallery which re-creates British Columbia's rocky coastline and mountainous interior. Vancouver's history is explored from the culture of the aboriginal people of the area to the city's pioneering days, celebrated in a series of delightful black-and-white photographs. The museum is particularly noted for its depiction of everyday life, with exhibits such as an 1880s Canadian Pacific Railroad car, 1930s clothes, and classic Vancouver street signs.

Part of the museum, the Pacific Space Centre is particularly popular with children. The Cosmic Courtyard is an interactive gallery that focuses on space exploration, including Canada's involvement in space research and astronomy. Here, visitors can launch a rocket or play at being an astronaut in the Virtual Voyages simulator.

Granville Island ❽

1398 Cartwright St. (604) 666
5784. Central Station. Central
Station. 51. Market: 9am–6pm
daily; other stores: 10am–6pm daily.

TODAY, THIS once down trodden industrial district has a glorious array of stores, galleries, and artists' studios in its brightly painted warehouses and tin sheds. The fire of 1886 destroyed almost all of fledgling Vancouver and drove people south across the water to Granville Island and beyond. Many of the early buildings were constructed on land reclaimed in 1915 to cope with the burgeoning lumber and iron industries.

Granville Island Brewing Company sign

There are no chain stores on the island, and the smaller stores are known for their variety, originality, and quality, displaying a range of local arts and crafts such as rugs, jewelry, and textiles.

The island is also a center for the performing arts and boasts several music, dance, and theater companies.

A daily public market offers a cornucopia of foods that reflect Vancouver's ethnic diversity. Waterside cafés and restaurants occupy the False Creek Shore where there was once a string of sawmills.

Queen Elizabeth Park and Bloedel Conservatory ❾

Cambie St. Conservatory: (604)
257 8584. 15. Conservatory:
May–Sep: 9am–8pm Mon–Fri; 10am–
9pm Sat & Sun; Oct–Apr: 10am–
5:30pm daily. for Conservatory.

QUEEN ELIZABETH PARK is located on Little Mountain, Vancouver's highest hill (152-m/499-ft), and has fine views of the city. Despite being built on the site of two former stone quarries, the park's gardens are continually in bloom, beginning in early spring when multicolor tulips cover the hillsides.

The plastic-domed Bloedel Conservatory is perched on top of the hill, and grows plants from many climactic zones in the world, from rainforest plants and trees to desert cacti. There are also free-flying colorful tropical birds and fishponds filled with Japanese carp.

The plastic dome of the Bloedel Conservatory in Queen Elizabeth Park

A dazzling fall display of reds and oranges, one of many attractions in Stanley Park

Van Dusen Botanical Gardens ❿

5251 Oak St. 【 *(604) 257 8666.* 🚉 *Central Station.* 🚍 *Central Station.* 🚌 *17.* ◯ *year round; call ahead for hours.* 🏞 ♿

SITUATED IN the center of Vancouver, this 22-ha (55-acre) garden was opened in 1975. In 1960 the land was under threat from its original owners, the Canadian Pacific Railroad, who wanted to build high-rise apartments there. It took a campaign by local people and a donation from Mr W.J. Van Dusen, a wealthy local businessman, to save the site for the gardens.

Marble statue in Botanical Gardens

Today, visitors enjoy a spectacular year-round display of plants from six continents, set among lakes and marble sculptures. In spring there are narcissi, crocuses, and thousands of flowering rhododendrons. The Perennial Garden is filled with roses in summer, while September heralds the blazing reds and oranges of fall.

University of British Columbia Museum of Anthropology ⓫

See pp274–5.

Old Hastings Mill Store ⓬

1575 Alma Rd. 【 *(604) 734 1212.* 🚍 *4th Ave. route.* ◯ *Jul & Aug: 11am–4pm Tue–Sun; Sep–Jun: 1–4pm Sat & Sun.* **Donation.** ♿

THE OLD HASTINGS Mill Store was Vancouver's first general store and one of the few wooden buildings to survive the Great Fire of 1886. Built in 1865, it was moved by barge from its original site at Gastown in 1930 to the shores of Jericho Beach and then to its present home on Alma Street, at the corner of Point Grey Road. The building was intended to be used as a yacht club, but in the 1940s local people contributed a variety of historic artifacts, and today the house is an interesting small museum. Behind the pretty clapboard exterior, the museum's exhibits include a range of Victorian artifacts such as a horse-drawn cab, several

The Old Hastings Mill Store, one of Vancouver's oldest buildings

antique sewing machines, and an extensive collection of native artifacts including an impressive range of hand-woven baskets.

Stanley Park ⓭

2099 Beach Ave. 【 *(604) 257 8400.* 🚉 *Central Station.* 🚍 *Central Station.* 🚌 *135, 123.* ⛴ *Horseshoe Bay.* ◯ *daily.* ♿

THIS IS A magnificent 404-ha (1,000-acre) park of tamed wilderness, just a few blocks from downtown, that was originally home to the Musqueam and Squamish native Canadians. Named after Lord Stanley, Governor General of Canada, the land was made a park by the local council in 1886. It offers visitors the opportunity to experience a range of typical Vancouver attractions. There are beaches, hiking trails, and fir and cedar woods as well as wonderful views of the harbor, English Bay, and the coastal mountains. Bicycles can be rented near the entrance to the park for the popular ride around the 10-km (6.5-mile) perimeter seawall. The park is also home to the **Vancouver Aquarium** where visitors can watch orca and beluga whales through the glass of enormous tanks.

🐟 **Vancouver Aquarium**
Stanley Park. 【 *(604) 659 3474.* ◯ *Jun–Sep: 9:30am–8pm daily; Oct–Apr: 10am–5:30pm daily.* 🏞 🎦 ♿

University of British Columbia Museum of Anthropology ⓫

Founded in 1947, this outstanding museum houses one of the world's finest collections of Northwest coast native peoples' art. Designed by Canadian architect Arthur Erickson in 1976, the museum is housed in a stunning building overlooking mountains and sea. The tall posts and huge windows of the Great Hall were inspired by the post-and-beam architecture of Haida houses and are a fitting home for a display of full-size totem poles, canoes, and feast dishes. Through the windows of the Great Hall, the visitor can see the magnificent outdoor sculpture complex, which includes two houses designed by contemporary Haida artist Bill Reid.

★ **The Great Hall**
The imposing glass and concrete structure of the Great Hall is the perfect setting for totem poles, canoes, and sculptures.

OUTDOOR HAIDA HOUSES AND TOTEM POLES

Set overlooking the water, these two Haida houses and collection of totem poles are faithful to the artistic tradition of the Haida and other tribes of the Pacific northwest, such as the Salish, Tsimshan, and Kwakiutl. Animals and mythic creatures representing various clans are carved in cedar on these poles and houses, made between 1959 and 1963 by Vancouver's favorite contemporary Haida artist Bill Reid and Namgis artist Doug Cranmer.

Carved red cedar totem poles

Climbing figures
These climbing figures are thought to have decorated the interior of First Nations family houses. Carved from cedar planks, the spare style is typical of Coast Salish sculpture.

Ceramic jug
This beautifully decorated jug was made in Central Europe in 1674 by members of the Anabaptist religious sect. The foliage motifs are in contrast to the freely sketched animals that run around the base.

STAR EXHIBITS

★ **The Great Hall**

★ **The Raven and the First Men by Bill Reid**

★ The Raven and the First Men *(1980)*
Carved in laminated yellow cedar by Bill Reid, this modern interpretation of a Haida creation myth depicts the raven, a wise and wily trick-ster, trying to coax mankind out into the world from a giant clamshell.

VISITORS' CHECKLIST

6393 NW Marine Drive.
☎ (604) 822 5087. 🚌 4 UBC,
10 UBC. ☐ Jun–Sep: 10am–5pm
Wed–Sun, 10am–9pm Tue;
Oct–May: 11am–5pm Wed–Sun,
11am–9pm Tue. ● Mon, Dec
25–26. 🎟 📷 ♿ 🍴 🏛

GALLERY GUIDE
The Museum's collections are arranged on one level. The Ramp gallery leads to the Great Hall, which features the cultures of Northwest coast First Nations peoples. The Visible Storage gallery contains artifacts from other cultures, and a range of 15th- to 19th-century European ceramics is housed in the Koerner Ceramics gallery.

Wooden Frontlet
Decorated with abalone shell, this wooden frontlet was a cere-monial head-dress worn only on important occasions such as births and marriages.

Red cedar carved front doors
This detail comes from the set of stunning carved red cedar doors that guard the entrance to the museum. Created in 1976 by a group of First Nations artists from the 'Ksan cultural center near Hazelton, the doors show the history of the first people of the Skeena River region in British Columbia.

KEY

☐	The Ramp gallery
☐	The Great Hall
☐	The Rotunda
☐	Visible storage/Research collection
☐	Archeological gallery
☐	Koerner Ceramics gallery
☐	Temporary exhibition space
☐	Theatre gallery
☐	Nonexhibition space

The restored Royal Hudson Steam Train takes visitors to Squamish

Royal Hudson Steam Train ⓮

BC Rail Station, 1311 W. First St.
📞 *(604) 984 5246.* 🕐 *mid-May–Sep: Wed–Sun.* 🎫 *book in advance.* ♿

ONE OF GREATER Vancouver's prime attractions, the Royal Hudson Steam Train was built in 1940 especially for use in British Columbia. A replica of the Royal Hudson that carried King George VI and Queen Elizabeth across Canada in 1939, the train was restored for summer trips to Squamish in 1974. The two-hour ride offers stunning views of the forests and rocky seascapes of British Columbia's coastline from a viewing car. The interior of the Parlor Class dining coach has authentic 1940s wooden and leather furnishings so passengers can dine in style. From Squamish, visitors can tour Shannon Falls or the West Coast Railway Heritage Museum nearby. An alternative to returning on the train is the M.V. *Britannia*, which offers a return cruise through Howe Sound.

Lonsdale Quay Market ⓯

123 Carrie Cates Ct. 📞 *(604) 985 6261.* 🚉 *Central Station.* 🚉 *Central Station.* ⛴ *Waterfront.* 🕐 *9:30am–6:30pm Sat–Thu, 9:30–9pm Sun.* ♿

OPENED IN 1986, this striking concrete-and-glass building forms part of the North Shore SeaBus terminal. The Lonsdale Quay Market has a floor devoted to food, with a market selling everything from fresh-baked bread to blueberries, as well as an array of cafés and restaurants serving every type of ethnic food. Specialty shops offering a wide choice of hand-crafted products such as jewelry, pottery, and textiles occupy the second floor. The complex includes a five-star hotel, a pub, and a nightclub.

There are music festivals here in the summer when visitors take advantage of the building's open walkways to take in the view of the port.

Lynn Canyon Park and Ecology Centre ⓰

3663 Lynn Canyon Park Rd. 📞 *(604) 981 3103.* 🚉 *Central Station.* 🚉 *Hastings.* 🚌 *228, 229.* ⛴ *Horseshoe Bay.* 🕐 *Apr–Sep: 10am–5pm daily; Oct–Mar: noon–4pm.* ⚫ *Dec 25, 26; Jan 1.* **Donation** 🎫 ♿ *limited.*

LOCATED BETWEEN Mount Seymour and Grouse Mountain, Lynn Canyon Park is noted for its forests. This is a popular spot for hiking and there are several marked trails, some of which are steep and rugged and take the visitor past waterfalls and cliffs. However, many of the trails are gentle strolls through Douglas fir, western hemlock, and western red cedar. If you venture far enough into the forest it is possible to see black bears, cougars, and blacktail deer, but most visitors keep to the main trails where they are more likely to see squirrels, jays, and woodpeckers. There are wonderful views from the 70-m (230-ft) high suspension bridge that crosses the canyon.

The nearby Ecology Centre offers guided walks, shows natural history films, and features interesting displays on the ecology of the area.

Grouse Mountain ⓱

6400 Nancy Greene Way. 📞 *(604) 984 0661.* 🚉 *Lonsdale Quay.* 🚌 *236.* 🕐 *9am–10pm daily.* 🅿 ♿

FROM THE SUMMIT of Grouse Mountain visitors experience the grandeur of British Columbia's dramatic landscape and stunning views of Vancouver. On a clear day it is possible to see as far as Vancouver Island in the west, the Coastal Mountains to the north and toward the Columbia Mountains in the east.

Although there is a tough 3-km (2-mile) trail that goes to the top of the 1,211-m (3,973-ft) mountain, it is easier to take the Skyride cable-car. At the summit there are all the amenities of a ski resort, including ski schools, a dozen ski runs, equipment rental, and snowboarding as well as restaurants with great views. At night the mountain is brightly illuminated and is popular with locals taking evening skiing lessons.

There are other hiking trails from the mountain top, but they can be demanding. In both summer and winter the resort offers a multitude of activities including mountain bike tours, guided tours for sightings of wildlife, and

Magnificent forests of Douglas fir and red cedar in Lynn Canyon Park

Panoramic view of Vancouver's skyline from Grouse Mountain

hang-gliding competitions, not to mention logger sports such as chain-saw sculpture shows. A cinema shows films on the history of Vancouver.

Capilano Suspension Bridge ⑱

3735 Capilano Rd, North Vancouver. 📞 (604) 985 7474. 🚇 Central Station. 🚌 Highlands 246. ☐ daily (call ahead as hours vary according to season). ● Dec 25. 🅿 ☑ May – Oct. ♿ limited.

THE CAPILANO Suspension Bridge has been a popular tourist attraction since it was built in 1889. Pioneering Scotsman George Grant Mackay, drawn by the wild beauty of the place, had already built a small cabin overlooking the Capilano Canyon. Access to the river below was almost impossible from the cabin and it is said that Mackay built the bridge so that his son, who loved fishing, could easily reach the Capilano River.

The present bridge, the fourth to be constructed here, is 70 m (230 ft) above the Canyon, and attracts thousands of visitors every year. Nature lovers are drawn by the views and the chance to wander through old-growth woods (old trees that have never been felled) past trout ponds and a 61-m (200-ft) waterfall. Visitors are told the history of the area by guides. The original 1911 tea house is now a gift shop.

Lighthouse Park ⑲

Off Beacon Lane, West Vancouver. 📞 (604) 925 7200. 🚇 Central Station. 🚌 Central Station. 🚢 Horseshoe Bay. ☐ daily.

NAMED AFTER the hexagonal lighthouse built at the mouth of Burrard Inlet in 1910 to guide ships through the foggy channel, Lighthouse Park is an unspoiled area with 75 ha (185 acres) of old growth forest and wild, rocky coast. The trees here have never been logged and some of the majestic Douglas firs are over 500 years old.

There is a variety of hiking trails in the park, some leading to the viewpoint near the

Lighthouse Park's Point Atkinson Lighthouse

18-m (60-ft) Point Atkinson Lighthouse. Here one can see stunning vistas across the Strait of Georgia all the way to Vancouver Island. A typical two-hour hike covers about 5 km (3 miles) of old-growth forests, taking the visitor through the fairly rugged terrain of moss-covered gulleys and steep rocky outcrops where there are good vantage points for watching seabirds wheeling above the sea. Closer to the shoreline, it is possible to sunbathe on smooth rocks.

The Capilano Suspension Bridge crossing the dramatic and tree-covered Capilano Canyon

Victoria ⑳

A QUIET, ATTRACTIVE CITY, Victoria's reputation for having an old-fashioned, seaside-town atmosphere is enhanced in the summer by the abundance of flowers in hanging baskets and window boxes that decorate every lampost, balcony, and storefront. Established as a Hudson's Bay Company fur-trading post in 1843 by James Douglas, Victoria had its risqué moments during its gold rush years (1858–63), when thousands of prospectors drank in 60 or more saloons on Market Square. Victoria was established as the provincial capital of British Columbia in 1871 but was soon outgrown by Vancouver, now BC's largest city. Today, Victoria is still the province's political center as well as one of its most popular attractions for visitors.

Fishing boats and pleasure craft moored in Victoria's Inner Harbour

Exploring Victoria

A stroll along Victoria's Inner Harbour takes in many of the city's main attractions, such as the excellent Royal British Columbia Museum with its dramatic depictions of the geology and native cultures of the region. Dominating the area are two late 19th-century buildings: the Empress Hotel and the Parliament Buildings, which were designed by noted architect, and Victoria's adopted son, Francis Rattenbury. Between Fort Street and View Street is the four-story shopping mall, the Eaton Centre. Bastion Square, with its restaurants and boutiques, lies to the west of Market Square and its restored 1850s buildings.

🏛 Parliament Buildings

501 Belleville St. 📞 *(250) 387 3046.*
⭘ *8:30am–5pm daily.* ⬤ *Dec 25, Jan 1.* ♿ ✉

Looking out toward the water at Inner Harbour, Victoria's many-domed Parliament Buildings are an impressive sight, particularly at night when the façades are illuminated by thousands of lights. Designed by Francis Rattenbury in 1892, the buildings were completed in 1897. Rattenbury, a 25-year-old British architect who had arrived in British Columbia only the year before, won a

SIGHTS AT A GLANCE

The Parliament Buildings illuminate the waters of Inner Harbour

national competition to design the new Parliament Buildings. He went on to design several of the province's structures including the nearby Empress Hotel and the Crystal Garden.

British Columbia's history is depicted throughout the buildings. A statue of explorer Captain George Vancouver is perched on top of the main dome. Inside, large murals show scenes from the past.

♛ Empress Hotel

721 Government St. ℂ (250) 384 8111. ◯ daily. ♿

Completed in 1905 to a Francis Rattenbury design, the Empress is one of Victoria's best-loved sights. Close to the Parliament Buildings, the Empress Hotel overlooks Inner Harbour and dominates the skyline with its ivy-covered Gothic splendor. Visitors are welcome to sample the luxurious decor of the

VISITORS' CHECKLIST

🏠 71,500. ✈ Victoria Airport. 25 km (15 miles) N of city. 🚉 Via Station, 450 Pandora Avenue. 🚌 Pacific Coach Lines, 1150 Terminal Avenue. ⛴ BC ferries. 🛈 812 Wharf Street. ℂ (250) 953 2033. 🎷 Jazz Fest Inter-national, (Jun); Victoria Shakespeare Festival, (Jul & Aug); First People's Festival, Royal BC Museum (Aug).

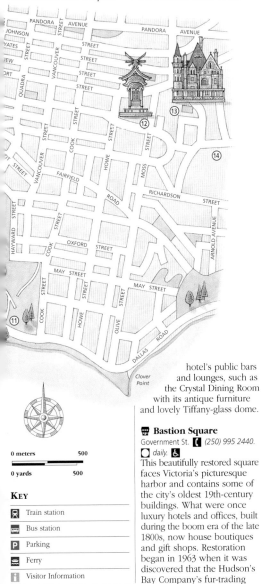

Bastion Square is a popular lunch spot for locals and visitors

post Fort Victoria, established in 1843, once stood on this site. Today, this pedestrian square includes the MacDonald Block building, built in 1863 in Italianate style, with elegant cast-iron columns and arched windows. The old courthouse, built in 1889, houses the BC Maritime Museum. In summer, both visitors and workers lunch in the courtyard cafés.

♛ Market Square

560 Johnson St. ℂ (250) 386 2441. ◯ 10am–5pm daily. ● Dec 25, Jan 1. ♿ limited.

Two blocks north of Bastion Square on the corner of John-son Street, Market Square has some of the finest Victorian saloon, hotel, and store façades in Victoria. Most of the build-ings were built in the 1880s and 1890s, during the boom period of the Klondike Gold Rush. After decades of neglect, the area received a much-needed face-lift in 1975. Today, the square is a shoppers' par-adise, with a variety of stores selling everything from books and jewelry to musical instru-ments and other arts and crafts.

hotel's public bars and lounges, such as the Crystal Dining Room with its antique furniture and lovely Tiffany-glass dome.

♛ Bastion Square

Government St. ℂ (250) 995 2440. ◯ daily. ♿

This beautifully restored square faces Victoria's picturesque harbor and contains some of the city's oldest 19th-century buildings. What were once luxury hotels and offices, built during the boom era of the late 1800s, now house boutiques and gift shops. Restoration began in 1963 when it was discovered that the Hudson's Bay Company's fur-trading

0 meters   500

0 yards   500

KEY

🚉 Train station

🚌 Bus station

P Parking

⛴ Ferry

🛈 Visitor Information

One of the giant totem poles on display at Thunderbird Park

♣ Thunderbird Park

cnr Belleville & Douglas Streets.
This compact park lies at the entrance to the Royal British Columbia Museum *(see pp282–3)* and is home to an imposing collection of plain and painted giant totem poles. During the summer months it is possible to watch native artists in the Thunderbird Park Carving Studio producing these handsome carved totems. The poles show and preserve the legends of many different tribes from the aboriginal peoples of the Northwest Coast.

🏛 Helmcken House

10 Elliot St. Square. 📞 (250) 387 4697. ◯ May–Oct: 11am–5pm daily; Nov–Apr: noon–4pm daily; Dec: special functions only. ● Jan. 🗺 🚻 ☑
Located in Elliot Square in the Inner Harbour area, the home of Hudson's Bay Company employee Dr. John Sebastian Helmcken was built in 1852 and is thought to be British Columbia's oldest house. The young doctor built his house with Douglas fir trees felled in the surrounding forest. This simple but elegantly designed clapboard dwelling contains many of the original furnishings including the piano,

which visitors are permitted to play. Other exhibits include a collection of antique dolls and the family's personal belongings such as clothes, shoes, and toiletries.

♣ Crystal Garden

713 Douglas St.
📞 (250) 381 1213. ◯ daily. 🚻
Built in 1925 to house Canada's largest salt-water swimming pool, the Crystal Garden was inspired by London's Crystal Palace and was designed by the architect Francis Rattenbury. The swimming pool has now been replaced by lush tropical gardens whose junglelike foliage provides a refuge for some 65 different species of rare monkey and tropical bird. There are also hosts of colorful free-flying butterflies to see while taking tea in the conservatory.

Parrot in the Crystal Gardens

🏛 Eaton Centre

Government St. 📞 (250) 389 2228. ◯ 9:30am–6pm Mon, Tue & Sat; 9:30am–9pm Wed–Fri; 11am–5pm Sun. 🚻
The Eaton Centre is a shopping mall within walking distance of the Inner Harbour and was built behind the façades of several historic buildings on Government Street. The Driard Hotel, designed in 1892 by

John Wright, was saved from demolition by a public campaign, as were the fronts of the 1910 Times Building and the fine, 19th-century Lettice and Sears Building. Behind these elegant façades, there are three floors of stores selling everything from fashion and gifts to handmade chocolates and gourmet food.

🏛 Carr House

207 Government St. 📞 (250) 383 5843. ◯ mid-May–mid-Oct: 10am–5pm daily. 🗺 🚻 ☑
Emily Carr, one of Canada's best-known artists *(see pp28–29)*, was born in 1871 in this charming, yellow clapboard house. It was built in 1864 by prominent architects Wright and Saunders, under instruction from Emily's father, Richard Carr. Located just a few minutes walk from Inner Harbour, at 207 Government Street, both the house and its English-style garden are open to visitors. All the rooms are appropriately furnished in late 19th-century period style, with some original family pieces. Visitors can see the dining room where Emily taught her first art classes to local children. Emily's drawing of her father still sits upon the mantel in the sitting room where, as an eight-year-old, she made her first sketches.

The Carr House where renowned painter Emily Carr was born

♣ Beacon Hill Park

Douglas St. ((250) 361 0600.
☐ daily. &

In the late 19th century this delightful park was used for stabling horses, but in 1888 John Blair, a Scottish landscape gardener, redesigned the park to include two lakes and initiated extensive tree planting. Once a favorite haunt of artist Emily Carr, this peaceful 74.5-ha (184-acre) park is now renowned for its lofty old trees (including the rare Garry oaks, some of which are over 400 years old), picturesque duck ponds, and a 100-year-old cricket pitch.

⚏ Art Gallery of Greater Victoria

1040 Moss St. ((250) 384 4101.
☐ 10am–5pm Mon–Wed, Fri, & Sat, 10am–9pm Thu, 1–5pm Sun. ⚐

This popular gallery's eclectic collection is housed in an impressive Victorian mansion on Moss Street, east of the downtown area, and a few blocks west of Craigdorrach Castle. Inside, fine wood moldings, original fireplaces, and tall ceilings provide a home for an array of exhibits, including a wideranging collection of Chinese and Japanese painting, ceramics, and pottery. The gallery also has the only authentic Shinto (a Japanese religion worshiping ancestor spirits) shrine in North America. The collection of contemporary Canadian painting includes the work of famous local artist Emily Carr. Executed between the 1900s and 1930s, Carr's paintings are among the most popular exhibits, with their haunting evocation of the stormy northwest and the lives of native peoples.

Shinto shrine detail at the Art Gallery

♠ Craigdarroch Castle

1050 Joan St. ((250) 592 5323.
☐ Jun–Sep: 9am–7pm daily; Oct–May: 10am–4:30pm daily.
● Dec 25, 26, Jan 1. ⚐

Completed in 1889, Craigdarroch Castle was the pet project of respected local coal millionaire, Robert Dunsmuir.

Although not a real castle, the design of this large house was based on that of his ancestral home in Scotland and mixes several architectural styles such as Roman and French Gothic.

When the castle was threatened with demolition in 1959, a group of local citizens formed a society that successfully battled for its restoration. Today, the restored interior of the house is a museum that offers an insight into the lifestyle of a wealthy Canadian entrepreneur.

The castle is noted for having one of the finest collections of Art Nouveau lead-glass windows in North America, and many of the rooms and hallways retain their patterned wood parquet floors and carved paneling in white oak, cedar, and mahogany. Every room is filled with opulent Victorian furnishings from the late 19th century and decorated in original colors such as deep greens, pinks, and rusts. Several layers of the paint have been painstakingly removed from the drawing room ceiling to reveal the original hand-painted, stencilled decorations beneath, including wonderfully detailed butterflies and lions.

A tower at Craigdarroch Castle in the French Gothic style of a château

♛ Government House

1401 Rockland Ave. ((250) 387 2080. ☐ daily (gardens only). &

The present Government House building was completed in 1959 after fire destroyed the 1903 building, which was designed by renowned architect Francis Rattenbury.

As the official residence of the Lieutenant-Governor of British Columbia, the Queen's representative to the province, the house is not open to the public, but visitors can view 5.6 ha (14 acres) of stunning public gardens with beautiful lawns, ponds, an English country garden, and a Victorian rose garden. Marvelous views of the grounds are available from Pearke's Peak, a mount formed from the rocky outcrops that surround the property and which contain rock gardens.

The 1959 Government House, built with blue and pink granite

The Royal British Columbia Museum

THE ROYAL BRITISH COLUMBIA MUSEUM tells the story of this region through its natural history, geology, and peoples. The museum is regarded as one of the best in Canada for the striking way it presents its exhibits. A series of imaginative dioramas re-create the sights, sounds, and even smells of areas such as the Pacific seashore, the ocean, and the rainforest, all of which occupy the second floor Natural History Gallery.

Every aspect of the region's history is presented on the third floor, including a reconstruction of an early 20th-century town. Visitors can experience the street life of the time in a saloon and a cinema showing silent films. The superb collection of native art and culture includes a ceremonial Big House.

Third Floor

19th-century Chinatown
As part of an 1875 street scene, this Chinese herbalist's store displays a variety of herbs used in traditional Chinese medicine.

★ First People's Gallery
Made of cedar bark and spruce root in around 1897, this hat bears the mountain goat crest of the raven clan.

First Nations' Ceremonial Masks
The mouse, raccoon, and kingfisher are carved on these masks, belonging to the Mungo family who wore them to dance on ceremonial occasions.

KEY TO FLOORPLAN

- ☐ First People's gallery
- ☐ Modern History gallery
- ☐ Feature exhibits
- ☐ Natural History gallery
- ☐ Museum theater
- ☐ National Geographic IMAX theater
- ☐ Nonexhibition space

Exterior of the museum
The museum's main exhibits building was opened in 1968 after years of having to occupy several sites in and around the Legislative Buildings. The museum also houses an archives building, and a Heritage Court.

Modern History Gallery

A variety of streets, stores and public buildings, from the 1700s to 1990s, are re-created in this gallery. Here, the Grand Hotel occupies an authentic wooden sidewalk.

★ Natural History Gallery

A full-size prehistoric tusked mammoth guards the entrance to the Natural History gallery which includes several lifelike dioramas that re-create British Columbia's coastal forests and ocean life since the last Ice Age.

Second Floor

★ Pacific Seashore Diorama

This diorama uses sound, film, lighting, and realistic animals such as this northern sea lion.

GALLERY GUIDE

The main exhibits of the museum are housed on the second and third floors. The Natural History gallery, on the second floor, reconstructs a range of environments from the Open Ocean to the Boreal Forest displays. The third floor has the First People's and Modern History galleries.

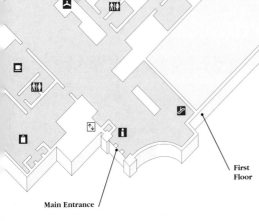

First Floor

Main Entrance

STAR EXHIBITS

★ **Pacific Seashore Diorama**

★ **Natural History Gallery**

★ **First People's Gallery**

The lily pond in the formal Italian garden at Butchart Gardens

Butchart Gardens ㉑

800 Benvenuto Ave., Brentwood Bay.
📞 *(250) 652 4422.* 🚌 *Victoria.*
🚆 *Victoria.* ⏱ *9am daily; closing times vary by season.* 🍴 ♿

T HESE BEAUTIFUL gardens were
begun in 1904 by Mrs.
Jennie Butchart, the wife of a
cement manufacturer. When
her husband moved west to
quarry limestone near Victoria,
Mrs. Butchart began to design
a new garden, which would
stretch down to the water at
Tod Inlet. When the limestone
deposits ran out, Mrs Butchart
decided to add to her burgeoning garden by landscaping the
quarry site into a sunken garden which now boasts a lake
overhung by willow and other
trees laden with blossom in
spring. A huge rock left in
the quarry was turned into a
towering rock garden. Today
visitors can climb stone steps
to see stunning views from
the top. As their popularity
grew, so the gardens were
filled with thousands of rare
plants collected from around
the world by Mrs Butchart.
Today, the gardens are
arranged into distinct areas.
There is a formal Italian
garden with a lily pond that
features a fountain bought in
Italy by the Butcharts in 1924.
The rose garden is filled with
the scent of hundreds of
different blooms in summer.
During the summer the
gardens are illuminated and
play host to evening jazz
and classical music concerts.

Port Renfrew ㉒

🚶 *300.* ℹ *2070 Phillips Rd., Sooke (250) 642 6351.*

P ORT RENFREW IS a small,
friendly fishing village and
ex-logging town. A popular
daytrip from Victoria, the
town offers visitors access
to Botanical Beach where a
unique sandstone shelf leaves
rock pools filled with marine
life such as starfish at low tide.
Port Renfrew is famed for its
hiking along old logging roads:
the Sandbar Trail goes through
a Douglas fir plantation to a
large river sandbar where it is
possible to swim at low tide.
A more serious hike is the
48-km (30-mile) Juan de Fuca
Marine Trail from Port Renfrew
to China Beach. This trail offers
a range of hikes, from treks
lasting several days to short
beach walks. The town is one
of two starting points for the
West Coast Trail in Pacific Rim
National Park *(see pp286–7).*

Cowichan District ㉓

🚆 & 🚌 *from Duncan.* ℹ *381A Trans-Canada Hwy, Duncan (250) 746 4636.*

L OCATED ON the south central
coast of Vancouver Island,
about 60 km (37 miles) north
of Victoria, the Cowichan
District incorporates both the
Chemainus and Cowichan
Valleys. Cowichan means
"warm land" in the language
of the Cowichan peoples, one
of British Columbia's largest
First Nations groups; the area's
mild climate means the waters
of Cowichan Lake are warm
enough to swim in during the

summer months. The largest
freshwater lake on the island,
Lake Cowichan offers excellent
fishing, canoeing, and hiking.
Between the town of Duncan
and the lake lies the Valley
Demonstration Forest which
has scenic lookouts and signs
explaining forest management.
Duncan is known as the City
of Totems as it displays several
poles along the highway. The
Cowichan Native Village is a
heritage center which shows
films on the history of the
Cowichan Tribe. The gift
shop sells traditional artifacts
including Cowichan sweaters.
At the large carving shed visitors can see sculptors creating
the poles while guides tell the
stories behind the images.

Stunning vista over Lake Cowichan in the Cowichan Valley

Chemainus ㉔

🚶 *4,000.* 🚆 🚌 ⚓ ℹ *9796 Willow St. (250) 246 3944.*

W HEN THE LOCAL sawmill
closed in 1983, the pic-
turesque town of Chemainus
transformed itself into a major
attraction with the painting of
giant murals around the town
that depict the history of the
region. Local artists continued
the project and today there
are more than 32 murals on
specially built panels, based on
real events in the town's past.

First Nations' faces looking down from a Chemainus town mural

Pleasure craft and fishing boats moored in Nanaimo harbor

Larger-than-life images of Cowichan natives, pioneers, and loggers dominate Chemainus and have revitalized the town. Visitors enjoy browsing in the town's various antique stores and relaxing in the many pleasant sidewalk cafés, espresso bars, and tearooms.

ENVIRONS: Some 70 km (45 miles) south of Chemainus, Swartz Bay is the departure point on Vancouver Island for ferries to the Southern Gulf Islands. Visitors are drawn to the 200 mostly uninhabited islands by their tranquillity and natural beauty. It is possible to stroll along empty beaches where sightings of eagles and turkey vultures are common. There are fishing charters for visitors who enjoy catching salmon and cod as well as kayaking tours offering stops on isolated shores to view otters, seals, and marine birds.

Salt Spring is the most populated island, with about 10,000 inhabitants. In the summer, visitors come to wander around the pretty Ganges Village, where a busy marina surrounds the wooden pier. The village offers stores, cafés, and galleries as well as colorful markets.

Nanaimo ㉕

🚶 75,000. ✈ 🚌 🚇 🚢 ℹ 2270 Bowen Rd. (250) 756 0106.

ORIGINALLY THE site of five Coast Salish native villages, Nanaimo was established as a coal-mining town in the 1850s. As the second largest city on Vancouver Island, Nanaimo has plenty of malls and businesses along the Island Highway, but it is the Old City Quarter that is most popular with visitors.

The Old City Quarter has many 19th-century buildings, including the Nanaimo Court House, designed by Francis Rattenbury in 1895. The **Nanaimo District Museum** is located at Piker's Park and has a re-creation of Victoria's 19th-century Chinatown, complete with wooden sidewalks, a general store, a barber shop, and a schoolroom. There is also a lifelike replica of a coal mine. Other exhibits include native artifacts displayed in a village diorama.

A carved eagle soars over Port Alberni Pier

🏛 Nanaimo District Museum
100 Cameron Rd. 📞 (250) 753 1821. 🕐 9am–5pm daily. 🔴 Sep–May; Mon all year. 🎫 ♿ 📷 book in advance.

Port Alberni ㉖

🚶 26,800. ✈ 🚌 🚢 ℹ Site 215, C10, RR2 (250) 724 6535.

PORT ALBERNI sits at the head of Alberni Inlet, which stretches 48 km (30 miles) from the interior of Vancouver Island to the Pacific Ocean in the west. The town depends upon the lumber and fishing industries and is a popular haunt for salmon fishers. Every year the Salmon Derby and Festival offers 5,000 Canadian dollars for the biggest fish caught during the last weekend in August. The town's other attractions include a 1929 locomotive offering train rides along the waterfront during the summer from the restored 1912 Port Alberni Railway Station by the Alberni Harbour Quay. Many visitors come to Port Alberni to cruise on one of two freighters, the 40-year-old M.V. *Lady Rose* and the M.V. *Frances Barkley*. The ships deliver mail all the way down the inlet, as well as offering trips for visitors to Ucluelet near the Pacific Rim National Park. The boats also carry kayaks and canoes for those hoping to sail around the Broken Islands Group (*see p286*).

Just east of Port Alberni, it is possible to hike among awe-inspiring old growth Douglas firs and red cedars in the outstanding MacMillan Cathedral Grove Provincial Park.

A 1929 locomotive offering rides along Port Alberni's waterfront

Gold River ㉗

🏘 *1,900.* ℹ️ *Highway 28 (250) 283 2418.*

GOLD RIVER IS a logging village located at the end of the picturesque Hwy 28, near Muchalat Inlet. The village is a popular center for caving, containing over 50 caves in its environs. Just 16 km (10 miles) west of Gold River, the unique crystalline formations of the Upana Caves and the deeper grottos of White Ridge draw hundreds of visitors every summer.

Summer cruises on a converted World War II minesweeper, *M.V. Uchuck III,* take visitors

to Friendly Cove where Captain Cook is said to have been the first European to meet local native peoples in 1778.

Gold River is a good base from which to explore **Strathcona Provincial Park** which lies in the center of Vancouver Island. Established in 1911, this rugged wilderness is BC's oldest provincial park and encompasses 250,000 ha

Mountain view at Strathcona Provincial Park

(617,750 acres) of impressive mountains, as well as lakes and ancient forests. However, much of the park's outstanding scenery can be explored only by experienced hikers.

🍁 **Strathcona Provincial Park**
Off Hwy 28. 📞 *(250) 337 2400.*
⏰ *daily.* 🏕 *for campsites.* ♿ *limited.*
🎫 *Jul & Aug: call ahead for details.*

Campbell River ㉙

🏘 *30,000.* ℹ️ *1235 Shoppers Row (250) 287 4636.*

LOCATED ON THE northeast shore of Vancouver Island, Campbell River is renowned as a center for salmon fishing. The waters of Discovery

Pacific Rim National Park Reserve ㉘

THE PACIFIC RIM NATIONAL PARK RESERVE is composed of three distinct areas: Long Beach, the West Coast Trail, and the Broken Group Islands, all of which occupy a 130-km (80-mile) strip of Vancouver Island's west coast. The park is a world famous area for whale-watching, and the Wikaninnish Centre off Hwy 4 has the latest information on their movements. Long Beach offers a range of hiking trails, with parking lots located at all trail heads and beach accesses. The most challenging hike is the 77-km (48-mile) West Coast Trail, between the towns of Port Renfrew and Bamfield. The Broken Group Islands are popular with kayakers.

The Broken Group Islands
This is an archipelago of some 100 islets popular with kayakers and scuba divers.

The Schooner Trail is one of nine scenic and easy-to-follow trails along the sands of Long Beach.

The Wikaninnish Centre has viewing platforms and telescopes for whale-watching.

Long Beach
The rugged, windswept sands of Long Beach are renowned for their wild beauty, with crashing Pacific rollers, unbeatable surfing opportunities, rock pools filled with marine life, and scattered driftwood.

Dodd Island
Turret Island
Effingham Island

The crashing waters of Elk Falls along the Campbell River

As well as renting one of the many available fishing boats, visitors can try their luck catching fish from the 200-m (656-ft) Discovery Pier in the town.

Just 10 km (6 miles) northwest of Campbell River, Elk Falls Provincial Park houses large Douglas Fir forests and several waterfalls, including the impressive Elk Falls.

Telegraph Cove ⑳

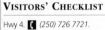 *100.* Port McNeill. Port Hardy (250) 949 7622.

LOCATED ON THE northern tip of Vancouver Island, Telegraph Cove is a small, picturesque boardwalk village, with distinctive high wooden houses built on stilts that look over the waters of Johnson Strait. In summer, about 300 killer whales, drawn to the area by the migrating salmon, come to cavort and scratch their bellies on the gravel beds in the shallow waters of Robson Bight, an ecological preserve established in 1982. Visitors may view the antics of the whales from tour boats or from the village pier.

Killer whales in the clean waters of Johnson Strait, Vancouver Island

Passage are on the migration route for five major species of salmon, including the giant Chinook. There are boat tours, which follow the fish up river.

WHALE WATCHING

Migrating gray whales

More than 20 species of whale are found in British Columbia's coastal waters. Around 17,000 gray whales migrate annually from their feeding grounds in the Arctic Ocean to breed off the coast of Mexico. The whales tend to stay near to the coast and often move close enough to Vancouver Island's west shore to be sighted from land. From March to August there are daily whale-watching trips from Tofino and Ucluelet.

VISITORS' CHECKLIST

Hwy 4. (250) 726 7721. from Port Alberni. daily. Jun–Sep.

KEY

▬▬ Major road

= Minor road

== West Coast Trail

— National Park boundary

— Rivers

Ⓐ Camping

Picnic areas

Tourist information

Viewpoint

West Coast Trail
This trail passes stunning scenery, including moss-draped rainforest and deep, rocky gullies.

At the Nitinat Narrows hikers on the West Coast Trail must take a short ferry ride across this pretty waterway. The trail is open from May to September.

Bamfield

Port Renfrew

0 km   10

0 miles   10

THE ROCKY MOUNTAINS

THE CANADIAN ROCKIES occupy a band of the provinces of British Columbia and Alberta nearly 805 km (500 miles) wide, and are part of the range that extends from Mexico through the United States into Canada. Between 65 and 100 million years ago, a slow but massive upheaval of the Earth's crust caused the rise of the Rocky Mountains and the dramatic, jagged appearance of their peaks, 30 of which are over 3,048-m (10,000-ft) high. A region of spectacular beauty, the landscape of the Rockies is dominated by snow-topped peaks, luminous glaciers, and iridescent glacial lakes, now protected in a series of national parks. The discovery of natural hot springs at Banff in 1883 prompted the federal government to create Canada's first national park. Since 1985 Banff, Jasper, Yoho, and Kootenay parks have become UNESCO World Heritage sites.

SIGHTS AT A GLANCE

Historic Towns and Cities
Calgary **1**
Cranbrook **7**
Fernie **5**
Fort Macleod **2**
Fort Nelson **19**
Fort St. John **18**
Grande Prairie **17**
Prince George **16**
Radium Hot Springs **10**

National and Provincial Parks
Banff National Park **13**
Glacier National Park **9**
Jasper National Park **15**
Kootenay National Park **11**
Muncho Lake Provincial Park **20**
Waterton Lakes National Park **3**
Yoho National Park **14**

Historical Sites and Places of Natural Beauty
Crowsnest Pass **4**
Fort Steele Heritage Town **6**
Kananaskis Country **12**
The Purcell Mountains **8**

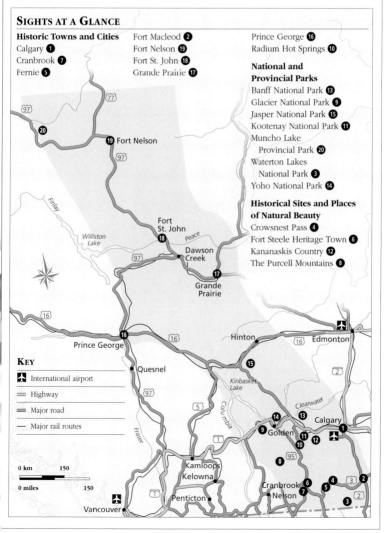

KEY

✈ International airport

═ Highway

▬ Major road

— Major rail routes

0 km   150

0 miles   150

◁ **Skilled horsemanship on display at the Calgary Exhibition and Stampede**

Calgary ➊

Blackfoot shirt in Glenbow Museum

Established in 1875, Calgary is famous for hosting the Winter Olympics of 1988, and for its Stampede. Calgary covers the largest area of any city in Alberta, and lies between the eastern foothills of the Rockies and the Prairies. It is a sophisticated place, with skyscrapers, galleries, and theaters, but it retains the air of a frontier town where pick-up trucks and cowboy boots are not out of place. The city's western atmosphere belies the fact that its modern skyline has grown since the oil boom of the 1960s. Noted for its proximity to Banff National Park, Calgary's center, with its offices and stores, is 120 km (75 miles) east of Banff Townsite *(see p301)*.

Calgary Tower surrounded by the skyscrapers of the city's skyline

Calgary Tower

9th Ave. & Centre St. SW. ☎ *(403) 266 7171.* ◯ *daily.* ♿

The Calgary Tower is the third-tallest structure in Calgary, with 18 elevators, which hurtle to the top in 62 seconds, and two emergency staircases composed of 762 steps apiece. From street level to the top, the tower measures 191 m (327 ft). At the top there is a restaurant and an observation deck, which offer some half-a-million tourists each year incredible views across to the Rockies and eastward over the vast plains of the Prairies.

❀ Devonian Gardens

317 7th Ave. SW. ☎ *(403) 268 3830.* ◯ *9am–9pm daily.* ♿

Devonian Gardens is a 1 ha (2.5 acre) indoor garden located downtown on the fourth floor of the Toronto Dominion Square complex. Reached by a glass-walled elevator from 8th Avenue, the gardens are a popular lunchtime haunt for office workers, offering a quiet

Secluded spot with fountains and fish pond in Devonian Gardens

sanctuary from the bustle of downtown. More than 135 varieties of tropical and native Albertan plants are intersected by winding pathways. There are waterfalls, fountains, and a pool that becomes an ice rink during the winter.

Shopping at a designer boutique in downtown Eau Claire Market

🏠 Eau Claire Market

End 3rd St. SW. ☎ *(403) 264 6450.* ◯ *daily.* ♿

Housed in a brightly colored warehouse, Eau Claire Market provides a welcome contrast to the surrounding office blocks downtown. Located on the Bow River, opposite Prince's Island Park, the market offers specialty stores selling a fine variety of gourmet foods, contemporary arts, street entertainers, craft markets, cinemas, cafés, and restaurants with outdoor terraces. A network of walkways connects to a footbridge that leads to Prince's Island Park.

| EAU CLAIRE AVE. |
| 2ND AVENUE SW |
| 3RD AVENUE SW |
| 4TH AVENUE SW |
| 5TH AVENUE SW |
| 6TH AVENUE SW |
| 7TH AVENUE SW |
| 8TH AVENUE SW |
| 9TH AVENUE |
| 10TH AVENUE SW |

Calgary Science Centre

Canada Olympic Park

↓ Heritage Park Historic Village

Sights at a Glance

Calgary Tower ➅
Calgary Centre for Performing Arts ➃
Calgary Chinese Cultural Centre ➇
Devonian Gardens ➆
Eau Claire Market ➈
Fort Calgary ➁
Glenbow Museum ➄
Hunt House and Deane House ➂
Prince's Island Park ➉
Saint George's Island ➀

⚘ Prince's Island Park

The pretty Prince's Island Park lies close to the city center on the banks of the Bow River. This tiny island is connected to the city via a pedestrian bridge at the end of 4th Street SW. During hot summers, visitors and locals picnic under the cool shade of the park's many trees, as well as using its walking and cycling trails.

🏯 Calgary Chinese Cultural Centre

197 1st St. SW. ☎ (403) 262 5071. ◯ daily. 🖼 for museum. ♿
Located in downtown Calgary, the Chinese Cultural Centre was completed in 1993. It is modeled on the 1420 Temple of Heaven in Beijing, which was used exclusively by emperors. The center was

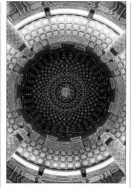

Blue tiles inside the dome of the Calgary Chinese Cultural Centre

built by artisans from China using traditional skills. The Dr. Henry Fok Cultural Hall is the highlight of the building with its 21-m-high (70-ft) ceiling and dome adorned with dragons and phoenixes. Each of the dome's four supporting columns is decorated with lavish gold designs, which represent the four seasons.

VISITORS' CHECKLIST

🏃 819,700. ✈ 16 km (10 miles) NE of city. 🚌 Greyhound Bus Station, 877 Greyhound Way SW. ℹ Calgary Convention and Visitors Bureau, 237 8th Avenue SE (403) 263 8510. 🎭 Calgary Stampede (Jul); Calgary Folk Festival (Jul); International Native Arts Festival (Aug).

🏛 Glenbow Museum

130 9th Ave. SE. ☎ (403) 268 4100. ◯ daily. 🖼 ♿
Located in the heart of downtown Calgary, the Glenbow Museum is western Canada's largest museum. The vast gallery houses an excellent collection of both European and contemporary Canadian art, as well as a wide range of objects that chronicle the history of the Canadian West. Laid out over four floors, the gallery's permanent displays include both native and pioneer artifacts, ranging from settlers' wagons to a stunning collection of First Nations' dress and jewelry. The fourth floor is devoted to five centuries of military history, with exhibits of medieval armor and Samurai swords.

🎭 Calgary Centre for Performing Arts

205 8th Ave. SE. ☎ (403) 294 7455. FAX (403) 294 7457. ◯ daily. 🖼
Opened in 1985, this large complex houses four theaters and a concert hall, as well as having five rental boardrooms. Located in the heart of the city on Olympic Plaza, the center has staged events as diverse as k.d. lang concerts and the High Performance Rodeo.

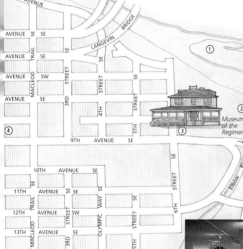

Bow River

ONT AVENUE

AVENUE SE
AVENUE SE
AVENUE SW
AVENUE SE
MACLEOD TRAIL SE
3RD STREET
4TH STREET
5TH STREET SE
LANGEVIN BRIDGE
①
②
③
Museum of the Regiments
④
9TH AVENUE SE
10TH AVENUE SE
11TH AVENUE SE SE
12TH AVENUE SW
MACLEOD TRAIL STREET SW
OLYMPIC WAY SW
13TH AVENUE SE
3RD STREET
5TH STREET
6TH STREET SE
Elbow River
14TH AVENUE SE

Stampede Park

0 meters 100
0 yards 100

KEY

🅿 Parking

🚉 Railroad station

ℹ Visitor information

The lobby of the Calgary Centre for Performing Arts

Mountie's cabin in the Interpretive Centre at Fort Calgary Historic Park

⚏ Hunt House and Deane House

750 9th Ave. SE. ☎ *(403) 290 1875.* ◯ *Deane House: daily.* ♿

The Hunt House lies across the Elbow River from the Fort Calgary Interpretive Centre. This small log house is one of the few buildings left from the original settlement of Calgary in the early 1880s.

Nearby Deane House was built for the Superintendent of Fort Calgary, Captain Richard Burton Deane, in 1906. Today, the house is a restaurant where visitors can enjoy a meal in a delightful period setting.

⚏ Fort Calgary Historic Park

750 9th Ave. SE. ☎ *(403) 290 1875.* ◯ *May–Oct: daily.* ♿ ♿

Fort Calgary was built by the North West Mounted Police in 1875 along the banks of the Bow River. The Grand Trunk Pacific Railway (later amalgamated with the CPR), arrived in 1883, and the tiny fort town grew to over 400 residents in a year. In 1886, a fire destroyed several of the settlement's key buildings and a new town was built out of the more fire-resistant sandstone. In 1911 the land was bought by the Grand Trunk Pacific Railway and the fort was leveled. Pieces of the fort were discovered during an archeological dig in 1970, and the well-restored site was opened to the public in 1978.

Today, the reconstructed fort offers an interpretive center, which houses a re-created quartermaster's store and carpenter's workshop. There are also delightful walks along the river. Costumed guides participate in dramatic reenactments such as an exciting jailbreak.

♣ Saint George's Island

Saint George's Island sits on the edge of the Bow River near downtown Calgary. The island houses the magnificent Calgary Zoo, the Botanical Gardens, and Prehistoric Park.

The zoo prides itself on the exciting presentation of its animals, which can be seen in their appropriate habitats. A series of environments called The Canadian Wilds has been created, highlighting the diversity of both the Canadian landscape and its wildlife. There are aspen woodlands where it is possible to see the endangered woodland caribou, and visitors can wander the pathways of the boreal forest environment, maybe spotting the rare whooping crane feeding in the shallow wetlands area.

The zoo is surrounded by the Botanical Gardens, which has a vast greenhouse displaying plants from different climate zones from around the world.

The Prehistoric Park offers a reconstructed Mesozoic landscape, where visitors can picnic among 22 life-size dinosaurs.

The stately whooping crane at Calgary Zoo, Saint George's Island

♣ Stampede Park

140 Olympic Way SE. ☎ *(403) 261 0422.* ◯ *daily.* ♿ *some events.* ♿

Famous as the site of the Calgary Stampede, the park offers year-round leisure and conference facilities. There is a permanent horse racetrack, as well as two ice-hockey stadiums, one of which is housed inside the striking Saddledome, named for its saddle-shaped roof. Trade shows, such as antiques and home improvements, are also held here.

CALGARY STAMPEDE

An exuberant ten-day festival of all things western, the Calgary Stampede is held every July in Stampede Park. Originally established as an agricultural fair in 1886, the Stampede of 1912 attracted 14,000 people. In the 1920s one of its still-popular highlights, the risky but exciting covered wagon races, became part of the show.

Today's festival has an array of spectacular entertainments that dramatize scenes from western history. They can be seen both on site and in Calgary itself. The fair starts with a dazzling parade through the city, and then features bull riding, calf roping, and cow tackling. The main events are the *Half-Million Dollar Rodeo*, and chuck-wagon racing which have combined prize money of over Can$1.2 million.

Heritage Park Historic Village houses some 70 historic buildings

bobsleds and luge tracks. The views toward the Rockies and over Calgary from the 90-m (295-ft) high Olympic Ski Jump Tower are truly stunning.

Visitors can experience the thrills of the downhill ski run and the bobsleds on the simulators housed in the Olympic Hall of Fame and Museum.

🏛 Calgary Science Centre

701 11th St. SW. 【 (403) 221 3700.
◯ Jun–Sep: daily; Sep–May: Tue–Sun. 📷 ♿
The Calgary Science Centre is a popular interactive museum, with over 35 exhibits of scientific wonders such as frozen shadows, laser shows, and holograms. One of the highlights is the Discovery Dome where the latest multimedia technology brings all kinds of images to life on the enormous domed screen. Fascinating shows include detailed explorations of everything from an ordinary backyard to the solar system. On Friday evenings, visitors can observe the stars using the high-powered telescopes in the observatory.

🏛 Museum of the Regiments

4520 Crowchild Trail SW. 【 (403) 974 2850. ◯ 10am–4pm daily. ● Wed. 📷 **Donation** ♿
Opened in 1990, the Museum of the Regiments is devoted to the history of the Canadian Armed Forces. The largest of its kind in western Canada, it focuses on four regiments and includes realistic displays that depict actual battle situations.

♣ Fish Creek Provincial Park

Bow Bottom Trail SE. 【 (403) 297 5293. ◯ daily. ♿ partial.
Established in 1975, Fish Creek Provincial Park is one of the world's largest urban parks, covering 1,189 ha (2,938 acres) of forest and wilderness along the Fish Creek valley. Park guides hold slide shows on both the ecology and history of the region, detailing the park's many archeological sites, such as buffalo jumps dated between 750 BC and 1800 AD.

The park's forest is a mix of white spruce, aspen, and balsam poplar. In winter, many of the hiking trails become cross-country ski trails, popular with locals and visitors alike. The Canada goose, the great blue heron, and the bald eagle are among a variety of birds that visit the park during both summer and winter.

🏛 Heritage Park Historic Village

1900 Heritage Drive. 【 (403) 259 1900. ◯ May–Sep: daily; Sep–Dec: weekends only. ● Jan–Apr. 📷 ♿
Heritage Park Historic Village sits on the shore of Glenmore Reservoir, and contains over 83 historic buildings, from outhouses to a two-story hotel, which have been brought here from sites all over western Canada. The buildings have been organized into time periods, which range from an 1880s fur trading post to the shops and homes of a small town between 1900 and 1914. Most of the 45,000 artifacts that furnish and decorate the village have been donated by residents of Calgary and the surrounding towns, and vary from teacups to steam trains. Among the most thrilling of

the exhibits, a working 19th-century amusement park has several rides, and three original operating steam locomotives. A replica of the SS *Moyie*, a charming sternwheeler paddle boat, takes visitors on 30-minute cruises around the Glenmore Reservoir. One of the most popular experiences is to ride one of two vintage electric streetcars to the park's front gates. The sense of stepping back in time is enhanced by the all-pervasive clip-clopping of horse-drawn carriages, and by the smells and sounds of shops such as the working bakery and the blacksmith's shop, all staffed by costumed guides.

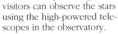

Victorian drink container at Heritage Park

♣ Canada Olympic Park

88 Canada Olympic Rd. SW. 【 (403) 247 5452. ◯ 9am–9pm daily. 📷 ♿
Canada Olympic Park was the site of the 1988 XV Olympic Winter Games, where events such as bobsledding and ski jumping took place. Today, both locals and visitors can enjoy the facilities all year round, including riding on the

Sherman tank on display outside the Museum of the Regiments

The mountain-ringed Lake Waterton in Waterton Lakes National Park

Fort Macleod ②

🏛 3,100. 🚌 ℹ *Fort Macleod Museum, 25th St. (403) 553 4703.*

ALBERTA'S OLDEST settlement, Fort Macleod was established in 1874 as the first North West Mounted Police outpost in the west. Sent to control lawless whiskey traders at the Fort Whoop-up trading post, the Mounties set up Fort Macleod nearby (*see p230*).

Today's town retains over 30 of its historic buildings, and the reconstructed fort palisades (completed in 1957) house the fort's museum, which tells the story of the Mounties' journey.

The world's oldest and best preserved buffalo jump lies just 16 km (10 miles) northwest of Fort Macleod. **Head-Smashed-In-Buffalo Jump** was made a UN World Heritage site in 1987. This way of hunting buffalo, where as many as 500 men wearing buffalo skins stampeded herds of the animals to their deaths over a cliff, was perfected by the Blackfoot tribe. The site takes its name from the brave whose head was smashed in when he decided to watch the kill from below the cliff!

⋔ **Head-Smashed-In-Buffalo Jump**
Rte 785, off Hwy 2. 📞 *(403) 553 2731.* 🕐 *daily.* 📷 ♿

Waterton Lakes National Park ③

🚌 *Calgary.* ℹ *Park Info Centre, open mid-May–Sep (403) 859 5133.* 🕐 *daily.* 📷 ♿ *partial.*

SCENERY AS AMAZING as any of that found in the Rockies' other national parks characterizes the less-known Waterton Lakes National Park. Located in the southwest corner of Alberta along the US border, the park is an International Peace Park and manages a shared ecosystem with Glacier National Park in the US.

The park owes its unique beauty to the geological phenomenon of the Lewis Overthurst, which was forged over a billion years ago (before the formation of the Rockies)

when ancient rock was pushed over newer deposits. Thus, the peaks of the mountains rise up sharply out of the flat prairies.

Waterton's mix of lowland and alpine habitats means it has the widest variety of wild-life of any of Canada's parks, from bears to bighorn sheep, and from waterfowl to nesting species such as sapsuckers.

Crowsnest Pass ④

🚌 *Calgary.* ℹ *Frank Slide Interpretive Centre (403) 562 7388.*

CROWSNEST PASS is located on Highway 3, in Alberta close to the border with British Columbia. Like most Rocky Mountain passes, it is enclosed by snowcapped mountains.

Visitors on an underground tour of Bellevue Mine at Crowsnest Pass

In the early 1900s this area was dominated by the coal-mining industry and was the site of Canada's worst mine disaster. In 1903, a huge mass of rock slid off Turtle Mountain into the valley below, hitting part of the town of Frank, and scooping up rocks and trees, killing 70 people. The Frank Slide Interpretive Centre offers an award-winning audio/visual presentation called "In The Mountain's Shadow." A trail through the valley is marked with numbered stops and leads hikers to the debris left by the disaster. Visitors can learn more about the history of local mining communities at the Bellevue Mine, which offers underground tours through the same narrow tunnels that working miners took daily between 1903 and 1961. Tours are available of Leitch Collieries, a fascinating early mining complex.

The Rocky Mountains tower over houses in the town of Fernie

Fernie ❺

🏔 4,877. 🚌 🛈 Hwy 3 & Dicken Rd. (250) 423 6868.

FERNIE IS AN attractive, tree-lined town beautifully set amid a circle of pointed peaks on the British Columbia side of Crowsnest Pass. The town owes its handsome appearance to a fire that burned it to the ground in 1908, since when all buildings have been constructed from brick and stone. Among several historic buildings, the 1911 courthouse stands out as the only château-style courthouse in BC.

Fernie is known for its winter sports, and boasts the best powder snow in the Rockies. The skiing season runs from November to April. The nearby Fernie Alpine Resort is huge and is capable of taking around 12,300 skiers up the mountain every hour. During the summer, the Mount Fernie Provincial Park offers a broad range of hiking trails through its magnificent mountain scenery. Boat trips on the many nearby lakes and rivers are popular, as is the fishing.

Various companies offer helicopter sightseeing trips that take visitors close to the mountains to see the formations and granite cliffs particular to this region of the Rockies.

Fort Steele Heritage Town ❻

Hwy 95. 📞 (250) 489 3351.
⭘ daily. 🅿 ♿

A RE-CREATION OF a 19th-century pioneering supply town, this settlement was established in 1864, when gold was discovered at Wild Horse Creek. Thousands of prospectors and entrepreneurs arrived by the Dewdney Trail, which linked Hope to the gold fields. The town was named after the North West Mounted Police Superintendent, Samuel

19th-century barber's shop at Fort Steele Heritage Town

Steele, who arrived in 1887 to restore peace between warring groups of Ktunaxa native peoples and European settlers. The town underwent a brief boom with the discovery of lead and silver, but the main-line railroad was routed through Cranbrook instead, and by the early 1900s Fort Steele was a ghost town.

Today, there are over 60 reconstructed or restored buildings, staffed by guides in period costume, including the general store, livery stable, and Mountie officers' quarters, where personal items such as family photographs, swords, and uniforms create the illusion of recent occupation. Demonstrations of traditional crafts such as quilt- and ice cream-making are also held here. Tours at the nearby Wild Horse Creek Historic Site include the chance to pan for gold.

THE BUFFALO

The large, shaggy-headed type of cattle known as buffalo are really North American bison. These apparently cumbersome beasts (a mature bull can weigh as much as 900 kg/1,980 lbs) are agile, fast, and unpredictable.

Before European settlers began moving west to the plains, in the 18th and 19th centuries, the buffalo lived in immense herds of hundreds of thousands. It is estimated that as many as 60,000,000 roamed here. Initially hunted only by the Plains Indians, who respected the beasts as a source of food, shelter, and tools, the buffalo were subsequently hunted almost to extinction by Europeans. By 1900 less than 1,000 animals remained. In 1874 a rancher called Walking Coyote bred a small herd of just 716 plains bison whose descendants now roam several Canadian national parks.

A North American plains bison

The luxurious dining car on a restored train at Cranbrook's rail museum

Cranbrook ❼

🏛 18,050. ✕ 🚆 ℹ 2279
Cranbrook St. N. (250) 426 2279.

CRANBROOK IS the largest town in southeast BC and lies between the Purcell and the Rocky Mountain ranges. A major transportation hub for the Rocky Mountain region, Cranbrook is within easy reach of a variety of scenic delights, including alpine forest and the lush, green valleys of the mountain foothills. A range of wildlife such as elk, wolves, cougar, and the highest density of grizzlies in the Rockies, may be spotted on one of many hikes available here.

The town's main attraction is the **Canadian Museum of Rail Travel**. Housed in the restored 1900 station, the museum possesses an archive of papers and photographs illustrating the history of the railroad. Outside, visitors can explore the lavish interiors of its collection of original trains.

🏛 **The Canadian Museum of Rail Travel**
Hwy 3/95 & Baker St. ☎ (250) 489 3918. ⊙ Apr–mid-Oct: daily; late Oct–Apr: Tue–Sat. 🎦 🚹

The Purcell Mountains ❽

🚆 Kamloops. ℹ Hwy 95, Golden (250) 344 7125.

THE RUGGED and beautiful Purcell Mountains face the Rockies across the broad Columbia River Valley. The region is one of the most remote in the Rockies and attracts hunters and skiers from across the globe. A high range of granite spires, called the Bugaboos, also draws mountain climbers. In the north of the Purcell range, and in one of its few accessible areas, the Purcell Wilderness Conservancy, covers a vast 32,600 ha (80,554 acres). Carefully regulated hunting expeditions for bear, mountain goats, and elk are permitted here.

From the nearby pretty town of Invermere, it is possible to access one of the most difficult trails in Canada; the Earl Grey Pass Trail extends some 56 km (35 miles) over the Purcell Mountains. It is named after Earl Grey, Canada's Governor General from 1904 to 1911, who chose the Purcell range as the place to build a vacation cabin for his family in 1909. The trail he traveled followed an established native route used by the Kinbasket natives of the Shuswap First Nations. Today the trail is notoriously dangerous; bears, avalanches, and fallen trees are often hazards along the way. Hiking along it requires skill and experience and should not be attempted by a novice.

Glacier National Park ❾

🚆 Revelstoke/Golden. ℹ Revelstoke (250) 837 7500. ⊙ daily. 🎦 🚹 🚻

GLACIER NATIONAL PARK covers 1,350 sq km (520 sq miles) of wilderness in the Selkirk Range of the Columbia Mountains. The park was established in 1886, and its growth was linked to

The Purcell Mountains are noted for remote rivers, forests, and mountains

The Illecillewaet Glacier is one of 420 glaciers in Glacier National Park

the growth of the railroad, which was routed through Roger's Pass in 1885. Today, many of the park's most accessible walking trails follow abandoned railroad lines. Other trails offer visitors stunning views of the park's 420 glaciers, including the Great Glacier, now known as the Illecillewaet Glacier.

The park is known for its very wet weather in summer and almost daily snowfalls in winter, when as much as 23 m (75 ft) of snow may fall in one season. The threat of avalanche is serious here, and skiers and climbers are monitored by the Park's Service.

The Roger's Pass line was abandoned by the CPR because of the frequent avalanches, and a tunnel was built underneath it instead. The Trans-Canada Highway (Hwy 1) follows the route of the pass as it bisects the park, en route to the lovely town of Revelstoke. From here, visitors may access the forests and jagged peaks of Mount Revelstoke National Park.

Radium Hot Springs ⑩

🏨 1,000. 🛈 Chamber of Commerce (250) 347 9331.

T HE SMALL TOWN of Radium Hot Springs is famous for its mineral springs and is a good base for exploring the nearby Kootenay National

Park. During the summer, flower-filled pots decorate the storefronts of the many coffee shops and pubs along the main street, and the town has more motel rooms than residents. Many of the 1.2 million annual visitors come to bathe in the healing waters of the springs. There are two pools, a hot soaking pool for relaxing in, and a cooler swimming pool. Locker rooms, swimsuits, showers, and towels can all be rented, and massages are readily available. Visitors can also explore the nearby Columbia Valley Wetlands. Fed by glacial waters from the Purcell and Rocky mountains, the Columbia River meanders through these extensive marsh lands, which provide an important habitat for over 250 migratory waterfowl such as Canada geese and tundra swans.

Taking the waters at Radium Hot Springs

Kootenay National Park ⑪

🚌 Banff. 🛈 Park Info Centre, open May–Sep (250) 347 9505. ◻ daily. 🅿️ ♿ 🚻

K OOTENAY NATIONAL PARK covers 1,406 sq km (543 sq miles) of the most diverse terrain in the Rockies. Much of this scenery can be seen from the Kootenay Parkway (Hwy 93), which cuts through the park from north to south following the Vermilion and Kootenay rivers. Most of the

park's attractions can be seen from the many short trails that lead from the highway.

The road winds westward through Sinclair Pass where the high red walls of Sinclair Canyon, a deep limestone gorge, lead to the crashing Sinclair Falls, and the Redwall Fault where rust-colored cliffs form a natural gateway across the highway. Farther north, the magical Paint Pots are reached by a short trail from the road. They are a group of small ochre and red-colored pools that have been formed from iron-rich undergound mineral springs. Farther on lies the high gray granite walls of the stunning Marble Canyon.

The ochre-colored Paint Pot pools in Kootenay National Park

Kananaskis Country ⑫

🚌 Canmore. 🛈 Suite 201, 800 Railway Ave., Canmore. (403) 678 5508.

K ANANASKIS COUNTRY is a verdant region of the Rocky Mountain foothills, with mountain peaks, lakes, rivers, and alpine meadows. Located southwest of Calgary on the boundary of Banff National Park, this 5,000 sq km (1,930 sq miles) of wilderness is a popular haunt for both visitors and locals to hike and view wildlife such as eagles, wolves, and bears. The town of Canmore serves as the center of this large recreational area, and has plenty of accommodations, as well as information on outdoor activities such as wildlife tours.

Banff National Park ⓭

THE BEST KNOWN OF the Rockies' national parks, Banff was also Canada's first. The park was established in 1885, after the discovery of natural hot springs by three Canadian Pacific Railroad workers in 1883. Centuries before the arrival of the railroad, Blackfoot, Stoney, and Kootenay native peoples lived in the valleys around Banff. Today, Banff National Park covers an area of 6,641 sq km (2,564 sq miles) of some of the most sublime scenery in the country. The park encompasses impressive mountain peaks, forests, glacial lakes, and mighty rivers. Some five million visitors a year enjoy a range of activities, from hiking and canoeing in summer, to skiing in winter.

Peyto Lake
One of the most rewarding walks in Banff is a short stroll from the Icefields Parkway, near Bow Summit, which leads to a vista over the ice-blue waters of Peyto Lake.

Parker Ridge

JASPER

Saskatchewan River

93

0 km 5

0 miles 5

Mistaya Lake

93

Bow Lake

View from Icefields Parkway
Renowned for its stunning views of high peaks, forests, lakes, and glaciers, this 230-km (143-mile) road runs between Lake Louise and Jasper.

Saskatchewan River Crossing lies at the junction of three rivers, along the route used by 19th-century explorer David Thompson.

BEAR SAFETY

Both grizzly and black bears are found in the Rockies' national parks. Although sightings are rare, visitors should observe the rules posted at campgrounds by the park wardens. A leaflet, *You are in Bear Country*, is published by the park's service detailing safety tips for encounters with bears. The fundamental rules are: don't approach the animals, never feed them, and don't run. Bears have an excellent sense of smell, so if camping be sure to lock food or trash inside a car or in the bear-proof boxes provided.

Grizzly bear in Banff

Valley of the Ten Peaks
A scenic road from Lake Louise winds to Moraine Lake, which is ringed by ten peaks each over 3,000 m (10,000 ft) high.

Johnston Canyon

This spectacular gorge boasts two impressive waterfalls, and is one of the most popular trails in the park. The walk can be reached from the Bow Valley Parkway (see p300), and has a paved trail with wheelchair access, as well as walkways close to the falls. Displays along the way explain the canyon's geology.

KEY

══ Highway

▬▬ Major road

— Rivers

Ⓐ Camping

ℹ️ Visitor information

☆ Viewpoint

Lake Minnewanka

is Banff's largest lake and is a popular place for picnics and boat trips.

Bankhead

An interpretive hiking trail displaying historic photographs leads visitors around this coal mine and ghost town.

Lake Louise

The turquoise waters of Lake Louise are an abiding symbol of the beauty of the Rockies. It was here that one of the first resorts was established in Banff. A giant finger of ice from the Victoria Glacier stretches to the lakeshore.

Red Deer River

Panther River

MMOND
CIER

VERMILION RANGE

Shadow Lake

YOHO NP
VANCOUVER

Banff

SUNDANCE RANGE

93

1A

1

Exploring Banff National Park

Wild goat by the Icefields Parkway

I T IS IMPOSSIBLE TO TRAVEL through Banff National Park and not be filled with awe. There are some 25 peaks that rise over 3,000 m (10,000 ft) in Banff, which are magically reflected in the turquoise waters of the park's many lakes. Banff townsite offers visitors a full range of facilities, including the therapeutic hot springs that inspired the founding of the park, and is an excellent base for exploring the surrounding country. Even the highway is counted an attraction here. The Icefields Parkway (Hwy 93) winds through stunning mountain vistas and connects Banff to Jasper National Park, beginning from the renowned Lake Louise.

Icefields Parkway (Highway 93)

The Icefields Parkway is a 230-km (143-mile) scenic mountain highway that twists and turns through the jagged spines of the Rocky Mountains. The road is a wonder in itself, where every turn offers yet another incredible view as it climbs through high passes from Lake Louise to Jasper.

The road was built during the Depression of the 1930s, as a work creation project. Designed for sightseeing, the highway was extended to its present length in 1960, with plenty of pull-offs to allow visitors to take in the views.

Bow Summit is the highest point on the highway, at 2,068 m (6,785 ft), and has a side road that leads to the **Peyto Lake** viewpoint, which looks over snow-topped peaks mirrored in the brilliant blue of the lake. In summer, Bow Summit's mountain meadows are covered with alpine flowers. From here, it is also possible to see the Crowfoot Glacier, a striking chunk of ice in the shape of a crow's foot, hanging over a cliff-face. Farther north a trail leads down from a parking lot to **Mistaya Canyon** with its vertical walls, potholes, and an impressive natural arch. The highway passes close by the Icefields (which cross the park boundaries into Jasper National Park), and the Athabasca Glacier is clearly visible from the road. Mountain goats and bighorn sheep are drawn to the mineral deposits by the roadside.

The Bow Valley Parkway passing scenic country along the river

The Bow Valley Parkway

The Bow Valley Parkway is a 55-km (35-mile) long scenic alternative to the Trans-Canada Highway, running between Banff and Lake Louise. The road follows the Bow River Valley and offers visitors the chance to explore the gentle country of the valley with many interpretive signs and viewpoints along the way. From the road it is possible to see the abundant wildlife such as bears, elk, and coyotes.

About 19 km (12 miles) west of Banff, one of the best short walks leads from the roadside to the **Johnston Canyon** trail. A paved path leads to the canyon and two impressive waterfalls. The path to the lower falls is wheelchair accessible, and the upper falls are a slightly longer 2.7-km (1.5-mile) hike. A boardwalk along the rock wall leads to the floor of the canyon, offering valley views close to the railroad crossing through the mountains. One of the most striking natural phenomena in the canyon is the Ink Pots, a series of pools where vivid blue-green water bubbles up from underground springs. Interpretive signs explain how this fascinating canyon took shape, and how the water created its unique rock formations.

Lake Minnewanka Drive

This narrow, winding 14-km (8.5-mile) loop road begins at the Minnewanka interchange on the Trans-Canada Highway. From here it is a pleasant drive to picnic sites, hiking trails, and three lakes. Lake Minnewanka is Banff's biggest lake, almost 20 km (13 miles) long.

A popular short trail leads to **Bankhead**, the site of an abandoned coal mine that was the first settlement in Banff and whose heyday was in the first half of the 19th century. The footpath displays old photographs and notices which depict the life of the miners.

Lake Minnewanka, the largest lake in Banff National Park

Banff Springs Hotel, styled after the baronial castles of Scotland

Banff

The town of Banff grew up around the hot springs that were discovered here in the 1880s. The Canadian Pacific Railroad's manager, William Cornelius Van Horne, realized the springs would attract visitors, so he built the grand Banff Springs Hotel in 1888. The resort was very popular, and the town expanded to accommodate the influx. Located at the foot of Sulphur Mountain, The **Cave and Basin National Historic Site** is the site of the original spring found by the railroad workers in 1883 and is now a museum telling the story of Banff's development. The **Upper Hot Springs Pool**, also at the base of Sulphur Mountain, is a popular resort where visitors can relieve their aches in the mineral-rich, healing waters.

At 2,282 m (7,486 ft) above sea level, Sulphur Mountain is the highest mountain in the town. Although there is a 5-km (3-mile) trail to the top, a glass-enclosed gondola (cable car) carries visitors to the summit in eight minutes. Here the viewing platforms offer beautiful vistas of the Rockies.

Banff is busy all year round. In winter snow sports from skiing to dog-sledding are available, while summer visitors include hikers, bicyclists, and mountaineers. The **Banff Park Museum** was built in 1903 and houses specimens of animals, birds, and insects.

Banff Park Museum

93 Banff Ave. *(403) 762 2291.* *daily.* *from Sep–Jun: Mon; Dec 25, Jan 1.*

Gondolas or cable cars taking visitors up Sulphur Mountain

Lake Louise

by Samson Mall (403) 522 3833.
One of Banff National Park's major draws, the beauty of Lake Louise is an enduring image of the Rockies. Famed for the blueness of its water and the snow-capped peaks that surround it, Lake Louise also boasts the Victoria Glacier, which stretches almost to the water's edge. Trails around the lake offer exhibits that explain the lake's formation some 10,000 years ago, at the end of the last Ice Age. The amazing color of the water of this and other lakes in the park comes from deposits of glacial silt, known as rock flour, suspended just beneath the surface. Dominating the landscape at one end of the lake is the imposing hotel Château Lake Louise, built in 1894.

During the summer, a gondola carries visitors up to Mount Whitehorn for stunning views of the glacier and the lake. In winter, the area attracts large numbers of skiers, ice-climbers, and snowboarders.

In Lake Louise village visitors can stock up on supplies, such as food, clothes, and gas.

Moraine Lake

Less well known than Lake Louise, Moraine Lake is every bit as beautiful, with its shimmering turquoise color. The lake has a pretty waterside lodge that offers accommodations, meals, and canoe rentals. There are several trails that all start at the lake: one lakeside path follows the north shore for 1.5 km (1 mile), while the climb, which leads up Larch Valley-Sentinel Pass trail, offers more stunning vistas, ending at one of the park's highest passes.

Yoho National Park ⑭

INSPIRED BY THE BEAUTY of the park's mountains, lakes, waterfalls, and distinctive rock formations, this area was named Yoho, for the Cree word meaning "awe and wonder." Yoho National Park lies on the western side of the Rockies range in BC, next to Banff and Kootenay National Parks. The Park offers a wide range of activities, from climbing and hiking to boating or skiing. The park also houses the Burgess Shale fossil beds, an extraordinary find of perfectly preserved marine creatures from the prehistoric Cambrian period, over 500 million years ago. Access to the fossil beds is by guided hike and is limited to 15 people each trip.

Shooting star flower

W A P T A
I C E F I E L D

Emerald Lake
The rustic Emerald Lake Lodge provides facilities at this quiet, secluded place in the middle of the park. The lake, which is named for the intense color of its waters, is a popular spot for canoeing, walking, and riding horses.

Natural Bridge
Found in the center of the park, over the waters of the Kicking Horse River, Natural Bridge is a rock bridge formed by centuries of erosion, which have worn a channel through solid rock. The bridge is a short walk from Highway 1.

VANCOUVER,
GLACIER
NATIONAL
PARK

KEY

▬	Highway
▬	Major road
▬	Rivers
Ⓐ	Campsite
🏕	Picnic
ℹ	Visitor information
☀	Viewpoint

Hoodoo Creek
These fabulous, mushroom-like towers of rock have been created by erosion and can be accessed from a short off-highway trail.

The Yoho Valley is noted for its stunning scenery, including the Takakkaw Falls.

VISITORS' CHECKLIST

Hwy 1. 🛈 Park Information Centre, Field (250) 343 6783.
🚌 to Field. ◯ daily. 📷 ♿ 🍴
💳 📷 ⛺

Takakkaw Falls
Takakkaw means "it is wonderful" in the language of the local natives, and these are among the most impressive falls in Canada, having a drop of 254 m (833 ft). The falls can be accessed along the Yoho Valley Road.

Burgess Shale is a UN World Heritage Site set up to protect two fossil beds. Day-long guided hikes here are by reservation only.

CALGARY, BANFF NATIONAL PARK

Kicking Horse River
This wild river rushes through Yoho alongside the original 1880s railroad. Today the tracks carry freight and the "Rocky Mountaineer" tourist train (see p407).

NBURY ACIER

Lake O'Hara
Shadowed by the majestic peaks of Mounts Victoria and Lefroy, Lake O'Hara is astonishingly beautiful. However, guests wishing to use the area's excellent hiking trails must book in advance as access is limited to protect this fragile environment.

0 km   3
0 miles   3

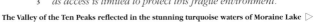

The Valley of the Ten Peaks reflected in the stunning turquoise waters of Moraine Lake ▷

Jasper National Park

T HE LARGEST AND MOST NORTHERLY of the four Rocky
Mountain national parks, Jasper is also the most
rugged. Covering an area of 10,878 sq km (4,199 sq
miles) of high peaks and valleys dotted with glacial
lakes, Jasper encompasses the Columbia Icefield (see
p308), a vast area of 400-year-old ice that is 900 m
(2,953 ft) thick in places. From the icefield, fingers of
ice reach down through many of Jasper's valleys.

Some of the most accessible hiking trails in the park
start from the Maligne Lake and Canyon, and Jasper
town. The town is located roughly in the park's center
and is the starting point for many of the most popular
walks and sights here, including the Miette Hot Springs.

Pyramid Lake
*Ringed by jagged peaks, both
Pyramid and nearby Patricia
Lake lie close to Jasper town.*

**The Jasper
Tramway**
*Only a few kilometers
out of Jasper town is the
popular Jasper Tramway,
which takes visitors to a
viewing platform near the
summit of Whistler's Mountain at 2,285 m (7,497 ft).
Panoramic vistas take in the
park's mountains, forests, and lakes.*

VICTORIA
CROSS
RANGE

VANCOUVER   16

0 km	20

0 miles	20

KEY

— Major road

= Minor road

— Rivers

Ⓐ Camping

Picnic

ℹ Visitor information

❄ Viewpoint

**Mount Edith
Cavell**
*It is possible to drive
up this mountain
as far as Cavell
Lake from where
the trail leads to
Angel Glacier and
to the flower-strewn
Cavell Meadows.*

Maligne Canyon

One of the most beautiful canyons in the Rockies, its sheer limestone walls and several impressive waterfalls can be seen from the many footbridges that are built both along and across its walls.

Miette Hot Springs

Visitors here enjoy relaxing in the warmest spring waters in the Rockies. The springs are said to have healing effects because of their high mineral content.

EDMONTON

Medicine Lake

Renowned for its varying water levels, Medicine Lake is drained by a series of underground tunnels and caves. It is also one of Jasper's prettiest lakes.

Maligne Lake

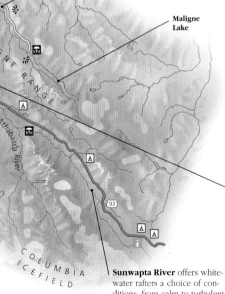

Sunwapta River offers whitewater rafters a choice of conditions, from calm to turbulent.

Athabasca Falls

The dramatic, rushing waters of these falls are the result of the Athabasca River being forced through a narrow gorge.

Exploring Jasper

Established in 1907, Jasper National Park is as staggeringly beautiful as anywhere in the Rockies, but it is distinguished by having more remote wilderness than the other national parks. These areas can be reached only on foot, horseback, or by canoe, and backpackers need passes from the Park Trail Office for hikes that last more than one day. Jasper also has a reputation for more sightings of wildlife such as bear, moose, and elk than any of the other Rockies' parks.

Although most of the park services are closed between October and Easter, visitors who brave the winter season have an opportunity to cross-country ski on breathtaking trails that skirt frozen lakes. In addition, they can go ice fishing, downhill skiing, or on guided walking tours on frozen rivers. In the summertime there are a range of daytrips which are easily accessible from the park's main town of Jasper.

Downhill skiing is just one of the outdoor activities around Jasper

Columbia Icefield and Icefield Centre

Icefields Parkway. [(403) 852 6288.] May–Oct: daily. [

The Columbia Icefield straddles both Banff and Jasper National Parks and forms the largest area of ice in the Rockies. The Icefield covers 325 sq km (125 sq miles) and were created during the last Ice Age.

Around 10,000 years ago, ice filled the region, sculpting out wide valleys, sheer mountain faces, and sharp ridges. Although the glaciers have retreated over the last few hundred years, during the early years of the 20th century ice covered the area where the Icefields Parkway now passes.

The Icefields Centre has an interpretive centre that explains the Ice Age and the impact of the glaciers on the landscape of the Rockies. Tours of the Athabasca Glacier, in specially designed 4-wheel drive Sno-coaches, are available from the Icefield Centre, which also has information on trails in the area.

Athabasca Falls

Located at the junction of highways 93 and 93A, where the Athabasca River plunges 23 m (75 ft) to the river bed below, these are among the most dramatic waterfalls in the park. Despite being a short drop compared with other falls in the Rockies, the force of the waters of the Athabasca River being pushed through a narrow, quartz-rich gorge transforms these waters into a powerful, foaming torrent.

Jasper

The town of Jasper was established in 1911 as a settlement for Grand Trunk Pacific Railroad workers, who were laying track along the Athabasca River Valley. As with Banff, the coming of the railroad and the growth of the parks as resorts went hand-in-hand, and the town expanded to include hotels, restaurants, and a visitor center. Today, many of the park's main attractions are close to the town, which is located at the center of the park, on both Highway 16 and Icefields Parkway (Hwy 93).

Just 7 km (4.5 miles) out of town is the Jasper Tramway station, from where visitors may take a brisk, seven-minute ride up **Whistlers Mountain**. The trip whisks visitors up to the upper terminal at 2,285 m (7,497 ft), where there is a clearly marked trail leading to

The wild waters of Athabasca River make it a popular venue for white-water rafting

the summit at 2,470 m (8,100 ft). On a clear day the view is incomparable. For those who would rather walk than ride the tram, there is a 2.8-km (1.7-mile) trail to the top of the mountain. The trail winds upward, offering panoramic views of both the Miette and Athabasca valleys, and, in July, the lush meadows are blanketed with colorful wild flowers.

Patricia and Pyramid Lakes
North of Jasper townsite, the attractive Patricia and Pyramid lakes nestle beneath the 2,763-m (9,065-ft) high Pyramid Mountain. A popular daytrip from the town, the lakes are noted for windsurfing and sailing. Equipment rental is available from two lakeside lodges.

The deep blue waters of Pyramid Lake beneath Pyramid Mountain

Maligne Lake Drive
Maligne Lake Drive begins 5 km (3 miles) north of Jasper townsite and leads off Hwy 16, following the valley floor between the Maligne and the Queen Elizabeth ranges. This scenic road travels past one magnificent sight after another, with viewpoints along the way, offering visitors panoramas of Maligne Valley. Among the route's most spectacular sights is the Maligne Canyon, reached by a 4-km (2.5-mile) interpretive hiking trail which explains the special geological features behind the gorge's formation. One of the most beautiful in the Rockies, Maligne Canyon has sheer limestone walls as high as 50 m (150 ft) and many waterfalls, which can be seen from several foot bridges. The

A boat cruise on Maligne Lake, the largest natural lake in the Rockies

road ends at the impressive Maligne Lake. The largest natural lake in the Rockies, Maligne is 22 km (14 miles) long and surrounded by snow-capped mountains. There are several scenic trails around the lake, one of which leads to the Opal Hills and amazing views of the area. Guided walks around here can be organized from Jasper, and it is possible to rent fishing tackle and canoes and kayaks to go out on the lake.

Medicine Lake
Medicine Lake is also reached from a side road off Maligne Lake Drive. The lake is noted for its widely varying water levels. In autumn the lake is reduced to a trickle, but in springtime the waters rise, fed by the fast-flowing Maligne River. A vast network of underground caves and channels are responsible for this event.

Miette Springs
☎ *(403) 866 3939.* ◯ *mid-May–Sep: daily.* 🏊 ♿
Located 61 km (38 miles) north of Jasper along the attractive Miette Springs Road, these

springs are the hottest in the Rockies, reaching temperatures as high as 53.9°C (129°F). However, the thermal baths are cooled to a more reasonable 39°C (102°F) for bathers. The waters are held to be both relaxing and healthy – they are rich in minerals, such as calcium, sulfates, and small amounts of hydrogen sulfide (which smells like rotten eggs).
The resort of Miette Springs now houses two new pools, including one suitable for children. The springs are part of a leisure complex that offers both restaurants and hotels.

Mount Edith Cavell
Named after World War I heroine nurse, this mountain is located 30 km (18.5 miles) south of Jasper townsite, and the scenic road that climbs it is well worth the drive. The road ends at Cavell Lake by the north face of the mountain. From here, a guided trail leads to a small lake beneath the Angel Glacier. A three-hour walk across the flower strewn Cavell meadows has views of the glacier's icy tongue.

A peninsula of ice from Angel Glacier seen from Mount Edith Cavell

Typical kitchen of the early 1900s at Grande Prairie Museum

Prince George ⑯

🏛 70,000. ☒ 🚌 🚏 🛈 1198 Victoria St. (250) 562 3700.

THE LARGEST town in northeastern British Columbia, Prince George is a bustling supply-and-transportation center for the region. Two major highways pass through here, the Yellowhead (Hwy 16) and Highway 97, which becomes the Alaska Highway at Dawson Creek. Established in 1807 as Fort George, a fur-trading post at the confluence of the Nechako and Fraser rivers, the town is well placed for exploring the province.

Today, Prince George has all the facilities of a larger city, including a new university specializing in First Nations' history and culture, as well as its own symphony orchestra and several art galleries. The **Fort George Regional Museum** lies on the site of the original Fort, within the 26-ha (65-acre) Fort George Park, and has a small collection of artifacts from native cultures, European pioneers, and early settlers to the region.

An important center for the lumber industry, the town offers a range of free tours of local pulp mills, which take visitors through the process of wood production, from vast fields of young seedlings to hill-sized piles of planks and raw timber.

🏛 **Fort George Regional Museum**
20th Ave. & Queensway. ☎ (250) 562 1612. ◻ daily. ● Dec 25, Jan 1. 🎫 **donation.** ♿

Grande Prairie ⑰

🏛 28,250. ☒ 🚏 🛈 10632 102nd Ave. (403) 532 5340.

GRANDE PRAIRIE is a large, modern city in the northwest corner of Alberta. Surrounded by fertile farming country, the city is a popular stop for travelers heading north toward Dawson Creek and the Alaska Highway (see pp260–1). The city is the hub of the Peace River region; it offers extensive opportunities for shopping in its giant malls and many downtown specialty stores, with the added draw of having no provincial sales tax (see p380).

Running through the city center is the attractive wilderness of Muskoseepi Park. Covering 45 ha (111 acres), the park offers a variety of outdoor activities including walking and biking trails, and cross-country skiing. Boating is very popular with both visitors and locals, and it is possible to rent canoes and

rowboats to take out onto the Bear Creek Reservoir. The **Grande Prairie Museum** is also housed in the park and has ten buildings containing over 16,000 historical artifacts. There are several reconstructions, including a 1911 schoolhouse, a rural post office, and a church. A renowned display of dinosaur bones recovered from the Peace River Valley can also be seen here.

Peace River runs through a broad, flat valley over which stand high, ravine-filled canyon walls. The valley is a magnet for bird-watchers, and sightings of eagles are common. The Peace River wetlands, particularly those at Crystal Lake in the northeast corner of the city, contain one of the few breeding grounds for the rare trumpeter swan.

🏛 **Grande Prairie Museum**
cnr 102nd St. & 102nd Ave. ☎ (403) 532 5482. ◻ May–Sep: daily; Oct–Apr: Sun–Fri. ● Dec 25, Jan 1. 🎫 ♿

Fort St. John ⑱

🏛 14,800. ☒ 🚏 🛈 9323, 100th St. (250) 785 6037.

FORT ST. JOHN is located at Mile 47 of the Alaska Highway among the rolling hills of the Peace River Valley. During the construction of the Highway in 1942, the tiny town dramatically expanded from a population of about 800 to 6,000. When completed, the highway turned Fort St. John into a busy supply center that caters to visitors

Lush farmland along the Peace River in northern British Columbia

The green waters of Muncho Lake framed by mountains in Muncho Lake Provincial Park

exploring the area, as well as supporting the growth of agriculture in the surrounding countryside. However, the town boomed when oil was found here in the 1950s, in what proved to be the largest oil field in the province. Today, Fort St. John's pride in its industrial heritage is reflected in the local museum, which has a 43-m (140-ft) high oil derrick at its entrance and a range of exhibits that tell the story of the local oil industry.

Fort Nelson ⓲

🏠 6,000. ✕ 🚌 🅸 5319 50th Ave. Sth. (250) 774 2541.

D ESPITE THE growth of the oil, gas, and lumber industries in the 1960s and 70s, Fort Nelson retains the atmosphere of a northern frontier town. Before the building of the Alaska Highway in the 1940s, Fort Nelson was an important stop on route for the Yukon and Alaska, and until the 1950s was without telephones, running water, or electricity. Fur trading was the main activity until the energy

boom; even today both native and white trappers hunt wolf, beaver, and lynx, for both their fur and their meat.

Today, the town has an air and bus service, a hospital, and good visitor facilities such as motels, restaurants, and gas stations. Local people are famous for their friendliness, and during the busy summer months run a program of free talks describing life in the north to visitors. A small museum displays photographs and artifacts that tell the story of the building of the 2,394-km (1,488-mile) Alaska Highway.

Lynx near Fort Nelson

Muncho Lake Provincial Park ⓴

Off Hwy 97. 🅲 (250) 232 5460. ◯ mid-May–Sep: daily.

O NE OF THREE provincial parks (including Stone Mountain and Liard Hot Springs) that were established after the building of the Alaska Highway in 1942, Muncho Lake occupies the most scenic

section of the road. The park encompasses the bare peaks of the northern Rockies, whose stark limestone slopes incorporate the faults, alluvial fans, and hoodoos that are a testament to thousands of years of glacial erosion. The Highway skirts the eastern shoreline of the 12-km (7.5-mile) long Muncho Lake before crossing the Liard River where the Mackenzie Mountain range begins. In early summer, passing motorists are likely to see moose grazing among meadows filled with colorful wildflowers. The park's bogs are popular with botanists eager to see the rare yellow Lady's Slipper orchid. The roadside also attracts goats, sheep, and caribou, drawn by delicious deposits of sodium, known as mineral licks.

Visitors may stay in the park at one of the campgrounds or lodges in order to explore its 88,000 ha (194,000 acres) of wilderness. The deep waters of Muncho Lake house a good supply of trout for anglers.

SOUTHERN AND NORTHERN BRITISH COLUMBIA

SOUTHERN BRITISH Columbia covers the region south of Prince George, down to the US border. There is a vast variety of natural beauty here, including the forests and waterfalls of Wells Gray Provincial Park, and the lush valleys, wineries, and lake resorts of the Okanagan Valley. One of the most stunning wildernesses in North America, northern British Columbia spreads north of Prince Rupert, between the Coast Mountains in the west, the Rockies in the east, and the Yukon. Its dramatic landscape, from the volcanic terrain around Mount Edziza with its lava flows and cinder cones to the frozen forests of Atlin Provincial Park, can be reached from the scenic Cassiar Highway. Some of the best sights can be enjoyed on the boat trip to Queen Charlotte Islands. For 10,000 years the archipelago has been home to the Haida people, famous for their totem-carving.

SIGHTS AT A GLANCE

Historic Towns and Cities
Castlegar ❺
Hope ❸
Kamloops ❾
'Ksan Village ⓭
Nakusp ❼

Nelson ❻
Prince Rupert ⓮
Quesnel ⓬
Sicamous ❽
Whistler ❶

National and Provincial Parks
Bowron Lake Provincial Park ⑪
Northern Parks ⑯
Wells Gray Provincial Park ⑩

Historic Sites and Areas of Natural Beauty
Fraser River ❷
Okanagan Valley ❹
Queen Charlotte Islands ⑮

KEY

✈ International airport

▬ Highway

▭ Major road

— Major rail routes

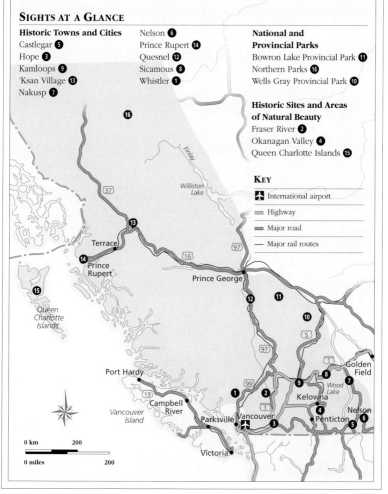

◁ The Fraser River flowing through Fraser River Canyon in the midst of wooded winter scenery

The Trans-Canada Highway overlooking the Fraser Canyon along the Fraser River

Whistler ➊

4,450. *4010 Whistler Way. (604) 932 2394.*

WHISTLER IS THE largest ski resort in Canada. Set among the spectacular Coast Mountains, just 120 km (75 miles) north of Vancouver, the resort is divided into four distinct areas: Whistler Village, Village North, Upper Village, and Creekside. Whistler and Blackcomb mountains have the greatest vertical rises of any ski runs in North America. The skiing here can be among the best in the world with mild Pacific weather, and reliable winter snow. In summer there is skiing on Blackcomb's Hortsman Glacier.

Although the resort is relatively new (the first ski lift was opened in 1961), Whistler Village offers visitors a full range of facilities. There are lots of places to stay, from comfortable bed-and-breakfasts, to luxurious five-star hotels. Café-lined cobbled squares and cozy bars and restaurants cater to a diversity of tastes, while a variety of stores sell everything from ski wear to native arts and crafts in this friendly alpine village.

Fraser River ➋

Vancouver (604) 739 0823.

THE MAJESTIC Fraser River travels 1,368 km (850 miles) through some of BC's most stunning scenery. The river flows from its source in the Yellowhead Lake, near Jasper, to the Strait of Georgia, near Vancouver. Along the way, it heads north through the Rocky Mountain trench before turning south near the town of Prince George. It continues by the Coast Mountains, then west to Hope through the steep walls of the Fraser Canyon, and on toward Yale.

It was Fraser Canyon that legendary explorer Simon Fraser found the most daunting when he followed the river's course in 1808. However, when gold was discovered near the town of Yale 50 years later, thousands of prospectors swarmed up the valley. Today, Yale is a small town with a population of 200 and the delightful **Yale Museum**, where exhibits focus on the history of the gold rush, as well as telling the epic story of the building of the Canadian Pacific Railroad through the canyon. This section of river is also a popular whitewater rafting area, and trips can be arranged from the small town of Boston Bar. At Hell's Gate the river thunders through the Canyon's narrow walls, which are only 34 m (112 ft) apart.

🏛 Yale Museum
Douglas St. *(604) 863 2324.* Jun–Sep: 10am–5pm daily.

Hope ➌

3,150. *919 Water Ave. (604) 869 2021.*

LOCATED AT THE southern end of the Fraser Canyon, Hope is crossed by several highways, including Hwy 1 (the Trans-Canada) and Hwy 3. Hope is an excellent base for exploring the Fraser Canyon and southern BC, as well as being within easy reach of several provincial parks. The beautiful country of Manning Provincial Park, with its lakes mountains, and rivers, is noted for its outdoor activities. During summer swimming, hiking, fishing, and sailing are popular: in winter there is both downhill and cross-country skiing.

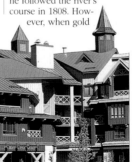

The ski resort at alpine Whistler village in British Columbia

Okanagan Valley Tour [4]

Okanagan wine

The Okanagan Valley is actually a series of valleys, linked by a string of lakes, that stretches for 250 km (155 miles) from Osoyoos in the south, to Vernon in the north. The main towns here are connected by Highway 97, which passes through the desert landscape near Lake Osoyoos, and on to the lush green orchards and vineyards for which the valley is most noted. Mild winters and hot summers have made the Okanagan one of Canada's favorite vacation destinations.

Tips for Drivers

Starting point: *On Highway 97 from Vernon in the north: Osoyoos in the south.*
Length: *230 km (143 miles).*
Highlights: *Blossom and fruit festivals are held in spring and summer, when roadside stalls offer a cornucopia of fruit, and wine tours are available year-round.*

Kelowna 4
The biggest city in the Okanagan, Kelowna lies on the shores of Lake Okanagan between Penticton and Vernon, and is the center of the wine- and fruit-growing industries.

Vernon 5
Surrounded by farms and orchards, Vernon owes its lush look to the growth of irrigation in 1908. Several small resorts are set around the nearby lakes.

Summerland 3
This small but charming lakeside resort boasts several 19th-century buildings and stunning views from the top of Giant's Head Mountain.

O'Keefe Historic Ranch 6
Founded by the O'Keefe family in 1867, this historic ranch displays original artifacts belonging to the family who lived here until 1977. The original log cabin remains, as does the church and store.

Penticton 2
This sunny lakeside town is known for the long Okanagan Beach, windsurfing, and local winery tours, as well as for its Peach Festival, held every August.

0 km 25
0 miles 25

Osoyoos 1
Visitors are drawn here by hot summers, the warm waters and sandy beaches of Lake Osoyoos, and the nearby pocket desert.

Key

Tour route
Other roads
Viewpoint

Impressive and historic stone buildings in the attractive town of Nelson

Castlegar ❺

🏃 *7,200.* ✈ 🚌 ℹ *1995 6th Ave.*
☎ *(250) 365 6313.*

LOCATED IN southeastern BC, Castlegar is a busy transportation hub. The town is crossed by two major highways, the Crowsnest and Hwy 22, and lies at the junction of the important Kootenay and Columbia rivers.

In the early 1900s, a steady influx of Doukhobors (Russian religious dissenters fleeing persecution) began arriving here. The **Doukhobor Village Museum** reflects the group's heritage and houses a variety of traditional clothes and tools, and antique farm machinery.

Traditional Doukhobor tunic

🏛 **Doukhobor Village Museum**
Jct Hwy 3 & 3A. ☎ *(250) 365 6622.*
◯ *May–Sep: daily.* 🖼 ♿

Nelson ❻

🏃 *9,000.* 🚌 ℹ *225 Hall St.*
☎ *(250) 352 3433.*

ONE OF THE MOST attractive towns in southern British Columbia, Nelson overlooks Kootenay Lake. Established in the 1880s as a mining town, with the coming of the railroad in the 1890s, Nelson flourished as a center for transporting ore and timber. The town owes its good looks to its location on the shores of the lake and to the large number of public buildings and houses that were constructed between 1895 and 1920. In 1986 the town was chosen as the location for the Steve Martin comedy film, *Roxanne.* British Columbia's best-known architect, Francis Rattenbury *(see p278),* played a part in the design of some of the town's most prestigious and beautiful structures, such as the elegant Burns building which was built in 1899 for millionaire cattle rancher and meat packer, Patrick Burns. Rattenbury also designed the Nelson Court House in 1908, a stately stone building with towers and gables.

Today, the town has a thriving cultural scene, with some 16 art galleries, as well as numerous cafés, book, and craft shops. Visitors also enjoy the short ride on Car 23, a 1906 streetcar that operated in the town between 1924 and 1949 (it was restored in 1992) and which today travels along Nelson's delightful waterfront. The infocenter provides visitors with a map and guide for the heritage walking tour of the town's historic buildings.

Nakusp ❼

🏃 *1,700.* ℹ *92 W. 6th Ave.*
☎ *(250) 265 4234.*

WITH THE snow-topped Selkirk Mountains as a backdrop, and overlooking the waters of Upper Arrow Lake, Nakusp is a charming town. Originally developed as a mining settlement, the town is now known for its mineral hot springs. There are two resorts close to town; the Nakusp and Halcyon Hot Springs, both of which provide therapeutic bathing in hot waters, rich in sulfates, calcium, and hydrogen sulfide, said to be good for everyday aches, as well as arthritis and rheumatism.

The town of Nakusp overlooks picturesque Upper Arrow Lake

Roughly 40 km (25 miles) to the south of Nakusp, in the Slocan Valley, are two fascinating abandoned silver mining towns, New Denver and Sandon. Sandon had 5,000 inhabitants at the height of the mining boom in 1892. It also had 29 hotels, 28 saloons, and several brothels and gambling halls. A fire in 1900, poor metal prices, and dwindling ore reserves crippled the mines, and Sandon became a ghost town. Today, the town has been declared an historic site, and its homes and businesses are being carefully restored. The nearby town of New Denver suffered a fate similar to Sandon's, but is also noted as the site of an internment camp for the Japanese during World War II. The Nikkei Internment Centre on Josephine Street is the only center in Canada devoted to telling the story of the internment of over 20,000 Japanese Canadians. The center is surrounded by a formal Japanese garden.

Houseboats moored along the waterfront at Sicamous

Sicamous ⑧

🏠 3,088. 🚉 🛈 110 Finlayson St. 📞 (250) 836 3313.

SICAMOUS IS an appealing waterfront village known for its 3,000 houseboats, as well as its charming cobblestone streets hung with flower-filled planters. Located between Mara and Shuswap lakes, at the junction of the Trans-Canada Highway and Highway 97A, the town is ideally placed for touring the lakes, and the resort of Salmon Arm, at the northern end of the Okanagan Valley (see p315). Over 250 houseboats are available for renting in the summer, and there are 12 marinas and a houseboat store. From the boats it is possible to view the inlets and forested landscape of Lake Shuswap where wildlife such as black bear, deer, moose, coyote, and bobcat have been spotted along the shore. In summer, visitors

and locals enjoy both the good public beach on the lake, as well as the pleasant walk along a marked waterfront trail.

Kamloops ⑨

🏠 80,000. ✈ 🚉 🚌 🛈 1290 W. Trans-Canada Hwy. 📞 (250) 372 7770.

KAMLOOPS MEANS "where the rivers meet" in the language of the Secwepemc First Nations. The largest town by area in BC's southern interior, it lies at the crossroads of the north and south Thompson Rivers. Three major highways also meet here; the Trans-Canada, Hwy 5, and Hwy 97 to the Okanagan Valley, as do the Canadian Pacific and Canadian National railroad.

European settlement began in 1812, when fur traders started doing business with local natives. The **Museum and Native Heritage Park** in Kamloops focuses on the cultural history of the Secwepemc First Nations and has a variety of artifacts, including a birch-bark canoe, hunting equipment, and cooking utensils. Outside, short trails lead visitors through the archeological remains of a 2,000-year-old Shuswap winter village site, which includes four authentically reconstructed winter pit houses and a summer camp. The village has a hunting shack, a fish-drying

A horse's snow shoe on display at Kamloops

rack, and a smoke house. The museum store sells pine-needle and birch-bark baskets, moccasins, and a wide variety of beaded and silver jewelry.

In the town center, the Art Gallery has a small but striking collection that features landscape sketches by A.Y. Jackson, one of the renowned Group of Seven painters (see pp160–61).

🏛 Museum and Native Heritage Park
353 Yellowhead Hwy. 📞 (250) 828 9801. ⊙ Jun–Sep: daily; Sep–May: 8:30am–4:30pm Mon–Fri. 🚫 ♿

Wells Gray Provincial Park ⑩

📞 (250) 851 3100. 🚉 Clearwater. 🚌 Clearwater. ⊙ daily.

WELLS GRAY Provincial Park is one of the most beautiful wildernesses in British Columbia, and offers wonders comparable to the Rockies in the east. The park was established in 1939 and is distinguished by alpine meadows, thundering waterfalls, and glacier-topped peaks that rise as high as 2,575-m (8,450 ft). The Canadian National Railroad and Hwy 5 follow the Thompson River along the park's western edge, and both routes offer travelers stunning views.

From the Clearwater Valley Road, off Hwy 5, there are several trails, from easy walks to arduous overnight hikes in remote country. A selection of small trails, just a few minutes from the road, lead to the spectacular sight of Dawson Falls.

Bowron Lake Provincial Park ⓫

C (250) 398 4414. **R** Quesnel. **R** Quesnel. **O** daily (weather permitting). **&** partial.

BOWRON LAKE Provincial Park is located about 113 km (70 miles) east of Quesnel on Highway 26 in the Cariboo Mountains. The park is renowned for having a 112-km (70-mile) rectangular waterway composed of nine lakes, three rivers, streams, small lakes, and many portages (trails linking the waterways). There is a week-long canoe trip here, but it is limited to 50 canoeists at a time, and passes must be obtained from the visitor center. It is a special trip that allows visitors to come quietly upon wildlife such as moose or beaver. In late summer, bears come to feed on the spawning sockeye salmon in the Bowron River.

A grizzly bear standing up

Quesnel ⓬

A 23,000. **X** **R** **R** **i** 705 Carson Ave. (250) 992 4922.

QUESNEL IS A busy logging town that started life as a gold rush settlement between 1858 and 1861. The town was the last along the Gold Rush Trail, or Cariboo Road (now Hwy 97), which was lined with mining towns between here and Kamloops. Quesnel occupies an attractive position in a triangle formed by the Fraser and Quesnel rivers. The town's sights include the Riverfront Park Trail System, a tree-lined 5-km (3-mile) path that runs along the banks of both rivers. Just outside the town's limits, Pinnacle Provincial Park features the geological wonder of hoodoos, rocky columns formed 12 million years ago when the volcanic surface was eroded by Ice Age meltwaters.

From Quesnel, 87 km (54 miles) east on Hwy 26, lies the historic mining town of **Barkerville**. The town was born when Englishman Billy Barker dug up a handful of gold nuggets in 1862. Today, it is a good example of a perfectly preserved 19th-century mining town, with more than 120 restored or reconstructed buildings and costumed guides. Visitors can see a blacksmith at work in his forge, see showgirls put on the kind of display the miners would have seen at the theater, or take a ride on a stagecoach.

🚇 Barkerville

85 km E. of Quesnel, Hwy 26.
C (250) 994 3302. **O** daily. 📷 **&**

A 19th-century horse and carriage in the streets of Barkerville

'Ksan Village ⓭

C (250) 842 5544. **O** grounds: year round; houses: Apr–Sep: daily. 📷 **&**

SOME 290 km (180 miles) east of Prince Rupert, 'Ksan Village is a re-creation of an 1870 native settlement, established in the 1950s to preserve the culture of the Gitxsan First Nations. Gitxsan natives have lived in the area for thousands of years, particularly along the beautiful Skeena River valley. Their way of life was threatened by an influx of white settlers who arrived in the 1850s at Prince Rupert to work their way up river to mine or farm. Noted for their skill in creating carved and painted masks, totems, and canoes, Gitxsan elders are now schooling new

Gitxsan carved cedarwood totem pole in 'Ksan Indian village

generations in these skills at 'Ksan Village. Within the complex there are seven traditional long houses containing a carving school, a museum, and a gift shop.

Prince Rupert ⓮

A 16,000. **X** **R** **R** **🚢** **i** 100 1st Ave. W. (250) 624 5637.

PRINCE RUPERT IS A vibrant port city, and the second-largest on BC's coast. Located on Kaien Island, at the mouth of the Skeena River, the city is circled by forests and mountains, and overlooks the beautiful fjord-studded coastline. The harbor is busy with cruise ships, ferries, and fishing boats and is the main access point for the rugged Queen Charlotte Islands and Alaska.

Like many of BC's major towns, Prince Rupert's development is linked to the growth of the railroad. Housed in the 1914 Grand Trunk Railroad Station, the Kwinitsa Railway Museum tells the story of businessman Charles Hay's big plans for the town, which were largely unfulfilled: he went down with the *Titanic* in 1912.

Tsimshian First Nations were the first occupants of the area, and as recently as 150 years ago the harbor was lined with their large cedar houses and carved totems. The excellent **Museum of Northern British Columbia** focuses on Tsimshian history and culture and offers archaeological tours, including the Tsimshian village of Metlakatla, describing their culture over 10,000 years.

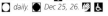

Museum of Northern British Columbia
100 1st Ave. W. *(250) 624 3207.* ○ *daily.* ● *Dec 25, 26.*

Queen Charlotte Islands ⑮

🚉 *Prince Rupert.* 🚌 *Prince Rupert.* 🛈 *3220 Wharf St., Queen Charlotte. (250) 559 8316 (open May–Sep).*

Atlin Lake in remote Atlin Provincial Park

SHAPED LIKE A bent ice-cream cone, the Queen Charlotte Islands, also known as Haida Gwaii, are an archipelago of about 150 islands across from the city of Prince Rupert.

The Queen Charlotte Islands were left untouched by the last Ice Age, and have an ecosystem unique to Canada. The forests house distinctive species of mammal such as the dusky shrew and short-tailed weasel. The islands are also home to a large population of bald eagles, and the spring brings hundreds of migrating gray whales past their shores.

The islands have been the home of the Haida people for thousands of years. Today, the Haida are recognized for their artistic talents, particularly their carvings and sculptures from cedar wood and argillite (a black slatelike stone found only on these islands).

It was the Haida who led environmental campaigns against the logging companies in the 1980s, which led to the founding of the **Gwaii Haanas National Park Reserve** in 1988. The park houses centuries-old rainforest, including 1,000-year-old Sitka spruce, red cedar, and western hemlock.

♣ Gwaii Haanas National Park Reserve
(250) 559 8818. ○ *May–Sep.*

Northern Parks ⑯

Mount Edziza, Spatsizi; Hwy 37. Atlin; Hwy 7. 🛈 *(250) 624 5637.*

THE PROVINCIAL parks of northern British Columbia comprise Mount Edziza Provincial Park, Spatsizi Plateau Wilderness Provincial Park, and, farther north, Atlin Provincial Park. These offer remote landscapes, with high peaks, icefields, and tundra.

Established in 1972, Mount Edziza Provincial Park is distinguished by its volcanic landscape which includes lava rivers, basalt plateaus, and cinder cones. The park can be reached by a minor road off the Cassiar Highway (Hwy 37). There is no vehicle access within the park, and only long, rugged overland trails or chartered float planes take visitors through open meadows, arctic birch woods, and over creeks.

Across the highway lies the even more rugged country of Spatsizi Plateau Wilderness Provincial Park, which includes the snow-capped peaks of the Skeena Mountains. Gladys Lake, a small lake in the center of the park, is an ecological reserve for the study of sheep and mountain goats. Access to the park is again limited to a small road leading from the village of Tatogga along Hwy 37. The village also offers guides and float plane hire.

The spectacular Atlin Provincial Park is only accessible from the Yukon on Hwy 7, off the Alaska Hwy. About one-third of the park is covered by large icefields and glaciers.

Massett, one of three major towns on Graham Island, the most populous of the Queen Charlotte Islands

Northern
Canada

Introducing Northern Canada

NORTHERN CANADA COVERS the Yukon, Northwest Territories, and Nunavut, and stretches up to within 800 km (500 miles) of the North Pole, and from the Atlantic Ocean west to the Pacific, 37 percent of Canada's total area. The landscape is incredibly harsh: barren, treeless, frozen tundra dominates most of the year, with subarctic forest, mountains, glaciers, and icy lakes and rivers. Nonetheless, an abundance of wildlife flourishes, with musk ox, caribou, polar bears, and seals. At the height of the brief summer the "midnight sun" provides 24-hour days, while the Aurora Borealis *(see p335)* illuminates dark winters with ribbons of colored light. Development in the far north has occurred only where conditions are hospitable, often where the land is most scenic and varied. Populated by First Nations people some 25,000 years ago and the Inuit about 3000 BC, this uniquely dramatic land is enjoyed by 500,000 visitors a year.

BANKS ISLAND

VICTORIA ISLAND

INUVIK

DAWSON

YUKON

MAYO

HAINES JUNCTION

WHITEHORSE

NORTHWEST TERRITORIES

Great Bear Lake

COPPERMINE

FORT SIMPSON

FORT PROVIDENCE

YELLOWKNIFE

Great Slave Lake

HAY RIVER

Glorious flaming fall colors rise above the evergreens in the north of the Yukon

GETTING AROUND

The watchword when traveling in this region is cost; trips, accommodations, and even food are all far more expensive than in the rest of the country. In the Yukon all major towns are connected by bus, but the most flexible way to travel around is by car. Air is the best means of traveling in Nunavut and the Northwest Territories. There are 600 landing strips and small airports here. Visitors should be aware that accommodations are equally restricted. In many settlements only one hotel is available, but the Yukon towns are well-equipped with places to stay.

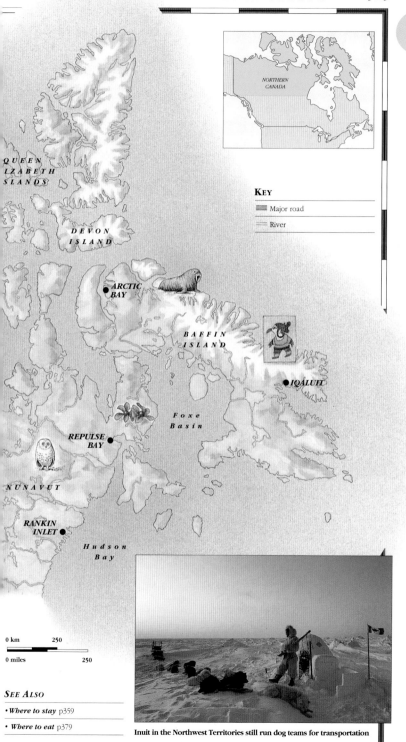

NORTHERN
CANADA

KEY

| | Major road |
| | River |

*QUEEN
ELIZABETH
ISLANDS*

*DEVON
ISLAND*

● *ARCTIC
BAY*

*BAFFIN
ISLAND*

● *IQALUIT*

*Foxe
Basin*

*REPULSE
BAY* ●

NUNAVUT

*RANKIN
INLET* ●

*Hudson
Bay*

0 km   250

0 miles   250

SEE ALSO

• *Where to stay* p359

• *Where to eat* p379

Inuit in the Northwest Territories still run dog teams for transportation

Inuit Art and Culture

For CENTURIES, the hunting and trapping lifestyle has created a distinct culture for the Inuit. Their customs have remained largely the same throughout the communities of eastern and central Northern Canada, although regional differences can be seen in the varied artforms. The Inuit have a limited written tradition, and much of 21st-century culture is still oral. It might seem surprising, given the outstandingly harsh environment and limited natural resources, that their communities offer a flourishing artistic output, but it is the hardship of northern life that has promoted artistic achievement. For example, the Inuit use their tool-making skills for sculpture. Inuit culture is closely tied to their lansdcape and environment, which has inspired many artists and mythmakers.

This woodblock print of a girl meeting a polar bear represents an artform developed in the 1950s. Stone cuts and stencils are also used to interpret drawings by older artists.

Warm clothing is both functional and decorative. Often painstakingly handwoven from scraps from the remains of a kill, women dress their families mostly in fur and wool.

Inuit beadwork and jewelry was made in earlier times from bone and ivory; colored stones and beads are now used. Each piece shows birds, animals, or people, and is unique. Western influences include new designs in silver and gold.

This soapstone carving represents Inuk, the human superhero of many pre-Christian Inuit legends, with a friendly seal companion.

INUIT WOMAN PREPARING CHAR
The outdated, if not offensive, name for the Inuit people is "eskimo," a native Cree word meaning "eaters of raw meat." The Inuit traditionally eat their meat uncooked, as the Arctic has no trees for firewood. Much of the caribou, polar bear, and fish was sundried or mixed with sauces made from summer fruits and berries. The arrival of the stone and modern fuels has changed the menu somewhat, although tradition remains at the heart of the community's eating habits.

These dancing costume ornaments are carved from ivory or whalebone and worn by Inuit dancers to celebrate ceremonial events. As with clothing, Arctic bird feathers are used for decoration.

Inuit father and son in parkas, *which are traditionally made by the women of the family. They use caribou, wolf, and polar bear fur. Today, imported Western fabrics are added for decoration.*

Inuit Homes are no longer the traditional igloo. Most people have moved to camps or community housing.

Inuit fishermen *have made the best possible use of their often limited natural resources and still rely largely on small-scale fishing for food.*

INUIT MYTH

Carving of Inuk fighting his spirit

Set on the very fringes of the habitable world, the Inuit guarded against the threat of starvation with a supernatural belief system based on the respect of the animals they hunted, being careful to guard against divine retribution. Their myths promote the belief that every living creature has a soul, and that the village shaman could travel between the upper and lower worlds to commune with, and appease, the spirits in control of the hunt and the weather. Since earliest times hunting tools and weapons have been carved with the representations of the appropriate guardian spirit, and singers and musicians are well versed in legends of sea spirits and human heroes.

Traditional hunting and fishing remains at the core of Inuit culture, although in the 1960s the Ottawa government unsuccessfully tried to stop these ancient practices.

Drum dancing *is one of the varied forms of traditional music, and plays an important part in most of life's great events: births, weddings, a successful hunt, and honoring a person who has died. Another form of music, throat singing, is usually performed by two women facing one another to recount a legend, life event, or myth.*

NORTHERN CANADA

STILL ONE of the most remote destinations on Earth, Northern Canada's Arctic beauty is now accessible to adventurous travelers in search of untouched terrain for superlative, challenging hiking and exploring. Many of the settlements at this brink of the world were established only in the 20th century. Some of the first towns grew up around RCMP outposts, established to monitor trappers, explorers, and whalers in Canadian territory; more recently defense outposts have developed new settlements. Local Inuit communities have gradually given up their nomadic life, and many are now settled around these outposts. These small towns are bases for exploring the stunning surroundings. In the winter the north is cold, descending to -50°C (-58°F), yet in summer warm air sweeps over the cold land, and the tundra bursts into bloom. The thaw acts in defiance of eight long months of winter when everything is draped in a blanket of white. This is a startlingly beautiful land with deserted plains, icy trails, rare wildlife, and gentle people, and is ripe for discovery.

SIGHTS AT A GLANCE

Historic Towns and Cities
Burwash Landing **5**
Carcross **2**
Dawson City **7**
Fort Providence **11**
Haines Junction **3**
Hay River **12**
Inuvik **8**

Norman Wells **9**
Stewart Crossing **6**
Whitehorse **1**
Yellowknife **13**

National Parks
Kluane National Park **4**
Nahanni National
  Park Reserve **10**

Areas of Natural Beauty
Baffin Island **17**
Baker Lake **15**
Banks Island and
  Victoria Island **16**
Rankin Inlet **14**

KEY

✈ International airport

▬ Major road

— Major rail route

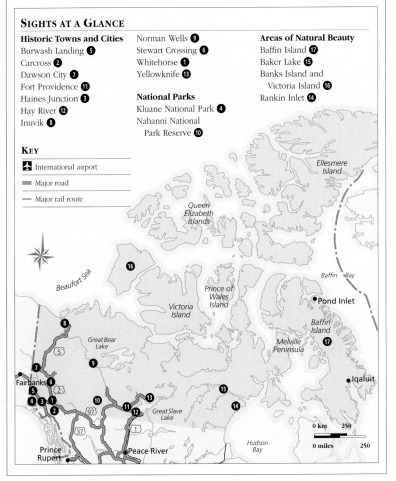

◁ **The frozen seas surrounding the coast of Baffin Island**

Whitehorse ❶

WHITEHORSE TAKES ITS NAME from the local rapids on the Yukon River that reminded miners in the gold rush of "the flowing manes of albino Appaloosas." The town evolved when 2,500 stampeders on the hunt for gold braved the arduous Chilkoot and White Pass trails on foot in the winter of 1897–98 and set up camp here by the banks of Lindeman and Bennett Lakes. Boatmen made over 7,000 trips through the rapids during the spring thaw of 1898 before a tramway was built around them. On the spot where gold miners could catch a boat downstream to the mines of the Klondike and the glittering nightlife of Dawson City in the Yukon, a tent town sprang up and Whitehorse was born. This regional capital is the fastest-growing town in the northern territories, but despite all modern amenities, the wilderness is always only a few moments away.

🏛 MacBride Museum
First Avenue & Wood St. ☎ (867) 667 2709. ◯ late May–Sep: daily; Sep–May: noon–4pm Tue–Thu. ⬚ ⬚
The MacBride Museum is housed in a log cabin at the corner of Wood Street and First Avenue along the river. Here the exciting history of the Yukon is revealed in its glory, with galleries featuring the gold rush, Whitehorse, natural history, the Mounties (RCMP), and native peoples of the region. Special features include an engine from the White Pass and Yukon Railroad, and a log cabin complete with recorded poetry readings from Yukon poet Robert Service *(see p31)*. Also included is the restored old government telegraph office, originally built in 1899 and used as the focus for the new museum in the 1950s.

🏢 Log Skyscrapers
Lambert St. & Third St. ℹ (867) 667 3084.
Two blocks away from the Old Log Church Museum on Elliott Street are the unique log skyscrapers. Now several decades old, these log cabins have two or three floors. They are still used as apartments and offices, and one was home to a Yukon member of parliament. Worth a detour, the cabins offer a pleasing diversion from the rather functional architecture that characterizes much of the rest of town.

🏛 Old Log Church Museum
Elliott St. & Third Ave. ☎ (867) 668 2555. ◯ 9am–6pm Mon–Sat; noon–4pm Sun. ⬚ ⬚
In 1900 Whitehorse's first priest lived and held services in a tent in the town – by 1901 the Old Log Church and Rectory had been built. They are now among the few buildings here remaining from the gold rush period. The church was the Roman Catholic cathedral for the diocese and is the only wooden cathedral in the world. Fully restored and now also open as a museum, the church displays exhibits of pre-contact life of the native peoples, as well as early explorers and exploration, the gold rush, long-standing missionary work with the natives in the region, and the church's history.

The Old Log Church, constructed entirely from local timber

🏛 S.S. Klondike
End Second Ave. ☎ (867) 667 4511. ◯ mid-May–mid-Sep: 9am–7pm daily. ⬚ ⬚
Originally built in 1929, the S.S. *Klondike* paddle-steamer sank in 1936. Rebuilt from its wreckage, the *Klondike* made 15 supply trips each season to Dawson City. In the early 1950s, bridges along the road to Dawson were built too low, blocking the passage of the sternwheelers, so all journeys stopped. The *Klondike* ceased

The city center of Whitehorse, sheltered in the Yukon River valley

S.S. *Klondike* in its permanent home in Whitehorse

operating in 1955 and was beached forever in Whitehorse. It is now restored to its heyday in every detail, right down to the 1937 *Life* magazines on the tables and authentic staff uniforms. Although no longer operational, the boat is a National Historic Site, with regular guided tours of the interior on offer.

🦌 Lake Laberge

Klondike Hwy. 🎫 (867) 668 3225. ⭕ daily, weather permitting.

Largest of the lakes in the area, Lake Laberge is 62 km (39 miles) from Whitehorse along the Klondike Hwy. Frozen for most of the year, with temperatures dropping below -30°C (-22°F), this popular summer swimming, fishing, and boating destination comes to life during the annual thaw. The lake is famous among locals as the site of the funeral pyre of Yukon poet Robert Service's Cremation of Sam Mc Gee, which relates the true-life demise of a local hero. Trout fishing is excellent; fish were barged here by the ton during the Klondike gold rush to feed the hordes of hopeful miners.

Local mountain goat

🦌 Yukon Wildlife Reserve

Takhini Hot Springs Rd.

🎫 (867) 668 3992. ⭕ daily. 🅿

This sanctuary was set up in 1965 for research and breeding purposes and lies about 25 km (16 miles) from the town off the Klondike Hwy on the Takhini Hot Springs Road. A beautiful reserve of forest, grassland, meadows, and water areas, it has many indigenous animals of the far north roaming free in their natural settings. Moose, bison, elk, caribou, mountain goats, deer, Dall sheep, as well as musk ox can all be seen here protected in the 280-ha (700-acre) parkland of their natural roaming habitat.

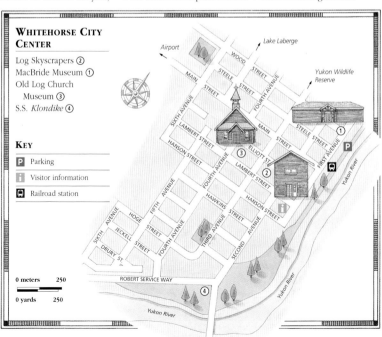

WHITEHORSE CITY CENTER

Log Skyscrapers ②
MacBride Museum ①
Old Log Church
   Museum ③
S.S. *Klondike* ④

KEY

🅿 Parking

ℹ Visitor information

🚉 Railroad station

0 meters 250
0 yards 250

Male caribou resting near Carcross, as herds migrate across the Yukon

Carcross ❷

🏃 250. 🚌 🛈 (867) 821 4431,
🕐 mid–May–Sep daily.

Carcross is a small village that lies at the picturesque confluence of Bennet and Tagish Lakes, an hour's drive south of Yukon's regional capital, Whitehorse. Early miners crossing the arduous Chilkoot Pass on their journey to the bounty of the gold mines in the north named the site "Caribou Crossing" after herds of caribou stormed their way through the pass between the two lakes on their biannual migration. The town was established in 1898 in the height of the gold rush with the arrival of the White Pass and Yukon railroad. "Caribou Crossing" was abbreviated officially to Carcross to avoid duplication of names in Alaska, British Colombia, and a town in the Klondike.

Carcross has a strong native tradition, and was once an important caribou hunting ground for the Tagish tribe. Tagish guides worked for US Army surveyors during the building of the Alaska Highway in 1942 *(see pp 260–61)*.

Traveling just 2 km (1 mile) north, there is a chance to see the smallest desert in the world, Carcross Desert. Blasted by strong winds, the sandy plain is barren, and the only remnant of a glacial lake that dried up after the last Ice Age. The strength of the winds allows little vegetation to grow, but the spot is memorable.

Haines Junction ❸

🏃 862. 🚌 🛈 Kluane National Park
Visitor Information Centre (867) 634
2345.

A useful service center on the Alaska and Haines highways, Haines Junction is a handy fuel and food stop for visitors on the way to the impressive Kluane National Park. The town has a post office, restaurant, and hotels. Trips into the park for rafting, canoeing, and various hiking excursions can be organized from the town, as the park's administrative headquarters are here. Haines Junction was once a base camp for the US Army engineers who in 1942 built much of the Alcan Highway (now known as the Alaska Highway) that links Fairbanks in Alaska to the south of Canada. The St. Elias Mountains tower above the town, and air trips can be taken from here to admire the views of the frozen scenery, glaciers, and icy peaks of this wilderness.

Kaskawulsh Glacier rising over Kluane National Park

Kluane National Park ❹

📞 (867) 634 2345. 🚌 Haines
Junction. 🕐 year round. 🏞 🅰 ✓

This superb wilderness area is a United Nations World Heritage Site. Covering 22,000 square km (8,500 square miles) of the southwest corner of the Yukon, the park shares the St. Elias mountain range, the highest in Canada, with Alaska. The whole park comprises the largest nonpolar icefield in the world.

Two-thirds of the park is glacial, filled with valleys and lakes that are frozen year-round, broken up by alpine forests, meadows, and tundra. The landscape is one of the last surviving examples of an Ice Age environment, which disappeared in the rest of the world around 5–10,000 BC. Mount Logan, at over 5,950 m (18,500 ft), is Canada's tallest peak. Numerous well-marked and established trails make for excellent hiking here, and

The St. Elias range dominates the small town of Haines Junction

Kluane National Park displays radiant foliage in fall, as seen here in the Alsek River area

several conveniently start from the main road. There are some less defined routes, which follow the old mining trails. There are trails to suit both the novice and experienced hiker, ranging from a two-hour stroll to a ten-day guided trek.

Kluane's combination of striking scenery and an abundance of wildlife, including moose, Dall sheep, and grizzly bears, make it the Yukon's most attractive wilderness destination. Trips into the park are organized mostly from nearby Haines Junction. Due to the hazardous weather, untamed wildlife, and isolated conditions, safety measures are mandatory here.

Burwash Landing ❺

🏛 88. 🛈 *Whitehorse (867) 667 3084.*

Northwest of Haines Junction by 124 km (77 miles), this little village at the western end of Kluane Lake lies just outside Kluane National Park on the Alaska Hwy. A community was established here in 1905, after a gold strike in a local creek, and Burwash Landing is now a service center. Visitors can also enjoy stunning panoramas of Kluane Lake to the south.

The village is noted for its Kluane Museum, with many animal-related exhibits, including a mammoth's tooth and numerous displays on local

natural history. Focus is also given to the traditional lifestyle of the region's tribe of Southern Tutchone native people.

🏛 **Kluane Museum**
Burwash Junction. 📞 (867) 841 5561. 🕐 *mid-May–mid-Sep: 9am–9pm daily.* 🍽 ♿

Stewart Crossing ❻

🏛 25. 🚗 🛈 *Whitehorse (867) 667 3084.*

Approximately 180 km (113 miles) east of Dawson City (*see p334*), Stewart Crossing is a small community at the junction of the Klondike Hwy and the Silver Trail, which leads to the small mining settlements of Mayo, Elsa, and Keno, once famous for their silver trade. During the gold rush in the late 19th century, the area was referred to as the "grubstake," because enough gold could be panned from the river sandbars here during the summer to buy the following

year's stake. Stewart Crossing is a modest service center that also operates as the starting-point for canoe trails on the Stewart River. Unusual for this wild terrain, these boat trips are suitable for children and beginners. Trips should be organized in Whitehorse or Dawson City.

Above the community is a scenic viewpoint that overlooks the spectacular Klondike River valley and the **Tintina Trench**. Providing in a glance visible proof of the geological theory of plate tectonics, the trench itself stretches for several hundred kilometers across the Yukon, with layers of millennia-old rock gaping open to the skies. "Tintina" means "chief" in the local native language, and this is one of the largest geological faults in the Yukon system. Stewart Crossing is an ideal place to view the trench, which runs up to here along the route of the Klondike Hwy, from a course parallel with the Yukon River that begins at Fortymile village.

Broad Valley by Stewart Crossing near the Yukon River, Yukon

The stunning beauty of a Yukon river valley in summer ▷

The Gaslight Follies Theatre in Dawson City

Dawson City ⑦

2,150. ✗ 🚗 🚻 **ℹ** *cnr Front & King Sts. (867) 993 5566.*

THE TOWN OF Dawson City came into prominence during the Klondike gold rush of 1898 (*see pp46–7*), when the population boomed and the city grew from a moose pasture into a bustling metropolis of some 30–40,000 people, all seeking their fortune in the new "Paris of the North." Dawson City continues to mine gold, but tourism is now the town's most reliable source of income.

Inuvik welcomes its visitors

Dawson City Museum has exhibits on the Klondike, with features on the gold rush and artifacts from that period. A popular attraction is **Diamond Tooth Gertie's**, the gambling hall complete with a honky-tonk piano and can-can girls.

🏛 **Dawson City Museum**
5th Ave. **ℹ** *(867) 993 5291.*
🕐 *mid-May–Sep: 10am–6pm daily; late Sep–May: by appointment.* 💳 ♿
🎰 **Diamond Tooth Gertie's**
cnr 4th Ave. & Queen St. **ℹ** *(867) 993 5575.* 🕐 *mid-May–mid-Sep: 7pm–2am daily.* 💳 ♿

Inuvik ⑧

3,300. ✗ **ℹ** *W. Arctic Regional Visitors' Centre (867) 777 4727.*

ABOUT 770 KM (480 miles) north of Dawson City, Inuvik lies at the tip the Dempster Hwy, the most northerly road in Canada. At the heart of the Mackenzie River delta, Inuvik has only a very recent history. Founded in the 1950s as a supply center for military projects in the NWT, the town prospered in the oil boom of the 1970s. Full of functional contemporary architecture, Inuvik's charm lies more in its location as a very good visitors' center for the region – there are a few hotels and several shops, no mean feat for a town that boasts just a single traffic light. It is, nonetheless, the most visited town in the northern Arctic, popular as a craft center for the Inuit and as a starting point for a tour of the far north.

ENVIRONS: The settlement of Paulatuk lies 400 km (250 miles) east of Inuvik and is one of the smallest communities in the territory. It is well placed for hunting, fishing, and trapping game; these activities remain its staple support for many centuries. Its location is also useful as a stepping-stone to the wilderness. Tourism is becoming popular, and trips leave from here with Inuit guides in search of wildlife. Visitors also come to see the unusual Smoking Hills nearby, which are composed of sulfide-rich slate and coal.

Norman Wells ⑨

800. ✗ **ℹ** *NWT Tourism Office, 52nd St., Yellowknife (867) 873 7200.*

IN 1919 CRUDE OIL discoveries were made here near a small Inuit settlement. Oil production surged in World War II when the US estabishd a pipeline to supply oil to the Alaska Highway while it was being built, and the town grew. The wells closed down in 1996 for economic reasons.

Today Norman Wells is the starting point for the Canol Heritage Route, a long-distance path of wilderness trail through to the Canol Road above the Ross River in the Yukon Territory, which links up with the Yukon Highway system. There are few facilities along the trail, making it one of the toughest trekking paths in the world. Despite the difficulties, this is a popular destination with experienced hikers.

Nahanni National Park Reserve ⑩

ℹ *(867) 695 2713.* ✗ *Fort Simpson.* 🕐 *year round.* 💳 **ℹ** *Nahanni National Park Reserve, Post Bag 300, Fort Simpson, NWT.*

NAHANNI NATIONAL Park Reserve sits astride the South Nahanni River between the border with the Yukon and the small settlement of Fort Simpson. In 1978, it was

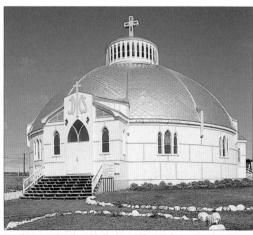

Inuvik's town church and hall, shaped like an igloo against the climate

The vast expanses of Nahanni National Park in summer

Hay River ⑫

🚶 3,600. ✈ 🚌 ⓘ *MacKenzie Hwy (867) 874 3180.* ☐ *Jun–Sep.*

SET ON THE BANKS of Great Slave Lake, the small community of Hay River is the major port in the Northwest Territories. A lifeline, the town supplies the High Arctic settlements and the northernmost towns in the country, particularly Inuvik, with essentials. When the river thaws in spring, it supplies freight. The town looks designed for the purpose it serves – the wharves are lined with barges and tugs, as well as the local fishing fleet.

Unusually for this area, Hay River's history stretches back over a millennium. The Dene moved here centuries ago, lured by the town's strategic position at the southern shore of the Great Slave Lake, for its hunting and fishing. Attractions here are based on local industry; as a shipping center, the harbor is a bustling place to spot barges. The original Dene settlement, now a village of 260 people, sits across the river north from the Old Town and welcomes visitors.

the first place in the world to be designated a UN World Heritage Site to protect its wildlife. The park is a great wilderness with four vast river canyons, hot springs, and North America's most spectacular undeveloped waterfall, Virginia Falls. The falls, at 90 m (295 ft), are twice the height of Niagara but have less volume, and boast excellent flora and fauna. At least 13 species of fish enjoy the cascades, and more than 120 varieties of bird live overhead. Wolves, grizzly bears, and woodland caribou move freely in the park.

The park's main activities are, surprisingly, not wildlife-watching but whitewater rafting and canoeing. In summer, watersports take precedence over walking tours as the rivers thaw and the landscape bursts into bloom with wild flowers. The park can be reached by boat along the Nahanni River.

the local Dene First Nations people settled here permanently. Today the town is a Dene handicrafts center.

Immediately north of the village lies the Mackenzie Bison Sanctuary. The sanctuary is home to the world's largest herd of 2,000 rare pure wood bison. The park stretches for 100 km (60 miles) north along the banks of Great Slave Lake, and bison can be seen along the road by drivers.

Fort Providence ⑪

🚶 750. 🚌 ⓘ *NWT Tourism Office, 52nd St., Yellowknife (867) 873 7200.*

THE DENE PEOPLE call this village "zhahti koe," which means mission house in their native tongue. Fort Providence began life as a Catholic mission and was later enlarged by the Hudson's Bay Company (*see pp158–9*), which set up an outpost here in the late 19th century. Attracted by this and the prospect of employment,

THE NORTHERN LIGHTS

The Northern Lights, or *aurora borealis*, are believed to be the result of solar winds entering the Earth's ionosphere some 160 km (100 miles) above the surface of the planet. Emanating from the sun, these winds collide with the gases present in the Earth's upper atmosphere, releasing energy that becomes visible in the night sky. The stunning consequences are visible in the Yukon and the NWT, most often from August to October. Some Inuit groups attach religious significance to the Lights, believing them to be the spirits of dead hunters, while 19th-century gold prospectors mistook them for vapors given off by ore deposits. Whatever one's beliefs, the sparkling ribbons of light are an awesome sight.

Yellowknife ⑬

ORIGINALLY A NATIVE Dene settlement, Yellowknife is named after the yellow-bladed copper hunting knives used by its first residents. The Hudson's Bay Company closed its outpost here in 1823 due to failing profits, but the Old Town thrived again with gold mining in the 1930s and again after 1945. With improved road communications, the city became the regional capital of the Northwest Territories in 1967. Growing bureaucratic needs and the occasional successful goldmine guaranteed that Yellowknife has flourished ever since the 1960s.

VISITORS' CHECKLIST

🏠 15,200. ✈ ℹ The Northern Frontier Regional Visitors' Centre, 4804 49th St. (867) 873 4262. 🎭 The Caribou Carnival (Mar); Festival of the Midnight Sun (Jul); Folk on the Rocks (Jul).

Makeshift houseboats built from empty oildrums on the Great Slave Lake

here on Yellowknife Bay, many living on makeshift houseboats. Also interesting is the variety of older architecture that can be seen from a stroll around this now residential area. Shops and accomodations are found farther south in the New Town. A good vantage point from which to survey the area is the Bush Pilot's Monument (a blue Bristol airplane) at the north end of Franklin Avenue.

The Old Town

Just 1 km (0.5 mile) north of downtown, the Old Town is situated on an island and a rocky peninsula on the Great Slave Lake. By 1947 Yellowknife had outgrown itself, and the New Town rose from the sandy plain southward. An unusual community thrives

The Wildcat Café

Wiley Road. 📞 (867) 669 2200. ☐ Jun–Sep: 11am–9pm daily. ♿ The oldest restaurant in Yellowknife, this institution is open only during the summer. A true frontier stop, the sagging log cabin is set under the hill

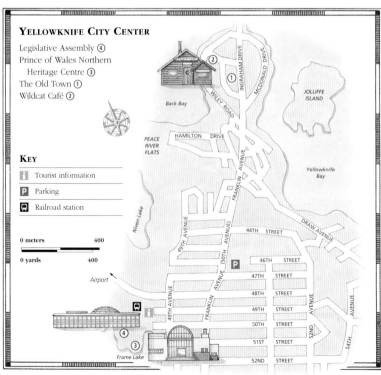

YELLOWKNIFE CITY CENTER

Legislative Assembly ④
Prince of Wales Northern
   Heritage Centre ③
The Old Town ①
Wildcat Café ②

KEY

ℹ   Tourist information

🅿   Parking

🚉   Railroad station

0 meters   400
0 yards   400

of the Old Town and has been refurbished in 1930s style. Its atmospheric interior is reminiscent of the pioneer days. Rather showing its age, this establishment is the most photographed building in Yellowknife. It is also the most popular eating place – top dishes include hearty stew and fish.

Sampling the fare at the Wildcat Café is a truly northern experience

🏛 The Prince of Wales Heritage Centre

49th Street. ◀ (867) 873 7551. ◯ daily. ● public holidays. ♿
This excellent local museum is a good introduction to the history of the Northwest Territories. There is a display on the lifestyles of the Dene and Inuit peoples, followed by one describing European development of the area. Another gallery retells the history of aviation in the Territories, with exhibits on natural sciences.

🏛 The Legislative Assembly

Frame Lake. ◀ (867) 669 2200. ◯ Mon–Fri. ♿ ☑ Jul & Aug.
Built in 1993, this headquarters of local government has a tall domed roof that stands out in the area. Signifying equal rights for all ethnic groups, the government chamber is the only round one of its kind in the country, with a large oval table to give all delegates equal responsibility, in the manner practiced by aboriginals. Decorated with paintings and Inuit art, the chamber is graced with a large polar bear rug. The official public government rooms can be toured when the council is not in session.

Rankin Inlet ❶

🏛 2,058. 🛈 (867) 645 3838. ✈

FOUNDED IN 1955 when North Rankin Nickel Mine opened, Rankin Inlet is the largest community in the stony plateau of Keewatin, the mainly Inuit district of Nunavut that stretches east of the Canadian Shield to Hudson Bay. This small town is the government center for the Keewatin region, whose population, now 85 percent aboriginal, has settled mainly on the coast. The Inlet is also the local tourism center.

This region is characterized by its historic rural way of life and stunning Arctic scenery. **Meliadine Park**, 10 km (6 miles) from the town center, contains a traditional Thule (ancestor of the Inuit) restored native site with stone tent rings, meat stores, and semi-subterranean winter houses.

🍁 Meliadine Park

10 km (6 miles) northwest of Rankin Inlet. ◀ (867) 645 3838. ◯ daily, weather permitting.

Baker Lake ❶

🏛 1,385. ✈ 🛈 (867) 793 2456.

BAKER LAKE IS geographically at the center of Canada and is the country's only inland Inuit community. Located at the source of the Thelon River, the area has always been a traditional summer gathering place for different Inuit peoples. Today it is an important center for Inuit art, especially textiles.

Heading westward, the **Thelon Game Sanctuary** can also be visited. Visitors can see herds of musk ox in their natural habitat and glimpse other indigenous animals and birds.

🦌 Thelon Game Sanctuary

300 km (200 miles) w. of Baker Lake. ◀ (867) 873 4262. ◯ daily.

Banks Island and Victoria Island ❶

🛈 (867) 645 3838.

LOCATED IN THE Arctic Ocean, Banks Island is home to the largest herds of musk ox in the world. They dwell in **Aulavik National Park**, on the remote northern tip of the island. This numbers among the world's most remote wildlife destinations, and is accessible only by plane. In common with large areas of the far north, trips are mostly undertaken by the wealthy and adventurous.

Split between the Northwest Territories and Nunavut, Victoria Island has a town in each – Holman in NWT and the Inuit Cambridge Bay in Nunavut, where local native people traveled each summer for char fishing and caribou and seal hunting. The town today is a service center for locals and visitors along the Arctic coast. Polar bears, musk ox, wolves, and Arctic birds live nearby.

🍁 Aulavik National Park

Sachs Harbour. ◀ (867) 690 3904. ◯ daily, weather permitting. ☑

An Inuit igloo builder near Baker Lake, practicing this traditional skill

Baffin Island

Purple Saxifrage in summer

P ART OF NUNAVUT, Baffin Island is one of the most remote places in North America. At 500,000 square km (193,000 square miles), the island is the fifth largest on the planet, with more than 60 percent of its landmass lying above the Arctic Circle. Sparsely populated, the island is inhabited by just 11,000 people, 9,000 of whom are Inuit. Most people live in one of nine settlements scattered throughout the island, the chief of which is Iqaluit, capital of the province of Nunavut.

With its spectacular fjords and knife-edged mountains sparkling with glaciers, Baffin Island offers a chance to experience all the outdoor activities of the Arctic. Canoeing, kayaking, trekking, and thrilling glacial walks are all unbeatable here. Many of the activities often take place in the company of abundant wildlife, including polar bears and whales.

Nanisivik is a mining settlement founded in 1974 to exploit lead and zinc, which can only be shipped when the inlet's sea thaws in summer.

ARCTIC BAY

BRODEUR PENINSULA

BYLOT ISLAND

BORDEN PENINSULA

Pond Inlet

Pond Inlet is a jewel in Nunavut's twinkling crown. Blessed with stunning scenery of mountains, glaciers, and icebergs, the town is surrounded by abundant Arctic marine life. Snowmobiling and dogsled rides to the floe's edge are popular.

PRIN CHAR ISLA

AUYUITTUQ NATIONAL PARK

Auyuittuq is the third-largest national park in Canada at 21,470 square km (8,300 square miles). It is a rarity as one of the few national parks above the Arctic Circle on Earth. A spectacular destination, the park displays a pristine wilderness of mountains, valleys, and fjords. In spring the meadows thaw out from under their snowy coverlets, and wildflowers burst into bloom. Within the park borders, wildlife abounds, with animals ranging from snow geese and arctic foxes to polar bears sharing the territory. Even in the brief summer, the weather can be tricky with the risk of heavy snow. Temperatures are low year-round. The nearby town of Pangnirtung is a craft center.

Wildflowers flourish beneath Auyuittuq's frozen peaks

| 0 km | 100 |
| 0 miles | 100 |

Cape Dorset is of interest archeologically as predecessors of the modern Inuit, the Thule and Dorset peoples, lived in this area.

KEY

— Rivers

— National Park boundary

❄ Viewpoint

☒ Domestic airport

Pangnirtung

This little town of 1,100 residents sits at the southern end of the Pangnirtung Pass, the 100-km (62-mile) hiking trail which is the most popular on Baffin. During the summer the Pass is free of snow and can be negotiated quite easily. Views of the fjord below are stupendous.

VISITORS'

11,400. Nu... Tourism, Iqaluit (867)...
w www.nunanet.com/...
Toonik Tyme (Apr), Iqalu...

ACCESSING CANADA'S NORTH

While tourism to the Northwest Territories increases every year, visitors should be aware of severely limited travel and communications. The only access to these remote settlements is by air, which is very expensive compared to mainline routes. Despite the cost, the region has over 600 airports and small landing strips covering the region.

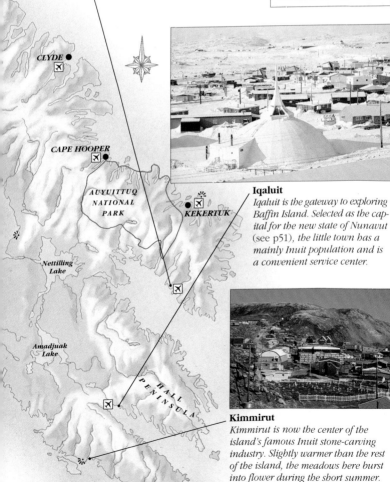

Iqaluit

Iqaluit is the gateway to exploring Baffin Island. Selected as the capital for the new state of Nunavut (see p51), the little town has a mainly Inuit population and is a convenient service center.

Kimmirut

Kimmirut is now the center of the island's famous Inuit stone-carving industry. Slightly warmer than the rest of the island, the meadows here burst into flower during the short summer.

ACCESSING CANADA'S NORTH

While tourism to the Northwest Territories increases every year, visitors should be aware of severely limited travel and communications. The only access to these remote settlements is by air, which is very expensive compared to mainline routes. Despite the cost, the region has over 600 airports and small landing strips covering the region.

Pangnirtung

This little town of 1,100 residents sits at the southern end of the Pangnirtung Pass, the 100-km (62-mile) hiking trail which is the most popular on Baffin. During the summer the Pass is free of snow and can be negotiated quite easily. Views of the fjord below are stupendous.

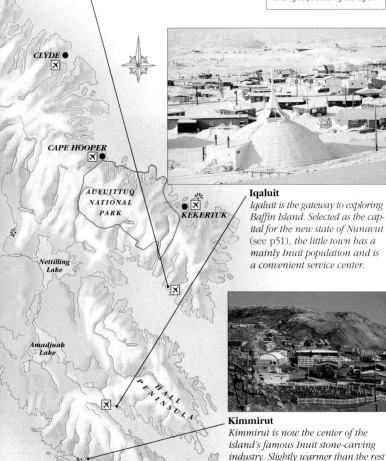

Iqaluit

Iqaluit is the gateway to exploring Baffin Island. Selected as the capital for the new state of Nunavut (see p51), the little town has a mainly Inuit population and is a convenient service center.

Kimmirut

Kimmirut is now the center of the island's famous Inuit stone-carving industry. Slightly warmer than the rest of the island, the meadows here burst into flower during the short summer.

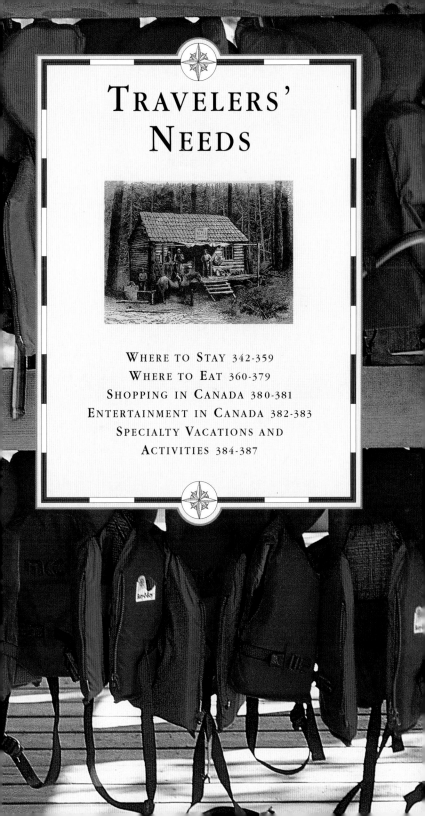

TRAVELERS' NEEDS

WHERE TO STAY

AS ONE MIGHT expect in a country of its size, Canada has a wide range of places in which to stay: from stately, world-famous hotels such as the Château Frontenac in Quebec City, to family-run bed-and-breakfasts in the countryside, the variety is immense. Canada offers excellent middle-range accommodations, and you will find rural inns, cottages to rent in scenic spots, elegant town apartments, hostels, houseboats, and the most popular choice of all, the convenient motel. Whether you need a mid-journey bed for the night or a seasonal rental, you can always find the right place and may not even need to book in advance. The listings on *pp344–59* describe in full a selection of destinations for every taste and budget.

Hotel doorman

A rental lodge in Banff National Park

GRADING AND FACILITIES

THERE IS NO government-sponsored hotel grading system in Canada, but the voluntary program "Canada Select" is usually very accurate. Each establishment is rated by numbers of stars. It is worth bearing in mind, however, that a 4-star hotel in a large city such as Toronto, for example, might not have the same level of facilities as one with the same rating in a small upscale resort with a château hotel.

The Canadian Automobile Association also operates an assessment system, mostly for hotels and motels along main highways, and these, while also non-official, are largely recognized as consistent and accurate. Air-conditioning comes as standard in most of the country during summer, except in national park lodges and cooler coastal and northern regions. Central heating country-wide is efficient. Cable TV, radio, irons and ironing boards, and coffee-making facilities are standard. Private bathrooms are usual, but you will need to specify a bathtub or shower – also remember to ask for double or twin beds when booking a double room.

PRICES

WITH SUCH A wide range of accommodations, prices vary hugely. In a major town, the top hotel's presidential suite may command a daily rate in excess of Can$1,000, while a hiker's hostel will provide a dormitory bed for under Can$25. Budget hotels and B-and-Bs charge Can$50–75 a night per person. Some prices rise in high season, but rates are discounted in low season.

RESERVATIONS

ADVANCE reservations are always recommended in the main cities, where festivals, conventions, meetings, and major sports and musical events are held year-round (*see pp34–7*). Provincial tourist offices or airlines (*see p393*) will assist in suggesting and arranging bookings.

CHILDREN

TRAVELING WITH children is relatively easy. Nearly every property will supply a cot or junior-sized bed in a parents' room. Major hotels offer baby-sitting services. A lone parent traveling with children may need written consent from the other parent under anti-abduction regulations.

DISABLED TRAVELERS

CANADA'S BUILDING laws require all new and renovated public buildings to provide wheelchair facilities with ramps, wide doors, and straight access to rooms. However, as many rural hotels date from the 19th century, facilities should always be checked in advance.

The imposing façade of The Royal York Hotel in Toronto (*see p351*)

LUXURY HOTELS

ALTHOUGH CANADA has few five-star hotels, the major cities boast some truly world-class establishments. The railroad age of the late 19th

Bedroom at Elmwood Inn, a B-and-B, Prince Edward Island *(see p345)*

century ushered in château-style hotels, which are unique Canadian architectural features. Nowadays, most of the castle-hotels, including the Château Frontenac, are owned and operated by Canadian Pacific Hotels. Luxury chains are well represented: the Four Seasons, the Hilton, the Radisson, the Sheraton, and Westin chains operate in Toronto, Montreal, Calgary, and Vancouver.

CHAIN HOTELS

CANADA OFFERS numerous franchise and chain hotels and motels. Reliable and comfortable, if occasionally a little bland, chains vary in style and price from grand resort areas to the less expensive but equally well-known Best Western, Comfort, and Super 8. Popular with families and business travelers, many of the properties have offices for use, including fax, e-mail, and telegraph equipment. Children's facilities are usually good.

EFFICIENCY APARTMENTS

THERE IS A tremendous variety of these options available in Canada in addition to the traditional cottage rental industry. Motorhomes or RVs (Recreational Vehicles) are gaining in popularity and can be leased in all the major cities. Most nowadays have air-conditioning, refrigerators, ovens, and bathrooms. Campgrounds are found all over the country, from lush fields in the fertile southern national parks to well-insulated zones partly inhabited by the Inuit

in the north. The proliferation of this choice guarantees high quality and a well-priced stay: electrical connections, as well as laundry facilities, general store, and sports programs are often available for all ages.

For many, the cottage or cabin option is traditionally Canadian. Ontario is famous for its selection of rural vacation homes, again very well equipped, which are available weekly, monthly, or seasonally, and are always well located for nearby attractions. National parks also rent lodges and offer campgrounds.

BED-AND-BREAKFASTS

THE GROWING number of bed-and-breakfasts across Canada is testimony to their popularity. From historic inns to rustic quarters on vacation farms, each provides personalized service, a friendly local face, and insight into the region's way of life. Atlantic Canada is renowned for its

B-and-Bs, with many located in the elegant Victorian homes of historic towns. Call the provincial tourist office for a detailed list with tariffs. Most establishments have up to four rooms for rent.

ACCOMMODATIONS TAXES

BEAR IN MIND that accommodations of almost every kind are subject to two taxes on top of the basic tariff. The first, provincial sales tax, varies from province to province from about 4–9 percent. It must be paid on accommodations as well as on goods and other services. Rules vary slightly between provinces: Alberta levies only the PST on hotel and motel stays, with campsites, B-and-Bs, and guesthouses tax-free. Manitoba and Quebec offer partial rebates on accommodations tax to foreigners on production of the receipt. Forms are available from **Revenue Canada**, Visitors' Rebate Program, 275 Pope Rd., Summerside, PEI, C1N 6C6. Most provinces charge for every stay and do not offer a rebate of the PST.

The Goods and Services Tax (GST) is a standard national charge of 7 percent throughout the country; this affects most accommodation classes. In some provinces the GST and PST are combined as "general sales tax" of approximately 15 percent. Smaller hotels may not charge the GST, so inquire on arrival. However, the GST is entirely refundable to visitors. Keep receipts and contact Revenue Canada for a refund.

A bed-and-breakfast in the Rocky Mountains

Choosing a Hotel

THE HOTELS in this guide have been selected for their good value, excellent facilities, or location. This chart lists the hotels by region in the same order as the rest of the guide. The color codes of each region are shown on the thumb tabs. Entries are alphabetical within price category. For restaurant listings, see pages 364–79.

		NUMBER OF ROOMS	RESTAURANT	CHILDREN'S FACILITIES	GARDEN/TERRACE	SWIMMING POOL
NEWFOUNDLAND AND LABRADOR						
GRAND FALLS: *Mount Peyton Hotel* 214 Lincoln Rd., NFD A2A 1P8. ☎ *(709) 489 2251.* FAX *(709) 489 6365.* This friendly family and business hotel offers hospitable service and one of the better restaurants in central Newfoundland. 🖪 📺 ♿ 🅿 🥂	$	150	●			
HAPPY VALLEY-GOOSE BAY: *Labrador Inn* 380 Hamilton Rd., LAB AUP 1CO. ☎ *(709) 896 3351.* FAX *(709) 896 3927.* The staff are big on northern hospitality here. The decor is *faux* Tudor, and the restaurant serves regional specialties. 🖪 📺 ♿ 🅿 🥂	$	74	●			
L'ANSE AU CLAIR: *Northern Light Inn* 58 Main St., NFD A0K 3K0. ☎ *(709) 931 2332.* FAX *(709) 931 2708.* This family-style hotel overlooks the bay. The restaurant serves local favorites, including Caribou. 🖪 📺 ♿ 🅿	$$	59	●			
NORRIS POINT: *Sugar Hill Inn* 115–129 Route 431, NFD A0K 4N0. ☎ *(709) 458 2147.* FAX *(709) 458 2166.* A quality inn located in the heart of Gros Morne National Park, near Lobster Point Lighthouse. The meals feature local seafood. 🖪 📺 🅿 🥂	$$	7	●			
ST. ANTHONY: *Haven Inn* Goose Cove Rd., NFD A0K 4S0. ☎ *(709) 454 9100.* FAX *(709) 454 2270.* This modern hillside motel offers great views of St. Anthony's harbor. There are cozy fireplaces in the lounge and dining room. 🖪 📺 ♿ 🅿 🥂	$	29	●			
ST. JOHN'S: *Balmoral Inn* 38 Queens Rd., NFD A1C 2AS. ☎ *(709) 754 5721.* FAX *(709) 722 8111.* This heritage property features elegant Queen Anne architecture, high ceilings, and attractive rooms decorated with antiques. 🖪 📺 🅿 🥂	$	5				
ST. JOHN'S: *Hotel Newfoundland* Cavendish Square, NFD A1C 5W8. ☎ *(709) 726 4980.* FAX *(709) 726 2025.* One of the Canadian Pacific chain, it offers views of Signal Hill and the harbor, as well as three on-site restaurants. 🖪 24 📺 ♿ 🅿 🍴 🥂	$$$$	301	●	■		■
TRINITY BAY: *Campbell House* High St., Trinity, NFD A1C 2Z1. ☎ *(709) 464 3377.* FAX *(709) 464 3377.* Two of these three waterfront homes are registered heritage properties. The oldest, built in 1842, has period antiques and decor. 🖪 📺 ♿ 🅿 🥂	$	5			●	
NEW BRUNSWICK, NOVA SCOTIA, AND PRINCE EDWARD ISLAND						
BAY FORTUNE: *The Inn at Bay Fortune* RR4, Souris, PEI C0A 2B0. ☎ *(902) 687 3745.* FAX *(902) 687 3540.* This elegant seaside inn is the perfect place to get away from it all. It is also home to one of Canada's finest restaurants *(see p364).* 🖪 ♿ 🅿 🥂	$$$$	18	●		●	
BOUCTOUCHE: *Le Vieux Presbytère* 157 Chemin du Couvent, NB E0A 1G0. ☎ *(506) 743 5568.* FAX *(506) 743 5566.* This charming Acadian country inn was built in 1880 and has gardens overlooking Bouctouche River. 🖪 📺 🅿 🥂	$	22	●		●	
BRIER ISLAND: *Brier Island Lodge* Westport, NS B0V 1H0. ☎ *(902) 839 2300.* FAX *(902) 839 2006.* Located on a tiny island in the Bay of Fundy, this small lodge is ideally situated for coastal walks and whale-watching. 🖪 📺 ♿ 🅿 🥂	$	40	●			
CAPE D'OR: *Cape d'Or Lighthousekeeper's Guesthouse* Cape d'Or Lighthouse, NS B0M 1S0. ☎ *(902) 670 0534.* This remote destination is near coastal cliffs and trails on the Minas Basin. The rooms have spectacular views. 🖪 🅿 🥂	$	4	●			

Price categories for a standard double room per night, including breakfast (where served), taxes, and any extra service charges:

$ under Can$100
$$ Can$100–$150
$$$ Can$150–$200
$$$$ Can$200–$250
$$$$$ over Can$250

RESTAURANT
Hotel restaurant or dining room, usually open to non-residents unless otherwise stated.

CHILDREN'S FACILITIES
Indicates child cribs and/or a baby-sitting service available. A few hotels also provide children's portions and high chairs in the restaurant.

GARDEN/TERRACE
Hotel with a garden, courtyard, or terrace often available for eating outside.

SWIMMING POOL
Hotel with an indoor or outdoor swimming pool.

	Price	Number of Rooms	Restaurant	Children's Facilities	Garden/Terrace	Swimming Pool
CARAQUET: *Hotel Paulin* 143 Blvd. St-Pierre west, NB E1W 1B6. (506) 727 9981. Innkeeper Gerard Paulin is the third generation of Paulins to operate this historic seaside hotel built in 1891.	$	8	●			
CAVENDISH: *Kindred Spirits Country Inn and Cottages* Route 6, PEI C0A 1N0. (902) 963 2434. FAX (902) 963 2434. This charming inn is located next to Green Gables House *(see p76)*. An oasis of peace amid this busy tourist destination. ● Nov–Apr.	$$	39				■
CHARLOTTETOWN: *Elmwood Inn* 121 North River Road, PEI P1A 3K7. (902) 368 3310. FAX (902) 628 8457. Based in Charlottetown's historic district, this is one of Canada's famous B-and-Bs. Beautifully furnished, it offers delicious food.	$$$	6			●	
CHARLOTTETOWN: *Prince Edward Hotel* 18 Queen St., PEI C1A 8B9. (902) 566 2222. FAX (902) 566 2282. One of the Canadian Pacific Hotels, the Prince Edward overlooks Charlottetown Marina. There are three on-site eateries, including a waterfront café.	$$$	213	●	■		■
EDMUNDSTON: *Howard Johnson Hotel and Convention Centre* 100 Rice St., NB E3V 1T4. (506) 739 7321. FAX (506) 735 9101. Clean, friendly, and family-oriented, this hotel is attached to a 22-store mall and well located for Edmundston's attractions.	$$	103	●	■		■
GRAND TRACADIE: *Dalvay-by-the-Sea* PEI National Park, PEI C0A 1P0. (902) 672 2048. FAX (902) 672 2741. This mansion was built by oil tycoon Alexander MacDonald in 1895. The restaurant specializes in island seafood *(see p365)*.	$$$$	32	●	■		
HALIFAX: *Delta Barrington* 1875 Barrington St., NS B3J 3L6. (902) 429 7410. FAX (902) 420 6524. Located in the heart of the city's historic downtown, this upscale business hotel is friendly and efficient.	$$	202	●	■		
HALIFAX: *Waverly Inn* 1266 Barrington St., NS B3J 1Y5. (902) 423 9346. FAX (902) 425 0167. This heritage inn opened in 1876, and its guests have included Oscar Wilde and P.T. Barnum. It is just a few minutes' walk from the historic downtown of this maritime city.	$$	32				
INGONISH BEACH: *Keltic Lodge* Middle Head Peninsula, NS B0C 1L0. (902) 285 2880. FAX (902) 285 2859. This grand resort is located on a rocky bluff overlooking Ingonish Harbour. Prices include a four-course dinner.	$$$$$	81	●	■	●	■
LOUISBOURG: *Cranberry Cove Inn* 12 Wolfe St., NS B0A 1M0. (902) 733 2171. FAX (902) 733 2449. This attractive inn was originally a private residence built in 1904. Today it offers chic accommodations and European-style cuisine using the best of the local produce.	$$	7	●			
LUNENBURG: *Lunenburg Inn* 26 Dufferin St., NS B0J 2C0. (902) 634 3963. FAX (902) 634 9419. Built in 1893, this beautiful Victorian building is located at the edge of Lunenburg's historic Old Town.	$$	7				
MARGAREE VALLEY: *Normaway Inn* Egypt Rd., NS B0E 2C0. (902) 248 2987. FAX (902) 248 2600. Located along the legendary Cabot Trail, this elegant 1920s resort is set on 100 ha (250 acres) in the heart of the Margaree Valley. It offers superb fishing, barn concerts, tennis, and a fine restaurant.	$$	29	●	■	●	

For key to symbols see back flap

Price categories for a standard double room per night, including breakfast (where served), taxes, and any extra service charges:
$ under Can$100
$$ Can$100–$150
$$$ Can$150–$200
$$$$ Can$200–$250
$$$$$ over Can$250

RESTAURANT
Hotel restaurant or dining room, usually open to non-residents unless otherwise stated.

CHILDREN'S FACILITIES
Indicates child cribs and/or a baby-sitting service available. A few hotels also provide children's portions and high chairs in the restaurant.

GARDEN/TERRACE
Hotel with a garden, courtyard, or terrace often available for eating outside.

SWIMMING POOL
Hotel with an indoor or outdoor swimming pool.

	Price	NUMBER OF ROOMS	RESTAURANT	CHILDREN'S FACILITIES	GARDEN/TERRACE	SWIMMING POOL
MONCTON: *Comfort Inn* 2495 Mountain Rd., NB E1A 6P9. ((506) 384 3175. FAX (506) 853 7307. A chain motel that offers better-than-average accommodations. Close to Magnetic Hill and the Trans-Canada Highway. 🖼 📺 & P 🌿	$	59				
ST. ANDREWS: *Algonquin Resort* 184 Adolphus St., NB E0G 2X0. ((506) 529 8823. FAX (506) 529 7162. This classic resort offers great views of Passamaquoddy Bay. Plenty of amenities, including an 18-hole golf course. 🖼 📺 & P 🛏 🌿	$$$	238	●	■	●	■
ST. ANDREWS: *Kingsbrae Arms, Relais & Châteaux* 219 King St., NB E0G 2X0. ((506) 529 1897. FAX (506) 529 1197. This elegant old-world inn is a member of the Relais & Chateaux group. Beautiful rooms with antiques, and superb dining. 🖼 24 📺 P 🌿	$$$$	8	●		●	■
SAINT JOHN: *Parkerhouse Inn and Restaurant* 71 Sydney St., NB E2L 1L5. ((506) 652 5054. FAX (506) 636 8076. Located in a Victorian mansion in the historic downtown area, a beautiful stained-glass conservatory is just one of the features. 🖼 📺 P 🌿	$	9	●		●	
SAINT JOHN: *Country Inn and Suites* 1011 Fairville Blvd., NB E2M 5T9. ((506) 635 0400. FAX (506) 635 3818. Clean, spacious accommodation and a homey atmosphere enhanced by country-style decor and a wood fire in the lounge. 🖼 📺 & P 🌿	$$	60				
SUMMERSIDE: *Loyalist Country Inn* 195 Harbour Drive, PEI C1N 5R1. ((902) 436 3333. FAX (902) 436 4304. This is a well-appointed family hotel close to the marina. The hotel is located just 20 minutes from Confederation Bridge. 🖼 📺 & P 🛏 🌿	$$$	103	●			■
WEST POINT: *West Point Lighthouse* O'Leary, RR2, PEI C0B 1V0. ((902) 859 3605. Canada's only inn in a functioning coast guard lighthouse surrounded by the sea, with country decor, crafts, and antiques. 🖼 📺 P 🌿	$	9	●			
WOLFVILLE: *Blomidon Inn* 127 Main St., NS B0P 1X0. ((902) 542 2291. FAX (902) 452 7461. This Victorian mansion is set back from the main street amid landscaped lawns. The inn is one of Nova Scotia's finest. 🖼 P 🌿	$	26	●		●	

MONTREAL

	Price	NUMBER OF ROOMS	RESTAURANT	CHILDREN'S FACILITIES	GARDEN/TERRACE	SWIMMING POOL
CHINATOWN: *Holiday Inn Sélect Montréal Centre-Ville* 99 Ave. Viger, QUE H2Z 1E9. ((514) 878 9888. FAX (514) 878 6341. Two pagodas on the roof help this modern hotel blend seamlessly into its surroundings. Miniature ponds, Chinese gardens, and the *Chez Chine* restaurant dominate the lobby. 🖼 📺 & P 🛏 🌿	$$$	235	●			■
DOWNTOWN: *Hôtel Viger* 1001 Rue Saint-Hubert, QUE H2L 3Y3. ((514) 845 6058. FAX (514) 844 6068. The rooms are basic, but the rates at this small hotel are low; the location is near Vieux-Montréal, Chinatown, and Mont-Royal. 🖼 📺 P 🌿	$	21				
DOWNTOWN: *Hôtel Château & Tour Versailles* 1808 Ouest Rue Sherbrooke, QUE H3H 1E5. ((514) 933 8111. FAX (514) 933 6867. The "château" part of this hotel is housed in two Victorian homes; the "tour" is a modern tower across the street. Rooms are comfortable, and the hotel's French restaurant is very good. 🖼 24 📺 P 🌿	$$	177	●			
DOWNTOWN: *Hôtel du Parc* 3625 Ave. du Parc, QUE H2X 3P8. ((514) 288 6666. Rooms decorated in blond wood and pastels overlook Parc Mont-Royal. A comfortable bar dominates the lobby. 🖼 📺 & P 🛏 🌿	$$	459	●			

DOWNTOWN: *Hôtel de Paris* 901 Est Rue Sherbrooke, QUE H2L 1L3. *(514) 522 6861.* FAX *(514) 522 1387.* The old graystone building with its fanciful turret is a short walk from the nightlife of Rue St. Denis. The rooms are comfortable. TV P	$$	39	●		●	
DOWNTOWN: *Hôtel-Suites Le Riche Bourg* 2170 Ave. Lincoln, QUE H3H 3N5. *(514) 935 9224.* FAX *(514) 935 5049.* All suites have kitchens and dining areas, which make them ideal for families or for longer stays. TV P	$$	221	●	■		■
DOWNTOWN: *Le Nouvel Hôtel* 1740 Ouest Blvd. René Lévesque, QUE H3H 1R3. *(514) 931 8841.* FAX *(514) 931 3233.* Montreal's amateur comics test their talent at the Comedy Nest, the cabaret of this comfortable, modern hotel near the *Centre Canadien d'Architecture.* TV P	$$	162	●	■	●	■
DOWNTOWN: *Delta Montréal* 475 Ave. Président Kennedy, QUE H3A 2TA. *(514) 286 1986.* FAX *(514) 284 4342.* This modern hotel has large comfortable rooms. Place des Arts and Montreal's department stores are nearby. 24 TV P	$$$	453	●	■		■
DOWNTOWN: *Hôtel du Fort* 1390 Rue du Fort, QUE H3H 2R7. *(514) 958 8333.* FAX *(514) 938 3123.* Most of the elegant rooms with kitchen facilities in this modern tower have good views of the harbor or Mont-Royal. TV P	$$$	126				
DOWNTOWN: *L'Hôtel de la Montagne* 1430 Rue de la Montagne, QUE H3G 1Z5. *(514) 288 5656.* FAX *(514) 288 9658.* A flamboyantly decorated lobby and rooftop pool, as well as its trendy downtown neighborhood, make this hotel popular. TV P	$$$	134	●		●	■
DOWNTOWN: *Marriott Château Champlain* 1 Place du Canada, QUE H3B 4C9. *(514) 878 9000.* FAX *(514) 878 6761.* This tall white tower with arch-shaped windows has excellent views of Mont-Royal and the harbor. TV P	$$$	611	●			■
DOWNTOWN: *Montréal Bonaventure Hilton* 1 Place Bonaventure, QUE H5A 1B4. *(514) 878 2332.* FAX *(514) 878 3881.* Built around a pleasant garden with an open-air pool that is open winter and summer, this hotel is located over the Place Bonaventure exhibition halls. TV P	$$$	395	●	■	●	■
DOWNTOWN: *Residence Inn by Marriott-Montréal* 2045 Rue Peel, QUE H3A 1T6. *(514) 982 6064.* FAX *(514) 844 8631.* All suites in this downtown hotel have fully equipped kitchens. The hotel also has a library with a fireplace. TV P	$$$	190	●		●	■
DOWNTOWN: *Hôtel La Reine Elizabeth* 900 Ouest Blvd. René Lévesque, QUE H3B 4A5. *(514) 861 3511.* FAX *(514) 954 2256.* This busy convention hotel is well located with comfortable rooms. The Beaver Club restaurant is on the ground floor. 24 TV P	$$$$	1042	●			■
DOWNTOWN: *Hôtel Ritz Carlton* 1228 Ouest Rue Sherbrooke, QUE H3G 1H6. *(514) 842 4212.* FAX *(514) 842 4907.* Richard Burton and Elizabeth Taylor had one of their two weddings in this Edwardian-style hotel. The Ritz Garden is a good place for tea, and the Café de Paris is a fine French restaurant. 24 TV P	$$$$	229	●		●	
DOWNTOWN: *Loews Hôtel Vogue* 1425 Rue de la Montagne, QUE H3G 1Z3. *(514) 285 5555.* FAX *(514) 849 8903.* The Vogue's elegantly decorated lobby looks out onto one of Montreal's trendiest streets. Its rooms are large and well furnished, each equipped with a whirlpool bath. 24 TV P	$$$$	142	●	■		
DOWNTOWN: *Omni Montreal* 1050 Ouest Rue Sherbrooke, QUE H3A 2R6. *(514) 284 1110.* FAX *(514) 845 3025.* The marble lobby of this modern hotel has a wonderful restaurant/bar with windows overlooking the street. 24 TV P	$$$$	300	●			■
PLATEAU MONT-ROYAL: *Hôtel de l'Institut* 3535 Rue Saint-Denis, QUE H2X 3P1. *(514) 282 5120.* FAX *(514) 873 9893.* Students at the *Institut de Tourisme et d'Hôtelerie du Québec* hone their skills by serving guests in the hotel on the upper floors of their college. TV P	$	42	●			

For key to symbols see back flap

						NUMBER OF ROOMS	RESTAURANT	CHILDREN'S FACILITIES	GARDEN/TERRACE	SWIMMING POOL

Price categories for a standard double room per night, including breakfast (where served), taxes, and any extra service charges:
$ under Can$100
$$ Can$100–$150
$$$ Can$150–$200
$$$$ Can$200–$250
$$$$$ over Can$250

RESTAURANT
Hotel restaurant or dining room, usually open to non-residents unless otherwise stated.

CHILDREN'S FACILITIES
Indicates child cribs and/or a baby-sitting service available. A few hotels also provide children's portions and high chairs in the restaurant.

GARDEN/TERRACE
Hotel with a garden, courtyard, or terrace often available for eating outside.

SWIMMING POOL
Hotel with an indoor or outdoor swimming pool.

Hotel	Price	Rooms	Rest.	Child.	Garden	Pool
PLATEAU MONT-ROYAL: *Hôtel Le Saint-André* 1285 Rue Saint-André, QUE H2L 3T1. (514) 849 7070. FAX (514) 849 8167. Guests get a surprising amount of style for a very modest fee at this little hotel near the bistros and bars of Rue Saint-Denis. 📷 TV P 🔲	$	65				
PLATEAU MONT-ROYAL: *Auberge de la Fontaine* 1301 East Rue St. Rachel, QUE H2J 2K1. (514) 597 0166. FAX (514) 597 0496. An adjoining pair of Second-Empire homes have been converted into a small hotel with stylish, eccentrically decorated rooms. 📷 TV & P 🔲	$$	21			●	
PLATEAU MONT-ROYAL: *Le Jardin d'Antoine* 2024 Rue St.-Denis, QUE H2X 3K7. (514) 843 4506. FAX (514) 281 1491. The pretty garden that gives this hotel its name offers a peaceful respite from the nearby cafés and nightclubs. The more deluxe rooms at the back overlook the garden. 📷 TV P 🔲	$$	25			●	
VIEUX MONTRÉAL: *Auberge les Passants du Sans Soucy* 171 Ouest Rue Saint-Paul, QUE H2Y 1Z5. (514) 842 2634. FAX (514) 842 2912. The lobby of this tiny hotel is a functioning art gallery. The building is an 18th-century warehouse with exposed beams and antiques. 📷 TV 🔲	$$	9				
VIEUX MONTRÉAL: *Pierre du Calvet AD 1725* 405 Rue Bonsecours, QUE H2Y 3C3. (514) 282 1725. FAX (514) 282 0456. Fireplaces, marble bathrooms, antique furniture, and Oriental rugs grace this historic hotel's rooms. 📷 🔲	$$$	9	●		●	
VIEUX MONTRÉAL: *Auberge du Vieux-Port* 97 E. Rue de la Commune, QUE H2Y 1J1. (514) 876 0081. FAX (514) 876 8923. This romantic hotel is housed in a 19th-century building overlooking the Vieux Port. The roof terrace is ideal for drinks or tea. 📷 🔲	$$$$	27	●		●	
VIEUX MONTRÉAL: *Hôtel Inter-Continental Montréal* 360 Ouest Rue Saint-Antoine, QUE H2Y 3X4. (514) 987 9900. FAX (514) 847 8550. Roof turrets on this hotel help it blend into a row of 19th-century buildings. Its rooms are elegant and comfortable. 📷 24 TV P 🍴 🔲	$$$$	357	●	■		■

QUEBEC CITY AND THE ST. LAWRENCE RIVER

Hotel	Price	Rooms	Rest.	Child.	Garden	Pool
BAIE SAINT-PAUL: *Auberge La Maison Otis* 23 Rue Saint-Jean-Baptiste, QUE G0A 1B0. (418) 435 2255. FAX (418) 435 2464. At the heart of this inn is an old stone house with seven exquisitely decorated rooms and one of the finest restaurants in the area. 📷 TV P 🔲	$$	30	●	■	●	■
CÔTE NORD: *Hôtel Tadoussac* 165 Rue du Bord-de-l'Eau, Tadoussac, QUE G0T 2A0. (418) 235 4421. FAX (418) 235 4607. Canada Steamships built this hotel in 1942 for its passengers; the red roof still dominates the town's skyline. Rates include breakfast and dinner. ● *Oct–May.* 📷 24 TV P 🔲	$$$	149	●	■	●	■
GASPÉ: *La Gîte du Mont-Albert* Parc de la Gaspésie, QUE G0E 2G0. (418) 763 2288. FAX (418) 763 7803. This mountain inn looks like a hunting lodge, enhanced by its rustic decor. The hotel also rents cottages. ● *Oct–Feb.* 📷 & P 🔲	$$	48	●		●	■
ILES-DE-LA-MADELEINE: *Hôtel au Vieux Couvent* Havre-aux-Maisons, QUE G0B 1K0. (418) 969 2233. FAX (418) 969 4693. A former convent school, the dormitories have been converted into bedrooms, and the chapel is a seafood restaurant. ● *Sep–Jun.* 📷 P 🔲	$	7	●		●	
LAC-SAINT-JEAN: *Hôtel du Jardin* 1400 Blvd. du Jardin, Saint-Félicien, QUE G8K 2N8. (418) 679 8422. FAX (418) 679 4459. This comfortable modern hotel makes a good base for exploring the Lac-Saint-Jean area. 📷 TV & P 🔲	$$	84	●			■

PERCÉ: *Hôtel-Motel La Normandie* $$
221 Route 132 east, Cap de Foi, QUE G0C 2L0. **(** *(418) 782 2112.* **FAX** *(418) 782 2337.* Most of the rooms of this inn overlook the sea and Rocher Percé. A fine seafood restaurant is on site. ● *Oct–May.*
45

POINTE-AU-PIC: *Manoir Richelieu* $$$
181 Rue Richelieu, QUE G0T 1M0. **(** *(418) 665 3703.* **FAX** *(418) 665 7736.* This stone castle sits on a cliff surrounded by gardens overlooking the estuary.
405

QUEBEC CITY: *Hôtel Particulier Belley* $
249 Rue Saint-Paul, QUE G1K 3W5. **(** *(418) 692 1694.* **FAX** *(418) 692 1696.* This old tavern is next to the Marché du Vieux-Port. Some rooms have bare brick walls and others have skylights.
8

QUEBEC CITY: *Le Priori* $$
15 Rue Sault-au-Matelot, QUE G1K 3Y7. **(** *(418) 692 3992.* **FAX** *(418) 692 0883.* A whimsical little hotel at the foot of Cap Diamant. Many rooms have stone walls but modern furniture.
26

QUEBEC CITY: *Hôtel Clarendon* $$$
57 Rue Sainte-Anne, QUE G1R 3X4. **(** *(418) 692 2480.* **FAX** *(418) 692 4652.* The interior of this 1870 hotel is an Art Deco delight. There is live jazz in the lobby every evening.
151

QUEBEC CITY: *Hôtel Dominion* $$$
126 Rue Saint-Pierre, QUE G1K 4A8. **(** *(418) 692 2224.* **FAX** *(418) 692 4403.* Old photographs decorate the high-ceilinged rooms in this 1912 building. Dozens of attractive restaurants line the picturesque Rue du Petit Champlain nearby.
40

QUEBEC CITY: *Château Frontenac* $$$$
1 Rue des Carrières, QUE G1R 4A7. **(** *(418) 692 3861.* **FAX** *(418) 692 1751.* Probably the most photographed hotel in Canada. Its baronial exterior is reflected inside in the wide hallways, wood paneling, and stonework. The rooms on the river have magnificent views.
605

RIVIÈRE-DU-LOUP: *Hôtel Lévesque* $
171 Rue Fraser, QUE G5R 1E2. **(** *(418) 862 6927.* **FAX** *(418) 867 5827.* This waterfront hotel is ideal for families, with its pool, beach, and big rooms. It has two restaurants, one offering simple fare, the other specializing in gourmet menus.
93

SEPT-ILES: *Hôtel Sept-Iles* $
451 Ave. Arnaud, QUE G4R 3B3. **(** *(418) 962 2581.* **FAX** *(418) 962 6918.* In the 1960s and 70s Sept-Iles' workers were the highest paid in Canada and spent their wages in the restaurant in this bayside hotel.
113

SOUTHERN AND NORTHERN QUEBEC

HULL: *Auberge de la Gare* $$
205 Blvd. Saint-Joseph, QUE J8Y 3X3. **(** *(819) 778 8085.* **FAX** *(819) 595 2021.* Serviceable, comfortable hotel in the heart of downtown Hull, close to the bridge and the attractions of Ottawa.
42

LAURENTIAN MOUNTAINS: *Auberge Le Rouet* $$
1288 Rue Lavoie, Val-David, QUE J0J 2N0. **(** *(819) 322 3221.* Pine trees and cross-country ski trails surround this rustic lodge. The low rates include three meals served in a log-paneled dining room.
30

LAURENTIAN MOUNTAINS: *Hôtel Far Hills Inn* $$
Val-Morin, QUE J0T 2R0. **(** *(819) 322 2014.* **FAX** *(819) 322 1995.* This mountaintop resort has its own lake, tennis courts, and 130 km (80 miles) of hiking and cross-country ski trails.
72

LAURENTIAN MOUNTAINS: *Château Mont-Tremblant* $$$
Station-de-Ski Mont Tremblant, QUE J0T 1Z0. **(** *(819) 681 7000.* **FAX** *(819) 681 7007.* This Canadian Pacific hotel brings big-city amenities into the Laurentian wilderness – part of the huge four-season resort.
316

LAURENTIAN MOUNTAINS: *Auberge de la Montagne-Coupée* $$$$
1000 Chemin Montagne-Coupée, QUE J0K 2S0. **(** *(450) 886 3891.* **FAX** *(450) 886 5401.* This modern establishment has a glass wall that looks out onto the mountains. Rates include breakfast and dinner.
50

Price categories	
Price categories for a standard double room per night, including breakfast (where served), taxes, and any extra service charges:	
$ under Can$100	
$$ Can$100–$150	
$$$ Can$150–$200	
$$$$ Can$200–$250	
$$$$$ over Can$250	

RESTAURANT
Hotel restaurant or dining room, usually open to non-residents unless otherwise stated.

CHILDREN'S FACILITIES
Indicates child cribs and/or a baby-sitting service available. A few hotels also provide children's portions and high chairs in the restaurant.

GARDEN/TERRACE
Hotel with a garden, courtyard, or terrace often available for eating outside.

SWIMMING POOL
Hotel with an indoor or outdoor swimming pool.

	Price	NUMBER OF ROOMS	RESTAURANT	CHILDREN'S FACILITIES	GARDEN/TERRACE	SWIMMING POOL
MAGOG: *Auberge l'Étoile sur le Lac* 1150 Ouest Rue Principale, QUE J1X 2B8. ((819) 843 6521. FAX (819) 843 5007. Many of the rooms have balconies overlooking Lac Memphrémagog. In summer, meals are served on the lakeside terrace.	$$	26	●		●	■
NORTH HATLEY: *Auberge Hovey Manor* Route 108 E. (Chemin Hovey), QUE J0B 2C0. ((819) 842 2421. FAX (819) 842 2248. Modeled on George Washington's Virginia home, many of the rooms here have fireplaces and four-poster beds.	$$$$	40	●		●	●
NUNAVIK: *Auberge Kuujjuaq* Kuujjuaq, QUE J0M 1C0. ((819) 964 2903. FAX (819) 964 2031. Lodging in Quebec's far north tends to be scarce and expensive. Book well ahead for a room in this little hotel.	$$$$	22	●			
OUTAOUAIS: *Château Montebello* 392 Rue Notre-Dame, Montebello, QUE J0V 1L0. ((819) 423 6341. FAX (819) 423 5283. Canadian workers built one of the largest log structures in the world during the Depression. It is now part of this charming riverside resort with golf course, riding trails, and tennis courts.	$$$	211	●	■	●	■
RICHELIEU VALLEY: *Hostelerie Les Trois Tilleuls* 290 Rue Richelieu, Saint-Marc-sur-Richelieu, QUE J0L 2E0. ((514) 856 7787. This member of the Château & Relais organization is set in farm country one hour's drive from Montreal. Every room has a balcony overlooking the Richelieu River.	$$$	24	●		●	●
ROUYN-NORANDA: *Hôtel Albert* 84 Ave. Principale, QUE J9X 4P2. ((819) 762 3545. FAX (819) 762 7157. This old-fashioned downtown hotel was renovated in 1997 and has large comfortable rooms with some original features.	$	51	●			
TROIS-RIVIÈRES: *Delta Trois-Rivières* 1620 Rue Notre-Dame, QUE G9A 6E5. ((819) 376 1991. FAX (819) 372 5975. This modern hotel is just a short walk from the old section of Trois-Rivières and the walkways along the St. Lawrence River.	$$	159	●	■		■

TORONTO

	Price	NUMBER OF ROOMS	RESTAURANT	CHILDREN'S FACILITIES	GARDEN/TERRACE	SWIMMING POOL
AIRPORT: *Delta Toronto Airport Hotel* 801 Dixon Rd, ONT M9W 1J5. ((416) 675 6100. FAX (416) 675 4022. A well-maintained modern hotel offering easy access to the airport. It has a lot of pool tables.	$$	250	●	■	●	■
AIRPORT: *Regal Constellation Hotel* 900 Dixon Rd., ONT M9W 1J7. ((416) 675 1500. FAX (416) 675 1737. This appealing chain hotel, situated close to the airport, has a splendid seven-story glass lobby.	$$	710	●			■
DOWNTOWN: *Bond Place Hotel* 65 Dundas St. East, ONT M5B 2G8. ((416) 362 6061. FAX (416) 360 6406. Right in the center of downtown, a short walk from the Eaton Centre, this simple hotel is popular with package-tour operators.	$	286	●	■		
DOWNTOWN: *Days Inn Toronto Downtown* 30 Carlton St., ONT M5B 2E9. ((416) 977 6655. FAX (416) 977 0502. A standard hotel, which has competitively priced, plain but functional rooms. It occupies a high-rise near College subway.	$$	536	●			■
DOWNTOWN: *Quality Hotel Downtown* 111 Lombard St., ONT M5C 2T9. ((416) 367 5555. FAX (416) 367 3470. An unassuming city center hotel with spotless rooms, ideal for those on a budget. It is located on a quiet street.	$$	196				

DOWNTOWN: *Toronto Colony Hotel* $$ 721
89 Chestnut St., ONT M5G 1R1. (*(416) 977 0707.* FAX *(416) 585 3164.*
Occupying a central location, close to City Hall, the Colony has pleasant
double rooms furnished in a modern style. 🛏 TV P 🍴 🍽

DOWNTOWN: *Victoria Hotel* $$ 48
56 Yonge St., ONT M5E 1G5. (*(416) 363 1666.* FAX *(416) 363 7327.*
Pocket-sized hotel situated in the heart of the city. It has
pleasant, if rather small, rooms. 🛏 TV P 🍽

DOWNTOWN: *Delta Chelsea Inn* $$$ 1594
33 Gerrard St. W, ONT M5G 1Z4. (*(416) 595 1975.* FAX *(416) 585 4302.*
Located close to the Eaton Centre, this is the biggest hotel in
Toronto, with outstanding leisure facilities. The rooms are spacious
and attractively furnished. 🛏 24 TV 🍴 P 🍴 🍽

DOWNTOWN: *Novotel Toronto Centre* $$$ 262
45 The Esplanade, ONT M5E 1W2. (*(416) 367 8900.* FAX *(416) 360 8285.*
This stylish establishment occupies a beautiful converted Art Deco
building close to Union Station. 🛏 TV 🍴 P 🍴 🍽

DOWNTOWN: *Ramada Suites Hotel* $$$ 102
300 Jarvis St., ONT M5B 2C5. (*(416) 977 4823.* FAX *(416) 977 4830.*
A convenient, high-rise hotel located on bustling Jarvis Street,
five minutes' walk east of Yonge. The hotel is a popular spot
with visiting businessfolk. 🛏 TV P 🍴 🍽

DOWNTOWN: *Royal York* $$$ 1385
100 Front St. W, ONT M5J 1E3. (*(416) 368 2511.* FAX *(416) 368 8148.*
When it was completed in the 1920s, the Royal York was the largest
hotel in the British Empire. The public areas have now been refurbished
to their original grandeur. 🛏 24 TV 🍴 P 🍴 🍽

DOWNTOWN: *Sheraton Centre Toronto Hotel* $$$ 1382
123 Queen St. W, ONT M5H 2M9. (*(416) 361 1000.* FAX *(416) 947 4874.*
A massive hotel right in the center of Toronto. The plush public areas
lead to large rooms decorated in modern style. 🛏 24 TV 🍴 P 🍴 🍽

DOWNTOWN: *Sutton Place Hotel* $$$ 230
955 Bay St., ONT M5S 2A2. (*(416) 924 9221.* FAX *(416) 324 5617.*
This trendy hotel is popular with visiting actors and politicians alike.
The rooms are well appointed, and the city's gay and lesbian
neighborhood is a short walk away. 🛏 24 TV 🍴 P 🍴 🍽

DOWNTOWN: *Radisson Plaza Hotel Admiral* $$$$ 157
249 Queens Quay W., ONT M4W 1A7. (*(416) 203 3333.* FAX *(416) 203 3100.*
Prestigious, ultra-modern hotel occupying a prime waterfront location.
It has stylish, comfortable rooms. 🛏 24 TV 🍴 P 🍴 🍽

DOWNTOWN: *SkyDome Hotel* $$$$ 346
1 Blue Jay Way, ONT M5V 1J4. (*(416) 341 7100.* FAX *(416) 345 8733.*
Much loved by baseball fans, this ultra-modern hotel forms part of
the SkyDome sports stadium *(see p169)*. Some of the rooms actually
overlook the playing area. 🛏 24 TV 🍴 P 🍴 🍽

DOWNTOWN: *The Westin Harbour Castle* $$$$ 980
1 Harbour Square, ONT M5J 1A6. (*(416) 869 1600.* FAX *(416) 361 7448.*
A prestige waterfront hotel, many of the rooms offer views of Lake
Ontario. It also has a revolving rooftop restaurant. 🛏 24 TV 🍴 P 🍴 🍽

DOWNTOWN: *Toronto Marriott Eaton Centre* $$$$ 459
525 Bay St., ONT M5G 2L2. (*(416) 597 9200.* FAX *(416) 597 9211.*
Ardent shoppers need look no further than this elegant hotel
adjoining the Eaton Centre. 🛏 24 TV 🍴 P 🍴 🍽

DOWNTOWN: *King Edward Hotel* $$$$$ 294
37 King Street E., ONT M5C 1E9. (*(416) 863 3131.* FAX *(416) 367 5515.*
Elegant hotel with plush public areas and attractive rooms. The
doormen are the most stylish in town. 🛏 24 TV 🍴 🍽

DOWNTOWN: *Hotel Intercontinental Toronto* $$$$$ 209
220 Bloor Street W., ONT M5S 1T8. (*(416) 960 5200.* FAX *(416) 960 8269.*
This sleek modern hotel offers every amenity, including open fireplaces
in some of its suites. 🛏 24 TV 🍴 P 🍴 🍽

For key to symbols see back flap

Price categories for a standard double room per night, including breakfast (where served), taxes, and any extra service charges:
($) under Can$100
($)($) Can$100–$150
($)($)($) Can$150–$200
($)($)($)($) Can$200–$250
($)($)($)($)($) over Can$250

RESTAURANT
Hotel restaurant or dining room, usually open to non-residents unless otherwise stated.
CHILDREN'S FACILITIES
Indicates child cribs and/or a baby-sitting service available. A few hotels also provide children's portions and high chairs in the restaurant.
GARDEN/TERRACE
Hotel with a garden, courtyard, or terrace often available for eating outside.
SWIMMING POOL
Hotel with an indoor or outdoor swimming pool.

	Number of Rooms	Restaurant	Children's Facilities	Garden/Terrace	Swimming Pool
HIGH PARK: *High Park Bed & Breakfast* ($) 4 High Park Blvd., ONT M6R 1M4. ☎ *(416) 531 7963.* FAX *(416) 531 0060.* An attractive old house in the High Park suburb, 5 km (3 miles) west of downtown. The rooms are comfortable and the breakfasts superb. [P]	2			●	
NORTH YORK: *Holiday Inn Toronto, Don Valley* ($)($) 1100 Eglinton Ave. E, ONT M3C 1H8. ☎ *(416) 446 3700.* FAX *(416) 446 3701.* A pleasant chain hotel located next door to the Ontario Science Centre *(see p187)*. It specializes in free meals and discounted accommodations for children. 🛋 [TV] [P] 🍸 💳	298	●	■	●	■
SCARBOROUGH: *Howard Johnson Plaza Hotel* ($) 940 Progress Ave., ONT M1G 3T5. ☎ *(416) 439 6200.* FAX *(416) 439 0276.* Routine but perfectly adequate hotel in the center of Scarborough, a suburb to the east of the city's downtown area. 🛋 [TV] [P] 🍸 💳	186	●			■
YORKVILLE: *Howard Johnson Yorkville* ($)($) 89 Avenue Rd., ONT M5R 2G3. ☎ *(416) 964 1220.* FAX *(416) 964 8692.* This modest hotel has a good location on the edge of Yorkville. The modern rooms are well maintained and spacious. 🛋 [TV] 💳	71				
YORKVILLE: *Four Seasons Hotel* ($)($)($)($)($) 21 Avenue Rd., ONT M5R 2G1. ☎ *(416) 964 0411.* FAX *(416) 964 2301.* This luxurious hotel is popular with visiting celebrities. Located in chic Yorkville, a short walk north of Bloor Street. 🛋 [24] [TV] [P] 🍸 💳	380	●	■	●	■

OTTAWA AND EASTERN ONTARIO

	Number of Rooms	Restaurant	Children's Facilities	Garden/Terrace	Swimming Pool
ALGONQUIN PROVINCIAL PARK: *Arowhon Pines Hotel* ($)($)($) off Hwy 60, Algonquin Provincial Park, ONT P1H 2G5. ☎ *(705) 633 5661.* FAX *(705) 633 5795.* The food and service here inspire rave reviews. Rates include three meals a day. ● *Nov–Apr.* 🛋 [TV] ♿ [P] 💳	50	●	■		
BROCKVILLE: *Royal Brock Hotel and Resort* ($)($) 100 Stewart Blvd., ONT K6V 4W3. ☎ *(613) 345 1400.* FAX *(613) 345 5402.* Selected as one of the finest small hotels in Canada, the Brock offers award-winning cuisine prepared by a European chef. 🛋 [TV] [P] 🍸 💳	72	●			■
HALIBURTON: *Sir Sam's Inn* ($)($)($) Eagle Lake, ONT K0M 1N0. ☎ *(705) 754 2188.* FAX *(705) 754 4262.* This is an adults-only resort located in the heart of the highlands. Rates include a four-course dinner. ● *mid-Nov–mid-Dec, Easter.* 🛋 [TV] [P] 💳	25	●			■
KAWARTHA LAKES: *Eganridge Inn & Country Club* ($)($)($) RR3 Fenelon Falls, ONT K0M 1N0. ☎ *(705) 738 5111.* Originally an 18th-century country estate, Eganridge is now an elegant inn located on Sturgeon Lake, on the Trent-Seven Waterway. ● *Nov–Apr.* 🛋 [TV] ♿ [P] 💳	13	●	■	●	
KINGSTON: *Marine Museum of the Great Lakes* ($) 55 Ontario St., ONT K7L 2Y2. ☎ *(613) 542 2261.* FAX *(613) 542 0043.* These modest comfortable ship's cabins are a few blocks from the downtown area. ● *Oct–Apr.* [P] 💳	27				
KINGSTON: *Hochelaga Inn* ($)($) 24 Sydenham St., ONT K7L 3G9. ☎ *(613) 549 5534.* FAX *(613) 549 5534.* Located in the heart of historic Kingston, this lovely old Victorian manor hotel is the perfect place to pamper yourself. 🛋 [TV] [P] 💳	23				
KINGSTON: *Prince George Hotel* ($)($)($) 200 Ontario St., ONT K7L 2Y9. ☎ *(613) 547 9037.* FAX *(613) 547 0056.* Built as a private home in 1809, it has been operating as a hotel for more than 150 years. Within walking distance of all attractions. 🛋 [TV] 💳	26	●			

NORTH BAY: *Pinewood Park Inn and Conference Centre*   Ⓢ   118
201 Pinewood Park Drive, ONT P1B 8J8. 【 (705) 472 0810. FAX (705) 472 4427.
This well-kept motel has an electric train that fascinates children. It is five
minutes from the Dionne Quints Museum *(see p201)*. 🛏 TV 🛗 🍴 🏊

OTTAWA: *Gasthaus Switzerland Bed & Breakfast Inn*   Ⓢ   22
89 Daly Ave., ONT K1N 6E6. 【 (613) 237 0335. FAX (613) 594 3327.
A charming old stone house that offers Swiss hospitality just two blocks
south of Rideau St. and the Byward Market *(see p194)*. 🛏 🏊

OTTAWA: *Lord Elgin Hotel*   ⓈⓈ   312
100 Elgin St., ONT K1P 5K8. 【 (613) 235 3333. FAX (613) 235 3223.
This is a 1940s hotel offering a great value in a prime location
across from the National Arts Centre. 🛏 TV P 🏊

OTTAWA: *Château Laurier Hotel*   ⓈⓈⓈ   425
1 Rideau St., ONT K1N 8S7. 【 (613) 241 1414. FAX (613) 562 7031.
This famous old hotel looks like a French château and is close to
Parliament Hill. Popular with the politicians of Ottawa. 🛏 TV 🛗 🏊

OTTAWA: *Delta Inn*   ⓈⓈⓈ   328
361 Queen St., ONT K1R 7S9. 【 (613) 238 6000. FAX (613) 238 2290.
Spacious, modern rooms, and the lobby fireplace is particularly attractive.
🛏 TV 🛗 P 🍴 🏊

THE GREAT LAKES

BAYFIELD: *The Little Inn of Bayfield*   ⓈⓈ   30
Main Street, ONT N0M 1G0. 【 (519) 565 2611. FAX (519) 565 5474.
One of the most charming hotels in Ontario occupies a restored
19th-century timber-and-brick building on the shores of Lake Huron.
The rooms are decorated in period style. 🛏 TV 🛗 P 🏊

MIDLAND: *Park Villa Motel*   Ⓢ   41
751 Yonge St. W., ONT L4R 2E1. 【 (705) 526 2219. FAX (705) 526 1346.
Midland is short on amenities, but this standard motel, 2 km (1 mile) from
the waterfront, with air-conditioned rooms is pleasant. 🛏 TV P 🏊

NIAGARA FALLS: *Quality Inn Fallsway*   ⓈⓈⓈ   274
4946 Clifton Hill, ONT L2E 6S8. 【 (905) 358 3601. FAX (905) 358 3818.
This Quality Inn is a modern, motel-style place within earshot
of the Falls. The rooms are spacious. 🛏 TV P 🏊

NIAGARA FALLS: *Oakes Inn Fallsview*   ⓈⓈⓈⓈ   167
6546 Buchanan Ave., ONT L2G 3W2. 【 (905) 356 4514. FAX (905) 356 3651.
A dapper hotel by any standard, the Oakes Inn is a sprightly modern
high-rise offering great views of the Falls. 🛏 TV P 🍴 🏊

NIAGARA FALLS: *Sheraton Fallsview Hotel*   ⓈⓈⓈⓈ   295
6755 Oakes Drive, ONT L2G 3W7. 【 (905) 374 1077. FAX (905) 374 6224.
Luxurious hotel providing panoramic views of the Falls.
The restaurant is one of the best in town. 🛏 TV P 🍴 🏊

NIAGARA FALLS: *Skyline Foxhead Hotel*   ⓈⓈⓈⓈ   690
5875 Falls Ave., ONT L2E 6W7. 【 (905) 374 4444. FAX (905) 357 4804.
One of Niagara's older hotels, this pleasant establishment stands
at the foot of Clifton Hill. The bedrooms on the upper floors provide
spectacular views of the Falls. 🛏 TV P 🏊

NIAGARA-ON-THE-LAKE: *Nana's Iris Manor Bed and Breakfast*   ⓈⓈ   3
36 The Promenade, ONT L0S 1J0. 【 (905) 468 1593. FAX (905) 468 1592.
A charming bed-and-breakfast set in a delightful 19th-century-style
villa in the Old Town. Take time to enjoy a cool drink on the
veranda in summer. 🛏 P 🏊

NIAGARA-ON-THE-LAKE: *Prince of Wales Hotel*   ⓈⓈⓈⓈⓈ   101
6 Picton St., ONT L0S 1J0. 【 (905) 468 3246. FAX (905) 468 5521.
This stylish hotel occupies a tastefully refurbished old building right in
the center of town. The rooms are pleasantly decorated. 🛏 TV 🛗 P 🏊

SAULT STE. MARIE: *Quality Inn Bay Front*   Ⓢ   109
180 Bay Street, P6A 6S2. 【 (705) 945 9264. FAX (705) 945 9766.
This unpretentious hotel has a great location in the centre of town, near
several good restaurants and the prime tourist sights. 🛏 TV 🛗 P 🍴 🏊

Price categories for a standard double room per night, including breakfast (where served), taxes, and any extra service charges:

$ under Can$100
$$ Can$100–$150
$$$ Can$150–$200
$$$$ Can$200–$250
$$$$$ over Can$250

RESTAURANT
Hotel restaurant or dining room, usually open to non-residents unless otherwise stated.

CHILDREN'S FACILITIES
Indicates child cribs and/or a baby-sitting service available. A few hotels also provide children's portions and high chairs in the restaurant.

GARDEN/TERRACE
Hotel with a garden, courtyard, or terrace often available for eating outside.

SWIMMING POOL
Hotel with an indoor or outdoor swimming pool.

	Price	Number of Rooms	Restaurant	Children's Facilities	Garden/Terrace	Swimming Pool
SAULT STE. MARIE: *Holiday Inn Sault Ste. Marie* 208 St. Mary's River Drive, ONT P6A 5V4. 📞 (705) 949 0611. FAX (705) 945 6972. This is a bright, cheerful chain hotel situated within easy distance of all the attractions. The rooms are slick and modern.	$$$	195	●	■	●	■
THUNDER BAY: *Airlane Hotel* 698 W. Arthur St., ONT P7E 5R8. 📞 (807) 577 1181. FAX (807) 475 4852. This clean, new hotel has bright modern rooms that are cheerily decorated. The hotel is near the town's prime tourist attraction, Old Fort William *(see p223)*.	$$	154	●			■
TOBERMORY: *Blue Bay Motel* Front St., Little Tub, ONT N0H 2R0. 📞 (519) 596 2392. FAX (519) 596 2335. The small fishing village of Tobermory is an agreeable place to break a long journey. The Blue Bay provides simple lodgings.	$	16				

CENTRAL CANADA

	Price	Number of Rooms	Restaurant	Children's Facilities	Garden/Terrace	Swimming Pool
DRUMHELLER: *Newcastle Country Inn* 1130 Newcastle Trail, AB T0J 0Y2. 📞 (403) 823 8356. FAX (403) 823 8356. This three-star property is conveniently located close to downtown. A delicious breakfast is included in the price of the room.	$	11				
EDMONTON: *Glenora Bed & Breakfast* 12327–102 Ave., AB T5N 0L8. 📞 (780) 488 6766. FAX (780) 488 5168. Each room has a distinct look, furnished with period antiques in this restored 1912 building. The main floor has restaurants and shops. Close to downtown and Victoria Promenade.	$	21	●			
EDMONTON: *Fantasyland Hotel* 17700–87th Ave., West Edmonton Mall AB T5T 4V4. 📞 (780) 444 3000. FAX (780) 444 3294. Standard rooms have the usual amenities while theme rooms such as African, Hollywood, and Igloo have whirlpools.	$$$	355	●			
EDMONTON: *Union Bank Inn* 10053 Jasper Ave., AB T5J 1S5. 📞 (780) 423 3600. FAX (780) 423 4623. Conveniently located in the heart of downtown. Rates include breakfast and evening aperitif. The restaurant is highly recommended.	$$$	414	●			
FORT QU'APPELLE: *Company House Bed & Breakfast* Adjacent to Town Office, Company Ave., SASK S0G 1S0. 📞 (306) 332 6333. FAX (306) 332 6333. This charming early 20th-century home includes a guest sitting room, two tiled cherrywood fireplaces, and shared bathrooms.	$	3				
LETHBRIDGE: *Heidelberg Inn* 1303 Mayor Magrath Drive, AB T1K 2R1. 📞 (403) 329 0555. FAX (403) 328 8846. Heidelberg Inn has tastefully appointed rooms, a laundry service, and sauna. Near Nikka Yuko Japanese Garden.	$	67	●			
MOOSE JAW: *Temple Gardens Mineral Spa Hotel* 24 Fairford St. East, SASK S6H 0C7. 📞 (306) 694 5055. FAX (306) 694 8310. Located close to "Tunnels of Little Chicago," this hotel is connected to a mineral pool and spa center. Jacuzzi suites are available.	$	96	●			■
REGINA: *Fieldstone Inn* near Craven, PO Box 26038, SASK S4R 8R7. 📞 (306) 731 2377. FAX (306) 731 2369. Located in the lovely Qu'Appelle Valley, this award-winning farm home offers inclusive watersports. Guests are picked up from Regina.	$$	6	●	■	●	■
REGINA: *Hotel Saskatchewan Radisson Plaza* 2125 Victoria Ave., SASK S4P 0S3. 📞 (306) 522 7691. FAX (306) 522 8988. A deluxe hotel with well-appointed rooms and complementary airport pickup. Convenient for downtown stores.	$$	217	●			

RIDING MOUNTAIN NATIONAL PARK: *Clear Lake Lodge* Wasagaming, MAN R0J 2H0. ☎ *(204) 848 2345.* [FAX] *(204) 848 2209.* The lodge has a comfortable living room with fireplace and common kitchen where guests have their own refrigerator. ⚫ *Nov–Apr.* 👶 [P] 💳	$	16			●	■
SASKATOON: *Delta Bessborough Hotel* 601 Spadina Crescent East, SASK S7K 3G8. ☎ *(306) 244 5521.* [FAX] *(306) 653 2458.* The "castle on the river" is set on the picturesque South Saskatchewan River. Popular Japanese restaurant on site. 👶 [TV] ♿ [P] 🍴 💳	$	225	●			■
WINNIPEG: *Fraser's Grove* 110 Mossdale Ave., MAN R2K 0H5. ☎ *(204) 661 0971.* Located in a quiet residential area, this comfortable modern home is near the river, golf courses, downtown, and Lake Winnipeg beaches.	$	3				
WINNIPEG: *Crowne Plaza Winnipeg Downtown* 350 St. Mary Ave., MAN R3C 3J2. ☎ *(204) 942 0551.* [FAX] *(204) 943 8702.* Comfortable downtown hotel, conveniently close to department stores. Noted for its billiards room and restaurant. 👶 [TV] ♿ [P] 🍴 💳	$$$	389	●	■		■
WINNIPEG: *The Lombard* 2 Lombard Place, MAN R3B 0Y3. ☎ *(204) 957 1350.* [FAX] *(204) 956 1791.* Winnipeg's highest-rated hotel, in the heart of the business district. Rooms have data ports, Nintendo, and videos. 👶 [TV] ♿ 🍴 💳	$$$	350	●	■		■
VANCOUVER AND VANCOUVER ISLAND						
MALAHAT: *The Aerie* 600 Ebedora Lane, BC V0R 2L0. ☎ *(250) 743 7115.* [FAX] *(250) 743 4766.* Elegant terraced inn on a hillside, overlooking one of the island's most incredible vistas. Rooms are furnished with hot tubs, and the landscaped grounds contain ponds and fountains. 👶 [TV] [P] 🍴 💳	$$$	23	●		●	■
NORTH VANCOUVER: *Thistledown House* 3910 Capilano Rd., BC V7R 4J2. ☎ *(604) 986 7173.* [FAX] *(604) 980 2939.* A heritage property built in 1920. Rooms are furnished with antiques from all over the world. 👶 [P] 💳	$$$	5			●	
PORT ALBERNI: *Eagle Nook Resort* Box 575, Port Alberni, BC V9Y 7M9. ☎ *(250) 723 1000.* [FAX] *(250) 723 6604.* A resort accessible by water taxi or seaplane only. Soak in the hot tub before feasting on a gourmet meal. 👶 🍴 💳	$$$$	23	●		●	
SOOKE: *Sooke Harbour House* 1528 Whiffen Spit Rd., BC V0S 1N0. ☎ *(250) 642 3421.* [FAX] *(250) 642 6988.* Just 9 m (30 ft) from the sea and 35 km (23 miles) from Victoria, this clapboard inn perched on a bluff is a wonderful getaway. 👶 [P] 💳	$$$$$	28	●		●	
SURREY: *Best Western Pacific Inn* 1160 King George Hwy, BC V4A 4Z2. ☎ *(604) 535 1432.* [FAX] *(604) 531 6979.* This Mexican-style hotel has rooms facing a covered courtyard with a swimming pool in the center. 👶 [TV] ♿ [P] 🍴 💳	$$	150	●		●	■
TOFINO: *Middle Beach Lodge* 400 Mackenzie Beach Rd., BC V0R 2Z0. ☎ *(250) 725 2900.* [FAX] *(250) 725 2901.* Two rustic lodges set on 16 ha (40 acres) of secluded oceanfront scenery, with a private beach. One resort is for families with young children, one strictly for adults. 👶 [TV] ♿ [P] 💳	$$$	58		■	●	
TOFINO: *Clayoquot Wilderness Resort* off Osprey Lane, Chesterman's Beach, BC V0R 2Z0. ☎ *(250) 726 8235.* [FAX] *(250) 726 8558.* This floating inn and its surrounding wilderness is a paradise for ecologically minded tourists. Activities include horseback riding, hiking, and whale-watching. 👶 [P] 🍴 💳	$$$$	16	●			
TOFINO: *Wickaninnish Inn* Off Osprey Lane, Chesterman's Beach. Box 250, BC V0R 2Z0. ☎ *(250) 725 3100.* [FAX] *(250) 725 3110.* This luxury inn lies 10 miles north of Tofino by boat. Rooms boast hot tubs, fireplaces, and ocean views. 👶 [TV] ♿ [P] 💳	$$$$$	46	●		●	
VANCOUVER: *Days Inn Downtown* 921 W Pender St., BC V6C 1M2. ☎ *(604) 681 4335.* [FAX] *(604) 681 7808.* Off-season rates and passes to the nearby YWCA fitness facility are some of the extras available at this European-style hotel. 👶 [TV] [P] 💳	$	85	●			

For key to symbols see back flap

Price categories for a standard double room per night, including breakfast (where served), taxes, and any extra service charges:

$ under Can$100
$$ Can$100–$150
$$$ Can$150–$200
$$$$ Can$200–$250
$$$$$ over Can$250

RESTAURANT
Hotel restaurant or dining room, usually open to non-residents unless otherwise stated.

CHILDREN'S FACILITIES
Indicates child cribs and/or a baby-sitting service available. A few hotels also provide children's portions and high chairs in the restaurant.

GARDEN/TERRACE
Hotel with a garden, courtyard, or terrace often available for eating outside.

SWIMMING POOL
Hotel with an indoor or outdoor swimming pool.

	Number of Rooms	Restaurant	Children's Facilities	Garden/Terrace	Swimming Pool
VANCOUVER: *Best Western Sands Hotel* $$$ 1755 Davie St., BC V6G 1W5. ((604) 682 1831. FAX (604) 682 3546. Located close to English Bay and Stanley Park. The shops and bistros on Davie Street make this a pedestrian haven. ▫ TV ♿ P ⫶ ⊜	121	●			
VANCOUVER: *Georgian Court Hotel* $$$ 773 Beatty St., BC V6B 2M4. ((604) 682 5555. FAX (604) 682 8830. A small, intimate European-style hotel, with one of Vancouver's finest restaurants. It is close to the entertainment district. ▫ TV ♿ P ⫶ ⊜	180	●			
VANCOUVER: *Quality Hotel Downtown* $$$ 1335 Howe St., BC V6Z 1R7. ((604) 682 0229. FAX (604) 662 7566. Close to everything, this boutique hotel was recently awarded the Hotel of the Year by Choice Hotels. ▫ TV ♿ P ⊜	157	●			■
VANCOUVER: *Delta Vancouver Suite Hotel* $$$$ 550 West Hastings St., BC V6B 1L6. ((604) 689 8188. FAX (604) 605 8881. This downtown hotel has clean Scandinavian decor with sleek and modern lines, bedrooms off the lounge area, and full business facilities. ▫ 24 TV ♿ P ⫶ ⊜	227	●			■
VANCOUVER: *Hyatt Regency Vancouver* $$$$ 655 Burrard St., BC V6C 2R7. ((604) 683 1234. FAX (604) 643 5812. Upscale convention hotel close to shopping and sightseeing attractions, visited by traveling businessmen and other international guests. ▫ TV ♿ P ⊜	645	●		●	■
VANCOUVER: *Four Seasons* $$$$$ 791 West Georgia St., BC V6C 2T4. ((604) 689 9333. FAX (604) 684 4555. This hotel has achieved five stars for 24 consecutive years. Located in the business center, close to the Pacific Centre shops, the hotel also features the Chartwell restaurant. ▫ 24 TV ♿ P ⫶ ⊜	385	●	■		■
VANCOUVER: *Hotel Vancouver* $$$$$ 900 West Georgia St., BC V6C 2W6. ((604) 684 3131. FAX (604) 662 1929. This landmark hotel in the heart of the city has offered luxurious service under its green copper roof since 1939. ▫ 24 TV ♿ P ⫶ ⊜	555	●	■		■
VANCOUVER: *Metropolitan Hotel Vancouver* $$$$$ 645 Howe St., BC V6C 2Y9. ((604) 687 1122. FAX (604) 602 7846. Known for its intimacy, this hotel is one of only 107 members of the "Preferred Hotels & Resorts" worldwide. ▫ 24 TV ♿ P ⫶ ⊜	197	●	■		■
VANCOUVER: *Pan Pacific Hotel Vancouver* $$$$$ 999 Canada Place, BC V6C 3B5. ((604) 662 8111. FAX (604) 685 8690. Located on the waterfront next to Canada Place, this hotel draws a corporate and international clientele. ▫ 24 TV ♿ P ⫶ ⊜	506	●	■	●	■
VANCOUVER: *Sutton Place Hotel* $$$$$ 845 Burrard St., BC V6Z 2K6. ((604) 682 5511. FAX (604) 682 5513. An impressive property tailored to the needs of both business travelers and tourists. Located in the heart of the city, the hotel offers luxurious rooms and an excellent restaurant. ▫ 24 TV ♿ P ⫶ ⊜	397	●	■		■
VANCOUVER: *Waterfront Hotel* $$$$$ 900 Canada Place Way, BC V6C 3L5. ((604) 691 1991. FAX (604) 691 1999. Modern glass-and-steel hotel across from the World Trade Centre. First-class amenities and attention to detail. ▫ 24 TV ♿ P ⫶ ⊜	489	●	■	●	■
VICTORIA: *Days Inn* $$ 123 Gorge Rd. East, BC V9A 1L1. ((250) 386 1422. FAX (250) 386 1254. This inn is located five minutes' drive from downtown Victoria. The rooms are comfortable and peaceful. ▫ TV P ⊜	94	●			

VICTORIA: *Abigail's Hotel* $$$$ 906 McClure St., BC V8V 3E7. ☎ *(250) 388 5363.* [FAX] *(250) 388 7787.* A small Tudor-style inn built in the 1930s. Rooms are furnished with antiques, and there's a cozy library with a wood-burning fire. ❄ [P] 💳	23			●	
VICTORIA: *Empress Hotel* $$$$ 721 Government St., BC V8W 1W5. ☎ *(250) 384 8111.* [FAX] *(250) 381 4334.* This 1908 stately building overlooks the harbor, near the Parliament Buildings. High Tea is served in the grand lobby. ❄ [TV] ♿ [P] 🏋 💳	460	●	■	●	■
VICTORIA: *Ocean Point Resort* $$$$ 45 Songhees Rd., BC V9A 6T3. ☎ *(250) 360 2999.* [FAX] *(250) 360 1041.* Located on Victoria's famous Inner Harbor with only the boardwalk between the hotel and the water's edge. World-class European spa and business center on premises. ❄ [24] [TV] ♿ [P] 🏋 💳	246	●		●	■
VICTORIA: *Humboldt House Bed & Breakfast* $$$$$ 867 Humboldt St., BC V8V 2Z6. ☎ *(250) 383 0152.* [FAX] *(250) 383 6402.* A luxury romantic getaway. Gourmet breakfasts delivered to your room, complete with Jacuzzi and fireplace. ❄ 💳	5				
THE ROCKY MOUNTAINS					
BANFF: *Rundlestone Lodge* $$$ 537 Banff Ave., AB T0L 0C0. ☎ *(403) 762 2201.* [FAX] *(403) 762 4501.* Renovated in 1997, this lodge includes Jacuzzis and fireplaces in some rooms. The restaurant offers fine cuisine. ❄ [TV] ♿ [P] 🏋 💳	95	●			■
BANFF: *Banff Springs Hotel* $$$$$ 405 Spray Ave., AB T0L 0C0. ☎ *(403) 762 2211.* [FAX] *(403) 762 5755.* This landmark hotel features fireplaces, tennis courts, a pool, ice rink, golf course, spa, shops, and restaurants. ❄ [24] [TV] ♿ [P] 🏋 💳	777	●	■	●	■
CALGARY: *Elbow River Inn* $ 1919 Macleod Trail, AB T2G 4S1. ☎ *(403) 269 6771.* [FAX] *(403) 237 5181.* The only Hotel Casino in Alberta, this sprawling property offers non-smoking rooms. ❄ [TV] ♿ [P] 💳	75	●		●	
CALGARY: *Quality Inn Motel Village* $$ 2359 Banff Trail, AB T2M 4L2. ☎ *(403) 289 1973.* [FAX] *(403) 282 1241.* Newly renovated property with a modern lobby, a poolside restaurant, and on-site pub with pool tables and darts. ❄ [TV] ♿ [P] 🏋 💳	105	●			■
CANMORE: *Quality Resort Château Canmore* $$$ 1720 Bow Valley Trail, AB T1W 1P7. ☎ *(403) 678 6699.* [FAX] *(403) 678 6954.* Château Canmore consists of chalets and suites equipped with fireplace, living quarters, microwave, and coffee-maker. ❄ [TV] ♿ [P] 🏋 💳	120	●	■	●	■
CRANBROOK: *Kootenay Country Comfort Inn* $ 1111 Cranbrook St. North, BC V1C 3S4. ☎ *250 426 2296.* [FAX] *(250) 426 3533.* This inn is a firm favorite with anglers fishing for trout in the nearby Premier Lake. ❄ [TV] ♿ [P] 💳	36				
FORT NELSON: *The Blue Bell Inn* $ 4103 50th Ave. South, BC V0C 1R0. ☎ *(250) 774 6961.* [FAX] *(250) 774 6983.* A bright modern motel in a good location, the complex includes a 24-hour convenience store, a laundromat, and a fuel station. ❄ [TV] [P] 💳	46	●			
LAKE LOUISE: *Lake Louise Inn* $$$ 210 Village Rd., AB T0L 1E0. ☎ *(403) 522 3791.* [FAX] *(403) 522 2018.* Just five minutes from the ski hill and Lake Louise, the rooms in this renovated property range from economy to superior. The café displays artifacts from the hunting and mining era. ❄ [TV] ♿ [P] 💳	232	●			■
LAKE LOUISE: *Simpson's Num-Ti-Jah Lodge* $$$ Mile 22, Bow Lake Icefield Parkway, AB T0L 1E0. ☎ *(403) 522 2167.* [FAX] *(403) 522 2425.* A historic log lodge built on the shore of Bow Lake in 1937 by legendary guide Jimmy Simpson. The Elk Horn dining room offers the finest cuisine on the parkway. ❄ [P] 💳	25	●			
LAKE LOUISE: *Château Lake Louise* $$$$$ Lake Louise Shore, AB T0L 1E0. ☎ *(403) 522 3511.* [FAX] *(403) 522 3834.* With a bygone elegance, Château Lake Louise has been host to adventurers since 1890. Dining and shopping on site. ❄ [24] [TV] ♿ [P] 🏋 💳	489	●	■	●	■

For key to symbols see back flap

Price categories for a standard double room per night, including breakfast (where served), taxes, and any extra service charges:

$ under Can$100
$$ Can$100–$150
$$$ Can$150–$200
$$$$ Can$200–$250
$$$$$ over Can$250

RESTAURANT
Hotel restaurant or dining room, usually open to non-residents unless otherwise stated.

CHILDREN'S FACILITIES
Indicates child cribs and/or a baby-sitting service available. A few hotels also provide children's portions and high chairs in the restaurant.

GARDEN/TERRACE
Hotel with a garden, courtyard, or terrace often available for eating outside.

SWIMMING POOL
Hotel with an indoor or outdoor swimming pool.

Hotel	Price	Number of Rooms	Restaurant	Children's Facilities	Garden/Terrace	Swimming Pool
PRINCE GEORGE: *Econo Lodge* 1915 3rd Ave., BC V2L 1G6. (250) 563 7106. FAX (250) 561 7216. Very quiet downtown location close to all amenities, with a choice of smoking and non-smoking rooms.	$	30		■		■
RADIUM HOT SPRINGS: *The Springs at Radium Golf Resort* 8100 Golf Course Rd., Hwy 93/95, BC V0A 1M0. (250) 347 9311. FAX (250) 347 6299. This three-story boutique hotel offers views of the mountains, and all rooms face one of two golf courses.	$$	118	●		●	■
WATERTON LAKES: *Prince of Wales Hotel* Waterton Lakes National Park, AB T0K 2M0. (403) 859 2231. FAX (403) 859 2630. This historic hotel is at home amid the grandeur of the Rockies. Its alpine style has made it one of Canada's most photographed hotels. Enjoy high tea served by the kilted staff.	$$$$	37	●	■	●	

SOUTH AND NORTH BRITISH COLUMBIA

Hotel	Price	Number of Rooms	Restaurant	Children's Facilities	Garden/Terrace	Swimming Pool
BARKERVILLE: *Kelly House* 2nd St., BC V0K 1B0. (250) 994 3328. FAX (250) 994 3312. Lodging in two heritage buildings. Highlights include delicious breakfasts and the sound of music from the nearby theater.	$	6				
HOPE: *Manning Park Resort* Manning Provincial Park, BC V0X 1L0. (250) 840 8822. FAX (250) 840 8848. A year-round family-oriented resort offering cabins, chalets, lodge rooms, and group facilities.	$$	73	●	■		
KAMLOOPS: *Comfort Inn* 1810 Rogers Place, BC V1S 1T7. (250) 372 0987. FAX (250) 372 0967. The rooms are spacious in this three-storey stucco property. The water slide on the grounds makes this inn ideal for families.	$$	89		■		■
KELOWNA: *Lake Okanagan Resort* 2751 Westside Rd., BC V1Z 3T1. (250) 769 3511. FAX (250) 769 6665. This family-orientated destination borders a beach. There is horseback riding, golf, tennis, and a kids' camp in the summer.	$$	134	●	■		■
PENTICTON: *Penticton Lakeside Resort* 21 Lakeshore Drive West, BC V2A 7M5. (250) 493 8221. FAX (250) 493 0607. A modern resort located on Okanagan Lake. A private beach, pier, jet-skiing, and para-sailing make it particularly popular with families.	$$	204	●	■	●	■
PRINCE RUPERT: *Cow Bay Bed & Breakfast* 20 Cow Bay Rd., BC V8J 1A5. (250) 627 1804. FAX (250) 627 1919. A tastefully decorated family home within walking distance of museums and the harbor.	$	4				
QUESNEL: *Becker's Lodge* Bowron Lake Provincial Park, 342 Kinchant St., BC V2J 2R4. (250) 992 8864. FAX (250) 992 8893. Campsites, log cabins, and basic meals. Canoes are for rent for the circuit in the park (see p.318). Oct–Dec.	$$	9	●	■		
WELLS: *White Cap Motor Inn & RV Park* Ski Hill Rd., BC V0K 2R0. (250) 994 3489. FAX (250) 994 3426. Suites with kitchenettes, a children's playground, and an adjacent RV park. Trails to Barkerville and lake fishing start here.	$	34		■	●	
WHISTLER: *Delta Whistler Resort* 4050 Whistler Way, BC V0N 1B4. (604) 932 1982. FAX (604) 932 7332. Located next to a golf course and the Whistler and Blackcomb gondolas, this resort has luxury amenities.	$$$	292	●		●	■

WHISTLER: *Holiday Inn SunSpree Resort* $$$ 114
4295 Blackcomb Way, BC V0N 1V4. ((604) 938 0878. FAX (604) 938 9943.
In the heart of Whistler Village, minutes from Whistler and Blackcomb
mountains, shopping, and nightlife, the rooms are equipped with
kitchenettes, jetted soaker tubs, and fireplaces. 🛏 TV & P 🍴 🏊

WHISTLER: *Château Whistler* $$$$$ 558 ● ■ ● ■
4599 Château Boulevard, BC V0N 1V4. ((604) 938 8000. FAX (604) 938
2099.Located at the base of Blackcomb Mountain, the hotel features rooms
with fireplaces, Jacuzzis, and private check-ins. Golf courses and a health
club add to the luxury in this world-class resort. 🛏 24 TV & P 🍴 🏊

WHISTLER: *Pan Pacific Lodge Whistler* $$$$ 121 ● ● ■
4320 Sundial Crescent, BC V0N 1B4. ((604) 905 2999. FAX (604) 905
2995. A luxury property with floor-to-ceiling windows. The outdoor
pool has spectacular mountain views. 🛏 TV & P 🍴 🏊

NORTHERN CANADA

DAWSON CITY: *Midnight Sun Hotel* $$ 44 ●
3rd Avenue and Queen St., YT Y0B 1G0. ((867) 993 5495. FAX (867) 993 6485.
An attractive outdoor patio and lounge look over the historic setting of
the gold rush, and the hotel's cabins back onto the casino. 🛏 TV & P 🏊

FORT PROVIDENCE: *Snowshoe Inn* $ 35 ●
1 Mackenzie St., NT X0E 0L0. ((867) 699 3511. FAX (867) 699 4300.
Kitchenettes, satellite TV, and modern office facilities add to
the relaxing charm of this old-style inn. 🛏 TV P 🏊

FORT SIMPSON: *Nahanni Inn* $ 34 ● ●
Main St., Fort Simpson, X0E 0N0. ((819) 695 2201. FAX (819) 695 3000.
Centrally located, the hotel has suites as well as self-catering facilities in
addition to a bar. It is also famous for its delicious meals. 🏊 TV & P 🛏

HAINES JUNCTION: *Kluane Park Inn* $ 20
Mile 1016, Alaska Highway. ((867) 634 2261. FAX (867) 634 2273.
The most scenic hotel in the area, an outside deck overlooks dramatic
arctic scenery and is host to regular barbecues in summer. 🛏 TV P 🏊

HAY RIVER: *Caribou Motor Inn* $ 29 ■
912 Mackenzie Highway, NT X0E 0R8. ((867) 874 6706. FAX (867) 874 6704.
Conveniently located near this small town, many of the rooms feature
luxurious whirlpools, steam baths, and Jacuzzis. 🛏 TV P 🏊

INUVIK: *McKenzie Hotel* $$ 32 ●
185 MacKenzie Rd., X0E 0C0. ((867) 777 2861. FAX (867) 777 3317.
Friendly considerate staff, a jolly atmosphere and comfortable
rooms make this a popular choice. 24 🛏 TV P 🏊

VICTORIA ISLAND: *Arctic Islands Lodge* $$$ 25 ●
26 Omingnak St., Cambridge Bay, NT X0E 0C0. ((867) 983 2345. FAX (867) 983
2480. This excellent hotel is known for its helpful staff and comfortable
rooms. A fascinating range of sporting facilities, including guided hunting
trips in the icy wilderness, are offered by the hotel. 🛏 TV P 🏊

WHITEHORSE: *Best Western Gold Rush Inn* $$ 106 ●
411 Main St., YT Y1A 2B6. ((867) 668 4500. FAX 867 668 7432.
This efficient hotel with friendly staff has a lobby packed with antiques
from gold rush days and a vast stuffed moose head. 🛏 TV & P 🏊

WHITEHORSE: *High Country Inn* $$ 85 ●
4051 4th Ave., YT Y1A 2A7. ((867) 667 4471. FAX (867) 667 6457.
One of the province's most stylish and comfortable inns, a grand
piano and log fires add to the luxurious atmosphere. 🛏 TV & 🏊

YELLOWKNIFE: *Discovery Inn* $$ 41 ●
4701 Franklin Ave., X1A 2N6. ((867) 873 4151. FAX (867) 920 7948.
Rooms offer kitchenettes here, but there is also a very good
licensed restaurant in the evenings. 🛏 TV P 🏊

YELLOWKNIFE: *Explorer Hotel* $$$ 127 ● ■
4825 49th Avenue X1A 2RZ. ((867) 873 3531. FAX (867) 873 2789.
This luxury hotel boasts two restaurants, Berkeley's family dining
room, and the Sakura Japanese restaurant. 🛏 TV & P 🏊

For key to symbols see back flap

WHERE TO EAT

Seafood on offer in Atlantic Canada

W HAT MAKES Canadian cuisine unique is its regional specialties: Alberta beef, goldeye fish in Manitoba, salmon from BC, Nova Scotia lobster, and Quebec French pies and pastries. Game, including rabbit, caribou, and bison, which have been served in aboriginal homes for centuries, are now considered gourmet dishes at cosmopolitan restaurants. A tradition of French haute cuisine is evident in most of the country's major cities, particularly in top hotels. However, as Canada is a nation of immigrants, ethnic restaurants are common everywhere. German, Greek, Chinese, Thai, Indian, Ukrainian, African, and Italian cuisines, along with other international favorites, provide a wide range of choice at a price to suit every budget. Regional specialties can be sampled in their place of origin, but most of the larger towns will also offer a choice of the country's best local produce, and in some areas this includes Canadian wines and beers *(see p363)*. The listings on *pp364–79* describe a selection of restaurants chosen for their variety, service, and good value.

The top class Zoë's Restaurant in Château Laurier, Ottawa *(see p373)*

TYPES OF RESTAURANTS

E ATING OUT IN Canada is surprisingly easy on the pocket, particularly compared to European prices. This makes a trip to a top restaurant to sample international cuisine (often made with local produce) very worthwhile. Eating places are extremely varied, with the tearoom, bistro, brasserie, and theater café competing with the more usual café, restaurant, and fast food outlet. Many pubs also serve excellent bar food, at reasonable prices. More unusual, but no less worthwhile, is the uniquely Canadian dining experience of the delicious lobster supper. Held throughout the summer on Prince Edward Island, these lively gatherings usually take place in church grounds on wooden tables surrounded by local fishermen. Equally unique, though by no means public, are Inuit dinners. Traveling through the Arctic north may result in an invitation to join an Inuit family for the evening meal. Traditional dishes might include sun-dried caribou sweetened with berry sauces or smoked and dried local fish. These family dinners are usually alcohol-free and very lively.

VEGETARIAN

V EGETARIAN options are on the increase throughout the country. Expect to see at least one vegetarian dish on each menu. For those who eat fish, seafood has something of a national reputation. "Health Canada," the government plan for healthy eating, took effect in the 1990s. Restaurants that subscribe to the plan sign menus with a heart symbol denoting low-fat dishes. Anyone on a special or weight-loss diet can feel free to ask the chef to leave out certain high-calorie ingredients. Fresh fruits are easily obtained throughout the south of the country, and are abundant and often day-old in the main growing areas of Ontario and BC's Okanagan Valley. Some of the best berries and peaches in the world can be enjoyed here in the summer. It is worth remembering that most food in the Northwest Territories and Nunavut is imported, and largely canned or frozen; apart from Inuit game kills, fresh food is hard to obtain, and very expensive, in these distant Arctic regions.

Open-air dining in downtown Montreal *(see pp366–8)*

Arowhon Pines Lodge in Algonquin Provincial Park, Ontario *(see p372)*

ALCOHOL

THE MINIMUM age of public purchase and consumption of alcohol is 19 throughout the country, except in Quebec where it is 18. Canada produces some fine wines *(see p363)*, which are becoming more widely available. Visitors should know that tipping in bars should be left until the end of the evening rather than at each round.

It is worth noting that many towns in the Northwest Territories and Nunavut, particularly Inuit settlements, are dry – alcohol sale in stores and bars is heavily restricted due to high native alcoholism rates. Some towns, however, have a hotel bar for visitors.

EATING HOURS AND RESERVATIONS

LUNCH TABLES are usually available from noon to 2pm, and dinner reservations from 6pm to 9pm, although later bookings should be accepted in larger cities. Reserving a table in advance is generally a good idea. It is considered polite to call ahead and cancel if you are unable to make your reservation.

PAYING AND TIPPING

IT IS POSSIBLE to eat well in Canada for a bargain price. A snack in a café should cost less than Can$5 a person. In a good restaurant, a three-course meal and a shared bottle of wine often costs between Can$25–$50. Even gourmet dinners can start at Can$50. Fixed-priced menus are common. Luncheon items are generally less expensive, and are often similar to the evening menu without the linen and candles. Restaurant tax is the 7 percent GST (Goods and Services Tax), plus a varying provincial sales tax, applicable everywhere except Alberta. Taxes are included on the final check as percentages of the total. Tipping in most restaurants and cafés is expected, and should be about 10–15 percent of the check. Service charges are not usually included. Europeans should note that tipping is expected in bars and nightclubs. In common with most countries, a tip should increase if you are bringing a larger party to a restaurant and for any exceptional service. Penalizing staff for bad service is not common.

CHILDREN

CANADA IS A child-friendly society. Most restaurants offer high chairs or booster seats. The more upscale the venue, the more parents are required to keep children seated at table and to take noisy or upset youngsters outside until they calm down. A children's menu or half-portions may well be available for those under eight years old.

DISABLED FACILITIES

ALL NEW restaurants, as well as existing establishments undergoing renovation, have made their sites accessible to wheelchair users. A wide bathroom door and no interior steps from entrance to dining table are now compulsory across the country in new buildings. However, older, rural establishments should be checked out in advance.

DRESS CODE

VACATIONERS need not worry unduly about bringing formal clothes with them on a trip. Most restaurants operate "smart-casual" policy, especially at lunchtime, but exceptions to this can include sneakers (trainers), cut-off jeans, and dirty or ripped clothes. The rule generally runs as follows: the more expensive and exclusive the restaurant, the more formal the attire required. Evening dress is very rarely required in any venue.

SMOKING

OVER 70 PERCENT of Canadians do not smoke, but surprisingly this country is liberal in its attitude to the dwindling minority of smokers. Increasingly, though, restaurants have a no-smoking area, but this does not apply in bars or cafés. Cigars are generally not popular in restaurants, so ask before lighting up. A note of caution: when picnicking in a park, be sure to extinguish your cigarette for fear of starting a forest fire.

Café-bars in cities are always inexpensive and popular options

A Glossary of Typically Canadian Food

WITH A RICH HISTORY of multiculturalism, Canada's culinary heritage is as diverse as it is intriguing. Although there is no national cuisine as such, regional specialties have their own strong identities. The major cities, in particular Montreal and Toronto, are centers of international cuisine, with restaurants ranging from Italian to Caribbean and Asian at prices to suit every budget. French Canada offers haute cuisine at the country's top dining spots in Quebec City and Montreal.

Provincial specialties offer good value and the chance to sample some of Canada's own excellent fish, beef, and homegrown fruit and vegetables. Seafood dominates Atlantic Canada and BC menus, while steaks and burgers should be sampled in the ranching plains of Alberta and Saskatchewan. Old-style Acadian cuisine, reminiscent of French country food, is available in New Brunswick and Nova Scotia. Summer in Ontario brings fresh fruits and vegetables that take less than a day to reach the table. In Northern Canada, age-old Inuit techniques produce a variety of sundried caribou and fish dishes.

SEAFOOD

BORDERED BY oceans on three sides, Canada offers wonderful seafood, particularly on its east and west coasts. Produce from here is freshly caught and can easily make it from the ocean to the dinnerplate within 24 hours. **Oysters**, **clams**, and **scallops** are a main feature of East Coast menus. In New Brunswick, **fiddleheads** (fern shoots) and **dulse** (seaweed) are enjoyed sautéed as a vegetable accompaniment. Prince Edward Island is famous for its **lobster**, which is simply boiled, broiled (grilled), or served whole with corn on the cob at one of the many church socials that run through summer on the little island; those who don't like crustacea can try **Atlantic salmon**.

Pacific salmon, **crab**, **shellfish**, and **shrimp** (prawns) dominate British Columbian fare, along with the typically northern fish the **Arctic char**. More unusual dishes, often incorporating historic pickling and preserving methods, include **Solomon Grundy**

Lobster platter from Quebec City

(Nova Scotia's fine marinated herring), and **cod tongues**, as well as tasty **seal flipper pie** from Newfoundland. Since it was the fruits of the sea that tempted early explorers to this area, it is no surprise that **cod**, **clams**, and **mussels** are still much enjoyed for their quality, as are the newly-stylish fresh broiled **tuna** and **sardines**. Freshwater fish, both the farmed and wild versions, is caught in the two million lakes dotted across Canada, and offers a delicate contrast to seafood. In the west of the country, the tender **Winnipeg goldeye**, **trout**, and **pickerel**, which is often cooked over open fires at informal summer outdoor shore lunches throughout the central region, are a uniquely Canadian treat.

MEAT

BASED IN CALGARY, Alberta's cattle ranches are the source of Canada's finest beef. Huge **burgers** and **steaks** are exceptionally high-grade here. Most beef in rural areas is served simply, with salad and fries, but one much-loved local dish is **Calgary beef hash**, corned beef with baked beans and fried potatoes. Lamb and buffalo are also farmed, albeit in smaller numbers. The Yukon, Northwest Territories, and Nunavut supply much of the country's game; **caribou**, **musk ox**, and **moose** are all sent down south to be cooked in the European style. Local people, particularly the Inuit, smoke meat for the winter months. Their **smoked caribou** is delicious and very popular. Famous for making the most of a kill, native people use every part of the animal for either clothing or food; even **moose fleas** are something of a delicacy. **Goose**, **duck**, and fish are all smoked or sundried too, providing staples for the very long winter. Caribou and birds are preserved by being hung out on lines to dry in the Arctic sun. Sauces made from wild berries moisten the meat, and may be sweetened to taste.

FRUIT AND VEGETABLES

ONTARIO IS the fruitbowl of Canada. In addition to its burgeoning wine industry, the area is known continent-wide for its strawberries and cranberries. Peaches and apples are also cultivated here in large quantities, as are blueberries, which also flourish in Nova Scotia and Quebec.

A Chinese vegetable-seller in traditional dress in Toronto

Basket of apples from Ontario in Muskoka market

Many berries grow wild and can be picked while hiking for the evening meal. Corn, black beans, and the gourd vegetable squash (collectively known as the "three sisters") are produced in Ontario alongside zucchini (courgette), huge tomatoes, and fresh herbs, all of which are grown for domestic use and for export.

DESSERTS AND SWEETS

CANADA HAS produced a dessert food famous the world over: maple syrup. Usually eaten with American (buttermilk) pancakes, the syrup can also be served French-style with **trempettes**, fried bread soaked in syrup and covered with heavy cream. The syrup is also used in tarts, bread, and pies. It can also round off a meal as maple sugar in coffee or aromatic maple fudge. French-Canadians are known for their rich desserts; **tarte au sucre** (sugar pie) is popular, as is **pudding au chomeur** (literally "unemployed pudding"), an upside-down cake with a caramel base. Fruit tarts from Quebec are also delicious.

FAST FOOD

THE STAPLE North American fare of hamburgers, hot-dogs, French fries, fried chicken, and pizza provides a recognizable selection of snacks for most visitors. For the adventurous, Quebec has managed to break into the world of fast food with **pou-tine**, a snack of French fries dripping with melted cheese and a rich beef or onion gravy.

A recent explosion in specialty coffee shops has raised the standard of some outlets;

freshly brewed multi-flavored cappuccinos served with a wide choice of muffins and bagels are highly popular. Doughnuts of many varieties are an old favorite: Canadians joke that the easiest way to find a police officer is to visit a doughnut shop, because officers on patrol always seem to be taking a break in one.

FRENCH-CANADIAN FOOD

THE CENTER of French-style gourmet cuisine in Canada is Quebec. Dishes here are reminiscent of the best European food, and Montreal usually boasts at least two well-known French chefs working in its top restaurants at any time. *Canadien* cooks are changing with the times. Many of North America's most innovative chefs work in Montreal and Quebec City, blending elements of centuries-old farmers' traditions with the lighter cuisine of modern

Maple Syrup

Europe and America. For more traditional French-Canadian dishes, both cities and towns in the province usually serve specialties. These include **creton** (a spicy pork pâté), **tourtière**, (a pastry pie filled with ground pork or beef and cloves), and many varieties of **pâtisserie**. **Smoked beef** is another popular local delicacy.

The Maritime Provinces offer excellent, originally French, Acadian dishes from recipes which are hundreds of years old. As well as meat pies, patés, and stews, rich desserts and cakes feature in their hearty menus.

There are several top French restaurants in Canada, based largely in Montreal and Quebec City. Vieux-Montréal boasts a variety of French bistros offering traditional delights such as **snails in garlic**, **filet mignon** steak, and delicate **butter tarts** and pâtisserie; in true French tradition, the *prix-fixe* menus are always good value. Quebec City offers more classic country fare such as Quebec **French pea soup**, and **duck**. Breakfast French-style is a treat; local **brioches** and **croissants** are delicious with **café au lait**.

WHAT TO DRINK

Canada's two favorite beers, the lagers Molson "Canadian" and Labatt "blue", are known the world over and are drunk, chilled, by Canadians in preference to any other beer. The first Canadian wine was made in 1811 for commercial sale, but it is only in recent years that Canadians have developed a taste for the grape. Canada produces excellent wines from hybrid grapes, thanks largely to European wine makers who emigrated to Canada after rigorous special training. Most wine comes from two areas: a pocket in the southern Okanagan Valley of British Columbia *(see p315)*, and a 55-km (35-mile) strip along the Niagara Peninsula of southern Ontario, where the majority of grapes are grown. Familiar grape varieties such as the Chardonnays, Riesling, and Pinot Noir, are among the better known wines also produced in Ontario, and in the more temperate climate of British Columbia. Rye Whisky is distilled in BC; Canadian Club is the most popular brand, but local distilleries produce specialties.

Molson, the popular Canadian Beer

Choosing a Restaurant

T HE RESTAURANTS in this guide have been selected across
a wide range of price categories for their exceptional
food, good value, or interesting location. Entries are listed by
region, in alphabetical order within price category. The thumb
tabs on the pages use the same color-coding as the correspon-
ding regional chapters in the main section of this guide.

	OUTDOOR EATING	VEGETARIAN SPECIALTIES	BAR AREA	FIXED-PRICE MENU	CHILDREN'S FACILITIES
NEWFOUNDLAND AND LABRADOR					
CORNER BROOK: *The Wine Cellar* $$$$ Glyn Mill Inn, Cob Lane. **(** *(709) 634 5181.* This steakhouse has a strong local following. Try the char-grilled Alberta beef and desserts made from wild Newfoundland berries. 🔓 🖼		●	■		
L'ANSE AU CLAIR: *Northern Light Inn* $$ 58 Main St. **(** *(709) 931 2332.* In an area where there are few restaurants, Northern Light offers dining that is reliable and filling. Seafood and Labrador caribou are specials. 🔓 🖼		●	■		
ROCKY HARBOUR: *Ocean View Hotel* $$$ Main St. **(** *(709) 458 2730.* The dining room offers a spectacular view of Rocky Harbour. The menu features fresh seafood and home-made pies. 🔓 🎵 🖼		●	■		■
ST. JOHN'S: *Bruno's* $$$ 248 Water St. **(** *(709) 579 7662.* Owners Bruno and Gail Ortichello make everything in this tiny Italian restaurant by hand, including sausages, breads, and pastas. For dessert, the tiramisu is breathtaking. 🖼		●	■	●	■
ST. JOHN'S: *Bianca's* $$$$ 171 Water St. **(** *(709) 726 9016.* One of Atlantic Canada's finest restaurants, the extensive menu includes French-cut rack of lamb, baked musk ox, salmon in bittersweet chocolate sauce, and, for dessert, Belgian chocolate torte or apple strudel. 🔓 🍴 🖼	■	●	■		
SAINT-PIERRE & MIQUELON: *Le Caveau* $$$$ 2 Rue Maître Georges Lefevre. **(** *(508) 41 30 30.* Possibly the best restaurant on this very French island, Le Caveau's menu takes full advantage of the local seafood and French bakery goods. A local favorite is the *Brioche d'escargots* in Roquefort dressing. 🍴 🖼	■	●	■		
TERRA NOVA NATIONAL PARK: *Clode Sound Dining Room* $$$ Terra Nova Park Lodge. **(** *(709) 543 2525.* This family dining room features a wide variety of pastas, seafood, and steaks, and traditional Newfoundland dishes. 🔓 🖼	■	●	■		■
WITLESS BAY: *The Captain's Table* $ Hwy 10. **(** *(709) 334 2278.* Eat here after a boat tour of the fabulous Witless Bay Bird Sanctuary. The fish and chips are some of the best in Newfoundland, and the rich, creamy chowder is a secret family recipe. 🔓 🖼					■
NEW BRUNSWICK, NOVA SCOTIA, AND PRINCE EDWARD ISLAND					
ANTIGONISH: *Sunshine on Main* $$ 332 Main St. **(** *(902) 863 5851.* A favorite here is the Seafood Pot-au-Feu – lobster, shrimp, scallops, mussels, and haddock in a tomato and white wine broth. 🔓 🖼		●			■
BADDECK: *Telegraph House Inn* $$ Chebucto St. **(** *(902) 295 9988.* Located in a large Victorian mansion, this restaurant prepares traditional Nova Scotia lobster, trout, and salmon. 🔓 🖼					■
BAY FORTUNE: *Inn at Bay Fortune* $$$$ Hwy 310. **(** *(902) 687 3745.* Regularly listed among Canada's finest restaurants, the chef presents a menu of fresh island fish, lamb, and beef. Book the Chef's Table and enjoy seven specially prepared surprise courses. 🔓 🍴 🖼		●		●	■

Price categories for a three-course meal for one, including half a bottle of wine (where available) and service: $ under Can\$25 $$ Can\$25–\$35 $$$ Can\$35–\$50 $$$$ Can\$50–\$70 $$$$$ over Can\$70	**OUTDOOR EATING** Some tables on a patio or terrace. **VEGETARIAN SPECIALTIES** One menu always includes a selection of vegetarian dishes. **BAR AREA** There is a bar area or cocktail bar within the restaurant, available for drinks and/or bar snacks. **FIXED-PRICE MENU** A fixed-price menu available at a good rate, for lunch, dinner or both, usually with three courses. **CHILDREN'S FACILITIES** Small portions and/or high chairs available on request.	OUTDOOR EATING	VEGETARIAN SPECIALTIES	BAR AREA	FIXED-PRICE MENU	CHILDREN'S FACILITIES
BOUCTOUCHE: *Le Tire-Bouchon* 157 Chemin du Couvent. ((506) 743 5568. The dining room at this delightful inn overlooks the garden. Chowders, scallops, lobster, fresh fish, chicken, and duck are all regular offerings.	$$$			■	●	■
CARAQUET: *Hotel Paulin* 143 Bvld. St. Pierre Ouest. ((506) 727 9981. The restaurant in this family hotel serves regional fare, including fresh trout and salmon. For dessert, try the traditional sugar pie.	$$$			■		
CHARLOTTETOWN: *Siranella* 83 Water St. ((902) 628 2271. This Italian eatery is located a short stroll from pretty Peake's Wharf. Try the home-made spinach gnocchi served in cream sauce with gorgonzola and parmesan, or the herb-cured veal grilled in olive oil.	$$	■	●			
CHARLOTTETOWN: *Piece A Cake* 119 Grafton St. ((902) 894 4585. A lively bistro that serves up an eclectic combination of dishes. The open kitchen allows diners to watch as the chef works his magic.	$$$		●			
DALHOUSIE: *Manoir Adelaide* 385 Adelaide St. ((506) 684 5681. Part of the Best Western chain, but the dining is far better than the average hotel fare. Fresh fish is grilled, steamed, or poached.	$$$	■	●	■		
GRAND TRACADIE: *Dalvay-by-the-Sea* Prince Edward Island National Park. ((902) 672 2048. This historic inn *(see p345)* serves seafood dishes with an Australian flair including salmon with roasted seaweed and tomato salsa.	$$$$		●	■	●	■
HALIFAX: *Da Maurizio* 1496 Lower Water St. ((902) 423 0859. An elegant Italian restaurant. Creative offerings include pasta with a range of unusual sauces and luscious creamy desserts.	$$$$		●			
HALIFAX: *Sweet Basil Bistro* 1866 Upper Water St. ((902) 425 2133. A comfortable but sassy bistro across from the Historic Properties serves innovative dishes such as ravioli stuffed with butternut squash and fresh herbs, covered with a light parmesan and hazelnut sauce.	$$$	■	●			
LUNENBURG: *The Lion Inn* 33 Cornwallis St. ((902) 634 8988. This small restaurant in Lunenburg's historic Old Town has an equally small but excellent menu, including Nova Scotia rack of lamb.	$$$			■		
MABOU: *Duncregan Country Inn* Hwy 19. ((902) 945 2207. In this small dining room, Eleanor and Steven Mullendore offer creative takes on regional dishes. The favorite is the fresh salmon grilled over an open flame with a Dijon, lemon, and honey marinade.	$$$		●		●	■
MONTAGUE: *Windows on the Water* 106 Sackville St. ((902) 838 2080. This delightful spot overlooking Montague Harbour features creative sandwiches and first-class chowders.	$$$	■	●			■
OYSTER BED BRIDGE: *Café St-Jean* Route 6 at Oyster Bed Bridge. ((902) 963 3133. This restaurant takes full advantage of the local seafood, including fresh lobster from a nearby lobster pound, to present a menu of classic and Cajun dishes. The dessert crêpes are wonderful.	$$$	■	●		●	■

For key to symbols see back flap

Price categories for a three-course meal for one, including half a bottle of wine (where available) and service: **⑤** under Can$25 **⑤⑤** Can$25–$35 **⑤⑤⑤** Can$35–$50 **⑤⑤⑤⑤** Can$50–$70 **⑤⑤⑤⑤⑤** over Can$70	**OUTDOOR EATING** Some tables on a patio or terrace. **VEGETARIAN SPECIALTIES** One menu always includes a selection of vegetarian dishes. **BAR AREA** There is a bar area or cocktail bar within the restaurant, available for drinks and/or bar snacks. **FIXED-PRICE MENU** A fixed-price menu available at a good rate, for lunch, dinner or both, usually with three courses. **CHILDREN'S FACILITIES** Small portions and/or high chairs available on request.	OUTDOOR EATING	VEGETARIAN SPECIALTIES	BAR AREA	FIXED-PRICE MENU	CHILDREN'S FACILITIES
PARRSBORO: *Harbour View Restaurant* **⑤** 476 Pier Rd. **(** *(902) 254 3507.* This restaurant is a favorite with locals, serving great chowders, fish and chips, coffee, and home-made pies, all with harbor views.		■			●	■
PRINCE WILLIAM: *King's Head Inn* **⑤⑤** Kings Landing Historic Settlement. **(** *(506) 363 4999.* Set in the Historic Settlement, waiters wear period costumes, and all the recipes date from 1855, the year the inn was built. ● *Dinner.* 🎵 🍴		■	●	■		■
ST. ANDREWS: *The Europe* **⑤⑤⑤** 48 King St. **(** *(506) 529 3818.* After a day of beachcombing along the shores of the Passamaquoddy Bay, nothing is better than the hearty French, Swiss, and German dishes that chef-owner Anita Ludwig does so well. 🚻 🍴				■		
SAINT JOHN: *Beatty and the Bistro* **⑤⑤** 60 Charlotte St. **(** *(506) 652 3888.* Lamb is a specialty here, roasted and stuffed with cranberries, pecans, rosemary, and garlic. Another popular dish is Zorba the Chicken, stuffed with feta cheese, spinach, and garlic. 🚻 🎵 🍴			●			
SAINT JOHN: *Billy's* **⑤⑤⑤** Old City Market. **(** *(506) 672 3474.* Dinner is chosen from the display of halibut, shrimp, oysters, and other seafood, then drinks are served while it is cooked to order. 🍴		■	●	■		
SHELBURNE: *Charlotte's Lane Café* **⑤⑤⑤** 13 Charlotte Lane. **(** *(902) 875 3314.* Swiss-trained chef Roland Glauser presents delicious menu items such as chicken stuffed with camembert, asparagus, and garlic. 🍴		■	●			
SUSSEX: *Broadway Café* **⑤⑤** 73 Broad St. **(** *(506) 433 5414.* An innovative lunch spot with a tempting assortment of sandwiches and home-made soups. ● *Sun–Thu D.* 🍴		■	●			■
WOLFVILLE: *Acton's Café* **⑤⑤⑤** 268 Main St. **(** *(902) 542-7525.* Acton's German-trained chef has created an international cuisine featuring ingredients from the farms of the Annapolis Valley. 🍴 🍴		■	●	■	●	
MONTREAL						
CHINATOWN: *Maison Kam Fung* **⑤⑤** 1008 Rue Clark. **(** *(514) 878 2888.* This bright, airy restaurant serves the city's most reliable lunchtime dim sum. Dinnertime specialties are standard Cantonese. 🚻 🍴			●	■	●	■
DOWNTOWN: *Schwartz's (Montréal Hebrew) Delicatessen* **⑤** 2895 Blvd. Saint-Laurent. **(** *(514) 842 4813.* Jewish immigrants from Romania made smoked brisket a staple of the Montreal diet. This place excels in cooking it. No alcohol or credit cards. 🚻					●	■
DOWNTOWN: *Brasserie Magnan* **⑤⑤** 2602 Rue Saint-Patrick. **(** *(514) 935 9647.* This old-fashioned Montreal tavern serves roast beef, salmon pie, and huge steaks to a mixed clientele. Good selection of draft beers. 🚻 🍴		■		■	●	
DOWNTOWN: *Biddle's Jazz and Ribs* **⑤⑤** 2060 Rue Aylmer. **(** *(514) 842 8656.* Jazz musician Charlie Biddle built this restaurant so that his friends would have a place to play a little music and feast on barbecued ribs. 🎵 🍴		■		■		

DOWNTOWN: *Le Canard* $$
4631 Blvd. St. Laurent. ((514) 284 6009.
Brass platters and fish nets decorate this simple restaurant. It is known
for its *canard à l'orange*, but the seafood *paella* is equally good. 🍷 🍽

DOWNTOWN: *Phayathai* $$
1235 Rue Guy. ((514) 933 9949.
Classic Thai dishes served in a friendly ambience. Seafood and *galangal*
(ginger) soups are excellent, as is the roast duck in curry sauce. 🍽

DOWNTOWN: *L'Actuel* $$$
1194 Rue Peel. ((514) 866 1537.
This cheerful Belgian-style brasserie serves a few dozen variations on
the mussels and French fries theme, as well as other classic Belgian
dishes such as smoked herring with potatoes. 🍷 🍽

DOWNTOWN: *Le Caveau* $$$
2063 Rue Victoria. ((514) 844 1624.
Le Caveau's intimate dining rooms are spread over three floors
in an old brick house surrounded by glass and steel towers.
The praline gateau is particularly good. ♿ 🍷 🍽

DOWNTOWN: *L'Orchidée de Chine* $$$
2017 Peel St. ((514) 287 1878.
Diners in romantic little booths can feast on such Chinese delicacies as
softshell crab, sautéed lamb with spicy sauce, and crispy duck. ♿ 🍽

DOWNTOWN: *Moishe's* $$$
396 Blvd. Saint-Laurent. ((514) 845 3509.
This large noisy dining room is a carnivore's paradise. The Lighter
family have been serving their thick steaks for 50 years. ♿ 🍷 🍽

DOWNTOWN: *Restaurant Julien* $$$
1191 Rue Union. ((514) 871 1581.
A large canopied terrace makes this French restaurant a charming
summer dining spot. The duck-breast tournedos and the chocolate
marquise are delicious. ♿ 🍷 🍽

DOWNTOWN: *Café de Paris* $$$$
Ritz-Carlton Hotel, 1228 Ouest Rue Sherbrooke. ((514) 842 4212.
During the summer, the formal Edwardian dining room in this
upscale hotel spills over into the garden. The kitchen serves
classic French cuisine. ♿ 🎵 🍷 🍽

DOWNTOWN: *Le Passe Partout* $$$$
3857 Blvd. Décarie. ((514) 487 7750.
New York-born chef James MacGuire writes his own menu every day
according to his fresh ingredients. Examples include duck terrine,
sautéed veal, swordfish, and the best bread in Montreal. 🍷 🍽

DOWNTOWN: *Toqué!* $$$$
3842 Rue Saint-Denis. ((514) 499 2084.
Normand Laprise and Christin LaMarch have reigned as Montreal's
most innovative chefs for more than a decade. ♿ 🍷 🍽

DOWNTOWN: *Beaver Club* $$$$$
Hôtel La Reine-Elizabeth, 900 Ouest Blvd. René Lévesque. ((514) 861 3511.
An élite ambience with classic roast beef, grilled salmon,
and lamb, and the best martinis in town. ♿ 🍷 🍽

DOWNTOWN: *Chez la Mère Michel* $$$$$
1209 Rue Guy. ((514) 934 0473.
One of the oldest and most traditional French restaurants in the city.
The Dover sole, served *à la meunière* or with lobster, is wonderful. 🍷 🍽

DOWNTOWN: *Nuances* $$$$$
Casino de Montréal, 1 Ave. du Casino. ((514) 392 2708.
The Casino de Montréal's grilled tuna with basil-flavored polenta and
lamb with wine and thyme are as spectacular as the views. ♿ 🍷 🍽

ILE SAINTE-HELENE: *Hélène de Champlain* $$$
200 Tour de l'Isle. ((514) 395 2424.
It is hard to beat this setting – an old stone house in the heart of
the St. Lawrence River region. The food is good too. ♿ 🍷 🍽

	OUTDOOR EATING	**VEGETARIAN SPECIALTIES**	**BAR AREA**	**FIXED-PRICE MENU**	**CHILDREN'S FACILITIES**

Price categories for a three-course meal for one, including half a bottle of wine (where available) and service:

$ under Can$25
$$ Can$25–$35
$$$ Can$35–$50
$$$$ Can$50–$70
$$$$$ over Can$70

OUTDOOR EATING
Some tables on a patio or terrace.
VEGETARIAN SPECIALTIES
One menu always includes a selection of vegetarian dishes.
BAR AREA
There is a bar area or cocktail bar within the restaurant, available for drinks and/or bar snacks.
FIXED-PRICE MENU
A fixed-price menu available at a good rate, for lunch, dinner or both, usually with three courses.
CHILDREN'S FACILITIES
Small portions and/or high chairs available on request.

Restaurant	Price	Outdoor Eating	Vegetarian Specialties	Bar Area	Fixed-Price Menu	Children's Facilities
PLATEAU MONT-ROYAL: *Café Santropol* 3990 Rue Saint-Urbain. **(** (514) 842 3110. Quiches, thick sandwiches, and great soups in a trendy atmosphere. No alcohol, but the tea selection is wide and exotic. **&**	$	■	●		●	■
PLATEAU MONT-ROYAL: *L'Anecdote* 801 East Rue Rachel. **(** (514) 526 7967. Movie posters and chrome fittings give this burger joint a 1950s feel, but concessions to modern tastes include a vegetarian club sandwich.	$		●			■
PLATEAU MONT-ROYAL: *Restaurant Salle Gérard-Delage* 3535 Rue Saint-Denis. **(** (514) 282 5121. Part of the attraction of eating here is that the waiters and waitresses, like the cooks and bartenders, are students of the Institut de Tourisme et d' Hôtellerie du Québec. **& ¶ ⌂**	$$			■	●	■
PLATEAU MONT-ROYAL: *Faros* 362 Rue Fairmont. **(** (514) 270 8437. Fine fresh seafood prepared in Greek style. The cozy restaurant in blue-and-white decor is full of nooks and crannies. **♫ ⌂**	$$$	■	●		●	■
PLATEAU MONT-ROYAL: *L'Express* 3927 Rue Saint-Denis. **(** (514) 845 5333. This almost perfect re-creation of a Paris bistro is very popular. The ambience is lively, and the food good and reasonably priced. **& ¶ ⌂**	$$$	■	●	■	●	■
VIEUX MONTRÉAL: *Stash's Café Bazaar* 200 Ouest Rue Saint-Paul. **(** (514) 845 6611. Stash's Polish kitchen turns out hearty winter sustenance, such as hot *borscht*. Diners sit at pews from a demolished convent. **¶ ⌂**	$$$		●	■		
VIEUX MONTRÉAL: *Chez Delmo* 211 Rue Notre-Dame Ouest. **(** (514) 849 4061. Most patrons of this seafood restaurant sit at long bars of polished wood to slurp oysters, crack lobsters, and indulge in Arctic char. **& ¶ ⌂**	$$$$					
VIEUX MONTRÉAL: *Claude Postel* 443 Rue Saint-Vincent. **(** (514) 875 5067. Belle Epoque opulence hides behind the stone walls of this restaurant. Try broiled bream with parmesan, and, for dessert, berry sorbet. **¶ ⌂**	$$$$			■	●	
VIEUX MONTRÉAL: *Les Remparts* 93 Est Rue de la Commune. **(** (514) 392 1649. Part of the city's original stone walls form the foundations of this cellar restaurant. The chef offers delights such as plum-stuffed rabbit. **¶ ⌂**	$$$$	■	●	■		■

QUEBEC CITY AND THE ST. LAWRENCE RIVER

Restaurant	Price	Outdoor Eating	Vegetarian Specialties	Bar Area	Fixed-Price Menu	Children's Facilities
BAIE SAINT-PAUL: *Le Mouton Noir* 43 Rue Sainte-Anne. **(** (418) 240 3030. Overlooking the Gouffre River, this small restaurant marries French techniques with local delicacies in fish and poultry dishes. **& ⌂**	$$$	■		■	●	■
CHARLEVOIX: *Auberge Petite Madeleine* Port-au-Persil. **(** (418) 638 2460. This inn serves traditional recipes of Charlevoix, rich in local berries, maple syrup, and wild herbs. Grand views of the St. Lawrence accompany French-style dishes served with flair. **⌂**	$$	■	●		●	■
HAVRE-SAINT-PIERRE: *Restaurant Chez Julie* 1023 Rue Dulcinée. **(** (418) 538 3070. This popular local has no pretensions. Huge portions of local seafood – the seafood pizza with béchamel sauce is quite extraordinary. **⌂**	$		●		●	■

Iles-de-la-Madeleine: *La Saline* $$
1009 Route 199, La Grave, Havre-Aubert. (418) 937 2230.
Unpretentious seafood restaurant offers "*pot-en-pot*," a creamy mix of
fish, seafood, and potatoes with a flaky crust. ● *mid-Sep–mid-May.*

Iles-de-la-Madeleine: *Auberge Marie Blanc* $$$$
1112 Rue Commerciale, Notre-Dame-du-Lac. (418) 899 6747.
A Boston industrialist built this romantic lodge on the shores of Lake
Témiscouta for his beautiful Creole mistress. The menu focuses on local
lamb, venison, rabbit, and partridge. ● *mid-Oct–Jun.*

Ile d'Orléans: *Le Vieux-Presbytère* $$$$
1247 Ave. Msgr-d'Esgly, Saint Pierre. (418) 828 9723.
This former priests' residence offers lovely views of the St. Lawrence.
A game farm next door provides buffalo and elk steaks.

Lac-Saint-Jean: *La Volière* $$$
200 4ième Ave. Péribonka. (418) 374 2360.
Try local delicacies here such as grilled John Dory, *ouananiche* (land-
locked salmon), and blueberry pie. There are also views of the rapids.

Métis-sur-Mer: *Au Coin de la Baie* $$$$
1140 Route 132. (418) 936 3855.
The simple decor does not detract from the view of Métis Bay.
The scallops and cod fillets are excellent. ● *mid-Sep–mid-May.*

Percé: *Auberge du Gargantua* $$$
222 Route des Failles. (418) 782 2852.
The dining room looks out over the Gaspé interior, so it is appropriate
that the menu should list several game specialties from this wilderness
hunting area. ● *Dec–May.*

Quebec City: *Le Cochon Dingue* $$
46 Blvd. Champlain. (418) 692 2013.
This is a fun place, with eccentric decor, brisk service, and a menu
of mussels or steak with French fries and sinful desserts.

Quebec City: *À la Maison de Serge Bruyère* $$$
1200 Rue Saint-Jean. (418) 694-0618.
This old house has been converted into three dining rooms, ranging
from formal French to a lively Bavarian beer hall.

Quebec City: *Aux Anciens Canadiens* $$$$
34 Rue Saint-Louis. (418) 692 2835.
Venison in blueberry wine and ham in maple syrup are among
the Quebec dishes served in this 17th-century home.

Sept-Iles: *Café du Port* $$
495 Ave. Brochu. (418) 962 9311.
Soft colors, fresh seafood, and friendly service make this
modest little restaurant worth investigating.

SOUTHERN AND NORTHERN QUEBEC

Hull: *Café Henry Burger* $$$$
69 Rue Laurier. (819) 777 5646.
Despite its name, chef Robert Bourassa's specialties are lamb in madeira,
or delicately seasoned salmon, rather than hamburgers.

Laniel: *Pointe-aux-Pins* $$$
1955 Chemin du Ski. (819) 634 5211.
A four-course dinner is on offer for those staying in the chalet complex
from Thursday to Sunday. The ingredients range from piglet with blue
potatoes to lamb with pesto sauce. ● *Mon–Wed; mid-Oct–mid-May.*

Laurentian Mountains: *Rôtisserie au Petit Poucet* $$
1030 Route 117, Val-David. (819) 322 2246.
A rustic log restaurant serves huge meals of, among other dishes, roasted
ham, pork, and caribou. The restaurant also smokes its own meat.

Laurentian Mountains: *Auberge des Cèdres* $$$$
26 305ième Ave. Saint Hippolyte. (450) 563 2083.
A Montreal financier built this rambling lakeside home as a summer
retreat. Chef André Schoot is most renowned for his duck dishes.

Price categories for a three-course meal for one, including half a bottle of wine (where available) and service:
[$] under Can$25
[$][$] Can$25–$35
[$][$][$] Can$35–$50
[$][$][$][$] Can$50–$70
[$][$][$][$][$] over Can$70

Outdoor Eating
Some tables on a patio or terrace.
Vegetarian Specialties
One menu always includes a selection of vegetarian dishes.
Bar Area
There is a bar area or cocktail bar within the restaurant, available for drinks and/or bar snacks.
Fixed-Price Menu
A fixed-price menu available at a good rate, for lunch, dinner or both, usually with three courses.
Children's Facilities
Small portions and/or high chairs available on request.

Laurentian Mountains: *L'Eau à la Bouche* [$][$][$][$][$]
3003 Blvd. Sainte-Adèle, Sainte-Adèle. ☎ *(450) 229 2991/227 1416.*
Nouvelle cuisine and Quebec cooking are combined here to produce such marvels as roast veal in Cognac and Roquefort sauce. ♿ 👔 💳

Montérégie: *L'Auberge des Gallants* [$][$][$][$]
1171 Chemin Saint-Henri, Sainte-Marthe. ☎ *(450) 459 4241.*
The menu of this hilltop inn is rich with rabbit and game dishes, but also offers Atlantic lobster and mussels. ♿ 👔

North Hatley: *Auberge Hatley* [$][$][$][$][$]
325 Virgin Rd. ☎ *(819) 842 2451.*
Chef Alain Labrie has been voted the best in Quebec three times. He uses his homegrown vegetables and picks his own wild berries to make sherbert. The dining room overlooks Lake Massawippi. 🎵 👔 💳

Outaouais: *L'Orée du Bois* [$][$][$][$]
15 Chemin Kingsmere, Chelsea. ☎ *(819) 827 0332.*
Tall trees shade this house at the entrance to Gatineau Park. The seafood *pot-au-feu* and the rillettes of wild boar are menu highlights. ♿ 👔 💳

Rigaud: *Sucrerie de la Montagne* [$][$][$]
300 Rang Saint-Georges. ☎ *(450) 451 0831.*
This rustic barn specializes in such Quebec delicacies as pork and beans, maple-cured ham, and sugar pie, all with maple syrup *(see p146).* ♿ 🎵 💳

Rouyn-Noranda: *La Renaissance* [$][$][$]
199 Avenue Principale. ☎ *(819) 764 4422.*
After dinner in this popular storefront restaurant, diners can retreat to a pleasant lounge for cigars and malt whisky. ♿ 💳

Sherbrooke: *La Falaise Saint-Michel* [$][$][$]
100 Rue Webster. ☎ *(819) 346 6339.*
This welcoming restaurant serves wonderful French specialties – the Barbary duck is particularly good. 👔 💳

Trois-Rivières: *La Becquée* [$][$]
3600 Blvd. Royale. ☎ *(819) 379 3232.*
La Becquée's charming decor offers an evening a light romantic feel. Specialties are delicious French cuisine. ♿ 💳

Toronto

Bloor Street West: *Dang de Lion* [$]
549 Bloor St. W. ☎ *(416) 538 0190.*
One of the best Vietnamese restaurants in the city, the Dang de Lion is a popular and fashionable spot. The food is inexpensive and delicious. 💳

Bloor Street West: *Kensington Vegetarian Cafe* [$]
460 Bloor St. W. ☎ *(416) 534 1294.*
This exceptional café serves only organic, sugar-free preparations, with 14 different varieties of home-baked bread and tasty wholefoods on offer throughout the day. 💳

Cabbagetown: *Rashnaa* [$]
307 Wellesley St. E. ☎ *(416) 929 2099.*
Sri Lankan restaurants are very much in vogue in Toronto, and this little place is one of the most popular. The food is superb. 💳

Cabbagetown: *Real Jerk* [$][$]
709 Queen St. E. ☎ *(416) 463 6055.*
One of the most authentic Jamaican restaurants, offering traditional dishes such as red beans and rice as well as more original fare. ♿ 💳

Restaurant	Outdoor Eating	Vegetarian Specialties	Bar Area	Fixed-Price Menu	Children's Facilities
L'Eau à la Bouche	■	●	■	●	■
L'Auberge des Gallants	■	●	■	●	■
Auberge Hatley	■		■	●	
L'Orée du Bois		●	■	●	■
Sucrerie de la Montagne		●		●	■
La Renaissance			■	●	
La Falaise Saint-Michel		●	■	●	■
La Becquée		●	■	●	■
Dang de Lion		●		●	■
Kensington Vegetarian Cafe		●		●	■
Rashnaa	■	●		●	■
Real Jerk		●	■		■

CABBAGETOWN: *Margarita's Cantina & Tapas Mexicanas* $$$
229 Carlton St. (416) 929 6284.
A lively night out at this authentic Mexican restaurant might include tortillas and *fajitas*, washed down with huge margaritas.

CHINATOWN: *Il Fornello* $$
35 Elm St. (416) 588 9358.
Atmospheric Italian restaurant highly regarded for its mouth-watering pizzas. A popular spot with chic and attractive furnishings in ultra-modern style.

DOWNTOWN: *Juice for Life* $
336 Queen St. W. (416) 599 4442.
Youthful, mostly vegan café. It is not to everyone's taste – the soundtrack is very loud – but the food is tasty and good value.

DOWNTOWN: *Ethiopian House* $$
4 Irwin Ave. (416) 923 5438.
Ethiopian restaurants are a rarity, but this appealing establishment serves as an excellent introduction to the cuisine, scooped up by an unleavened piece of bread (*injera*) rather than traditional cutlery.

DOWNTOWN: *Goulash Party Haus* $$
498 Queen St. W. (416) 703 8056.
This homey café-restaurant serves up what is regarded as the best goulash in town. There are other Hungarian specialties too.

DOWNTOWN: *Hard Rock Café SkyDome* $$
1 Blue Jays Way. (416) 341 2388.
This burger bar and restaurant is part of the SkyDome sports complex (*see p169*) and is crowded with sports fans during games.

DOWNTOWN: *Shopsy's* $$
33 Yonge St. E. (416) 365 3333.
Shopsy's was founded as a delicatessen/diner shortly after World War II and has been popular ever since. The meat-loaded sandwiches are still delicious and the diner-style decor appealing.

DOWNTOWN: *Filet of Sole* $$$
11 Duncan St. (416) 598 3256.
Among the many seafood restaurants that dot downtown Toronto, this is one of the most popular, a lively affair situated in a converted warehouse with an emphasis on quantity.

DOWNTOWN: *Lai Wah Heen* $$$
Metropolitan Hotel, 108 Chestnut St. (416) 977 9899.
A chic and well-established restaurant, the Lai Wah Heen serves outstanding Cantonese cuisine from a menu of great originality and flair. Many locals swear by the dim sum.

DOWNTOWN: *Mata Hari Grill* $$$
39 Baldwin St. (416) 596 2832.
Malaysian restaurant with jazz as background music and a good choice of wines. Satays and curry are the house specialties.

DOWNTOWN: *Nami* $$$
55 Adelaide St. E. 416 362 7373.
Among Toronto's several Japanese restaurants, this is one of the best. Smoked eel is a particular specialty here.

DOWNTOWN: *Picante* $$$
326 Adelaide St. W. (416) 408 2958.
Gallant Spanish restaurant in the heart of downtown Toronto. The house specialties are *paella* and an appetizing range of *tapas*.

DOWNTOWN: *Boston Tavern* $$$$
4 Front St. E. (416) 860 0086.
Most Canadian restaurants are resolutely informal, but this is a punctilious place where the menu emphasizes local traditions with meat and fish. The seafood comes highly recommended.

DOWNTOWN: *Ematei Japanese Restaurant* $$$$
1st Floor, 30 St. Patrick St. (416) 340 0472.
This stylish and attractive Japanese place does a good line in *sushi*. It is located just to the east of the Art Gallery of Ontario (*see pp174–5*).

For key to symbols see back flap

Price categories for a three-course meal for one, including half a bottle of wine (where available) and service:

$ under Can$25
$$ Can$25–$35
$$$ Can$35–$50
$$$$ Can$50–$70
$$$$$ over Can$70

OUTDOOR EATING
Some tables on a patio or terrace.

VEGETARIAN SPECIALTIES
One menu always includes a selection of vegetarian dishes.

BAR AREA
There is a bar area or cocktail bar within the restaurant, available for drinks and/or bar snacks.

FIXED-PRICE MENU
A fixed-price menu available at a good rate, for lunch, dinner or both, usually with three courses.

CHILDREN'S FACILITIES
Small portions and/or high chairs available on request.

	OUTDOOR EATING	VEGETARIAN SPECIALTIES	BAR AREA	FIXED-PRICE MENU	CHILDREN'S FACILITIES
DOWNTOWN: *La Fenice* $$$$ 319 King St. W. ((416) 585 2377. This classy restaurant, with its chic modern furnishings, offers exquisite Italian cuisine with an imaginative blend of sauces and spices.		●	■		
DOWNTOWN: *Le Papillon* $$$$ 16 Church St. ((416) 363 0838. Quebecois cuisine is hard to find in Toronto, but the French pies and pastries at this first-rate establishment help to fill the gap.		●	■		■
DOWNTOWN: *Rodney's Oyster House* $$$$ 209 Adelaide St. E. ((416) 363 8105. Oysters galore at this long-established eatery where the bivalve rules supreme. It attracts a mixed crowd of tourists and businessfolk.			■		■
DOWNTOWN: *Canoe* $$$$$ Toronto Dominion Tower, 66 Wellington St. W. ((416) 364 0054. Canoe prides itself on its use of fresh Canadian ingredients such as Arctic char and caribou. The results are mouthwatering. It is situated on the 54th floor of the Toronto Dominion Tower office block.		●	■		
DOWNTOWN: *Senator* $$$$$ 253 Victoria St. ((416) 364 7517. This superb central restaurant makes fair claim to be the best steakhouse in the city. The Art Nouveau decor is striking.	■		■		
GREEKTOWN: *Avli* $$$$ 401 Danforth Ave. ((416) 461 9577. This Greek restaurant to the east of the city center is perhaps the best of its type, featuring wonderful casseroles and Greek classics.	■	●	■		
YORKVILLE: *Café Nervosa* $$$ 75 Yorkville Ave. ((416) 961 4642. This chic café-restaurant is located in Toronto's ritziest neighborhood. The cuisine is a light mix of salads, pastas, pizzas, and seafood.	■	●	■		■
LITTLE ITALY: *Corso Italia* $$$ 584 College St. ((416) 532 3635. Celebrated Italian restaurant featuring the best of home-made pastas, seafood, and an excellent range of Italian wines – very popular.	■	●	■		
OTTAWA AND EASTERN ONTARIO					
ALGONQUIN PROVINCIAL PARK: *Arowhon Pines* $$$$ off Hwy 60, Algonquin Provincial Park. ((705) 633 5661. Even if you're not staying here *(see p352)*, this one is worth the drive off the highway for a meal – the view from the six-sided log dining room is spectacular. Bring your own wine. ● *Nov–Apr.*		●		●	
KINGSTON: *Kingston Brewing Company* $ 34 Clarence St. ((613) 542 4978. A beautifully appointed, 65-seat restaurant, with an outdoor patio. There are no chemicals in the home-brewed ales and lagers.	■	●	■		■
KINGSTON: *Candlelight Dining* $$$ Fort Henry. ((613) 530 2550. To have dinner right inside Fort Henry *(see p198)* attended by soldier servants in period costume is a unique experience.	■	●	■	●	
KINGSTON: *General Wolfe Hotel* $$$ Wolfe Island. ((613) 385 2611. Getting here is half the fun, with a delightful free ride on the Wolfe Island ferry to Kingston's home of the gourmet dinner.		●	■	●	■

NORTH BAY: *Churchill's Prime Rib* $$$
631 Lakeshore Drive. ((705) 476 7777.
This comfortable lakeside spot with fine views draws rave reviews from
those who relish a hearty steak meal with local vegetables.

OTTAWA: *Heart & Crown* $
67 Clarence St. ((613) 562 0674.
Located in the trendy Byward Market, Heart & Crown specializes in
Irish pub fare. There's live Celtic music several nights a week and a
selection of Irish whiskies and beers.

OTTAWA: *Mamma Teresa Ristorante* $
300 Somerset W. ((613) 236 3023.
Traditional Italian fare is featured in addition to crispy pizzas, and this is
a great place to watch for MPs, cabinet ministers, and media types.

OTTAWA: *Royal Thai* $$
272 Dalhousie St. ((613) 562 8818.
The name says it all here – authentic Thai curries at very
reasonable prices served in the center of town.

OTTAWA: *The Ritz* $$
89 Clarence St. ((613) 789 9797.
Set in the popular Byward Market area with fine 19th-century decor and
excellent staff, this is a good spot to watch for local celebrities.

OTTAWA: *Big Daddy's Crab Shack & Oyster Bar* $$$
339 Elgin St. ((613) 228 7011.
Very popular with the younger crowd, this place serves lots of
Cajun-style cooking, as well as some more exotic fare.

OTTAWA: *Château Laurier Hotel* $$$
1 Rideau St. ((613) 241 1414.
This famous hotel (*see p193*) is a must; the twin restaurants of Zoë's
and Wilfrid's cater to a wide variety of upmarket diners.

PETERBOROUGH: *Parkhill Café* $$
655 Parkhill Rd. W. ((705) 743 8111.
Parkhill Café, with its fine large sandwiches and capuccinos, is rated
by locals and visitors as "the" place to eat in Peterborough.

THE GREAT LAKES

BAYFIELD: *The Little Inn of Bayfield* $$$$
Main St. ((519) 565 2611.
One of Ontario's finest restaurants, located in one of its best hotels.
The specialty is fish from Lake Huron – perch or pickerel.

GODERICH: *Robindale's Fine Dining* $$$$
80 Hamilton St. ((519) 524 4171.
Set in the pretty country town of Goderich, this first-rate restaurant
occupies a tastefully converted Victorian house. The wide-ranging menu
features local ingredients – the beef is mouthwatering.

NIAGARA FALLS: *Capri* $$
5438 Ferry St. ((905) 354 7519.
Something of a local institution, this family-run restaurant
provides excellent Italian fare in generous portions.

NIAGARA FALLS: *The Pinnacle Restaurant* $$$
6732 Oakes Drive. ((905) 356 1501.
Perched on top of the Minolta Tower, there are great
views of the Falls. The simpler dishes are tasty.

NIAGARA FALLS: *Yukiguni* $$$
5980 Buchanan Ave. ((905) 354 4440.
This popular Japanese restaurant offers some of the best food in town.
The sizzling dishes are served in style – try the salmon teriyaki.

NIAGARA FALLS: *Skylon Tower* $$$$
5200 Robinson St. ((905) 356 2651.
One of the busiest spots in town, the revolving restaurant on top of the
Skylon Tower provides unparalleled views of the Falls. Honeymooners
and young families alike enjoy favorites such as Caesar salad.

For key to symbols see back flap

Price categories for a three-course meal for one, including half a bottle of wine (where available) and service:

Ⓢ under Can$25
ⓈⓈ Can$25–$35
ⓈⓈⓈ Can$35–$50
ⓈⓈⓈⓈ Can$50–$70
ⓈⓈⓈⓈⓈ over Can$70

OUTDOOR EATING
Some tables on a patio or terrace.
VEGETARIAN SPECIALTIES
One menu always includes a selection of vegetarian dishes.
BAR AREA
There is a bar area or cocktail bar within the restaurant, available for drinks and/or bar snacks.
FIXED-PRICE MENU
A fixed-price menu available at a good rate, for lunch, dinner or both, usually with three courses.
CHILDREN'S FACILITIES
Small portions and/or high chairs available on request.

	OUTDOOR EATING	VEGETARIAN SPECIALTIES	BAR AREA	FIXED-PRICE MENU	CHILDREN'S FACILITIES
NIAGARA-ON-THE-LAKE: *Shaw Café and Wine Bar* ⓈⓈ 92 Queen St. 【 (905) 468 4772. Named after playwright George Bernard Shaw, this fashionable café-bar is much favored by theater-goers. The menu is Mediterranean. 🔊 🍴 🍽	■	●	■		■
NIAGARA-ON-THE-LAKE: *The Oban Inn* ⓈⓈⓈ 160 Front St. 【 (905) 468 2165. A classy affair of prettily folded napkins and highly polished cutlery. The food is great too – the poached salmon is recommended. 🔊 🍴 🍽		●	■	●	■
NIAGARA-ON-THE-LAKE: *The Olde Angel Inn* ⓈⓈⓈ 224 Regent St. 【 (905) 468 3411. Occupying a 19th-century roadhouse, the Olde Angel has a dining room and a tavern. Particular favorites include beef cooked in Guinness and roast duckling. 🍴 🍽		●	■		
PENETANGUISHENE: *Blue Sky Family Restaurant* Ⓢ 48 Main St. 【 (705) 549 8611. A traditional family-run diner, with bar stools, formica tables, and authentic fare – eggs and bacon, muffins, and the like. 🍽				●	■
SAULT STE. MARIE: *A Thymely Manner* ⓈⓈⓈⓈ 531 Albert St. 【 (705) 759 3262. This outstanding restaurant, easily the best in town, is noted for its locally raised lamb. The seafood is delicious too – try the lake trout. 🍴 🍽		●			
THUNDER BAY: *Hoito Restaurant* ⓈⓈ 314 Bay St. 【 (807) 345 6323. Hundreds of Finns emigrated to Thunder Bay in the early 20th century, and Hoito offers traditional Finnish food at reasonable prices. 🍽			■	●	
WINDSOR: *The Park Terrace* ⓈⓈⓈⓈ Windsor Hilton Hotel, 277 Riverside Drive W. 【 (519) 973 5555. This plush hotel restaurant combines excellent food made from top local produce with fine views of Detroit just across the river. 🔊 🍴 🍽		●	■	●	■
CENTRAL CANADA					
EDMONTON: *Bourbon Street* Ⓢ West Edmonton Mall. 【 (780) 423 0202. A collection of restaurants in a New Orleans-style street atmosphere, including Sherlock Holmes (noted for its beer), Albert's (Montreal-smoked meat), and Hooters (scantily-clad waitresses). 🔊 🍽	■	●	■	●	■
EDMONTON: *Unheardof Restaurant* ⓈⓈⓈ 9602 82nd Ave. 【 (780) 432 0480. Located in the Old Strathcona district, this popular restaurant's favorites include tenderloins of bison. ● *Mon.* 🔊 🍽		●		●	■
GULL HARBOUR: *Viking Dining Room* ⓈⓈ Gull Harbour Resort, Hecla Provincial Park. 【 (204) 279 2041. Icelandic fare includes Rulupsa lamb with molasses-based brown bread, fresh fish from Lake Winnipeg, and Vinarterta for dessert. 🔊 🍽	■	●	■		
MEDICINE HAT: *Mario's Ristorante* Ⓢ 439-5th Ave. SE. 【 (403) 529 2600. Located in historic downtown, Mario's serves traditional Italian pastas, veal, steak, chicken, and seafood, in a warm, classic atmosphere. 🔊 🍴 🍽		●	■	●	■
RED DEER: *Shauney's* Ⓢ 4909 48 St. 【 (403) 342 2404. Elegant dining in comfortable surroundings. Ostrich and bison are served, along with other exotic offerings. 🔊 🍽		●	■	●	■

REGINA: *The Harvest Eating House* ⓢ
379 Albert St. 【 *(306) 545 3777.*
Housed in a wooden building decorated with fig trees and rural
artifacts, this restaurant features prime rib steak and seafood.
The wagon bar is symbolic of Saskatchewan. 🔲 📧

REGINA: *The Diplomat* ⓢⓢⓢ
2032 Broad St. 【 *(306) 359 3366.*
This elegant restaurant features steak, seafood, and rack of lamb.
Paintings of Canada's prime ministers line the walls. 🔲 📧

SASKATOON: *The Granary* ⓢ
2806-8th St. East. 【 *(306) 373 6655.*
Designed like a country grain elevator, the restaurant features roast prime
rib of beef, plus seafood, chicken, and a bountiful salad wagon. 🔲 📧

SASKATOON: *Wanuskewin Restaurant* ⓢ
Wanuskewin Heritage Park. 【 *(306) 931 9932.*
Buffalo burgers, home-made soup, bannock bread, and Saskatoon
berry pie are served at this national historic site *(see p242).* 🔲 📧

SASKATOON: *Saskatoon Asian* ⓢⓢ
136 2nd Ave. South. 【 *(306) 665 5959.*
This restaurant specializes in Vietnamese dishes: rice-paper-wrapped
shrimps are a popular delicacy. 🔲 📧

STEINBACH: *Livery Barn Restaurant* ⓢ
Mennonite Heritage Village, Hwy 12 North. 【 *(204) 326 9661.*
Tasty Mennonite fare from traditional recipes, served in a pioneer setting.
The store sells local stone-ground coffee and old-fashioned candy. 🔲

WINNIPEG: *Nun's Kitchen* ⓢ
1033 Hwy 26, St. François Xavier. 【 *(204) 864 2306.*
Located in a former convent, the original kitchen of the Grey Nuns serves
buffalo burgers, chicken, and ribs. Reservations essential. 🔲 📧

WINNIPEG: *Suzy Q's* ⓢ
1887 Portage Ave. 【 *(204) 832 7814.*
A detailed re-creation of a 1950s-style lunch counter serves delicious
hamburgers, French fries, and super-thick milkshakes. 🔲

WINNIPEG: *Restaurant Dubrovnik* ⓢⓢⓢⓢ
390 Assiniboine Ave. 【 *(204) 944 0594.*
The restaurant is one of city's finest. Specialties include pork with mango
chutney and lobster with snow pea sauce. Reservations essential. 🔲 🍷 📧

VANCOUVER AND VANCOUVER ISLAND

CAMPBELL RIVER: *Legends Dining Room* ⓢⓢ
1625 McDonald Rd. 【 *(250) 286 1102.*
Overlooking Discovery Passage, patrons indulge on west coast fare while
watching ships cruise by. Brandy is served in the fireside lounge. 🔲 📧

MALAHAT: *The Aerie* ⓢⓢ
600 Ebedora Lane. 【 *(250) 743 7115.*
Sample an excellent menu of local meat and seafood overlooking
spectacular views of ocean fjords and mountains. 🔲 🎵 🍷 📧

NANAIMO: *Wesley Street Café* ⓢⓢ
321 Wesley St. 【 *(250) 753 4004.*
An intimate café for those who appreciate the light, fresh flavors
of contemporary west coast food. Live jazz at the weekends adds
a touch of sophistication. 🎵 🍷 📧

NANAIMO: *Mable House Restaurant* ⓢⓢⓢ
2104 Hemer Rd. 【 *(250) 722 3621.*
This 1904 farmhouse set in an English garden includes "Adventure
Wednesday" when the chef cooks a five-course surprise dinner. 🎵 🍷 🍷

NORTH VANCOUVER: *HiWus Feasthouse* ⓢⓢⓢⓢⓢ
6400 Nancy Greene Way. 【 *(604) 984 0661.*
A unique dinner-show experience in a Long House, combining
traditional native foods and authentic song and dance of the
Pacific Northwest Coast First Nations. 🔲 🎵

Price categories for a three-course meal for one, including half a bottle of wine (where available) and service:

$ under Can$25
$$ Can$25–$35
$$$ Can$35–$50
$$$$ Can$50–$70
$$$$$ over Can$70

OUTDOOR EATING
Some tables on a patio or terrace.
VEGETARIAN SPECIALTIES
One menu always includes a selection of vegetarian dishes.
BAR AREA
There is a bar area or cocktail bar within the restaurant, available for drinks and/or bar snacks.
FIXED-PRICE MENU
A fixed-price menu available at a good rate, for lunch, dinner or both, usually with three courses.
CHILDREN'S FACILITIES
Small portions and/or high chairs available on request.

	OUTDOOR EATING	VEGETARIAN SPECIALTIES	BAR AREA	FIXED-PRICE MENU	CHILDREN'S FACILITIES
NORTH VANCOUVER: *Pacific Starlight Dinner Train* $$$$$ BC Rail Station, 1311 W. 1st St. *(604) 984 5244.* Impress your significant other by inviting them for a romantic dinner on a train. The band plays when the train pulls into Porteau Cove.		●	■	●	
SALT SPRING ISLAND: *Hastings House* $$$$$ 160 Upper Ganges Rd. *(250) 597 2362.* A historic English manor estate overlooking Ganges' bustling harbor. Homegrown cuisine is served in elegant style in a wood-beamed dining room. Farm buildings have been restored for overnight guests.		●		●	
SOOKE: *Sooke Harbour House* $$$$ 1528 Whiffen Spit Rd. *(250) 642 6988.* The award-winning menu can include sea asparagus and sea urchins served with vegetables and herbs from the gardens on site.		●			■
TOFINO: *Wickaninnish Inn & Pointe Restaurant* $$$$ Osprey Lane at Chesterman's Beach. *(250) 725 3100.* A beautiful dining room with a circular fireplace and views of the Pacific. The menu includes fresh seafood and Pacific Northwest wines.	■	●	■	●	■
VANCOUVER: *Havana* $ 1212 Commercial Drive. *(604) 253 9119.* This authentic Cuban restaurant, with imported cocktails, is a lively slice of Havana in one of Vancouver's bustling neighborhoods.	■	●	■	●	■
VANCOUVER: *The Old Spaghetti House* $ 53 Water St. *(250) 684 1288.* Family dining in a lively atmosphere with friendly staff and a varied Italian menu. Dine outside in the heart of Gastown.	■	●	■	●	
VANCOUVER: *Cin Cin Restaurant* $$ 1154 Robson St. *(604) 688 7338.* Decorated in Italian Mediterranean style, with a clattering open kitchen and a sizzling alderwood grill, this restaurant fills with Vancouver's film types during the week and tourists on the weekend.	■	●	■	●	
VANCOUVER: *Cotton Club* $$ 200–1833 Anderson. *(604) 738 7465.* This dinner club serves North and Southwest American dishes to the sound of jazz played by internationally acclaimed musicians.	■	●	■	●	
VANCOUVER: *The Fish House* $$ 8901 Stanley Park Drive. *(604) 681 7275.* Located in Stanley Park, this fine fish restaurant is surrounded by greenery and panoramic views of English Bay. There is an early-bird special between 5 and 6pm.	■	●	■		■
VANCOUVER: *Villa De Loupa* $$ 869 Hamilton St. *(604) 688 7436.* Mouthwatering Italian food, such as risotto with fresh chives, free-range stuffed chicken, and olive-poached tomatoes.		●			
VANCOUVER: *900 West Hotel Vancouver* $$ 900 West Georgia St. *(604) 669 9378.* Guests can eat at the kitchen counter, or in the dining room at a table setting. Over 60 wines are on offer in the award-winning bar.		●	■	●	
VANCOUVER: *Diva at the Met* $$$ Metropolitan Hotel, 645 Howe St. *(604) 687 1122.* The terraced floors and open-style kitchen create a casual flair, and the award-winning menu includes pizza topped with barbecued chicken, salmon steaks, and pickled zucchini.		●	■	●	■

VANCOUVER: *Tojo's Japanese* $$$
777 West Broadway suite, 202. (604) 872 8050.
Since opening in 1988, Tojo's has consistently served award-winning
Japanese food. Most of the patrons are local media types.

VANCOUVER: *C Restaurant* $$$
2–1600 Howe St. (604) 681 1164.
A contemporary fish restaurant claiming the best seafood in town, with
a charming patio bedecked in white linen and white tiles.

VANCOUVER: *Piccolo Mondo Ristorante* $$$
850 Thurlow St. (604) 688 1633.
With 480 Italian wines in the cellar and family recipes to hand, guests can
expect delicious northern Italian food in a relaxed atmosphere.

VICTORIA: *Barb's Place* $
Fisherman's Wharf, Erie St. Float. (250) 384 6515.
A floating kitchen sitting on the docks of Victoria's harbor. Serves fish
and chips and other tasty fare to a happy clientele. Nov–Apr.

VICTORIA: *J & J Wonton Noodle House* $
1012 Fort St. (250) 383 0680.
Big room with cozy atmosphere serving fresh home-made noodles to
the locals and the lucky tourists who go out of their way to find it.

VICTORIA: *Empress Room* $$$
Empress Hotel, 721 Government St. (250) 384 8111.
Fine dining in a 1908 Edwardian dining room. An evening harpist
sets an elegant mood, and the menu includes swordfish.

VICTORIA: *Il Terrazzo* $$$
555 Johnson St. (250) 361 0028.
Located in the heart of Old Town, in an original 1890 building, this
restaurant boasts the best Italian food in Victoria. A beautiful courtyard
is warmed by six fireplaces, ten months of the year.

VICTORIA: *The Victorian* $$$
Ocean Point Resort, 45 Songhees Rd. (250) 360 2999.
Candlelight, fine wine, delicious Pacific Northwest cuisine and views
of the harbor can be expected at Victoria's premier resort.

THE ROCKY MOUNTAINS

BANFF: *Giorgio's Trattoria* $
219 Banff Avenue. (403) 762 5114.
An intimate restaurant located in the heart of town, the food is Italian
pastas and fresh pizza prepared in a wood-burning oven.

BANFF: *Buffalo Mountain Lodge Dining Room* $$$
Tunnel Mountain Rd. (403) 762 2400.
This wood-beamed dining room slightly off the beaten track serves
Canadian Rockies fare: venison, caribou, deer, lamb, and beef.

CALGARY: *Ranchman's* $
9615 McLeod Trail South. (403) 253 1100.
A Calgary tradition, this cowboy café and country music club displays
trophy rodeo saddles and a chuck wagon above the stage. The menu
features beef and chicken prepared in Texas-style smokers.

CALGARY: *Crosshouse Garden Café* $$
1240 8th Avenue SE (403) 531 2767.
The 1891 home of Calgary pioneer A.E. Cross offers Arctic char and
buffalo as well as many fish and chicken dishes.

CALGARY: *Mescalero Restaurant* $$
1315 1st St. SW. (403) 266 3339.
With southwestern US influences, the menu here includes enchiladas,
black bean soup, and seafood cooked in lime. The building looks like
a hacienda, with adobe-style walls and Mexican tile floor.

CRANBROOK: *The Art Café* $
20 7th Avenue South. (250) 426 4565.
Decorated with BC art and parquet floors, the Mexican and European
recipes are prepared in an open kitchen in view of the patrons.

Price categories for a three-course meal for one, including half a bottle of wine (where available) and service: ⓢ under Can$25 ⓢⓢ Can$25–$35 ⓢⓢⓢ Can$35–$50 ⓢⓢⓢⓢ Can$50–$70 ⓢⓢⓢⓢⓢ over Can$70	**OUTDOOR EATING** Some tables on a patio or terrace. **VEGETARIAN SPECIALTIES** One menu always includes a selection of vegetarian dishes. **BAR AREA** There is a bar area or cocktail bar within the restaurant, available for drinks and/or bar snacks. **FIXED-PRICE MENU** A fixed-price menu available at a good rate, for lunch, dinner or both, usually with three courses. **CHILDREN'S FACILITIES** Small portions and/or high chairs available on request.	OUTDOOR EATING	VEGETARIAN SPECIALTIES	BAR AREA	FIXED-PRICE MENU	CHILDREN'S FACILITIES
FAQUIER: *Mushroom Addition* ⓢ 129 Oak St. 〖 *(250) 269 7467.* Local wild mushrooms are served in nearly every dish. During the summer the place is adorned with fresh-cut flowers. 🚻 🖼		■	●			■
KIMBERLY: *The Old Bauernhaus* ⓢⓢ 280 Norton Avenue. 〖 *(250) 427 5133.* This 18th-century Bavarian barn was disassembled, shipped to Canada and rebuilt in the 1980s. The first floor is now the restaurant serving hearty German fare. ● *Oct–Nov, Apr–May.* 🚻 🎵 🖼		■	●			■
LAKE LOUISE: *Poppy Room* ⓢⓢ Chateau Lake Louise. 〖 *(403) 522 3511 ext 1189.* Every table has a view of Lake Louise in this busy dining room. Burgers, salads, pastas, and fish are offered on the menu. Breakfast is buffet-style with a choice of omelettes and waffles. 🚻 🖼			●			■
LAKE LOUISE: *Elkhorn Dining Room* ⓢⓢⓢ Mile 22 Bow Lake Icefield Parkway. 〖 *(403) 522 2167.* This historic building was built by artist Jimmy Simpson, and his watercolors adorn the walls. The cuisine focuses on local game. 🚻 🍷 🖼			●	■		■
NAKUSP: *Mattie's Family Restaurant* ⓢ Leland Hotel, 96th 4th Avenue SW. 〖 *(250) 265 3316.* Prime rib is the specialty in this restaurant overlooking Arrow Lake. Antique furniture and old photographs create an Edwardian feel. 🚻 🖼		■	●		●	■
NELSON: *The Outer Clove* ⓢ 536 Stanley St. 〖 *(250) 354 1667.* Chefs here use five pounds of garlic a day in a variety of ways, including the desserts, in this brightly painted old brick building. ● *Sun.* 🎵 🖼		■	●			
REVELSTOKE: *The Peak's Lodge Resort* ⓢⓢ Trans Canada Hwy 1. 〖 *(250) 837 2176.* Beneath Boulder Mountain, this old lodge is furnished with antiques. The menu offers Alberta beef and BC salmon smoked on site. 🍷 🖼		■	●	■	●	■
SOUTHERN AND NORTHERN BRITISH COLUMBIA						
FORT LANGLEY: *Bedford House* ⓢⓢ 9272 Glover. 〖 *(604) 888 2333.* Located in historic Fort Langley, enjoy good food in a relaxed atmosphere with attentive staff and fine wines. 🚻 🎵 🍷 🖼		■	●	■		■
KELOWNA: *Williams Inn* ⓢⓢ 526 Lawrence Avenue. 〖 *(250) 763 5136.* The menu in this romantic two-storey home is European-style game, steak, lamb, seafood, chicken, and home-made dessert. 🚻 🍷 🖼		■	●		●	
LADNER: *48th Avenue Restaurant* ⓢ 5047 48th Avenue. 〖 *(604) 946 2244.* A casual room with window seats overlooking the heritage buildings in this seaport village. West coast cuisine of seafood and pasta. 🚻 🖼		■	●	■		■
NARAMATA: *The Country Squire* ⓢⓢⓢ 3950 1st St. 〖 *(250) 496 5416.* Delicious five-course meals are served over the evening; walk around the garden with a glass of Okanagan wine between courses. 🚻 🍷 🖼			●	■	●	
OSOYOOS: *The Diamond Steak and Seafood House* ⓢⓢ 8903 Main St. 〖 *(250) 495 6223.* Three dining rooms specialize in Greek and Italian cuisine with a variety of steaks, seafood, pasta, and pizza. Prime rib is a favorite. 🚻 🍷 🖼			●	■	●	

PRINCE RUPERT: *Smile's Café* 1 Cow Bay Rd. ☎ *(250) 624 3072.* A family seafood restaurant in a 1930s wharf building, decorated in netting and old photographs. A coffee shop is also on site. ♿ 🍷 💳	$	■				■
WELLS: *Country Encounters* 4236 Jones Avenue. ☎ *(250) 994 2361.* Home-made breads, pastas, and luscious desserts. Popular with snow-mobilers in the winter; balcony seating in the summer. ● *Apr, Oct.* 💳	$	■	●		●	■
WHISTLER: *Black's Original Restaurant* 4270 Mountain Square. ☎ *(604) 932 6408.* An open-style restaurant located in the Westbrook Hotel at the base of the mountains. Turkey roast is served on Sundays and the British pub upstairs specializes in Guinness. ♿ 💳	$$	■	●	■	●	■
WHISTLER: *Bear Foot Bistro* 4121 Village Green. ☎ *(604) 932 3433.* The acid-washed cement floors, brown leather chairs, live jazz, and North America's largest selection of Cuban cigars create a sophisticated air. The food is innovative French. ♿ ♫ 🍷 💳	$$$$$		●	■	●	■
NORTHERN CANADA						
DAWSON CITY: *Bonanza Dining Room* Eldorado Hotel, 3rd & Princess Sts. ☎ *(867) 993 5451.* Two rustic restaurants in this hotel serve simple bar food. The specials change daily. ♫ 💳	$$		●	■		
DAWSON CITY: *Klondike Kate's* 3rd Avenue & King St. ☎ *(867) 993 6527.* This popular, friendly café, named after a Dawson City dance hall girl, serves the best breakfast in the Yukon. ● *winter.* 💳	$$	■			●	
FORT PROVIDENCE: *Snowshoe Inn* 1 Mackenzie St. ☎ *(867) 699 3511.* Home-cooking comes to the fore in the largest restaurant in town; sophisticated seafood is also on offer. ♿ 💳	$$			■		■
INUVIK: *MacKenzie Hotel* 186 MacKenzie Rd. ☎ *(867) 777 2861.* Inuit cooking, including char and caribou, can be sampled at this hotel restaurant *(see p359).* ♿ ♫ 💳	$$			■		
IQALUIT: *Kamotiq In Restaurant* 3506 Wiley Rd. ☎ *(867) 979 5937.* Two dining rooms, one shaped like an igloo, serve Arctic cuisine, steaks, seafood, and Mexican dishes. ♿ ♫ 💳	$$$		●	■		■
RANKIN INLET: *Siniktarvik Hotel* 3506 Wiley Rd. ☎ *(819) 645 2949* Warming stews and large steaks are available in this newly refurbished restaurant. 💳	$$		●	■	●	
WHITEHORSE: *The Cellar Dining Room* 101 Main St. ☎ *(867) 667 2572.* Part of the Edgewater Hotel, this cellar venue is popular with townspeople and has a great atmosphere and excellent food. 🍷 💳	$$		●	■	●	■
WHITEHORSE: *Yukon Mining Company* High Country Inn, 4051 4th Avenue. ☎ *(867) 667 4471.* Each evening an outdoor barbecue allows diners to appreciate the stunning scenery surrounding the hotel. Particularly popular are the salmon and halibut, as well as locally brewed beer. ♿ 🍷 💳	$$	■	●	■	●	■
YELLOWKNIFE: *The Prospector* 3506 Wiley Rd. ☎ *(867) 920 7620.* Seaplane docking is available for fly-in clients looking for a bite to eat in the summer months. ● winter. ♫ 💳	$$	■		■	●	
YELLOWKNIFE: *Wildcat Café* 3506 Wiley Road. ☎ *(867) 873 8850.* A real slice of wild Canadian life. Local food a speciality, in particular, hearty soups and casseroles *(see p336).* ● winter. 🍷	$$	■	●		●	■

SHOPPING IN CANADA

SHOPPING IN Canada offers more than the usual tourist fare of Mountie dolls and maple leaf T-shirts. Visitors can choose from a wide range of products, and buy everything from electronic equipment to clothes and jewelry. There is also a variety of goods unique to the country – maple syrup from Quebec, smoked salmon from British Columbia, and cowboy boots from Alberta, to

Doll from Charlottetown

name a few. Native art inspired by centuries-old tradition, includes carvings by west-coast peoples and Inuit paintings and tapestries. In each major city there are covered malls, chainstores, specialty shops, and galleries, as well as street markets to explore. In country areas, beautifully-made crafts by local people can be found. Be aware that sales taxes are added to the price of many items.

SHOPPING HOURS

STORE HOURS vary, but in larger cities most stores are open by 9am and close between 5pm and 9pm. However, some grocery and variety stores are open 24 hours a day, and in major towns several pharmacies are also open for 24 hours. In most towns, stores have late closing until 9pm on Friday evening. However, in smaller towns and villages you should not expect any store, including the gas station, to be open after 6pm. Sunday openings are increasing: usually hours run from noon to 5pm but vary from province to province. Check first, as many may be closed in rural areas.

HOW TO PAY

MOST CANADIAN stores accept all major credit cards, with VISA and Master-Card being the most popular. Some stores require a minimum purchase in order to use the card. They may limit the use of cards during summer and winter sales. Direct payment, or "Switch" transactions, are also widely used, with point-of-sale terminals for bank cards available in most supermarkets and department stores. Travelers' checks are readily accepted with proper identification; a valid passport or driver's license are the usually accepted forms.

US dollars are the only non-Canadian currency accepted in department stores. Bear in mind that the exchange rate is usually lower, sometimes as

much as 15 percent, than a bank will give. Large stores may offer money-changing facilities within the store.

SALES TAXES

CANADIANS LOVE to curse the national Goods and Services Tax (GST), which currently runs at 7 percent. It is added to most retail transactions; the major exception is basic food items. Visitors who are non-resident in Canada can apply for a GST rebate on most goods within 60 days of purchase. This excludes restaurant bills, drinks, tobacco, or transportation expenses. Refund forms are available in airports, duty free stores, hotels, and most Canadian Embassies. Include original receipts when sending the application to Revenue Canada (see p343) as photocopies are not accepted.

In addition to the GST, most provinces add a provincial sales tax, varying from 5–12 percent, on meals and store-bought items. Alberta, the Yukon, and the Northwest Territories do not impose this tax, and Quebec, Manitoba, Nova Scotia, and Newfoundland offer rebates to non-residents.

CONSUMER RIGHTS AND SERVICES

SMART SHOPPERS always check a store's refund policy before buying an item. Policies vary, some stores will refund money on unwanted items, others offer store vouchers, and many will not exchange or refund sale merchandise. Reputable stores will take back

defective merchandise within 28 days as long as it is accompanied by the original bill. As credit card fraud increases, it is wise to be cautious about buying by telephone using cards.

Native Canadian Wayne Carlick, carving soapstone, British Columbia

COMPLETELY CANADIAN

PRODUCTS MADE in Canada offer shoppers a wide variety of choice. Although most specialty items are on sale across the country, many goods are less expensive in their province of origin. Hand-knitted sweaters and pottery are particularly good value in Atlantic Canada, as is the much-praised Seagull pewter made in Nova Scotia. The Prairie provinces and Alberta specialize in cowboy attire; tooled belts, vests, cowboy hats, and boots. Farther west, British Columbian artisans produce elaborate carvings,

Shopkeeper at the Lonsdale Quay craft market in Vancouver *(see p276)*

MALLS AND SHOPPING CENTERS

SUBURBIA MAY not offer the most culture in Canada, but some of the malls are fine destinations in themselves. The renowned modernist Eaton Centre in Toronto is enclosed by a glass and steel arched roof, with a wonderful sculpted flock of geese soaring over shoppers. Over 42 million visitors annually enjoy this showcase of modern architecture, though it has been derided as "brutalism" by conservative Torontonians. Canada has the world's largest mall, the West Edmonton Mall in Edmonton, Alberta. Over 800 stores, more than 100 restaurants, 34 movie theaters, a huge water park, an amusement park, a theme hotel, a mini-golf course, an ice rink, and a zoo with dolphins are just some of the sights that draw Canadians and visitors alike to this retail paradise.

Exclusive stores are largely found in the country's retail capital, Toronto. Bloor Street and Yorkville Avenue are lined with status brands known the world over, such as Tiffany, Holt Renfrew, Ralph Lauren, and Gucci. Both Vancouver and Montreal have their own selection of world-class luxury stores. Montreal is notable as the fur capital of the country; good department stores will stock a selection of winter and summer furs at very reasonable prices. For those unable to travel to the north, Inuit art features highly in craft shops here.

including totem poles. Jade jewelry, from locally mined stone, is also reasonable here. Local specialties from Quebec and Ontario include maple syrup and sugar-related products. Quebec artisans make beautiful wood carvings too. In Ontario, native basketwork is good as a lasting souvenir. For those who need an extra suitcase to carry their finds home, the renowned Tilley travel cases and products are made and sold locally throughout Ontario.

Native carvings can be found across Canada, especially in the far north. Genuine Inuit carvings are inspected and stamped by the federal government. A sticker featuring an igloo marks a true piece; it will also be signed by the artist. Since the 1950s, the Inuit have been producing prints of traditional scenes, which are popular, as is native jewelry. Beautifully handmade parka jackets, embroidered panels, and soft deer hide moccasins make excellent gifts.

Contemporary Canadian art features highly in gift shops and galleries countrywide. Photographs and prints are recommended for the budget-conscious shopper. Recordings of Canadian music are freely available: Europeans will be pleased to find that tapes and CDs are at least 50 percent cheaper in Canada.

Modern sportswear and outerwear is both durable and beautifully designed. Camping, hiking, and boating equipment

are fine buys, as is fishing tackle. With such a strong tradition of outdoor life, a wide range of products is usually available at well below US and European prices.

DEPARTMENT STORES

THE BAY IS the major middle-range department store chain across the country. Canadian department stores have suffered financially during the last years of the 20th century. They are changing to meet the competition of US chains, such as Wal-Mart and discount stores, and membership stores including Costco and Price Club. Chains such as Sears and Zeller's occupy the middle to lower end of the market place. The Bay, Canada's own chain store, owned by the Hudson's Bay company, provides good bargains and quality products.

Pottery jar, Nova Scotia

The Underground City, with hundreds of boutiques, in Montreal

ENTERTAINMENT IN CANADA

ENTERTAINMENT in Canada boasts all the sophistication tourists have come to expect from a major North American country, coupled with delightful rural entertainments in relaxing local venues. Covering mainstream world-class productions in Ottawa and the larger cities, Canada also offers the latest in alternative acts and traditional artforms, particularly in its exceptional folk music heritage. Music of the highest quality, both classical and modern, is offered throughout the country, and major cities provide first-rate theater, dance, and film, not to mention many musical shows and film festivals.

Royal Winnipeg Ballerina

INFORMATION

PROVINCIAL DAILY newspapers are the most reliable sources of information about forthcoming events; the *Vancouver Sun*, *Montreal Gazette*, *Ottawa Citizen*, and *Toronto Star* are the most popular. Listings are usually published at least once a week. The *Globe & Mail* is issued in Toronto but is on sale countrywide and has an excellent arts section containing reviews of the latest attractions. Tourist offices *(see p393)* are helpful; some operators may assist in booking tickets. Visitor centers and hotel lobbies have weekly entertainment guides, such as *Where*, a magazine covering the Vancouver scene. In Quebec, French-language entertainment is chronicled by two papers, *La Presse* and *Le Devoir*. *Macleans* is a national weekly magazine with arts coverage.

BOOKING

TICKETMASTER outlets are found in many shopping malls and represent major halls across the country. Tickets to venues in Quebec are available from Admission Network. Different offices cater to different sports and artistic events in each city. Most venues, however, can be contacted directly for tickets.

DISABLED VISITORS

CANADIAN VENUES are usually very well equipped to deal with wheelchair users. All interior halls contain ramps and restroom access. Parking lots will have designated disabled spaces nearby. A hearing loop system is available at Ottawa's National Arts Centre *(see p195)*, and at most other major venues. Call ahead to check their availability. Outside ramps and elevators are provided to reach concerts halls and theaters at most large centers.

THEATER

TORONTO, OTTAWA, Vancouver, and Montreal are the four top theater centers in Canada (most of their productions are in English). Homegrown talent mixes here with shows imported from Europe and the US. Musicals and classical theater are always popular and tend to be fine quality. Shakespeare is popular, but there is a wide spectrum of shows – a stylish revival of the 1980s hit *Fame* was a long-running success in Toronto in the late 1990s. The main theaters listed opposite have a principal season from November to May, but summer attractions are on the increase. Musicals and historical reconstructions are always strong family entertainment; the best-known is the musical *Anne of Green Gables*, performed year-round since the 1950s in Charlottetown.

FILM

IMPORTED Hollywood blockbusters have no better chance of success than in Canada, where premieres are often parallel with the US, so visitors may well see films in advance of a showing in their own country. Huge IMAX™ and OMNIMAX™ movie theaters, often with up to 20 screens, are to be found in the center of major cities, particularly in Ottawa and Hull.

Canada has a fine history of filmmaking: the documentary genre was invented here, and more recently its art films have attracted a wider audience. The main centers to see the new trends are Montreal, Vancouver, and Toronto. Robert LePage, Canada's own theater and movie impresario, has an international following among the cognoscenti. The surrealist David Cronenberg, director of *eXistenz* (1999), is also Canadian. Quebec's Denys Arcand directed *Jesus of Montreal* (1986), a film that, despite some controversial scenes, was highly praised. The National Film

Façade of The Royal George Theatre, Niagara-on-the-Lake

The Ontario Place IMAX™ giant movie theater in Toronto

Board selects and releases a work by native talent each year, comprising feature films, animations, and documentaries. Ideal for spotting new talent in its birthplace, every year the Toronto Film Festival provides a lively magnet to moviegoers, as do parallel festivals held in Montreal and Vancouver.

CLASSICAL MUSIC BALLET, AND OPERA

CLASSICAL MUSIC and opera draw large audiences in Canada, and this is reflected by the high quality of performers and venues. The Canada Opera Company is based at the Hummingbird Centre for the Performing Arts *(see p176)* in Toronto, with a repertoire ranging from Mozart to cutting-edge pieces sung in English. The National Ballet of Canada is also based here, rival to the Royal Winnipeg Ballet; both companies feature period pieces and experimental work in their seasonal run. Fringe theater takes off in Toronto each summer with 400 shows selected by lottery. Well over 100,000 people annually visit the state-of-the-art Jack Singer Concert Hall in the Calgary Centre for the Performing Arts to hear the celebrated Calgary Philharmonic Orchestra. The Vancouver Symphony Orchestra plays at the Orpheum Theatre in Vancouver.

ROCK, FOLK, AND POP MUSIC

DURING THE 1990s, Canadian pop music acquired a credibility even its kindest supporters would admit had previously been lacking. Quebec's Celine Dion, risen to superstar status, performs often at the Molson Centre in Montreal and around the country. Alanis Morissette, a worthy successor to her country's heritage of folk rock, now tours the globe.

Canada is perhaps the best known for its folk music, with such stars as Leonard Cohen, Neil Young, and Joni Mitchell being the best-known faces from a centuries-old tradition. The product of an intensely musical rural people, the nature of Canadian song changes across the country,

Celine Dion, one of Canada's best-selling international artists

moving from the lonesome Celtic melodies on the east coast to the yodeling cowboys in the west. Atlantic Canada has numerous tiny, informal venues, where an excellent standard of music can be found. Prince Edward Island often offers a violin accompaniment to its lobster suppers, and New Brunswick's folk festival celebrates both music and dance. Quebec's French folksters include singer Gilles Vigneault *(see p24)* who is also admired in Europe. The Yukon's memories of the gold rush surface in 19th-century vaudeville, reenacted by dancing girls and a honky-tonk piano in Whitehorse.

DIRECTORY

TICKET AGENCIES

Admission Network
(613) 237 3800 Ottawa.
(514) 528 2828 Montreal.
(416) 861 1017 Toronto.

Ticketmaster
(416) 870 8000 Toronto.

MAJOR VENUES

Hummingbird Centre for the Performing Arts
(416) 393 7469.

The National Ballet of Canada
(416) 362 4670 Toronto.

Royal Winnipeg Ballet
(204) 956 0183.

The Newfoundland Symphony Orchestra
(709) 753 6492.

Calgary Centre for the Performing Arts
(403) 294 7455.

Jack Singer Concert Hall and Calgary Philharmonic Orchestra
(403) 571 0270.

Vancouver Symphony Orchestra
(604) 876 3434.

Orpheum Theatre
(604) 665 3050.

Molson Centre
(514) 932 2582.

SPECIALTY VACATIONS AND ACTIVITIES

THE SHEER VARIETY of the massive, unspoiled landscape is, in many ways, what attracts visitors to Canada. Taking advantage of the 38 national parks, several of which are UN World Heritage sites, most specialty vacations tend to revolve around Canada's spacious natural playgrounds. The range of activities

Hiking sign in National Parks

available in this single country is wide: sledding and snowmobiling with Inuit guides or cruising in the spring through the flower-filled Thousand Islands of Ontario are both possibilities. Other choices include scenic train rides through the Rockies, trout-fishing in pristine secluded lakes, and adventurous world-class hiking.

HIKING

CANADA IS ONE OF the world's top hiking destinations, with excellent facilities and a wide variety of terrain for beginners and experts alike. Hiking trails range from a leisurely two-hour nature walk to several days' physically demanding trek through starkly beautiful wilderness.

The preferred starting places for hiking trails in each national park are well marked. Accommodations for longer trips are often available in lodges or hostels within a park; alternatively you can bring your own tent or rent one in a nearby town. Large-scale maps of any area, including national and provincial parks, can be obtained from **Canadian Topographical Series** in Ottawa.

Most of the more popular hikes require little preparation and only basic training. The best-known hiking areas are found in Alberta and British

Columbia, in particular in and around the "big four parks" of Kootenay, Yoho, Jasper, and Banff, which encircle the Rocky Mountains. The variety of lands here, from the lush, gently rolling country near Calgary to craggy mountain peaks, reinforces the popularity of the area. More centrally, the prairie provinces offer a surprising variety of walking, from the arid badlands of Alberta's dinosaur country to the wilderness hiking in Prince Albert National Park. In the east the mountains resume; the steep scenery of the Quebec park of Gatineau and the untamed wilds of the eastern and central Gaspé Peninsula both have wonderful scenery.

In northern Canada the hiking is more demanding but equally rewarding. Most walking and hiking takes place from April to August, when temperatures do rise slightly, although drops to -30°C (-22°F) are not unusual. At best, the weather remains

Turquoise Lake O'Hara in Yoho National Park

unpredictable. The Chilkoot Pass is a 53-km (33-mile) trail that follows the path of early gold prospectors in the late 19th century from Bennett in northern British Columbia to Dyea in Alaska. For the area, this is a relatively easy path to follow and gives a good taste of northern scenery. More arduous, not to say dangerous, is the memorable Pangnirtung Trail through the southeast of Baffin Island, which even in the summer has a permanently frozen ice cap. Inuit guides will take hikers through the frozen wastes by arrangement.

Occasionally wildlife-watching hikes are available, and teams of husky dogs carry visitors on sleds across ice paths in the wilderness to reach remote destinations. An unforgettable experience, these tours are expensive due to their remoteness and a lack of other modes of transportation.

Hikers near Weasel River, Auyuittuq National Park, Baffin Island

SAFETY MEASURES

Training and safety procedures must be followed for any hike. Always contact the local park or provincial tourist office for their advice and route maps before setting off. Remember, however unlikely a meeting may seem, wildlife can be aggressive; following instructions on bear safety is a must (*see p298*). While less alarming, insects are a constant irritant: take all possible measures to repel blackflies and mosquitos. However clear and sparkling it may seem, do not drink stream or river water without thoroughly boiling it first as it may contain an intestinal parasite, which can lead to "beaver fever" or giardiasis.

In the far north, freezing weather conditions place a premium on safety measures. Never go on a trip without telling someone your planned route and expected time of arrival. Consult local wardens about wildlife and routes, and take the proper equipment. Even in the summer, freezing weather changes can be sudden, so be prepared. Those venturing into little-known territory must be accompanied by a trained guide or seek local advice on dealing with the unexpected.

EQUIPMENT

Most hiking areas offer rental outlets for tents and cold-weather clothing. Nonetheless, sturdy walking boots, rain gear, and a change of spare clothing are essentials that hikers have to bring themselves, or buy in a nearby town. Appropriate medication and a first-aid kit should also be taken, in particular bug

Rental lodge by Emerald Lake in Yoho National Park

repellent, and antihistamine. Exposure, resulting in either sunstroke or hypothermia, can be guarded against by using appropriate clothes and medication. On a long trip, carry energy-giving foods such as chocolate or trail mix.

NATIONAL PARKS

Canada's 38 national parks cover the country's most beautiful mountains, lakes, rivers, forests, and coastline. Areas of unspoiled peace, they are the ideal destination for those seeking an outdoor vacation filled with sports, activities, or even a natural spa. The most celebrated upland areas are the "big four" parks in Alberta and BC, Kluane in the Yukon, and the arctic

Swimmers at Radium Hot Springs in the Rockies

flower-filled tundra of Auyuittuq National Park in southern Baffin Island.

Most of the parks are administered by the government heritage body, **Parks Canada**, and each has a visitors' center or park office to welcome visitors. Here walking, hiking, canoeing, and fishing information is available, often from guides who know every detail of the terrain. These offices also issue permits for fishing, which are necessary in each park. Hunting of any kind and use of firearms are all strictly forbidden in national parks, as is feeding the wildlife and damaging any trees and plants. Most parks have camping facilities, or rustic lodges and cottages. The parks generally charge for these facilities, and most have a daily, weekly, or yearly entrance fee, but some are free. Season tickets are available from either the individual park or the Parks Canada office in Hull.

**Canoeists on Lake Wapizagonke,
Parc National de la Mauricie**

CANOEING

N ative canadians perfected the canoe to maneuver around the country's vast system of waterways for food and survival; today canoeing is a largely recreational pursuit. In provincial or national parks with many lakes and rivers, canoeists can portage (or trek) to the backwaters, getting away from the most populated areas at a gentle pace.

Over 250,000 lakes and 35,000 km (20,000 miles) of waterways in Ontario make this the most accessible canoeing destination. Rivers and lakes making up more than 25,000 km (16,000 miles) of canoe routes run through the Algonquin, Killarney, and Quetic parks. The Rideau Canal, which travels 190 km (120 miles) from Ottawa to Kingston is a favorite route through the province, taking in the capital, the sprinkling of tiny islands near the historic town of Kingston, and acres of fruit orchards by the fertile waterway. While traveling through the islands, be careful of the other marine traffic. The Canal connects with the St. Lawrence Seaway, the world's largest draft inland waterway, and shipping regulations are tight. Smaller craft may have to make way for tankers.

Most towns near canoeing routes will rent boats by the day, week, or month, and wetsuits, oars, and life jackets are usually available. Because of the popularity of watersports, Canada is an extremely reasonable place to buy fishing and canoeing equipment; many outfitters offer good-quality products at almost half European and US prices.

WHITEWATER RAFTING

W hitewater rafting may be attempted in the national parks of British Columbia. The Mackenzie River system, which runs from BC backwaters through the Northwest Territories, provides occasionally hair-raising rafting and canoeing. Most routes in the far north are for the experienced only. The toughest trek of all is the 300-km (180-mile) run of the South Nahanni River near Fort Simpson in the Northwest Territories. New roads here and in the Yukon have boosted the number of visitors to yet another grueling set of waterways, the Yukon River system.

Inexperienced boaters and rafters can take advantage of two-week basic training courses offered all over the country. Lake canoeing in Wells Gray Provincial Park is popular throughout the province for those seeking a more relaxing alternative.

**Windsurfing in Georgian Bay
Islands National Park, Lake Ontario**

OTHER WATERSPORTS

A lthough the season may be short, sailing has always been a popular summer pastime. Canada contains a large proportion of the world's fresh

Whitewater rafting on the Athabasca River, Jasper National Park in the Rocky Mountains

Snowmobiling in Ontario across virgin powder snow

water, and there are allegedly more boats per head here than anywhere else in the world. The Great Lakes are the prime sailing and windsurfing areas, as are both east and west coastal regions from May to September. Swimming is also a favorite in warm weather; beaches on Prince Edward Island and Cape Breton off the east coast offer warm waters and sandy beaches, while lakes in Ontario, such as Lake Huron, provide inland swims. Torontonians sometimes swim in Lake Ontario in the summer.

Fishing

OVER THREE MILLION square miles of inland waters go partway to justifying Canada's reputation as a paradise for anglers. There are countless varieties of sports fish (see p21), not to mention the charterboat ocean fishing for salmon off the Pacific coast. Almost all parks offer fishing, often in secluded, pristine lakes and rivers. Be sure to contact the park's main office to obtain a fishing license. While most visitors fish in summer, a tiny wooden structure that sits on the frozen lake makes winter fishing more comfortable. These huts sit over a hole in the ice and are often heated. It may be worth buying rods and reels at your destination; Canadian fishing equipment is very high quality, with a good choice, and is usually very reasonably priced.

Canadian snowboard

Skiing, Snowboarding, and Snowmobiling

NOT FOR NOTHING is Canada known as the Great White North, providing some of the world's best skiing. In the east, the Laurentian resorts of Mont Tremblant and Mont-Ste-Anne offer excellent skiing. Cross-country skiing is available through the Laurentian mountain range, around Gatineau, and throughout the Eastern Townships of Quebec. Moving west, the international resorts of Whistler, Lake Louise, and Banff provide unforgettable dramatic skiing. High in the Rockies, virgin powder snow awaits the adventurous; heli-skiing (lifting skiers by helicopter to pristine slopes) takes place on the deserted northern peaks. Many of the runs are higher than those in the European Alps, particularly in Banff and Lake Louise. These sites have held major competitions, in particular the Winter Olympics in 1976. Another advantage to skiing in Canada is the close proximity of the mountains to major cities; each of the main resorts is near a city, and it is perfectly possible to travel out for a day's skiing and to spend the evening dining out in the metropolis.

Snowboarding has become increasingly popular in snowsports centers across the country. In Northern Canada, there are now hotels that cater specifically to snowboarding parties – easily spotted because

Directory

Maps

Canadian Topographical Series
[C] 1 (800) 214 8524.

Canada Map Office
Ottawa
[C] (613) 952 7000.

Ulysses Travel Bookshop
Montreal (maps)
[C] (514) 843 9447.

Rand McNally (maps)
[C] 1 (800) 333 0136.

Useful Organizations

Parks Canada
[C] (819) 997 0055 Hull.

Cycling Canada
[C] (613) 748 5629.

Canadian Paraplegic Association
[C] (416) 422 5644.

Travel Operators

Air Canada Vacations
[C] (905) 615 8000 Toronto.
[C] (902) 425 1066 Halifax.
[C] (514) 876 4141 Montreal.

American Express
[C] 1 (800) 241 1700.

Cosmos/Globus
[C] 1 (800) 556 5454.

Trek America
[C] 1 (800) 221 0596.

Questers Worldwide Nature Tours
[C] 1 (800) 468 8668.

of the snowboard racks outside. Ontario is noted for its winter weekend deals. The province has almost 50,000 km (35,000 miles) of snowmobile trails. Seasoned riders can cover up to 500 km (300 miles) in two days.

More recently, snowmobiling has also established itself in British Columbia and is available in the principal ski resorts. Traveling in groups is preferable; there are many new and popular pitstops en route. These "snow inns" often offer package deals.

SURVIVAL
GUIDE

PRACTICAL INFORMATION

Whale-watching sign

Canada is a popular holiday destination, and offers visitors a mix of urban sophistication and outdoor pleasures. Visitors' facilities are generally excellent. Accommodations and restaurants are of international standard *(see pp342–79)*, public transportation is efficient *(see pp400–411)*, and tourist information centers are found nearly everywhere.

The following pages contain useful information for all visitors. Personal Security and Health *(see pp394–5)* details a number of recommended precautions, while Banking and Currency *(see p396)* answers the important financial queries, together with taxation details. There is also a section on how to use the Canadian telephone and postal services.

WHEN TO GO

WEATHER and geography dominate any visit to Canada. The vastness of the country means that most trips will be centered on one or the other of the major cities, Vancouver, Toronto, Ottawa, and Montreal, although it is possible to stay in remote areas such as the isolated Inuit settlements dotted west and north of Hudson Bay. Depending on each visitor's individual interests, the best time to go will be dictated by local climate and the time of year.

In general, the climates on both the west and east coasts are temperate, while harsher weather occurs in the center of the country, in Saskatchewan, Manitoba, and Alberta, where the summers are fine but the winters long and hard.

Northern Canada is at its most welcoming during July and August when the land thaws, and the temperature is more likely to climb above zero.

In eastern Canada, Nova Scotia, New Brunswick, and Prince Edward Island, there are four distinct seasons, with snowy winters, mild springs, and long, crisp falls; summer is still the best time to visit the provinces' resorts. Quebec and Ontario have hot, humid summers and cold winters, with snow lingering until late March. Spring and fall are brief but can be the most rewarding times to make a visit.

The northeastern province of Newfoundland and coastal Labrador have the most extreme temperatures, ranging on a winter's day from 0˚C (32°F) to -50˚C (-41°F) in St. John's on Newfoundland's

east coast. Winter visitors to British Columbia and the Rockies can enjoy some of the best skiing in the world. This region is also noted for its temperate weather but can be very wet in spring and fall as Pacific depressions roll in over the mountains.

ENTRY REQUIREMENTS

ALL VISITORS to Canada should have a passport valid for longer than the intended period of stay. Travelers from the UK, US, EU, and all British Commonwealth countries do not require a special visa to visit Canada. Tourists are issued with a visitor's visa on arrival if they satisfy immigration officials that they have a valid return ticket, and that they have sufficient funds for the duration of their stay.

Children play in the Kids' Village at the Waterpark, the Ontario Place leisure complex in Toronto

Visitors can stay up to six months, but to extend their stay they must apply to Citizenship and Immigration Canada in Ottawa before expiration of their authorized visit. As visa regulations are subject to change, it is wise to check with the nearest Canadian Consulate, Embassy, or High Commission before leaving home or buying tickets.

Anyone under the age of 18 who is traveling unaccompanied by an adult needs a letter of consent from a parent or guardian giving them permission to travel alone.

TOURIST INFORMATION

CANADIAN TOURIST offices are famous for the amount and quality of their information, offering everything from local maps to hotel, B-and-B, or campground bookings. Special tours such as wilderness camping, archaeological digs, and wildlife-watching can often be arranged through the tourism service. All the provincial and national parks have visitors' centers, which generally provide maps detailing hiking trails and canoe routes.

The national Canadian Tourism Commission is the central organization, and each province has its own tourism authority. Most smaller towns also have their own seasonal tourist offices, which offer good free maps and detailed information. Each of the large cities has a main office as well as extra booths and kiosks open during busy summer months. Accommodations can usually be booked at the booths found in airports and regional offices.

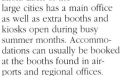
"The Small Apple" tourist booth in Ontario

OPENING HOURS AND ADMISSION PRICES

MOST MUSEUMS, parks, and other attractions throughout Canada charge an admission fee. The amount can vary enormously and many

CANADIAN TIME ZONES

Canada has six time zones spanning a four-and-a-half hour time difference from coast to coast. Between Vancouver and Halifax there are five zones; Pacific, Mountain, Central, Eastern, and Atlantic Standard Time, with an unusual half-hour difference between Newfoundland and Atlantic time. Every province except Saskatchewan uses Daylight Saving Time to give longer summer days, from the first Sunday in April to the last Sunday in October. Clocks go back an hour in October, forward an hour in April.

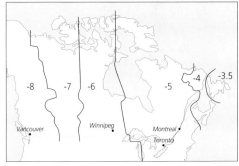

Time Zone	Hours minus GMT	Time Zone	Hours minus GMT
Pacific	-8	Eastern	-5
Mountain	-7	Atlantic	-4
Central	-6	Newfoundland	-3.5

sights offer a range of discount packages for families, children, and seniors. Tourist office leaflets, brochures, and local newspapers often carry discount coupons. Some galleries and museums have free-of-charge days, evenings, or a free hour daily before closing time.

Opening times vary according to the time of the year. As a rule, most of the sights are open for longer through summer but may close completely during the winter months. Many museums and galleries close one day each week, usually on a Monday or Tuesday, but not on weekends. Although many attractions are closed on major holidays, such as Christmas and New Year's Day, a surprising number are open all-year-round. School summer holidays in Canada are from June to Labor Day Weekend, which ends on the first Monday in September. Labor Day generally signifies the end of

summer. This is the weekend after which opening hours change over to shorter winter hours of operation. Rural sights generally have shorter hours year-round than those in cities.

SENIOR TRAVELERS

IN CANADA people over 60 are refered to as "seniors," and are offered a wide range of discounts. Reduced rates frequently apply to the cost of movie tickets, public transportation, entrance fees, and some restaurant menus. VIA Rail reduce their fares by 10 percent for seniors. When applicable, reductions range from 10 percent to 50 percent for people aged from 55, 60, or 65, depending on the province or attraction. If discounts are not advertised it is always a good idea to inquire.

Educational trips for senior citizens are run by **Elderhostel Canada**, a non-profit organization that offers good, cheap accommodation in university dorms. A typical holiday comprises morning lectures, guided tours in the afternoon, and a communal dinner.

Tourists enjoying the scenery of Niagara Falls

TRAVELING WITH CHILDREN

ALTHOUGH Canada lacks the numbers of theme parks of the US, its beach resorts, parks, and city centers have much to offer children and families. Most types of accommodations state whether or not they welcome children. Those hotels that do often do not charge for a child sharing a parent's room. They will also normally provide cribs and high chairs, and sometimes have baby-sitting services.

Restaurants now generally welcome children, and many offer kids' menus and high chairs, or will warm up milk and baby food. Some even have play areas. It is best to check in advance with the more upscale establishments.

Both international and internal airfares are often cheaper for children, and babies under two years old who are not taking up a seat may well travel free. On public transportation children under five travel free, and those under 12 have lower fares. If you are renting a car you can reserve one or two car seats for children from your rental firm (see p411).

ETIQUETTE

CANADA is very much a multicultural nation (see pp22–3), which welcomes and respects people and customs from the rest of the world. Native Canadians are never referred to as "Indians"; in general they are known as Canada's "First Nations" or "natives," while "eskimos" are always known as Inuit (see p27). In Quebec, be prepared to hear French spoken first. It is also appreciated if visitors show that they have tried to learn a few French words.

Canada's relaxed, informal atmosphere is evident in its dress codes, which tend to be practical and dependent on the climate. Canadians favor jeans and sweatshirts, and dress in layers so they can add or subtract clothing, especially when moving between well-heated malls and winter streets. However, in the cities and larger towns more formal clothing is expected, particularly in more stylish restaurants, theaters, and other formal places. Even the more humble eateries insist on proper attire, and the sign "no shoes, no shirt, no service" is frequently seen in many tourist areas. Topless sunbathing is generally frowned upon in Canada.

Drinking in non-licenced public places is illegal, and it is also illegal to have opened bottles of alcohol in the car when traveling. It is against the law to smoke on buses and trains, in most taxis, in all public buildings, and some restaurants, although some still have smoking areas. Unlike the US, Canada still tolerates smokers, and in some cities, such as Toronto, the rules have now been relaxed to accommodate them. Ask about smoking policies when booking a restaurant or hotel.

Unless a service charge is included in your check, the standard tip is 15 percent (more if the service is exceptional). Taxi drivers expect a similar tip, while barbers and hairdressers should receive about 10 percent of the total. Porters at airports and train stations, cloakroom attendants, bellhops, doormen, and hotel porters expect Can$1 per bag, and it is customary to leave something for the hotel maids. Tipping bar staff in bars and nightclubs is also expected. Anyone in charge of a large party of visitors should prepare to be generous.

STUDENT TRAVELERS

WITH AN International Student Identity Card (ISIC), full-time students are entitled to substantial discounts on travel as well as admission prices to movies, galleries, museums, and many other tourist attractions. The ISIC card should be purchased in the student's home country at a Student Travel Association (STA) office in the nearest city.

International student I.D. card

There are also a wide range of bus and rail discounts available to students, such as the "Go Canada" Accommodation and Coach Pass, which offers both reduced-cost travel and stays in youth hostels across the country. The pass can be booked through local agents specializing in student travel. VIA Rail also offers students the "Canrail Pass," which allows a period of unlimited travel on all routes. Reasonably priced accommodations are available on university campuses in the larger cities during local student vacations. There are also comfortable hostels throughout the country, most of which are affiliated to the International Youth Hostelling Federation (IYHF). Eating out is inexpensive, so students can easily find great food on a budget.

ELECTRICITY

CANADIAN electrical appliances come with either a two-prong or three-prong plug, and most sockets will accept either. The system is a 110-volt, 60-cycle system. You need a plug adaptor if you are visiting from outside North America. Batteries are universal and are readily available for all appliances. Bear in mind that bargain electrical goods purchased here will probably need modification for use in Europe.

Standard plug

TRAVELERS WITH DISABILITIES

TRAVELERS WITH physical disabilities can expect some of the best facilities in the world in Canada. Increasingly, large towns and cities offer wheelchair access in most public buildings, as well as on public transportation. Vancouver's buses all have low platforms, and VIA Rail trains can accommodate wheelchairs. Each province has varying requirements for disabled drivers, and information on this is available through the **Canadian Paraplegic Association (CPA)**. This Ottawa-based association also has details on companies that rent specially adapted cars and RV vehicles. Parking permits can be obtained in advance through the CPA but require a doctor's letter and a small processing fee.

There is a wide choice of hotels with disabled facilities in Canada. Most of the big chains such as Best Western and Holiday Inn are easily accessible, as are some luxury hotels and youth hostels. The CPA also has details on the most disabled-friendly attractions. Many of the national and provincial parks have interpretive centers, short nature trails, and boardwalks that are wheelchair accessible.

CONVERSION CHART

Imperial to Metric
1 inch = 2.54 centimeters
1 foot = 30 centimeters
1 mile = 1.6 kilometers
1 ounce = 28 grams
1 pound = 454 grams
1 pint = 0.6 liters
1 gallon = 4.6 liters

Metric to Imperial
1 centimeter = 0.4 inches
1 meter = 3 feet, 3 inches
1 kilometer = 0.6 miles
1 gram = 0.04 ounces
1 kilogram = 2.2 pounds
1 liter = 1.8 pints

DIRECTORY

IMMIGRATION

Canadian High Commission
Macdonald House,
38 Grosvenor Street,
London, W1X 0AA.
((0891) 616644.

Citizenship and Immigration Canada
Jean Edmonds Towers,
365 Laurier Ave. W,
Ottawa, ON K1A 1L1.
((613) 954 9019.

TOURIST INFORMATION

Canadian Tourism Commission
235 Queen St,
Ottawa, ON MSW 1A3.
((416) 973 8022.

Tourism Canada
501 Penn Ave.,
NW Washington DC, USA
((202) 682 1740.

Canadian Tourism Commission
Visit Canada Centre,
62–65 Trafalgar Square,
London, WC2N 5DY.
((0891) 715 000.

PROVINCIAL OFFICES

British Columbia
Tourism British Columbia
865 Hornby St., 8th floor,
Vancouver, BC VBZ 2G3.
((604) 660 2881.

Ontario
Ministry of Tourism
900 Bay St., 9th floor,
Hearst Block, Toronto,
ON M7A 2E1.
((416) 325 6666.

Travel Manitoba
155 Carlton St.,
7th Floor, Winnipeg,
MB R3C 3HB.
((204) 945 3796.

Tourism Saskatchewan
500–1900 Albert St.,
Regina, SK S4P 4L9.
(1(800) 667 7191.

Newfoundland and Labrador
Department of Tourism,
PO Box 8700,
St. John's, NF A1B 4J6.
((709) 729 2831.

Tourism New Brunswick
PO Box 6000,
Fredericton, NB E3B 5H1.
(1 (800) 561 0123.

Travel Alberta
Suite 500,
999–8 St. SW,
Calgary, AB T2R 1J5.
((403) 297 2700.

Tourism Prince Edward Island
PO Box 940,
Charlottetown,
PEI C1A 7M5.
(1 (800) 565 0201.

Nunavut Tourism
PO Box 1450,
Iqaluit, NT XOA OHO.
((867) 979 6551.

Northwest Territories
NWT Arctic Tourism
PO Box 1320, Yellowknife,
NWT X1A 2N5.
(1(800) 661 0788.

Tourism Nova Scotia
PO Box 519,
1800 Argyle St., Suite 605,
Halifax, NS B3J 2R7.
(1(800) 565 0000.

Tourism Yukon
PO Box 2703,
Whitehorse,
Yukon, Y1A 2C6.
((867) 667 5340.

Tourism Quebec
PO Box 979,
Montreal, PQ H3C 2W3.
((514) 873 2015.

SENIOR TRAVELERS

Elderhostel Canada
4 Cataraqui Street,
Kingston,
Ontario, K7K 1Z7.
((613) 530 2222.

STUDENT TRAVELERS

STA Travel
((0207) 361 6262 UK.
((800) 825 3001 Can.

DISABLED TRAVELERS

Canadian Paraplegic Association
National Office
1101 Prince of Wales Dr.,
Suite 230, Ottawa,
Ontario, K2C 3W7.
((613) 723 1033.

Personal Security and Health

WITH ITS COMPARATIVELY low crime rate, Canada is a safe country to visit. In contrast to many US cities, there is little street crime in the city centers, perhaps because so many Canadians live downtown that the cities are never empty at night. However, it is wise to be careful and to find out which parts of town are more dangerous than others. Avoid city parks after dark, and make sure cars are left locked. In the country's more remote areas visitors must observe sensible safety measures. In the remote country, wildlife and climatic dangers can be avoided by heeding local advice. If a serious problem does arise, contact one of the national emergency numbers in the telephone directory.

PERSONAL SAFETY

THERE ARE FEW off-limit areas in Canadian cities. Even the seedier districts tend to have a visible police presence, making them safer than the average suburban area at night. Always ask your hotelier, the local tourist information center, or the police, which areas to avoid. Although theft is rare in hotel rooms, it is a good idea to store any valuables in the hotel safe, as hotels will not guarantee the security of property left in rooms. Make sure you leave your hotel room key at the front desk.

Pickpockets can be a hazard at large public gatherings and popular tourist attractions, so it is a good idea to wear cameras and bags over one shoulder with the strap across your body. Try not to be seen with large amounts of cash, and if necessary use a coin purse and a wallet for larger bills. Keep your passport apart from your cash and traveler's checks. Never hang your purse over the back of your chair in restaurants; put it on the floor beside your feet with one foot over the strap, or pinned down by a chair leg. Male travelers should not carry their wallets in their back pocket, as this makes a very easy target. Safe options for both sexes are zippered purse belts.

LAW ENFORCEMENT

CANADA IS policed by a combination of forces. The Royal Canadian Mounted Police (RCMP) operate throughout most of the country, while Ontario and Quebec are looked after by provincial forces. There are also city police and native police on the reserves. For the most part, the officers are noted for their helpful attitude, but it is illegal to comment on (or joke about) safety, bombs, guns, and terrorism in places such as airports, where it is possible to be arrested for an off-the-cuff remark. Drinking and driving is also taken seriously here, and remember that open alcohol containers in a car are illegal. Narcotics users face criminal charges often followed by moves for deportation.

Canadian policemen on duty

LOST PROPERTY

AS SOON AS something is lost, report it to the police. They will issue a report with a number that you will need in order to make a claim on your insurance policy. If a credit card is missing, call the company's toll-free number and report it immediately. Lost or stolen traveler's checks must also be reported to the issuer. If you have kept a record of the checks' numbers, replacing them should be a painless experience, and new ones may be issued within 24 hours.

If you lose your passport, contact the nearest embassy or consulate. They will be able to issue a temporary replacement as visitors do not generally need a new passport if they will be returning directly to their home country. However, if you are traveling on to another destination, you will need a full passport. It is also useful to hold photocopies of your driver's license and birth certificate, as well as notarized passport photographs if you are contemplating an extended visit or need additional ID.

TRAVEL INSURANCE

TRAVEL INSURANCE is essential in Canada and should be arranged to cover health, trip-cancellation, and interruption, as well as theft and loss of valuable possessions.

Canadian health services are excellent, but if you do not wish to pay you will need insurance. If you already have private health insurance you should check to see if the coverage includes all emergency hospital and medical expenses such as physician's care, prescription drugs, and private duty-nursing. In case of a serious illness, separate coverage is also required to send a relative to your bedside or return a rented vehicle. Emergency dental treatment, and out-of-pocket expenses or loss of vacation costs also need their own policies. Your insurance company or travel agent should recommend the right policy, but beware of exclusions for pre-existing medical conditions.

MEDICAL TREATMENT

A COMPREHENSIVE range of treatment centers are available in Canada. For minor problems pharmacies are often a good source of advice, and walk-in clinics in the cities will treat visitors relatively quickly. In smaller communities, or in more difficult cases, go straight to the emergency room of the closest hospital, but be prepared for a long medical emergency dial 911 in most areas, or 0 for the operator, to summon an ambulance.

Anyone taking a prescription drug should ask their doctor for extra supplies when they travel, as well as a copy of the prescription in case more medication is needed on the trip. It is a good idea to take a simple first-aid kit, especially for longer trips in the more remote or Arctic areas of the country. Generally this should include aspirin (or paracetamol), antihistamine for bites or allergies, motion sickness pills, antiseptic and bandages or band aids, calamine lotion, and bug repellent. Antibiotic creams are useful for intrepid wilderness hikers.

All the provincial capitals have dental clinics that will provide emergency treatment. The Yellow Pages telephone book lists dentists in each area together with opticians and alternative health practitioners.

NATURAL HAZARDS

T HERE ARE times when Canada's mosquitoes and black flies can be so troublesome that moose and deer leave the woods for relief. Insects are a major irritant for tourists in rural areas. They are at their worst during annual breeding periods from late spring to midsummer, and allyear-round in Northern Canada. There are precautions one can take to alleviate the misery. Taking Vitamin B complex tablets for two weeks before traveling is thought to

affect the skin's chemistry and reduces the chance of bites considerably. Stick to light-colored clothes as the bugs are drawn to dark ones, and cover as much skin as possible with long sleeves, and pants tucked into boots and socks. It might even be worth investing in a gauze mask for your head and neck if you are planning to venture into deserted areas at peak breeding times.

Canada is notorious for cold winter weather, but tourists are not likely to suffer many serious problems. The media gives daily extensive coverage to the weather, and on days when frostbite is possible they offer detailed reports. Dressing in layers and wearing a hat is necessary. Sunscreen is needed in summer, even on overcast days.

Warning sign for motorists

BEARS

C ANADA'S national parks' service, particularly in the Rockies, supplies advice on bear safety *(see p298)*, but unless you are camping or hiking in the woods it is unlikely that you will come across them. Encounters can be avoided by following a few basic rules: never leave food or garbage near your tent, car, or RV, do not wear scent, and make a noise (many hikers blow whistles) as you walk, as

bears are more likely to attack if surprised. If you do come across a bear, do not scream or run as bears are very fast, and do not climb trees – they are even better at that. Instead, keep still, speak to them in a low voice, and put your luggage on the ground to try and distract them.

A polar bear approaching a tourist Tundra Buggy, northern Manitoba

Banking and Currency

ATM or banking machine sign

CANADIAN CURRENCY is based on the decimal system, and has 100 cents to the dollar. Two of the most useful coins are the 25-cent and $1 pieces which operate pay telephones, newspaper boxes, and vending machines. They are also handy for public transportation in the larger cities, where as a matter of policy bus drivers often do not carry any change. It is a good idea to arrive with some Canadian currency, around Can$50–100 including small change for tipping and taxis, but to carry most of your funds in Canadian dollar traveler's checks.

DIRECTORY

CURRENCY EXCHANGE AND WIRING MONEY

Thomas Cook
Check replacement, UK
C (0800) 622 101.
Canada and US
C 1 (800) 223 7373.

American Express
Check replacement,
Canada
C 1 (800) 221 7282.

Western Union
Wiring money, Canada
C 1 (800) 235 0000.

Sandstone façade of the Toronto Stock Exchange

BANKS

CANADA'S MAIN national banks are the Royal Bank of Canada, the Bank of Montréal, the Toronto Dominion, the Canadian Imperial Bank of Commerce, the Bank of Nova Scotia, and the National Bank. These banks generally accept ATM (automatic teller machine) cards, although it is wise to check with your bank first. ATMs can also be found at such places as grocery stores, shopping centers, gas stations, train and bus stations, and airports.

Banks are usually open Monday to Friday, from 9am to 5pm; some stay open later on Fridays, and a few open on Saturday mornings. All banks are closed on Sundays and on statutory holidays.

Toronto Dominion Bank logo

TRAVELER'S CHECKS

TRAVELER'S CHECKS issued in Canadian dollars are probably the safest and most convenient way to carry money for your vacation. They offer security because they can be easily replaced if they are lost or stolen. They are also accepted as cash in a vast range of gas stations, shops, and restaurants across the country. Buy checks in smaller denominations such as $20 as most retailers prefer not to give out large amounts of change. It is a good idea to find out which Canadian banks charge commission for changing traveler's checks, as many have arrangements with certain issuers of checks and make no charge. The Royal Bank of Canada, for example, charges no commission on American Express checks in Canadian dollars. A passport or other form of ID is needed to cash traveler's checks at a bank or at Bureaux de Changes offices such as American Express or Thomas Cook.

CREDIT CARDS

CREDIT CARDS are used extensively in Canada, and American Express, Diner's Club, MasterCard/Access, and VISA are widely accepted. Credit cards are often asked for as a form of ID, and for placing large deposits – most car rental companies in Canada insist on a credit card or require a substantial cash deposit. Some hotels also prefer prepayment by credit card.

Credit cards can also be used to secure cash advances, but you will be charged interest from the date of withdrawal.

WIRING MONEY

IF YOU RUN OUT of money or have an emergency it is possible to have cash wired from home in minutes using an electronic money service. Both American Express and Thomas Cook provide this service, as does Western Union which has 22,000 outlets all over North America.

WESTERN UNION | MONEY TRANSFER
The world's No. 1 money transfer service.

Western Union's familiar logo

COINS AND BANK NOTES

CANADIAN COINS are issued in denominations of one cent (the penny), five cents (the nickel), ten cents (the dime), 25 cents (the quarter), $1 (dubbed the "loonie" because it has an illustration of the bird, the Canadian loon on one side), and the $2 coin or "twonie," which replaced the old bank note in 1996.

Bank notes are printed in denominations of $5, $10, $20, $50, $100, $500, and $1,000. However, the larger denominations such as $50 or $100 dollar bills are sometimes viewed with suspicion as they are not used very often in small stores, or even in cafés and gas stations.

Media and Communications

THE BIRTHPLACE of the inventor of the telephone, Alexander Graham Bell, Canada now has some of the most sophisticated communication systems in the world. There are public payphones everywhere; in cafés, bars, public buildings, gas stations, and post offices. Most operate with coins or cards, and while local calls are a bargain, international calls can be expensive. It is also possible to send telegrams, faxes, and even documents via Intelpost, a satellite communications system.

Canada Post, the country's mail service, is famous for being slow, but it is reliable. It can be quick however, if you are willing to pay extra for priority service.

DIRECTORY

PROVINCIAL CODES

Alberta - *403 & 780.*
British Columbia - *604 & 250.*
Manitoba - *204.*
New Brunswick - *506.*
Northwest Territories - *867.*
Nova Scotia - *902.*
Newfoundland & Labrador - *709.*
Ontario - *416 & 905 (Toronto).*
 705 - (central and northeast).
 519 - (southwest peninsula).
 613 - (Ottawa region).
 807 - (northwest).
Prince Edward Island - *902.*
Quebec - *514 & 540 (Montreal).*
 819 - (north).
 418 - (east).
Saskatchewan - *306.*
Yukon & Nunavut- *867.*

PUBLIC TELEPHONES

PUBLIC TELEPHONES operate on 25 cent coins, although there is an increasing number of phones that accept both credit and phone cards. Rates are generally cheaper between 6pm and 8am, and on weekends. All local calls cost 25 cents (private subscribers have free local calls). For any call outside the local area, including international calls, the operator will tell you how much to pay for the initial period and will then ask for more money as your call progresses. It is usually easier to make long distance calls using card phones than to have the stacks of change required.

Public roadside telephones are found countrywide

POSTAL SERVICES

ALL MAIL FROM Canada to outside North America is by air and can take between one and five days to arrive. If you are sending mail within the country it can also take days, but it is faster if you include the postal code. To send mail, look for signs that say "Canada Post" since some post offices are located in malls.

MOBILE PHONES AND E-MAIL

IT IS POSSIBLE to rent a mobile phone while on vacation, or to have your own mobile tuned to local networks.

Visitors can use e-mail in the larger hotels or at one of many city-based Internet cafés.

FAX AND TELEGRAM SERVICES

IT IS POSSIBLE to send a fax from the commercial outlets found in most towns. Telegrams are dealt with by Canadian National Telecommunications (CNT) or Canadian Pacific (CP). There are two main services, Telepost, which provides first-class delivery, and Intelpost, which sends documents abroad via satellite.

MEDIA

THERE IS NO daily national newspaper as such in Canada, but Toronto's *The Globe and Mail* is distributed nationwide. There is also a national news weekly magazine called *MacLean's*. Most cities have their own daily newspapers and some, such as Toronto, have several. Many towns and areas have weeklies that are excellent for finding out about local events.

Canada has a national 24-hour public broadcasting corporation (CBC), 80 percent of whose programs are produced locally. CBC also provides an excellent radio service, and can be a good source of information on local happenings and weather for visitors. They also have a national service in French.

USEFUL INFORMATION

Canadian Post Customer Services line.
(*1 (800) 267 1177.*

REACHING THE RIGHT NUMBER

- For direct-dial calls to another area code: dial 1 followed by the area code and the 7-digit local number.
- For international direct-dial calls: dial **011** then the code of the country (Australia **61**, New Zealand **64**, the UK **44**) followed by the local area/city code (minus the first **0**) and the number. To call the US from Canada dial the state code, then the number.
- For international operator assistance dial **0**.
- For information on numbers within your local area dial **411**.
- For information on long distance numbers call **1** followed by the provincial code then **555 1212**.
- An **800** or **888** prefix means the call will be toll free.

TRAVEL INFORMATION

**Maple leaf
Air Canada logo**

THE MAJORITY OF visitors to Canada arrive by air, usually at one of the country's three largest international airports – Vancouver, Toronto, or Montreal. It is also possible to fly direct to cities such as Halifax, Winnipeg, Edmonton, Calgary, and St. John's, Newfoundland. The size of the country makes flying between locations popular with visitors who wish to see more than one part of Canada. For example, on a short stay, it could prove difficult to see Toronto and Montreal in the east, as well as the Rocky Mountains in the west without spending some time in the air. There are other transportation choices that allow visitors to see much of Canada. The national rail network, VIA Rail, links most major cities, while long-distance bus routes provide a delightful, and often less expensive, way to see the country. There are short cruises and ferry rides that take in some spectacular scenery. Exploring Canada by car is also a popular choice, enabling visitors to get to locations that can be difficult to reach any other way.

ARRIVING BY AIR

CANADA IS A destination for several international airlines, and the country's two major carriers, **Air Canada** and **Canadian Airlines**, are linked with national airlines around the world. All Europe's principal airlines fly into Toronto or Montreal, while Vancouver is a gateway for carriers such as Cathay Pacific, Quantas, and national airlines from the Far East. Visitors who intend to see parts of the US as well as Canada can find plenty of connecting flights to such principal US destinations as New York, Los Angeles, Dallas, Chicago, and Atlanta.

INTERNATIONAL FLIGHTS

FLIGHTS BETWEEN Canada and Europe take from seven to nine hours; from Asia or Australia, across the Pacific, you may be in transit for as long as 25 hours. Older travelers or those with children may wish to consider a stopover for the sake of comfort (Hawaii is a popular choice). It is also a good idea to plan flights so that they account for international time differences.

Canada has 13 international airports, the busiest being at Toronto, Montreal, and Vancouver. It is also possible to fly direct into airports in cities such as Edmonton, Halifax, Ottawa, Winnipeg, and St. Johns, Newfoundland. All the major cities are connected with airports in the US. Several leading airlines offer special deals that allow visitors to fly to one part of North America and leave from another.

AIR FARES

FLIGHTS TO Canada from Europe, Australia, and the US can be expensive, especially during peak holiday periods such as Christmas, New Year, and the summer months between July and mid-September. It is always cheaper to book an Apex

**Canadian Airlines plane displays
its new "proud wings" livery**

AIRPORT	INFORMATION
St. John's	📞 (709) 758 8500
Halifax	📞 (902) 873 1223
Montreal (Dorval)	📞 (514) 394 7377
Montreal (Mirabel)	📞 (514) 394 7377
Ottawa	📞 (613) 248 2100
Toronto	📞 (416) 247 7678
Winnipeg	📞 (204) 987 9402
Calgary	📞 (403) 735 1372
Edmonton	📞 (780) 890 8382
Vancouver	📞 (604) 276 6101

(Advanced Purchase Excursion) fare, which should be bought no less than seven days in advance, (most major airlines, including Air Canada and Canadian Airlines, offer them). These tickets generally impose such restrictions as a minimum (usually seven days) and maximum (of 3–6 months) length of stay. It can also be difficult to alter dates of travel, and it is worth considering insuring yourself against unforeseen delays or cancellations.

Charter flights sometimes offer a cheaper alternative, with savings of 20 percent on some tickets. Round-the-world fares are increasingly popular, as are package vacations which provide a variety of choices. The kinds of deals available range from fly/drive

vacations with a much reduced car rental as part of the price of the ticket, to a guided tour, including all accommodations, transportation, and meals.

ON ARRIVAL

JUST BEFORE landing in Canada you will be given customs and immigration documents to fill in. On arrival you will be asked to present them, along with your passport, to the appropriate customs and immigration officials.

The larger airports offer a better range of services, but most airports have shops, medical and postal services, foreign exchange bureaus, newsstands, and bookstores. The major car rental companies have outlets at the airport, and buses, limousines, and shuttle buses into town are available. Most terminals offer facilities for disabled travelers.

Visitors hoping to catch a connecting flight to another part of the country will have to claim and clear their baggage through customs before checking in

Roads to and from airports are well sign-posted

DIRECTORY

AIRLINES IN THE UK, US, AND CANADA

Air Canada
UK: (0990) 247 226.
CAN: (416) 323 1815
(for a list of provincial toll-free numbers).
US: (1 800) 813 9237.

Canadian Airlines
UK: (0208) 577 7722 (London).
(0345) 616 767 (outside London).
CAN: (1 800) 665 1177.
US: (1 800) 426 7000.

American Airlines
UK: (0345) 789789.
CAN: (1 800) 433 7300.
US: (1 800) 433 7300.

British Airways
UK: (0208) 897 4000.
CAN and US: (1 800) 247 9297.

with the connecting airline. Arrangements for transferring to domestic flights are usually made when you book your trip. It is a good idea to ask airline staff if you need more information; as in large airports such as Toronto's Pearson International there are three separate terminals.

DISTANCE FROM CITY	TAXI FARE TO CITY	BUS TRANSFER TO CITY
8 km (5 miles)	CAN$14	NO SERVICE
42 km (26 miles)	CAN$35	30–45 mins
22 km (14 miles)	CAN$25	25 mins
55 km (34 miles)	CAN$62	40–55 mins
18 km (11 miles)	CAN$35–40	20–30 mins
24 km (15 miles)	CAN$35	45–55 mins
10 km (6 miles)	CAN$15	20 mins
16 km (10 miles)	CAN$25	30 mins
31 km (19 miles)	CAN$35	45 mins
15 km (9 miles)	CAN$25–30	25–45 mins

Domestic Air Travel

BECAUSE OF THE DISTANCES involved, flying around the country has become an accepted part of Canadian life. There is a complex network of domestic flights, with over 75 local airlines, many of which are linked to Air Canada or Canadian Airlines. The smaller operators fly within provinces, and to remote locations where they are often the only means of transportation. In all there are some 125 domestic destinations. It is possible to book domestic flights with a travel agent before departure or, once in Canada, through local agents or the Yellow Pages. Domestic flights are not cheap, but there are often discounts advertised in the local press, or a range of pass deals exclusively for visitors from abroad. Light aircraft can also be chartered for fascinating but costly trips over far-flung landmarks such as Baffin Island.

Dash-7 aircraft during a trip in Canada's far north

AIR ROUTES AND AIRLINES

THE IMPRESSIVE array of domestic flights available here means that most of the nation's smaller urban areas are within reach of regular services. However, you will generally have to fly to the major city in the area, principally Vancouver, Toronto, or Montreal, and then take a connecting flight. Most of the smaller airlines are connected with Canada's two major carriers, Air Canada and Canadian Airlines, and it is often possible to book your connection through them.

The majority of the country's long-haul domestic routes run east-to-west, connecting the cities: from Halilfax on the east coast, through to Montreal, Toronto, Ottawa, Winnipeg, Calgary, and Edmonton to Vancouver in the west. Longer north-to-south flights to places such as the Yukon and Northwest Territories usually originate from Edmonton and Winnipeg. In the remote north, light aircraft are the best way to reach a destination such as Baffin Island, (which can be reached by boat only in good weather) with the exception of Churchill, Manitoba, which is connected by train.

APEX FARES AND OTHER DISCOUNTS

THERE ARE several kinds of bargain tickets available within Canada: through charter carriers, Apex (Advance Purchase Excursion) fares, and seat sales. Charter airlines such as Canada 3000, Royal, and Air Transat fly between Canadian cities much like scheduled airlines. However, they are usually up to 20% cheaper than scheduled tickets and can be booked through tour operators. To take advantage of the reductions available through Apex you must book between 7 and 21 days in advance: the earlier the booking, the larger the discount. Each fare will have its own set of rules, which include restrictions on length of stay and time of travel (such as between certain hours or on certain days). Be aware that refunds are seldom given and it might be difficult to change your dates.

Seat sales are another bargain option whereby an airline will advertise exceptionally cheap tickets to boost travel on popular routes during quiet times of the year. There is very little flexibility on these deals, and you have to fly within a specific period of time.

Both the major Canadian airlines offer pass deals for visitors who want to travel all over the country, as well as to the US. The passes are available only outside of North America. Most involve paying for a number of coupons (up to eight with Canadian Airlines), each of which represents a flight within either the continent or a specific region. The passes also specify a period of time (7 to 60 days) for which they are valid.

FLY-DRIVE DEALS

A GOOD WAY to make the most of a visit to Canada is to book a fly-drive vacation. The deal invariably involves a substantial cut in the cost of the car rental. Arrangements can also be made to pick up and drop off your vehicle in different places. It would be possible, for example, to pick up a car in Toronto, tour Ontario, dropping the car off in Ottawa before flying on to Vancouver on the west coast. Known as one-way car rental, these deals may involve large drop-off fees: from Toronto to Ottawa costs around Can$200. Travel agents offer a wide range of such packages.

BAGGAGE RESTRICTIONS

PASSENGERS traveling economy on domestic flights should be aware that there are restrictions on the amount and weight of baggage that can be taken on board. The type of aircraft determines what can be carried, and light aircraft usually accept only hand-baggage. In general, passengers are entitled to have two suitcases, each with an average weight of 32 kg (70 lb) per item. Hand-baggage must fit safely under aircraft seats or in overhead lockers. Garment bags may be carried on board some aircraft but must be soft-sided and comply with size restrictions – length 112 cm (45 ins), depth 11 cm (4.5 ins) – so remember to check with your airline or travel agent when puchasing your ticket.

CHECKING IN

SECURITY IS a necessity nowadays and can make the boarding procedure take longer. Within Canada you must check in at least 30 minutes prior to departure; for flights to the US, allow 60 minutes; and for international flights, leave at least 90 minutes. Visitors from other countries traveling within Canada should carry a passport to verify that he or she is the traveler named on the ticket.

It is also worth noting that the daily peaks at the larger Canadian airports are usually from 7am to 9am and from 3pm to 8pm. Passenger volume also increases significantly during the winter holiday season, March break, and the summer, so it is wise to allow extra time for parking, check-in, and security screening during these periods.

Canadian Airlines logo

PRINCIPAL DOMESTIC AIR ROUTES

Canada's two major airlines are Air Canada and Canadian Airlines. Together with a number of regional carriers, they link up to form a comprehensive domestic air network.

GETTING AROUND CANADA'S CITIES

Although the car is a popular way to travel in Canada, the country is noted for the fast, frequent, and efficient public transit systems of its cities. In general, the best way for visitors to explore Canada's urban centers is primarily on foot, using public transportation as a back up. The streets are clean and safe, and strolling through different neighborhoods is a pleasant way to get to know them. Most municipal transit systems are reasonably priced, with discounted multi-ticket deals and

Tourbus in Toronto

day passes. Driving around downtown areas can be daunting, particularly during the rush hour, and parking tends to be both difficult and expensive.

Most transit systems offer free maps, available at stations or tourist information centers. The following pages detail how to get around Canada's three largest cities, Vancouver, Toronto, and Montreal *(see endpaper for detailed transit maps)*, as well as other provincial capitals and the most often visited towns and communities.

MONTREAL

Montreal's bus and subway network is integrated so that the stations connect with bus routes and tickets can be used on either. Be sure to get a transfer ticket, which should take you anywhere in the city for one fare. Known as the Métro, Montreal's subway is clean, safe, and air-conditioned in summer and heated in the winter. It is by far the fastest and cheapest way to get around town *(see endpaper)*. Free maps are available at any of the ticket booths. Visitors can buy a Tourist Pass for one or three days at major hotels and at the Visitor Information Office downtown.

Driving is not recommended here, as the roads are busy and parking is severely restricted, especially in the old town. It is best to use the city's park-and-ride system. Cabs can be hailed in the street. They have a white or orange sign on the roof; the sign is lit up when the cab is available.

Many streets in Montreal now have bike lanes. The Great Montreal Bike Path-Guide is available free at the tourist office. Bikes can be taken on the Métro anytime except during rush hour, from about 7am to 10am and 5pm to 7pm on weekdays. There are some lovely bike paths, such as the waterfront trail on the historic Canal de Lachine, and those

that lead through Cité du Havre and across Pont de la Concorde to the islands. There are a number of bicycle shops offering daily or weekly rental; they generally require a deposit of Can$250 or more in addition to the daily rate.

TORONTO

The Toronto Transit Commission (TTC) operates a huge system of connecting subway, bus, and streetcar lines that serves the entire city. It is one of the safest and cleanest systems of its kind anywhere in the world. There are two major subway lines, with 60 stations along the way *(see endpaper)*. Be sure to get a free transfer pass if

Scenic riverside cyling path in Quebec City

you intend to continue your trip by bus or streetcar after you leave the subway.

To ride buses and streetcars, you must have exact change, a ticket, or a token. Tickets and tokens are on sale at subway entrances and stores. The "Pick up a Ride Guide" shows every major place of interest and how to reach it by public transit, and is available at most subway ticket offices. A Light Rapid Transit line connects downtown to the lakefront (called Harbourfront). The line starts at Union Station and terminates at Spadina/Bloor subway station.

It is easy to catch a cab in Toronto; they can be hailed in the street, called in advance, or found outside hotels. There are several outlets that rent bicycles, but as downtown Toronto is busy with traffic, it is best to confine your cycling to the parks. The Martin Goodman Trail is a well-marked scenic bicycle route along the long, scenic waterfront.

As in Vancouver, you will need the right coins for the bus. The regular adult fare is Can$2 across the whole system, and transfers are free for up to an hour. If you are going to be in Toronto for an extended period, it is worth considering a MetroPass for one month, or you can buy 10 tickets or tokens for Can$17. There are day passes for use during off-peak hours.

Toronto taxicabs gather at a taxi stand

Ferries to the Toronto Islands run several times an hour at peak times in summer and continue well into the evening. There is also a road bridge.

VANCOUVER

Vancouver's well-organized network of light rail (called SkyTrain), bus, and ferry services is run by BC Transit. An inexpensive Transit Guide is available from newsstands and information centers. It includes a map of the city showing all routes. Driving is not the best way to see the city as congestion is heavy, and you are unlikely to find a spot to park. There is a park-and-ride system, where commuters can leave their cars at certain points around the city center.

The SkyTrain is a light rail system of driverless trains that connects downtown Vancouver with the suburbs of Burnaby, New Westminster, and Surrey. It travels partially beneath ground and partially overground on a raised track. The main terminal is at Waterfront Station at the bottom of Seymour Street. An alternative to the SkyTrain is to use the city's downtown bus routes. These are worth riding as they offer delightful tours past the city's top attractions, although it is advisable to avoid rush hour traffic. Bus services end around midnight, but there is a scaled down "Night Owl" service.

One of the best ways to get around Vancouver is by water. The SeaBus is a 400-seat Catamaran that shuttles between Lonsdale Quay in North Vancouver and the downtown terminal at Waterfront Station. The trip takes around 15 minutes and includes wonderful views of the mountains and Vancouver skyline. Aquabus Ferries connect stations on False Creek, Granville Island, Stamp's Landing, and the Hornby Street Dock.

If you want to take a cab it is best to call one of the main companies such as Black Top or Yellow Cab, as hailing a taxi in the streets is rarely successful. However, Vancouver is a great city for cyclists, with plenty of bike paths, including the 10 km (6 mile) road around Stanley Park. There is a park-and-ride service for bikes here, similar to the one elsewhere for cars.

Fares are the same for bus, SkyTrain, and SeaBus in the Vancouver area, but the price varies according to time of day and the distance you travel. Adult fares are cheaper after 6:30pm, and all day Saturday, Sunday, and holidays. There are three zones in the city, and the price of the fare depends on how many zones you cross. The off-peak adult fare in zone one is Can$1.50. There are a wide variety of discounts available: a FareSaver book of 10 tickets or a day pass are good value. Children under 4 ride free, and those between the ages of 5 and 13 pay less (as do students with a valid GoCard), and seniors over 65 also get concessions. A transfer ticket is free and lasts for 90 minutes of travel.

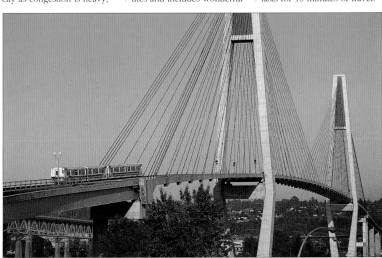

SkyTrain traveling over the city bridge in Vancouver on a summer evening

The scenic approach to Château Frontenac in Quebec City, best appreciated on foot

OTTAWA

FORTUNATELY for visitors, many of the capital city's major tourist attractions are within walking distance of Parliament Hill. Ottawa's sidewalks are both wide and clean, and you can do most of your sightseeing on foot, using public transportation to cover the longer distances. The region of Ottawa-Carlton operates **OC Transpo**, a 130-route bus network. Fares are among the most expensive in Canada, with a two-tier system that charges more for traveling during rush hour, Can$2.10 per ticket. You need the exact fare unless you buy tickets in advance. These are available at newsstands and corner stores. If you need to change buses, ask for a transfer, which can be used for up to an hour. It is possible to get a transfer for use on the separate Hull bus system across the Ottawa River, although you may have to pay a little more. All routes meet downtown at the Rideau Centre, and the stops are color-coded according to the route.

If you are using a car there are several reasonably priced municipal car lots – look for a green 'P' sign. Taxis can be booked by phone or hailed at stands outside major hotels.

Bicycles are a good way to explore a city that has some 150 km (93 miles) of scenic paths. The Rideau Canal, that crosses the city from north to south, is bordered by delightful walking and bike paths.

CALGARY

CALGARY TRANSIT operates buses and a light-rail transit system known as the C-Train. For a flat fare of Can$1.60 you can transfer to either using the same ticket, although day passes for around Can$5 are good value for visitors hoping to see several sights in one day. The C-Train travels north to the University and airport, and south to Macleod Trail. It is free in the downtown section between 10th Street and City Hall (buses are not). Maps are available from the **Calgary Transit** offices, where you can also buy tickets. C-Train tickets can be bought from machines located on the platforms.

If you wish to travel mostly within the city center, walking and public transportation are

Logo for the C-Train in Calgary

your best options. However, the city's blocks are long, (Calgary is Canada's second largest city by area) and any trip to the outskirts and beyond requires a car. There are several rental companies, including all the major outlets, and charges are around Can$50 per day, although weekend rates are much cheaper. Cabs are expensive here and cannot be hailed on the street, but they can be picked up at hotels or ordered by telephone.

WINNIPEG

MANY OF Winnipeg's attractions are within a 20-minute walk of one another in the downtown area, centered on the crossroads of Portage and Main Streets. **Winnipeg City Transit** operates an efficient bus system, which is also ideal for reaching farther-placed sights. There is a flat fare of Can$1.55, or you can purchase a book of 10 tickets for Can$15 from the Transit Service Centre based in the underground concourse at Portage and Main. (A transfer, valid for an hour, is available from the driver if you are changing buses.) The center is open weekdays between 8:30 am and 4:30 pm, and offers detailed information and a free route map of the city. There are also several pleasant bicycle paths that run through the city as well as to outlying districts.

QUEBEC CITY

T HE CHARMING narrow streets of the old city are best seen on foot, especially since most of the historic sights are located within a small area of the walled city. If you need to travel farther to see one of the more distant sights such as the Musée du Québec, the bus system is frequent and reliable. Fares are cheaper if you buy a ticket before boarding and are on sale at several outlets in grocery stores and supermarkets. There are also one-day passes for Can$4.60. The bus station is in the Lower Town on Boulevard Charest Est. Most of the main routes stop centrally on the Place d'Youville in the Old Town.

Taxi stands are located in front of the major hotels or outside city hall. Horse-drawn carriages or *calèches* may be hired for a gentle trot around the Old Town, but expect to pay Can$50 for 40 minutes.

HALIFAX

T HE COMPACT CITY of Halifax is best explored on foot or bicycle, which can be hired for a half or full day. Driving around is difficult: parking is hard to come by and expensive. To reach outlying districts there is the **Halifax Metro Transit** bus system. Fares are cheap, with a flat fare downtown of Can$1.30 or $1.50 to Dartmouth and other outer zones. It is also possible to purchase budget books of 20 tickets. In the city from Monday to Saturday, a free bus service called "Fred" circles the downtown area about every 20 minutes.

CHARLOTTETOWN

S INCE THE completion of the Confederation Bridge in 1997, Prince Edward Island has become easily accessible by bus and car. Travelers still use the ferry service, which

runs from New Glasgow, Nova Scotia between May and November. There is a shuttle bus service from Halifax that travels to the island by ferry. The island's public transportation system is limited to a bus service in Charlottetown run by **Trius Tours**, which operates only during the summer months. However, touring by car is most popular, and it is a good idea to reserve a car during July and August. Several companies offer organized bus, walking, and cycling tours.

Driving over Confederation Bridge to Prince Edward Island

ST. JOHN'S, NEWFOUNDLAND

I N COMPARISON to most of Canada's cities, parking is easy in St. John's. It is possible to buy a parking permit from one of many well-placed machines. They take quarters (25 cents) or dollar coins. Car rental here is less expensive than in many other Canadian cities and there is a good choice of companies.

The local bus service is run by Metrobus, and tickets cost Can$1.50 every trip. If you are planning on spending some

time here it is worth investing in a book of 10 tickets for Can$12.50. By riding on two routes, such as one downtown and one suburban bus, you get a bargain tour of the city.

Bus traveling over Harbour Bridge in St. John's, Newfoundland

Train Travel in Canada

THE CANADIAN RAIL network is run by the government-owned VIA Rail. The service has been significantly reduced since the late 1980s when many cross-country services, along with other lines, were cut. VIA Rail still provides a service on the famed 1950s *Canadian*, a beautifully restored train that travels across the country between Toronto and Vancouver, passing through stunning Rockies' scenery between Jasper and Kamloops.

Increasingly, Canadians fly long distances or use their cars to cover most of the shorter hauls. For visitors, traveling by train remains a wonderful way to see large parts of Canada (especially in those trains that have glass-domed observation cars). Smaller commuter networks around the major cities are also useful for visitors who wish to explore an area in detail.

Specialty trips on the Rocky Mountaineer travel through the Rockies

THE CANADIAN RAIL NETWORK

VIA RAIL CANADA INC. operates Canada's national passenger rail service. Despite the closing of several lines there are still 400 trains every week, which cover some 13,000 km (8,000 miles) on major routes between Vancouver and Toronto, traveling on to Montreal, Quebec, and Halifax. It is possible to cross the country by train – a trip that takes five days – by connecting up with these lines. The longest continuous route remains the Vancouver–Toronto trip on board the stylish and luxurious 1950s *Canadian*, with its observation and dining cars. Places with no road link, such as the town of Churchill in northern Manitoba, rely on the railroad. The line between Winnipeg and Churchill is

mostly used by visitors in October, heading north to see the polar bears *(see p251)*.

VIA Rail operates both long-haul trains in eastern and western Canada, as well as inter-city trains in the populous Ontario Corridor, from Quebec City to Windsor, passing through Kingston, Montreal, Niagara Falls, Ottawa, and Toronto. This is a fast service that offers snacks and drinks on board most trains.

It is easy to travel onward to the United States, as VIA connects with the American rail network, Amtrak, at both Montreal and Vancouver. VIA Rail and Amtrak jointly run the Toronto–New York line through Niagara Falls, and Toronto–Chicago trains through Sarnia/Port Huron. The VIA station in Windsor is only a few kilometers from the Amtrak station in Detroit.

SMALLER NETWORKS

VISITORS SHOULD also be aware that VIA is not the only passenger rail service in Canada. The larger cities all have useful local commuter lines. Vancouver has **BC Rail** and the West Coast Express to Prince Rupert, while Toronto's Go Transit covers the city's outlying suburbs as far as Milton, Bradford, Richmond Hill, and Stouffville, and Montreal has AMT *(see p405)*.

SPECIALTY TRIPS

THERE ARE several lines that offer visitors the chance to enjoy Canada's best scenery in comfortable, often luxurious trains. Among the best trips is the **Algoma Central Railway** in Ontario *(see p223)*, which runs from Sault Ste. Marie to Hearst and has an excursion train from Sault Ste. Marie to the Agawa Canyon through spectacular landscapes from early June to October. There is a Snow Train excursion on weekends from late December to early March, also from Sault Ste. Marie.

Ontario Northland Railway operates both freight and passenger services on its main line from North Bay to Moosonee. *The Polar Bear Express* is a summer excursion to Moosonee, which provides a close-up look at the northern wilderness. The passenger service continues south of North Bay to Toronto.

The Cariboo Prospector train, run by BC Rail, travels from North Vancouver to Prince George, through gold rush country in comfortable, air-conditioned cars. An additional summer train, the *Whistler Explorer*, running between Whistler and Kelly Lake, is popular with tour groups from the US and overseas. BC Rail also operates the historic steam train excursion, *The Royal Hudson*, from Vancouver to Squamish between June and September.

The most spectacular train ride in Canada is probably in British Columbia, where, from mid-May until early October, **Rocky Mountaineer Railtours** runs two-day excursions from Vancouver to Calgary via Banff or Jasper. The *Rocky Mountaineer* follows the original route of the Canadian Pacific Railroad. These trips operate entirely in daylight, and the package includes a night in Kamloops plus meals. There is also a dome car for viewing the stunning scenery that lies around every bend.

TRAVEL CLASSES

O N LONG-distance routes there are two main classes of travel available, Economy and a variety of Sleeper classes, known as VIA 1. Economy Class offers comfortable, reclining seats in cars with wide aisles and large windows, as well as blankets and pillows for overnight trips. Passengers in Economy class also generally have access to one of the onboard snack bars or restaurants. Sleeper classes offer a range of options from double- and single-berth bunks to double bedrooms, which convert to luxurious sitting rooms by day. VIA

services in Western Canada such as the *Canadian*, offer the choice of "Silver & Blue" first-class cars that have access to a private observation car, as well as plush dining cars.

TICKETS AND BOOKINGS

R ESERVATIONS FOR rail travel can be made through travel agents or direct through VIA Rail. There are a variety of discounts available on both economy and sleeper classes if you book round-trip tickets or in advance. Reductions on Ontario corridor lines are available if you book five days in advance (on most other routes you need to reserve tickets seven days in advance.) There are also discounts for bookings made for travel during the off-peak period between October and December, and from January until the end of May.

The CANRAILPASS gives you 12 days of unlimited travel in economy class during a 30-day period. Just show your CANRAILPASS each time you obtain a ticket. The card is

Maple leaf on VIA Rail logo

valid on all VIA Rail routes, and you can make as many stops as you like during your trip. Up to three extra days' travel can be added, which can be bought in advance or at any time during the 30-day validity period. It is a good idea to reserve seats in advance during the summer as there are a limited number for pass holders. Throughout the VIA system, travelers over 60 are entitled to an additional ten percent reduction on fares.

PRINCIPAL RAIL ROUTES

VIA Rail is the main provider of passenger rail services throughout Canada. It is possible to reach all the major centers of the country, and regional operators link up with most town's outlying districts.

0 km 500

0 miles 500

Iqaluit

Rankin Inlet

Whitehorse   Yellowknife

Churchill   Labrador City

Lynn Lake

Prince Rupert   Prince George   Thompson   Gaspé

Jasper   Edmonton   The Pas   Mont-Joli   Charlottetown

Lilleoet   Saskatoon   Sioux Lookout   Senneterre   Jonquière   Moncton

Courtenay   Banff   Hearst   Cochrane   Hervey   Halifax

Nanaimo   Kamloops   Calgary   White River   Sudbury   QUEBEC CITY

VANCOUVER   Winnipeg   Sault   North   OTTAWA   Levis   Montreal

Victoria   Ste. Marie   Bay   Kingston

Windsor   Hamilton   TORONTO

Chicago   Detroit   New York

Traveling by Bus

BUSES ARE THE least expensive way to get around Canada. The majority of bus routes west of Toronto are run by Greyhound Canada, including the epic trip along the Trans-Canada Highway (Hwy 1) between Toronto and Vancouver. East of Toronto there are several smaller companies that cover most areas. Although a long bus trip can mean one or more nights spent sitting upright, the buses are generally clean and comfortable, and offer plenty of rest stops. The network is also reliable and efficient with buses usually arriving on time. In more remote regions, check timetables in advance as there may be no service or only one bus a week.

LONG-DISTANCE BUSES

LONG-DISTANCE buses provide a cheaper and often faster option than the railroad. The main operator, Greyhound Canada, carries more than two million passengers each year to most of the towns and cities across the country. Although Greyhound lines operate in the west and center of the country, many routes are linked to bus lines in the east, and in the United States. West of Vancouver, Greyhound links up with Pacific and Maverick Coach Lines, east of Ottawa, with Voyageur Colonial, Orleans Express, and Acadian SMP. Greyhound's express services offer a faster, highway-based service on buses that have more leg room, movies, music, and snacks.

Although smoking is prohibited, most long-haul buses stop every three to four hours so that travelers can leave the bus for a rest break. Rest breaks or driver changes take place at both bus and service stations, where you will find a variety of facilities ranging from restaurants and cafés to snack vending machines. All the buses are air-conditioned and have washrooms. Buses also offer passengers the advantage of picking up and arriving in convenient downtown areas.

DISCOUNTS AND PASSES

THERE IS A variety of discounted bus passes available to visitors. Children under five usually travel free, and travelers over 60 are entitled to discounts on both return tickets and pass deals. Fares are also cheaper if you book in advance or travel during the off-peak season, from January to June or from October to December.

The Greyhound Canada Pass offers unlimited travel on both Greyhound and many other lines, such as those running eastward between Ontario and Quebec or across Saskatchewan, for a range of time periods: 7 days travel within 10 days, 15 days in 20, 30 days in 40, and 60 days in 80. Prices range from approximately Can$247 for 7 days to Can$547 for 60. The Canada Coach Pass Plus is similar, with the bonus of including travel across the country to Montreal, Quebec City, Halifax, St. John, and Charlottetown, as well as to New York City in the US. Some pass deals include accommodation in more than 80 hostels from coast to coast such as the Go Canada Budget Travel Pass. This pass can also be used to travel on VIA Rail between Toronto, Ottawa, and Montreal. Exchange a coupon for a rail ticket at any VIA station for travel on a specified route.

Rout-Passes offer access to some 35 intercity bus companies in Ontario and Quebec from mid-April to mid-November. Passengers do not need to decide on their itinerary in advance, and reservations are not necessary. There is a wide range of Rout-Passes to choose from, and some include accommodation vouchers. The 16-day Rout-Pass can be bought only by members of the International Hostelling Association.

BUS STATIONS AND RESERVATIONS

BUSES FROM different carriers all operate from the same stations, making it easy to connect with other bus lines and municipal transit services. Reservations are not usually needed since buses are filled on a first-come, first-served basis. Passengers are advised to be there at least an hour ahead of departure time, leaving plenty of time to buy tickets and check their luggage. Do not panic if the bus fills up; it will generally be replaced with another one right away. Buying tickets in advance does not guarantee you a seat, and you will still have to line up to board the bus.

Most bus stations have a small restaurant or café where reasonably priced snacks and meals can be purchased. On long-distance journeys it is a

Greyhound bus logo

Boarding the bus on Ottawa's Parliament Hill

Tourists on a bus trip to the Athabasca Glacier in Jasper

good idea to take some food with you, otherwise you will have to rely on the sometimes over-priced, unappealing food available in service stations. At the larger stations it is possible to rent luggage lockers, leaving you free to explore unencumbered by suitcases. In the major cities such as Toronto, you have the choice of boarding in the suburbs or in the city center. Choose the city center since the bus may be full by the time it reaches outlying

districts. Always ask if there is an express or direct service to your destination; as some trips involve countless stops en route and can seem very long. A small pillow or traveling cushion, a sweater (to counter the sometimes fierce air-conditioning), and a good book or magazine can often help to make a long trip more comfortable.

BUS TOURS

THERE ARE SEVERAL tour companies that offer package deals on a variety of trips. An extensive range of tours is available, from city sightseeing and day trips to particular attractions, to expensive luxury, multi-day tours including guides, meals, and accommodations. There are specialized tours that focus on such activities as glacier hikes, white-water rafting, and horseback riding. A typical ten-day tour of the Rockies may take in everything from a cruise to Victoria, a hike in Banff, and a picnic on Lake Louise, to a trip to the Columbia Icefield, or a look at the history of gold rush country in the Cariboo

region. Most companies will send you detailed itineraries in advance, and it is a good idea to make sure that there are no hidden extras such as tips, sales taxes, and entry fees, as these are often included in the price of the package. Some of the most beautiful scenery can also be seen on regular Greyhound routes, such as those in the Rockies.

DIRECTORY

Greyhound Canada Inquiries
(1 800 661 8747.

Timetable Information
from Canada and US
(1 800 661 8747.
from the UK
((44) 0891 633 269.

Bookings (passes only)
(UK) (01342 317317.

BUS TOUR COMPANIES

Brewster Transportation
for tours in the west
((800) 661 1152.

Great Canadian Holidays
for tours in the east
((519) 896 8687.

BUS ROUTES

This map shows the main bus routes across Canada. It is possible to travel right across the country along the Trans-Canada Highway using Greyhound Canada and the bus companies that operate east of Toronto.

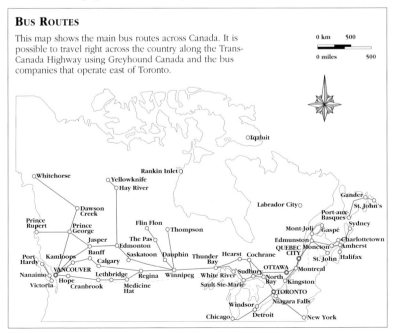

0 km   500

0 miles   500

Iqaluit

Whitehorse
Rankin Inlet
Yellowknife
Hay River
Dawson Creek
Prince Rupert
Prince George
Jasper
Edmonton
Flin Flon
Thompson
The Pas
Labrador City
Gander
St. John's
Port-aux-Basques
Mont-Joli
Gaspé
Sydney
Edmonton
QUEBEC Moncton Charlottetown
CITY Amherst
St. John Halifax
Port Hardy
Kamloops
Banff
Saskatoon
Dauphin
Thunder Bay
Hearst
Cochrane
VANCOUVER
Calgary
Nanaimo
Lethbridge
Regina
Winnipeg
White River
Sudbury
OTTAWA
Montreal
Hope
North Bay
Kingston
Victoria
Cranbrook
Medicine Hat
Sault Ste-Marie
TORONTO
Niagara Falls
Windsor
New York
Chicago
Detroit

Driving in Canada

Driving Route tour sign

I⸏ IS A GOOD IDEA to rent a car when visiting Canada. Other modes of transportation will get you around the cities and from one rural town to another, but once you arrive in a remote country area, a car is the best way of exploring. Tours of regions such as Quebec's wild Gaspé Peninsula *(see pp140–41)*, or British Columbia's Okanagan Valley *(see p315)* are best made by car. Several aspects of Canadian life reflect the fact that this is a driver's country: there is an excellent, well-maintained highway network, and many places have huge out-of-town malls. However, city-center traffic congestion means that visitors to the major cities of Toronto, Vancouver, Montreal, and Ottawa may find that public transportation is quicker and cheaper than driving.

ARRIVING BY CAR

M⸏ANY PEOPLE drive to Canada from the US. The border here is the longest in the world. There are 13 crossing points, the two busiest being from Detroit to Windsor and at Niagara Falls. Most of the highways entering Canada connect to the Trans-Canada Highway (Hwy 1), which is the longest highway through the country, running for some 5,000 km (8,045 miles) from Victoria, BC, to St. John's in Newfoundland. Customs control ask that visitors declare their citizenship, their place of residence, and proposed length of stay. You may be asked to show your passport and visa *(see pp390–91)*. It is a good idea to fill up with less expensive fuel on the US side. It is also possible to enter the country from the Alaska side by the famed Alaska Highway *(see pp260–61)*, which crosses the Yukon and ends in British Columbia at Dawson City.

DRIVER'S LICENSES

A⸏N UP-TO-DATE driver's license from your own country usually entitles you to drive in Canada for up to three months. There are some provincial variations: in British Columbia, Quebec, and New Brunswick your license will be valid for up to six months, in Prince Edward Island four months, and in the Yukon only one month. It is advisable to carry an International Driving Permit (IDP) with your license in case of problems with traffic officials or the police.

INSURANCE

W⸏HETHER driving a rental or your own car you will need proof of insurance coverage, which is compulsory in Canada. If you are using your own car it is advisable to check whether your insurance is valid in Canada, as this may save money. The minimum liability cover is Can$200,000, except in Quebec, where it starts at Can$50,000. Most rental companies offer collision damage waiver and personal accident insurance for an additional charge; it is a good idea to have both. If you are driving a private car that is not registered in your own name, you will need to carry a letter from the owner that authorizes your use of the vehicle. For a rental vehicle you must carry the company's official documentation for the same reason. Arranging summer rentals and insurance in advance is recommended.

A Recreational Vehicle passes mountains and forests on a trip through Banff National Park, Alberta

Car Rental

RENTAL CARS are available just about everywhere in Canada. Most major rental car dealers such as Hertz, Avis, and Tilden, have offices at airports and in towns and cities across the country. Among the less expensive options are booking a fly-drive package from home, or there may be discounts if you rent your car in advance. The cost varies greatly depending on the season, type of vehicle, and length of rental. Ask about hidden costs such as drop-off charges, provincial sales tax, and the Goods and Services Tax (GST). When picking up your car you may be asked to show your passport and return airline ticket. The minimum age for renting a car is usually 25 or, in some cases, 21. You will need a credit card for the deposit as it is all but impossible to rent a car in Canada without one. Children under 18 kg (40 lbs) require a child seat fixed in place with a seat belt. Most companies will arrange for one with a little notice. The biggest rental companies offer a wide choice of vehicles, ranging from two-door economy cars to four-door luxury models. Most cars come with a radio and air-conditioning. Bear in mind that nearly all rental cars in Canada have automatic transmission. Manual models are unusual, although cars with specially adapted hand controls for disabled drivers are available from some of the larger companies. RVs (Recreational Vehicles) or camper vans can also be rented, but they are more expensive. They should be booked well in advance if you intend to travel in summer.

Fuel and Service Stations

FUEL PRICES are slightly higher than in the US and half the price you pay in the UK, especially in cities and large towns, although rural areas often charge more. Unleaded gas and diesel only are available in Canada. Rental companies generally provide a full tank on departure, and give you the choice of paying for the fuel in advance or on return. Service stations are often self-service, which can be a problem if you need a mechanic. In major cities some stations are open for 24 hours, but in rural areas they often close at 6pm and are few and far between, especially in northerly regions. It is a good idea to fill up before setting off. Credit cards and traveler's checks are widely accepted.

Rules of the Road

CANADA's Highway system is well maintained and has mostly two-lane all-weather roads. They are all clearly numbered and signed. Most highway signs are in English, and some bilingual, except for those in Quebec where they are only in French. A good road map is essential and can be obtained from any auto club such as the **Canadian Automobile Association (CAA)**, which is affiliated with other similar clubs in the world. It is worth checking the rules of the road with them as there are numerous small provincial variations. In Canada you drive on the right.

Moose warning sign on highway

You can turn right on a red light everywhere, except in Quebec. The speed limits are posted in kilometers-per-hour (km/h) and range from 30–40 km/h (18–30 mph) in urban areas to 80–100 km/h (50–60 mph) on highways. On multi-lane highways you pass on the right for safety. Some provinces require cars to keep their headlights on for extended periods after dawn and before sunset, for safety reasons. Seat belts are compulsory for both drivers and passengers.

Driving in the north involves special procedures because most of the roads are extremely hazardous due to ice, and are passable only during the summer months.

Winter Driving and Safety

CANADIAN winters are harsh, and you should always check road conditions and weather forecasts before setting out on trips. Drifting snow and black ice are frequent hazards in winter or in northern regions. When driving in remote areas, make sure you have a full gas tank, and carry blankets, some sand, a shovel, and emergency food, such as chocolate bars, in case you get stuck. Jumper cables are also useful because extreme cold can drain a car battery quickly. Studded tires are allowed year-round in the Yukon, the Northwest Territories, Alberta, and Saskatchewan and are permitted in winter in most other provinces. Check with local tourist offices.

During the summer months animals such as bears and moose can be a hazard, especially in parts of British Columbia. They can suddenly appear on roads when they rush out of the woods to escape the blackflies during spring and summer. Watch for road signs, and take extra care when you see deer or moose road signs as these indicate an area where animals are most likely to appear suddenly.

General Index

Acknowledgments

DORLING KINDERSLEY would like to thank the following people whose contributions and assistance have made the book possible:

MAIN CONTRIBUTORS

Paul Franklin has recently completed Nova Scotia's provincial travel guide, commissioned by the Government of Nova Scotia. A writer and photographer for both Canadian and world travel guides, he lives in Nova Scotia.

Sam Ion and **Cam Norton** live and work in Burlington, Ontario. A successful travel-writing team, they contribute to newspapers, magazines, and brochures as well as their most recent work, the Ontario Government's millenium website, celebrating the province.

Philip Lee has worked as a travel writer for over a decade, and is the author of numerous articles and travel books about countries throughout the world. He has lived and traveled extensively through the US and Canada and is now based in Nottingham, England.

Lorry Patton lives and works in British Columbia, having recently been travel editor of BC Woman magazine. She currently runs an online travel magazine which includes BC, and lives on the Gulf Islands just outside Vancouver.

Geoffrey Roy is an award-winning freelance travel writer and photographer, based in Surrey, England. He has published numerous articles on Northern Canada.

Donald Telfer is a Saskatchewan-based travel writer with over 20 years' writing experience of Central Canada. He contributes regularly to a variety of Canadian and international newspapers and magazines.

Paul Waters is a Montreal-based journalist who has lived and worked in several cities in Quebec and has written extensively on the province. He is currently the travel editor for *The Gazette*, a popular Montreal English-language daily.

ADDITIONAL CONTRIBUTORS

Alan Chan, Michael Snook.

ADDITIONAL PHOTOGRAPHY

James Jackson, Matthew Ward.

ADDITIONAL ILLUSTRATIONS

Stephen Conlin, Eugene Fleury, Steve Gyapay, Chris Orr, Mel Pickering, Peter Ross.

CARTOGRAPHY

ERA-Maptec Ltd, Dublin, Ireland.

PROOF READER

Sam Merrell.

INDEXER

Hilary Bird.

DESIGN AND EDITORIAL ASSISTANCE

Gillian Allen, Louise Bolton, Vivien Crump, Joy Fitzsimmons, Emily Green, Marie Ingledew, Steve Knowlden, Lee Redmond, Ellen Root, Anna Streiffert.

SPECIAL ASSISTANCE

Canada Map Office, Ontario; Canadian Tourism Office, London, UK; Claude Guerin and Danielle Legentil, Musée d'art contemporain de Montreal; Jim Kemshead, Tourism Yukon; Wendy Kraushaar, RCMP Museum, Regina, Saskatchewan; 'Ksan Historical Indian Village & Museum, Hazleton, BC; Leila Jamieson, Art Gallery of Ontario, Toronto; Antonio Landry, Village Historique Acadien, New Brunswick; Marty Hickie, Royal Tyrrell Museum, Drumheller, Alberta; Mary Mandley, Information Office, Sainte-Marie among the Hurons; National Air Photo Library, Ottawa, Ontario; Liette Roberts, Manitoba Museum of Man and Nature, Winnipeg; Mark Sayers; Ernest D. Scullion, Aeriel Photography Services, Scarborough, Ontario; Visit Canada office, London, UK; Jennifer Webb, UBC Museum of Anthropology, Vancouver, BC.

PHOTOGRAPHY PERMISSIONS

Dorling Kindersley would like to thank everyone for their assistance and kind permission to photograph at their establishments.

Placement Key - t = top; tl = top left; tlc = top left centre; tc = top centre; trc = top right centre; tr = top right; cla = centre left above; ca = centre above; cra = centre right above; cl = centre left; c = centre; cr = centre right; clb = centre left below; cb = centre below; crb = centre right below; bl = bottom left; b = bottom; bc = bottom centre; bcl = bottom centre left; bottom centre right = bcr; br = bottom right; d = detail.

Works of art have been produced with the permission of the following copyright holders: The work illustrated on page 172c is reproduced by permission of the Henry Moore Foundation; © Bill Vazan *Shabagua Shard*, 1989 sandblasted sheild granite 187c.

The publishers would like to thank the following individuals, companies, and picture libraries for their kind permission to reproduce their photographs:

AIR CANADA: 49b, 398t; AKG, London: 47b; BRYAN AND CHERRY ALEXANDER: 16c, 20t, 21cr, 23c/cr/bl, 26t, 37t, 51c/b, 153t, 321c, 322, 324cb, 324-5, 325c, 332-3, 334t, 338t, 339t/c; ALLSPORT: Scott Halleran 32b; Elsa Hasch 17c; Jed Jacobson 33t; Jamie Squire 35b; Rick Stewart 32c; ANCHORAGE MUSEUM OF HISTORY AND ART, Anchorage, Alaska: B74.1.25 46t; courtesy of THE ANNE OF GREEN GABLES MUSEUM, Silver Bush, Park Corner, Prince Edward Island: 79b; ART GALLERY OF ONTARIO: Karoo Ashevak, Canadian: Inuit 1940–74, *Shaman with Spirit Helper* 1972, whalebone; ivory; dark greystone; sinew 47.7 x 23.6 x 16.6 cm, Gift of Samuel and Esther Sarick, Toronto 1996 © Palaejook Eskimo Co-op Ltd. 175ca; Pieter Brueghel the Younger, Flemish 1564–1638 THE PEASANTS WEDDING n.d., oil on cradled oak panel 36.2 x 44.2 cm 175cb(d); Paul Gaugin French 1848–1903, HINA AND FATU c.1892, tamanu wood, 32.7 cm height, Gift of the Volunteer Committee

DORLING KINDERSLEY SPECIAL EDITIONS

Dorling Kindersley books can be purchased in bulk quantities at discounted prices for use in promotions or as premiums. We are also able to offer special editions and personalized jackets, corporate imprints, and excerpts from all of our books, tailored specifically to meet your own needs.

To find out more, please contact: (in the United Kingdom) – SPECIAL SALES, DORLING KINDERSLEY LIMITED, 9 HENRIETTA STREET, COVENT GARDEN, LONDON WC2E 8PS; TEL. 020 7753 3572;

(in the United States) – SPECIAL MARKETS DEPARTMENT, DORLING KINDERSLEY, INC., 95 MADISON AVENUE, NEW YORK, NY 10016.

Fund, 1980 174tl; Lawren H. Harris Canadian 1885–1970 *Above Lake Superior* c.1922 oil on canvas 121.9 x 152.4 cm Gift from Ruben and Kate Leonard Canadian Fund 1929 © Mrs. James H Knox 160b; J.E.H. MacDonald Canadian (1873–1932) *Falls, Montreal River* 1920 oil on canvas 121.9 x 153cm Purchase 1933 Acc no 2109 Photo Larry Ostrom 161t; Henry Moore British (1898–1986) *Draped Reclining Figure* 1952 - 53 original plaster 100.4 x 160.4x 68.6 cm Gift of Henry Moore, 1974. The work illustrated on page 174ca is reproduced by permission of the Henry Moore Foundation; Robert Gray Murray (b1936) To 1963 painted aluminium, 2 units, tubular column H271.1cm planar column 275.0cm Gift from the Junior Women's Committee Fund 1966 65/60.1-2 29cb; Claes Oldenburg, American b.1929 *Floor Burger* 1962, canvas filled with foam rubber and cardboard boxes, painted with latex and liquidtex 132.1 x 213.4 m, purchased 1967 174cb; Photographic Resources 28b; Tom Thomson Canadian 1887-1917 *The West Wind* 1917 oil on canvas 120.7 x 137.2 cm Gift of the Canadian Club of Toronto, 1926 175t; E.P Taylor Research Library and Archives 160tl; AXIOM: Chris Coe 3c, 18c, 22tl, 23tr, 45bc, 84c, 203b, 232, 235t/c, 237c/br, 240c, 245t, 252-253, 275t, 276t, 308t, 315t, 330c/b, 361b.

BRIDGEMAN ART LIBRARY, London: Art Gallery of Ontario Paul Kane (1810–71) *Indian Encampment on Lake Huron* 6-7, Emily Carr (1871–1945) *Skidgate, Graham Island, British Columbia* 1928 (oil on canvas) Gift of the J.S. Mclean Collection by Canada Packers Inc. 1990 29t, Maurice Galbraith Cullen (1866–1934) *On the Saint Lawrence* 1897 (oil on canvas) Gift of the Reuben and Kate Leonard Canadian Fund, 1926 28c; British Library portolan by Pierre Descaliers Canada: *from the voyage of Jacques Cartier* (1491–1557) and his followers c.1534–41 40c, *Jacques Cartier* (1491–1557) *French navigator and discoverer of Canadian River St. Lawrence* (steel engraving after a portrait in St. Malo) 40b; Hudson Bay Company Lieutenant Smyth (19th Century) *Incidents on Trading Journey: HMS Terror Making Fast to an Iceberg in Hudson's Strait*, August 18th, 1836 159t; Private Collection "British Boys learn how to own your farm in Canada! Decide on Canada now" 26b, medal commemorating the British capture of Quebec, 1759 (bronze) 43b; engraving by Jean Antoine Theodore Gudin (1802–80) *Jacques Cartier* (1491–1557) on the St. Lawrence River, 1535 t; engraved by Charles Maurand by French School (19th century) *Delaware Indians Killing Bison* in the 1860's photo Ken Welsh 225c, litho by Howard Pyle (1853–1911) *The Capitualtion of Louisbourg, illustration from 'Colonies and Nation'* by Woodrow Wilson, pub. in Harper's Magazine, 1901 43t, Benjamin West (1738–1820) *Willaim Penn's Treaty with the Indians in November 1683* (oil on canvas) 22tr; Stapleton Collection engraved by Carl Vogel (1816–51) *Indian Hunting the Bison, plate 31 from volume 2 "Travels in the Interior of North America"*, 1844 (aquatint) engraved by Karl Bodmer (1809–93) (after) 22br, engraved by Charles Geoffroy (1832–82) *Assiniboin Indians, plate 32 from volume 2 of "Travels in the interior of North America 1832–34"*, 1844 (aquatint) by Karl Bodmer (1809-93) (after) 245b; BRITISH COLUMBIA ARCHIVES: Province of B.C. Photo 43cb.

Courtesy of CALGARY TRANSIT: 404c; Courtesy of CANADIAN AIRLINES: 401c, Cohn & Wolfe 398b; CEPHAS: Fred R. Palmer 98tr; Pascal Quittemelle 98b; TOP/Hervé Amiard 24b; BRUCE COLEMAN LTD.: John Cancalosi 243c; JEAN-LOUP CHARMET: 42t; COLORIFIC!: Randa Bishop 395b; Terence LeGoubin 223t; John Moss 262; Black Star/Richard Olsenius 68b; Jeff Perkell 60; Michael Saunders 99b; Geray Sweeneyt 19b; Focus/Eric Spiegelhalter 319t; CORBIS: 25t, 29b, 44b, 46c, 53c, 59br, 159br, 207, 209nl, 230bl, 248bl; Craig Aurness 230-1; David Bartruff 325b; Bettman 45bl, 47c, 48b; Bettman/UPI 201b; Peter Harholdt 324b; Hulton Deutsch collection 50cr/bl/br; Wolfang Kaehler 324ca; Lake County Museum 231c; Library of Congress 41t/cb,

155c; New York Public Library Picture Collection 40t; PEMCO-Webster & Stevens Collection Museum of History and Industry, Seattle 47tl; UPI 31c.

ADRIAN DORST: 254c, 286c, 287b.

ROBERT ESTALL PHOTO LIBRARY: 73b, 98-99,100c, 152b; MARY EVANS PICTURE LIBRARY: 43c, 47tr, 95c, 158tr, 253c, 341c, 389c.

P.M. FRANKLIN: 19t, 21tl, 56ca, 59tr/c, 70, 82-83, 91t; WINSTON FRASER PHOTOS: 8-9, 64b, 69b, 98c, 99c, 101tr, 226b, 136b, 248t, 334b, 397, 399; Black Star 153c; Canada In Stock 217tr; Ivy Images/Don Mills 36c, 56br, 58t, 59tl, 68c, 69t, 147c, 227, 238-9; Ivy Images/Don Mills/© Gilles Daigle 74t,/© Sylvain Grandadam 387t; /© Tony Mihok 34b/ © Dan Roitner 77b; T.Klassen Photography 236c, 240t, 251t.

Courtesy of GREYHOUND CANADA: 408t.

LYN HANCOCK: 336, 338b, 339b, 384b; ROBERT HARDING PICTURE LIBRARY: 21cl, 23tl, 256cl; Charles Bowman 103; Philip Craven 34t; Robert Francis 388-9; Jeff Greenberg 260cb; Norma Joseph Frgs 231b; Maurice Joseph Frgs, Arps 34c, 409; Paolo Kotch 101c; R. McLeod 319b; Roy Rainford 176t, Waltcr Rawlings 303c; Geoff Renner 229tl; Ian Tomlinson 35t, 288, 292b; Dr A.C. Waltham 328b; Tony Waltham 214-5; Explorer 152t;/Patrick Lorne 140b; Publiphoto Diffusion 20cl;/Paul G. Adam 136t;/Yves Marcoux 116-7, 139t; Bild Agenteur Schuster GMBH 94-5; DAVID HOUSER: 68t, 69c, 139b, 141bl; © Steve Cohen 95, 337t; HUDSON BAY COMPANY ARCHIVES, Toronto: 158tl; Provincial Archives of Manitoba 158b, 159c; HULTON GETTY COLLECTION: 50t, 91b, 100cb.

INUIT ART FOUNDATION, Ontario: Sarah Joe Qinuajua, Puvirnituq *A Polar Bear Meets A Woman* QC1985 Black Stone Cut 324t.

JASPER TOURISM AND COMMERCE: 306t; Hugh Levy 307tr;

WOLFGANG KAEHLER: 140t, 141br; ROBIN KARPAN: 15t, 27b, 224-225, 226t, 229c/b, 230tr, 234b, 236b, 241b, 242c/b, 243b, 244t/c/b, 246b, 247t/b, 248c, 249cl/cr/b, 329t, 337b; JOSEPH KING: 265, 270-1, 273t, 318b; KOBAL COLLECTION: 17b, *Rose Marie*, MGM 231tr; *Anne of Green Gables*, RKO 30c.

FRANK LANE PICTURE AGENCY: Dembinsky 20br; Michael Gore 57crb; John Hawkins 57br; FotoNatura/F.Hazelhoff 2-3; David Hosking 228cb,258t, 295b; Maslowski 20bcr; C. Mullen 139c; Mark Newman 21crb, 258cb; C.Rhodes 21br; M.Rhode 72c; Leonard Lee Rue 21clb, 152c, 311b; Sunset/Brake 72t, 338c;/T.Leeson 258bl; John Watkins 56bca; L.West 302t; David Whittaker 258ca: Terry Whittaker 20bl; LEISURAIL/VIA RAIL CANADA: 407.

courtesy of the MANITOBA MUSEUM OF MAN AND NATURE: 237bl; ARNOLD MATCHTINGER: 184b; McCORD MUSEUM OF CANADIAN HISTORY, Montreal: Notman Photographic Archives 49t; McMICHAEL CANADIAN ART COLLECTION: Photo Arthur Goss/Arts & Letters Club 161b; A.V Jackson (1882–1974) *The Red Maple*, 1914 oil on panel, 21.6 x 26.9cm Gift of Mr. S. Walter Stewart 1968.8.18 160tr; courtesy of MOLSON COMPANIES: 363b; MUSEE D'ART CONTEMPORAN DE MONTREAL: Natalie Roy *Les Dentelles de Montmirail*, 1995 (detail) Soutens-gorge et jupon sous acrylique et bois 32 x 300 x 35cm Denis Farley et Natalie Roy Du Compagnonnage du 2 Juin au Septembre 1999 ©SODART/DACS, 2000 112t; Richard Long *Niagra Sandstone Circle*, 1981 32 pierres de gres © Richard Long 112c; MUSEE DES BEAUX-ARTS DE MONTREAL: Laurent Arriot *Teapot* Photo Christine Guest 1952 DS 41 114b; El Greco *Portrait of a young Man* 1945.885 115c; Harmensz van Rijn Rembrandt *Portrait of a Young Lady* 1949-1006 114cl;

MONTREAL METRO

A single ticket covers connecting lines and bus trips. Running from early morning until 1am on weekdays, with a slightly slower service that finishes earlier on weekends, the métro is an efficient way to dodge the traffic in the busy city. Above ground stations are marked with large blue arrowed signs (see below).

HENRI-BOURASSA
Sauvé
Crémazie
Jarry
SAINT-MICHEL
D'Iberville
Fabre
JEAN-TALON
De Castelnau
Beaubien
Assor
Parc
Rosemont
Préfontaine
Laurier
Frontenac
Acadie
Mont-Royal
CÔTE-VERTU
Sherbrooke
Du Collège
Outremont
BERRI-UQAM
Beaudry
De la Savane
Université-de-Montréal
Édouard-Montpetit
Saint-Laurent
Namur
Place-des-Arts
Plamondon
Côte-des-Neiges
McGill
Champ-de-Mars
Côte-Sainte-Catherine
Peel
Place-d'Armes
SNOWDON
Guy-Concordia
Square-Victoria
Villa-Maria
Atwater
Bonaventure
Vendôme
Lucien-L'Allier
Place-Saint-Henri
Georges-Vanier
LIONEL-GROULX
Charlevoix
La Salle
Jolicoeur
De l'Église
Monk
ANGRIGNON
Verdun

Fleuve

KEY

— Ligne Verte (Green Line)
— Ligne Orange (Orange Line)
— Ligne Jaune (Yellow Line)
— Ligne Bleu (Blue Line)

LONDSALE QUAY

Burrard Inlet

Burrard
WATERFRONT
Granville
Stadium
Science World
Main Street
Broadway
Nanaimo

VANCOUVER SKYTRAIN

The SkyTrain runs from about 5am to after midnight on weekdays, with late trains on Saturdays. The correct fare is required as drivers carry no change, but tickets can be bought at corner booths and small stores. Tickets can be transfered from bus to train, but ferry tickets are sold separately.

29th Avenue
Joyce
Patterson
Metrotown
Edmonds
New Westminster
Royal Oak
Columbia
22nd Street

KEY

— SkyTrain
≡ SeaBus

Fraser River

Greater Vancouver Transportation Authority GVTA